Oxford School Shakespeare

The Merchant
of Venice

edited by

Roma Gill
M.A. *Cantab*. B.Litt. *Oxon*.

Oxford University Press

Oxford University Press, Walton Street, Oxford OX2 6DP

London New York Toronto
Delhi Bombay Calcutta Madras Karachi
Kuala Lumpur Singapore Hong Kong Tokyo
Nairobi Dar es Salaam Cape Town
Melbourne Auckland
and associated companies in
Beirut Berlin Ibadan Mexico City Nicosia

Oxford is a trade mark of Oxford University Press

© Oxford University Press, 1979

First published 1979
Reprinted 1980, 1981, 1982, 1983, 1984, 1985, 1987 (twice)

Illustrations by Coral Mula

Oxford School Shakespeare
edited by Roma Gill

A Midsummer Night's Dream

Romeo and Juliet

As You Like It

Macbeth

Julius Caesar

The Merchant of Venice

Henry IV Part I

Twelfth Night

Printed in Great Britain
at the University Printing House, Oxford

A letter to all students of this text

I want to say a few words of explanation to all those readers who are studying this text for examination purposes. I'm sure that Shakespeare would be very pleased with the kind of attention that you and I are going to give to the words of his play – but he would also be very surprised. He wrote his plays to be *acted*. He did not think that they would be *read* – and read more than 300 years after he had written them. He cared so little for *readers*, that many of his plays were not printed until after his death.

Act this play! Enjoy the characters, the situations, and the language. Don't worry too much if you don't fully understand the language at first. A modern poet, T. S. Eliot, has said that the best poetry will mean *something* to the reader before it is completely understood.

Shakespeare wrote the best poetry; but his language is not always easy to appreciate, even for those who are native speakers of English. There are three reasons for this.

Firstly, you will find that some words look odd because there is an apostrophe where you would expect a letter: the word 'ever', for instance, often appears as 'ere'. Many verbs appear in the past tense as (for example) 'look'd', which you have been properly taught to spell 'looked'. This is because of the length of Shakespeare's verse line, which has ten syllables (when it is regular).[1] By writing 'e'er' and not 'ever' the dramatist managed to save one syllable. It is almost the same with verbs in the past tense. Although today 'looked' is pronounced as one syllable, in Shakespeare's time it could have been two – 'look-ed'. The spelling 'look'd' instructs you to use a modern English pronunciation. When you find 'looked' in poetry, you should pronounce the second syllable as well as the first. This care for the rhythm of the lines is not needed in the prose parts of the play, and so the spelling there is the spelling of modern English.

The second problem is that we no longer speak the English of Shakespeare's time. Many words have changed their meaning. When the Servant tells Portia that her visitor has brought 'sensible regreets' (*Act 2*, Scene 9, line 88), we need to be told that 'regreets' (a word no longer in use) meant 'greetings', and that 'sensible' could also mean 'generous, substantial' – the visitor has come bringing more than mere words of greeting; he has rich presents for Portia.

Finally, it is sometimes hard to understand what a character is saying. This is because Shakespeare had a very powerful mind, and his thoughts are not always easy to understand. As well as this, he liked to play with words, as we see when Shylock tells us that he hates Antonio 'for that in low simplicity He lends out money gratis' (*Act 1*, Scene 3, lines 39–40). Here the words 'low and 'simplicity' have, each of them, two meanings. Shylock scorns Antonio for his wretched stupidity in lending money without demanding interest; but readers who are sympathetic to the generous Antonio will praise his humble honesty and fair dealing.

Don't think a lot about the past. It is true that Shakespeare was writing in the sixteenth and early seventeenth centuries, as you will see from the Table on p. 103. Yet soon after his death Ben Jonson, who was a friend of Shakespeare's and a playwright himself, said of him that 'He was not of an age, but for all time'. The characters that Shakespeare has created, and the feelings that he has described, are alive in *our* world. You must know of girls who fall in love, and of young men who go to great lengths to win the girl of their dreams. And our century can provide many examples of racial hatred and religious intolerance. These, and many others, are the characters and topics of Shakespeare's plays.

Study this play then; and act it. Read it aloud. You owe it to yourselves and to your teachers to do as well as you can in the examinations. You also have a debt to Shakespeare, and you can pay this debt by *acting* the play, and enjoying it – just as he intended it to be acted and enjoyed. You need no fancy costumes or expensive scenery. Shakespeare's own professional actors had very little scenery. Their clothes had often been given to them by rich courtiers who were tired of them. There were no women among these actors, for it was not thought respectable for women to act. Boys played the parts of the female characters.

This play is given to you as it would be given to a company of actors. You are told when each character comes on to the stage ('*Enter* Shylock'), and when he leaves ('*Exit*'). It is traditional in the theatre to use Latin here, saying 'exit' for 'he goes out' or 'exeunt' for 'they go out'. Sometimes you will find a stage direction telling you that a noise is heard 'within'. This simply means that the noise is off-stage.

In the Introduction and the Notes I have tried to help you as much as I can. But I may well have missed something that you could tell me about. if this happens, please write to me at the local office of the Oxford University Press. Your letters will be forwarded to me, and I shall be very happy to hear from you.

Roma Gill

---

[1]The technical term for this is 'iambic pentameter'. The lines should be read as rhythmically as possible. When you are reading (either aloud or silently) you will find that it is usually necessary to put a strong stress on alternate syllables. Portia's description of the 'quality of mercy' should be stressed like this:

But mércy ís abóve this scéptred sway,
It ís enthróned ín the héarts of kíngs,
It ís an áttribúte to Gód himsélf . . .

(iv,1,191–3)

Contents

Prejudice in *The Merchant of Venice*

Shylock, the money-lender who is hated because he is a Jew, explains how prejudice works. He calls it 'affection',[1] and shows the relationship between prejudice and the emotions:

> affection,
> Master of passion, sways it to the mood
> Of what it likes and loathes.

If we are prejudiced, we may dislike someone for no other reason than that he is different from us in nationality, religion, colour, or social class. In England today there are laws that attempt to control the effects of prejudice: it is an offence in law, for instance, for an employer to refuse a job simply because the applicant is coloured, or female, or Jewish. If *The Merchant of Venice* were a new play, written in 1978, it would probably be banned by the English censor. The topics it presents—racial hatred, colour prejudice, class distinction, and the position of women in society—are all capable of provoking intense feelings in an audience; but this would not be the reason for the censor's disapproval. He would be suspicious of Shakespeare's attitude to these matters, as it is communicated through the characters and the action. Shakespeare seems to accept the prejudices of some of his characters. Only occasionally do they ever question the justice of their positions, and usually a satisfactory answer is to be found in subsequent events of the play.

Portia is one character who, at the beginning of the play, resents the situation in which she is placed. Her father, who is now dead, devised a test for selecting the man that his daughter should marry; in Portia's words, 'the will of a living daughter [is] curbed by the will of a dead father'. English girls today would find this intolerable, but Portia only grumbles: she does not rebel. Fortunately for Portia, the right man makes the right choice, and she is given to the man she loves. Portia does not think to question a man's rights to the ownership of all his wife's possessions; in fact, she seems glad when she tells Bassanio,

[1] The word *affection* was quite often used in Shakespeare's time with this sense of 'prejudice'.

> But now I was the lord
> Of this fair mansion, master of my servants,
> Queen o'er myself; and even now, but now,
> This house, these servants, and this same myself
> Are your's, my lord's.

Only for the past hundred years has a woman in England been allowed to keep her own property when she marries, and even now there is some discrimination against the sex. Because I am a woman, I cannot borrow from a money-lender unless some man will act as guarantor for me, just as Antonio does for Bassanio.

The different social classes are clearly indicated in *The Merchant of Venice*, but the linguistic 'markers' that Shakespeare uses are not as familiar to a twentieth-century audience as they were to Shakespeare's contemporaries. The pronouns 'you' and 'thou' are very significant, and almost imperceptibly define the relationships between the characters. 'You' is neutral, formal, and polite, whilst 'thou' is affectionate, condescending, or contemptuous. Bassanio always speaks to Antonio as 'you', but to Gratiano as 'thou'; Antonio mostly uses the formal word, but with Bassanio he allows himself the occasional 'thou' of affection, and with Shylock the dismissive 'thou' of contempt. As long as Old Gobbo believes that he is speaking to a young gentleman, he adopts the 'you' which is appropriate when addressing a superior; but when he knows he is speaking to his son, his recognition is expressed through the pronoun: 'I'll be sworn if thou be Launcelot . . .'

It is by such small details that English social status is revealed. To show excessive care for position is ill-mannered, and the Prince of Arragon's lengthy discourse on rank shows him to be merely vulgar: he is himself the 'blinking idiot' that he finds in the casket.

Subtlety has no place, however, when colour is the object of the discrimination, and the Prince of Morocco wastes no words. He speaks proudly of his dark skin, the 'shadow'd livery of the burnish'd sun', and in his dignity we can feel Shakespeare's admiration for the character he has created and the people whom the Prince represents. Yet he is unacceptable as a suitor for Portia; her conversation with him leaves few doubts in our minds, and her relief when he chooses the wrong casket is unmistakeable: 'Let all of his complexion choose me so'.

The Prince of Morocco confronts Portia with a powerful argument against prejudice. Find a fair-skinned northern prince, he urges her, and let the two of them 'make incision' in their flesh. From both bodies, the blood that flows will be red. The argument is taken up in a later scene by Shylock, and the opening lines of Shylock's speech are often quoted to demonstrate Shakespeare's lack of prejudice and refusal to discriminate against individuals on grounds of race or religion.

> Hath not a Jew eyes? hath not a Jew hands, organs, dimensions, senses, affections, passions? Fed with the same food, hurt with the same weapons, subject to the same diseases, healed by the same means, warmed and cooled by the same winter and summer as a Christian is? If you prick us, do we not bleed?

But this can only serve as evidence when it is taken out of context— removed entirely from the play. *The Merchant of Venice* confirms Shylock as a villain, as monstrous a creature as any in the drama of Shakespeare's time. Indeed, English drama *since* the seventeenth century has failed to produce Shylock's equal.

The Jew was a figure hated and feared by the Elizabethans, but the reasons for their hatred are not at all simple. Superstition was a main one, arising out of medieval legends such as that of St. Hugh of Lincoln, a little boy who was said to have been crucified by Jews. True religious hostility was rare, but religion gave the English Christians a good excuse for persecuting the foreigners who had come to live amongst them. Dislike of the aliens was intensified by the prosperity of some Jews, whose success in business enterprises sometimes made the native English dependent on the immigrants. Parallel cases of suspicion and jealousy are not hard to find in the modern world.

Shylock's viciousness transcends his Jewishness, and it would be unfair to cite this character as an example of Shakespeare's racial prejudice. But we can find this surrounding Shylock's daughter. We are sympathetic to Jessica, yet we are never allowed to forget that she is a Jew. The reminders are always affectionate, and sometimes funny—as when Launcelot reproaches Lorenzo for converting Jessica, 'for in converting Jews to Christians you raise the price of pork'. Laughter can take away the cruelty of prejudice, but it helps to reinforce in an audience the awareness of difference.

In *The Merchant of Venice* Shakespeare acknowledges the existence of prejudice, and he makes use of it to suit his dramatic ends. He was an entertainer, not a reformer. His play cannot be read as propaganda for the abolition of prejudice; at most, it recommends that we should sometimes remember that there is a human being inside the skin.

Leading characters in the play

Antonio the merchant of the play's title. He is a good and generous man, who promises to pay Shylock the money borrowed by Bassanio or else allow Shylock to cut off a pound of his flesh. His part in the play is rather a passive one, and he reveals his character mainly in his generosity to his friend and in his hatred of the Jew.

Bassanio a younger man, who has already spent all his own money and now hopes to restore his fortunes by marrying an heiress. He needs to borrow money so that he can appear rich when he courts Portia, and it is for his sake that Antonio enters into the bond with Shylock. Bassanio is made to show good judgement when he makes his choice of the leaden casket and so wins Portia for his wife.

Gratiano a young man with a reputation for wild behaviour. He accompanies Bassanio to Belmont, and wins the love of Portia's lady-in-waiting, Nerissa.

Lorenzo He is in love with Jessica, and plans to steal her from her father's house.

Portia the most important character in the play. She is an heiress, and is in love with Bassanio; but her father has devised a test with three caskets, and Portia must marry the man who chooses the right casket. Portia is intelligent as well as beautiful; dressed as a lawyer she goes to Venice and saves Antonio from being killed by Shylock. Her home is Belmont, and the peace and harmony here contrast with the tense business world of Venice.

Nerissa Portia's lady-in-waiting, who falls in love with Gratiano. When Portia goes to Venice as a lawyer, Nerissa accompanies her, dressed as a lawyer's clerk.

Shylock a money-lender, who is hated for his greed and because he is a Jew. He is Antonio's enemy, and when Bassanio's money is not repaid he demands the pound of flesh that Antonio promised as a forfeit. (See also p. xxvii.)

Jessica   Shylock's daughter; she disguises herself as a boy in order to run away from her father's house, where she is unhappy. She is in love with the Christian Lorenzo.

Launcelot Gobbo   the comedian of the play. He is at first Shylock's servant, then goes to work for Bassanio. His clowning often takes the form of misusing the English language; it is sometimes a welcome break from the tense or romantic scenes.

The Merchant of Venice: commentary

The action of the play takes place in Venice and in Belmont. Belmont is imaginary, but Venice is real. The city is located on the sea coast in the north of Italy, and is in fact built over a lagoon. Its main streets are canals, and the only vehicles are boats (see illustration page 13). In the sixteenth century, Venice was the centre for international trade, importing goods from all corners of the earth, and exporting them in the same way. We are told that Antonio, the greatest of the merchants, is waiting for his ships to return

> From Tripolis, from Mexico, and England,
> From Lisbon, Barbary, and India.   (3, 2, 267–8)

To be successful, a merchant had to invest his money wisely—and have luck on his side. Trading by sea was hazardous, and a sudden storm, or unseen rocks, could easily wreck a ship and drown the merchant's hopes along with the cargo.

Act 1

Scene 1   When his friends see that Antonio is depressed, they immediately think that he is worried about his ships at sea. They are sympathetic, and Solanio does his best to make light of the situation by exaggerating his fears to make his friend smile. But Antonio is sad for some other reason, and when we meet his dearest friend, Bassanio, we begin to guess at this reason. Bassanio is a carefree young man, who cheerfully admits that he has spent all of his own money and a good deal of Antonio's. However, Bassanio now has a scheme for acquiring more wealth. Before he gives any details, he explains his theory: a lost arrow (he says) can often be found by shooting another arrow in the same direction, and watching carefully to see where it falls. The theory is, as Bassanio acknowledges, a 'childhood proof'; he believed it when he was a schoolboy, and now he wants to put it to the test again, spending more money in the hope of winning back what he has lost. This is not a very sensible, or responsible, way to act, but Bassanio emphasizes his youth and innocence. Perhaps he hopes that Antonio will treat him as though he were a child, and ignore the irresponsibility of his demand for more money to spend.

Bassanio next tells Antonio of an heiress, who has already given him some unspoken encouragement. Her name is Portia, and Bassanio claims to have fallen in love with her. He may be speaking the truth, but it is clear that the lady's wealth is a very attractive feature for him. Antonio promises aid, but all the money he possesses is tied up in his own business ventures. Still, his 'credit' is good, and Bassanio can borrow all the ducats he needs to present himself to Portia as an eligible suitor, giving Antonio's name as security—that is, promising that Antonio will repay the debt if he himself is unable to do so.

Our feelings towards Bassanio at the end of this scene cannot be wholly favourable, despite his youthful optimism. He has wasted a lot of money, both his own and his friend's. It seems that he wants to marry Portia not just because of love but also because of her money. But he himself, perhaps unconsciously, shows what we should feel about him when he explains that his youth has been 'something too prodigal'. Repeated phrases throughout the play compare Bassanio with the Prodigal Son of Christ's parable (St. Luke 15: 11-32), who spent all his inheritance in 'riotous living'. When he was penniless and starving, he went repentantly back to his father's house, where he was welcomed with rejoicing. Bassanio has been 'prodigal'; now he asks for a chance to redeem himself.

Like the Prodigal Son's father, Antonio has shown the loving and forgiving generosity of his nature, but he remains a mysterious character. Early in the scene he tells Gratiano that he thinks of the world as 'A stage where every man must play a part, And mine a sad one'. It is his changing relationship with Bassanio that causes his melancholy. Some Elizabethans thought—as the Greeks and Romans did—that the friendship between two men was a more spiritual bond, and should be more highly esteemed, than the love between a man and a woman. Knowing that Bassanio is interested in a lady (see lines 119-21), Antonio may be secretly grieving for the inevitable end to a friendship.

Scene 2   From the hearty, but anxious, masculine world of Venice, we move to the feminine peace of Belmont. Even here there is anxiety, as Portia's opening sigh indicates. It is now Nerissa who tries to cheer Portia, but she cannot take her mistress's mind off the situation where she is surrounded by suitors and yet 'cannot choose one, nor refuse none'. Shakespeare has to communicate to his audience a lot of information about the trial that Portia's father devised for the men who wish to marry her. The information is given gradually, in five separate scenes, so that we seem to discover the facts just as the suitors do. For the moment, we are merely told that each candidate must make a choice between three caskets.

Nerissa explains why Portia must obey this somewhat absurd commandment when she says that 'holy men at their death have good inspirations'. It was proverbially believed that a good man would be divinely inspired, and might even speak prophetically, when he was close to death. To disobey or disregard such an utterance was almost sacrilege.

The two young women amuse themselves by gossiping about the suitors who have already assembled at Belmont. Although Portia and Nerissa are Italian, they share a sense of humour which is undoubtedly English. As they laugh about each man's peculiarities, we can learn something of what the Elizabethan Englishmen thought of their continental neighbours—and also of how they could laugh at themselves. The 'young baron of England' is a caricature of the Englishman abroad, in the twentieth century as well as in the sixteenth: the English have never been good at speaking foreign languages! Nor is there a 'national dress' for England, such as many other countries possess; the Englishman was always content (it seems) to imitate the costumes of other countries. The joke about the Scottish lord would have a topical significance for Shakespeare's audience. At this time England and Scotland were separate kingdoms, and in their frequent quarrels the French always promised to aid the Scots (but rarely kept their promises).

We are never allowed to see this 'parcel of wooers', for Nerissa tells Portia that they have all decided to return home, not trying their luck with the caskets. There is no doubt that Portia is glad they are leaving. Nerissa reminds her of a young Venetian whom Portia met whilst her father was alive, and the promptness with which Portia recalls Bassanio's name is enough to tell us that she remembers him with pleasure. Bassanio is described by Nerissa as 'a scholar and a soldier'. These qualities made up the ideal courtier in Elizabethan eyes, and the description may help to prepare us for a Bassanio who is rather different from the one we left in Venice.

Portia's enthusiasm dies away, and her weary resignation returns, when she is told that a new suitor is approaching Belmont. It is the Prince of Morocco, and the title arouses her prejudice as she goes inside to prepare for his coming.

Scene 3   Meanwhile, in Venice, Bassanio has found a usurer who can lend the money he needs. Shylock is very cautious, repeating each of Bassanio's demands to make sure that they are perfectly understood. His deliberation makes Bassanio nervous, and he shows irritation when Shylock says that 'Antonio is a good man'. The word 'good' has different implications: Bassanio thinks that it refers to Antonio's character, and he is angry that such a man as Shylock should presume to judge his friend. Shylock, having succeeded in annoying Bassanio, hastens to explain that by 'good' he meant only 'sufficient'—financially sound. The two disagree again over the interpretation of 'assur'd', by which Bassanio means that Shylock may trust Antonio; Shylock says that he will indeed be 'assur'd', meaning that he will take all precautions to protect himself and his money.

Bassanio's polite invitation to dinner is refused by Shylock in words that introduce the theme of racial hatred: he thinks he would be asked 'to smell pork', a meat forbidden to Jews by their religion. Shylock perhaps speaks these words '*aside*', not talking directly to Bassanio but uttering his thoughts aloud for the audience alone to hear them, just as only the audience hears the soliloquy in which Shylock reveals his attitude to Antonio. Religious feeling has some part in this attitude, but a minor one compared with the enmity he bears towards a business rival.

We learn that Antonio disapproves morally of lending money for interest (and it is a mark of his affection for Bassanio that he is prepared now to break his own rules). Shylock justifies his activities by telling the story of Jacob from the Old Testament (Genesis 30: 31–43). Jacob was angry with Laban, his uncle, and tried to outwit him, using his skill as a shepherd. He believed that the ewes, seeing the striped twigs in front of them when they conceived, would give birth to striped or spotted lambs, which Laban had agreed should become Jacob's wages. This indeed happened, but whereas Shylock applauds Jacob's cunning, Antonio (and most devout Jews) ascribes the success to the hand of God.

The merchant and the usurer engage in passionate argument. Shylock reveals the cruel insults he has had to suffer from Antonio in the past, but Antonio stands firm in his contempt for the Jew.

He refuses to borrow the money as a friend, but urges Shylock, with words that he will regret, to

> lend it rather to thine enemy;
> Who if he break, thou may'st with better face
> Exact the penalty.

Shylock proposes 'a merry sport' which Antonio, surprisingly, is willing to accept. He agrees to the forfeit that Shylock suggests— 'an equal pound of your fair flesh'—to be given if the money cannot be properly repaid.

The words 'kind' and 'kindness' are repeated several times at the end of this scene. They have a surface meaning—'generous' and 'generosity'—which Antonio accepts, and an ironic double meaning. If Shylock 'grows kind' in this second sense, he will become even more like himself, true to his nature. And we have already, in his soliloquy, seen what this is.

Act 2

Scene 1   Prejudice is the subject of the short episode in Belmont, where we see Portia's reception of the Prince of Morocco. The prince's appearance shows that he is an exotic figure: a note, probably written by Shakespeare himself, describes him as 'a tawny [brown] Moor, all in white'. His first speech reinforces our sense that he is excitingly different from the Europeans that we have seen so far, but it does not change Portia's mind. She is polite, but we understand, better than Morocco can, what she means when she tells him that, in her eyes, he is 'as fair As any comer I have look'd on yet'. We have heard what Portia thought of her other suitors. The Prince's reply to this ambiguous remark does not encourage our good opinion of him. He boasts of his own valour and achievements in very exaggerated language, and so loses some of our sympathy.

We are given a new piece of information concerning the casket test. The men who choose wrongly must never again think of marrying. It is now clear why the earlier suitors left Belmont without trying their luck; Morocco, however, is not deterred, and prepares to make his choice.

Whilst Morocco is taking his oath in the 'temple'—many great houses at this time had their own private chapels—Shakespeare returns us to Venice. The next five scenes will send Bassanio from Venice to Belmont, and introduce a sub-plot, connected to the main plot through Jessica, Shylock's daughter. First, Shakespeare creates a role for the leading comedian of his acting company: he is to be Launcelot Gobbo, Shylock's servant.

Scene 2   Comedy scenes such as this are the most difficult and unrewarding to read; they need to be performed, so that the actor can introduce the visual effects that the lines demand. When Launcelot pretends to be torn between his conscience and the devil, he might (for instance) jump to the left when the devil is speaking—because devils traditionally appeared on the left—and to the right when 'conscience' replies. There could be humour in the difference between Launcelot's appearance (as the miserly Shylock's servant he would not be well dressed) and his grand manner of speech to the old man; this would emphasize the comedy of the 'mistaken identity' situation. When Old Gobbo feels his son's head and comments on his 'beard', it is obvious from Launcelot's reply that he has got hold of the hair tied at the back of his neck; and if Launcelot passes his father's hand across his fingers, implying that they are his ribs ('You may tell every finger I have with my ribs'), the comedy will increase with the old man's bewilderment.

The English language is a very complicated one, and Englishmen themselves are not always very good at speaking it! There are many words that sound grand—but sometimes the people who use them do not understand their meanings, or else confuse one word with another that sounds similar. This is especially likely to happen when the speakers are trying to create a good impression of themselves. Launcelot and his father are doing this when they address Bassanio. They are conscious that Bassanio is a gentleman, whilst they are only peasants, and they try to use what they think is the proper language of gentlemen. Even in the twentieth century, when class distinctions are much less clearly marked than they were in the sixteenth, the writers of television comedy still find subjects for laughter in our linguistic snobbishness. Lorenzo's comment is valid today: 'How every fool can play upon the word' (3, 5, 42).

Bassanio is in a good temper, and responds well to Launcelot's fooling; he agrees to employ him and give him 'a livery More guarded than his fellows'. A 'guarded' uniform—one decorated with yellow braid—was often worn by the professional fool in a gentleman's household; perhaps this is the function that Bassanio intends for Launcelot when he becomes 'The follower of so poor a gentleman'.

Even though he admits he is poor, Bassanio is already behaving with his former extravagance, now that he has got Shylock's money. He is planning to give a party before he leaves Venice. However, he shows a more sedate side of his character when Gratiano asks to accompany him to Belmont. Gratiano turns Bassanio's solemn warning into comedy. He promises to behave in a way that is very sober, but at the same time quite ridiculous, and he probably accompanies his speech with exaggerated gestures.

Scene 3   Quickly, Shakespeare presents his new plot when Jessica gives to Launcelot the letter she has written to Lorenzo. The short scene takes the plot one small step further, and it also serves to increase our dislike for Shylock. We learn that his 'house is hell', and that Jessica is 'asham'd to be [her] father's child', although she recognizes that it is a 'heinous sin' for a daughter to have such feelings.

Scene 4   The letter is delivered to Lorenzo when he and his friends are discussing their costumes for Bassanio's party. It was quite usual, in Shakespeare's time, for a small band of the guests at a grand feast to disguise themselves in elaborate costumes and entertain the other guests with a masque—a performance with singing and dancing. Page-boys carried torches for the masquers, and Lorenzo suddenly realizes how he can steal Jessica away from her father's house: she can be disguised as his page.

Scene 5   There can scarcely be a greater contrast than that between the lively young men planning their evening's entertainment, and the surly Shylock. He takes no pleasure in the feast, but has decided to 'go in hate, to feed upon The prodigal Christian' (yet another comparison of Bassanio with the Prodigal Son). Shylock is determined to do all he can to ruin Bassanio, and he even considers that Launcelot's change of employer might 'help to waste His borrow'd purse'.

Scene 6   Gratiano's reference to the 'penthouse' under which they are standing is one of many remarks in Elizabethan drama that help us to reconstruct, in imagination, the kind of stage that Shakespeare was writing for. It seems that there was always a balcony, which allowed 'split-level' acting. In this scene the young men assemble on the main stage, underneath the 'penthouse' formed by the balcony on which Jessica appears, dressed as a boy. She is shy, because in Elizabethan times women *never* wore men's clothes. Her embarrassment is expressed with great delicacy, and it is easy to forget that Shakespeare and his contemporaries would probably have been a little amused by the situation. In many plays of this period the female characters put on masculine clothing, and a gentle comedy arises out of the fact that female characters were always played by boy actors: the boys dress up as girls, and then the 'girls' turn into boys.

Waiting for Jessica has made the masquers late for the feast, and now Antonio comes in search of Gratiano. The wind has changed, and it is time to set sail for Belmont.

Scene 7 Whilst all the activity of Jessica's elopement was taking place in Venice, the Prince of Morocco at Belmont has dined, and sworn an oath never to look for a wife if he fails the casket test. At last we see the caskets that we have heard so much about. Each one bears an inscription, which Morocco reads aloud. The gold and silver caskets make promises, but the leaden one is menacing. Morocco refuses to be threatened, and passes to the silver casket, which assures him that he 'shall get as much as he deserves'. We heard in *Act 2*, scene 1 that he has a good opinion of himself, and he is naturally tempted to choose silver. The golden casket, however, offers 'what many men desire', and Morocco decides that this refers to Portia, because 'all the world desires her'. It would be an insult to Portia (he concludes) to associate her with lead, or even with silver; so he opens the golden casket.

The casket contains a skull, the emblem of death—which indeed many unhappy men do desire. Shocked and saddened, the Prince of Morocco departs immediately.

Scene 8 In Venice, Shylock has discovered that his daughter is missing —and she has taken a lot of his money with her. Solanio gives a comical account of the Jew's confusion, when Shylock apparently did not know which loss to lament more. It is important that we do not *see* Shylock here, because his distress might create too much sympathy for him. Instead, we join Salerio and Solanio in their laughter.

But not everything in this scene is comic: there is bad news for Antonio. A ship has been wrecked in the English Channel, and it may well be his. The conversation becomes sober, as the two friends think of Antonio's generosity—'A kinder gentleman treads not the earth'—and remind us of his great affection for Bassanio: 'I think he only loves the world for him'.

Scene 9 Yet another suitor, the Prince of Arragon, has arrived at Belmont; he repeats the three promises that he has sworn to keep, and goes to make his choice of the three caskets. Like the Prince of Morocco, he reads the inscriptions, and speaks his thoughts aloud.

The Prince of Arragon is excessively conscious of his social position, and insists that he is different from other men: he will not 'jump with common spirits', and look in the golden casket for 'what many men desire'. He is attracted by the promise of the silver casket: 'Who chooseth me shall get as much as he deserves'. For a time he meditates on the subject of nobility and merit, deploring the fact that 'low peasantry' (men of humble birth) can be found among noblemen—'the true seed of honour'. Having convinced *himself* that he deserves to win Portia, he opens the silver casket. We are not surprised that this is the wrong choice, for Arragon has convinced *us* that he is far too conceited—although perhaps he deserves something better than 'the portrait of a blinking idiot'.

As soon as the Prince of Arragon has left, news is brought that another suitor is approaching. He has already made a good impression on Portia's servants with the 'Gifts of rich value' that he has sent to announce his coming; and we recognize the extravagance that is characteristic of Bassanio. Portia and Nerissa are hopeful.

Act 3

Scene 1   The optimism of Belmont gives place to the darkening atmosphere of Venice. There is still no confirmation that the ship wrecked in the English Channel is indeed Antonio's, but Solanio believes the rumour to be true. Shylock also has heard the report, and his anger over his daughter's flight is forgotten for a moment as he gives expression to his hatred and resentment of Antonio. He has had to suppress his feelings for years, but now they explode violently. His passion increases, and so too does the sympathy of the audience. He appeals to common humanity: 'Hath not a Jew eyes? hath not a Jew hands . . . if you poison us, do we not die?' He becomes almost a hero, and certainly a human being—then suddenly he changes back into a monster: 'and if you wrong us, shall we not revenge?'

Salerio and Solanio are fortunately saved from having to reply to this tirade; they leave Shylock with another Jew, Tubal, who has news of Jessica.

Shylock experiences another confusion of emotions as Tubal imparts various pieces of information in an incoherent manner. Jessica is spending her father's money recklessly, and in exchange for a pet monkey she has given away the ring that was a token of betrothal from her mother to her father. Grief and anger conflict with malicious glee when Shylock hears of Antonio's misfortunes, and it is clear that he will take revenge for the loss of his daughter and his ring when he claims the forfeit from Antonio.

Scene 2   Portia is happy in Bassanio's company, and she tries to persuade him to stay at Belmont for a few days before making his choice of the caskets. Her happiness is mingled with modesty, for she is too shy to tell Bassanio that she loves him. Bassanio too has fallen in love, but he cannot endure the uncertainty and feels that he must try his luck as soon as possible. So Portia orders Nerissa and the servants to stand aside, away from the caskets. Portia and Bassanio seem to be alone on the stage. Music is playing, whilst Portia watches the man she loves as he tries to make the decision that will bring happiness to both of them.

The song that helps to create a magic atmosphere also introduces Bassanio's meditation on appearance and reality. He is speaking only to himself; Portia does not hear him, just as he did not hear her speech before the song. The audience, of course, knows which casket Bassanio must choose, because Shakespeare has already shown us the contents of the gold and silver caskets.

Portia is almost overcome with delight when Bassanio selects the 'meagre lead'; and when Bassanio finds 'Fair Portia's counterfeit' in the casket he is ecstatically happy. He praises the picture rapturously, and for a time cannot believe his luck.

A rather more materialistic note is heard in the metaphorical language when Portia wishes to 'stand high in [Bassanio's] *account*', and offers him 'the full *sum*' of herself; it is repeated when Gratiano refers to the '*bargain*' of their faith. But to balance this there is the ritual moment when Portia gives away all that she owns (including 'this same myself') and as a token places a ring on Bassanio's finger. Bassanio accepts the token, and binds himself to Portia:

> when this ring
> Parts from this finger, then parts life from hence.

Gratiano and Nerissa announce their intention of imitating Bassanio and Portia; and the happiness of the moment is complete.

It is now time to change the direction of the scene, and Shakespeare switches the mood with a bawdy joke (in prose).

The arrival of Salerio, Lorenzo, and Jessica is a welcome surprise, but the letter that Salerio has brought from Venice 'steals the colour from Bassanio's cheek'. Things have gone very badly for Antonio: he is ruined. Salerio can tell of Shylock's eagerness to claim his bond from Antonio, and Jessica is able to bear witness of her father's fiendish malice: 'he would rather have Antonio's flesh Than twenty times the value of the sum That he did owe him'. Portia is more than able to pay back the three thousand ducats, but we can take no comfort from her offer. The situation seems hopeless, and when Antonio's pathetic letter is read aloud it destroys the last remaining scrap of the happiness established in the scene.

Scene 3   A short scene shows us what the letter described. Antonio, in the custody of a gaoler, meets Shylock. The Jew will hear no pleas for mercy, and Antonio knows that it is useless to speak to him. Solanio hopes that the Duke will be able to intervene in the dispute, but Antonio knows the importance of strict justice in the mercantile world of which Venice is the head. This is a subject that will be mentioned at Antonio's trial.

Scene 4   Lorenzo has been telling Portia about Antonio, and Portia has decided that she and Nerissa will go away for a few days, leaving Belmont in the care of Lorenzo. She sends a servant to her cousin in Padua, asking for some 'notes and garments'. We understand the request for clothes when Portia explains to Nerissa that they are going to dress up as men, and that she herself will imitate all the mannerisms of a brash young man—including the voice that is 'between the change of man and boy'.

Scene 5   The next scene, still at Belmont, does nothing to develop any plot. But it encourages the audience to imagine that enough time has passed to allow Portia and Nerissa to travel from Belmont to Venice; on a practical level, it gives the actors time to change from their female dresses to the male costumes required in the following scene. In addition, it provides an opportunity for the comedian, in the part of Launcelot, to deliver some more of his word-play jokes. Launcelot, of course, accompanied his new master when Bassanio came to Belmont.

Act 4

Scene 1   The trial scene in *The Merchant of Venice* is the most famous scene in English drama. It has given a phrase to the English language: people who have never read the play—and perhaps never even heard of it—understand what it means to want one's 'pound of flesh'.

The conversation between the Duke and Antonio, before Shylock comes on to the stage, shows the hopeless resignation with which Antonio faces Shylock's wrath. The Duke makes a further plea for mercy, but Shylock is unmoved. He will admit that his hatred for Antonio is irrational and emotional: just as some people hate cats, or the sound of bagpipes, so (he says)

> can I give no reason, nor I will not,
> More than a lodg'd hate and a certain loathing
> I bear Antonio.

Antonio is not intimidated, and shows his contempt for Shylock's 'Jewish heart'. Bassanio offers to repay twice the money that he borrowed, but Shylock will not yield, and reminds the court that the pound of flesh is his by law. If the Duke refuses to grant this, it will appear that 'There is no force in the decrees of Venice'. We remember Antonio's words (*3*, *3*, *27–31*), and realize that, if the law is not observed, Venice will suffer in its reputation as the centre of international trade.

The Duke has made a final attempt to save Antonio legally. He has asked for the opinion of a famous lawyer, Bellario, and the court waits to hear this man's judgement. Bassanio is optimistic, but the tension of the situation has made Antonio even more resigned to his fate; he almost feels that he deserves to die.

The lawyer's clerk has brought a letter from Bellario, and whilst the Duke reads the letter, Shylock sharpens his knife. Gratiano cannot bear to see this sight, and he begins to abuse Shylock. The Jew appears to be unaffected by his insults, for he knows the strength of his position: 'I stand here for law'.

Bellario is sick, and cannot come to Venice; instead he has sent a legal colleague, 'a young doctor of Rome', who is fully acquainted with the case. The audience recognizes this 'doctor': it is Portia, and the 'clerk' was Nerissa. The other characters of the play, however, cannot penetrate the disguise.

Portia upholds Venetian law, but she urges Shylock to show

mercy. She describes the 'quality of mercy' as a divine blessing, which benefits both the man who shows mercy and the man who receives it. The petition in the Lord's Prayer, 'forgive us our trespasses', comes to mind when Portia explains how mercy belongs to God; if this were not so, the whole human race would be damned for its sins. But this is Christian doctrine, and Shylock's religion is of the Old Testament, which emphasizes the importance of the law, just as Shylock does now: 'I crave the law'.

Once again Bassanio offers the money; again Shylock refuses it; and once more we are reminded that a general principle lies beneath this particular instance:

> 'Twill be recorded for a precedent,
> And many an error by the same example
> Will rush into the state.

The statement is harsh, but it is correct. Portia has earned Shylock's praise 'A Daniel come to judgement'. Daniel was 'a young youth', according to 'The Story of Susanna' in the *Apocrypha*. He was inspired by God to give judgement when the chaste Susanna was accused of adultery by two lascivious 'elders' who had tried to rape her.

Portia continues to win Shylock's approval as she instructs the court about the penalty that Antonio must pay. The knife is sharpened, and the scales are ready; Antonio prepares for death. He speaks a few words of comfort to Bassanio, ending with a wry jest about the debt:

> For if the Jew do cut but deep enough,
> I'll pay it instantly with all my heart.

The tension is broken, but only for a moment, when Bassanio and Gratiano refer to their wives. The 'lawyer' and his 'clerk' are amused.

Just when Shylock is ready to cut into Antonio's flesh, Portia stops the proceedings. She reveals to Shylock the single flaw in his carefully worded bond: he is entitled to his pound of flesh, but has made no provision for a single drop of blood.

Gratiano exults over Shylock, repeating ironically all the words of praise that the Jew bestowed on the 'learned judge', and agreeing that he is indeed 'A second Daniel'. Like Portia, Daniel was not expected in the court, and the verdict he gave saved Susanna and condemned her accusers. The comparison is more apt now than it was when Shylock introduced it.

Shylock realizes that he cannot have his pound of flesh, and he tries to take the money that Bassanio is still offering. Now it is Portia's turn to be inflexible, and she insists that Shylock can have 'merely justice, and his bond'. When Shylock proposes to leave the court, Portia calls him back. The law of Venice has a strict penalty that must be paid by any 'alien'—foreigner—who tries to murder a Venetian. Shylock has thus offended, and for this crime his possessions are confiscated and his life is in danger. Antonio, of course, shows his generosity. Half of Shylock's wealth is forfeited to him, but he is willing to renounce his personal share and take the money on loan, keeping it in trust for Lorenzo, 'the gentleman That lately stole his daughter'. He makes two conditions: firstly, Shylock must become a Christian; and, secondly, he must make a will leaving all that he possesses to Jessica and Lorenzo. Shylock is utterly defeated. He asks for permission to leave the court, and indicates his agreement to Antonio's conditions: 'send the deed after me And I will sign it'.

For a long time Bassanio has been silent, perhaps because the events have affected him very deeply and prevented him from sharing in Gratiano's expressions of triumph. Sometimes Gratiano's speeches seem rather cruel, for although Shylock undoubtedly deserves punishment, it is hard that he should lose everything, including his right to believe in the Jewish faith. Gratiano, however, shows the character that Bassanio rebuked him for before the two men went to Belmont—'bold of voice' and with a 'skipping spirit' (2, 2, 173; 179). Bassanio and Antonio are more dignified in their behaviour.

It is only necessary now to pay the 'lawyer', and then Bassanio can take Antonio home to Belmont, to meet his new wife. The 'lawyer' refuses payment, then suddenly catches sight of a ring on Bassanio's finger, and requests this as a keepsake. It is the ring that Portia gave to Bassanio, telling him that if he should ever part with it for any reason, it would 'presage the ruin of [his] love'. Remembering this, Bassanio refuses; the 'lawyer' departs, apparently angry. Antonio begs Bassanio not to withhold the ring, and Bassanio cannot refuse the friend who risked so much for him.

Scene 2   Gratiano hurries after Portia to give her Bassanio's ring. Nerissa, still disguised as the lawyer's clerk, whispers to Portia that she will use a similar trick to get her own ring from Gratiano. The two girls laugh in anticipation of their husbands' embarrassment when they return to Belmont.

Act 5

Scene 1   Moonlight and music emphasize the tranquillity of Belmont and its contrast with the harsh legal world of Venice. Lorenzo and Jessica are relaxed here, and Jessica's escape from the 'hell' of her father's house seems to be almost as remote in time as the mythological lovers who are recalled by the moonlight. The mood of the scene is saved from being over-romantic when the couple start to tease each other, and when the messengers break in with their news. Harmony is restored, however, when Lorenzo and Jessica are alone again. Lorenzo starts to explain the theory of the music of the spheres, which Plato (a Greek philosopher) described. The music was made as the spheres touched each other in their constant motion, but could not be heard by human ears, which are deafened by the noises of earthly life.

Portia's musicians appear, probably on the balcony, to 'draw [their mistress] home with music'. The beauty of Lorenzo's speech (when he describes the 'patens of bright gold', and the 'young-eyed cherubins') blends with the playing of the musicians to re-create, in human terms, the heavenly harmony. Lorenzo and Jessica fall silent; perhaps they are asleep.

Portia and Nerissa come from the opposite side of the stage as they approach Belmont from Venice. Their chatter breaks into the music, and the dream world becomes real. A trumpet announces the arrival of Bassanio, just as day is breaking. The missing rings provide a final gentle comedy, as the two embarrassed husbands try to justify their actions to wives who are trying to hide their amusement.

In the end, of course, all is happiness. Lorenzo and Jessica join the other two couples, and Portia gives Antonio a last surprise —the news that three of his ships 'Are richly come to harbour suddenly'. There can be no reaction from the audience other than Antonio's 'I am dumb', and final applause for Shakespeare. He has taken three main strands—the casket story, the bond story, and the ring story—and woven them into a single plot, which brings all three stories to a successful conclusion, and ensures that all the characters—with one exception—'live happily ever after', just as fairy-tale characters ought to do.

Shylock

A happy ending for the leading characters is essential for a romantic comedy such as *The Merchant of Venice*. But one very important character is left out of the general rejoicing in Act 5. Shylock has been defeated of his bond, robbed of his ducats, and deserted by his daughter; he is even compelled to give up his birthright, his Jewish religion, and become one of the Christians whom he so much hates. Does he deserve this fate? Is *The Merchant of Venice* a comedy for all the other characters, but a tragedy for Shylock?

Shakespeare took the story of Shylock's bond from an Italian novel, but the money-lending Jew in this source has no personality, and no daughter. Consequently, we can assume that Shylock is Shakespeare's own creation: all the personality traits that we find in him were deliberately worked out by the dramatist, and not borrowed accidentally along with the plot.

Shylock starts from a double disadvantage, as far as an Elizabethan audience was concerned. He is a Jew, and he is a money-lender. There were not many Jews in England, but in the Middle Ages English Christians hated the Jews, and this feeling was still strong in the sixteenth century. The Elizabethans also hated the traditional Jewish profession of usury—the lending of money for profit. Jews were often forbidden to own land or to engage in trade in England; consequently the only lucrative profession open to them was money-lending. The Christians deplored this—in theory. In practice, the expanding economy of the times demanded that money should be readily available. Francis Bacon, who was Lord Chancellor of England in 1618, claimed that

> to speak of the abolishing of usury is idle. All states have ever had it, in one kind, or rate, or other. So as that opinion must be sent to Utopia. (Essay 'Of Usury')

Certainly, the usurer is necessary to the world of *The Merchant of Venice*. Shylock's wealth is evidence of his professional success, which could only come from satisfying a social need.

Shylock first appears as the cautious businessman, thinking carefully before he invests his three thousand ducats in Bassanio's

enterprise. His reaction to the polite invitation to dinner is un-
expected in its venom, which increases as he tells the audience of
his hatred for Antonio. Religious differences 'seem to be less
important than professional jealousy:

> I hate him for he is a Christian;
> But more for that in low simplicity
> He lends out money gratis.

To some extent Shylock justifies his hostility when he describes
how he has been treated by Antonio—insulted, spat upon, and
kicked out of the way like 'a stranger cur'. Because of this, we
sympathize with him. When the scene ends, we are left with two
conflicting opinions of Shylock and his 'merry sport'. Are we to
share Antonio's surprise, 'And say there is much kindness in the
Jew'? Or is Bassanio right to be suspicious of 'fair terms and a
villain's mind'?

The scene with Antonio and Bassanio shows Shylock in his
professional, public, life. Next, we hear what he is like at home.
His comic servant, Launcelot Gobbo, exaggerates (with a characteristic misuse of the English language) when he says that 'the Jew
is the very devil incarnation'. But this opinion is echoed by Shylock's daughter, Jessica, when she sighs 'Our house is hell'. Jessica
is 'asham'd to be [her] father's child', although she knows that it
is a 'heinous sin' for a daughter to have such feelings. We can
understand Jessica's misery when her father gives instructions
about locking up his house whilst he is away. Jessica is forbidden
even to look out of the window to watch the masquers going to
Bassanio's feast. Shylock is a kill-joy—and he has also killed his
daughter's natural affection for him.

Shakespeare does not let us see Shylock in his first frenzy of
distress when he finds that Jessica is missing, because this would
surely arouse our sympathy. Instead, Solanio describes the scene,
and the audience is encouraged to share in his laughter. From
Solanio's account, it seems that Shylock's grief over the loss of his
daughter is equalled (perhaps even surpassed) by his anger at the
theft of his money. He utters 'a passion so confus'd':

> My daughter! O my ducats! O my daughter!
> Fled with a Christian! O my Christian ducats!

When Shylock next appears (*Act 3*, scene 1) the passion is subdued
into an intense and malevolent bitterness; yet the jesting of the

two Christians is cruel. The loss of a daughter is a real cause for
sorrow, and Shylock earns some pity (from the audience) when he
tells Solanio and Salerio that 'my daughter is my flesh and my
blood'.

It is with very mixed feelings, then, that we are led up to the
powerful speech in which Shylock catalogues the abuses he has had
to suffer from Christians in general, and from Antonio in particular.
There is only one reason that he can see for this treatment: 'I am
a Jew'. It is easy to respond to the rhetorical questions that follow:

> Hath not a Jew eyes? hath not a Jew hands, organs, dimen-
> sions, senses, affections, passions? fed with the same food,
> hurt with the same weapons, subject to the same diseases,
> healed by the same means, warmed and cooled by the same
> winter and summer, as a Christian is? if you prick us, do we
> not bleed? if you tickle us, do we not laugh? if you poison us,
> do we not die?

Shylock appeals to our common humanity. To give a negative
answer to his questions would deny not *his* humanity, but our own.
The speech, however, continues:

> and if you wrong us, shall we not revenge? If we are like you
> in the rest, we will resemble you in that . . . The villainy you
> teach me I will execute, and it shall go hard but I will better
> the instruction.

Common humanity ignores all limitations of colour, race, or creed;
and this is strongly asserted in the first part of Shylock's speech.
But the assertions of these last lines show that the individual—
Shylock—is determined to ignore the limits of humanity. He will
'better the instruction', and prove himself to be not the *equal* of
the Christians in inflicting suffering on others, but their *superior*.

The events that follow do nothing to moderate the presentation of Shylock in the terms used by the Duke when he warns
Antonio, before the trial begins, that his adversary is

> an inhuman wretch
> Uncapable of pity, void and empty
> From any dram of mercy.

During the trial, Shylock loses the audience's sympathy, by his
words and by the action of sharpening the knife on the sole of his

shoe (which Gratiano observes in line 123). Neither insults nor pleading spoil the enjoyment of his triumph, and when sentence is given against Antonio, he repeats the words of the bond with a lingering relish:

> Ay, 'his breast':
> So says the bond—doth it not, noble judge?—
> 'Nearest his heart'—those are the very words.

Shylock demanded a strict observance of the law, and (in poetic justice) it is precisely this that defeats him. Gratiano exults over his downfall, but the other characters in the court speak no unnecessary words and show no satisfaction until Shylock has left the court. Even then, conversation is formal, occupied only with thanks and payment. It does not obliterate the memory of Shylock's parting words:

> I pray you give me leave to go from hence:
> I am not well.

A snarl of frustrated wrath can deliver this line; or else it can be spoken with the anguish of a man who has lost everything—his daughter, his wealth, his religious freedom, and the engagement ring given to him by his wife.

Recent English productions of *The Merchant of Venice* have emphasized the suffering human being, but I do not think that this is what Shakespeare intended. Shylock is more complex than any of the other characters in the play: we can think of him as a 'real' person, whose words and deeds are motivated by thoughts and feelings that we can discover from the play, and that we can understand when we have discovered them. We cannot think of Bassanio (for instance) in this way. Yet in admiring Shakespeare's achievement in the creation of Shylock, we must beware of danger. Often, when we know a person well, and understand why he acts as he does, we become sympathetic to him; in *The Merchant of Venice* we are further encouraged to sympathize with Shylock also by the fact that other leading characters (such as Bassanio) do *not* compel our sympathies. Sympathy can give rise to affection, and affection often tempts us to withhold moral judgement, or at least be gentle in our censure. Shylock's conduct merits condemnation. We can only refrain from condemning it because we know that he has suffered for being a Jew; and this, surely, is another form of prejudice?

Characters in the play

The Duke of Venice

Antonio	*a merchant of Venice*
Bassanio	*his best friend, in love with Portia*
Gratiano	*another friend, in love with Nerissa*
Lorenzo	*another friend, in love with Jessica*

Salerio	
Solanio	*other friends*

Leonardo   *servant to Bassanio*

Shylock	*a Jew, and a money-lender*
Jessica	*his daughter*
Tubal	*another Jew, Shylock's friend*
Launcelot Gobbo	*servant to Shylock*
Old Gobbo	*Launcelot's father*

Portia	*an heiress of Belmont*
Nerissa	*her lady-in-waiting*

Prince of Morocco	
Prince of Arragon	*suitors to Portia*

Balthazar	
Stephano	*servants to Portia*

Merchants, Officers of the Court of Justice, Gaoler, Musicians, Servants

Act 1

Act 1 Scene 1

Antonio, the great merchant, is sad, but
he cannot tell his friends the reason for
his sadness. They suggest various
possible causes for anxiety, and try to
make him laugh. Antonio is waiting to
meet his best friend, Bassanio, who
confesses to Antonio that he has spent
a great deal of money, and also that he
is in love with Portia, a rich heiress.
Antonio has no more money to lend
to Bassanio at present, but promises to
help him to borrow from the money-
lenders so that he can visit Portia.

1   *In sooth*: truly.
2   *It*: his sadness.
3   *came by*: got.
5   *am to learn*: do not know.
6   *want-wit*: idiot.
7   *ado*: trouble.

Scene 1 *Venice. A street*

Enter Antonio, Salerio, *and* Solanio

Antonio
In sooth, I know not why I am so sad:
It wearies me; you say it wearies you;
But how I caught it, found it, or came by it,
What stuff 'tis made of, whereof it is born,
5 I am to learn;
And such a want-wit sadness makes of me,
That I have much ado to know myself.
    Salerio
Your mind is tossing on the ocean,
There, where your argosies with portly sail,
10 Like signiors and rich burghers on the flood,
Or, as it were, the pageants of the sea,
Do overpeer the petty traffickers,

9   *argosies*: merchant ships.
     portly: stately.
10   *signiors*: gentlemen (the modern
     Italian word is *signori*).
     burghers: citizens.
     flood: sea.
11   *pageants*: decorated carts in
     carnival processions.
12   *overpeer*: look over the heads of.
     petty traffickers: small commercial
     boats.
13   *That . . . reverence*: that bob up
     and down, as if they were showing
     respect.
15   *had . . . forth*: if I had such
     business abroad.
16   *affections*: concerns.
17   *still*: always.
18   *Plucking . . . wind*: holding up a
     blade of grass to see in which direction
     the wind is blowing.
19   *roads*: harbours.
21   *out of doubt*: without doubt,
     certainly.
22   *wind*: breath.
     broth: soup.
23   *ague*: fit of shivering.
25   *sandy hour-glass*. Two spheres of
     glass were joined together, with a tiny
     hole between them; sand ran from one
     sphere to the other, taking just an hour
     to do so.
26   *shallows*: shallow waters.
     flats: sandbanks.
27   *Andrew*: a common name for a
     big ship at this time; despite the mascu-
     line name, the ship—like all English
     ships—is referred to as feminine.
     dock'd: run ashore.
28   *Vailing her high-top*: lowering
     her mast.
     ribs: the wooden sides of the
     ship.
29   *burial*: the sand in which the
     ship is being buried.
31   *straight*: immediately.
32   *touching but*: only by touching.
     vessel: both 'ship' and 'con-
     tainer'.

That curtsy to them, do them reverence,
As they fly by them with their woven wings.

Solanio
15   Believe me, sir, had I such venture forth,
     The better part of my affections would
     Be with my hopes abroad. I should be still
     Plucking the grass to know where sits the wind;
     Peering in maps for ports, and piers, and roads;
20   And every object that might make me fear
     Misfortune to my ventures, out of doubt
     Would make me sad.

Salerio   My wind, cooling my broth,
     Would blow me to an ague, when I thought
     What harm a wind too great might do at sea.
25   I should not see the sandy hour-glass run
     But I should think of shallows and of flats,
     And see my wealthy Andrew dock'd in sand
     Vailing her high-top lower than her ribs
     To kiss her burial. Should I go to church
30   And see the holy edifice of stone,
     And not bethink me straight of dangerous rocks,
     Which touching but my gentle vessel's side

33-4 *spices . . . silks*: i.e. the cargo.
34 *Enrobe*: clothe.
35 *in a word*: briefly.
35-6 *but . . . nothing*: just a moment ago the cargo was so valuable, and now it is worth nothing.
36-8 *Shall . . . sad*: if I have the imagination to think that this could happen, shall I not also have the imagination to think that, if it happened ('bechanc'd') it would make me sad?
41 *fortune*: both 'luck' and 'wealth'.
42 *ventures*: business.
   bottom: ship.
44 *fortune*: chance.

46 *Fie, fie*: nonsense.

50 *Janus*: a Roman god, always placed above doorways, with one head looking inwards and the other looking out.
51 *fram'd*: constructed.
52 *evermore*: always.
   peep . . . eyes: wrinkle their faces in laughter, so that their eyes appear to be peeping through the folds.
53 *parrots at a bag-piper*. Bagpipes make a dreary noise, and only someone as brainless as a parrot will laugh at it.
54 *vinegar*: bitter.
   aspect: nature.
56 *Nestor*: an old and solemn Greek general, who fought in the Trojan War; a joke must have been very funny if Nestor laughed at it.
57 *kinsman*: probably Solanio means 'friend' and not 'relative'.
62 *regard*: esteem.
63 *calls on*: needs.
64 *embrace th' occasion*: are glad of the chance.

Would scatter all her spices on the stream,
Enrobe the roaring waters with my silks;
35 And, in a word, but even now worth this,
And now worth nothing? Shall I have the thought
To think on this, and shall I lack the thought
That such a thing bechanc'd would make me sad?
But tell not me: I know Antonio
40 Is sad to think upon his merchandise.
   Antonio
Believe me, no: I thank my fortune for it,
My ventures are not in one bottom trusted,
Nor to one place; nor is my whole estate
Upon the fortune of this present year:
45 Therefore, my merchandise makes me not sad.
   Solanio
Why, then you are in love.
   Antonio   Fie, fie!
   Salerio
Not in love neither? Then let us say you are sad
Because you are not merry: and 'twere as easy
For you to laugh and leap, and say you are merry
50 Because you are not sad. Now, by two-headed Janus,
Nature hath fram'd strange fellows in her time:
Some that will evermore peep through their eyes,
And laugh like parrots at a bag-piper;
And other of such vinegar aspect
55 That they'll not show their teeth in way of smile,
Though Nestor swear the jest be laughable.

   Enter Bassanio, Lorenzo, *and* Gratiano
   Solanio
Here comes Bassanio, your most noble kinsman,
Gratiano, and Lorenzo. Fare ye well:
We leave you now with better company.
   Salerio
60 I would have stay'd till I had made you merry,
If worthier friends had not prevented me.
   Antonio
Your worth is very dear in my regard.
I take it, your own business calls on you,
And you embrace th' occasion to depart.

66   *laugh*: meet to enjoy ourselves.
67   *You . . . strange*: we don't see
you very often.
68   We will have time to spare whenever you do.
71   *have in mind*: remember.
74   You worry about the world too
much.
75   Those who spend a lot of time
worrying about worldly matters (such
as success and happiness) are never
really successful or happy.
76   *you . . . chang'd*: your appearance has changed a great deal.
77   *hold*: think of.
81   *liver*. The Elizabethans believed
that there were four basic character-
types—the choleric, the melancholy,
the phlegmatic, and the sanguine—and
that these types were in part physio-
logically determined, by the digestion
of food in the liver. A liver heated by
wine would produce rich blood, and so
a lively, sanguine personality.
82   *heart . . . groans*. The Elizabethans thought that sighs and groans
caused the blood to drain away from
the heart.
      mortifying: killing.
84   *like . . . alabaster*: like the white
stone statue on his grandfather's tomb.
85   *Sleep . . . wakes*: be as still and
silent during the day as if he were
asleep.
      jaundice: a disease that turns the
skin yellow; it was thought by the
Elizabethans to be associated with
jealousy and bad temper (peevishness).
87   *'tis . . . speaks*: I am saying this
because I love you.
88-9 *whose . . . pond*: whose faces are
covered in a mask as white and thick as
the film on a stagnant pond.
90   *do . . . entertain*: deliberately
(wilfully) put on an air of solemnity.
91   *With purpose*: in order.
      to be . . . opinion: to gain a
reputation.
92   *profound conceit*: deep thought.

Salerio

65 Good morrow, my good lords.

Bassanio

Good signiors both, when shall we laugh? say,
      when?
You grow exceeding strange: must it be so?

Salerio

We'll make our leisures to attend on yours.

[*Exeunt* Salerio *and* Solanio

Lorenzo

My Lord Bassanio, since you have found Antonio,

70 We two will leave you; but, at dinner-time,
I pray you, have in mind where we must meet.

Bassanio

I will not fail you.

Gratiano

You look not well, Signior Antonio;
You have too much respect upon the world:

75 They lose it that do buy it with much care.
Believe me, you are marvellously chang'd.

Antonio

I hold the world but as the world, Gratiano;
A stage where every man must play a part,
And mine a sad one.

Gratiano   Let me play the fool:

80 With mirth and laughter let old wrinkles come,
And let my liver rather heat with wine
Than my heart cool with mortifying groans.
Why should a man, whose blood is warm within,
Sit like his grandsire cut in alabaster,

85 Sleep when he wakes, and creep into the jaundice
By being peevish? I tell thee what, Antonio—
I love thee, and 'tis my love that speaks—
There are a sort of men whose visages
Do cream and mantle like a standing pond,

90 And do a wilful stillness entertain,
With purpose to be dress'd in an opinion
Of wisdom, gravity, profound conceit,

93   *As who should say*: as though he
were to say.

      I am Sir Oracle: I speak with the
authority of the Greek oracle. The
oracle was the voice of the gods, speaking through the mouths of priests.

94   *ope*: open.

96-7   *That . . . nothing*: who have a
reputation for being wise only because
they never say anything.

98-9   If they were to speak, their
listeners would say they were fools, and
for saying this the listeners would be
damned (because the Bible says that
'whosoever shall say to his brother . . .
"Thou fool", shall be in danger of hell
fire'; St. Matthew 5: 22).

101-2   Don't try to use this sadness to
get such a reputation which is like a
silly little fish (not worth having).

104   *exhortation*: sermon.

110   *grow*: become.
         for this gear: because of this
nonsense.

112   *a neat's tongue dried*: an ox-
tongue, preserved and ready to be
eaten.
         a maid not vendible: an old maid
(one whom no-one will buy—or
marry).

115   *reasons*: thoughts.

117   *ere*: before.

119   *the same*: she.

123   *disabled*: damaged.

124-5   By living in a rather grander
style ('port') than my means will permit
('grant continuance').

As who should say, 'I am Sir Oracle,
And when I ope my lips, let no dog bark!'
95 O my Antonio, I do know of these
That therefore only are reputed wise
For saying nothing; when, I am very sure,
If they should speak, would almost damn those ears
Which, hearing them, would call their brothers
      fools.
100 I'll tell thee more of this another time:
But fish not, with this melancholy bait,
For this fool-gudgeon, this opinion.
Come, good Lorenzo. Fare ye well awhile:
I'll end my exhortation after dinner.
      Lorenzo
105 Well, we will leave you then till dinner-time.
I must be one of these same dumb wise men,
For Gratiano never lets me speak.
      Gratiano
Well, keep me company but two years more,
Thou shalt not know the sound of thine own tongue.
      Antonio
110 Fare you well: I'll grow a talker for this gear.
      Gratiano
Thanks, i' faith; for silence is only commendable
In a neat's tongue dried and a maid not vendible.
      [*Exeunt* Gratiano *and* Lorenzo
      Antonio
Is that anything now?
      Bassanio
Gratiano speaks an infinite deal of nothing, more
115 than any man in all Venice. His reasons are as two
grains of wheat hid in two bushels of chaff: you shall
seek all day ere you find them, and when you have
them, they are not worth the search.
      Antonio
Well, tell me now, what lady is the same
120 To whom you swore a secret pilgrimage,
That you today promis'd to tell me of?
      Bassanio
'Tis not unknown to you, Antonio,
How much I have disabled mine estate,
By something showing a more swelling port

126   *make moan*: complain.
    to be abridg'd: because I have
been forced to cut down my expenses.

127   *care*: concern.

129   *my time . . . prodigal*: my youth,
which has been rather too lavish;
Bassanio is comparing himself to the
Prodigal Son in Christ's parable (St.
Luke, chapter 15).

130   *gag'd*: in debt.

132-4   Because I know you love me,
I feel that I have your permission
('warranty') to set out before you all my
plans to free myself from the debts
I owe.

135   *it*: Bassanio's plan.

136-7   *stand . . . Within the eye of
honour*: looks honourable.

139   *Lie . . . occasions*: are all at your
disposal.

140   *shaft*: arrow.

141   *I . . . flight*: I shot an identical
arrow.

142   *The self-same*: exactly the same.
    more advised watch: watching it
more carefully.

143   *To . . . forth*: to find out the
other.
    adventuring: risking.

144   *urge*: offer.
    proof: example.

148   *self*: same.

150   *As . . . aim*: because I will take
care ('watch') with what I am doing.

150-1   *or . . . Or*: either . . . or.

151   *latter hazard*: the second loan
you have risked.

152   *thankfully rest debtor*: gratefully
remain in debt to you.

153   *spend but time*: only waste time.

154   To approach my love in such an
indirect, complicated way.

155   *out of doubt*: indeed.

156   In doubting that I will do everything I can.

157   *made waste of*: destroyed.

160   *prest unto it*: quite ready to do it.

161   *richly left*: who has inherited
great wealth.

162   *fairer than that word*: better than
fair.

125   Than my faint means would grant continuance:
    Nor do I now make moan to be abridg'd
    From such a noble rate; but my chief care
    Is, to come fairly off from the great debts
    Wherein my time, something too prodigal,
130   Hath left me gag'd. To you, Antonio,
    I owe the most, in money and in love;
    And from your love I have a warranty
    To unburden all my plots and purposes
    How to get clear of all the debts I owe.

Antonio

135   I pray you, good Bassanio, let me know it;
    And if it stand, as you yourself still do,
    Within the eye of honour, be assur'd,
    My purse, my person, my extremest means,
    Lie all unlock'd to your occasions.

Bassanio

140   In my school-days, when I had lost one shaft,
    I shot his fellow of the self-same flight
    The self-same way with more advised watch,
    To find the other forth; and by adventuring both,
    I oft found both. I urge this childhood proof,
145   Because what follows is pure innocence.
    I owe you much, and (like a wilful youth)
    That which I owe is lost; but if you please
    To shoot another arrow that self way
    Which you did shoot the first, I do not doubt,
150   (As I will watch the aim) or to find both,
    Or bring your latter hazard back again,
    And thankfully rest debtor for the first.

Antonio

    You know me well, and herein spend but time
    To wind about my love with circumstance;
155   And out of doubt you do me now more wrong
    In making question of my uttermost
    Than if you had made waste of all I have.
    Then do but say to me what I should do
    That in your knowledge may by me be done,
160   And I am prest unto it: therefore speak.

Bassanio

    In Belmont is a lady richly left,
    And she is fair, and, fairer than that word,
    Of wondrous virtues: sometimes from her eyes

164   *speechless*: unspoken.
165-6 *nothing undervalu'd To*: no less
       worthy than.
166   *Portia*: the daughter of a brave
       and noble Roman general, Portia was a
       tender and loving wife to Brutus (who
       led the conspiracy against Julius
       Caesar).
169   *locks*: hair.
170   *golden fleece*. In Greek mytho-
       logy, Jason led an expedition to
       Colchis in search of the golden ram's
       fleece.
171   *seat*: house.
       strand: shore.
172   *quest*: search.
173-4 *had I . . . them*: if I could become
       a rival with these suitors.
175   *presages*: prophesies.
       thrift: profitable success.
176   *questionless*: without doubt.
177   *fortunes*: wealth.
178   *commodity*: goods, security for a
       loan.
179   *a present sum*: cash.
180   See how much you can borrow
       in Venice, giving me as your security.
181   *rack'd*: stretched.
182   *furnish thee to Belmont*: provide
       what is necessary for you to go to
       Belmont.
183   *presently*: at once.
184-5 *I . . . sake*: I have no doubt but
       that you will be able to borrow money
       either formally on my credit, or for
       friendship's sake.

I did receive fair speechless messages:
165 Her name is Portia; nothing undervalu'd
To Cato's daughter, Brutus' Portia;
Nor is the wide world ignorant of her worth,
For the four winds blow in from every coast
Renowned suitors; and her sunny locks
170 Hang on her temples like a golden fleece;
Which makes her seat of Belmont Colchis' strand,
And many Jasons come in quest of her.
O my Antonio, had I but the means
To hold a rival place with one of them,
175 I have a mind presages me such thrift
That I should questionless be fortunate.
    Antonio
Thou know'st that all my fortunes are at sea;
Neither have I money, nor commodity
To raise a present sum: therefore go forth,
180 Try what my credit can in Venice do:
That shall be rack'd, even to the uttermost,
To furnish thee to Belmont, to fair Portia.
Go, presently inquire, and so will I,
Where money is, and I no question make
185 To have it of my trust or for my sake.   [*Exeunt*

Act 1   Scene 2

Portia and Nerissa talk about the test which Portia's suitors must take. Some men have already come to Belmont in the hope of marrying her, but when Portia describes them she makes fun of them and shows her dislike. Finally Nerissa reminds her of Bassanio.

1   *troth*: faith.
     aweary: tired.

4   *in the same abundance*: as plentiful.

5   *aught*: anything.
     surfeit: eat excessively.

7   *no mean happiness*: no little happiness.

7-8   *seated in the mean*: placed in the middle; Nerissa is playing with the two senses of 'mean'.

Scene 2 *Belmont. A room in Portia's house*

Enter Portia *and* Nerissa

Portia

By my troth, Nerissa, my little body is aweary of this great world.

Nerissa

You would be, sweet madam, if your miseries were in the same abundance as your good fortunes are:
5 and yet, for aught I see, they are as sick that surfeit with too much as they that starve with nothing. It is no mean happiness therefore, to be seated in the mean: superfluity comes sooner by white hairs, but competency lives longer.

Portia

10 Good sentences, and well pronounced.

8-9　Those who have too much (a 'superfluity') grow old quickly, but those who have just enough (a 'competency') live longer.

10　*sentences*: proverbs.
　pronounced: spoken. Portia is also hinting at the legal use of 'sentences' which are technically 'pronounced' by judges.

11　*followed*: obeyed.

13　*had been*: would have been.

14　*divine*: preacher.

18　*blood*: will. Portia is making the distinction between reason and will, or mind and body.

19-20　Youthful high spirits are like a hare, which easily leaps over the nets ('meshes') of limping good advice.

21　*reasoning*: wise talk.
　in the fashion: the right way.

22　*O me*: oh dear.

23　*I would*: I like.

24　*the will*: Portia plays with the two meanings, 'desire' and 'testament'.
　curbed: restrained.

27　*ever*: always.

30-1　*his meaning*: the one that Portia's father meant him to choose.

32　*rightly*: Nerissa plays with the two meanings, 'correctly' and 'truly'.

36　*over-name them*: call out their names.

38　*level*: guess.

39-98　For an explanation of the comedy of these lines, see Introduction, p. xiv.

39　*Neapolitan*: from Naples.

40　*colt*: awkward young man (like a young horse).

41-2　*a great . . . parts*: point in his own favour.

43　*afeard*: afraid.

44　*smith*: blacksmith.

45　*County Palatine*: a count who reigned over territory which in other countries would be ruled by a king.

Nerissa
They would be better if well followed.

Portia
If to do were as easy as to know what were good to do, chapels had been churches, and poor men's cottages princes' palaces. It is a good divine that
15　follows his own instructions: I can easier teach twenty what were good to be done, than be one of the twenty to follow mine own teaching. The brain may devise laws for the blood, but a hot temper leaps o'er a cold decree: such a hare is madness (the youth),
20　to skip o'er the meshes of good counsel (the cripple). But this reasoning is not in the fashion to choose me a husband. O me, the word 'choose'! I may neither choose who I would nor refuse who I dislike; so is the will of a living daughter curbed by the will of
25　a dead father. Is it not hard, Nerissa, that I cannot choose one, nor refuse none?

Nerissa
Your father was ever virtuous, and holy men at their death have good inspirations; therefore, the lottery that he hath devised in these three chests of
30　gold, silver, and lead, whereof who chooses his meaning chooses you, will, no doubt, never be chosen by any rightly but one who you shall rightly love. But what warmth is there in your affection towards any of these princely suitors that are
35　already come?

Portia
I pray thee, over-name them, and as thou namest them, I will describe them; and, according to my description, level at my affection.

Nerissa
First there is the Neapolitan prince.

Portia
40　Ay, that's a colt indeed, for he doth nothing but talk of his horse; and he makes it a great appropriation to his own good parts that he can shoe him himself. I am much afeard my lady his mother played false with a smith.

Nerissa
45　Then is there the County Palatine.

46   *as who should say*: as if he were to say.
47   *choose*: pick anyone you will.
48   *prove*: become like.
48-9   *the weeping philosopher*: Heraclitus of Ephesus, who went to live alone in the mountains because he was so distressed by mankind's stupidity.
50   *unmannerly*: rude.
51   *death's-head*: skull.

54   *How say you by*: what do you think of?

56   *pass for*: be accepted as.
57   *to be mocker*: to mock at.

60   *he is . . . no man*: he has everybody else's characteristics and no personality of his own.
61   *throstle*: thrush.
        falls straight a-capering: immediately starts jumping up and down (to the music).

70   *come into court*: bear witness.
71   *poor pennyworth*: not very much (as much as could be bought for a penny).
72   *proper man's picture*: the appearance of a handsome man.
73   *a dumb-show*: a mime, acting without words.
74   *suited*: dressed.
        doublet: tunic.
75   *round hose*: breeches.
76   *behaviour*: manners.
79   *borrowed . . . of*: received . . . from.
        a box of the ear: a blow on the ear.
81   *became his surety*: guaranteed that he would repay the debt.
        sealed under: signed his name underneath the Scotsman's signature on the (imaginary) bond.

Portia

He doth nothing but frown, as who should say, 'And you will not have me, choose.' He hears merry tales, and smiles not: I fear he will prove the weeping philosopher when he grows old, being so full of
50 unmannerly sadness in his youth. I had rather be married to a death's-head with a bone in his mouth than to either of these. God defend me from these two!

Nerissa

How say you by the French lord, Monsieur Le
55 Bon?

Portia

God made him, and therefore let him pass for a man. In truth, I know it is a sin to be mocker; but, he! why, he hath a horse better than the Neapolitan's, a better bad habit of frowning than
60 the Count Palatine; he is every man in no man; if a throstle sing, he falls straight a-capering; he will fence with his own shadow. If I should marry him, I should marry twenty husbands: if he would despise me, I would forgive him, for if he loves
65 me to madness, I shall never requite him.

Nerissa

What say you, then, to Falconbridge, the young baron of England?

Portia

You know I say nothing to him, for he understands not me, nor I him: he hath neither Latin, French,
70 nor Italian; and you will come into the court and swear that I have a poor pennyworth in the English. He is a proper man's picture, but, alas! who can converse with a dumb-show? How oddly he is suited! I think he bought his doublet in Italy, his
75 round hose in France, his bonnet in Germany, and his behaviour everywhere.

Nerissa

What think you of the Scottish lord, his neighbour?

Portia

That he hath a neighbourly charity in him, for he borrowed a box of the ear of the Englishman, and
80 swore he would pay him again when he was able: I think the Frenchman became his surety and sealed under for another.

88-9   *And . . . fell*: if ('And') the worst that ever happened ('fell') should happen ('fall').
89   *make shift*: manage.

91   *offer*: decide.

95   *Rhenish wine*: German white wine, from the district of the Rhine.
        contrary: other.

99   *the having*: that you will have to accept.
100   *acquainted me with*: informed me of.
        determinations: decisions.
103   *sort*: way.

105   *Sibylla*: the Sibyl of Cumae, a prophetess in classical mythology; Apollo granted her as many years of life as the number of grains of sand that she held in her hand.
106   *Diana*: the goddess of virginity in classical mythology.
107   *parcel*: set.

Nerissa

How like you the young German, the Duke of Saxony's nephew?

Portia

85 Very vilely in the morning, when he is sober, and most vilely in the afternoon, when he is drunk: when he is best, he is a little worse than a man, and when he is worst, he is little better than a beast. And the worst fall that ever fell, I hope I shall make shift
90 to go without him.

Nerissa

If he should offer to choose, and choose the right casket, you should refuse to perform your father's will, if you should refuse to accept him.

Portia

Therefore, for fear of the worst, I pray thee, set a
95 deep glass of Rhenish wine on the contrary casket, for, if the devil be within and that temptation without, I know he will choose it. I will do anything, Nerissa, ere I will be married to a sponge.

Nerissa

You need not fear, lady, the having any of these
100 lords: they have acquainted me with their determinations; which is, indeed, to return to their home and to trouble you with no more suit, unless you may be won by some other sort than your father's imposition depending on the caskets.

Portia

105 If I live to be as old as Sibylla, I will die as chaste as Diana, unless I be obtained by the manner of my father's will. I am glad this parcel of wooers are so reasonable, for there is not one among them but I dote on his very absence, and I pray God grant
110 them a fair departure.

Nerissa

Do you not remember, lady, in your father's time, a Venetian, a scholar and a soldier, that came hither in company of the Marquis of Montferrat?

Portia

Yes, yes: it was Bassanio—as I think so was he
115 called.

True, madam: he of all the men that ever my foolish
eyes looked upon, was the best deserving a fair
lady.
    Portia
I remember him well, and I remember him worthy
120 of thy praise.

    Enter a Servant
How now, what news?
    Servant
The four strangers seek for you, madam, to take
their leave; and there is a forerunner come from a
fifth, the Prince of Morocco, who brings word the
125 prince his master will be here tonight.
    Portia
If I could bid the fifth welcome with so good heart
as I can bid the other four farewell, I should be glad
of his approach: if he have the condition of a saint
and the complexion of a devil, I had rather he
130 should shrive me than wive me.
Come, Nerissa. [*To Attendant*] Sirrah, go before.
Whiles we shut the gate upon one wooer, another
    knocks at the door.   [*Exeunt*

Scene 3 *Venice. A public place*

    Enter Bassanio *and* Shylock
    Shylock
Three thousand ducats; well.
    Bassanio
Ay, sir, for three months.
    Shylock
For three months; well.
    Bassanio
For the which, as I told you, Antonio shall be
5 bound.
    Shylock
Antonio shall become bound; well.

122   *four*. Shakespeare seems to have
forgotten that six suitors have been
discussed.
123   *fore-runner*: messenger who came
ahead of his master, herald.

128   *condition*: nature.
129   *complexion*: appearance.
130   *shrive me*: hear my confession
and give absolutions—as a holy man or
'saint' would.
    wive me: make me his wife.

Act 1   Scene 3
Shylock is able to lend money to
Bassanio, but he makes it clear that he
hates Antonio. Shylock and Antonio
argue about the morality of making a
profit from money-lending, and
Shylock reminds Antonio of his past
insults. However, he agrees to lend the
money; but he asks for an unusual
bond.
1   *ducats*: Venetian gold coins.

5   *bound*: as security.

7   *stead*: supply.

Bassanio

May you stead me? Will you pleasure me? Shall
I know your answer?

Shylock

Three thousand ducats, for three months, and
10 Antonio bound.

Bassanio

Your answer to that?

Shylock

Antonio is a good man.

Bassanio

Have you heard any imputation to the contrary?

Shylock

Ho, no, no, no, no; my meaning in saying he is
15 a good man is to have you understand me that he is
sufficient. Yet his means are in supposition: he hath
an argosy bound to Tripolis, another to the Indies;
I understand moreover, upon the Rialto, he hath
a third at Mexico, a fourth for England, and other
20 ventures he hath squandered abroad. But ships are
but boards, sailors but men: there be land-rats and
water-rats, water-thieves and land-thieves—I mean
pirates—and then there is the peril of waters, winds,
and rocks. The man is, notwithstanding, sufficient.
25 Three thousand ducats; I think I may take his bond.

16   *sufficient*: financially adequate.
are in supposition: have to be
taken on trust (because his property is
all outside Venice, as Shylock goes on
to explain).
17   *argosy*: merchant ship.
18   *the Rialto*: the Venetian Stock
Exchange; the name is often used
today for the bridge leading to the
Exchange.
20   *squandered*: scattered lavishly.

Bassanio

Be assured you may.

Shylock

I will be assured I may; and, that I may be assured,
I will bethink me. May I speak with Antonio?

Bassanio

If it please you to dine with us.

Shylock

30 Yes, to smell pork; to eat of the habitation which
your prophet the Nazarite conjured the devil into.
I will buy with you, sell with you, talk with you,
walk with you, and so following; but I will not eat
with you, drink with you, nor pray with you. What
35 news on the Rialto? Who is he comes here?

30   *pork*: meat forbidden to the
Jews.
30-1   *the habitation . . . into*: Jesus
('the Nazarite') healed a madman by
ordering the devils that possessed his
mind to leave the man and enter into
a herd of pigs (St. Mark 5: 1-13).
33   *and so following*: etc.

Enter Antonio

Bassanio

This is Signior Antonio

Shylock

[*Aside*] How like a fawning publican he looks!
I hate him for he is a Christian;

37   *fawning*: servile.
publican: innkeeper.
38   *for*: because.

39	*low*: base.
	simplicity: foolishness.
40	*gratis*: free of interest.
41	*usance*: usury, money-lending.
42	*upon the hip*: off his guard, at a disadvantage.
43	*feed fat*: i.e. as though the grudge were an animal to be looked after.
44	*rails*: abuses.
46	*thrift*: success.
47	*interest*: profit.
49	*debating of*: reckoning up.
	present store: ready money.
50	*near*: close.
51	*gross*: whole sum.
54	*furnish*: supply.
	soft: wait a minute.
56	*in our mouths*: that we were talking about.
57	*albeit*: although.
58	*excess*: interest (an amount exceeding the original sum lent or borrowed).
59	*ripe*: urgent.
60	*possess'd*: informed.
61	*would*: want.
66	*Upon advantage*: with interest.
	I do never use it: I have never done it.
67–84	There are two stories about Jacob in the Book of Genesis. The first (chapters 25 and 27) tell how, with the aid of 'his wise mother', he tricked his elder brother of his birth-right, and so became the heir to his father and to his grandfather, Abraham, the founder of the Jewish race. The second story (chapter 30) tells of Jacob's cunning trick with Laban's sheep; Shylock recounts this episode.
67	*graz'd*: shepherded.
69	*wrought*: devised.

But more for that in low simplicity
40 He lends out money gratis, and brings down
The rate of usance here with us in Venice.
If I can catch him once upon the hip,
I will feed fat the ancient grudge I bear him.
He hates our sacred nation, and he rails,
45 Even there where merchants most do congregate,
On me, my bargains, and my well-won thrift,
Which he calls interest. Cursed be my tribe,
If I forgive him!

Bassanio   Shylock, do you hear?

Shylock
I am debating of my present store,
50 And, by the near guess of my memory,
I cannot instantly raise up the gross
Of full three thousand ducats. What of that?
Tubal, a wealthy Hebrew of my tribe,
Will furnish me. But soft! how many months
55 Do you desire? [*To* Antonio] Rest you fair, good
        signior;
Your worship was the last man in our mouths.

Antonio
Shylock, albeit I neither lend nor borrow
By taking nor by giving of excess,
Yet, to supply the ripe wants of my friend,
60 I'll break a custom. [*To* Bassanio] Is he yet possess'd
How much ye would?

Shylock   Ay, ay, three thousand ducats.

Antonio
And for three months.

Shylock
I had forgot; three months; you told me so.
Well then, your bond; and let me see—but hear you;
65 Methought you said, you neither lend nor borrow
Upon advantage.

Antonio   I do never use it.

Shylock
When Jacob graz'd his uncle Laban's sheep—
This Jacob from our holy Abram was,
As his wise mother wrought in his behalf,
70 The third possessor: ay, he was the third—

Antonio
And what of him? did he take interest?

Shylock
No, not take interest; not, as you would say,
Directly interest: mark what Jacob did.
When Laban and himself were compromis'd,
75 That all the eanlings which were streak'd and pied
Should fall as Jacob's hire, the ewes, being rank,
In end of autumn turned to the rams;
And, when the work of generation was
Between these woolly breeders in the act,
80 The skilful shepherd pill'd me certain wands,
And, in the doing of the deed of kind,
He stuck them up before the fulsome ewes,
Who, then conceiving, did in eaning time
Fall parti-colour'd lambs, and those were Jacob's.
85 This was a way to thrive, and he was blest:
And thrift is blessing, if men steal it not.

Antonio
This was a venture, sir, that Jacob serv'd for;
A thing not in his power to bring to pass,
But sway'd and fashion'd by the hand of heaven.
90 Was this inserted to make interest good?
Or is your gold and silver ewes and rams?

Shylock
I cannot tell; I make it breed as fast:
But note me, signior.—

Antonio   Mark you this, Bassanio,
The devil can cite Scripture for his purpose.
95 An evil soul, producing holy witness,
Is like a villain with a smiling cheek,
A goodly apple rotten at the heart.
O what a goodly outside falsehood hath!

Shylock
Three thousand ducats; 'tis a good round sum.
100 Three months from twelve: then, let me see, the
rate—

Antonio
Well, Shylock, shall we be beholding to you?

Shylock
Signior Antonio, many a time and oft
In the Rialto you have rated me
About my moneys and my usances:
105 Still have I borne it with a patient shrug,
For sufferance is the badge of all our tribe.

---

74   *compromis'd*: agreed.
75   *eanlings*: new-born lambs.
      streak'd and pied: with fleeces of two colours.
76   *fall as Jacob's hire*: be counted as Jacob's wages.
      rank: on heat, ready for mating.
80   *pill'd . . . wands*: peeled the bark from some twigs (so that they appeared to be striped).
81   *deed of kind*: act of breeding.
82   *fulsome*: passionate.
83   *eaning*: lambing.
84   *Fall*: give birth to.
86   *thrift*: profit.

87   *venture*: enterprise.
      serv'd for: was a servant for.
88   *sway'd*: ruled.
      fashion'd: shaped.
90   Did you introduce this story as a justification of usury?

94   *cite*: quote.

101   *beholding*: indebted.

102   *oft*: often.
103   *rated*: scolded.
104   *usances*: financial deals.
105   *Still*: always.
106   *sufferance*: long-suffering.
      badge: characteristic.

107   *misbeliever*: heretic, unbeliever.

108   *gaberdine*: long loose coat, worn traditionally by Jews.

111   *Go to, then*: and now what are you doing (an expression of exasperation).

112   *moneys*. The plural form may be Shakespeare's attempt to indicate some Jewish speech habit.

113   *void your rheum*: spit.

114   *foot*: kick.

115   *suit*: request.

119   *key*: tone.

120   *With bated breath*: anxiously.

126   *as like*: just as likely.

130   *A breed ... metal*: a product of sterile metal.

132   *break*: fail to keep his bond.

136   *doit*: jot (a very small amount).

137   *usance*: interest.

138   *kind*: kindness; but see Introduction, p. xvi.

140   *notary*: solicitor.
      seal me: sign for me.

141   *single*: simple.
      in a merry sport: as a joke.

144   *Express'd in the condition*: set down in the formal agreement.

145   *nominated for*: named as.
      equal: accurate.

You call me misbeliever, cut-throat dog,
And spit upon my Jewish gaberdine,
And all for use of that which is mine own.
110 Well then, it now appears you need my help:
Go to then; you come to me, and you say,
'Shylock, we would have moneys:' you say so;
You, that did void your rheum upon my beard,
And foot me as you spurn a stranger cur
115 Over your threshold. Moneys is your suit.
What should I say to you? Should I not say,
'Hath a dog money? Is it possible
A cur can lend three thousand ducats?' or
Shall I bend low, and in a bondman's key,
120 With bated breath, and whispering humbleness,
Say this:
'Fair sir, you spat on me on Wednesday last;
You spurn'd me such a day; another time
You call'd me dog—and for these courtesies
125 I'll lend you thus much moneys'?

   Antonio
I am as like to call thee so again,
To spit on thee again, to spurn thee too.
If thou wilt lend this money, lend it not
As to thy friends, for when did friendship take
130 A breed for barren metal of his friend?
But lend it rather to thine enemy;
Who if he break, thou may'st with better face
Exact the penalty.

   Shylock   Why, look you, how you storm!
I would be friends with you, and have your love,
135 Forget the shames that you have stain'd me with,
Supply your present wants, and take no doit
Of usance for my moneys, and you'll not hear me:
This is kind I offer.

   Bassanio
This were kindness.

   Shylock   This kindness will I show.
140 Go with me to a notary, seal me there
Your single bond; and, in a merry sport,
If you repay me not on such a day,
In such a place, such sum or sums as are
Express'd in the condition, let the forfeit
145 Be nominated for an equal pound

Of your fair flesh, to be cut off and taken
In what part of your body pleaseth me.
Antonio
Content, in faith: I'll seal to such a bond,
And say there is much kindness in the Jew.
Bassanio
150 You shall not seal to such a bond for me:
I'll rather dwell in my necessity.
Antonio
Why, fear not, man, I will not forfeit it:
Within these two months, that's a month before
This bond expires, I do expect return
155 Of thrice three times the value of this bond.
Shylock
O father Abram, what these Christians are,
Whose own hard dealings teaches them suspect
The thoughts of others! Pray you, tell me this:
If he should break his day, what should I gain
160 By the exaction of the forfeiture?
A pound of man's flesh, taken from a man,
Is not so estimable, profitable neither,
As flesh of muttons, beefs, or goats. I say,
To buy his favour, I extend this friendship:
165 If he will take it, so; if not, adieu;
And, for my love, I pray you wrong me not.
Antonio
Yes, Shylock, I will seal unto this bond.
Shylock
Then meet me forthwith at the notary's;
Give him direction for this merry bond.
170 And I will go and purse the ducats straight,
See to my house, left in the fearful guard
Of an unthrifty knave, and presently
I'll be with you.   [*Exit* Shylock
Antonio   Hie thee, gentle Jew.
The Hebrew will turn Christian: he grows kind.
Bassanio
175 I like not fair terms and a villain's mind.
Antonio
Come on: in this there can be no dismay;
My ships come home a month before the day.
                                        [*Exeunt*

151   *dwell*: remain.

157   *hard*: tough.
       suspect: be suspicious of.

159   *break his day*: fail to pay on the
       agreed date.

170   *purse the ducats*: put the ducats
       in a purse.
171   *fearful*: not to be trusted.
172   *unthrifty*: careless.
       knave: lad, servant.

Act 2

Act 2   Scene 1
Portia meets the Prince of Morocco, who wants to marry her; he chooses to try his luck with the caskets, although she warns him of the penalty he must pay if he makes the wrong choice.

1   *Mislike*: dislike.
2   *shadow'd*: dark.
     livery: uniform.
3   *near bred*: closely related.
4   *fairest*: both 'most handsome' and 'with the palest skin'.
5   *Phœbus*: the classical sun-god.
6   And let us [himself and the fair northern prince] cut ourselves for love of you.
7   *whose blood is reddest*: the Elizabethans believed that red blood was a sign of good spirits and courage; see note to *1, 1, 80*.
8   *aspect*: appearance.
9   *fear'd*: frightened.
10   *regarded*: esteemed.
     clime: climate, country.
11   *hue*: colour.
12   *steal your thoughts*: win your affections.
13   *In terms of choice*: in the matter of choosing.
13-14 *I am . . . eyes*: I am not influenced only by what my eyes (which are not easy to please—'nice') tell me to do.
15   *the lottery of my destiny*: the fact that my fate depends upon luck.

Scene 1 *Belmont. A room in Portia's house*

Enter the Prince of Morocco, *and his* Followers; Portia *and* Nerissa

Morocco
Mislike me not for my complexion,
The shadow'd livery of the burnish'd sun,
To whom I am a neighbour, and near bred.
Bring me the fairest creature northward born,
5 Where Phœbus' fire scarce thaws the icicles,
And let us make incision for your love,
To prove whose blood is reddest, his or mine.
I tell thee, lady, this aspect of mine
Hath fear'd the valiant: by my love, I swear
10 The best regarded virgins of our clime
Have lov'd it too: I would not change this hue,
Except to steal your thoughts, my gentle queen.

Portia
In terms of choice I am not solely led
By nice direction of a maiden's eyes;
15 Besides, the lottery of my destiny
Bars me the right of voluntary choosing:
But if my father had not scanted me
And hedg'd me by his wit, to yield myself
His wife who wins me by that means I told you,
20 Yourself, renowned prince, then stood as fair
As any comer I have look'd on yet
For my affection.

Morocco   Even for that I thank you:
Therefore, I pray you, lead me to the caskets

16   *Bars*: forbids.
    voluntary choosing: choosing
what I want.
17   *scanted*: restricted.
18   *hedg'd me*: bound me in.
    wit: wisdom.
18-19   *to yield myself His wife*: to give
myself as a wife to that man.
20   *stood as fair*: had as good a
chance (with, also, a play on 'fair' =
fair-skinned).
21   *any comer*: anyone who has
come.
24   *scimitar*: short, curved sword.
25   *Sophy*: Emperor of Persia.
26   *of*: from.
    Sultan Solyman: leader of the
Turks against the Persians in 1535.
27   *o'erstare*: outface, defy.
31   *alas the while*: Morocco sighs.
32   *Hercules and Lichas*: Hercules
was the super-man of classical mythology and Lichas was his servant.
33   *Which . . . man*: to find out
which is the better man.
35   *Alcides*: another name for
Hercules, meaning 'son of Alcaeus'.
42   *In way of*: on the subject of.
    advis'd: warned.
43   *Nor will not*: I will not ask anyone else to marry me.
    chance: fate, trial.
44   *forward*: let us go forward.
45   *hazard*: gamble.
46   *cursed'st*: most cursed.

Act 2   Scene 2

Launcelot Gobbo, Shylock's servant, is
wondering whether he ought to run
away from his master. Old Gobbo, his
father, comes on to the stage in search
of his son; because he is blind he does
not recognize Launcelot, who plays a
rather cruel trick on him. Old Gobbo
asks Bassanio to give employment to
Launcelot, which Bassanio agrees to do.
Gratiano also asks a favour from
Bassanio: he wants to accompany him
to Belmont. Bassanio agrees, but he
warns Gratiano that he must behave
properly.

To try my fortune. By this scimitar—
25 That slew the Sophy, and a Persian prince
That won three fields of Sultan Solyman—
I would o'erstare the sternest eyes that look;
Outbrave the heart most daring on the earth;
Pluck the young sucking cubs from the she-bear;
30 Yea, mock the lion when he roars for prey,
To win thee, lady. But, alas the while!
If Hercules and Lichas play at dice
Which is the better man, the greater throw
May turn by fortune from the weaker hand:
35 So is Alcides beaten by his page;
And so may I, blind fortune leading me,
Miss that which one unworthier may attain,
And die with grieving.
    Portia   You must take your chance;
And either not attempt to choose at all,
40 Or swear before you choose, if you choose wrong,
Never to speak to lady afterward
In way of marriage: therefore be advis'd.
    Morocco
Nor will not: come, bring me unto my chance.
    Portia
First, forward to the temple: after dinner
45 Your hazard shall be made.
    Morocco   Good fortune then!
To make me blest or cursed'st among men!
                      [Exeunt

Scene 2 *Venice. The street outside Shylock's house*

Enter Launcelot Gobbo
    Launcelot
Certainly my conscience will serve me to run from
this Jew my master. The fiend is at mine elbow,
and tempts me, saying to me, 'Gobbo, Launcelot
Gobbo, good Launcelot,' or 'good Gobbo,' or 'good
5 Launcelot Gobbo, use your legs, take the start, run
away.' My conscience says, 'No; take heed, honest
Launcelot; take heed, honest Gobbo;' or, as afore-
said, 'honest Launcelot Gobbo; do not run; scorn
running with thy heels.' Well, the most courageous

1 *serve*: assist.

6 *heed*: care.

8–9 *scorn . . . heels*: both 'be utterly contemptuous of running' and 'be contemptuous of using your legs to run away'.

10 *pack*: hurry off.
  Via: on your way (Latin).

11 *for the heavens*: for heaven's sake.
  rouse up: awaken.

13 *hanging . . . heart*: clinging to my heart (like a wife with her arms round his neck).

15–16 *honest woman*: virtuous woman.

16–17 *my father . . . grow to*: Launcelot hints, without completing the suggestion, that his father enjoyed the company of women other than his wife.

18 *budge*: move.

23 *God bless the mark*: a phrase meaning, roughly, 'if I may say so'.

25 *saving your reverence*: a phrase meaning, roughly, 'with all due respect'. Launcelot is apologizing to the audience for using such strong language ('the devil').

27 *incarnation*: Launcelot's error for 'incarnate' (= in the flesh).
  in my conscience: to speak truly.

28 *hard*: strict.

34 *true-begotten father*: a joke, because it is the father who begets the son.

35 *sand-blind*: half-blind.
  high gravel-blind: almost completely blind (which would be 'stone-blind').

36 *try confusions*: try out a test on him.

40 *marry*: by the Virgin Mary (a mild oath).

---

10 fiend bids me pack: '*Via!*' says the fiend; 'away!' says the fiend; 'for the heavens, rouse up a brave mind,' says the fiend, 'and run.' Well, my conscience, hanging about the neck of my heart, says very wisely to me, 'My honest friend Launcelot, 15 being an honest man's son,'—or rather an honest woman's son, for, indeed, my father did something smack, something grow to, he had a kind of taste— well, my conscience says, 'Launcelot, budge not.' 'Budge!' says the fiend. 'Budge not!' says my 20 conscience. 'Conscience,' say I, 'you counsel well;' 'Fiend,' say I, 'you counsel well.' To be ruled by my conscience, I should stay with the Jew my master, who (God bless the mark!) is a kind of devil; and, to run away from the Jew, I should be ruled 25 by the fiend, who (saving your reverence) is the devil himself. Certainly, the Jew is the very devil incarnation; and, in my conscience, my conscience is but a kind of hard conscience, to offer to counsel me to stay with the Jew. The fiend gives the more 30 friendly counsel: I will run, fiend; my heels are at your commandment; I will run.

Enter Old Gobbo, *with a basket*

Gobbo

Master young man, you; I pray you, which is the way to Master Jew's?

Launcelot

[*Aside*] O heavens! this is my true-begotten father, 35 who, being more than sand-blind, high gravel-blind, knows me not: I will try confusions with him.

Gobbo

Master young gentleman, I pray you, which is the way to Master Jew's?

Launcelot

Turn up on your right hand at the next turning, 40 but, at the next turning of all, on your left; marry, at the very next turning, turn of no hand, but turn down indirectly to the Jew's house.

43   *sonties*: saints (Old Gobbo speaks a country dialect).
      hit: find.
44   *one Launcelot*: a certain Launcelot.

47   *raise the waters*: bring tears to his eyes.

51   *well to live*: in good health.

52   *'a*: he.

55   *ergo*: Latin for 'therefore'—but Launcelot does not know the meaning, and uses the word merely to bewilder the old man.
57   *an 't*: if it.
      mastership: Gobbo invents the word, as being suitable for one who so insists on calling Launcelot 'master' (compare 'lordship' and 'ladyship').
59   *father*: a common way of addressing an old man; Launcelot uses it for comedy.
61   *the sisters three*: the Fates, three goddesses in classical mythology who controlled human destiny.

66   *hovel-post*: main timber supporting a poor dwelling.

68   *Alack the day*: Old Gobbo groans.

Gobbo
By God's sonties, 'twill be a hard way to hit. Can you tell me whether one Launcelot, that dwells with
45 him, dwell with him or no?
Launcelot
Talk you of young Master Launcelot? [*Aside*] Mark me now; now will I raise the waters. Talk you of young Master Launcelot?
Gobbo
No 'master', sir, but a poor man's son; his father,
50 though I say 't, is an honest, exceeding poor man, and, God be thanked, well to live.
Launcelot
Well, let his father be what 'a will, we talk of young Master Launcelot.
Gobbo
Your worship's friend, and Launcelot, sir.
Launcelot
55 But I pray you, *ergo*, old man, *ergo*, I beseech you, talk you of young Master Launcelot?
Gobbo
Of Launcelot, an 't please your mastership.
Launcelot
Ergo, Master Launcelot. Talk not of Master Launcelot, father; for the young gentleman (accord-
60 ing to fates and destinies and such odd sayings, the sisters three and such branches of learning) is, indeed, deceased; or, as you would say in plain terms, gone to heaven.
Gobbo
Marry, God forbid! the boy was the very staff of
65 my age, my very prop.
Launcelot
[*Aside*] Do I look like a cudgel or a hovel-post, a staff or a prop? Do you know me, father?
Gobbo
Alack the day! I know you not, young gentleman: but I pray you, tell me, is my boy—God rest his
70 soul!—alive or dead?

Launcelot

Do you not know me, father?

Gobbo

Alack, sir, I am sand-blind; I know you not.

Launcelot

Nay, indeed, if you had your eyes, you might fail
of the knowing me: it is a wise father that knows his
75 own child. Well, old man, I will tell you news of
your son. [*Kneels*] Give me your blessing: truth
will come to light; murder cannot be hid long;
a man's son may, but, in the end, truth will out.

Gobbo

Pray you, sir, stand up. I am sure you are not
80 Launcelot, my boy.

Launcelot

Pray you, let's have no more fooling about it, but
give me your blessing: I am Launcelot, your boy
that was, your son that is, your child that shall be.

Gobbo

I cannot think you are my son.

Launcelot

85 I know not what I shall think of that; but I am
Launcelot, the Jew's man, and I am sure Margery
your wife is my mother.

Gobbo

Her name is Margery, indeed: I'll be sworn, if thou
be Launcelot, thou art mine own flesh and blood.
90 Lord worshipped might he be! what a beard hast
thou got! thou hast got more hair on thy chin than
Dobbin my fill-horse has on his tail.

Launcelot

It should seem then that Dobbin's tail grows backward: I am sure he had more hair of his tail than
95 I have of my face, when I last saw him.

Gobbo

Lord, how art thou changed! How dost thou and
thy master agree? I have brought him a present.
How 'gree you now?

74-5   *it is . . . child*: Launcelot inverts
the proverb 'it is a wise child that
knows his own father'.

78   *out*: come out.

90   *Lord . . . be*: the Lord be praised.

92   *fill-horse*: cart-horse (one that
works in the 'fills' or shafts).

93   *backward*: i.e. shorter.

94   *of*: on.

97   *agree*: suit each other.

98   *'gree*: agree.

99   *for mine own part*: as far as I am concerned.

99-100   *set up my rest*: made up my mind.

101   *ground*: distance.

102   *halter*: i.e. a rope to hang himself with.

103   *tell*: count.

103-4   *finger . . . ribs*: another of Launcelot's reversals; perhaps he spreads his own hand over his chest, and runs his father's hand across the fingers as though they were his ribs.

104-5   *give me your present*: just give your present.

106   *liveries*: uniforms, jobs.

110   *hasted*: speeded up.

112   *put . . . making*: arrange for the uniforms to be made.

113   *anon*: at once.

114   *To him*: speak to him.

116   *Gramercy*: many thanks (from the French *grand merci*).

120   *infection*: Gobbo's mistake for 'affection' = desire.

122   *the short and the long*: all that needs to be said (the more usual idiom is 'the long and the short').

Launcelot

Well, well: but, for mine own part, as I have set
100 up my rest to run away, so I will not rest till I have
run some ground. My master's a very Jew: give him
a present? give him a halter! I am famished in his
service; you may tell every finger I have with my
ribs. Father, I am glad you are come: give me your
105 present to one Master Bassanio, who, indeed, gives
rare new liveries. If I serve not him, I will run as
far as God has any ground. O rare fortune! here
comes the man: to him, father; for I am a Jew, if
I serve the Jew any longer.

Enter Bassanio, *with* Leonardo, *and other*
Servants

Bassanio

110 You may do so; but let it be so hasted that supper
be ready at the farthest by five of the clock. See
these letters delivered; put the liveries to making;
and desire Gratiano to come anon to my lodging.
[*Exit a* Servant

Launcelot

To him, father.

Gobbo

115 God bless your worship!

Bassanio

Gramercy! wouldst thou aught with me?

Gobbo

Here's my son, sir, a poor boy—

Launcelot

Not a poor boy, sir, but the rich Jew's man; that
would, sir—as my father shall specify—

Gobbo

120 He hath a great infection, sir (as one would say) to
serve—

Launcelot

Indeed, the short and the long is, I serve the Jew,
and have a desire, as my father shall specify—

124   *saving . . . reverence*: with respect
to you, sir (an apology for the dialect
expression that he is going to use).

125   *cater-cousins*: good friends (fellow
bread-eaters).

128   *frutify*: fructify (bear fruit);
Launcelot really means 'notify'.

129   *dish of doves*: doves ready for
eating; the gift is a kind of bribe to
persuade Bassanio to grant his request
('suit').

131   *impertinent*: impudent—the very
opposite of what Launcelot means to
say, which is 'pertinent' (= relevant).

137   *defect*: Old Gobbo means to say
'effect' (= conclusion).

138   *thou . . . suit*: your request is
granted.

140   *preferr'd*: recommended.
preferment: promotion.

143   *The old proverb*: the proverb is
'The grace of God is gear enough',
meaning that the man who has the
grace of God has all he needs for
salvation. As a Christian, Bassanio
should have 'the grace of God', and as
a rich man, Shylock has 'enough'.
parted: divided.

147-8   *inquire . . . out*: make your way
to my house.

149   *More . . . fellows*: with more gold
braid on it than the uniforms of the
other servants, his mates. The
additional decoration might indicate
that Launcelot is to be Bassanio's
jester.

Gobbo

His master and he (saving your worship's reverence)
125 are scarce cater-cousins.

Launcelot

To be brief, the very truth is that the Jew having
done me wrong, doth cause me—as my father,
being, I hope, an old man, shall frutify unto you—

Gobbo

I have here a dish of doves that I would bestow
130 upon your worship, and my suit is—

Launcelot

In very brief, the suit is impertinent to myself, as
your worship shall know by this honest old man;
and, though I say it, though old man, yet (poor
man) my father.

Bassanio

135 One speak for both. What would you?

Launcelot

Serve you, sir.

Gobbo

That is the very defect of the matter, sir.

Bassanio

I know thee well; thou hast obtain'd thy suit:
Shylock thy master spoke with me this day,
140 And hath preferr'd thee, if it be preferment
To leave a rich Jew's service, to become
The follower of so poor a gentleman.

Launcelot

The old proverb is very well parted between my
master Shylock and you, sir: you have 'the grace of
145 God', sir, and he hath 'enough'.

Bassanio

Thou speak'st it well. Go, father, with thy son.
Take leave of thy old master, and inquire
My lodging out. [*To his* Servants] Give him a livery
More guarded than his fellows': see it done.

150   *in*: go inside—off the stage and, by implication, into Bassanio's house.

150-1   *I cannot . . . head*: Launcelot is joking by saying—here and in the rest of the speech—the opposite of what he means.

152   *table*: palm of the hand; Launcelot pretends to be a palmist, telling his fortune by looking at his hand.
    offer: promise.

153   *to swear upon a book*: to swear a legal oath it is customary to lay one's right hand on the Bible.

154   *line of life*: on the palm of the hand, a line passes round the ball of the thumb, and in palmistry this is called the line of life. Unbroken lines joining the base of the thumb to this line of life are said to indicate the number of wives that a man will have.
    trifle: minor matter.

156   *maids*: virgins.
    simple coming-in: modest income (Launcelot thinks of the dowries his wives will bring him).

157   *'scape*: escape.

159   *if Fortune be a woman*: the personification of Fortune is female, to indicate the inconstancy of Fate.

160   *gear*: business.

161   *in the twinkling*: in the twinkling of an eye (the time it takes to wink).

163   *orderly*: in order.
    bestow'd: put away (presumably on the boat for Belmont).

164   *feast*: give a banquet for.

166   *endeavours*: efforts.

170   *have a suit to you*: have a favour to ask you.

173   *rude*: unmannerly.

174   *Parts*: qualities.
    become thee: suit you.

177   *Something too liberal*: rather too freely.
    pain: care.

Launcelot

150   Father, in. I cannot get a service, no! I have ne'er
a tongue in my head. Well, [*Looking at his hand*] if
any man in Italy have a fairer table which doth offer
to swear upon a book, I shall have good fortune. Go
to; here's a simple line of life: here's a small trifle of
155   wives: alas! fifteen wives is nothing: eleven widows
and nine maids is a simple coming-in for one man;
and then to 'scape drowning thrice, and to be in
peril of my life with the edge of a feather-bed; here
are simple 'scapes. Well, if Fortune be a woman,
160   she's a good wench for this gear. Father, come; I'll
take my leave of the Jew in the twinkling.

        [*Exeunt Launcelot and Old Gobbo*

Bassanio

I pray thee, good Leonardo, think on this.
These things being bought, and orderly bestow'd,
Return in haste, for I do feast tonight
165   My best-esteem'd acquaintance. Hie thee, go.

Leonardo

My best endeavours shall be done herein.

Enter Gratiano

Gratiano

Where's your master?

Leonardo   Yonder, sir, he walks.

                                     [*Exit*

Gratiano

Signior Bassanio!

Bassanio

Gratiano!

Gratiano

170   I have a suit to you.

Bassanio   You have obtain'd it.

Gratiano

You must not deny me: I must go with you to
Belmont.

Bassanio

Why, then you must. But hear thee, Gratiano;
Thou art too wild, too rude, and bold of voice—
Parts that become thee happily enough,
175   And in such eyes as ours appear not faults—
But where thou art not known, why, there they show
Something too liberal. Pray thee, take pain

To allay with some cold drops of modesty
Thy skipping spirit, lest, through thy wild behaviour,
180 I be misconster'd in the place I go to,
And lose my hopes.
   Gratiano   Signior Bassanio, hear me:
If I do not put on a sober habit,
Talk with respect, and swear but now and then,
Wear prayer-books in my pocket, look demurely,
185 Nay more, while grace is saying, hood mine eyes
Thus with my hat, and sigh, and say 'amen',
Use all the observance of civility,
Like one well studied in a sad ostent
To please his grandam, never trust me more.
   Bassanio
190 Well, we shall see your bearing.
   Gratiano
Nay, but I bar tonight; you shall not gauge me
By what we do tonight.
   Bassanio   No, that were pity:
I would entreat you rather to put on
Your boldest suit of mirth, for we have friends
195 That purpose merriment. But fare you well:
I have some business.
   Gratiano
And I must to Lorenzo and the rest;
But we will visit you at supper-time.   [*Exeunt*

Scene 3   *Venice. The street outside Shylock's house*

Enter Jessica *and* Launcelot
   Jessica
I am sorry thou wilt leave my father so:
Our house is hell, and thou, a merry devil,
Didst rob it of some taste of tediousness.
But fare thee well; there is a ducat for thee—
5 And, Launcelot, soon at supper shalt thou see
Lorenzo, who is thy new master's guest:
Give him this letter—do it secretly.
And so farewell: I would not have my father
See me in talk with thee.

---

178   To damp down with a drop of decency.
179   *skipping*: boisterous.
180   *misconster'd*: misunderstood.

182   *a sober habit*: both 'respectable clothes' and 'a serious manner'.
183   *but*: only.
185   *saying*: being said.
      hood: cover (hats were worn at meals in polite society).
187   *observance*: outward forms.
      civility: good manners.
188   *studied*: practised.
      sad: serious.
      ostent: appearance.
189   *grandam*: grandmother.
190   *bearing*: conduct.
191   *bar*: make an exception of.
      gauge: judge.
192   *were pity*: would be a pity.

194   *suit of mirth*: both 'amusing manner' and 'party dress'.
195   *purpose*: intend.

Act 2   Scene 3
Launcelot says goodbye to Shylock's daughter, Jessica, who is sorry to see him go.

3   *taste*: part.

10   *Adieu*: goodbye (French).
      exhibit: Launcelot means 'inhibit my tongue' (= prevent me from speaking).

13   *something*: somewhat, rather.

16   *heinous*: hateful.

19   *not to his manners*: not like him in behaviour.
20   *keep promise*: keep your promise.

Act 2   Scene 4
Bassanio's friends have planned some kind of entertainment to amuse the guests at dinner. Launcelot gives Lorenzo the letter from Jessica, and Lorenzo explains his intentions to the audience.

5   *spoke us*: ordered.

6   *quaintly order'd*: done with style.

9   *To furnish us*: to get ourselves ready.

10   *And*: if.
      break up this: break the seal on the letter.
11   *seem to signify*: inform you.
12   *know the hand*: recognize the handwriting—but then Lorenzo goes on to talk about 'the hand that writ' (wrote) the letter.

Launcelot

10 Adieu! tears exhibit my tongue. Most beautiful pagan, most sweet Jew! If a Christian do not play the knave and get thee, I am much deceived. But, adieu! these foolish drops do something drown my manly spirit: adieu!

Jessica

15 Farewell, good Launcelot.   [*Exit* Launcelot
    Alack, what heinous sin is it in me
    To be asham'd to be my father's child!
    But though I am a daughter to his blood,
    I am not to his manners. O Lorenzo,
20 If thou keep promise, I shall end this strife,
    Become a Christian, and thy loving wife.   [*Exit*

Scene 4 *Venice. The street outside Shylock's house*

        Enter Gratiano, Lorenzo, Salerio, *and* Solanio

Lorenzo

Nay, we will slink away in supper-time,
Disguise us at my lodging, and return
All in an hour.

Gratiano

We have not made good preparation.

Salerio

5 We have not spoke us yet of torch-bearers.

Solanio

'Tis vile unless it may be quaintly order'd,
And better, in my mind, not undertook.

Lorenzo

'Tis now but four o'clock: we have two hours
To furnish us.

        Enter Launcelot, *with a letter*
                Friend Launcelot, what's the news?

Launcelot

10 And it shall please you to break up this, it shall seem to signify.

Lorenzo

I know the hand: in faith, 'tis a fair hand;
And whiter than the paper it writ on
Is the fair hand that writ.

	Gratiano　　　　　　Love news, in faith.
	Launcelot
15　*By your leave*: with your per- mission (Launcelot asks if he may go).	15　By your leave, sir.
	Lorenzo
	Whither goest thou?
	Launcelot
17　*sup*: dine.	Marry, sir, to bid my old master, the Jew, to sup tonight with my new master, the Christian.
	Lorenzo
	Hold here, take this: tell gentle Jessica
	20　I will not fail her; speak it privately.
	Go, gentlemen,　　　　　　[*Exit* Launcelot
	Will you prepare you for this masque tonight?
23　*provided of*: supplied with.	I am provided of a torch-bearer.
	Salerio
24　*straight*: immediately.	Ay, marry, I'll be gone about it straight.
	Solanio
	25　And so will I.
	Lorenzo　　　　　　Meet me and Gratiano
	At Gratiano's lodging some hour hence.
	Salerio
	'Tis good we do so.
	[*Exeunt* Salerio *and* Solanio
	Gratiano
	Was not that letter from fair Jessica?
	Lorenzo
29　*I must needs tell thee all*: I've just *got* to tell you everything. 　　*directed*: instructed.	I must needs tell thee all. She hath directed
	30　How I shall take her from her father's house;
31　*furnish'd* supplied.	What gold and jewels she is furnish'd with;
	What page's suit she hath in readiness.
	If e'er the Jew her father come to heaven,
34　*gentle*: Launcelot makes a pun with 'gentile' (a non-Jewish person).	It will be for his gentle daughter's sake;
35　*foot*: path.	35　And never dare misfortune cross her foot,
36　*she*: i.e. misfortune (personified as female).	Unless she do it under this excuse,
under: with.	That she is issue to a faithless Jew.
37　*she is . . . Jew*: Jessica is the offspring of a Jew who does not believe in the Christian faith.	Come, go with me: peruse this as thou goest.
38　*peruse*: study.	Fair Jessica shall be my torch-bearer.　　　[*Exeunt*

Act 2   Scene 5
Shylock instructs Jessica to lock up the
house carefully; he then goes off to
have dinner with Bassanio.

2   *of*: between.
3   *gormandize*: over-eat.

5   *rend apparel out*: wear holes in
your clothes.

8   *wont*: accustomed.

11   *bid forth*: invited out.
12   *wherefore*: why.

15   *prodigal*: wasteful; see note to
1, 1, 129.
16   *Look to*: take care of.
        right loath: very reluctant.
17   There is some evil being plotted
against my peace of mind.

20   *reproach*: Launcelot means
'approach'.

21   *So do I his*: i.e. his reproach;
Shylock takes Launcelot's word, not
his meaning.

23–7   *it was . . . afternoon*: Launcelot's
nonsense, making fun of prophesying
by omens: *Black Monday* is Easter
Monday, and *Ash Wednesday* the first
day of Lent.

Scene 5 *Venice. The street outside Shylock's house*

Enter Shylock *and* Launcelot
Shylock
Well, thou shalt see, thy eyes shall be thy judge
The difference of old Shylock and Bassanio—
What, Jessica!—thou shalt not gormandize
As thou hast done with me—What, Jessica!—
5   And sleep and snore, and rend apparel out—
Why, Jessica, I say!
Launcelot   Why, Jessica!
Shylock
Who bids thee call? I do not bid thee call.
Launcelot
Your worship was wont to tell me that I could do
nothing without bidding.

Enter Jessica
Jessica
10 Call you? What is your will?
Shylock
I am bid forth to supper, Jessica;
There are my keys. But wherefore should I go?
I am not bid for love: they flatter me.
But yet I'll go in hate, to feed upon
15 The prodigal Christian. Jessica, my girl,
Look to my house. I am right loath to go:
There is some ill a-brewing towards my rest,
For I did dream of money-bags tonight.
Launcelot
I beseech you, sir, go: my young master doth expect
20 your reproach.
Shylock
So do I his.
Launcelot
And they have conspired together: I will not say
you shall see a masque; but if you do, then it was
not for nothing that my nose fell a-bleeding on
25 Black Monday last, at six o'clock i' the morning,
falling out that year on Ash Wednesday was four
year in th' afternoon.

Shylock
What, are there masques? Hear you me, Jessica:
Lock up my doors, and when you hear the drum
30 And the vile squealing of the wry-neck'd fife,
Clamber not you up to the casements then,
Nor thrust your head into the public street
To gaze on Christian fools with varnish'd faces,
But stop my house's ears—I mean my casements—
35 Let not the sound of shallow foppery enter
My sober house. By Jacob's staff I swear
I have no mind of feasting forth tonight;
But I will go. Go you before me, sirrah;
Say I will come.
Launcelot
40 I will go before, sir. Mistress, look out at window,
for all this:

There will come a Christian by,
Will be worth a Jewess' eye.
                                        [*Exit* Launcelot
Shylock
What says that fool of Hagar's offspring, ha?
Jessica
45 His words were, 'Farewell, mistress'; nothing else.
Shylock
The patch is kind enough, but a huge feeder;
Snail-slow in profit, and he sleeps by day
More than the wild cat: drones hive not with me;
Therefore I part with him, and part with him
50 To one that I would have him help to waste
His borrow'd purse. Well, Jessica, go in—
Perhaps I will return immediately—
Do as I bid you; shut doors after you:
'Fast bind, fast find',
55 A proverb never stale in thrifty mind.   [*Exit*
Jessica
Farewell; and if my fortune be not cross'd,
I have a father, you a daughter, lost.   [*Exit*

---

30   *wry-neck'd fife*: a fife is a small pipe which is played sideways, giving the player a twisted ('wry') neck.

31   *casements*: windows.

33   *varnish'd*: painted, or wearing masks.

35   *shallow foppery*: frivolity.

36   *Jacob's staff*: in Genesis 32: 10 Jacob boasts that he had only his staff when he crossed the river Jordan, yet he returned with two companies of men.

37   *forth*: away from home.

43   'Worth a Jew's eye' was a proverbial expression to indicate great value.

44   *Hagar*: the maid to Abraham's wife. Abraham was the father of her son, but he rejected the boy and sent him with his mother into the wilderness (Genesis, chapter 21).

46   *patch*: fool.
huge feeder: he eats a lot.

47   *Snail-slow*: as slow as a snail.
profit: learning his job.

48   *drones*: bees who do no work.
hive: live (as in a bee-hive).

50   *waste*: ruin.

54   He who takes care of what he has will prosper.

56   *cross'd*: thwarted.

Act 2   Scene 6
Lorenzo and his friends meet outside
Shylock's house. Jessica appears on the
balcony, rather embarrassed because
she is dressed as a boy.

1   *penthouse*: porch.
2   *make stand*: wait.

4   Lovers always come before their
appointed hour.

5–7   Lovers are always in a greater
hurry to keep a new engagement than
they are to keep their marriage vows
('obliged faith') unbroken ('unforfeited').

5   *Venus' pigeons*: the classical
goddess of love rode in a chariot drawn
by doves.

8   *That ever holds*: that is always
true.

10   *untread*: retrace.

11   *tedious measures*: boring steps in
a formal riding exercise (which we now
call 'dressage').
unbated: undiminished.

12   *pace*: perform.

14   *younger*: younger son, such as the
Prodigal Son in the parable (see note
to *1, 1*, 129).

15   *scarfed bark*: ship decorated with
flags and pennants.

16   *strumpet wind*: the wind is like
an unfaithful woman because it changes
so easily; the metaphor continues the
'Prodigal Son' allusion, because the son
wasted his money on prostitutes.

18   *over-weather'd ribs*: weather-
beaten sides.

19   *rent*: torn.
21   *abode*: delay.

Scene 6 *Venice. The street outside Shylock's house*

Enter Gratiano *and* Salerio *dressed as
masquers*

Gratiano
This is the penthouse under which Lorenzo
Desir'd us to make stand.
Salerio   His hour is almost past.
Gratiano
And it is marvel he out-dwells his hour,
For lovers ever run before the clock.
Salerio
5   O ten times faster Venus' pigeons fly
To seal love's bonds new-made, than they are wont
To keep obliged faith unforfeited!
Gratiano
That ever holds: who riseth from a feast
With that keen appetite that he sits down?
10   Where is the horse that doth untread again
His tedious measures with the unbated fire
That he did pace them first? All things that are,
Are with more spirit chased than enjoy'd.
How like a younger or a prodigal
15   The scarfed bark puts from her native bay,
Hugg'd and embraced by the strumpet wind!
How like the prodigal doth she return,
With over-weather'd ribs and ragged sails,
Lean, rent, and beggar'd by the strumpet wind!

Enter Lorenzo

Salerio
20   Here comes Lorenzo: more of this hereafter.
Lorenzo
Sweet friends, your patience for my long abode;
Not I but my affairs have made you wait:
When you shall please to play the thieves for wives,
I'll watch as long for you then. Approach;
25   Here dwells my father Jew. Ho! who's within?

27   *tongue*: voice.

Enter Jessica *on the balcony, dressed as a boy*

Jessica
Who are you? Tell me, for more certainty,
Albeit I'll swear that I do know your tongue.
Lorenzo
Lorenzo, and thy love.
Jessica
Lorenzo, certain; and my love indeed,
30 For who love I so much? And now who knows
But you, Lorenzo, whether I am yours?
Lorenzo
Heaven and thy thoughts are witness that thou art.
Jessica
Here, catch this casket; it is worth the pains.
I am glad 'tis night, you do not look on me,

35   *exchange*: i.e. of clothes.

35 For I am much asham'd of my exchange:
But love is blind, and lovers cannot see
The pretty follies that themselves commit;
For if they could, Cupid himself would blush
To see me thus transformed to a boy.

Lorenzo

40 Descend, for you must be my torch-bearer.

Jessica

What! must I hold a candle to my shames?
They in themselves, good sooth, are too too light.
Why, 'tis an office of discovery, love,
And I should be obscur'd.

Lorenzo   So are you, sweet,

45 Even in the lovely garnish of a boy,
But come at once;
For the close night doth play the runaway,
And we are stay'd for at Bassanio's feast.

Jessica

I will make fast the doors, and gild myself

50 With some more ducats, and be with you straight.

                                        [*Exit above*

Gratiano

Now, by my hood, a gentle, and no Jew.

Lorenzo

Beshrew me, but I love her heartily;
For she is wise, if I can judge of her;
And fair she is, if that mine eyes be true;

55 And true she is, as she hath prov'd herself;
And therefore, like herself, wise, fair, and true,
Shall she be placed in my constant soul.

                Enter Jessica

What, art thou come? On, gentlemen; away!
Our masquing mates by this time for us stay.

                        [*Exeunt, except* Gratiano

                Enter Antonio

Antonio

60 Who's there?

Gratiano

Signior Antonio!

Antonio

Fie, fie, Gratiano! where are all the rest?
'Tis nine o'clock; our friends all stay for you.
No masque tonight: the wind is come about;

65 Bassanio presently will go aboard:
I have sent twenty out to seek for you.

Gratiano

I am glad on't: I desire no more delight
Than to be under sail and gone tonight.   [*Exeunt*

---

42   *good sooth*: indeed.
     light: both 'obvious' and 'wanton'.

43   *an office of discovery*: a torch-bearer's job is to light up and reveal things.

44   *obscur'd*: concealed.

45   *garnish*: costume.

47   *close night*: night that hides our secret.
     doth play the runaway: is slipping away.

48   *stay'd*: waited.

49   *make fast*: lock.
     gild: adorn with gold.

50   *straight*: at once.

51   *by my hood*: upon my word.
     gentle: both 'gentle lady' and 'gentile'.

52   *Beshrew me*: curse me (a very mild oath, added only to intensify the declaration of love).
     heartily: with all my heart.

54   *be true*: see truly.

57   She shall always have a place in my soul.

63   *stay*: wait.

64   *is come about*: has changed direction.

65   *presently*: now.
     aboard: on to his ship.

68   *to be under sail*: to sail.

Act 2   Scene 7
The Prince of Morocco has come to
examine the caskets. He reads aloud the
inscription on each one, and tries to
puzzle out the meanings. At last he
makes his choice.

1   *discover*: reveal.
2   *several*: different.

8   *as blunt*: as dull as the lead.
9   *hazard*: risk.

12   *withal*: with the casket.

14   *back again*: in reverse order.

Scene 7 *Belmont. A room in Portia's house*

Enter Portia, *with the* Prince of Morocco,
and their Servants

Portia
Go, draw aside the curtains, and discover
The several caskets to this noble prince.
                    [*The curtains are drawn back*
Now make your choice.

Morocco
The first, of gold, who this inscription bears:
5 '*Who chooseth me shall gain what many men desire*'.
The second, silver, which this promise carries:
'*Who chooseth me shall get as much as he deserves*'.
This third, dull lead, with warning all as blunt:
'*Who chooseth me must give and hazard all he hath*'.
10 How shall I know if I do choose the right?

Portia
The one of them contains my picture, prince:
If you choose that, then I am yours withal.

Morocco
Some god direct my judgment! Let me see:
I will survey th' inscriptions back again:
15 What says this leaden casket?
'*Who chooseth me must give and hazard all he hath*.'

19   *fair advantages*: good returns.
20   *dross*: rubbish (impure metal).
21   *nor . . . nor*: neither . . . nor.
22   *virgin hue*: colour of purity
(white).

25   *even*: steady.
26   *rated*: assessed.
       thy estimation: your own
estimation.

29-30   *to be . . . myself*: to be unsure of
what I deserve is a sign of weakness,
bringing discredit on ('disabling')
myself.

36   *grav'd*: engraved.
       in gold: on the gold casket.

40   *mortal*: living.
41   *Hyrcanian deserts*: a savage
region to the south of the Caspian Sea.
       vasty wilds: immense wilder-
nesses.
42   *throughfares*: main roads.
44   *The watery kingdom*: the ocean.
44-5   *whose . . . heaven*: whose waves
surge up as though they wanted to
touch the sky, throwing spray (spitting)
into the clouds.
45   *bar*: obstacle.
46   *foreign spirits*: suitors from
abroad.
49   *Is 't like*: is it likely?
50-1   *it were . . . cerecloth*: lead would
be too crude to enfold ('rib') the
winding-sheet when she is buried.
52   *immur'd*: walled in.
53   *undervalu'd to*: less value than.
       tried: tested (without impurities).
54-5   Jewels as precious as Portia are
never set in worse metal than gold.

Must give! For what? for lead? hazard for lead?
This casket threatens. Men that hazard all
Do it in hope of fair advantages:
20 A golden mind stoops not to shows of dross;
I'll then nor give nor hazard aught for lead.
What says the silver with her virgin hue?
'*Who chooseth me shall get as much as he deserves*'.
As much as he deserves! Pause there, Morocco,
25 And weigh thy value with an even hand.
If thou be'st rated by thy estimation,
Thou dost deserve enough; and yet enough
May not extend so far as to the lady:
And yet to be afeard of my deserving
30 Were but a weak disabling of myself.
As much as I deserve! Why, that's the lady:
I do in birth deserve her, and in fortunes,
In graces, and in qualities of breeding;
But more than these, in love I do deserve.
35 What if I stray'd no further, but chose here?
Let's see once more this saying grav'd in gold:
'*Who chooseth me shall gain what many men desire*'.
Why, that's the lady: all the world desires her;
From the four corners of the earth they come,
40 To kiss this shrine, this mortal breathing saint:
The Hyrcanian deserts and the vasty wilds
Of wide Arabia are as throughfares now
For princes to come view fair Portia:
The watery kingdom, whose ambitious head
45 Spits in the face of heaven, is no bar
To stop the foreign spirits, but they come,
As o'er a brook, to see fair Portia.
One of these three contains her heavenly picture.
Is 't like that lead contains her? 'Twere damnation
50 To think so base a thought: it were too gross
To rib her cerecloth in the obscure grave.
Or shall I think in silver she's immur'd,
Being ten times undervalu'd to tried gold?
O sinful thought! Never so rich a gem
55 Was set in worse than gold. They have in England

56   *A coin . . . angel*: the gold coin was in fact known as an 'angel'.

57   *insculp'd upon*: engraved on the surface of the coin.

61   *form*: picture.

63   *A carrion Death*: a skull.

65   *glisters*: glitters.
67   *his life hath sold*: has given his whole life.
68   *my outside*: the gilded outside of the casket.
69   *worms*: that feed on the bodies inside the 'Gilded tombs'.
71   *old*: experienced.
72   You would not have been given the answer written on this scroll.
73   *your suit is cold*: your hopes are dead.
77   *tedious*: lengthy, formal.
      part: depart.
78   *A gentle riddance*: a happy deliverance.
79   *complexion*: both 'colour' and 'personality'.

Act 2   Scene 8
Salerio and Solanio discuss a mystery—where is Lorenzo? Shylock (they have heard) has lost his daughter and been robbed of some money. There is bad news for Antonio.

1   *under sail*: set sail.
4   *raised*: roused from sleep (it was nine o'clock in scene 6, line 63).

A coin that bears the figure of an angel
Stamp'd in gold, but that's insculp'd upon;
But here an angel in a golden bed
Lies all within. Deliver me the key:
60   Here do I choose, and thrive I as I may!
     Portia
There, take it, prince; and if my form lie there,
Then I am yours.
                              [*He unlocks the golden casket*
     Morocco   O hell! what have we here?
A carrion Death, within whose empty eye
There is a written scroll. I'll read the writing.
65   *All that glisters is not gold;*
      Often have you heard that told:
      Many a man his life hath sold
      But my outside to behold:
      Gilded tombs do worms infold.
70   *Had you been as wise as bold,*
      Young in limbs, in judgment old,
      Your answer had not been inscroll'd.
      Fare you well, your suit is cold.

Cold, indeed; and labour lost:
75   Then farewell heat, and welcome, frost!
Portia, adieu. I have too griev'd a heart
To take a tedious leave: thus losers part.
                              [*Exit with his* Servants
     Portia
A gentle riddance. Draw the curtains: go.
Let all of his complexion choose me so.   [*Exeunt*

Scene 8 *Venice. A street*

        Enter Salerio *and* Solanio
     Salerio
Why, man, I saw Bassanio under sail,
With him is Gratiano gone along;
And in their ship I am sure Lorenzo is not.
     Solanio
The villain Jew with outcries rais'd the duke,
5   Who went with him to search Bassanio's ship.

Salerio

He came too late, the ship was under sail,
But there the duke was given to understand
That in a gondola were seen together
Lorenzo and his amorous Jessica.

10 Besides, Antonio certified the duke
They were not with Bassanio in his ship.

Solanio

I never heard a passion so confus'd,
So strange, outrageous, and so variable,
As the dog Jew did utter in the streets:

15 'My daughter! O my ducats! O my daughter!
Fled with a Christian! O my Christian ducats!
Justice! the law! my ducats, and my daughter!
A sealed bag, two sealed bags of ducats,
Of double ducats, stol'n from me by my daughter!

20 And jewels! two stones, two rich and precious
   stones,
Stol'n by my daughter! Justice! find the girl!
She hath the stones upon her, and the ducats.'

Salerio

Why, all the boys in Venice follow him,
Crying his stones, his daughter, and his ducats.

Solanio

25 Let good Antonio look he keep his day,
Or he shall pay for this.

Salerio   Marry, well remember'd.

I reason'd with a Frenchman yesterday,
Who told me, in the narrow seas that part
The French and English, there miscarried

30 A vessel of our country richly fraught.

---

7   *given to understand*: told.

8   *gondola*: a flat-bottomed boat used on the canals of Venice.

10   *certified*: assured.

13   *variable*: because Shylock was crying for his daughter, his ducats, and revenge.

19   *double ducats*: worth double the value of ducats.

25   *look he keep his day*: be careful to pay his debt on the appointed day.

27   *reason'd*: talked.

28   *the narrow seas*: the English Channel.
      part: separate.

29   *miscarried*: perished.

30   *vessel*: ship.
      fraught: laden.

I thought upon Antonio when he told me,
And wish'd in silence that it were not his.

Solanio

You were best to tell Antonio what you hear;
Yet do not suddenly, for it may grieve him.

Salerio

35 A kinder gentleman treads not the earth.
I saw Bassanio and Antonio part:
Bassanio told him he would make some speed
Of his return: he answer'd, 'Do not so;
Slubber not business for my sake, Bassanio,
40 But stay the very riping of the time;
And for the Jew's bond which he hath of me,
Let it not enter in your mind of love:
Be merry, and employ your chiefest thoughts
To courtship and such fair ostents of love
45 As shall conveniently become you there.'
And even there, his eye being big with tears,
Turning his face, he put his hand behind him,
And with affection wondrous sensible
He wrung Bassanio's hand; and so they parted.

Solanio

50 I think he only loves the world for him.
I pray thee, let us go and find him out,
And quicken his embraced heaviness
With some delight or other.

Salerio   Do we so.
                                                    [*Exeunt*

Scene 9 *Belmont. A room in Portia's house*

Enter Nerissa, *with a* Servant

Nerissa

Quick, quick, I pray thee; draw the curtain straight:
The Prince of Arragon hath ta'en his oath,
And comes to his election presently.

                            [*Curtains drawn to reveal caskets*

Enter the Prince of Arragon, Portia, *and*
Servants

Portia

Behold, there stand the caskets, noble prince:
5 If you choose that wherein I am contain'd,
Straight shall our nuptial rites be solemniz'd;

---

39   *Slubber not business*: do not
hurry your business carelessly.

40   *the . . . time*: until the time is
ripe, until the right moment.

41   *for*: as for.

42   Don't let it enter your head,
which should be full of love.

44   *ostents*: demonstrations.

45   As shall be suitable and do you
credit there.

46   *even there*: then and there.

47   *Turning*: turning away.

48   *wondrous sensible*: wonderfully
tender.

50   I think he loves nothing else in
the world so much as Bassanio.

52   *quicken*: enliven.
       his embraced heaviness: the sad-
ness that he is indulging in.

Act 2   Scene 9

Another suitor, the Prince of Arragon,
is to make his choice of the caskets. He
reads the inscriptions, and meditates on
what he deserves, before he opens one
of the caskets. Just as he has read the
scroll, news is brought that Bassanio is
coming to Belmont.

1   *straight*: at once.

3   *to his election*: to make his choice.
       presently: now.

6   *solemniz'd*: performed.

9   *enjoin'd*: bound.
         observe: promise.
10   *unfold*: disclose.
14   *do fail . . . of*: am unlucky in.
17   *hazard*: gamble.
18   *so have I address'd me*: I have
prepared in this way (by making the
promises).
24-5   *that . . . multitude*: that word
'many' may refer to the foolish masses.
25   *show*: appearance.
26   Never knowing more than the
foolish ('fond') eye can see.
27   *pries not*: does not look more
closely.
         th'interior: the heart of the
matter.
27-8   *the martlet . . . wall*: the house-
martin, a bird that builds its nest in the
open air ('weather') on the outside wall
of a building.
29   Just in the way of accidents.
31   *jump*: go along with.
32   *rank me*: join.
37   *cozen*: cheat.
37-8   *be . . . merit*: pretend to be noble
when he cannot show that he is worthy.
39   To put on nobleness (like a
cloak) which he is not entitled to.
40   *estates*: positions of rank (such as
lordships and knighthoods).
         degrees: social positions in an
established hierarchy (an earl, for
example, is superior to a viscount, and
a viscount is superior to a baron).
         offices: appointments.
41   *deriv'd corruptly*: obtained by
foul means.
42   *the wearer*: the holder of the
titles. The clothing metaphor arises
from the fact that on ceremonious
occasions the members of different
ranks wore (and still wear) distinctive
robes.
43   *cover*: keep their hats on.
         bare: bareheaded, as a mark of
respect to superiors—those who 'cover'.
45-6   *How . . . honour*: how many of
those who should really be poor
peasants could be picked out from the
true sons of the nobility.

But if you fail, without more speech, my lord,
You must be gone from hence immediately.
      Arragon
I am enjoin'd by oath to observe three things:
10   First, never to unfold to any one
Which casket 'twas I chose; next, if I fail
Of the right casket, never in my life
To woo a maid in way of marriage; lastly,
If I do fail in fortune of my choice,
15   Immediately to leave you and be gone.
      Portia
To these injunctions every one doth swear
That comes to hazard for my worthless self.
      Arragon
And so have I address'd me. Fortune now
To my heart's hope! Gold, silver, and base lead.
20   '*Who chooseth me must give and hazard all he hath.*'
You shall look fairer, ere I give or hazard.
What says the golden chest? ha! let me see:
'*Who chooseth me shall gain what many men desire*'.
What many men desire! that 'many' may be meant
25   By the fool multitude, that choose by show,
Not learning more than the fond eye doth teach,
Which pries not to th' interior, but, like the martlet,
Builds in the weather on the outward wall,
Even in the force and road of casualty.
30   I will not choose what many men desire,
Because I will not jump with common spirits
And rank me with the barbarous multitudes.
Why, then to thee, thou silver treasure-house;
Tell me once more what title thou dost bear:
35   '*Who chooseth me shall get as much as he deserves*'.
And well said too; for who shall go about
To cozen fortune, and be honourable
Without the stamp of merit? Let none presume
To wear an undeserved dignity.
40   O that estates, degrees, and offices
Were not deriv'd corruptly, and that clear honour
Were purchas'd by the merit of the wearer.
How many then should cover that stand bare!
How many be commanded that command!
45   How much low peasantry would then be glean'd

46-8   *how much . . . new varnish'd*: how
much that is truly noble could be
sorted out from the modern rubbish
and restored to its original splendour.
48   *but to*: I must return to.
50   *I will . . . desert*: I will claim to
be deserving.
52   *Too long a pause.* Arragon is
speechless.
53   *blinking*: with goggling eyes.

54   *schedule*: scroll.
55   *thou*: i.e. the picture of the idiot.
60   To commit an offence and to
pass judgement on the offence are quite
separate actions (Arragon has done
wrong—in choosing the wrong casket
—but he is unable to judge himself).
62   *The fire . . . this*: for purification,
silver is refined in a furnace seven
times.
63-4   Perfect judgement, that never
makes a mistake, must be as refined as
silver.
64   *amiss*: wrongly.
65   *shadows kiss*: embrace illusions,
believe in what is not real.
66   *a shadow's bliss*: the illusion of
happiness.
67   *iwis*: indeed.
68   *Silver'd o'er*: covered in silver
(so that their folly is hidden).
69   *Take . . . bed.* This seems to
contradict the condition that the
unlucky suitor should never marry.
70   You will always be a fool.
71   *sped*: finished.
72-3   The longer I stay here, the
bigger fool I shall appear.

From the true seed of honour! and how much
  honour
Pick'd from the chaff and ruin of the times
To be new varnish'd! Well, but to my choice:
'*Who chooseth me shall get as much as he deserves*'.
50 I will assume desert. Give me a key for this,
And instantly unlock my fortunes here.

[*He opens the silver casket*

Portia
Too long a pause for that which you find there.

Arragon
What's here? the portrait of a blinking idiot,
Presenting me a schedule! I will read it.
55 How much unlike art thou to Portia!
How much unlike my hopes and my deservings!
'*Who chooseth me shall have as much as he deserves*'.
Did I deserve no more than a fool's head?
Is that my prize? are my deserts no better?

Portia
60 To offend, and judge, are distinct offices,
And of opposed natures.

Arragon   What is here?

The fire seven times tried this:
Seven times tried that judgment is
That did never choose amiss.
65 *Some there be that shadows kiss:*
Such have but a shadow's bliss.
There be fools alive, iwis,
Silver'd o'er; and so was this.
Take what wife you will to bed,
70 *I will ever be your head.*
So be gone: you are sped.

Still more fool I shall appear
By the time I linger here:
With one fool's head I came to woo,
75 But I go away with two.
Sweet, adieu. I'll keep my oath,
Patiently to bear my wrath.

[*Exit Arragon with his* Servants

78   *sing'd*: burned.
79   *deliberate fools*: fools who try to give reasons for their actions.
80   Their reasoning ('wit') gives them enough intelligence ('wisdom') to make the wrong choice, and lose.
81   *ancient saying*: proverb.
      heresy: falsehood.
82   *wiving*: marrying.

84   *what . . . lord*: what does my lord want? Portia is joking with her servant.
85   *alighted*: dismounted from his horse.
86   *before*: in advance.
87   *signify*: announce.
88   *sensible*: substantial (not simply words of greeting, but gifts).
      regreets: greetings.
89   *To wit*: that is to say.
      commends: compliments.
      breath: words.
91   *likely*: hopeful.
92   *A day in April*: in England this is sometimes quite warm and sunny, with a few green leaves on the trees, and flowers in bud.
93   *costly*: rich.
      at hand: coming soon.
94   *fore-spurrer*: herald, one who spurs on his horse on advance of the main party.
95   *afeard*: afraid.
96   *anon*: presently.
      some kin to thee: one of your relations.
97   *high-day wit*: special invention, suitable for a holiday.
99   *Cupid*: the classical god of love
      post: messenger.
      mannerly: courteously.
100   *Bassanio*: may it be Bassanio.

Portia
Thus hath the candle sing'd the moth.
O these deliberate fools! when they do choose,
80 They have the wisdom by their wit to lose.
    Nerissa
The ancient saying is no heresy:
'Hanging and wiving goes by destiny.'
    Portia
Come, draw the curtain, Nerissa.

            Enter a Servant
    Servant
Where is my lady?
    Portia   Here; what would my lord?
    Servant
85 Madam, there is alighted at your gate
A young Venetian, one that comes before
To signify th' approaching of his lord;
From whom he bringeth sensible regreets,
To wit, besides commends and courteous breath,
90 Gifts of rich value. Yet I have not seen
So likely an ambassador of love.
A day in April never came so sweet
To show how costly summer was at hand,
As this fore-spurrer comes before his lord.
    Portia
95 No more, I pray thee: I am half afeard
Thou wilt say anon he is some kin to thee,
Thou spend'st such high-day wit in praising him.
Come, come, Nerissa; for I long to see
Quick Cupid's post that comes so mannerly.
    Nerissa
100 Bassanio, lord Love, if thy will it be!   [*Exeunt*

Act 3

Act 3   Scene 1
Salerio has heard bad news about one
of Antonio's ships. Shylock threatens
Antonio, and when Shylock and Tubal
are left on the stage together he gloats
over Antonio's danger. Shylock's
pleasure over this matter is equal to the
pain he suffers in the loss of his
daughter.

2   *yet it lives there*: there is still
a rumour.
        unchecked: undenied.
3   *lading*: cargo.
        the narrow seas: the English
Channel.
4   *the Goodwins*: the Goodwin
Sands, in the very middle of the
Channel.
5   *flat*: sandbank.
6   *tall*: fine.
6–7   *my gossip Report*: old mother
Rumour.
8   *gossip*: old woman.
        that: that report.
9   *knapped*: chewed.
        ginger. In Elizabethan drama old
people are often said to eat ginger, but
no-one seems to know why; perhaps it
warmed their stomachs, or aided
digestion.
11   *without . . . prolixity*: without
using any long and boring phrases.
11–12 *crossing . . . talk*: departing from
the straight line of conversation.

Scene 1   *Venice. A street*

Enter Solanio *and* Salerio

Solanio
Now, what news on the Rialto?
Salerio
Why, yet it lives there unchecked that Antonio hath
a ship of rich lading wrecked on the narrow seas—
the Goodwins, I think they call the place, a very
dangerous flat, and fatal, where the carcasses of   5
many a tall ship lie buried, as they say, if my gossip
Report be an honest woman of her word.
Solanio
I would she were as lying a gossip in that as ever
knapped ginger, or made her neighbours believe
she wept for the death of a third husband. But it is   10
true—without any slips of prolixity or crossing the
plain highway of talk—that the good Antonio, the
honest Antonio—O, that I had a title good enough
to keep his name company!
Salerio
Come, the full stop.   15
Solanio
Ha! what say'st thou? Why, the end is, he hath lost
a ship.
Salerio
I would it might prove the end of his losses.

15   *the full stop*: both 'come to the point' (in punctuation), and (from the technical terms of horse management) 'bring your horse from full gallop to a standstill'.

19-20   *Let . . . prayer*: when they say 'amen' (= so be it) at the end of a prayer, some Christians make the sign of the cross. Solanio puns on this meaning of 'cross' and the meaning 'frustrate', which is what the devil would do to his hopes for Antonio.

19   *betimes*: immediately.

26   *withal*: with.

28   *fledge*: fledged, having grown feathers on its wings.
      complexion: nature.

29   *dam*: mother.

31   *the devil*: i.e. Shylock himself (Salerio refers back to line 20).

33   *Out . . . carrion*: you dirty old man. Solanio pretends to think that Shylock meant his own body, rebelling in lust against the control of reason.

37   *Rhenish*: expensive white German wine.

39   *no*: not.

40   *match*: bargain.

42   *so smug*: looking so pleased with himself.

43   *mart*: stock exchange, the Rialto.
      look to: take care of.

44   *wont*: accustomed.

Solanio

Let me say 'amen' betimes, lest the devil cross my
20 prayer, for here he comes in the likeness of a Jew.

      Enter Shylock

How now, Shylock! what news among the
merchants?

Shylock

You knew, none so well, none so well as you, of my
daughter's flight.

Salerio

25 That's certain: I, for my part, knew the tailor that
made the wings she flew withal.

Solanio

And Shylock, for his own part, knew the bird was
fledge; and then it is the complexion of them all to
leave the dam.

Shylock

30 She is damned for it.

Salerio

That's certain, if the devil may be her judge.

Shylock

My own flesh and blood to rebel!

Solanio

Out upon it, old carrion! rebels it at these years?

Shylock

I say my daughter is my flesh and my blood.

Salerio

35 There is more difference between thy flesh and hers
than between jet and ivory; more between your
bloods than there is between red wine and Rhenish.
But tell us, do you hear whether Antonio have had
any loss at sea or no?

Shylock

40 There I have another bad match: a bankrupt,
a prodigal, who dare scarce show his head on the
Rialto; a beggar, that was used to come so smug
upon the mart. Let him look to his bond! he was
wont to call me usurer. Let him look to his bond!

49 *To bait fish*: to use as bait for fishing.
50 *disgraced*: dishonoured.
51 *hindered ... million*: prevented me from making half a million (ducats) profit.
53 *bargains*: business deals.
 cooled: diminished their affections.
 heated: encouraged their hatred.
56 *dimensions*: parts of the body.

65 *what is his humility*: what does the Christian (who ought to bear his sufferings with humility) do?
66-7 *what ... be*: how should he endure it?
68-9 *it shall ... instruction*: if you are not very careful, I shall do even more harm than you have taught me to do.

72 We have been looking everywhere for him.

73-4 *a third ... matched*: there is not another Jew to equal these two.

45 he was wont to lend money for a Christian courtesy. Let him look to his bond!

Salerio

Why, I am sure, if he forfeit thou wilt not take his flesh: what's that good for?

Shylock

To bait fish withal: if it will feed nothing else, it
50 will feed my revenge. He hath disgraced me, and hindered me half a million, laughed at my losses, mocked at my gains, scorned my nation, thwarted my bargains, cooled my friends, heated mine enemies; and what's his reason? I am a Jew. Hath
55 not a Jew eyes? hath not a Jew hands, organs, dimensions, senses, affections, passions? fed with the same food, hurt with the same weapons, subject to the same diseases, healed by the same means, warmed and cooled by the same winter and
60 summer, as a Christian is? If you prick us, do we not bleed? if you tickle us, do we not laugh? if you poison us, do we not die? and if you wrong us, shall we not revenge? If we are like you in the rest, we will resemble you in that. If a Jew wrong a
65 Christian, what is his humility? Revenge! If a Christian wrong a Jew, what should his sufferance be by Christian example? Why, revenge! The villainy you teach me I will execute, and it shall go hard but I will better the instruction.

Enter a Servant

Servant

70 Gentlemen, my master Antonio is at his house, and desires to speak with you both.

Salerio

We have been up and down to seek him.

Enter Tubal

Solanio

Here comes another of the tribe: a third cannot be matched, unless the devil himself turn Jew.

    [*Exeunt* Solanio, Salerio *and* Servant

Shylock

75 How now, Tubal! what news from Genoa? Hast
thou found my daughter?

Tubal

I often came where I did hear of her, but cannot
find her.

Shylock

Why there, there, there, there! a diamond gone,
80 cost me two thousand ducats in Frankfurt! The
curse never fell upon our nation till now; I never
felt it till now: two thousand ducats in that, and
other precious, precious jewels. I would my
daughter were dead at my foot, and the jewels in
85 her ear! would she were hearsed at my foot, and the
ducats in her coffin! No news of them—why so?
and I know not what's spent in the search. Why
thou—loss upon loss! the thief gone with so much,
and so much to find the thief; and no satisfaction,
90 no revenge: nor no ill luck stirring but what lights
o' my shoulders; no sighs but o' my breathing;
no tears but o' my shedding.

Tubal

Yes, other men have ill luck too. Antonio, as I
heard in Genoa—

Shylock

95 What, what, what? ill luck? ill luck?

Tubal

—hath an argosy cast away, coming from Tripolis.

Shylock

I thank God! I thank God! Is it true? is it true?

Tubal

I spoke with some of the sailors that escaped the
wreck.

Shylock

100 I thank thee, good Tubal. Good news, good news!
ha, ha! Heard in Genoa?

Tubal

Your daughter spent in Genoa, as I heard, one
night, fourscore ducats.

80-1   *The curse . . . nation*: God cursed
the Jews because they disobeyed His
law, and condemned them to exile
(Daniel 9:11).

85   *hearsed*: laid in her coffin.

90   *lights o'*: lands on.
91   *but o' my breathing*: except the
sighs that I breathe.

96   *argosy*: merchant ship.
       cast away: wrecked.

102-3   *one night*: on one night.

105   *at a sitting*: on a single occasion.

107   *divers*: several.
107-8   *in my company*: along with me.
109   *break*: go bankrupt.

112   *of*: from.

114   *Out upon her*: damn her.
115   *had it of Leah*: it was a present
         from Leah (his wife—now presumably
         dead).

119-20   *fee me an officer*: hire a sheriff's
         officer for me. This was the normal
         procedure for arresting a debtor—
         Shylock is *not* suggesting a bribe.
120   *bespeak . . . before*: order him to
         be ready two weeks before Antonio's
         debt is due to be repaid.
122   *merchandise*: business.
123   *synagogue*: the Jewish temple.

Shylock
Thou stick'st a dagger in me: I shall never see my
gold again: fourscore ducats at a sitting! fourscore
ducats!
Tubal
There came divers of Antonio's creditors in my
company to Venice, that swear he cannot choose
but break.
Shylock
I am very glad of it: I'll plague him; I'll torture
him: I am glad of it.
Tubal
One of them showed me a ring that he had of your
daughter for a monkey.
Shylock
Out upon her! Thou torturest me, Tubal: it was
my turquoise; I had it of Leah when I was a
bachelor: I would not have given it for a wilderness
of monkeys.
Tubal
But Antonio is certainly undone.
Shylock
Nay, that's true, that's very true. Go, Tubal, fee
me an officer; bespeak him a fortnight before. I will
have the heart of him, if he forfeit; for, were he out
of Venice, I can make what merchandise I will. Go,
Tubal, and meet me at our synagogue; go, good
Tubal; at our synagogue, Tubal.

[*Exeunt in different directions*

Act 3   Scene 2
Portia has fallen in love with Bassanio
and wants him to wait a few days
before making his choice of the caskets.
But Bassanio refuses to wait. He
meditates aloud on the difference
between appearance and reality, and
then chooses the leaden casket and
wins Portia for his wife. Nerissa and
Gratiano congratulate him, and
Gratiano declares his own marriage
plans. Lorenzo and Jessica arrive at
Belmont, together with Salerio, who
has brought a letter from Antonio.
Antonio has written to say that he is in
Shylock's power.

1   *tarry*: wait.
2   *hazard*: take this risk.
5   *I would not*: I don't want to.
6   Hatred does not give this kind of
advice.
8   Portia seems to be saying that
her speech should be easily understood
because it is a simple expression of her
thoughts (without the obscurities
created by elaborate language).
10   *venture for me*: try to win me.
11   *I am forsworn*: I would have
broken my promise.
12   *miss*: lose.
13–14 *wish . . . forsworn*: wish I had
committed the sin of breaking my
promise.
14   *Beshrew*: shame on.
15   *o'erlook'd*: bewitched.
18–19 *O these . . . rights*: in these
wicked times there are obstacles to
prevent owners from taking possession
of the things they own.
20   *Prove it so*: if this proves to be
the case (i.e. that Bassanio cannot
possess her).
21   It will be fortune's fault, not
mine.
22   *peise*: measure out.
23   *eke it*: add to it.
24   *To . . . election*: to hold you back
from making your choice.
25   *the rack*: an instrument of torture
which stretched the victim's body (as
Portia is trying to stretch out the time)
until he confessed his crimes—usually
of treason to the state.

Scene 2 *Belmont. A room in Portia's house*

Enter Bassanio, Portia, Gratiano, Nerissa,
and Servants

Portia
I pray you, tarry, pause a day or two
Before you hazard; for, in choosing wrong,
I lose your company: therefore, forbear awhile.
There's something tells me (but it is not love)
5 I would not lose you; and you know yourself,
Hate counsels not in such a quality.
But lest you should not understand me well—
And yet a maiden hath no tongue but thought—
I would detain you here some month or two
10 Before you venture for me. I could teach you
How to choose right, but then I am forsworn;
So will I never be: so may you miss me—
But if you do, you'll make me wish a sin,
That I had been forsworn. Beshrew your eyes,
15 They have o'erlook'd me and divided me:
One half of me is yours, the other half yours—
Mine own, I would say; but if mine, then yours,
And so all yours. O these naughty times
Put bars between the owners and their rights;
20 And so, though yours, not yours. Prove it so,
Let fortune go to hell for it, not I.
I speak too long; but 'tis to peise the time,
To eke it and to draw it out in length,
To stay you from election.
Bassanio   Let me choose;
25 For as I am, I live upon the rack.
Portia
Upon the rack, Bassanio! then confess
What treason there is mingled with your love.
Bassanio
None but that ugly treason of mistrust,
Which makes me fear th' enjoying of my love:
30 There may as well be amity and life
'Tween snow and fire, as treason and my love.
Portia
Ay, but I fear you speak upon the rack,
Where men enforced do speak anything.

29   *fear th' enjoying of my love*: afraid that I shall not have the one I love for my wife.

30   *amity*: friendship.

33   *enforced*: compelled (by torture).

35   *confess, and live*: this was offered to traitors on the rack, as the alternative to dying with their secrets.

36   Would be all that I have to confess.

38   *for deliverance*: to be released.

42   *aloof*: out of the way.

44   *a swan-like end*: the Elizabethans believed that the swan (which has no voice at all) sings only once, just before it dies.

45   *Fading*: dying.

46   *stand more proper*: fit more exactly.

46–7   *my eye ... for him*: I shall weep, so he will seem to drown in my tears.

49   *flourish*: ceremonial fanfare on trumpets.

51   *dulcet*: sweet.
   in: at.

54   *presence*: handsome appearance.

55   *Alcides*: Hercules (son of Alcaeus). He rescued a Trojan princess, Hesione, who was being sacrificed (a 'virgin tribute') to a sea-monster. His motive was not love, however: he wanted her father's horses.

58   *aloof*: apart.
   Dardanian: Trojan (the descendants of Dardanus, who founded Troy).

59   *bleared visages*: tear-stained faces.

60   *issue*: outcome.

61   *Live thou*: if you live.
   dismay: alarm.

62   *fray*: fighting.

63   *fancy*: attraction.

64   *Or ... or*: either ... or.

67–9   Appearance is what first attracts one person to another, and the attraction grows stronger the more the couple look at each other. But fancy has a very short life.

Bassanio
Promise me life, and I'll confess the truth.
   Portia
35 Well, then, confess, and live.
   Bassanio   'Confess and love'
Had been the very sum of my confession:
O happy torment, when my torturer
Doth teach me answers for deliverance!
But let me to my fortune and the caskets.
   Portia
40 Away then! I am lock'd in one of them:
If you do love me, you will find me out.
Nerissa and the rest, stand all aloof.
Let music sound while he doth make his choice;
Then, if he lose, he makes a swan-like end,
45 Fading in music: that the comparison
May stand more proper, my eye shall be the stream
And watery death-bed for him. He may win;
And what is music then? then music is
Even as the flourish when true subjects bow
50 To a new-crowned monarch: such it is
As are those dulcet sounds in break of day
That creep into the dreaming bridegroom's ear,
And summon him to marriage. Now he goes,
With no less presence, but with much more love,
55 Than young Alcides, when he did redeem
The virgin tribute paid by howling Troy
To the sea-monster: I stand for sacrifice;
The rest aloof are the Dardanian wives,
With bleared visages come forth to view
60 The issue of th' exploit. Go, Hercules!
Live thou, I live: with much, much more dismay
I view the fight than thou that mak'st the fray.
   [*A Song, whilst* Bassanio *comments on the caskets to*
                               himself

     Tell me where is fancy bred,
     Or in the heart or in the head?
65   *How begot, how nourished?*
        Reply, reply.
     It is engend'red in the eyes,
     With gazing fed; and fancy dies
     In the cradle where it lies.
70   *Let us all ring fancy's knell:*
       I'll begin it—Ding, dong, bell.
     Ding, dong, bell.

70	*knell*: funeral bell.
73	*least themselves*: not at all what they appear to be.
74	*The world*: people.
75-7	*In law . . . evil*: in legal matters, the most rotten case can be presented so well that the presentation conceals the evil (just as bad—'tainted'—meat can be spiced—'seasoned'—to hide the real taste).
78-9	*What . . . text*: a great sin ('damned error') can be committed by a man with a pious appearance ('sober brow') who is able to quote the Bible and excuse ('approve') what he is doing (see also *1, 3, 94*).
81	*There . . . simple*: both 'no vice is so plain' and 'no vicious man is so foolish'.
81-2	*but . . . parts*: that the vice (or the vicious man) does not have the outward appearance of virtue.
84	*stairs of sand*: sandbanks. *yet*: nevertheless.
85	*Hercules*: the superman of classical mythology. *Mars*: the classical god of war.
86	*inward search'd*: if their intestines are examined. *livers . . . milk*: a brave man's liver should (the Elizabethans thought) be red with blood (see note on *1, 1, 80*).
87	*valour's excrement*: the hairy growth ('beards') of courage.
88	*render them redoubted*: make them seem terrible. *beauty*: cosmetics.
89-91	Those who wear the heaviest make-up which has been bought by the ounce ('purchas'd by the weight') are the most immoral ('lightest'). The two senses of 'light' (in weight and in morals) allow Bassanio to point out the paradox, the 'miracle in nature'.
92-6	The golden curls on a woman's head may be no more than a wig, made from the hair of some other woman, now dead. The adjective 'snaky' implies a comparison with the head of Medusa, who had snakes for hair; anyone who looked at Medusa was turned to stone.

Bassanio

So may the outward shows be least themselves:
The world is still deceiv'd with ornament.
75 In law, what plea so tainted and corrupt
But, being season'd with a gracious voice,
Obscures the show of evil? In religion,
What damned error, but some sober brow
Will bless it and approve it with a text,
80 Hiding the grossness with fair ornament?
There is no vice so simple but assumes
Some mark of virtue on his outward parts.
How many cowards, whose hearts are all as false
As stairs of sand, wear yet upon their chins
85 The beards of Hercules and frowning Mars,
Who, inward search'd, have livers white as milk;
And these assume but valour's excrement
To render them redoubted. Look on beauty,
And you shall see 'tis purchas'd by the weight;
90 Which therein works a miracle in nature,
Making them lightest that wear most of it:
So are those crisped snaky golden locks
Which make such wanton gambols with the wind,
Upon supposed fairness, often known
95 To be the dowry of a second head,
The skull that bred them in the sepulchre.
Thus ornament is but the guiled shore
To a most dangerous sea, the beauteous scarf
Veiling an Indian beauty; in a word,
100 The seeming truth which cunning times put on
To entrap the wisest. Therefore, thou gaudy gold,
Hard food for Midas, I will none of thee;
Nor none of thee, thou pale and common drudge
'Tween man and man: but thou, thou meagre lead,
105 Which rather threaten'st than dost promise aught,
Thy paleness moves me more than eloquence,
And here choose I: joy be the consequence!
      Portia
[*Aside*] How all the other passions fleet to air,
As doubtful thoughts, and rash-embrac'd despair,

92 *crisped*: curled.

95 *dowry of*: endowment (legacy) from.

97 *guiled*: treacherous.

99 *Indian*: dark-skinned. The Elizabethan ideal of beauty was blonde, with a fair skin; 'an Indian beauty' would be almost a contradiction in terms.

99 *in a word*: briefly.

102 *Midas*: in Greek mythology, Midas was granted his wish that everything he touched should be turned to gold; food became a problem for him.
will none of thee: will not have anything to do with you.

104 *meagre*: unattractive.

105 Who makes threats rather than promises (in the inscription on the casket).

107 *consequence*: i.e. of the choice.

108 *fleet to*: vanish into.

109 *As*: such as.
rash-embrac'd: too quickly accepted.

110 *green eyed*: green was the colour associated with jealousy (in England we still say 'green with envy').

111 *allay*: diminish.

112 *measure*: moderation.
scant: restrain.

115 *counterfeit*: image.

115-16 *What . . . creation*: the artist must have been almost divine, because he has made a picture which is so like life.
Move these eyes: do the eyes move.

117-18 Or is it rather that, because they seem to be fixed ('riding') on my own eyeballs, they appear to be moving.

118 *sever'd*: parted.

119-20 *so sweet . . . friends*: it is right that such a sweet barrier (Portia's breath) should separate such sweet friends (her lips).

120-3 *Here . . . cobwebs*: in this picture, the painter has been like a spider, because the hair is like a golden network ('mesh'), which traps men's hearts just as gnats are caught in spiders' webs.

110 And shuddering fear, and green-eyed jealousy.
O love be moderate, allay thy ecstasy,
In measure rain thy joy, scant this excess,
I feel too much thy blessing; make it less,
For fear I surfeit!

Bassanio   What find I here?
[*He opens the leaden casket*

115 Fair Portia's counterfeit! What demi-god
Hath come so near creation? Move these eyes?
Or whether, riding on the balls of mine,
Seem they in motion? Here are sever'd lips,
Parted with sugar breath; so sweet a bar

120 Should sunder such sweet friends. Here in her hairs
The painter plays the spider, and hath woven
A golden mesh t' entrap the hearts of men
Faster than gnats in cobwebs: but her eyes!
How could he see to do them? having made one,

125 Methinks it should have power to steal both his
And leave itself unfurnish'd: yet look how far
The substance of my praise doth wrong this shadow
In underprizing it, so far this shadow
Doth limp behind the substance. Here's the scroll,

130 The continent and summary of my fortune.

You that choose not by the view,
Chance as fair, and choose as true!
Since this fortune falls to you,
Be content and seek no new.
135 *If you be well pleas'd with this*
And hold your fortune for your bliss,
Turn you where your lady is
And claim her with a loving kiss.

A gentle scroll. Fair lady, by your leave;
[*Kissing her*
140 I come by note, to give and to receive.
Like one of two contending in a prize,

124-6   *having . . . unfurnis'd*: I think that when one eye had been painted, it would have the power (with its beauty) to blind the painter (stealing away his eyes) so that he could not paint the second eye.

126   *unfurnish'd*: not provided with a companion.

126-9   *yet look . . . substance*: I know that my praise is inadequate ('doth wrong') the portrait (which is only a sketch—'shadow' of Portia), and cannot speak its true worth (underprizes it). In the same way, the portrait ('shadow') is far behind the real thing.

130   *continent*: container.

131   *by the view*: from the outside appearance.

132   May you always have such good fortune ('Chance') and choose as well (as you have done this time).

136   And think ('hold') that your luck ('fortune') means happiness.

140   *by note*: as instructed.

143   *universal shout*: shouts of approval from everyone.

144   *Giddy in spirit*: dazed.

145   *his or no*: for him or not.

148   *ratified*: validated, given authority.

155   *That only*: only in order to.
       account: estimation.

156   *livings*: possessions.

157   *Exceed account*: be worth more than can be reckoned.

157-9   *but . . . unpractis'd*: the full amount of me is no more than the full amount of something that, at best ('to term in gross'), is a girl with no education, no training, no experience.

160   *Happy*: fortunate.

162   *is not bred so dull*: was not born so stupid.

166-7   *Myself . . . converted*: I now belong, with all that I possess, to you.

167   *but now*: just a moment ago.

174   *vantage*: opportunity.
       exclaim on: accuse.

175   *bereft me of*: stolen from me.

176   *my blood speaks*: Bassanio is blushing.

That thinks he hath done well in people's eyes,
Hearing applause and universal shout,
Giddy in spirit, still gazing in a doubt
145 Whether those peals of praise be his or no;
So, thrice-fair lady, stand I, even so,
As doubtful whether what I see be true,
Until confirm'd, sign'd, ratified by you.

     Portia

You see me, Lord Bassanio, where I stand,
150 Such as I am: though for myself alone
I would not be ambitious in my wish,
To wish myself much better; yet, for you,
I would be trebled twenty times myself;
A thousand times more fair, ten thousand times more
     rich;
155 That only to stand high in your account,
I might in virtues, beauties, livings, friends,
Exceed account: but the full sum of me
Is sum of something, which, to term in gross,
Is an unlesson'd girl, unschool'd, unpractis'd;
160 Happy in this, she is not yet so old
But she may learn; happier than this,
She is not bred so dull but she can learn;
Happiest of all, is that her gentle spirit
Commits itself to yours to be directed
165 As from her lord, her governor, her king.
Myself and what is mine, to you and yours
Is now converted: but now I was the lord
Of this fair mansion, master of my servants,
Queen o'er myself; and even now, but now,
170 This house, these servants, and this same myself
Are yours, my lord's. I give them with this ring;
Which when you part from, lose, or give away,
Let it presage the ruin of your love,
And be my vantage to exclaim on you.

     Bassanio

175 Madam, you have bereft me of all words,
Only my blood speaks to you in my veins;
And there is such confusion in my powers,
As, after some oration fairly spoke
By a beloved prince, there doth appear
180 Among the buzzing pleased multitude;

177-80   My thoughts are confused, just
     like a crowd of happy, murmuring
     citizens who have heard a fine speech
     from a much-loved ruler.
181-2   When everything is so mixed up
     that it becomes a wilderness where
     nothing can be distinguished except
     ('save of') joy.

187   *prosper*: be fulfilled.

190   I hope that you will have all the
     happiness that you can wish for your-
     selves.
191   You cannot wish for any more
     than I wish for you.
192   *solemnize*: celebrate formally.
193   *bargain of your faith*: contract of
     your love.
194   *Even at that time*: at that very
     same time
195   *so*: provided that.

199-200   *intermission . . . you*: time-
     wasting no more belongs to me than
     to you—I don't waste any more time
     than you do.
201   *stood*: depended.
202   *as the matter falls*: as it happens.
203   *until I sweat again*: so hard that
     I was sweating.
204   *swearing*: declaring my love.
     roof: i.e. the roof of his mouth.
205   *if promise last*: if she keeps her
     promise. Gratiano puns with two
     senses of a word, here and in line 211.
206   *of*: from.

209   *so*: if.
     stand: are.

211   *faith*: in good faith.

213-14   We'll bet them that whoever gets
     the first son wins a thousand ducats.

Where every something, being blent together,
Turns to a wild of nothing, save of joy,
Express'd, and not express'd. But when this ring
Parts from this finger, then parts life from hence:
185 O then be bold to say Bassanio's dead.
     Nerissa
My lord and lady, it is now our time,
That have stood by and seen our wishes prosper,
To cry, good joy. Good joy, my lord and lady!
     Gratiano
My Lord Bassanio, and my gentle lady,
190 I wish you all the joy that you can wish;
For I am sure you can wish none from me.
And when your honours mean to solemnize
The bargain of your faith, I do beseech you,
Even at that time I may be married too.
     Bassanio
195 With all my heart, so thou canst get a wife.
     Gratiano
I thank your lordship, you have got me one.
My eyes, my lord, can look as swift as yours:
You saw the mistress, I beheld the maid;
You lov'd, I lov'd: for intermission
200 No more pertains to me, my lord, than you.
Your fortune stood upon the caskets there,
And so did mine too, as the matter falls;
For wooing here until I sweat again,
And swearing till my very roof was dry
205 With oaths of love, at last (if promise last)
I got a promise of this fair one here
To have her love, provided that your fortune
Achiev'd her mistress.
     Portia   Is this true, Nerissa?
     Nerissa
Madam, it is, so you stand pleas'd withal.
     Bassanio
210 And do you, Gratiano, mean good faith?
     Gratiano
Yes, faith, my lord.
     Bassanio
Our feast shall be much honour'd in your marriage.
     Gratiano
We'll play with them the first boy for a thousand
ducats.

215   *and stake down*: with our money
down on the table (to show that the
bet is serious). Gratiano replies with a
bawdy joke, pretending that Nerissa
means 'with weapon down'.

217   *infidel*: non-believer (a reference
to Jessica's Jewishness).

220-1   If I have the right ('power') to
welcome you here, since my claim
('interest') to this place is so new
(young).

222   *very*: true.

226   *My purpose was not*: I did not
intend.

227   *by the way*: by chance.

228   *past . . . nay*: and would not let
me refuse.

231   *Commends him*: sends his
greetings.

235   *estate*: condition.

236   *yond*: yonder.

238   *royal*: honourable.

240   *Jasons*: see note on *1, 1, 170*.

Nerissa

215 What, and stake down?

Gratiano

No, we shall ne'er win at that sport and stake down!
But who comes here? Lorenzo and his infidel!
What! and my old Venetian friend, Salerio?

Enter Lorenzo, Jessica, *and* Salerio

Bassanio

Lorenzo, and Salerio, welcome hither,

220 If that the youth of my new interest here
Have power to bid you welcome. By your leave,
I bid my very friends and countrymen,
Sweet Portia, welcome.

Portia   So do I, my lord:
They are entirely welcome.

Lorenzo

225 I thank your honour. For my part, my lord,
My purpose was not to have seen you here,
But meeting with Salerio by the way,
He did entreat me, past all saying nay,
To come with him along.

Salerio   I did, my lord,

230 And I have reason for it. Signior Antonio
Commends him to you.   [*Gives* Bassanio *a letter*

Bassanio   Ere I ope his letter,
I pray you, tell me how my good friend doth.

Salerio

Not sick, my lord, unless it be in mind;
Nor well, unless in mind: his letter there

235 Will show you his estate.

                              [Bassanio *opens the letter*

Gratiano

Nerissa, cheer yond stranger; bid her welcome.
Your hand, Salerio. What's the news from Venice?
How doth that royal merchant, good Antonio?
I know he will be glad of our success;

240 We are the Jasons, we have won the fleece.

Salerio

I would you had won the fleece that he hath lost.

Portia

There are some shrewd contents in yond same
    paper,
That steals the colour from Bassanio's cheek:
Some dear friend dead, else nothing in the world
245 Could turn so much the constitution
Of any constant man. What, worse and worse!
With leave, Bassanio; I am half yourself,
And I must freely have the half of anything
That this same paper brings you.

Bassanio   O sweet Portia!
250 Here are a few of the unpleasant'st words
That ever blotted paper. Gentle lady,
When I did first impart my love to you,
I freely told you all the wealth I had
Ran in my veins—I was a gentleman—
255 And then I told you true; and yet, dear lady,
Rating myself at nothing, you shall see
How much I was a braggart. When I told you
My state was nothing, I should then have told you
That I was worse than nothing; for, indeed,
260 I have engag'd myself to a dear friend,
Engag'd my friend to his mere enemy,
To feed my means. Here is a letter, lady;
The paper as the body of my friend,
And every word in it a gaping wound,
265 Issuing life-blood. But is it true, Salerio?
Hath all his ventures fail'd? What, not one hit?
From Tripolis, from Mexico, and England,
From Lisbon, Barbary, and India?
And not one vessel 'scape the dreadful touch
270 Of merchant-marring rocks?

Salerio   Not one, my lord.
Besides, it should appear, that if he had
The present money to discharge the Jew,
He would not take it. Never did I know
A creature, that did bear the shape of man,
275 So keen and greedy to confound a man.
He plies the duke at morning and at night,
And doth impeach the freedom of the state,
If they deny him justice: twenty merchants,
The duke himself, and the magnificoes
280 Of greatest port, have all persuaded with him;

---

242 *shrewd*: bitter.

245 *constitution*: complexion.
246 *constant*: normal.
247 *With leave*: excuse me.

251 *blotted paper*: spoiled a paper
    with ink.
253 *freely*: honestly.
254 *Ran in my veins*: was in my
    blood.
256 *Rating*: valuing.
257 *was a braggart*: boasted.
258 *state*: estate, fortune.

260 *engag'd*: bound.
261 *mere*: absolute.
262 *To feed my means*: to get the
    money I needed.
263 *as*: is like.

265 *Issuing life-blood*: from which his
    life-blood pours.
266 *ventures*: business speculations.
    hit: success.

270 *merchant-marring rocks*: rocks
    that ruin merchants.

272 *present*: ready.
    discharge: pay his debt to.

275 *confound*: ruin.
276 *plies*: urges his case on.
277 *impeach*: question.
    freedom of the state: the integrity
    of the law in Venice.
279 *magnificoes*: noblemen.
280 *port*: authority.

281   *drive him from*: persuade him to give up.
        envious plea: malicious claim.

284   *his countrymen*: fellow Jews.

288   *deny not*: do not prevent it.
289   *hard*: badly.

292-3   *The . . . courtesies*: a man whose spirit is the most willing and untiring in helping others.
294   *The ancient Roman honour*: i.e. loyalty to friends and country.

298   *deface*: cancel.

302   *call me wife*: make me your wife.

310   *shall hence*: must go away from here.
311   *cheer*: face.
312   *dear bought*: expensively purchased.

But none can drive him from the envious plea
Of forfeiture, of justice, and his bond.
    Jessica
When I was with him, I have heard him swear
To Tubal and to Chus, his countrymen,
That he would rather have Antonio's flesh
Than twenty times the value of the sum
That he did owe him; and I know, my lord,
If law, authority, and power deny not,
It will go hard with poor Antonio.
    Portia
Is it your dear friend that is thus in trouble?
    Bassanio
The dearest friend to me, the kindest man,
The best-condition'd and unwearied spirit
In doing courtesies, and one in whom
The ancient Roman honour more appears
Than any that draws breath in Italy.
    Portia
What sum owes he the Jew?
    Bassanio
For me, three thousand ducats.
    Portia   What, no more?
Pay him six thousand, and deface the bond;
Double six thousand, and then treble that,
Before a friend of this description
Shall lose a hair through Bassanio's fault.
First go with me to church and call me wife,
And then away to Venice to your friend;
For never shall you lie by Portia's side
With an unquiet soul. You shall have gold
To pay the petty debt twenty times over:
When it is paid, bring your true friend along.
My maid Nerissa and myself meantime
Will live as maids and widows. Come, away!
For you shall hence upon your wedding-day.
Bid your friends welcome, show a merry cheer;
Since you are dear bought, I will love you dear.
But let me hear the letter of your friend.

285

290

295

300

305

310

314   *miscarried*: been lost.

317   *cleared*: cancelled.
318   *but*: only.
319   *use your pleasure*: do as you please.

321   *O love*: Portia speaks as though Antonio's reference to Bassanio's 'love' was meant for her.
      dispatch: hurry up with.
322   *good leave*: kind permission.
324–5   I shall not go to bed, and not even rest shall come between us.
325   *twain*: two.

Act 3   Scene 3
Antonio has been arrested and taken to prison. Shylock threatens him, but Antonio is patient.

1   *look to him*: guard him carefully.
2   *gratis*: free of interest.

4   *speak not*: don't argue.

9   *naughty*: worthless.
    fond: foolish.
10 *abroad*: out of the prison.

14 *dull-eyed*: stupid.

16 *intercessors*: pleaders.

Bassanio

Sweet Bassanio, my ships have all miscarried, my
315 *creditors grow cruel, my estate is very low, my bond to*
the Jew is forfeit; and since, in paying it, it is impossible
I should live, all debts are cleared between you and
I, if I might but see you at my death. Notwithstanding,
use your pleasure: if your love do not persuade you
320 *to come, let not my letter.*

Portia

O love, dispatch all business, and be gone!

Bassanio

Since I have your good leave to go away,
I will make haste; but, till I come again,
No bed shall e'er be guilty of my stay,
325 Nor rest be interposer 'twixt us twain.   [*Exeunt*

Scene 3 *Venice. A street*

Enter Shylock, Solanio, Antonio, *and*
Gaoler

Shylock

Gaoler, look to him: tell not me of mercy;
This is the fool that lent out money gratis:
Gaoler, look to him.

Antonio   Hear me yet, good Shylock.

Shylock

I'll have my bond; speak not against my bond:
5 I have sworn an oath that I will have my bond.
Thou call'dst me dog before thou hadst a cause,
But, since I am a dog, beware my fangs:
The duke shall grant me justice. I do wonder,
Thou naughty gaoler, that thou art so fond
10 To come abroad with him at his request.

Antonio

I pray thee, hear me speak.

Shylock

I'll have my bond; I will not hear thee speak:
I'll have my bond, and therefore speak no more.
I'll not be made a soft and dull-eyed fool,
15 To shake the head, relent, and sigh, and yield
To Christian intercessors. Follow not;
I'll have no speaking; I will have my bond.   [*Exit*

18   *impenetrable*: hard-hearted.
19   *kept with*: lived among.

20   *follow*: appeal to.
      bootless: useless.

22   *deliver'd*: rescued.
      forfeitures: actions against those
who could not pay their debts;
Antonio himself is now enduring one
of these 'forfeitures'.
23   *made moan*: appealed.
25   Will never agree that Shylock
should be allowed to make his demand
(for the pound of flesh).
26   *the course of law*: that law must
take its course.
27–31 Because if 'the course of law' is
not allowed ('denied'), then the rights
('commodity') of foreigners
('strangers') will make them doubt
('impeach') Venetian justice; and this
will be a serious matter, because the
city's prosperity ('profit') depends on
international trade.
32   *so bated me*: made me lose so
much weight.
34   *bloody*: blood-thirsty.

Solanio
It is the most impenetrable cur
That ever kept with men.
Antonio   Let him alone:
20 I'll follow him no more with bootless prayers.
He seeks my life; his reason well I know.
I oft deliver'd from his forfeitures
Many that have at times made moan to me;
Therefore he hates me.
Solanio   I am sure the duke
25 Will never grant this forfeiture to hold.
Antonio
The duke cannot deny the course of law:
For the commodity that strangers have
With us in Venice, if it be denied,
Will much impeach the justice of the state,
30 Since that the trade and profit of the city
Consisteth of all nations. Therefore, go:
These griefs and losses have so bated me,
That I shall hardly spare a pound of flesh
Tomorrow to my bloody creditor.
35 Well, gaoler, on. Pray God, Bassanio come
To see me pay his debt, and then I care not!
                                      [*Exeunt*

Act 3   Scene 4
Portia asks Lorenzo to look after her
house until she and Nerissa return.
They are going to Venice, and plan to
dress as men to play a trick on their
husbands.

2   *conceit*: understanding.

3   *amity*: friendship.

5   *to whom*: i.e. Antonio.

7   *lover*: friend.

8–9   *you would . . . you*: you would be
more proud that you had done this
deed than you are of your usual acts of
kindness ('bounty').

Scene 4 *Belmont. A room in Portia's house*

Enter Portia, Nerissa, Lorenzo, Jessica,
and Balthazar
Lorenzo
Madam, although I speak it in your presence,
You have a noble and a true conceit
Of god-like amity; which appears most strongly
In bearing thus the absence of your lord.
5 But if you knew to whom you show this honour,
How true a gentleman you send relief,
How dear a lover of my lord your husband,
I know you would be prouder of the work
Than customary bounty can enforce you.

Portia

10 I never did repent for doing good,
Nor shall not now: for in companions
That do converse and waste the time together,
Whose souls do bear an equal yoke of love,
There must be needs a like proportion
15 Of lineaments, of manners, and of spirit;
Which makes me think that this Antonio,
Being the bosom lover of my lord,
Must needs be like my lord. If it be so,
How little is the cost I have bestow'd
20 In purchasing the semblance of my soul
From out the state of hellish cruelty!
This comes too near the praising of myself;
Therefore, no more of it: hear other things.
Lorenzo, I commit into your hands
25 The husbandry and manage of my house
Until my lord's return: for mine own part,
I have toward heaven breath'd a secret vow
To live in prayer and contemplation,
Only attended by Nerissa here,
30 Until her husband and my lord's return.
There is a monastery two miles off,
And there we will abide. I do desire you
Not to deny this imposition,
The which my love and some necessity
35 Now lays upon you.

Lorenzo   Madam, with all my heart:
I shall obey you in all fair commands.

Portia

My people do already know my mind,
And will acknowledge you and Jessica
In place of Lord Bassanio and myself.
40 So fare you well till we shall meet again.

Lorenzo

Fair thoughts and happy hours attend on you!

Jessica

I wish your ladyship all heart's content.

Portia

I thank you for your wish, and am well pleas'd
To wish it back on you: fare you well, Jessica.
[*Exeunt* Jessica *and* Lorenzo

12   *waste*: spend.
13   Whose souls are joined together by the same bond of marriage (as oxen are joined by a yoke).
14   *be needs*: necessarily be.
         a like: the same.
15   *lineaments*: characteristics.
17   *bosom lover*: close friend.
19   *bestow'd*: spent.
20   *the . . . soul*: Portia has argued that lovers must be like each other in soul, and that close friends must also resemble each other; therefore Antonio must be like Bassanio, whose soul resembles Portia's own.
22   *comes too near*: is too like.
25   *husbandry and manage*: careful management.

33   *deny*: refuse.
         imposition: task.

37   *my mind*: what I intend.
38   *acknowledge*: recognize your authority.

44   *it back on you*: the same to you.

<table>
<tr><td>

46   *ever*: always.
     honest-true: honest and trust-
worthy.
47   *So . . . still*: may I continue to
find you so.
48   *all . . . man*: go as fast as a man
can.
49   *render*: give.
51   *And look*: and take care of.
52   *imagin'd speed*: all conceivable
speed.
53   *traject*: landing-place.
54   *trades*: carries passengers for
hire.
56   *convenient speed*: as fast as I can.

57   *work in hand*: a plan in my mind.

59   *think of us*: expect to see us.

60   *habit*: costume.
61   *accomplished*: equipped.
62   *that we lack*: i.e. the attributes of
masculinity.
        wager: bet.
63   *accoutered*: dressed up.
64   *prettier*: smarter.
66   *between . . . boy*: as though my
voice were breaking (changing from a
boy's voice to a man's voice).
67   *reed*: squeaky.
        mincing: dainty, lady-like.
68   *frays*: fights.
69   *bragging*: boastful.
        quaint: elaborate.
72   *I . . . withal*: I could not do any-
thing about it.
74   *puny*: feeble, silly.
75–6   *I have . . . twelvemonth*: that it is
a year since I left school.
77   *raw*: crude.
        jacks: fellows.
78   *turn to men*: change into men.
Portia pretends to think that Nerissa
means 'take men for lovers'.

</td></tr>
</table>

45 Now, Balthazar,
As I have ever found thee honest-true,
So let me find thee still. Take this same letter,
And use thou all th' endeavour of a man
In speed to Padua: see thou render this
50 Into my cousin's hand, Doctor Bellario;
And look what notes and garments he doth give
     thee,
Bring them, I pray thee, with imagin'd speed
Unto the traject, to the common ferry
Which trades to Venice. Waste no time in words,
55 But get thee gone: I shall be there before thee.
　　　　Balthazar
Madam, I go with all convenient speed.　　　[*Exit*
　　　　Portia
Come on, Nerissa: I have work in hand
That you yet know not of: we'll see our husbands
Before they think of us.
　　　　Nerissa　　　　　　　　Shall they see us?
　　　　Portia
60 They shall, Nerissa; but in such a habit
That they shall think we are accomplished
With that we lack. I'll hold thee any wager,
When we are both accoutered like young men,
I'll prove the prettier fellow of the two,
65 And wear my dagger with the braver grace,
And speak between the change of man and boy
With a reed voice, and turn two mincing steps
Into a manly stride, and speak of frays
Like a fine bragging youth, and tell quaint lies,
70 How honourable ladies sought my love,
Which I denying, they fell sick and died—
I could not do withal; then I'll repent,
And wish, for all that, that I had not kill'd them.
And twenty of these puny lies I'll tell,
75 That men shall swear I have discontinu'd school
Above a twelvemonth. I have within my mind
A thousand raw tricks of these bragging jacks,
Which I will practise.
　　　　Nerissa　　　　Why, shall we turn to men?

Portia
Fie, what a question's that,
80 If thou wert near a lewd interpreter!
But come: I'll tell thee all my whole device
When I am in my coach, which stays for us
At the park gate; and therefore haste away,
For we must measure twenty miles today.

[*Exeunt*

Scene 5 *Belmont. Portia's garden*

Enter Launcelot *and* Jessica

Launcelot
Yes, truly; for, look you, the sins of the father are
to be laid upon the children; therefore, I promise
you, I fear you. I was always plain with you, and
so now I speak my agitation of the matter: therefore
5 be o' good cheer; for, truly, I think you are damned.
There is but one hope in it that can do you any
good, and that is but a kind of bastard hope
neither.

Jessica
And what hope is that, I pray thee?

Launcelot
10 Marry, you may partly hope that your father got
you not, that you are not the Jew's daughter.

Jessica
That were a kind of bastard hope, indeed: so the
sins of my mother should be visited upon me.

Launcelot
Truly then I fear you are damned both by father
15 and mother: thus when I shun Scylla (your father)
I fall into Charybdis (your mother): well, you are
gone both ways.

Jessica
I shall be saved by my husband; he hath made
me a Christian.

Launcelot
20 Truly the more to blame he: we were Christians
enow before; e'en as many as could well live one by
another. This making of Christians will raise the
price of hogs: if we grow all to be pork-eaters, we
shall not shortly have a rasher on the coals for
25 money.

---

80   *lewd interpreter*: someone with a dirty mind.
81   *device*: plan.

84   *measure*: travel.

Act 3   Scene 5
Launcelot Gobbo teases Jessica about her Jewish nationality. Her husband Lorenzo joins in the fun.
1   *look you*: you see.
     the sins of the father: Launcelot is quoting the first of the Ten Commandments (Exodus 20: 5).
2   *laid upon*: revenged upon.
3   *I fear you*: I fear for you.
     plain: honest.
4   *agitation*: Launcelot means 'cogitation' (= considered opinion).
7   *bastard hope*: both 'false hope' and 'hope that you are a bastard'.
7-8   *but . . . neither*: only.
10-11   *got you not*: did not beget you.
12   *so*: if that were the case.
13   *should . . . me*: I should be punished for.
15-16   *Scylla . . . Charybdis*: monsters of classical legend, taking the form of rocks and a whirlpool on either side of the straits between Italy and Sicily; sailors who escaped one were usually caught by the other.
17   *gone*: doomed.
18   Jessica refers to 1 Corinthians 7: 14: 'the unbelieving wife is sanctified by the husband'.
20-1   *we . . . before*: there were enough of us Christians before he converted you.
21   *e'en*: quite.
21-2   *one by another*: together.
22-3   *raise . . . hogs*: because as Christians they will be allowed to eat pork, which is forbidden to Jews.
24   *rasher on the coals*: slice of bacon cooking on the fire.
24-5   *for money*: at any price.

Enter Lorenzo

Jessica

I'll tell my husband, Launcelot, what you say: here he comes.

Lorenzo

I shall grow jealous of you shortly, Launcelot, if you thus get my wife into corners.

Jessica

30 Nay, you need not fear us, Lorenzo: Launcelot and I are out. He tells me flatly there's no mercy for me in heaven, because I am a Jew's daughter: and he says you are no good member of the commonwealth, for, in converting Jews to Christians, you

35 raise the price of pork.

Lorenzo

I shall answer that better to the commonwealth than you can the getting up of the negro's belly: the Moor is with child by you, Launcelot.

Launcelot

It is much that the Moor should be more than

40 reason; but if she be less than an honest woman, she is indeed more than I took her for.

Lorenzo

How every fool can play upon the word! I think the best grace of wit will shortly turn into silence, and discourse grow commendable in none only but

45 parrots. Go in, sirrah: bid them prepare for dinner.

Launcelot

That is done, sir; they have all stomachs.

Lorenzo

Goodly Lord, what a wit-snapper are you! then bid them prepare dinner.

Launcelot

That is done too, sir; only 'cover' is the word.

Lorenzo

50 Will you cover, then, sir?

Launcelot

Not so, sir, neither; I know my duty.

Lorenzo

Yet more quarrelling with occasion! Wilt thou show the whole wealth of thy wit in an instant? I pray thee, understand a plain man in his plain

29   *into corners*: i.e. where you can whisper together, and flirt.

31   *are out*: have fallen out, have quarrelled.
       flatly: certainly.

37   *getting up*: swelling.
38   *Moor*: Moorish (woman); Launcelot's reply puns on 'Moor' and 'more'.
39–40   *more than reason*: bigger than she ought to be.
40–1   *but if . . . for*: even if she is not quite an honest woman, she is nevertheless better than I thought her to be (presumably he thought she was a whore).
43   *the best . . . silence*: soon, the best way to show one's cleverness will be by keeping silent.
44–5   *discourse . . . parrots*: talking will be something to admire only in parrots.
46   *they have all stomachs*: they are all hungry (with a pun on 'stomachs' = appetites, and = digestions).
47   *wit-snapper*: comedian.
49   *'cover' is the word*: you ought to say 'lay the table'; but when Lorenzo does use the word 'cover', Launcelot pretends to think he intends another meaning—'put on your hat'.
51   *my duty*: respect; inferiors stood bare-headed in the presence of their superiors.
52   *quarrelling with occasion*: taking every opportunity to make a play on words.

58   For the table: as far as the food is concerned (Launcelot pretends to mistake Lorenzo's 'table').

59   covered: i.e. to keep it hot.

60-1   as . . . govern: as your whims and fancies please you.

62   O dear . . . suited: Lorenzo laughs at Launcelot's ability to distinguish different meanings of a word, and fit them for his purpose.

65   A many: a lot of.
       stand in better place: have better positions (perhaps as professional fools).

66   Garnish'd: supplied with a stock of words; perhaps Lorenzo also refers to the extra gold braid on Launcelot's livery (see 2, 2, 149) which makes him look like a court jester.
       tricksy: clever.

67   Defy the matter: confuse the sense of what they are saying.
       How cheer'st thou: are you happy?

70   Past all expressing: I can't find words to say how good she is.
       meet: necessary.

71   upright: honourable.

75   In reason: it is only reasonable that.

77-80 If each of these gods should give a human woman as his bet ('wager'), and one of these women was Portia, something else would have to be gambled ('Pawn'd') with the other woman, for no woman in the world is Portia's equal ('fellow').

83   anon: shortly.

84   stomach: both 'appetite for dinner' and 'desire to praise you'.

85   table-talk: conversation during the meal.

86   howsome'er: however.

87   set you forth: put you in your place.

---

55 meaning: go to thy fellows; bid them cover the table, serve in the meat, and we will come in to dinner.

Launcelot

For the table, sir, it shall be served in; for the meat, sir, it shall be covered; for your coming in to dinner,

60 sir, why, let it be as humours and conceits shall govern.   [*Exit*

Lorenzo

O dear discretion, how his words are suited!
The fool hath planted in his memory
An army of good words, and I do know

65 A many fools, that stand in better place,
Garnish'd like him, that for a tricksy word
Defy the matter. How cheer'st thou, Jessica?
And now, good sweet, say thy opinion;
How dost thou like the Lord Bassanio's wife?

Jessica

70 Past all expressing. It is very meet
The Lord Bassanio live an upright life,
For, having such a blessing in his lady,
He finds the joys of heaven here on earth;
And if on earth he do not merit it,

75 In reason he should never come to heaven.
Why, if two gods should play some heavenly match,
And on the wager lay two earthly women,
And Portia one, there must be something else
Pawn'd with the other, for the poor rude world

80 Hath not her fellow.

Lorenzo   Even such a husband
Hast thou of me, as she is for a wife.

Jessica

Nay, but ask my opinion too of that.

Lorenzo

I will anon; first, let us go to dinner.

Jessica

Nay, let me praise you while I have a stomach.

Lorenzo

85 No, pray thee, let it serve for table-talk;
Then howsome'er thou speak'st, 'mong other things
I shall digest it.

Jessica   Well, I'll set you forth.
                                                    [*Exeunt*

Act 4

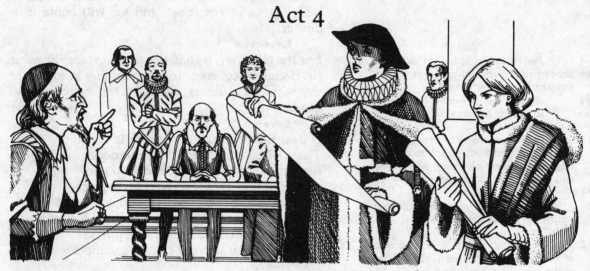

Act 4   Scene 1

The Duke asks Shylock to show mercy
to Antonio, but Shylock refuses and
insists on having his pound of flesh.
A young lawyer comes into the court—
it is Portia in disguise, with Nerissa as
the lawyer's clerk. Portia makes a
speech in praise of mercy, but Shylock
is unmoved. Portia agrees that he is
legally entitled to a pound of Antonio's
flesh, and Antonio prepares to die. At
the last moment Portia finds a way of
escape for Antonio. Bassanio is very
grateful because his friend's life has
been saved, and he offers to reward
the young lawyer. Portia asks for a
ring.

5   *void*: empty.
6   *dram*: a tiny measure.
7   *qualify*: moderate.
8   *stands obdurate*: remains hard-
hearted.

11   *arm'd*: prepared.

Scene 1 *Venice. A court of justice*

Enter the Duke, *the* Merchants, Antonio,
Bassanio, Gratiano, Salerio, *and* Officers
of the Court

Duke
What, is Antonio here?
   Antonio
Ready, so please your Grace.
   Duke
I am sorry for thee: thou art come to answer
A stony adversary, an inhuman wretch
5 Uncapable of pity, void and empty
From any dram of mercy.
   Antonio   I have heard
Your Grace hath ta'en great pains to qualify
His rigorous course; but since he stands obdurate,
And that no lawful means can carry me
10 Out of his envy's reach, I do oppose
My patience to his fury, and am arm'd
To suffer with a quietness of spirit
The very tyranny and rage of his.
   Duke
Go one, and call the Jew into the court.
   Salerio
15 He is ready at the door: he comes, my lord.

Enter Shylock

Duke

Make room, and let him stand before our face.
Shylock, the world thinks, and I think so too,
That thou but lead'st this fashion of thy malice
To the last hour of act; and then 'tis thought
20 Thou'lt show thy mercy and remorse more strange
Than is thy strange apparent cruelty;
And where thou now exact'st the penalty—
Which is a pound of this poor merchant's flesh—
Thou wilt not only loose the forfeiture,
25 But, touch'd with human gentleness and love,
Forgive a moiety of the principal,
Glancing an eye of pity on his losses,
That have of late so huddled on his back,
Enow to press a royal merchant down,
30 And pluck commiseration of his state
From brassy bosoms and rough hearts of flints,
From stubborn Turks and Tartars, never train'd
To offices of tender courtesy.
We all expect a gentle answer, Jew.

Shylock

35 I have possess'd your Grace of what I purpose;
And by our holy Sabbath have I sworn
To have the due and forfeit of my bond:
If you deny it, let the danger light
Upon your charter and your city's freedom.
40 You'll ask me, why I rather choose to have
A weight of carrion flesh than to receive
Three thousand ducats. I'll not answer that,
But say it is my humour. Is it answer'd?
What if my house be troubled with a rat,
45 And I be pleas'd to give ten thousand ducats
To have it ban'd? What, are you answer'd yet?
Some men there are love not a gaping pig;
Some, that are mad if they behold a cat;
And others, when the bagpipe sings i' the nose,
50 Cannot contain their urine: for affection,
Master of passion, sways it to the mood
Of what it likes, or loathes. Now, for your answer:
As there is no firm reason to be render'd,

18-19 *thou ... act*: you intend to carry on with this show of cruelty until the last moment.
20 *more strange*: which will be more strange.
21 *apparent*: as it appears now.
22 *exact'st*: insist on having.
24 *loose the forfeiture*: refuse to accept the penalty that Antonio should pay.
26 Allow him to keep a part of the original sum he borrowed.
29 *Enow*: enough.
royal: noble.
30 *commiseration of*: sympathy for.
31 *brassy bosoms*: hearts as hard as brass.
32 *stubborn*: unfeeling.
32-3 *train'd ... courtesy*: taught to behave with gentleness.
35 *possess'd*: informed.
36 *Sabbath*: the seventh day of the Jewish week, which was the holiest day (Genesis 2: 3).
37 *due ... bond*: the proper penalty for not repaying my loan.
38 *light*: descend.
39 *charter*: the document by which Venice was granted independence ('freedom').
41 *carrion*: rotten.
43 *it is my humour*: because I want it.
46 *ban'd*: poisoned.
47 *a gaping pig*: a pig's head, roasted, with the mouth open.
49 *sings i' the nose*: drones.
50-2 *affection ... loathes*: prejudice is stronger than any emotion ('passion'), and directs our emotion to love or hate the objects of our prejudice.

54-6   *he . . . he . . . he*: this man . . .
that man . . . the other man.

56   *woollen bagpipe*: the bag of the
pipes was covered in woollen material.

56-8   *but . . . offended*: but when he is
himself offended, he is compelled
(forced) to react in such a shameful
way that he must give offence to
others.

60   *lodg'd*: deep-rooted.

62   *A losing suit*: a legal case where
I must lose money.

64   *current*: outpouring.

Why he cannot abide a gaping pig;
55 Why he, a harmless necessary cat;
Why he, a woollen bagpipe, but of force
Must yield to such inevitable shame
As to offend, himself being offended;
So can I give no reason, nor I will not,
60 More than a lodg'd hate and a certain loathing
I bear Antonio, that I follow thus
A losing suit against him. Are you answer'd?
   Bassanio
This is no answer, thou unfeeling man,
To excuse the current of thy cruelty.
   Shylock
65 I am not bound to please thee with my answers.
   Bassanio
Do all men kill the things they do not love?
   Shylock
Hates any man the thing he would not kill?
   Bassanio
Every offence is not a hate at first.
   Shylock

68   A single offence is not a cause
for hatred.

What! wouldst thou have a serpent sting thee
twice?
   Antonio

70   *think . . . Jew*: remember that
you are arguing with the Jew.

72   *main flood*: ocean tide.
       bate: reduce.

73   *use question with*: ask.

70 I pray you, think you question with the Jew:
You may as well go stand upon the beach,
And bid the main flood bate his usual height;
You may as well use question with the wolf,
Why he hath made the ewe bleat for the lamb;
75 You may as well forbid the mountain pines
To wag their high tops, and to make no noise
When they are fretten with the gusts of heaven;
You may as well do anything most hard,
As seek to soften that—than which what's harder?—

76   *wag*: wave.

77   *fretten*: blown.

80 His Jewish heart: therefore, I do beseech you,
Make no more offers, use no farther means;
But with all brief and plain conveniency,
Let me have judgment, and the Jew his will.
   Bassanio
For thy three thousand ducats here is six.
   Shylock

82   But as quickly and simply as
you can.

85 If every ducat in six thousand ducats
Were in six parts, and every part a ducat,
I would not draw them. I would have my bond.

87   *draw*: accept.

Duke
How shalt thou hope for mercy, rendering none?
Shylock
What judgment shall I dread, doing no wrong?
90 You have among you many a purchas'd slave,
Which, like your asses and your dogs and mules,
You use in abject and in slavish parts,
Because you bought them: shall I say to you,
'Let them be free, marry them to your heirs?
95 Why sweat they under burdens? let their beds
Be made as soft as yours, and let their palates
Be season'd with such viands?' You will answer,
'The slaves are ours'. So do I answer you:
The pound of flesh which I demand of him,
100 Is dearly bought; 'tis mine and I will have it.
If you deny me, fie upon your law!
There is no force in the decrees of Venice.
I stand for judgment. Answer—shall I have it?
Duke
Upon my power I may dismiss this court,
105 Unless Bellario, a learned doctor,
Whom I have sent for to determine this,
Come here today.
Salerio   My lord, here stays without
A messenger with letters from the doctor,
New come from Padua.
Duke
110 Bring us the letters: call the messenger.
Bassanio
Good cheer, Antonio! What, man, courage yet!
The Jew shall have my flesh, blood, bones, and all,
Ere thou shalt lose for me one drop of blood.
Antonio
I am a tainted wether of the flock,
115 Meetest for death: the weakest kind of fruit
Drops earliest to the ground; and so let me.
You cannot better be employ'd, Bassanio,
Than to live still, and write mine epitaph.

Enter Nerissa, *dressed like a lawyer's clerk*
Duke
Came you from Padua, from Bellario?

90   *purchas'd slave*: slave that you
have bought.

92   *in abject . . . parts*: for lowly and
servile tasks.

97   *Be season'd . . . viands*: be treated
with the same food as your own.

101   *fie*: shame.
102   *force*: power.

104   *Upon my power*: with my
authority.

107   *stays without*: waits outside.

114   *tainted wether*: diseased ram.
115   *Meetest*: most suitable.

118   *live still*: go on living.

Nerissa

120 From both, my lord. Bellario greets your Grace.

[*Presents a letter*

Bassanio

Why dost thou whet thy knife so earnestly?

Shylock

To cut the forfeiture from that bankrupt there.

Gratiano

Not on thy sole, but on thy soul, harsh Jew,

Thou mak'st thy knife keen; but no metal can,

125 No, not the hangman's axe, bear half the keenness

Of thy sharp envy. Can no prayers pierce thee?

Shylock

No, none that thou hast wit enough to make.

Gratiano

O, be thou damn'd, inexorable dog!

And for thy life let justice be accus'd.

130 Thou almost mak'st me waver in my faith

To hold opinion with Pythagoras,

That souls of animals infuse themselves

Into the trunks of men: thy currish spirit

Govern'd a wolf, who, hang'd for human slaughter,

135 Even from the gallows did his fell soul fleet,

And whilst thou lay'st in thy unhallow'd dam,

Infus'd itself in thee; for thy desires

Are wolvish, bloody, starv'd, and ravenous.

Shylock

Till thou canst rail the seal from off my bond.

140 Thou but offend'st thy lungs to speak so loud:

Repair thy wit, good youth, or it will fall

To cureless ruin. I stand here for law.

Duke

This letter from Bellario doth commend

A young and learned doctor to our court.

145 Where is he?

Nerissa   He attendeth here hard by,

To know your answer, whether you'll admit him.

Duke

With all my heart: some three or four of you

Go give him courteous conduct to this place.

[*Exeunt* Officers

Meantime, the court shall hear Bellario's letter.

121   *whet*: sharpen. Bassanio's comment in line 123 shows that Shylock is using the sole of his shoe for sharpening the knife.

128   *inexorable*: relentless.

129   Let justice be said to be guilty that you are alive.

131   *hold opinion*: agree.
       Pythagoras: a Greek philosopher who believed (as Bassanio explains) that the souls of men and of animals passed into other bodies.

132   *infuse*: pour.

133   *currish*: like a cur—a mongrel dog.

134   *hang'd for human slaughter*: this was in fact a means of destroying killer animals.

135   *Even*: directly.
       fell: cruel.
       fleet: speed away.

136   *unhallow'd*: unsanctified (because non-Christian).
       dam: mother.

139   *rail*: shout.

140   *offend'st*: trouble.

142   *cureless*: incurable.

145   *hard*: near.

148   *give him courteous conduct*: lead him politely.

150 *Your Grace shall understand that at the receipt of*
your letter I am very sick; but in the instant that your
messenger came, in loving visitation was with me a
young doctor of Rome; his name is Balthazar.
I acquainted him with the cause in controversy
155 *between the Jew and Antonio the merchant. We*
turned o'er many books together. He is furnished with
my opinion; which, bettered with his own learning—
the greatness whereof I cannot enough commend—
comes with him, at my importunity, to fill up your
160 *Grace's request in my stead. I beseech you, let his lack*
of years be no impediment to let him lack a reverend
estimation, for I never knew so young a body with so
old a head. I leave him to your gracious acceptance,
whose trial shall better publish his commendation.

> *Enter* Portia, *dressed like a doctor of law*

165 You hear the learn'd Bellario, what he writes:
And here, I take it, is the doctor come.
Give me your hand. Come you from old Bellario?

Portia

I did, my lord.

Duke   You are welcome: take your place.
Are you acquainted with the difference
170 That holds this present question in the court?

Portia

I am informed throughly of the cause.
Which is the merchant here, and which the Jew?

Duke

Antonio and old Shylock, both stand forth.

Portia

Is your name Shylock?

Shylock   Shylock is my name.

Portia

175 Of a strange nature is the suit you follow;
Yet in such rule, that the Venetian law
Cannot impugn you as you do proceed.
[*To* Antonio] You stand within his danger, do you
    not?

Antonio

Ay, so he says.

Portia   Do you confess the bond?

Antonio

180 I do.

154   *cause*: matter.
    controversy: dispute.

156   *turned o'er*: looked through.
    is furnished: has been given.

157   *bettered*: improved.

159   *importunity*: earnest request.

160   *in my stead*: instead of me.

160-2   *let . . . estimation*: do not think
    poorly of him because he is young.

164   *whose . . . commendation*: try him,
    and you will see how much better he is
    than my praise.

169-70   *the difference . . . court*: the
    dispute that is at present on trial in
    this court.

171   *throughly*: thoroughly.

176   *in such rule*: so correctly.

177   Cannot find any fault in your
    proceedings.

178   *within his danger*: in danger from
    him.

181   *On . . . I*: what will compel me and force me to do it?

182   *is not strain'd*: cannot be forced (constrained).

186   *'Tis . . . mightiest*: both 'mercy is seen at its most powerful in the men with most power', and 'mercy is the most powerful weapon that the most powerful men possess'.
       becomes: suits.

188-9   The king's sceptre symbolizes his earthly ('temporal') power, which is the proper characteristic ('attribute') of a royal man ('majesty') who commands respect ('awe').

191   *this sceptred sway*: this world that is ruled by men with sceptres.

193   *attribute to*: quality belonging to.

195   *seasons*: moderates.

196   *Though . . . plea*: although you are asking for justice.

197-8   *in . . . salvation*: if we were all to get what we deserve, in the strict course of justice none of us would be saved.

201   To ask you to soften your demand for justice.

203   *Must needs*: is compelled.

204   *My . . . head*: I will take the responsibility for what I am doing.
       crave: ask for.

206   *discharge*: repay.

207   *tender*: offer.

209   *be bound*: make a legal promise.

212   *bears down*: overcomes.

213   *Wrest*: twist.
       once: on this one occasion.
       to: with.

215   *curb*: restrain.

Portia   Then must the Jew be merciful.

Shylock

On what compulsion must I? tell me that.

Portia

The quality of mercy is not strain'd;
It droppeth as the gentle rain from heaven
Upon the place beneath: it is twice bless'd;

185 It blesseth him that gives and him that takes.
'Tis mightiest in the mightiest: it becomes
The throned monarch better than his crown;
His sceptre shows the force of temporal power,
The attribute to awe and majesty,

190 Wherein doth sit the dread and fear of kings:
But mercy is above this sceptred sway,
It is enthroned in the hearts of kings,
It is an attribute to God himself,
And earthly power doth then show likest God's

195 When mercy seasons justice. Therefore, Jew,
Though justice be thy plea, consider this,
That in the course of justice none of us
Should see salvation: we do pray for mercy,
And that same prayer doth teach us all to render

200 The deeds of mercy. I have spoke thus much
To mitigate the justice of thy plea,
Which if thou follow, this strict court of Venice
Must needs give sentence 'gainst the merchant there.

Shylock

My deeds upon my head! I crave the law,

205 The penalty and forfeit of my bond.

Portia

Is he not able to discharge the money?

Bassanio

Yes, here I tender it for him in the court;
Yea, twice the sum: if that will not suffice,
I will be bound to pay it ten times o'er,

210 On forfeit of my hands, my head, my heart.
If this will not suffice, it must appear
That malice bears down truth. And, I beseech you,
Wrest once the law to your authority:
To do a great right, do a little wrong,

215 And curb this cruel devil of his will.

Portia
It must not be. There is no power in Venice
Can alter a decree established:
'Twill be recorded for a precedent,
And many an error by the same example
220 Will rush into the state. It cannot be.
Shylock
A Daniel come to judgment! yea, a Daniel!
O wise young judge, how I do honour thee!
Portia
I pray you, let me look upon the bond.
Shylock
Here 'tis, most reverend doctor, here it is.
Portia
225 Shylock, there's thrice thy money offer'd thee.
Shylock
An oath, an oath, I have an oath in heaven;
Shall I lay perjury upon my soul?
No, not for Venice.
Portia   Why, this bond is forfeit;
And lawfully by this the Jew may claim
230 A pound of flesh, to be by him cut off
Nearest the merchant's heart. Be merciful:
Take thrice thy money; bid me tear the bond.
Shylock
When it is paid according to the tenour.
It doth appear you are a worthy judge;
235 You know the law, your exposition
Hath been most sound: I charge you by the law,
Whereof you are a well-deserving pillar,
Proceed to judgment: by my soul I swear
There is no power in the tongue of man
240 To alter me. I stay here on my bond.

Most heartily I do beseech the court
To give the judgment.
Portia   Why then, thus it is:
You must prepare your bosom for his knife.
Shylock
O noble judge! O excellent young man!
Portia
245 For, the intent and purpose of the law

221   *Daniel*: the 'History of Susanna' in the Apocrypha tells how God sent Daniel, 'a young youth', to give judgement against the elders.

233   *tenour*: actual wording.

235   *exposition*: understanding of the case.

237   *pillar*: support.

241   *Most heartily*: with all my heart.

246 *Hath full relation*: entirely
     supports.

249 *elder*: more mature.

253 *balance*: scales.
255 *on your charge*: at your expense.
257 *nominated*: specified.

262 *arm'd*: i.e. spiritually.

266 *still her use*: usually her custom.

273 *speak . . . death*: speak kindly of
     me when I am dead.

276 *Repent but you*: you must only
     regret.

Hath full relation to the penalty,
Which here appeareth due upon the bond.
Shylock
'Tis very true! O wise and upright judge!
How much more elder art thou than thy looks!
Portia
250 Therefore lay bare your bosom.
Shylock   Ay, 'his breast':
So says the bond:—doth it not, noble judge?—
'Nearest his heart'—those are the very words.
Portia
It is so. Are there balance here to weigh
The flesh?
Shylock   I have them ready.
Portia
255 Have by some surgeon, Shylock, on your charge,
To stop his wounds, lest he do bleed to death.
Shylock
Is it so nominated in the bond?
Portia
It is not so express'd; but what of that?
'Twere good you do so much for charity.
Shylock
260 I cannot find it: 'tis not in the bond.
Portia
You, merchant, have you anything to say?
Antonio
But little: I am arm'd and well prepar'd.
Give me your hand, Bassanio: fare you well!
Grieve not that I am fall'n to this for you,
265 For herein Fortune shows herself more kind
Than is her custom: it is still her use
To let the wretched man outlive his wealth,
To view with hollow eye and wrinkled brow
An age of poverty; from which lingering penance
270 Of such misery doth she cut me off.
Commend me to your honourable wife.
Tell her the process of Antonio's end;
Say how I lov'd you, speak me fair in death;
And, when the tale is told, bid her be judge
275 Whether Bassanio had not once a love.
Repent but you that you shall lose your friend,

And he repents not that he pays your debt;
For if the Jew do cut but deep enough,
I'll pay it instantly with all my heart.
Bassanio
280 Antonio, I am married to a wife

281 *Which*: who.

Which is as dear to me as life itself;
But life itself, my wife, and all the world,
Are not with me esteem'd above thy life:
I would lose all, ay, sacrifice them all,

285 *deliver*: save.

285 Here to this devil, to deliver you.
Portia
Your wife would give you little thanks for that,
If she were by to hear you make the offer.
Gratiano
I have a wife, who, I protest, I love:
I would she were in heaven, so she could
290 Entreat some power to change this currish Jew.
Nerissa
'Tis well you offer it behind her back;
The wish would make else an unquiet house.
Shylock
These be the Christian husbands! I have a
daughter;
Would any of the stock of Barabas

294 *stock*: breed.
Barabas: the thief who was released when Christ was crucified (St. John 18: 40).
296 *trifle time*: waste time in trivialities.
pursue: go on with.

295 Had been her husband rather than a Christian!
We trifle time; I pray thee, pursue sentence.
Portia
A pound of that same merchant's flesh is thine:
The court awards it, and the law doth give it.
Shylock
Most rightful judge!
Portia
300 And you must cut this flesh from off his breast:
The law allows it, and the court awards it.
Shylock
Most learned judge! A sentence! come, prepare!
Portia

303 *Tarry*: wait.
304 *jot*: drop.

Tarry a little: there is something else.
This bond doth give thee here no jot of blood;
305 The words expressly are 'a pound of flesh':
Take then thy bond, take thou thy pound of flesh;

But, in the cutting it, if thou dost shed
One drop of Christian blood, thy lands and goods
Are, by the laws of Venice, confiscate
310 Unto the state of Venice.

Gratiano

O upright judge! Mark, Jew: O learned judge!

Shylock

Is that the law?

Portia   Thyself shalt see the act;
For, as thou urgest justice, be assur'd
Thou shalt have justice more than thou desir'st.

Gratiano

315 O learned judge! Mark, Jew: a learned judge!

Shylock

I take this offer then: pay the bond thrice,
And let the Christian go.

Bassanio   Here is the money.

Portia

Soft!
The Jew shall have all justice; soft! no haste:—
320 He shall have nothing but the penalty.

Gratiano

O Jew! an upright judge, a learned judge!

Portia

Therefore prepare thee to cut off the flesh.
Shed thou no blood; nor cut thou less, nor more,
But just a pound of flesh: if thou tak'st more,
325 Or less, than a just pound, be it but so much
As makes it light or heavy in the substance,
Or the division of the twentieth part
Of one poor scruple, nay, if the scale do turn
But in the estimation of a hair,
330 Thou diest, and all thy goods are confiscate.

Gratiano

A second Daniel, a Daniel, Jew!
Now, infidel, I have you on the hip.

Portia

Why doth the Jew pause? take thy forfeiture.

Shylock

Give me my principal, and let me go.

Bassanio

335 I have it ready for thee; here it is.

312 *act*: the legal act confirming the law.

313 *urgest*: demand.

321 *upright*: honest.

326 *substance*: weight.

328 *scruple*: a weight unit (used by the old apothecaries) of 20 grains.

329 *estimation*: weight.

332 *on the hip*: at my mercy.

334 *principal*: the original sum borrowed.

Portia
He hath refus'd it in the open court:
He shall have merely justice, and his bond.

Gratiano
A Daniel, still say I; a second Daniel!
I thank thee, Jew, for teaching me that word.

Shylock
340 Shall I not have barely my principal?

Portia
Thou shalt have nothing but the forfeiture,
To be so taken at thy peril, Jew.

Shylock
Why, then the devil give him good of it!
I'll stay no longer question.

Portia   Tarry, Jew:
345 The law hath yet another hold on you.
It is enacted in the laws of Venice,
If it be prov'd against an alien
That by direct or indirect attempts
He seek the life of any citizen,
350 The party 'gainst the which he doth contrive
Shall seize one half his goods; the other half
Comes to the privy coffer of the state;
And the offender's life lies in the mercy
Of the duke only, 'gainst all other voice.
355 In which predicament, I say, thou stand'st;
For it appears by manifest proceeding,
That indirectly, and directly too,
Thou hast contriv'd against the very life
Of the defendant; and thou hast incurr'd
360 The danger formerly by me rehears'd.
Down therefore and beg mercy of the duke.

Gratiano
Beg that thou may'st have leave to hang thyself—
And yet, thy wealth being forfeit to the state,
Thou hast not left the value of a cord;
365 Therefore thou must be hang'd at the state's charge.

Duke
That thou shalt see the difference of our spirit,
I pardon thee thy life before thou ask it.
For half thy wealth, it is Antonio's;
The other half comes to the general state,
370 Which humbleness may drive unto a fine.

344 *question*: to argue.

346 *enacted*: decreed.

350 *party*: person (Portia uses the correct legal term, still used today).
     contrive: plot.
352 *privy coffer*: treasury.

354 *'gainst all other voice*: no matter what anyone else says.

356 *manifest proceeding*: quite clearly from what has happened.

360 *rehears'd*: declared.

369 *general state*: general use of the state.
370 And if you are humble this may be reduced to a fine.

371   *not for Antonio*: the money due
to Antonio will not be reduced.

Portia
Ay, for the state; not for Antonio.
Shylock
Nay, take my life and all; pardon not that:
You take my house, when you do take the prop
That doth sustain my house; you take my life
375 When you do take the means whereby I live.
Portia
What mercy can you render him, Antonio?
Gratiano
A halter gratis; nothing else, for God's sake!

377   *halter*: rope to hang himself with.
gratis: free of interest.

378   *So please*: if it pleases.

379   *quit*: be satisfied with.
for: instead of.

380   *so*: if.

381   *in use*: on trust—to use as
Antonio now describes.

Antonio
So please my lord the duke, and all the court,
To quit the fine for one half of his goods,
380 I am content so he will let me have
The other half in use, to render it,
Upon his death, unto the gentleman
That lately stole his daughter.
Two things provided more, that, for this favour,

385   *presently*: immediately.

385 He presently become a Christian;
The other, that he do record a gift,

387   *all he dies possess'd*: all that he
owns when he dies.

Here in the court, of all he dies possess'd,
Unto his son Lorenzo and his daughter.
Duke
He shall do this, or else I do recant

389   *recant*: withdraw.

390 The pardon that I late pronounced here.
Portia
Art thou contented, Jew? what dost thou say?
Shylock
I am content.
Portia   Clerk, draw a deed of gift.
Shylock
I pray you give me leave to go from hence:
I am not well. Send the deed after me,
395 And I will sign it.
Duke   Get thee gone, but do it.
Gratiano
In christening shalt thou have two god-fathers;
Had I been judge, thou shouldst have had ten more,
To bring thee to the gallows, not to the font.
                              [*Exit* Shylock

396   *god-fathers*: these take the
responsibility for seeing that the
baptized child is properly educated in
the Christian faith; 'god-fathers' was
also a joking name for the members of
a jury—a body of twelve men who
were needed to pass sentence on a
criminal. Gratiano suggests that a jury
would have condemned Shylock to
death.

Duke
Sir, I entreat you home with me to dinner.

Portia

400 I humbly do desire your Grace of pardon:
I must away this night toward Padua,
And it is meet I presently set forth.

Duke

I am sorry that your leisure serves you not.
Antonio, gratify this gentleman,
405 For, in my mind, you are much bound to him.

[*Exeunt* Duke, Merchants, *and* Officers of the Court

Bassanio

Most worthy gentleman, I and my friend
Have by your wisdom been this day acquitted
Of grievous penalties, in lieu whereof,
Three thousand ducats, due unto the Jew,
410 We freely cope your courteous pains withal.

Antonio

And stand indebted, over and above,
In love and service to you evermore.

Portia

He is well paid that is well satisfied,
And I, delivering you, am satisfied,
415 And therein do account myself well paid:
My mind was never yet more mercenary.
I pray you, know me when we meet again:
I wish you well, and so I take my leave.

Bassanio

Dear sir, of force I must attempt you further:
420 Take some remembrance of us as a tribute,
Not as a fee. Grant me two things, I pray you,
Not to deny me, and to pardon me.

Portia

You press me far, and therefore I will yield.
Give me your gloves, I'll wear them for your sake;
425 And (for your love) I'll take this ring from you.
Do not draw back your hand; I'll take no more,
And you in love shall not deny me this.

Bassanio

This ring, good sir? alas! it is a trifle,
I will not shame myself to give you this.

Portia

430 I will have nothing else but only this;
And now methinks I have a mind to it.

---

402   *meet*: necessary.

403   *your leisure serves you not*: you do not have time to spare.
404   *gratify*: show your gratitude to.
405   *bound*: indebted.

408   *in lieu whereof*: in payment for this.

410   *freely*: most willingly.
       cope: reward.
       pains: trouble.
411   *over and above*: in addition.

416   *mercenary*: interested in money.
417   *know*: recognize.

419   *of force*: it is necessary.
       attempt you further: try harder to persuade you.
420   *some remembrance*: something to remind you.
       tribute: token of respect.
422   Not to refuse my request, and to forgive me for making it.
423   *You press me far*: you are very insistent.
424   *for your sake*: to acknowledge your politeness.
425   *for your love*: to acknowledge your love.

431   And now I really do want it.

Bassanio
There's more depends on this than on the value.
The dearest ring in Venice will I give you,
And find it out by proclamation:
435 Only for this, I pray you, pardon me.
    Portia
I see, sir, you are liberal in offers:
You taught me first to beg, and now methinks
You teach me how a beggar should be answer'd.
    Bassanio
Good sir, this ring was given me by my wife,
440 And, when she put it on, she made me vow
That I should neither sell, nor give, nor lose it.
    Portia
That 'scuse serves many men to save their gifts.
And if your wife be not a mad-woman,
And know how well I have deserv'd this ring,
445 She would not hold out enemy for ever,
For giving it to me. Well, peace be with you.
                    [*Exeunt* Portia *and* Nerissa
    Antonio
My Lord Bassanio, let him have the ring:
Let his deservings and my love withal
Be valu'd 'gainst your wife's commandèment.
    Bassanio
450 Go, Gratiano; run and overtake him;
Give him the ring, and bring him, if thou canst,
Unto Antonio's house. Away, make haste.
                    [*Exit* Gratiano
Come, you and I will thither presently,
And in the morning early will we both
455 Fly toward Belmont. Come, Antonio.   [*Exeunt*

434   *by proclamation*: by public
announcement that I will buy the most
expensive ring in Venice.
435   *for this*: i.e. this ring.
436   *liberal in offers*: generous only in
making offers (not in fulfilling them).

442   *'scuse*: excuse.

445   *hold out enemy*: be angry with
you.

449   *'gainst*: more highly than.
commandèment: the extra *è* is for
the sake of the rhythm.

Act 4   Scene 2
Gratiano gives Bassanio's ring to
Portia, who is still disguised as the
young lawyer and accompanied by
Nerissa as her 'clerk'. Nerissa plans to
get her own ring from Gratiano.
1   *Inquire . . . out*: find out where
the Jew's house is.
this deed: the document in which
he promises to make Lorenzo his heir.

Scene 2 *Venice. A street*

Enter Portia *and* Nerissa
    Portia
Inquire the Jew's house out, give him this deed,
And let him sign it. We'll away tonight,
And be a day before our husbands home:
This deed will be well welcome to Lorenzo.

Enter Gratiano

Gratiano

5 Fair sir, you are well o'erta'en.

My Lord Bassanio, upon more advice,

Hath sent you here this ring, and doth entreat

Your company at dinner.

Portia   That cannot be.

His ring I do accept most thankfully,

10 And so, I pray you, tell him: furthermore,

I pray you, show my youth old Shylock's house.

Gratiano

That will I do.

Nerissa   Sir, I would speak with you.

[*Aside to* Portia] I'll see if I can get my husband's

ring.

Which I did make him swear to keep for ever.

Portia

15 Thou may'st, I warrant. We shall have old swearing

That they did give the rings away to men;

But we'll outface them, and outswear them too.

Away, make haste! thou know'st where I will tarry.

Nerissa

Come, good sir, will you show me to this house?

[*Exeunt*

---

6   *upon more advice*: having thought more about the matter.

15   *Thou may'st, I warrant*: I'm sure you will be able to do it.
    old: a lot of.

18   *tarry*: wait.

Act 5

Act 5   Scene 1

Lorenzo and Jessica talk lovingly in
the moonlight. Messages are brought,
telling them that Portia and Bassanio
are (separately) on their way home.
After a short time, Portia and Nerissa
arrive at Belmont; a little later, as day
breaks, Bassanio and Gratiano appear.
The wives ask their husbands for the
rings, and pretend to be angry; at last
they reveal the truth.

4   *Troilus*: in the Trojan War,
Troilus was separated from his love,
Cressida, when she was taken into the
enemy (Greek) camp. Shakespeare
wrote a play, *Troilus and Cressida*, on
this subject.

Scene 1 *Belmont. The garden in front of Portia's
house*

Enter Lorenzo *and* Jessica

Lorenzo

The moon shines bright: in such a night as this,
When the sweet wind did gently kiss the trees,
And they did make no noise, in such a night
Troilus methinks mounted the Trojan walls,
5 And sigh'd his soul toward the Grecian tents,
Where Cressid lay that night.

Jessica   In such a night
Did Thisbe fearfully o'ertrip the dew,
And saw the lion's shadow ere himself,

7   *Thisbe*: when she saw the lion, Thisbe ran away, dropping her scarf which the lion mauled. Seeing the bloody scarf, her lover Pyramus thought Thisbe had been killed, and stabbed himself. This episode is made comic in Shakespeare's *A Midsummer Night's Dream*.

    o'ertrip: walk lightly over.

8   *ere himself*: before she saw the lion.

10   *Dido*: the Queen of Carthage, who was deserted by her lover Aeneas when he sailed to Italy. Shakespeare's great contemporary, Christopher Marlowe, wrote a tragedy on this subject.

11   *waft*: waved to.

13   *Medea*: the enchantress who loved Jason and helped him to win the golden fleece (see note on *1*, *1*, *170*); she restored Aeson (Jason's father) to youth with her magic herbs.

15   *steal*: both 'run away' and 'rob'.

16   *unthrift love*: both 'careless devotion' and 'penniless lover'.

19   *Stealing*: gaining possession.

21   *shrew*: scolding woman.

23   *out-night you*: beat you at this game of 'in such a night'; the word is invented.

    did nobody come: if there were not somebody coming.

24   *footing*: footsteps.

31   *holy crosses*: small shrines set by the roadside for travellers to pray; there are few in England now, but many remain in Italy.

And ran dismay'd away.

Lorenzo   In such a night
10 Stood Dido with a willow in her hand
Upon the wild sea-banks, and waft her love
To come again to Carthage.

Jessica   In such a night
Medea gather'd the enchanted herbs
That did renew old Æson.

Lorenzo   In such a night
15 Did Jessica steal from the wealthy Jew,
And with an unthrift love did run from Venice,
As far as Belmont.

Jessica   In such a night
Did young Lorenzo swear he lov'd her well,
Stealing her soul with many vows of faith,
20 And ne'er a true one.

Lorenzo   In such a night
Did pretty Jessica, like a little shrew,
Slander her love, and he forgave it her.

Jessica
I would out-night you, did nobody come;
But, hark! I hear the footing of a man.

Enter Stephano

Lorenzo
25 Who comes so fast in silence of the night?

Stephano
A friend.

Lorenzo
A friend! what friend? your name, I pray you, friend.

Stephano
Stephano is my name; and I bring word
My mistress will before the break of day
30 Be here at Belmont: she doth stray about
By holy crosses, where she kneels and prays
For happy wedlock hours.

Lorenzo   Who comes with her?

Stephano
None but a holy hermit and her maid.
I pray you, is my master yet return'd?

Lorenzo

35 He is not, nor we have not heard from him.
But go we in, I pray thee, Jessica,
And ceremoniously let us prepare
Some welcome for the mistress of the house.

Enter Launcelot

Launcelot
Sola, sola! wo ha, ho! sola, sola!

Lorenzo

40 Who calls?

Launcelot
Sola! did you see Master Lorenzo? Master
Lorenzo! sola, sola!

Lorenzo
Leave hollowing, man; here.

Launcelot
Sola! where? where?

Lorenzo

45 Here.

Launcelot
Tell him there's a post come from my master, with
his horn full of good news: my master will be here
ere morning.   [*Exit*

Lorenzo
Sweet soul, let's in, and there expect their coming.

50 And yet no matter; why should we go in?
My friend Stephano, signify, I pray you,
Within the house, your mistress is at hand;
And bring your music forth into the air.
                                         [*Exit* Stephano
How sweet the moonlight sleeps upon this bank!

55 Here will we sit, and let the sounds of music
Creep in our ears: soft stillness and the night
Become the touches of sweet harmony.
Sit, Jessica—look how the floor of heaven
Is thick inlaid with patens of bright gold:

60 There's not the smallest orb which thou behold'st
But in his motion like an angel sings,
Still quiring to the young-eyed cherubins;
Such harmony is in immortal souls,
But whilst this muddy vesture of decay

65 Doth grossly close it in, we cannot hear it.

37–8   *ceremoniously . . . welcome*: let us prepare some ceremony of welcome.

39   Launcelot is pretending to be a messenger-boy blowing his horn.

43   *Leave hollowing*: stop shouting.

46   *post*: messenger.

51   *signify*: announce.

57   *Become*: suit.
59   *patens*: small pieces of shiny metal—the stars.
60   *orb*: planet.
61   *motion*: movement. The Elizabethans believed that as the planets moved they created heavenly harmony but (as Lorenzo explains) human beings could not hear it.
62   *quiring*: serenading.
     young-eyed cherubins: angels whose eyes are always young.
64   *vesture of decay*: clothing of mortality—the human body.
65   *grossly*: roughly.

	Enter Musicians
66 *Diana*: the classical goddess of the moon, who fell in love with the beautiful Endymion and came down from heaven every night to sleep with him (see also line 109).	Come, ho! and wake Diana with a hymn: With sweetest touches pierce your mistress' ear, And draw her home with music. [*Music*
	Jessica
	I am never merry when I hear sweet music.
	Lorenzo
70 *attentive*: receptive.	70 The reason is, your spirits are attentive: For do but note a wild and wanton herd,
72 *race*: breed. *unhandled*: unbroken, untrained.	Or race of youthful and unhandled colts, Fetching mad bounds, bellowing and neighing loud,
74 Which it is in the nature of their wild blood to do.	Which is the hot condition of their blood;
75 *perchance*: perhaps.	75 If they but hear perchance a trumpet sound, Or any air of music touch their ears,
77 *make a mutual stand*: all stand still at once.	You shall perceive them make a mutual stand,
78 *modest*: gentle.	Their savage eyes turn'd to a modest gaze
79–80 *the poet . . . floods*: the Roman poet Ovid told how Orpheus, a Greek musician, charmed even lifeless objects with his music.	By the sweet power of music: therefore the poet 80 Did feign that Orpheus drew trees, stones, and floods;
81 *naught*: nothing. *stockish*: stubborn.	Since naught so stockish, hard, and full of rage, But music for the time doth change his nature. The man that hath no music in himself,
84 *concord*: harmony.	Nor is not mov'd with concord of sweet sounds,
85 *stratagems*: plots. *spoils*: destruction.	85 Is fit for treasons, stratagems, and spoils;
86 *motions*: movements.	The motions of his spirit are dull as night,
87 *Erebus*: a dark place in the Greek underworld.	And his affections dark as Erebus:
88 *Mark*: pay attention to.	Let no such man be trusted. Mark the music.
	Enter Portia *and* Nerissa
	Portia
	That light we see is burning in my hall.
	90 How far that little candle throws his beams!
91 *naughty*: wicked.	So shines a good deed in a naughty world.
	Nerissa
	When the moon shone, we did not see the candle.
	Portia
94 *substitute*: deputy.	So doth the greater glory dim the less:
95 *by*: present.	A substitute shines brightly as a king
95–6 *his state Empties itself*: his glory vanishes.	95 Until a king be by, and then his state Empties itself, as doth an inland brook
97 *main of waters*: sea.	Into the main of waters. Music! hark!
98 *music . . . of the house*: a small company of musicians, belonging to Portia's household of servants.	**Nerissa** It is your music, madam, of the house.

Portia
Nothing is good, I see, without respect:
100 Methinks it sounds much sweeter than by day.
Nerissa
Silence bestows that virtue on it, madam.
Portia
The crow doth sing as sweetly as the lark
When neither is attended, and I think
The nightingale, if she should sing by day
105 When every goose is cackling, would be thought
No better a musician than the wren.
How many things by season season'd are
To their right praise and true perfection!
Peace, ho! the moon sleeps with Endymion,
110 And would not be awak'd!
                     [*Music ceases*
Lorenzo   That is the voice,
Or I am much deceiv'd, of Portia.
Portia
He knows me, as the blind man knows the cuckoo,
By the bad voice.
Lorenzo   Dear lady, welcome home.
Portia
We have been praying for our husbands' welfare,
115 Which speed, we hope, the better for our words.
Are they return'd?
Lorenzo   Madam, they are not yet;
But there is come a messenger before,
To signify their coming.
Portia   Go in, Nerissa:
Give order to my servants that they take
120 No note at all of our being absent hence;
Nor you, Lorenzo; Jessica, nor you.
                   [*A trumpet sounds*
Lorenzo
Your husband is at hand, I hear his trumpet;
We are no tell-tales, madam, fear you not.
Portia
This night methinks is but the daylight sick;
125 It looks a little paler: 'tis a day,
Such as the day is when the sun is hid.

      Enter Bassanio, Antonio, Gratiano, *and*
      their Servants
Bassanio
We should hold day with the Antipodes,
If you would walk in absence of the sun.

---

99   Nothing is good in itself alone, without taking circumstances into consideration.

103   *attended*: listened to.
104   *nightingale*: a bird that sings only at night, when all other birds are silent.

107-8   *by season . . . perfection*: what a lot of things are given their proper value and excellence by the fact that they come at the right time.
109   *Endymion*: see note on 5, 1, 66.

115   And we hope that they have had some benefit from our prayers.

119-20   *take No note*: make no mention.

123   *tell-tales*: tellers of secrets.

127-8   It would be daytime here when it is in Australia ('the Antipodes' = the other side of the world) if you [Portia] would walk here when the sun is away.

129	*be light*: be faithless.
130	*heavy*: sorrowful.
131	*for me*: because of what I have done.
132	*sort all*: decide everything.
135	*bound*: indebted.
137	*bound*: in chains as a prisoner.
138	*acquitted of*: repaid for (with the love of Bassanio and the gratitude of Portia).
141	*scant*: cut short. *breathing courtesy*: verbal politeness.
144	*Would . . . gelt*: I wish he had been castrated. *for my part*: as far as I am concerned.
145	Since it seems to mean so much to you.
148	*posy*: words engraved on a ring.
149	*cutler's poetry*: doggerel verse, engraved by a knife-maker ('cutler') on his knives.
151	*What*: why?
155	*for me*: for my sake.
156	*respective*: careful of your honour.
158	*wear hair on's face*: grow a beard.
159	*and if*: if ever.

Portia
Let me give light, but let me not be light;
130 For a light wife doth make a heavy husband,
And never be Bassanio so for me:
But God sort all! You are welcome home, my lord.
Bassanio
I thank you, madam. Give welcome to my friend:
This is the man, this is Antonio,
135 To whom I am so infinitely bound.
Portia
You should in all sense be much bound to him,
For, as I hear, he was much bound for you.
Antonio
No more than I am well acquitted of.
Portia
Sir, you are very welcome to our house:
140 It must appear in other ways than words,
Therefore I scant this breathing courtesy.
Gratiano
[*To* Nerissa] By yonder moon I swear you do me
                wrong;
In faith, I gave it to the judge's clerk;
Would he were gelt that had it, for my part,
145 Since you do take it, love, so much at heart.
Portia
A quarrel, ho, already! what's the matter?
Gratiano
About a hoop of gold, a paltry ring
That she did give me, whose posy was
For all the world like cutler's poetry
150 Upon a knife, 'Love me, and leave me not'.
Nerissa
What talk you of the posy, or the value?
You swore to me, when I did give it you,
That you would wear it till your hour of death,
And that it should lie with you in your grave:
155 Though not for me, yet for your vehement oaths,
You should have been respective and have kept it.
Gave it a judge's clerk! no, God's my judge,
The clerk will ne'er wear hair on's face that had it.
Gratiano
He will, and if he live to be a man.

Nerissa

160 Ay, if a woman live to be a man.

Gratiano

Now, by this hand, I gave it to a youth,

162 *scrubbed*: stunted.

A kind of boy, a little scrubbed boy,

No higher than thyself, the judge's clerk.

164 *prating*: chattering.

A prating boy that begg'd it as a fee:

165 I could not for my heart deny it him.

Portia

You were to blame—I must be plain with you—

To part so slightly with your wife's first gift;

A thing stuck on with oaths upon your finger,

And so riveted with faith unto your flesh.

170 I gave my love a ring and made him swear

Never to part with it: and here he stands;

172 *leave*: part with.

I dare be sworn for him he would not leave it,

Nor pluck it from his finger, for the wealth

174 *masters*: is master of.

That the world masters. Now, in faith, Gratiano,

175 You give your wife too unkind a cause of grief:

176 *And 'twere to me*: if it had been done to me.

And 'twere to me, I should be mad at it.

Bassanio

[*Aside*] Why, I were best to cut my left hand off,

And swear I lost the ring defending it.

Gratiano

My Lord Bassanio gave his ring away

180 Unto the judge that begg'd it, and indeed

Deserv'd it too; and then the boy, his clerk,

182 *pains*: care.

That took some pains in writing, he begg'd mine;

And neither man nor master would take aught

But the two rings.

Portia   What ring gave you, my lord?

185 Not that, I hope, which you receiv'd of me.

Bassanio

If I could add a lie unto a fault,

I would deny it; but you see my finger

Hath not the ring upon it—it is gone.

Portia

189 *void*: empty.

Even so void is your false heart of truth.

190 By heaven, I will ne'er come in your bed

Until I see the ring.

Nerissa   Nor I in yours,

Till I again see mine.

Bassanio   Sweet Portia,
If you did know to whom I gave the ring,
If you did know for whom I gave the ring,
195 And would conceive for what I gave the ring,
And how unwillingly I left the ring,
When naught would be accepted but the ring,
You would abate the strength of your displeasure.

Portia
If you had known the virtue of the ring,
200 Or half her worthiness that gave the ring,
Or your own honour to contain the ring,
You would not then have parted with the ring.
What man is there so much unreasonable,
If you had pleas'd to have defended it
205 With any terms of zeal, wanted the modesty
To urge the thing held as a ceremony?
Nerissa teaches me what to believe:
I'll die for 't, but some woman had the ring.

Bassanio
No, by my honour, madam, by my soul,
210 No woman had it, but a civil doctor,
Which did refuse three thousand ducats of me,
And begg'd the ring, the which I did deny him,
And suffer'd him to go displeas'd away;
Even he that had held up the very life
215 Of my dear friend. What should I say, sweet lady?
I was enforc'd to send it after him.
I was beset with shame and courtesy;
My honour would not let ingratitude
So much besmear it. Pardon me, good lady,
220 For by these blessed candles of the night,
Had you been there, I think you would have
  begg'd
The ring of me to give the worthy doctor.

Portia
Let not that doctor e'er come near my house.
Since he hath got the jewel that I lov'd,
225 And that which you did swear to keep for me;
I will become as liberal as you—
I'll not deny him anything I have,
No, not my body, nor my husband's bed.
Know him I shall, I am well sure of it.
230 Lie not a night from home; watch me like Argus:

199   *virtue*: magic power.

201   Or how it was a matter of honour
  that you should keep the ring.

205   *terms of zeal*: determination.
205-6   *wanted . . . ceremony*: would have
  been so lacking in good manners as to
  insist on having something that you
  thought sacred.
208   *I'll die for 't*: I am ready to die
  for my belief.
210   *civil doctor*: doctor of civil law.

213   *suffer'd*: allowed.
214   *held up*: saved.

217   *beset*: overcome.

219   *besmear*: stain.
220   *candles of the night*: i.e. the stars.

222   *of*: from.

230   *Argus*: in classical mythology,
  a monster with a hundred eyes.

If you do not, if I be left alone,
Now by mine honour, which is yet mine own,
I'll have that doctor for my bedfellow.
Nerissa
And I his clerk; therefore be well advis'd

234   *be well advis'd*: take good care.
235   *to mine own protection*: to look after my own honour.
236   *take*: catch.
237   *I'll mar . . . pen*: I'll ruin his equipment.

235 How you do leave me to mine own protection.
Gratiano
Well, do you so: let not me take him, then,
For if I do, I'll mar the young clerk's pen.
Antonio
I am th' unhappy subject of these quarrels.
Portia
Sir, grieve not you; you are welcome notwith-
standing.
Bassanio

240   *this enforced wrong*: this injury that I was compelled to do.

240 Portia, forgive me this enforced wrong;
And in the hearing of these many friends,
I swear to thee, even by thine own fair eyes,
Wherein I see myself—
Portia   Mark you but that!
In both my eyes he doubly sees himself;

246   *of credit*: that can be believed.

245 In each eye, one: swear by your double self,
And there's an oath of credit.
Bassanio   Nay, but hear me:
Pardon this fault, and by my soul I swear
I never more will break an oath with thee.
Antonio

249   *wealth*: well-being, happiness.

I once did lend my body for his wealth,

251   *miscarried*: been lost.
252   *My . . . forfeit*: at the risk of forfeiting my soul.
253   *advisedly*: deliberately.
254   *surety*: security.

250 Which, but for him that had your husband's ring,
Had quite miscarried: I dare be bound again,
My soul upon the forfeit, that your lord
Will never more break faith advisedly.
Portia
Then you shall be his surety. Give him this,
255 And bid him keep it better than the other.
Antonio
Here, Lord Bassanio; swear to keep this ring.
Bassanio
By heaven! it is the same I gave the doctor!
Portia
I had it of him: pardon me, Bassanio,
For, by this ring, the doctor lay with me.

262 *In lieu of*: in return for.
263-4 Newly-married wives should not need to take lovers—any more than roads should need mending in summer.
265 *cuckolds*: men whose wives are unfaithful to them.
deserv'd it: i.e. by showing themselves to be unsatisfactory lovers.
266 *grossly*: coarsely.

275 *soon*: at once.
276 *argosies*: merchant ships.

288 *road*: anchorage.

Nerissa
260 And pardon me, my gentle Gratiano;
For that same scrubbed boy, the doctor's clerk,
In lieu of this, last night did lie with me.
Gratiano
Why, this is like the mending of highways
In summer, where the ways are fair enough!
265 What, are we cuckolds ere we have deserv'd it?
Portia
Speak not so grossly. You are all amaz'd:
Here is a letter, read it at your leisure,
It comes from Padua, from Bellario:
There you shall find that Portia was the doctor,
270 Nerissa there her clerk. Lorenzo here
Shall witness I set forth as soon as you,
And even but now return'd; I have not yet
Enter'd my house. Antonio, you are welcome;
And I have better news in store for you
275 Than you expect: unseal this letter soon;
There you shall find three of your argosies
Are richly come to harbour suddenly.
You shall not know by what strange accident
I chanced on this letter.
Antonio   I am dumb.
Bassanio
280 Were you the doctor, and I knew you not?
Gratiano
Were you the clerk that is to make me cuckold?
Nerissa
Ay, but the clerk that never means to do it,
Unless he live until he be a man.
Bassanio
Sweet doctor, you shall be my bedfellow:
285 When I am absent, then lie with my wife.
Antonio
Sweet lady, you have given me life and living;
For here I read for certain that my ships
Are safely come to road.
Portia   How now, Lorenzo!
My clerk hath some good comforts too for you.

Nerissa

290 Ay, and I'll give them him without a fee.
There do I give to you and Jessica,
From the rich Jew, a special deed of gift,
After his death, of all he dies possess'd of.

Lorenzo

Fair ladies, you drop manna in the way
295 Of starved people.

Portia   It is almost morning,
And yet I am sure you are not satisfied
Of these events at full. Let us go in;
And charge us there upon inter'gatories,
And we will answer all things faithfully.

Gratiano

300 Let it be so: the first inter'gatory
That my Nerissa shall be sworn on is,
Whether till the next night she had rather stay,
Or go to bed now, being two hours to day:
But were the day come, I should wish it dark,
305 That I were couching with the doctor's clerk.
Well, while I live, I'll fear no other thing
So sore as keeping safe Nerissa's ring.   [*Exeunt*

294   *manna*: food which the Israelites found when they were starving in the wilderness and which they believed to have been sent from heaven (Exodus 16: 14).

298   *at full*: in detail.

299   Ask us for our information (interrogate us) as though we were witnesses in court.

305   *couching*: going to bed.

306   *while I live*: as long as I live.

306-7   *I'll . . . ring*: I'll take care of nothing so much as guarding Nerissa's ring [and also her honour].

Examinations

I know that many of you will have been studying *The Merchant of Venice* for examination purposes, and I want now to offer some suggestions about the techniques of answering examination questions.

First of all, you must know the play well: that is, you must know what happens in it, what the characters are like, and what the words mean. Then, the most important rule in any kind of examination is: *answer the question.* You will always have far more information to offer than the question asks for; but the aim of the examination is not simply to test what you know. The examiners want to find out how well you can *use* what you know—how you can select information that is relevant to the question, and how you can organize your material into a coherent and logical argument.

Different Examining Boards set different kinds of questions; your teacher will be able to tell you which sort is favoured by your Board. Looking through past papers, I have found three kinds of question—'context' questions, 'comprehension' questions, and essays. I have taken recent specimens of each one of these and tried to show you how I would answer them. Following my 'answers' is a range of questions such as I would set if I were an examiner.

Specimen Answers

A Context questions

These questions present you with short passages from the play, and ask you to explain them. Usually you have to make a choice of passages: there may be five on the paper, and you are asked to choose three. Be very sure that you know exactly how many passages you must choose. Study the ones offered to you, and select those you feel most certain of.

Question

> *Gratiano:*
> If I do not put on a sober habit,
> Talk with respect, and swear but now and then,

Wear prayer-books in my pocket, look demurely,
Nay more, while grace is saying, hood mine eyes
Thus with my hat, and sigh, and say 'amen'!
Use all the observance of civility,
Like one well studied in a sad ostent
To please his grandam, never trust me more.

(i) To whom is Gratiano speaking? What accusations has this person made against Gratiano? For what reason has this person asked Gratiano to change?

(ii) What is the effect of Gratiano's speech on the person being addressed?

(iii) Quote two of the comments, made earlier in the play, on Gratiano's behaviour. Later, at Shylock's trial, we see Gratiano in a different mood. Say what you can of his mood at that time.

Suggested answer

(i) Bassanio. He has accused Gratiano of being wild and talking loudly and rudely. Bassanio does not want to create a bad impression when he goes to Belmont.

(ii) Bassanio laughs and says that he will wait to see how Gratiano behaves later, but that he can be merry at the feast.

(iii) Bassanio says that Gratiano 'speaks an infinite deal of nothing', and Lorenzo says that Gratiano will never let him speak.

At the trial Gratiano first insults Shylock, and then he is sarcastic when he rejoices over the Jew's defeat.

Question

Solanio:
I would she were as lying a gossip in that as ever knapped ginger, or made her neighbours believe she wept for the death of a third husband. But it is true—without any slips of prolixity or crossing the plain highway of talk—that the good Antonio, the honest Antonio—O that I had a title good enough to keep his name company!

(i) To whom does the 'she' in the first line refer? Who is being spoken to?

(ii) Explain the phrase: 'crossing the plain highway'. What is the news that Solanio is trying to give?

(iii) A third person arrives. Who is it? How does his own news coupled with the news in (ii) affect this third person who has just arrived?

Suggested answer
   (i) Rumour. Salerio.
   (ii) Leaving the direct subject of (the conversation). That Antonio's ship has been wrecked.
   (iii) Shylock. His daughter has stolen some of his money and run away from him. It makes Shylock more determined to get his pound of flesh from Antonio.

B Comprehension questions

These also present passages from the play and ask questions about them, and again you often have a choice of passages. But the extracts are much longer than those presented as context questions. A detailed knowledge of the language of the play is asked for here, and you must be able to express unusual or archaic phrases in your own words; you may also be asked to comment critically on the effectiveness of Shakespeare's language.

Question
Read the following passage, and answer all the questions printed beneath it.

Jessica: Who are you? Tell me, for more certainty,
Albeit I'll swear that I do know your tongue.
Lorenzo: Lorenzo, and thy love.
Jessica: Lorenzo, certain; and my love indeed,
For whom love I so much? And now who knows   5
But you, Lorenzo, whether I am yours?
Lorenzo: Heaven and thy thoughts are witness that thou art.
Jessica: Here, catch this casket; it is worth the pains.
I am glad 'tis night, you do not look on me,
For I am much asham'd of my exchange;   10
But love is blind, and lovers cannot see
The pretty follies that themselves commit;
For if they could, Cupid himself would blush
To see me thus transformed to a boy.
Lorenzo: Descend, for you must be my torch-bearer.   15
Jessica: What! must I hold a candle to my shames?
They in themselves, good sooth, are too too light.

Why, 'tis an office of discovery, love,
And I should be obscur'd.
Lorenzo :   So you are, sweet,
Even in the lovely garnish of a boy.   20
But come at once;
For the close night doth play the runaway,
And we are stay'd for at Bassanio's feast.
Jessica : I will make fast the doors, and gild myself
With some more ducats, and be with you straight.   25
                                                    [*Exit above*
Gratiano : Now, by my hood, a Gentile, and no Jew.
Lorenzo : Beshrew me, but I love her heartily;
For she is wise, if I can judge of her,
And fair she is, if that mine eyes be true,
And true she is, as she hath prov'd herself;   30
And therefore, like herself, wise, fair, and true,
Shall she be placed in my constant soul.

(i) Say concisely where in the play the passage occurs.

(ii) Give the meaning of *garnish* (line 20) and *Gentile* (line 26).

(iii) Bring out in your own words the meaning of lines 18–19 (*Why, 'tis an office . . . obscur'd*) and lines 22–3 (*For the close . . . feast*).

(iv) Explain the reason for the *exchange* referred to in line 10.

(v) What do you learn of Lorenzo and Jessica from the passage?

Suggested answer

(i) During the feast which Bassanio gives *after* he has borrowed the money from Shylock, and *before* he goes to Belmont.

(ii) Clothing. Someone who is not a Jew; also, because there is a pun with 'gentle', a charming woman.

(iii) A torch-bearer's job is to reveal things with the light of his torch, but Jessica ought to be kept in the dark.

The night, which allows us to be secret, is getting late, and they are waiting for us at Bassanio's party.

(iv) Jessica has exchanged her girl's clothing for boy's costume, so that in this disguise she will be able to escape from her father.

(v) Jessica is a little bit uncertain at first about Lorenzo's love. She is also shy because she is dressed as a boy, but she is very much in love with Lorenzo. She is sensible, and has taken care to get some of her father's jewels in the casket; she is also going to steal some money. Lorenzo thinks that she is beautiful, clever, and faithful, and he is determined to be true to her.

C Essays These questions always give you a specific topic to discuss. They *never* want you to tell the story of the whole play—so don't. The examiner has read the play, and does not need to be reminded of it. Give him only what he asks for.

Question

Give a full account of Bassanio's wooing and winning of Portia.

Suggested approach to an answer

First, make a list of the material you can draw on for this answer; then make a plan. The plan should be no more than an outline: you do not have time in the examination to write a rough draft of your essay and copy it out. Your plan might look like this:

1. Before the choice of caskets
   B's first mention of P, when he tells Ant. about her.
   P's attitude to B and attempt to make him delay choice—gives him encouragement.
2. Choosing casket
   B's thoughts about appearance and reality—shows he deserves P.
   Does P give any help (e.g. with song about fancy)?
3. Right choice
   Praise of picture and P's beauty.
   B cannot believe that he has won.
   P gives him ring, and he promises not to lose it.

———————

Can you remember any of the actual words of the play? If you can, it will help you to make your points more strongly, and show the examiner that you have indeed studied *the play*, and not just a prose account of the action and characters. But quotations must always be relevant. If they are not relevant, it is a waste of time writing them out; you will get no marks for this.

Specimen Questions

A Context questions   1.   The patch is kind enough, but a huge feeder;
Snail-slow in profit, and he sleeps by day
More than the wild-cat: drones hive not with me;
Therefore I part with him, and part with him
To one that I would have him help to waste
His borrow'd purse.

(i) Who is speaking, and to whom does he speak?

(ii) Who is being discussed, and what has this person decided to do?

(iii) How does the person addressed feel towards the speaker?

2.   You know me well, and herein spend but time
            To wind about my love with circumstance;
            And out of doubt you do me now more wrong
            In making question of my uttermost
            Than if you had made waste of all I have.
            Then do but say to me what I should do.

(i) Who is speaking, and to whom does he speak?

(ii) What is the speaker accusing the other person of?

(iii) What does the person addressed want the speaker to do, and why?

3.   O, be thou damn'd, inexorable dog!
            And for thy life let justice be accus'd.
            Thou almost mak'st me waver in my faith
            To hold opinion with Pythagoras,
            That souls of animals infuse themselves
            Into the trunks of men: thy currish spirit
            Govern'd a wolf.

(i) Who is speaking, and on what occasion?

(ii) What has the person addressed been doing to cause this outburst?

(iii) What effect does this speech have on the person addressed?

4.   Lock up my doors, and when you hear the drum
            And the vile squealing of the wry-neck'd fife,
            Clamber not you up to the casements then,
            Nor thrust your head into the public street
            To gaze on Christian fools with varnish'd faces,
            But stop my house's ears—I mean my casements—
            Let not the sound of shallow fopp'ry enter
            My sober house.

(i) Who is speaking, and to whom does he speak?

(ii) Where is the speaker going?

(iii) How will the 'Christian fools with varnish'd faces' help the person addressed?

5.   You swore to me when I did give it you,
      That you would wear it till your hour of death,
      And that it should lie with you in your grave:
      Though not for me, yet for your vehement oaths,
      You should have been respective and have kept it.
      Gave it a judge's clerk! no, God's my judge,
      The clerk will ne'er wear hair on's face that had it.

   (i) Two people are quarrelling: who are they?
   (ii) What does 'it' refer to?
   (iii) Will the 'clerk' ever 'wear hair' on his face? Why?

6.   I am as like to call thee so again,
      To spit on thee again, to spurn thee too.
      If thou wilt lend this money, lend it not
      As to thy friends, for when did friendship take
      A breed for barren metal of his friend?
      But lend it rather to thine enemy;
      Who if he break, thou may'st with better face
      Exact the penalty.

   (i) Who is speaking, and to whom does he speak?
   (ii) Why will the speaker spit on the man he addresses?
   (iii) What is meant by 'if he break'? Will the speaker ever
'break'?

B Comprehension   7.   *Portia:*
       questions   You see me, Lord Bassanio, where I stand,
                              Such as I am: though for myself alone
                              I would not be ambitious in my wish,
                              To wish myself much better; yet, for you,
                              I would be trebled twenty times myself;   5
                              A thousand times more fair, ten thousand times
                                    more rich;
                              That only to stand high in your account,
                              I might in virtues, beauties, livings, friends,
                              Exceed account: but the full sum of me
                              Is sum of something, which, to term in gross,   10
                              Is an unlesson'd girl, unschool'd, unpractis'd,
                              Happy in this, she is not yet so old

But she may learn; happier than this,
She is not bred so dull but she can learn;
Happiest of all, is that her gentle spirit   15
Commits itself to yours to be directed
As from her lord, her governor, her king.
Myself and what is mine, to you and yours
Is now converted: but now I was the lord
Of this fair mansion, master of my servants,   20
Queen o'er myself; and even now, but now,
This house, these servants, and this same myself
Are yours, my lord's. I give them with this ring;
Which when you part from, lose, or give away,
Let it presage the ruin of your love,   25
And be my vantage to exclaim on you.

(i) Say exactly where in the play this passage occurs.

(ii) Give the meaning of *livings* (line 8), *happy* (line 12), *but now* (line 19), and *presage* (line 25).

(iii) Express in your own words the meaning of line 7 (*only . . . account*), lines 18–19 (*Myself . . . converted*), and line 26 (*be my vantage . . . you*).

(iv) What happens to the ring that Portia gives to Bassanio in line 23?

(v) What impression of the relationship between Portia and Bassanio do you get from this passage?

8. *Arragon:*
I will not choose what many men desire,
Because I will not jump with common spirits
And rank me with the barbarous multitudes.
Why, then to thee, thou silver treasure house;
Tell me once more what title thou dost bear: 5
'*Who chooseth me shall get as much as he deserves*'.
And well said too; for who shall go about
To cozen fortune, and be honourable
Without the stamp of merit? Let none presume
To wear an undeserved dignity.   10
O that estates, degrees, and offices
Were not deriv'd corruptly, and that clear honour
Were purchas'd by the merit of the wearer.
How many then should cover that stand bare!
How many be commanded that command!   15
How much low peasantry would then be glean'd

From the true seed of honour! and how much honour
Pick'd from the chaff and ruin of the times
To be new varnish'd! Well, but to my choice:
'*Who chooseth me shall get as much as he deserves*'.   20
I will assume desert. Give me the key for this,
And instantly unlock my fortunes here.

(i) What does the Prince of Arragon find in the casket?

(ii) Give the meaning of *title* (line 5), *cozen* (line 8), and *assume desert* (line 21).

(iii) Express in your own words the meaning of lines 2–3 (*Because . . . multitudes*), line 14 (*How . . . bare*), lines 16–17 (*How much . . . honour*), and lines 17–19 (*and how much honour . . . varnish'd*).

(iv) What is the dramatic necessity for the scene in which this speech occurs?

(v) Describe the Prince of Arragon's character as it is revealed in this speech and elsewhere in the scene.

9.   *Lorenzo :*
How sweet the moonlight sleeps upon this bank!
Here will we sit, and let the sounds of music
Creep in our ears: soft stillness and the night
Become the touches of sweet harmony.
Sit, Jessica—look how the floor of heaven   5
Is thick inlaid with patens of bright gold:
There's not the smallest orb which thou behold'st
But in his motion like an angel sings,
Still quiring to the young-eyed cherubins;
Such harmony is in immortal souls,   10
But whilst this muddy vesture of decay
Doth grossly close it in, we cannot hear it.
            Enter Musicians
Come, ho! and wake Diana with a hymn:
With sweetest touches pierce your mistress' ear,
And draw her home with music.   15

(i) Say exactly where in the play this speech occurs.

(ii) Give the meaning of *Become* (line 4), *patens* (line 6), *quiring* (line 9), and *cherubins* (line 9).

(iii) Explain the meaning of lines 7–8 (*There's not . . . sings*), lines 11–12 (*But whilst . . . hear it*), and line 13 (*wake Diana with a hymn*).

(iv) What are Jessica and Lorenzo doing at Belmont?

(v) What is the dramatic function of the first part of the scene in which this speech occurs?

C   Essays

10. Do you agree that 'Portia is the most important character in the play'?

11. Show how Shakespeare makes a contrast between Venice and Belmont.

12. 'I have much ado to know myself'; these are Antonio's words at the beginning of the play. Explain what we learn about him as the play progresses.

13. With detailed reference to the text of the play, describe the conflict between Antonio and Shylock.

14. Describe *three* of Portia's suitors (other than Bassanio) and her attitudes towards them.

15. Describe the character of Gratiano, and say what you think he contributes to the play.

16. Is there, in your opinion, any inconsistency between the character of Bassanio as he appears in Venice, and as he behaves at Belmont?

17. Try to explain the dramatic function of Launcelot Gobbo in *The Merchant of Venice*.

18. In what ways is the sub-plot of Jessica and Lorenzo necessary to *The Merchant of Venice*?

19. In Shakespeare's day, an alternative title for *The Merchant of Venice* was *The Jew of Venice*; which title do you think is the more appropriate?

William Shakespeare, 1564–1616

Elizabeth I was Queen of England when Shakespeare was born in 1564. He was the son of a tradesman who made and sold gloves in the small town of Stratford-upon-Avon, and he was educated at the grammar school in that town. Shakespeare did not go to university when he left school, but worked, perhaps, in his father's business. When he was eighteen he married Anne Hathaway, who became the mother of his daughter, Susanna, in 1583, and of twins in 1585.

There is nothing exciting, or even unusual, in this story; and from 1585 until 1592 there are no documents that can tell us anything at all about Shakespeare. But we have learned that in 1592 he was known in London, and that he had become both an actor and a playwright.

We do not know when Shakespeare wrote his first play, and indeed we are not sure of the order in which he wrote his works. If you look on page 103 at the list of his writings and their approximate dates, you will see how he started by writing plays on subjects taken from the history of England. No doubt this was partly because he was always an intensely patriotic man—but he was also a very shrewd business-man. He could see that the theatre audiences enjoyed being shown their own history, and it was certain that he would make a profit from this kind of drama.

The plays in the next group are mainly comedies, with romantic love stories of young people who fall in love with one another, and at the end of the play marry and live happily ever after.

At the end of the sixteenth century the happiness disappears, and Shakespeare's plays become melancholy, bitter, and tragic. This change may have been caused by some sadness in the writer's life (one of his twins died in 1596). Shakespeare, however, was not the only writer whose works at this time were very serious. The whole of England was facing a crisis. Queen Elizabeth I was growing old. She was greatly loved, and the people were sad to think she must soon die; they were also afraid, for the Queen had never married, and so there was no child to succeed her.

When James I came to the throne in 1603, Shakespeare continued to write serious drama—the great tragedies and the plays based on Roman history (such as *Julius Caesar*) for which he is most famous. Finally, before he retired from the theatre, he wrote another set of comedies. These all have the same theme: they tell of happiness which is lost, and then found again.

Shakespeare returned from London to Stratford, his home town. He was rich and successful, and he owned one of the biggest houses in the town. He died in 1616.

Shakespeare also wrote two long poems, and a collection of sonnets. The sonnets describe two love-affairs, but we do not know who the lovers were. Although there are many public documents concerned with his career as a writer and a business-man, Shakespeare has hidden his personal life from us. A nineteenth-century poet, Matthew Arnold, addressed Shakespeare in a poem, and wrote 'We ask and ask—Thou smilest, and art still'.

There is not even a trustworthy portrait of the world's greatest dramatist.

Approximate order of composition of Shakespeare's works

Period	Comedies	History plays	Tragedies	Poems
I	Comedy of Errors Taming of the Shrew Two Gentlemen of Verona Love's Labour's Lost	Henry VI, part 1 Henry VI, part 2 Henry VI, part 3 Richard III King John	Titus Andronicus	Venus and Adonis Rape of Lucrece
1594				
II	Midsummer Night's Dream Merchant of Venice Merry Wives of Windsor Much Ado About Nothing As You Like It	Richard II Henry IV, part 1 Henry IV, part 2 Henry V	Romeo and Juliet	Sonnets
1599				
III	Twelfth Night Troilus and Cressida Measure for Measure All's Well That Ends Well		Julius Caesar Hamlet Othello Timon of Athens King Lear Macbeth Antony and Cleopatra Coriolanus	
1608				
IV	Pericles Cymbeline A Winter's Tale The Tempest	Henry VIII		
1613				

An Introduction to
MODERN
ARABIC

An Introduction to
MODERN
ARABIC

Farhat J. Ziadeh
and
R. Bayly Winder

DOVER PUBLICATIONS, INC.
Mineola, New York

Bibliographical Note

This Dover edition, first published in 2003, is an unabridged reprint of the work published by Princeton University Press, Princeton, New Jersey, in 1957.

Library of Congress Cataloging-in-Publication Data

Ziadeh, Farhat Jacob.
    An introduction to modern Arabic / Farhat J. Ziadeh and R. Bayly Winder.
      p. cm.
    Includes indexes.
    ISBN 0-486-42870-2 (pbk.)
    1. Arabic language—Grammar. I. Winder, R. Bayly (Richard Bayly), 1920– II. Title.

PJ6307 .Z5 2003
492.7'82'421—dc21

2002041311

Manufactured in the United States of America
Dover Publications, Inc., 31 East 2nd Street, Mineola, N.Y. 11501

PREFACE

Until a decade or so ago Arabic was taught almost exclusively to students on the graduate level and from books written by European scholars using technical expressions and Latin terms which, especially to an undergraduate, were forbidding. Now the English-speaking student has available to him a book designed to meet his particular needs as one encountering for the first time a language that is truly foreign—French, German, Latin, or any other language that he might have studied being members of the same family to which English belongs. The attempt embodies years of teaching experience and involves years of work on the part of the authors. The joint authorship represents a happy combination of one in whose blood Arabic flows and one who having "suffered...is able to succour them that are tempted." Far from claiming to be the "seal" (*khātam*) of all Arabic grammars, or challenging the validity of the biblical assertion that "of making many books there is no end"—though the writer could not have had grammars in mind—this *Introduction to Modern Arabic* hopes to simplify the intricacies and endear the niceties of the "tongue of the angels" (*lisān al-malā'ikah*) to the would-be Arabist. If it does, then all the efforts of the authors and, behind them, of the Department of Oriental Studies of Princeton, will not have been in vain.

Philip K. Hitti

April 1, 1957

INTRODUCTION

The purpose of this book is to introduce the student, particularly the student with relatively little experience in studying languages, to modern literary Arabic with concentration on the style employed in newspapers. The book does not pretend to cover all the fine points of the language or to be an advanced reference grammar. Further, we have not thought of it as a "teach-yourself" book though the experience of some users indicates that it may be satisfactory for that purpose.

Our approach centers on two themes. The first is to analyze the morphological and syntactical patterns of the language inductively after they have been used. Thus normal progression is from the specific to the general, although this has not in all cases seemed wise—notably in the introductory material and in the chapter on numbers. In general, no patterns or usages occur prior to the chapter which deals with them, and an attempt has been made to limit the amount of new material in any one chapter.

The second major point is an extremely careful control of vocabulary, which is the most difficult hurdle at almost every stage in learning literary Arabic. To this end every occurrence of every word was recorded and, when the first draft was completed, those words which were used less than four or five times were for the most part either eliminated or used more often. To assure high frequency, we checked the vocabulary with Moshe Brill's *The Basic Word List of the Arabic Daily Newspaper* (Jerusalem: The Hebrew University Press Association, 1940), although we did not follow it slavishly. We also adopted Brill's criteria for defining a vocabulary unit. The great majority of words used are of high frequency in the Brill count, though inevitably there are some common words which do not occur. The result is that the student who has gone through the book carefully has a small, selected, and compact vocabulary. The total number of words in the book is 1,013.

A typical chapter contains four sections. Section I consists of a text—with parallel translation—in which the new grammatical points to be exemplified, whether syntactical and/or morphological, are presented as well as new vocabulary. Section II consists of an analysis of these new points plus generalizations based on them. In some cases supplementary notes are also included. Usually, once a point is made, knowledge of it is thereafter assumed. Section III contains a second text, with parallel translation, in which the new points that the chapter deals with are again stressed, and new vocabulary is again introduced. Section IV consists of isolated sentences in English and Arabic to be translated. These sentences are intended to make the student use the constructions exemplified in the chapter and to repeat some of the vocabulary units, without introducing new vocabulary. Exceptions to the practice of not introducing new patterns or usages prior to the chapter that deals with them were made in the case of simple maṣdars and proper names.

Two other points may clarify the use of the book. First, in the English translations, parentheses are used not only to enclose genuinely parenthetic material such as the literal meaning of a word, but also to indicate words which have no equivalent in the Arabic text but which are necessary in the English. Brackets show words which do not represent English usage but which do appear in the Arabic. Second, vowels and other signs are progressively omitted as follows: starting with Chapter XXVIII vowels before their lengtheners; with Chapter XXXI the fatḥah before tā' marbūṭah and the waṣlah and sukūn of the definite article; with Chapter XXXII the shaddah on a "Sun letter" following the definite article; with Chapter XXXIII the vowels of prepositions and the conjunctions ﻭ, ...ﻓَ and ﺃَﻭْ, and the vowels of maṣdars and participles except for the vowel which distinguishes between active and passive participles; with Chapter XXXIV fatḥah tanwīn when alif is present, vowels of the ﻣَﻔْﻌُﻮﻝ, ﻓَﺎﻋِﻞ, and ﻓَﻌِﻴﻞ patterns, the shaddah on the yā' of nisbah, the final vowels of sound masculine plurals and of duals, the vowels of pronominal suffixes, the vowels of demonstrative and personal pronouns and of the relatives ﺃَﻟَّﺬِﻱ and ﺃَﻟَّﺘِﻲ, and all waṣlahs. In Chapter XXXV only the few vowels which seemed essential for clarity were used.

The content of the texts for the most part needs no comment; however, it might be worth observing that it is intended to impart some knowledge of the Middle East area and that it is largely political and in some cases deliberately nationalistic. It is also generally of a simple narrative type.

The appendices, indices, and vocabularies are largely self-explanatory. The paradigms, in contrast to those found in most books, are complete in the active voice. Their arrangement, it is hoped, will aid the student to observe the variations among different classes of verbs with greater ease than is possible in the traditional layout. Appendix II, "Verbs and Their Prepositions," fulfills, we think, a long-felt need and draws together information otherwise available only in dictionaries or the "breasts of men."

Some liberties of various sorts have been taken and may require explanation. The English translations are frequently stilted and unidiomatic because of a desire to stay relatively close to the Arabic. The aim here has been pedagogical not literary. On the Arabic side liberties have also been taken, e.g. listing فَعْلَانُ as فَعْلَانٌ (Chapter XI, section II, note B), and there are various conscious omissions which the expert will detect, especially some accusatives such as the مَفْعُولٌ مَعَهُ, the مُسْتَثْنَى, and the مَا ٱلتَّعَجُّبِ. One other observation is that the limitation placed upon us by the gradual presentation of grammatical points made the style of the texts embodying those points, especially in the first part of the book, sound somewhat rigid and not as smooth and natural as we would have liked.

The list of those who have helped us is a long one. First place on it goes to Professor Philip K. Hitti of Princeton, who originally proposed to us the idea of writing the book (it represents in fact, to a considerable extent, a crystallization of teaching methods developed by him during his long and distinguished academic career at Princeton); who sustained and encouraged us with his characteristic friendliness and interest over the long period of time we have engaged in the undertaking; who looked over almost every chapter (and detected numerous slips we had missed) before it went to press; and who only rebelled when a student assistant, in our absence, unduly pestered him with queries about obscure verb forms for the paradigms. Others who gave of their time and thought were Professor H. A. R. Gibb of Harvard, who advised us on the problem of accent; Professor Wilfred C. Smith of McGill, who supplied us with our rule for the chair which hamzah takes in the middle of a word; Professor Samuel Atkins of Princeton, who read critically Chapter VII and advised on other points; and Messrs. Stanford Shaw, John Joseph, Fadlou Shehadeh, Oleg Grabar, Caesar Farah, Richard Debs, John

Williams, George Scanlon, and Nicholas Heer—all of whom made contributions of various types. Naturally, none of these gentlemen bears the slightest responsibility for anything in the book. Another group to whom we are most grateful are those somewhat intrepid gentlemen who agreed to use the preliminary, xerographed version of the book—sight unseen—in their teaching, for our benefit. These include: Professors Kenneth Cragg, S. D. Goitein, Meyer Bravmann, F. R. C. Bagley and Mr. Majed Saʿid. From them, as well as from our own students, have come many valuable suggestions. We are also particularly grateful to the compositors of the Cambridge University Press and to the publisher, Princeton University Press, for their co-operation and skill in completing a most exacting task. Finally, we wish to thank the Department of Oriental Studies of Princeton University, under the chairmanship of Professor T. Cuyler Young, for making possible the publication of this book.

To our wives we owe a debt of gratitude far beyond that which authors normally owe. Due to unusual circumstances we had to work— over a five year period—almost wholly at night and away from our homes. We asked too much, but they gave freely.

Princeton, New Jersey　　　　　　　　　　　　　　F. J. Z.
　　October, 1956　　　　　　　　　　　　　　　　R. B. W.

TABLE OF CONTENTS

TABLE OF CONTENTS

AN INTRODUCTION TO
MODERN ARABIC

THE ALPHABET: TRANSLITERATION AND PRONUNCIATION. THE NUMERALS

I. The Arabic alphabet consists of twenty-eight characters, written from right to left. All twenty-eight characters represent consonants. In addition there are vowel signs and various other orthographic signs.

The consonants, as they appear when standing alone, are as follows:

NAME OF LETTER	SYMBOL	TRANSLITERATION
hamzah[1]	ء	ʾ
bā'	ب	b
tā'	ت	t
thā'	ث	th
jīm	ج	j
ḥā'	ح	ḥ
khā'	خ	kh
dāl	د	d
dhāl	ذ	dh
rā'	ر	r
zā' *or* zāy	ز	z
sīn	س	s
shīn	ش	sh
ṣād	ص	ṣ
ḍād	ض	ḍ
ṭā'	ط	ṭ
ẓā'	ظ	ẓ
'ayn	ع	ʿ
ghayn	غ	gh
fā'	ف	f
qāf	ق	q
kāf	ك	k
lām	ل	l
mīm	م	m
nūn	ن	n
hā'	ه	h
wāw	و	w
yā'	ي	y

[1] Many grammars give *alif* (ا) as the first letter in the alphabet. In reality alif is only a "chair" on top of which the hamzah "sits" thus آ, and as such has no phonetic

II. The pronunciation of the consonants is as follows:[2]

ء : The hamzah represents a glottal stop produced by completely closing the vocal chords and then by suddenly separating them. The sound is frequently made in English at the beginning of a word with an initial vowel, particularly if emphasized, e.g. *absolutely essential!* It is the same sound that is heard at the beginning of the second syllable in the Scotch pronunciation of *bottle.*

ب : Bā' represents the same sound as does English *b.*

ت : Tā' represents almost the same sound as does English *t,* but the tongue does not, as in English *t,* come into contact with the gum behind the upper teeth but with the upper teeth themselves. The *t* of *eighth* is perhaps most like tā'.

ث : Thā' represents the same sound as does the unvoiced *th* of English *mouth* or *thing.*

ج : In literary Arabic, jīm represents the same sound as does the *j* of English *jam.* The most important variants are: in Egypt where the hard *g* of *gas* or *lag* predominates, and in Lebanon and other adjacent areas where it is the voiced correlative of *sh,* equivalent to the ʒ in *azure.*

ح : Ḥā' represents an unvoiced pharyngeal fricative formed further back and lower than khā' (خ; see below) and entirely without velar vibration. The back of the tongue is depressed to almost the same extent it is when a doctor examines the throat and depresses it artificially. The sound may be mastered by realizing that it is similar to a stage whisper, but formed farther back. It can be produced by whispering *ha* as loudly as possible.

خ : Khā' represents an unvoiced velar fricative, similar to the *ch* of German *ach.* The sound can be produced by pronouncing the syllables *ik, ak,* and *uk* in succession and noting the point of contact with the soft palate in each case, which, it will be found, recedes from front to back. If the student then causes the tongue to approach any of these *k*-positions, but, before contact occurs, forces breath through the narrowed orifice, khā' will result. The "scrape" which is essential to khā' is due to agitation of the velum by the breath forced through the narrow orifice.

---

value. However, in unvowelled texts alif only is written, hamzah being understood; and in reciting the alphabet, one says *alif, bā',* etc., not *hamzah, bā',* etc.

[2] These simplified descriptions of the sounds represented by Arabic consonants are largely based on the full treatment of the subject found in W. H. T. Gairdner, *The Phonetics of Arabic* (London: Oxford University Press, 1925).

د :   Dāl represents almost the same sound as does English *d*, but with the same reservations made for tā' (ت) above. The *d* of *width* is perhaps most like dāl.

ذ :   Dhāl represents the same sound as does the voiced *th* of English *to mouth* or *this*.

ر :   Rā' represents the rolled *r*, i.e. there are a rapid succession of taps by the tip of the tongue on the teeth ridge. Two taps are usually sufficient. It should be emphasized, however, that the unrolled *r*, in which the tip of the tongue is curved back toward the hard palate, as in western American *farm*, is to be avoided.

ز :   Zā' represents the same sound as does English *z*.

س :   Sīn represents the same sound as does English *s*.

ش: Shīn represents the same sound as does the English combination *sh*.

ص: Ṣād represents an "emphatic" velarized correlative of sīn (س). Ṣād is formed by placing the tip of the tongue in approximately the same position as for sīn and raising the back of the tongue toward the velum.

ض: Dād represents an "emphatic" velarized correlative of dāl (د), formed in the same way as is ṣād (ص).

ط :   Ṭā' represents an "emphatic" velarized correlative of tā' (ت), formed in the same way as is ṣād.

ظ :   Ẓā' properly represents an "emphatic" velarized correlative of dhāl (ذ), but in Egypt and Syria this sound is often replaced by that of the emphatic velarized correlative of zā' (ز).

ع :   'Ayn is a very difficult sound for the average Westerner to produce, and it is best mastered in connection with a native speaker. It is generally regarded that 'ayn is a voiced correlative of ḥā' (ح). This supposition is partially true, for if 'ayn is unvoiced, something close to ḥā' results. However, if the process is reversed, and ḥā' is voiced, it will be found that the general tenseness in the pharynx is greatly increased; there may be other physical modifications as well.

غ :   Ghayn, a voiced velar fricative, is almost the voiced correlative of khā' (خ), but the correlation is not exact, for in ghayn there is no velar scrape. This sound, which is similar to the Parisian *r*, may be produced by pronouncing the *ch* of Scottish *loch* (without velar scrape) and then by voicing that fricative.

ف :   Fā' represents the same sound as does English *f*.

ق :   Qāf is a voiceless uvular stop which can be reproduced by taking the point of contact in the *ik, ak, uk* series (see above under khā' [خ]) one stage further back so that contact may be made at the

5

extremity of the velum. In various areas, especially the Persian Gulf, qāf is pronounced like the hard *g* in *gas*.

ك : Kāf represents the same sound as does English *k*.

ل : Essentially, lām represents the same sound as does English *l*. However, it is worth noting that lām is velarized in the word *Allāh* (unless preceded by an *i* vowel) and when it is influenced by velarized sounds such as ṣād (ص), ḍād (ض), and ṭā' (ط). In these cases lām is formed in the same way as is ṣād.

م : Mīm represents the same sound as does English *m*.

ن : Nūn represents the same sound as does English *n*.

ه : Hā' represents the same sound as does English *h*. It is only difficult in Arabic when final because it does not so occur in English. To master it in this position, say *aha* or *uhu*; gradually diminish the length of the second vowel; and finally eliminate it altogether.

و : Wāw represents the same sound as does the consonantal English *w*.

ي : Yā' represents the same sound as does the consonantal English *y*.

NOTE: The form ة, called *tā' marbūṭah*, is a combination of the letter tā' (ت) and the letter hā' (ه). It only occurs at the end of words. When vocalized, it is pronounced as is tā'; when not vocalized it is pronounced as is hā'. (For use of this ending, see Chapter IX, section II, 2.)

III. The numerals are as follows:

٠	٩	٨	٧	٦	٥	٤	٣	٢	١
0	9	8	7	6	5	4	3	2	1

In combination, however, they are arranged as in English, thus

١٩٤٨ = 1948,   ١٩٥٠ = 1950,   ١٩٥٥ = 1955.

EXERCISE

Identify the following:

أ   ب   ج   د   ه   د   و   ز   ح   ط   ي   ك   ل   م   ن   س   ع   ف

ص   ق   ر   ش   ت   ث   خ   ذ   ض   ظ   غ   ة

CHAPTER II

VOWELS AND LETTERS IN
CONNECTED FORM

I. The vowels in Arabic are three: *a*, *u*, and *i*. The signs of these three vowels are respectively:

1. *Fatḥah*, a small diagonal stroke above a consonant, as in بَ [ba].

2. *Ḍammah*, a small waw (و) above a consonant, as in بُ [bu].

3. *Kasrah*, a small diagonal stroke under a consonant, as in بِ [bi].
   When hamzah bears kasrah, both hamzah and kasrah are written under alif (إ).

The pronunciation of the fatḥah is the same as that of the *a* in English *fat* or *add*.[1] The pronunciation of the ḍammah is similar to that of the *oo* in *boot*, but much shorter. The pronunciation of the kasrah is the same as that of the *i* in *admit* or *habit*.

In addition to the three vowel signs there is another sign called *sukūn* which indicates the absence of a vowel after a consonant. It consists of a small circle written above the consonant as بْ [b].

EXERCISE

Recite aloud:

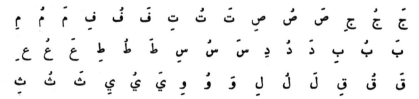

---

[1] The sounds represented by the vowel signs are of course all influenced by those of surrounding consonants. It is to be especially noted that when the fatḥah is above one of the velarized consonants, ص, ض, ط, ظ, ق and above the ر, its sound tends to be that of the *a* in *sofa* or *abound*. In other cases, it tends to be that of the *e* in *end*. The question of vowel variations usually settles itself automatically because of the mechanics of proper consonant production. For a thorough treatment of the subject consult Gairdner, *op. cit.*, pp. 32–51.

7

نَ نُ نِ نْ هَ هُ هِ ذَ ذُ ذِ ذْ حَ حِ حُ إِ أُ أَ زَ زُ زِ زِ

ظَ ظُ ظِ ظْ غَ غُ غِ شَ شُ شِ زَ زُ زِ خَ خُ خِ خِ

ضَ ضُ ضِ كَ كُ كِ

II. Most of the consonants are written in slightly different forms according to whether they stand alone, or are joined to a following letter only (initial), or are joined to a following and a preceding letter (medial), or are joined to a preceding letter only (final). In addition the six letters و ز ر ذ د ا cannot be joined to following letters. The following chart shows these variations.

TERMINAL	MEDIAL	INITIAL	ALONE
‍ا...	‍ا...	ا	ا
‍ب...	...ب...	ب...	ب
‍ت...	...ت...	ت...	ت
‍ث...	...ث...	ث...	ث
‍ج...	...ج...	ج...	ج
‍ح...	...ح...	ح...	ح
‍خ...	...خ...	خ...	خ
‍د...	‍د...	د...	د
‍ذ...	‍ذ...	ذ...	ذ
‍ر...	‍ر...	ر...	ر
‍ز...	‍ز...	ز...	ز
‍س...	...س...	س...	س
‍ش...	...ش...	ش...	ش
‍ص...	...ص...	ص...	ص
‍ض...	...ض...	ض...	ض
‍ط...	...ط...	ط...	ط
‍ظ...	...ظ...	ظ...	ظ
‍ع...	...ع...	ع...	ع
‍غ...	...غ...	غ...	غ
‍ف...	...ف...	ف...	ف
‍ق...	...ق...	ق...	ق

TERMINAL	MEDIAL	INITIAL	ALONE
...كـ	...كـ...	كـ...	ك
...لـ	...لـ...	لـ...	ل
...مـ	...مـ...	مـ...	م
...نـ	...نـ...	نـ...	ن
...هـ	...هـ...	هـ...	ه
...و	و...	و	و
...ي	...يـ...	يـ...	ي

When alif follows an initial or a medial ل, they are written thus لا, ﻼ, respectively. Furthermore, the student must familiarize himself with a number of common ligatures, some of which appear in the Exercise.

EXERCISE

Recite aloud:

حَبْ بُدْ تَمْ قَدْ بَطْ تَلْ كَمْ لَمْ قُمْ فَمْ بِعْ كُلْ دَعْ رَبْ

ذَمْ أَخْ وَجْ قَطْ زِدْ قِسْ عَمْ غَمْ هَلْ حَلْ خَلْ دَفْ كَفْ

رَفْ رُحْ مُتْ فِرْ خُذْ ثُمْ نِدْ يَمْ سَمْ طِبْ شَمْ ظِلْ جَلْ

ضَبْ صَكْ هُمْ حَجْ لَكْ بِكْ

CHAPTER III

ACCENT AND SHADDAH

I. Words of two syllables are accented on the first syllable.

EXERCISE

Recite aloud:

إِسْمْ بَحْرْ عِلْمْ مِصْرْ نَهْرْ دَرْسْ قَصْرْ بَغْلْ كَسْرْ دَمْعْ لَحْمْ

حَجْمْ جَمْعْ تَمْرْ نَفْسْ طَبْعْ صِنْعْ قُرْصْ فَرْسْ نِصْفْ قُدْسْ

سَمَكْ ضَعْفْ خُبْزْ ثَغْرْ نَمِرْ بَدْرْ تِبْنْ جِسْرْ ظَهْرْ بَعْدْ

شَحْمْ حَبْلْ خَمْرْ دَرْبْ وَعْدْ يُسْرْ قُطْرْ طَبْلْ ظَبْي زَهْرْ لَعْبْ

نَحْوَ عِنْدَ تَحْتَ أَبْ أَخْ رَأْي

II. Three syllable words are accented on the first syllable unless the middle syllable is closed, in which case it receives the accent. A closed syllable may be defined as one which consists of a consonant, a short vowel, and a vowelless consonant; an open syllable, as one which consists of a consonant and a short vowel.

EXERCISE

Recite aloud:

قَتَلَ كَسَرَ لَعِبَ عَلِمَ فَهِمَ جَمَعَ دَرَسَ رَكَضَ حَلِمَ نَصَحَ

قَدِمَ ذَهَبَ رَكِبَ سَمِعَ عَمِلَ أَكَلَ شَرِبَ ظَلَمَ طَبَعَ ثِقَةً صِلَةً

غَفْلَةً سَنَةً كَتَبْتَ كَتَبْتُ كَتَبْتُمْ رَغْبَةً نَكْتُبْ يَكْتُبْنَ عَمَلُ قَلَمْ

بَقَرْ شَجَرْ ذَنَبْ جَمَلْ حَمَلَ وَلَدْ حَجَرْ بَدَنْ كُتُبْ عُمَرُ حَلَبْ

عَجَبْ قَدَمْ فَرَسْ مُهْرْ وَطَنْ وَرَقْ عَدَدْ قُطُرْ عِلَبْ فِتَنْ ذِمَمْ

عِنَبْ قَلْعَةً قَرْيَةً عَلِمْتُمْ ضَرَبْتَ سَمِعْتَ دَرَسْنَ

10

III. When a consonant occurs twice without a vowel between, it is written only once and the sign ˮ, called *shaddah*, is written above it, as in قَتَّلَ. Letters which have shaddah above them are commonly said to be doubled. However, there is not, as in French *cette table*, an implosion and explosion for each *t*. Rather, as in English *hot time*, there is only one closure; but the length of time between implosion and explosion is long, and in addition the implosion is slightly emphasized because the accent is on it.

EXERCISE

Recite aloud:

كَسَّرَ عَلَّمَ قَدَّمَ دَخَّنَ وَدَّعَ سَلَّمَ وَجَّهَ كَلَّمَ ظَنَّ قَلَّ قَلَّ عَدَّ وَدَّ

سَدَّ شَدَّ لَمَّ جَرَّدَ جَمَّعَ حَلَّ رَدَّ عِزَّةُ سِكَّةُ

CHAPTER IV

LONG VOWELS AND DIPHTHONGS

I. The letters alif (ا), wāw (و), and yā' (ي) are known as weak (i.e. irregular) letters. In addition to the function of alif as a chair for the hamzah (ء) and to the function of wāw and yā' as consonants,[1] these three letters have the additional function of lengthening the vowels to which they respectively correspond, namely, fatḥah, ḍammah, and kasrah. Thus, دَارُ [dāru] as opposed to دَرُ [daru], نُورُ [nūru] as opposed to نُرُ [nuru], and نِيرُ [nīru] as opposed to نِرُ [niru]. When the weak letters are used as lengtheners, they do not bear any sign. However, from the point of view of accent a syllable consisting of a consonant, a vowel, and a lengthener is considered to be a closed syllable. (See Chapter III, section II.)

The pronunciation of the long vowels is as follows:

ـَا:　　This combination represents the same sound as does the *a* of *acid* when none of the letters ظ ط ض ص or ق ر is in juxtaposition with it. When these consonants are juxtaposed, it represents the same sound as does the *a* of *father*. In both cases the sound is long.

ـُو:　　This combination represents a sound similar to that of the *oo* in *boot*, but much longer. There is no diphthongization.

ـِي:　　This combination represents a sound similar to that of the *ee* in *sleep*, though much longer. There is no diphthongization.

A final long vowel is shortened, however, before a pause or when it forms one syllable with the beginning of a succeeding word.

EXERCISE

Recite aloud:

دَارُ نَارُ جَارُ قُولُ بُوقُ عُودُ دِينُ فِيلُ عِيدُ بُومُ بِيدُ كَارُ

حَالُ سُودُ نِيرُ طُورُ تِينُ بَابُ دَارِي جَارِي بُوقِي عُودِي دِينِي

عِيدِي فِينَا سِينَا.

---

[1] Wāw and yā' may also be chairs for hamzah under certain conditions; see Chapter V, section I.

12

طُورُ سِينَاَ فِي مِصْرَ. بَابُ دَارِي عَالِي. بُوقِي مِنْ جَارِي.

خَالِي فِي دَارِي.

كَانَ قَامَ بَاعَ سِيرَةٌ سَاعَةٌ نَاقَةٌ كِتَابُ كَاتِبُ قَتِيلُ قَاتِلُ

جَامِعُ سَلِيمُ سَالِمُ.

II. There are two diphthongs in Arabic represented by the combinations وْ — and يْ — transliterated respectively [aw] and [ay]. The sound represented by the former is similar to that of the *ow* in *fowl*. The sound represented by the latter is similar to that of the word *eye*. However, in literary Arabic diphthongs, the glide is carried all the way to the consonant positions of the *w* and *y* respectively. Diphthongs are closed syllables.

EXERCISE

Recite aloud:

قَوْلُ نَوْمُ بَيْعُ عَيْبُ صَوْمُ دَيْنُ مَوْتُ بَيْتُ لَوْمُ عَيْنُ زَيْنُ

بَيْرُوتُ صَوْتُ خَوْفُ رَيْبُ كُلَيْبُ لَيْلَةُ رَوْضَةُ بَيَّنَ بَيْعَ قَوْمُ

بَوَّبَ حَيَّرَ سَيَّرَ عَوَّدَ لَوَّعَ طَيَّرَ

CHAPTER V

HAMZAH AND THREE TYPES OF
LONG ALIF

I. It has already been stated (Chapter I, footnote 1) that alif (ا) is used as a chair for hamzah. In addition, however, one of the other weak letters, yāʾ (ى, without dots) and wāw (و), may be the chair. Further, hamzah sometimes occurs without a chair and is then written either over the line connecting the letters on either side of it or by itself.

The rules governing the chair of the hamzah may be summarized as follows:

1. At the beginning of a word the chair is always alif.

2. In the middle of a word:

   (a) If only one of the vowels ― or ― or ― (or two identical vowels) is contiguous to the hamzah (i.e. precedes or is borne by it), the chair will be, respectively, ى or و or ا (e.g. يَسْئَلُ يَسْأَلُ سُؤْلُ سُؤُولُ).

   (b) If two different vowels are contiguous to the hamzah, the vowel which determines the chair (in accordance with the correspondence given in I, 2a) is governed by the following order of preference: ― ― ― (e.g. سَئِمَ سُؤَالٌ سُئِلَ; in the first example the contiguous vowels are ― and ―, the ― takes preference, and therefore the chair is ى).

   (c) If the hamzah is preceded by a long vowel and bears ―, it has no chair (e.g. خَطِيئَةٌ مُرُوءَةٌ سَاءَلَ). If, however, the hamzah is preceded by a long vowel and bears ― or ―, the chair usually corresponds to the vowel the hamzah bears (e.g. سَائِلٌ تَسَاؤُلٌ).

3. At the end of a word:

   (a) The preceding vowel determines the chair (in accordance with the correspondence given in I, 2 (a), e.g. بَدَأَ دَفُؤَ فَتِئَ).

14

(*b*) If there is no preceding short vowel (i.e. if there is sukūn or a long vowel), there is no chair (e.g. بَطِيءٌ شَيْءٌ).

EXERCISE

Copy the following, putting in the correct chair for the hamzah if one is necessary; join letters as required:

ءَكَلَ ءَخَذَ ءَمَنَ ءَرَخَ ءَرَخَ قَعَلَ ءَكَّدَ ءُسْمُ ءُخْتُ سَءَلَ وَءَدَ رَءْسُ

يَسءَلُ مُءْمِنُ سُءَالُ فُءَادُ لُءْمُ سُءِلَ رَءِيسُ بِءْرُ يَءِسَ

يَبءُسُ تَسَاءَلَ خَاءِلُ نَشَءَ مَلَءَ قَرَءَ هَدَءَ دَفَءُ بَطَءَ فَتَءَ هَزَءَ

مَرَءُ يَنشِءُ يَبرِءُ جُزءُ شَيْءُ ضَوْءُ بَطِيءُ جَرِيءُ بَرِيءُ سَمَاءُ جَزَاءُ

دُعَاءُ

II. If alif-hamzah-fatḥah is followed by a lengthening alif (i.e. أَا), then the hamzah and its vowel are dropped, one alif only is written, and above this alif is written the sign ~, called *maddah*. The pronunciation is not changed. Similarly, if alif-hamzah-fatḥah is followed by a hamzah with sukūn above it (i.e. أَاْ), alif-maddah is written and the pronunciation is as in the previous case.

EXERCISE

Recite aloud:

ءَامَنَ ءَانَسَ ءَاكَلَ ءَاذَنَ قُرءَانُ ءَالَامُ رَءَاهُ ءَاخَرُ مِرءَاةُ ءَابَارُ ءَالءَانَ

III. In a few words ا— is expressed by a short vertical stroke (in reality a miniature alif), known as "dagger" alif, written above the consonant instead of the fatḥah. The pronunciation is not changed.

EXERCISE

Recite aloud:

هٰذَا ذٰلِكَ لٰكِنْ لٰكِنَّ رَحْمٰنُ هٰؤُلَاءِ سَمٰوَاتُ إِبرٰهِيمُ

15

IV. At the end of some words ‍ا‍— is expressed by ‍ی‍—. This alif, in the form of yā' (without dots), is called *alif maqṣūrah*. Whenever, for inflectional reasons, an alif maqṣūrah ceases to be final, it returns to the regular form. Thus رَمَى, but رَمَاهُ .

EXERCISE

Recite aloud:

فَتَى إِلَى عَلَى جَرَى أَلْقَى تَلَقَّى وُسْطَى كُبْرَى ذِكْرَى غَضْبَى

أَقْصَى أَدْنَى لَدَى أُخْرَى أَعْلَى عُظْمَى صُغْرَى

CHAPTER VI

THE DEFINITE ARTICLE. SUN LETTERS.
WAṢLAH. NŪNATION. ACCENT.
MISCELLANEOUS

I. The definite article for all genders and numbers is اَلْ.... It is prefixed to every noun that it limits. It does not affect the accentuation of the noun.

EXERCISE

Recite aloud:

الْفَقْر الْغَد الْعَيْن الْخَمْر الْحِبْر الْجَبَل الْبَيْت بَيْت الْأَب أَب

الْفِيل الْجَار الْقَوْل الْمُؤْمِن الْيَسَر الْوَلَد الْهَمّ الْمَطَر الْكُفْر الْقَمَر

الْقَلْعَة الْمُدَّة الْهَمْزَة الْخَبْز الْقَصْر الْعَدَد الْفَرَس الْكُتُب الْبُوق

الْقَرْيَة الْعِزَّة الْغَفْلَة

II. The consonants are, on phonetic grounds, divided into "Sun letters" and "Moon letters."[1] The Sun letters are the dentals: ت ث د ذ ر ز س ش ص ض ط ظ ل and ن. The Moon letters are all the others.

When the definite article limits a word beginning with a Sun letter, the lām of the article, being itself a dental, is assimilated by the Sun letter, which is "doubled" in pronunciation. However, the lām is retained in writing without either vowel or sukūn. In addition shaddah is written over the initial Sun letter to show the assimilation. Thus الرَّجُل is pronounced *ar-rajulu.*

EXERCISE

Recite aloud:

الصَّدْر الشَّمْس الزَّمَن الرَّبّ الذَّنْب الدَّم الثَّمَن ثَمَن التَّمْر تَمْر

---

[1] This terminology is based on the fact that the Arabic word for *sun* begins with a Sun letter and the Arabic word for *moon* begins with a Moon letter.

الضَّرْبُ الطَّعْمُ الظُّهْرُ الظِّهْرُ اللَّيْلُ النَّوْمُ النِّيرُ النَّارُ النُّورُ النُّورُ التَّاجُ الطُّورُ
الدَّيْنُ الصَّوْمُ اللَّيْلَةُ السَّنَةُ النَّاقَةُ الرَّوْضَةُ

III. In some cases initial hamzah is not an essential part of the word. In these cases, when the initial hamzah is preceded by another word, the hamzah and its vowel are dropped, the sign ‿, called *waṣlah*, is written in their place over the alif, and one elides from the last vowel of the preceding word directly to the letter following the waṣlah. If the preceding word does not end in a vowel, then one is given it in order to make elision possible. A hamzah which can change in this way is called *hamzat al-waṣl*.

The hamzah of the definite article is hamzat al-waṣl and is, therefore, elided. Thus عَبْدُ ٱلْمَلِك not عَبْدُ أَلْمَلِك.

If the first letter of the word which the definite article limits is a Sun letter, then one elides from the last vowel of the preceding word to the Sun letter. Thus عَبْدُ ٱلرَّحْمٰن not عَبْدُ أَلرَّحْمٰن.

EXERCISE

Recite aloud:

إِسْمِي عُمَرُ. عَرَفَ ٱلرَّجُلُ ٱسْمِي. ٱلْبَيْتُ لِأَبِي. دَخَلْتُ ٱلْبَيْتَ.
أُدْرُسْ دَرْسَكَ. أُكْتُبْ دَرْسَكَ وَٱدْرُسْهُ. جَاءَ ٱلْأُسْتَاذُ وَقَرَأَ ٱلْأَسْمَاءَ وَبَدَأَ
ٱلدَّرْسَ.

IV. At the end of indefinite nouns and adjectives the three vowel signs are in most cases written double, thus ً or ٌ, ٍ, and ٍ. When this occurs, an *n* sound is added to that of the vowel and they are, therefore, pronounced *un*, *an*, and *in*, respectively. This ending is called *tanwīn* or *nūnation*. In addition, fatḥah tanwīn requires an alif (not pronounced) after it unless the word ends in tā' marbūṭah (ة) or hamzah (ء).[2]

A word may not simultaneously have both tanwīn and the definite article.

---

[2] An alif is required after hamzah if the letter preceding the hamzah is one which can be joined to a following letter, e.g. شَيْئًا. Note that in this case the hamzah is written over the connecting line.

EXERCISE

Recite aloud:

أَبُ ٱلْأَبِ . بَيْتُ ٱلْبَيْتِ . ضَرَبَ ٱلرَّجُلَ . ضَرَبَ رَجُلاً . ضَرَبَ ٱلْخَادِمَةَ .

ضَرَبَ خَادِمَةً . ذَهَبَ إِلَى ٱلْبَيْتِ . ذَهَبَ إِلَى بَيْتٍ . شَمْسُ شَمْسًا شَمْسٍ .

لَيْلَةً لَيْلَةَ لَيْلَةٍ . رَوْضَةٌ رَوْضَةً رَوْضَةٍ . مَلِكُ مَلِكًا مَلِكٍ . جُزْءٌ جُزْءًا جُزْءٍ .

V. In words of four or more syllables the accent goes back to the first closed syllable, but never further than the third from the end. If there is no closed syllable, the accent is on the third from the end.

EXERCISE

Recite aloud:

خَيَّاطُونَ أَخْبَرْنَاكُمْ مَشُورَةٌ مُكَاتَبَةٌ مَدْرَسَةٌ كَتَبْتُهُمَا مِصْرِيَّةٌ مُؤَرِّخٌ

خَشَبَةٌ إِنْفَعَلَ يَسْتَفْعِلُ كَاتِبَتَانِ دَقِيقَةٌ مَمْلُوكَةٌ فَاطِمَةُ قَبِيلَةٌ

VI. Sentence accentuation is best learned in connection with a native speaker.

There are no capital letters in Arabic, and proper names can, therefore, only be distinguished by the context.

Punctuation is a recent innovation and is for the most part rather chaotic in its use. In this book it is used sparingly. In general, marks of punctuation are a reversal of their form in English, i.e. a comma is written ، , a question mark ؟ .

CHAPTER VII

THE ARABIC LANGUAGE IN GENERAL

The beginning student of Arabic who has had no previous acquaintance with Semitic languages, will be impressed by the difference between the structure of Arabic and that of English or other Indo-European languages which he may know.[1] The most characteristic feature of the Arabic language is that the great majority of its words are built up from (or can be analyzed down into) roots each of which consists of three consonants or radicals. By using these radicals as a base and by varying the three vowels and adding prefixes, infixes, and suffixes, according to certain patterns, the actual words are produced. The triconsonantal root is loosely equated with the third person masculine singular perfect of the verb which is the citation form. Thus the root *qtl*, which contains the idea of killing, is referred to as *qatala* although *qatala* actually means 'he killed.'

In general it may also be observed that Arabic like Latin is a synthetic, or inflectional, language rather than a language like English which is predominantly analytic. In simple terms this means that the syntactical relationship of nouns is indicated by case endings and that verbs are inflected by means of prefixes, infixes, and suffixes to indicate the various persons, numbers, genders, derived forms, moods, and tenses, in contrast to English where, for example, a separate word (noun or pronoun) is required to indicate the person.

Orthodox Arabic grammarians recognize only three parts of speech: verbs, nouns, and particles. The concept of a verb is the same in Arabic as in English; but adjectives, adverbs, and pronouns (in addition to nouns proper) are classified as nouns; particles include conjunctions, prepositions, and interjections. Although this system has a certain convenience once one has mastered Arabic, it tends to be confusing to a beginner and accordingly this book uses traditional English terminology for parts of speech. In general the transfer of grammatical terminology from one language (not to say language family) to another is likely to be misleading. The student must, therefore, be on his guard to catch the subtle changes of meaning which occur when an old term is applied to a new situation.

[1] The student is not necessarily expected to master this chapter on first reading. It is intended to serve as a basis for interpreting the details which will confront him as he proceeds in his study. It is hoped that by referring back to it he will obtain a fuller insight into the language.

In other problems of terminology a middle course is steered. Arabic terms are used only when no English term seems to cover the situation.

Verbs. In addition to the simple verb each root has the potentiality of expanding, by the systematic addition of one or more affixes, into any one of nine[2] "derived forms." Each of these derived forms bears a specific semantic relationship to the simple verb. Thus *qatala* means 'kill,' but *qattala* (with "doubling" of the middle radical) means 'slaughter,' for when the middle radical is doubled, the meaning of the root is intensified. Similarly *taqātala* (with prefixed *ta-* and a lengthening of the vowel of the first radical, *q*) means 'fight one another,' for when those changes are made in the simple verb, the action signified by the verb acquires a reciprocal meaning.

There are two additional facts to be noted about the derived verb forms. First, it is seldom in actual practice that all the derived forms of a given root are used. Second, in not a few cases the meanings of the derived forms have deviated considerably from what one might expect if he knew only the meaning of the root and the semantic increment which the particular derived form requires. English equivalents may obscure relationships even more. In these cases it is almost impossible to predict the meaning of the particular derived form. That is to say, the student must in many cases treat the root form and the verb forms derived from it as separate units of vocabulary.

Finally, we may note that Arabic verbs have only two "tenses,"[3] perfect and imperfect.[4] In reality these are not tenses, for the distinction between them is not basically that of time. Rather, they indicate whether action is complete or not. The perfect denotes completed action, and the imperfect denotes incomplete action—irrespective of time. It is usually the case that the Arabic perfect is equivalent to the English past and that the Arabic imperfect is equivalent to the English present or future, but exact equivalents must be determined by the context.

Nouns. In Arabic, nouns—like verbs—are distinguished by the wealth of derivatives from the root. For example, from the root *kataba*, 'write,' are formed, among others, the following nouns: *kātib* 'writer,' *maktūb* 'something written,' *kitābah* 'writing,' *kitāb* 'book,' *maktab* 'office' (place where one writes), *maktabah* 'library,' *mukātabah* 'correspondence.' This phenomenon, though much less widespread, is not unfamiliar in English, for we are accustomed to analogous affixation as for example: *writing, writer, writable, write-off, write-up, unwritten, re-write.*

---

[2] Considering the root form as number one, the derived forms are numbered two through ten. There are actually thirteen derived forms, but only nine are in common use.   [3] More precisely, aspects.

[4] More precisely, perfective and imperfective.

In Arabic the process of deriving nouns is relatively systematic. For instance, from both the root and each of the derived verb forms both an active and a passive participle[5] may be derived according to regular patterns. From the root *qatala*, for example, *qātil* 'killer' is the active participle and *maqtūl* 'killed one' is the passive participle. It will be noted that these two words correspond in form to *kātib* and *maktūb* cited from the root *kataba* above. According to other patterns, participles may be formed from each of the derived verb forms. Gerunds, or *maṣdars* (the term used in this book), may also be derived according to regular patterns from each verb form; in fact, from the root form there are potentially some forty maṣdar patterns.

Another aspect of the Arabic noun is less familiar, namely plural formation. In English most plurals are formed by the addition of the suffix *s*, although others are "irregular," such as *ox, oxen; mouse, mice; foot, feet; man, men; opus, opera*. In Arabic the situation is approximately reversed. There are "regular" plural suffixes (forming the so-called "sound" plurals), but the vast majority of Arabic plurals (the so-called "broken" plurals) are more analogous to the English "irregulars" in that they are formed by certain combinations of prefixes, infixes, suffixes, and vowel changes. A few common examples will illustrate the point: *walad, awlād* 'boy(s)'; *qalb, qulūb* 'heart(s)'; *kalb, kilāb* 'dog(s)'; *kitāb, kutub* 'book(s)'; *nahr, anhur* 'river(s).'

Pronouns. Pronouns should occasion no special problem. They are for the most part analogous to English pronouns and have approximately the same amount of inflection.

Adjectives. In Arabic the adjective is only a noun used to describe and is not considered a separate part of speech. In this book, however, words which are used adjectivally are called "adjectives." Not every noun pattern lends itself to this dual noun-adjective usage, but many do. Some of these patterns are in fact used primarily for adjectives, but even in these cases there are instances where the words are nouns. One of the commonest of these primarily-adjectival patterns is illustrated by the following: *jamīl* 'pretty,' *karīm* 'generous,' 'noble,' *marīḍ* 'sick,' and *kabīr* 'big,' 'old.' However, on the same pattern we find, for instance, the nouns *ṭarīq* 'road,' *sabīl* 'way,' 'path.'

Adverbs. In English the majority of adverbs are formed by adding the

[5] Good English terms for these patterns are lacking. The Latin terms *nomen agentis* (noun of the agent, or doer of the action) and *nomen patientis* (receiver of the action) fit the situation exactly, but seem inappropriate in a book of this type. The Arabic terms are also cumbersome. We, therefore, use "active participle" and "passive participle," but the student must understand that the transfer of meaning is very inexact.

suffix -*ly* to adjectives or participles (e.g. *seriously, knowingly*). In Arabic the roughly analogous process is to put nouns or adjectives in the accusative case. In addition there are a number of instances where in English an adverbial idea is usually expressed by a prepositional phrase, but where in Arabic a single word in the accusative is sufficient. Some particles also are adverbial in Arabic.

Particles. The particle should occasion little trouble. In addition to conjunctions, prepositions, and interjections there are particles which indicate that a sentence is interrogative or negative and others which have an adverbial force. None of them is inflected.

Faʿala. In order to describe the different noun or verb patterns the Arabs do not call them by generic terms signifying their function but instead refer to them by using the root *f'l* (فَعَلَ) as a model. Thus the active participle, *qātil* (قَاتِل), is said to be of the *fāʿil* (فَاعِل) pattern, the passive participle, *maqtūl* (مَقْتُول), is said to be of the *mafʿūl* (مَفْعُول) pattern, and the adjective, *karīm* (كَرِيم), is said to be of the *faʿīl* (فَعِيل) pattern. The present work uses this system in many instances but not when referring to the derived verb forms which are designated by number.

Sentence structure. Arabic syntax is not difficult, but it is sometimes quite different from English. There are two basic types of sentences: verbal and nominal. The verbal sentence, the dominant type, is one that is introduced by a verb. Thus, for example, in a verbal sentence, one says, *Reads Ahmad the book*, not *Ahmad reads the book*. This type of sentence is similar to the English sentence (or clause) in requiring a subject and a verb (with or without object or predicate adjective). The only important difference is that the verb always comes *before* its subject.

A nominal sentence is one that is introduced by a noun (or pronoun). In most cases the nominal sentence results from the facts that the present tense of the verb *to be* is not used and that Arabic has no verb corresponding to *to have*. Thus the sentence *The man is tall* would be expressed as *The man tall*. Nominal sentences have no verb by definition but only a subject and a predicate. However, it frequently happens that the predicate itself contains a verb. Thus, for instance, the sentence *The man came his father* would be a normal way of saying *The man's father came*. In this case the word *man* is the subject of the nominal sentence, and the whole clause, *came his father*, is the predicate. The clause itself is verbal (because it begins with a verb) and *father* is the subject of the verb. One may also say *The man came* where *man* is the subject and the clause *came* is the predicate. The clause is verbal with a verb and an understood subject referring back to *man*. In such nominal sentences the subject is used first for emphasis. There are three common varieties of predicate for nominal sentences:

1. The predicate may be a noun or adjective, e.g. *Muḥammad the prophet of God* (meaning *Muḥammad is the prophet of God*); *The man tall* (see analysis above).
2. The predicate may be a prepositional phrase, e.g. *Peace on you* (meaning *Peace be on you*); *To Aḥmad a book* (meaning *Aḥmad has a book*).[6]
3. The predicate may be a clause which may be:
   (*a*) Verbal, e.g. *The man came his father* or *The man came* (see analysis above).
   (*b*) Nominal, e.g. *The man his son intelligent* (meaning *The man's son is intelligent*). Here, the nominal clause, *his son intelligent*, is the predicate and contains within itself a subject *son* and a predicate *intelligent*.[7]

---

[6] In most cases when the predicate of a nominal sentence is a prepositional phrase, the subject and predicate are inverted. Note that in this sentence the "missing" verb is *to have*.

[7] Diagrams of all these illustrative sentences follow:

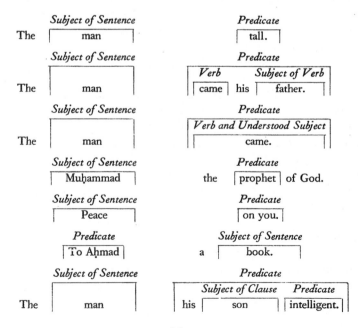

Vocabulary. Arabic grammar may at the beginning seem the most difficult problem in learning the language, but the authors believe that the student should be able to master the essentials of grammar during the first year and that ultimately it is vocabulary which causes the most difficulty. The student is advised, therefore, to pursue his study of vocabulary with industry.

Arabic has a wealth of literature, both medieval and modern. It is a living language for 80 million people and the "Latin" of 370 million Muslims. The potential proliferation of words from a single root makes it relatively adaptable to modern needs, even though it has only recently felt those needs, and is its most interesting structural feature. A student who learns it well will feel with new insight the force of the proverb كل لسان انسان and may in fact wish to interpret it as كل لسان انسانان.

NOMINAL SENTENCES: SUBJECT AND PREDICATE

I. ILLUSTRATIVE TEXT

1. The boy is young (small).	١. اَلْوَلَدُ صَغِيرٌ.
2. The man is learned (*literally*, a knower).	٢. اَلرَّجُلُ عَالِمٌ.
3. The king is generous.	٣. اَلْمَلِكُ كَرِيمٌ.
4. The prince is killed.	٤. اَلْأَمِيرُ مَقْتُولٌ.

II. GRAMMATICAL ANALYSIS

1. This is a nominal sentence because it begins with a noun. وَلَد is the subject, and صَغِير is the predicate. They are both in the nominative case. All nouns are in the nominative case unless there is a reason for them to be in another case.

اَلْوَلَدُ is composed of two words: the definite article ...أَلْ and the masculine noun وَلَد. The sign of the nominative is the final ḍammah. It is not nūnated because it is made definite by the article ...أَلْ. The word وَلَد is non-derived.

The predicate صَغِير is one word in the nominative case. The sign of the nominative is the final ḍammah. صَغِير is indefinite, a fact which is shown by the nūnation. In elliptical nominal sentences of this type the predicate must agree with the subject in gender and number. صَغِير is derived from the verb صَغُر 'to become small' on the adjectival pattern of فَعِيل.

In a nominal declarative sentence the verb *to be* is not required when the tense implied is the present tense.

2. This sentence is similar to sentence 1. The only essential difference is that the predicate عَالِمٌ is formed on the active participle pattern of فَاعِلٌ and derived from the verb عَلِمَ 'to know.' The active participle signifies the doer of the action.

3. This sentence is similar to sentence 1.

4. In this sentence, which is syntactically the same as sentence 1, the subject أَمِيرٌ is formed from the verb أَمَرَ 'to command' on the adjectival pattern of فَعِيلٌ. However, in this case the adjectival pattern is used as a noun.

The predicate مَقْتُولٌ is derived from the verb قَتَلَ 'to kill' on the passive participle pattern مَفْعُولٌ. The passive participle signifies the receiver of the action.

III. PRACTICE TEXT

1. The writer is learned.   ١. أَلْكَاتِبُ عَالِمٌ.

2. The man is old (*literally*, big).[1]   ٢. أَلرَّجُلُ كَبِيرٌ.

3. The boy is poor.   ٣. أَلْوَلَدُ فَقِيرٌ.

4. The dog is faithful.   ٤. أَلْكَلْبُ أَمِينٌ.

5. The prince is tall (long).   ٥. أَلْأَمِيرُ طَوِيلٌ.

6. The man is disliked.   ٦. أَلرَّجُلُ مَكْرُوهٌ.

IV. EXERCISES

Translate into English:

١. أَلْمَلِكُ صَغِيرٌ.

٢. أَلرَّجُلُ كَرِيمٌ.

٣. أَلْوَلَدُ مَقْتُولٌ.

---

[1] The word كَبِير means *old* only when referring to animate objects; otherwise, *big*. The word used for *old* in other cases is قَدِيم (see Chapter IX, section III, 5).

٤. اَلْأَمِيرُ عَالِمٌ.

٥. اَلْمَلِكُ مَقْتُولٌ.

٦. اَلرَّجُلُ صَغِيرٌ.

٧. اَلْوَلَدُ كَرِيمٌ.

٨. اَلْأَمِيرُ صَغِيرٌ.

٩. اَلْعَالِمُ كَرِيمٌ.

١٠. اَلرَّجُلُ مَقْتُولٌ.

Translate into Arabic:

1. The prince is generous.
2. The king is faithful.
3. The man is tall.
4. The dog is old.
5. The writer is poor.
6. The learned (man) is faithful.
7. The prince is a boy.
8. The man is a king.
9. The dog is killed.
10. The boy is disliked.

CHAPTER IX

GENDER

I. ILLUSTRATIVE TEXT

1. The prince is generous.	١. اَلْأَمِيرُ كَرِيمٌ.
2. The princess is generous.	٢. اَلْأَمِيرَةُ كَرِيمَةٌ.
3. Fāḍil is happy.	٣. فَاضِلٌ سَعِيدٌ.
4. Hind is happy.	٤. هِنْدٌ سَعِيدَةٌ.
5. The mother is beautiful.	٥. اَلْأُمُّ جَمِيلَةٌ.

II. GRAMMATICAL ANALYSIS

1. This nominal sentence, whose subject is masculine, is similar to those in the preceding lesson.

2. This is a nominal sentence because it begins with a noun. أَمِيرَةٌ is the subject, and كَرِيمَةٌ is the predicate. They are both in the nominative case.

اَلْأَمِيرَةُ is composed of two words: the definite article اَلْ... and the feminine noun أَمِيرَةٌ. The sign of the nominative is the final ḍammah. It is not nūnated because it is definite. أَمِيرَةٌ is the feminine of أَمِيرٌ which in turn is derived from the verb أَمَرَ on the adjectival pattern of فَعِيلٌ. The suffix ة... is the most common feminine ending.

The predicate كَرِيمَةٌ is one word in the nominative case. The sign of the nominative is the final ḍammah. It is nūnated because it is indefinite. كَرِيمَةٌ is the feminine of كَرِيمٌ, which is derived from the verb كَرُمَ on the adjectival pattern of فَعِيلٌ. The word كَرِيمَةٌ is feminine because the predicate must agree in gender with the subject.

29

Most feminines derived from the masculine are formed by substituting a fatḥah for the last vowel of the masculine, and by adding a ة. There are some noun patterns, however, which are feminine because they end with ة, but which have no equivalent masculines.

All Arabic nouns are either masculine or feminine. There is no neuter gender.

3. This sentence is like sentence 1 except that the subject فَاضِل is a proper name. Although a proper name, فَاضِل is a regularly derived noun from the verb فَضَل 'to become gracious' on the active participle pattern of فَاعِل. Nūnation does not make a proper name indefinite.

The predicate سَعِيد is masculine because the subject is masculine.

4. This sentence is like sentence 2 except that the subject هِنْد is a feminine proper name (although it does not have a feminine ending). Nouns referring to females which do not have a feminine ending are, nevertheless, feminine in gender.

The predicate سَعِيدَة is feminine because the subject is feminine.

5. This sentence is like sentence 4 except that the subject أُم is a common noun denoting a female.

III. PRACTICE TEXT

1. The room is large.	١. أَلْغُرْفَة كَبِيرَةٌ.
2. [The][1] Life is enjoyable.	٢. أَلْحَيَاةُ لَذِيذَةٌ.
3. The girl is beautiful.	٣. أَلْبِنْتُ جَمِيلَةٌ.
4. [The][1] Life is short.	٤. أَلْعُمْرُ قَصِيرٌ.
5. The city is old.	٥. أَلْمَدِينَةُ قَدِيمَةٌ.
6. The house is small.	٦. أَلْبَيْتُ صَغِيرٌ.

[1] Arabic, in contrast to English, uses the definite article with a noun expressing the abstract or the generic

IV. EXERCISES

Translate into English:

١. هِنْدٌ كَبِيرَةٌ .

٢. أَلْأُمُّ كَرِيمَةٌ .

٣. أَلْغُرْفَةُ صَغِيرَةٌ .

٤. أَلْكَاتِبُ عَالِمٌ .

٥. أَلْكَاتِبَةُ عَالِمَةٌ .

٦. أَلْكَلْبَةُ أَمِينَةٌ .

٧. أَلْأَمِيرَةُ مَكْرُوهَةٌ .

٨. أَلْبِنْتُ طَوِيلَةٌ .

٩. أَلْمَلَكَةُ سَعِيدَةٌ .

١٠. أَلْوَلَدُ طَوِيلٌ .

Translate into Arabic:

1. Hind is young.
2. The man is generous.
3. The girl is faithful.
4. The city is beautiful.
5. The prince is happy.
6. The room is beautiful.
7. The queen is generous.
8. The king is old.
9. The mother is poor.
10. The dog (f.) is killed.

CHAPTER X

THE CONSTRUCT PHRASE

I. ILLUSTRATIVE TEXT

1. The door of the house is large. ١. بَابُ ٱلدَّارِ كَبِيرٌ.

2. The palace of the king is grand. ٢. قَصْرُ ٱلْمَلِكِ عَظِيمٌ.

3. The rider of the mare is a cavalier. ٣. رَاكِبُ ٱلْفَرَسِ فَارِسٌ.

4. The generous of [the] spirit is happy. ٤. كَرِيمُ ٱلنَّفْسِ سَعِيدٌ.

5. The man is a rider of a mare. ٥. أَلرَّجُلُ رَاكِبُ فَرَسٍ.

II. GRAMMATICAL ANALYSIS

1. This is a nominal sentence because it begins with a noun. بَابُ the subject, is in the nominative case. It is not nūnated because it is rendered definite by the word دَار which limits it.

ٱلدَّار is composed of two words: the definite article ...ٱلْ and دَار. The word دَار is in the genitive case because it limits بَابُ. The sign of the genitive is the final kasrah.

When one noun immediately follows another in such a manner that the second limits or defines the first and renders it definite (though without the definite article), this combination is called a construct phrase. Characteristically, the second word of the construct phrase limits the first by signifying the possessor of the first (as is best shown in I, 2). However, possession is not the only type of relationship between members of a construct phrase as is shown in I, 3 (which shows an actor-object relationship) and in I, 4 (in which logically the first member adjectivally modifies the second). The final vowel of the second member of the construct is a kasrah, and the noun is said to be in the genitive case. The second member may be definite or indefinite.

Sentences 2, 3, and 4 are syntactically similar to sentence 1.

In sentence ٥ the predicate رَاكِبُ is the first member of a construct phrase. The second member فَرَسٍ is indefinite.[1]

III. PRACTICE TEXT

1. 'Abdullāh (*literally*, the servant of God) is a king.

١. عَبْدُ ٱللهِ مَلِكٌ .

2. The knowledge of 'Abdullāh is extensive.

٢. عِلْمُ عَبْدِ ٱللهِ وَاسِعٌ .

3. The student's book is new.

٣. كِتَابُ ٱلطَّالِبِ جَدِيدٌ .

4. The admiral (*literally*, the commander of the sea) is strong.

٤. أَمِيرُ ٱلْبَحْرِ شَدِيدٌ .

5. The color of the book of the student is beautiful.

٥. لَوْنُ كِتَابِ ٱلطَّالِبِ جَمِيلٌ .

IV. EXERCISES

Translate into English:

١. أُمُّ عَبْدِ ٱللهِ كَرِيمَةُ ٱلنَّفْسِ .

٢. غُرْفَةُ ٱلْأَمِيرِ وَاسِعَةٌ .

٣. حَيَاةُ ٱلرَّجُلِ قَصِيرَةٌ .

٤. أُمُّ هِنْدٍ جَمِيلَةٌ .

٥. قَصْرُ ٱلْأَمِيرَةِ صَغِيرٌ .

---

[1] Strictly speaking, when the second member of a construct phrase is indefinite, it renders the first member not definite but "specialized," in the same sense that an adjective "specializes" or limits a noun. This "specialized" first member, however, although indefinite in meaning, behaves like a definite noun in accepting neither nūnation nor the definite article.

Translate into Arabic:

1. The door of the palace of the king is large.

2. The boy's dog is small.

3. The prince of the city is great.

4. The king's daughter (girl) is beautiful.

5. Fāḍil's mare is killed.

CHAPTER XI

ADJECTIVES. COLLECTIVES

I. ILLUSTRATIVE TEXT

1. The small boy is faithful.	١. أَلْوَلَدُ ٱلصَّغِيرُ أَمِينٌ .
2. The generous girl is happy.	٢. أَلْبِنْتُ ٱلْكَرِيمَةُ سَعِيدَةٌ .
3. The new book of the student is long.	٣. كِتَابُ ٱلطَّالِبِ ٱلْجَدِيدُ طَوِيلٌ .
4. The learned man is liked.	٤. أَلرَّجُلُ ٱلْعَالِمُ مَحْبُوبٌ .
5. The king is a small boy.	٥. أَلْمَلِكُ وَلَدٌ صَغِيرٌ .
6. 'Abd al-'Azīz is a Nejdi king.	٦. عَبْدُ ٱلْعَزِيزِ مَلِكٌ نَجْدِيٌّ .
7. The lazy student is disliked.	٧. أَلطَّالِبُ ٱلْكَسْلَانُ مَكْرُوهٌ .
8. The good mare is fast.	٨. أَلْفَرَسُ ٱلْحَسَنَةُ سَرِيعَةٌ .
9. A generous people is beloved.	٩. أَلشَّعْبُ ٱلْكَرِيمُ مَحْبُوبٌ .
10. The Arabs are a generous people.	١٠. أَلْعَرَبُ شَعْبٌ كَرِيمٌ .
11. The Arab is a faithful man.	١١. أَلْعَرَبِيُّ رَجُلٌ أَمِينٌ .
12. Trees are beautiful.	١٢. أَلشَّجَرُ جَمِيلٌ .
13. The tree is tall.	١٣. أَلشَّجَرَةُ طَوِيلَةٌ .

II. GRAMMATICAL ANALYSIS

1. The subject of this nominal sentence is modified by the adjective صَغِيرٌ which agrees with it in case, gender, number, and definiteness.

2. This sentence is similar to sentence 1 except that the subject أَلْبِنْتُ is feminine, and, therefore, the adjective كَرِيمَة as well as the predicate سَعِيدَةٌ is feminine.

35

3. The subject كِتَاب of this sentence is the first member of a construct of which أَلطَّالِب is the second. The adjective جَدِيد modifies the subject and therefore agrees with it in case, gender, number, and definiteness. It may be noted that the subject is definite because of its position as first member of a construct phrase.

4. In this sentence the active participle عَالِم is used adjectivally.

5. In this sentence the adjective صَغِير modifies the predicate وَلَد.

6. In this sentence عَبْد is the subject and مَلِك is the predicate, which is modified by the word نَجْدِيّ. This word is formed by removing the final vowel of the word نَجْد and by suffixing ـِيّ. A word formed in this way is an adjective, and the ـِيّ is called the yā' of nisbah 'pertaining to.' If the original noun has the feminine ending ـَة, this ending is dropped in the formation of the nisbah.

7. The adjective كَسْلَان in this sentence is derived from the verb كَسِلَ on the adjectival pattern of فَعْلَان.

8. The adjective حَسَنَة is derived from the verb حَسُنَ on the adjectival pattern فَعَل. This adjective is feminine because the word it modifies is feminine.

9. In this sentence أَلشَّعْب, the subject, is a collective noun of the فَعْل pattern. When collectives of this pattern signify human beings, they can be treated grammatically either as masculine singular (as here) or as masculine plural.

10. In this sentence أَلعَرَب is another collective. Various proper nouns referring to peoples, tribes, religious or social groupings are collectives without being of any special pattern. The modern tendency is to treat these nouns as masculine plural (as here), although, when the collectivity is thought of, they can be considered as feminine singular.

11. The word أَلعَرَبِيّ is a nisbah adjective used as a noun formed from the collective عَرَب. The nisbah masculine and feminine forms of collectives mentioned in item 10 above denote the singular masculine and singular feminine, respectively.

12. The word أَلشَّجَر is a collective noun which designates the species known as trees. There are a number of such collectives designating

animals, insects, vegetables, minerals and the like (spontaneous natural groupings). The plurality idea is lacking in these nouns; what they represent are the species in abstraction. Grammatically they are treated as masculine singular; hence the predicate adjective جَمِيلٌ in this item is masculine singular.

13. The word ٱلشَّجَرَةُ indicates a single tree. The singular of most collectives of the type described in II, 12, above is formed by suffixing ـَة... to the collective. It is the only singular possible and is feminine in gender.

NOTE A: Collectives of the type mentioned in II, 12, above frequently take one or more plural forms when the plurality, and *not* the species, is intended.

NOTE B: The adjectival patterns used so far in this lesson are فَعِيلٌ فَاعِلٌ فَعْلَانٌ فَعَلٌ and the nisbah.

Other patterns used adjectivally are:

فَعُولٌ	which denotes intensity
أَفْعَلُ	for colors and defects
مَفْعُولٌ	
فَعِلٌ	
فَعُلٌ	
فَعْلَانٌ	
فَعَّالٌ	(see Chapter XXI)

III. PRACTICE TEXT

1. The playful student is lazy.

١. أَلطَّالِبُ ٱللَّعُوبُ كَسْلَانٌ .

2. The loved man is happy.

٢. أَلرَّجُلُ ٱلْمَحْبُوبُ سَعِيدٌ .

3. The difficult lesson is disliked.

٣. أَلدَّرْسُ ٱلصَّعْبُ مَكْرُوهٌ .

4. The Black Sea is wide (extensive).

٤. أَلْبَحْرُ ٱلْأَسْوَدُ وَاسِعٌ .

37

5. The green color is beautiful. ٥. اَللَّوْنُ ٱلْأَخْضَرُ جَمِيلٌ .

6. [The] Egyptian rice is delicious. ٦. أَلْأَرُزُّ ٱلْمِصْرِيُّ لَذِيذٌ .

7. The Arab people are generous. ٧. أَلشَّعْبُ ٱلْعَرَبِيُّ كَرِيمٌ .

8. The small tree is beautiful. ٨. أَلشَّجَرَةُ ٱلصَّغِيرَةُ جَمِيلَةٌ .

IV. EXERCISES

Translate into English:

١. أَلرَّجُلُ ٱلْمَقْتُولُ نَجْدِيٌّ .

٢. أَلْحَيَاةُ ٱلطَّوِيلَةُ لَذِيذَةٌ .

٣. أَلْمَدِينَةُ ٱلْعَظِيمَةُ قَدِيمَةٌ .

٤. أَلْبِنْتُ ٱلْمِصْرِيَّةُ جَمِيلَةٌ .

٥. بَابُ ٱلْقَصْرِ ٱلْأَخْضَرِ كَبِيرٌ .

٦. أَلشَّجَرُ ٱلْكَبِيرُ جَمِيلٌ .

Translate into Arabic:

1. The generous of spirit is happy.
2. The playful cavalier is an Egyptian.
3. The learned writer is great.
4. The faithful mother is beloved.
5. The room of the new house is small.
6. Tall trees are beloved.

CHAPTER XII

PRONOUNS

I. ILLUSTRATIVE TEXT

1. 'Abd al-'Azīz is the king of Nejd.	١. عَبْدُ ٱلْعَزِيزِ مَلِكُ نَجْدٍ .
2. He is an able man.	٢. هُوَ رَجُلٌ قَدِيرٌ .
3. And his importance is great.	٣. وَشَأْنُهُ عَظِيمٌ .
4. His capital is Riyadh.	٤. عَاصِمَتُهُ ٱلرِّيَاضُ .
5. And it is a Nejdi city.	٥. وَهِيَ مَدِينَةٌ نَجْدِيَّةٌ .
6. Its atmosphere is dry.	٦. جَوُّهَا جَافٌّ .
7. Its amīr is the son of the king.	٧. أَمِيرُهَا ٱبْنُ ٱلْمَلِكِ .
8. This amīr is a just ruler.	٨. هٰذَا ٱلْأَمِيرُ حَاكِمٌ عَادِلٌ .

II. GRAMMATICAL ANALYSIS

2. This is a nominal sentence because it begins with the separable personal pronoun هُوَ 'he,' 'it.' هُوَ is the subject, in the nominative case, but invariable, i.e. its final vowel does not change with the change of case.

3. This sentence is joined to the previous sentence by the inseparable co-ordinate conjunction ...وَ. The subject شَأْنُ is in construct with the pronominal suffix ...هُ 'his,' 'its' which is in the genitive, but invariable.

NOTE: Personal pronouns in Arabic are of two types: those which are separate words and those which are suffixes. The separate pronouns are used when the pronoun is in the nominative case. The pronominal

39

suffixes are used when the pronoun is in the genitive or accusative case (see Chapter XV, section II, note).

4. عَاصِمَتُهُ consists of two words: the noun عَاصِمَةٌ and the pronominal suffix هُ.... It is to be noticed that the tā' marbūṭah is written as an ordinary medial tā'. Whenever a word ending in ـة... has a suffix, this change takes place.

5. This nominal sentence begins with the separable pronoun هِيَ 'she,' 'it.'

6. The subject of this sentence, جَوُّ, is in construct with the pronominal suffix هَا 'her,' 'its,' 'it,' which is in the genitive but invariable. The predicate جَافٌّ is derived from the doubled verb جَفَّ (< * جَفَفَ) on the active participle pattern of فَاعِلٌ. It will be noted that in the case of doubled verbs, those whose second and third radicals are assimilated (i.e. written together with *shaddah*), this assimilation persists in the active participle pattern.

7. اِبْنٌ is one of eight nouns which begin with hamzat al-waṣl. Among the others are اِبْنَةٌ 'daughter', 'girl', اِمْرَأَةٌ 'woman,' and اِسْمٌ 'name.'

8. In this sentence أَمِيرٌ is the subject. It is preceded by هٰذَا 'this,' a demonstrative which modifies it, but does not affect it grammatically.

NOTE A: If a demonstrative modifies a succeeding word, the latter must carry the definite article. If it modifies the first member of a construct, it is placed after that construct. When used pronominally, demonstratives behave like separable pronouns.

NOTE B:

SEPARABLE PERSONAL PRONOUNS

		Singular		Dual		Plural	
3 M[1]	he, it	هُوَ	they			they	هُمْ
3 F	she, it	هِيَ	„	هُمَا		they	هُنَّ
2 M	you, thou	أَنْتَ	you		أَنْتُمَا	you	أَنْتُمْ
2 F	you, thou	أَنْتِ	„			you	أَنْتُنَّ
1 MF	I	أَنَا	—		—	we	نَحْنُ

[1] These abbreviations stand for "third person masculine," etc.

PRONOMINAL SUFFIXES

	Singular Gen.	Singular Acc.		Dual Gen.	Dual Acc.		Plural Gen.	Plural Acc.	
3 M	his, its	him, it	‫...ـهُ‬	their	them	‫...ـهِما‬	their	them	‫...ـهُمْ‬
3 F	her, its	her, it	‫...ـها‬	their	them		their	them	‫...ـهُنَّ‬
2 M	your, thy	you, thee	‫...ـكَ‬	your	you	‫...ـكُما‬	your	you	‫...ـكُمْ‬
2 F	your, thy	you, thee	‫...ـكِ‬	your	you		your	you	‫...ـكُنَّ‬
1 MF	my	‫...ـي‬	me	‫...ـنِي‬	—	—	—	our	us	‫...ـنا‬

NOTE C: The following are the most frequently used demonstratives:

THIS, THESE

	Singular M	Singular F	Dual M	Dual F	Plural M	Plural F
Nominative	‫هٰذا‬	‫هٰذِه‬	‫هٰذان‬	‫هٰتان‬	‫هٰؤُلاء‬	‫هٰؤُلاء‬
Accusative	„	„	‫هٰذَين‬	‫هٰتين‬	„	„
Genitive	„	„	„	„	„	„

THAT, THOSE

	Singular M	Singular F	Dual	Plural M	Plural F
All cases	‫ذٰلِكَ‬ ‫ذاكَ‬	‫تِلْكَ‬	rarely used	‫أُولائِكَ‬	‫أُولائِكَ‬

III. PRACTICE TEXT

1. This is Mount Hermon (*literally*, the mountain of the old man).

‫١. هٰذا جَبَلُ ٱلشَّيْخِ .‬

2. Its white top (*literally*, head) is magnificent.

‫٢. رَأْسُهُ ٱلأَبْيَضُ عَظيمٌ .‬

3. This village is large.

‫٣. هٰذِه ٱلقَرْيَةُ كَبيرَةٌ .‬

4. Its name is Sūq al-Gharb (*literally*, the market of the west).

‫٤. إِسْمُها سُوقُ ٱلغَرْبِ .‬

5. That wadi is beautiful.

٥. ذلِكَ ٱلْوَادِي جَمِيلٌ .

6. The water of that spring is light.

٦. تِلْكَ ٱلْعَيْنُ مَاؤُهَا خَفِيفٌ .

IV. EXERCISES

Translate into English:

١. هٰذَا ٱلشَّيْخُ فَقِيرٌ .

٢. هٰذَا ٱلدَّرْسُ صَعْبٌ .

٣. تِلْكَ ٱلْفَرَسُ سَرِيعَةٌ .

٤. لَوْنُهَا حَسَنٌ وَرَأْسُهَا صَغِيرٌ .

٥. هِيَ لَعُوبَةٌ وَأَمِينَةٌ .

٦. رَاكِبُهَا عَظِيمُ ٱلشَّأْنِ .

٧. وَهُوَ عَبْدُ ٱللهِ .

Translate into Arabic:

1. I am the son of 'Abdullāh.

2. My name is Ṭalāl.

3. He is my king and your (masc. sing.) king.

4. You are his faithful scribe.

5. Our capital is 'Ammān.

6. This is a big city, and it is old.

7. Its market is extensive.

8. That is the palace of Raghdān.

9. And that is my room.

CHAPTER XIII

PREPOSITIONS AND CONJUNCTIONS

I. ILLUSTRATIVE TEXT

1. I have a newspaper; in it is a beautiful picture.

١. عِنْدِي جَرِيدَةٌ فِيهَا صُورَةٌ جَمِيلَةٌ .

2. And under it is its name in the Arabic language.

٢. وَتَحْتَهَا ٱسْمُهَا بِٱللُّغَةِ ٱلْعَرَبِيَّةِ .

3. Above it is the title of the newspaper with its number.

٣. وَفَوْقَهَا عُنْوَانُ ٱلْجَرِيدَةِ مَعَ عَدَدِهَا .

4. Then after the picture, on the

second page, is a part about travel

from Iraq to America.

٤. ثُمَّ بَعْدَ ٱلصُّورَةِ عَلَى ٱلصَّفْحَةِ
ٱلثَّانِيَةِ قِسْمٌ عَنِ ٱلسَّفَرِ
مِنَ ٱلْعِرَاقِ إِلَى أَمْرِيكَا .

5. And I have (written) in it a section about the war between America and Germany.

٥. وَلِي فِيهَا قِسْمٌ عَنِ ٱلْحَرْبِ بَيْنَ
أَمْرِيكَا وَأَلْمَانِيَا .

II. GRAMMATICAL ANALYSIS

1. This item is composed of two sentences. The first is عِنْدِي جَرِيدَةٌ, and the second is فِيهَا صُورَةٌ جَمِيلَةٌ. The first is a nominal sentence in which the predicate عِنْدِي precedes the subject جَرِيدَةٌ (for this inversion see page 24, n. 6). The second is a nominal sentence in which the predicate فِيهَا precedes the subject صُورَةٌ, which is modified by the adjective جَمِيلَةٌ. The second sentence is a modifier of جَرِيدَةٌ. It is to be noted that in English the relationship of the second sentence to the first would be expressed

43

by a relative clause introduced by a relative pronoun. In Arabic when the modified noun is indefinite, no relative pronoun is used. (For the use of the relative pronoun in Arabic, see Chapter XVI, section II, 3, and Chapter XXV, section II, 6, note.)

In the first sentence the predicate عِنْدِي is composed of two words عِنْدَ and ـِي.... The word عِنْدَ (which has a meaning like that of *chez* in French) is an adverb of place used as a preposition and is in construct with the pronominal suffix ـِي..., which is, therefore, in the genitive case, but invariable. The combination عِنْدِي may be translated *I have*. Adverbs end with a fatḥah. (Fatḥah is the sign of the accusative, for which see Chapters XV–XVI.) The final fatḥah of عِنْدَ has been superseded by the kasrah which is an essential part of the first person singular pronominal suffix. This kasrah always supersedes the preceding vowel.

In the second sentence the predicate فِيهَا precedes the subject صُورَة. The predicate is composed of two words, the separable preposition فِي and the pronominal suffix هَا..., which is in the genitive case because it is object of the preposition, but هَا... does not have the genitive case ending (kasrah) because it is invariable. All objects of prepositions are in the genitive.

2. In this sentence the predicate تَحْتَهَا is composed of تَحْتَ which is an adverb of place used as a preposition and the pronominal suffix هَا..... The adverb تَحْتَ ends with a fatḥah.

The subject اِسْم is modified by the prepositional phrase بِٱللُّغَةِ ٱلْعَرَبِيَّةِ, which is composed of the inseparable preposition ...بِ, its object, ٱللُّغَة, and the nisbah adjective ٱلْعَرَبِيَّة which modifies ٱللُّغَة.

4. This nominal sentence is introduced by the separable conjunction ثُمَّ. The predicate is بَعْدَ ٱلصُّورَة, and the subject is قِسْم. The word أَمْرِيكَا though genitive is indeclinable because it ends with alif.

5. The predicate of this nominal sentence is لِي, and the subject is قِسْم. The predicate لِي is composed of two words, the inseparable preposition ...لِ, which means *to* (here in the sense of *belonging to*), and the first person singular pronominal suffix ـِي.... .

NOTE:

The most common prepositions, with their most basic meanings, are the following:		The most common co-ordinate conjunctions are the following:		The most common adverbs used as prepositions, with their most basic meanings, are the following:	
عَلَى	on, over	وَ...	and	أَمَام	in front of
فِي	in	فَ...	and, then	بَعْدَ	after
عَنْ	from, about[1]	أَوْ	or	بَيْنَ	between, among[3]
إِلَى	to, until	ثُمَّ	then	تَحْتَ	under, below
مَعَ	with	لٰكِنَّ (لٰكِنْ)	but	فَوْقَ	above, over
مِنْ	from, of[1]			حَوْلَ	around, about
حَتَّى	until			دُونَ	under, without
لِ...	for, to[2]			ضِدَّ	against
بِ...	by, with, in			عِنْدَ	chez, with, at
كَ...	as, like			قَبْلَ	before (essentially time, occasionally place)
				قُدَّام	before (place)
				لَدَى	with, at
				نَحْوَ	towards, approximately
				وَرَاءَ	behind

[1] When the prepositions عَنْ and مِنْ precede a hamzat al-waṣl, they receive a final vowel (عَنِ and مِنَ) to facilitate pronunciation.

[2] When this preposition precedes the definite article, the hamzat al-waṣl and its alif drop out in writing, and the two lāms are joined together, e.g. لِ... + اَلْمَلِك = لِلْمَلِك. With pronominal suffixes other than ...ـِي it takes a fatḥah, e.g. لَهُ, لَهَا.

[3] The adverb بَيْنَ is repeated if at least one of the two words dependent on it is a pronoun (see below III, 3, and Chapter XXXV, section II, 12).

III. PRACTICE TEXT

1. The Saudi Arabian state is in the Arabian peninsula (*literally*, island).

١. اَلدَّوْلَةُ الْعَرَبِيَّةُ السُّعُودِيَّةُ فِي الْجَزِيرَةِ الْعَرَبِيَّةِ .

2. It has a king (who is) like [the] lion in war.

٢. لَهَا مَلِكٌ كَالْأَسَدِ فِي الْحَرْبِ .

3. Between him and the people is a great love.

٣. بَيْنَهُ وَبَيْنَ الشَّعْبِ حُبٌّ عَظِيمٌ .

4. His palace is large; in front of it is a mosque.

٤. قَصْرُهُ كَبِيرٌ، أَمَامَهُ جَامِعٌ .

5. Above it is the green Saudi flag.

٥. وَفَوْقَهُ الْعَلَمُ الْأَخْضَرُ السُّعُودِيُّ .

IV. EXERCISES

Translate into English:

١. اَلْجَامِعُ الْكَبِيرُ فِي الْعَاصِمَةِ .

٢. حَوْلَهُ سُوقُ الْمَدِينَةِ .

٣. وَوَرَاءَهُ دَارُ جَرِيدَةِ "الْحَيَاةِ ."

٤. وَقُدَّامَهُ نَحْوَ الْغَرْبِ بَابٌ قَدِيمٌ .

٥. وَقَبْلَ الْبَابِ السُّوقُ الطَّوِيلَةُ .

Translate into Arabic:

1. The wadi is below the mountain.

2. In it is a spring; its water is light.

3. To the west of it is the sea.

4. Between the spring and the sea is a small village.

5. At its head is the village shaykh.

CHAPTER XIV

COMPARATIVE AND SUPERLATIVE. COPULA. DIPTOTES

I. ILLUSTRATIVE TEXT

1. *Al-Ahrām* (*literally*, the pyramids) is a large Egyptian newspaper, and it is larger than any newspaper in Lebanon.

١. "اَلْأَهْرَام" جَرِيدَةٌ مِصْرِيَّةٌ كَبِيرَةٌ، وَهِيَ أَكْبَرُ مِنْ أَيَّةِ جَرِيدَةٍ فِي لُبْنَانَ.

2. Its form (format) is good, but the format of the newspaper *Al-Miṣri* (*literally*, the Egyptian) is the best in the Arab world.

٢. شَكْلُهَا حَسَنٌ، لٰكِنْ شَكْلُ جَرِيدَةِ "اَلْمِصْرِيّ" هُوَ اَلْأَحْسَنُ فِي اَلْعَالَمِ اَلْعَرَبِيِّ.

3. The magazine *Al-Hilāl* (*literally*, the crescent) is the best magazine in Egypt and it is the largest magazine in the Middle East.

٣. مَجَلَّةُ "اَلْهِلَال" هِيَ أَفْضَلُ مَجَلَّةٍ فِي مِصْرَ وَهِيَ اَلْمَجَلَّةُ اَلْكُبْرَى فِي اَلشَّرْقِ اَلْأَوْسَطِ.

II. GRAMMATICAL ANALYSIS

1. In this sentence the word أَكْبَرُ is the comparative, formed on the pattern of أَفْعَل. It is followed by the word مِنْ, which when following a comparative, is the equivalent of the English *than*. The form أَفْعَل is used for both the masculine and the feminine. Although the comparative adjective أَفْعَل like any other noun may occur in any of the three cases, it takes only two case endings, the ḍammah for the nominative and the fatḥah for both the accusative and the genitive. Words which behave in this manner are known as diptotes, in contradistinction to regular nouns,

which are known as triptotes. Another characteristic of diptotes shown here is that they take no nūnation. However, if a diptote is definite, it is treated as a triptote.

The noun أَيَّةٌ is the feminine of أَيُّ (*any*).

The word لُبْنَانُ is in the genitive case because it is object of the preposition فِي. It takes a final fatḥah instead of kasrah because it is diptote.

The word لُبْنَانُ is a proper noun of foreign origin. Practically all proper nouns of foreign origin are diptote.

2. The word لٰكِنْ is a co-ordinate conjunction.

The pronoun هُوَ is used in this sentence to join the subject شَكْلُ to the predicate اَلْأَحْسَنُ and is, therefore, called a copula. It is used either to emphasize the subject or, as here, to indicate where the predicate begins.

The predicate اَلْأَحْسَنُ is composed of the definite article ...اَلْ and the word أَحْسَنُ which is of the comparative pattern. When the definite article ...اَلْ limits the comparative, the resulting combinaiion is the superlative.

3. The word مَجَلَّةٌ is not of a previously given pattern. It is of foreign origin. The word أَفْضَلُ, which is of the أَفْعَلُ pattern, is here rendered superlative because it is first member of a construct and therefore definite.

بِصَرُ is an example of a foreign proper name and is, therefore, diptote.

اَلْكُبْرَى is the feminine form of the superlative, اَلْأَكْبَرُ.

NOTE: Whereas the comparative has one form, أَفْعَلُ, for both the masculine and the feminine, the superlative has a separate form for each, اَلْأَفْعَلُ (m.) and اَلْفُعْلَى (f.).

If the superlative is formed by a construct relationship whereby the second member is singular indefinite, the masculine of the superlative is used regardless of the gender of the second member, e.g. أَفْضَلُ مَجَلَّةٍ in I, 3, above. If the second member is plural definite, the superlative may also agree in gender and number. When the superlative follows the noun modified, it agrees, like any other adjective, in gender, e.g. اَلْمَجَلَّةُ اَلْكُبْرَى in I, 3, above.

اَلْأَوْسَطُ is also superlative in form.

48

III. PRACTICE TEXT

1. Cairo is the greatest city in the Arab East.

١. اَلْقَاهِرَةُ أَعْظَمُ مَدِينَةٍ فِي ٱلشَّرْقِ ٱلْعَرَبِيّ.

2. And the most modern part of it is Heliopolis (*literally*, new Cairo).[1]

٢. وَأَحْدَثُ قِسْمٍ مِنْهَا مِصْرُ ٱلْجَدِيدَةُ.

3. Baghdad is smaller than Cairo, but is older than it.

٣. بَغْدَادُ أَصْغَرُ مِنَ ٱلْقَاهِرَةِ وَلٰكِنْ أَقْدَمُ مِنْهَا.

4. Ankara is the capital of Turkey, and it is in Asia Minor.

٤. أَنْقَرَةُ عَاصِمَةُ تُرْكِيَّا وَهِيَ فِي آسِيَا ٱلصُّغْرَى.

5. Samarkand is in Central Asia.

٥. سَمَرْقَنْدُ فِي آسِيَا ٱلْوُسْطَى.

IV. EXERCISES

Translate into English:

١. اَلْأَرُزُّ ٱلْعِرَاقِيُّ أَفْضَلُ مِنَ ٱلْأَرُزِّ ٱلْمِصْرِيِّ.

٢. اَلْأَسَدُ أَكْبَرُ مِنَ ٱلْكَلْبِ.

٣. اَلْأُمُّ أَجْمَلُ مِنْ بِنْتِهَا.

٤. حَاكِمُ ٱلْجَزِيرَةِ هُوَ أَعْدَلُ حَاكِمٍ.

٥. لُغَةُ نَجْدٍ أَجْمَلُ لُغَةٍ بَيْنَ ٱلْعَرَبِ.

٦. اَلسَّفَرُ بِٱلْبَحْرِ أَصْعَبُ مِنَ ٱلسَّفَرِ بِٱلْجَوِّ.

[1] The word مِصْر, like various other geographical terms, is used both for the country (Egypt) and its capital (Cairo).

Translate into Arabic:

1. The mare is quicker than the dog and more beautiful than the lion.

2. The head of a Nejdi mare is smaller than the head of an Egyptian mare.

3. The crescent of the Turkish flag is smaller than the crescent of the Egyptian flag.

4. The state of Egypt is the largest state in the Arab world.

5. Riyadh is the greatest city in Nejd.

CHAPTER XV

VERBS. VERBAL SENTENCES. SUBJECT
AND OBJECT OF VERB

I. ILLUSTRATIVE TEXT

1. Jamīl went to Cairo.	١. ذَهَبَ جَمِيلٌ إِلَى ٱلْقَاهِرَةِ.
2. And he stopped (*literally*, descended) at Shepheard's Hotel.	٢. وَنَزَلَ فِي فُنْدُقِ شَبَرْدْزَ.
3. Then he entered the old part of the city.	٣. ثُمَّ دَخَلَ ٱلْقِسْمَ ٱلْقَدِيمَ مِنَ ٱلْمَدِينَةِ.
4. And visited al-Azhar mosque,	٤. وَزَارَ ٱلْجَامِعَ ٱلْأَزْهَرَ.
5. where he met the rector of the mosque.	٥. حَيْثُ لَقِيَ شَيْخَ ٱلْجَامِعِ.
6. And the rector took him to the university,	٦. وَٱلشَّيْخُ أَخَذَهُ إِلَى ٱلْجَامِعَةِ.
7. and (there) he attended the Arabic language class (*literally*, study).	٧. فَحَضَرَ دَرْسَ ٱللُّغَةِ ٱلْعَرَبِيَّةِ.
8. And the class pleased him (*literally*, was fine in his eye).	٨. وَحَسُنَ ٱلدَّرْسُ فِي عَيْنِهِ.

II. GRAMMATICAL ANALYSIS

1. This is a verbal sentence because it begins with a verb, i.e. ذَهَبَ, which is of the root form فَعَلَ. The subject of the verb is جَمِيلٌ. It is in the nominative case because the subject of a verb is always in the nominative case. The subject of the verb is the doer of the action expressed by the verb and *must follow* the verb.

The verb ذَهَبَ is third person masculine singular perfect. The word *perfect* means that the action has been completed, in contradistinction to

51

the word *imperfect*, which means that the action has not been completed (see Chapter VII, page 21).

It is to be remembered (Chapter VII, page 20) that the third person masculine singular perfect is the citation form from which all derived forms, whether verbal or nominal, come.

2. This sentence is also verbal, for it begins with the third person masculine singular perfect verb نَزَلَ. Since the subject of the verb is not expressed, the subject is said to be hidden in the verb. When this situation obtains, the verb is said to consist of two words: the verb and the hidden subject. Thus sentence 2 is different from sentence 1 in that in sentence 1 the subject of the verb is expressed and, therefore, the verb is deemed to be one word, for a verb *can only have one subject*.

3. In this verbal sentence the verb دَخَلَ is transitive, and the noun ٱلْقِسْمَ is its object, and, therefore, is in the accusative case. The sign of the accusative is the final fatḥah. The word is not nūnated because it is definite.

ٱلْقَدِيمَ is an adjective modifying ٱلْقِسْمَ and, therefore, agrees with it in case.

The subject of the verb دَخَلَ, not being expressed, is hidden in it.

4. In this verbal sentence it will be noticed that the verb زَارَ differs from the regular trisyllabic verb form فَعَلَ in that it has only two syllables. Originally this verb did follow the regular pattern in that it was زَوَرَ*, but it changed to زَارَ for phonetic reasons. This type of verb is known as a *hollow* verb, and its conjugation is irregular (see Chapter XVIII).

5. The word حَيْثُ is an invariable adverb.

The verb لَقِيَ is of the root pattern فَعِلَ.

The root pattern may be either فَعَلَ or فَعَلَ or فَعُلَ.

6. Item 6 consists of two sentences. The first is a nominal sentence whose subject is ٱلشَّيْخُ and whose predicate is the rest of the item. This predicate itself is the second sentence. It is a verbal sentence because it begins with the verb أَخَذَ. Since the subject of the verb is not expressed, it is hidden in it. The pronominal suffix ـهُ... is the object of the verb to which it is attached and is in the accusative case although, being invariable, it does

not show it. Therefore the combination أَخَذَهُ consists of three words: the verb, its hidden subject, and its object.

NOTE: A pronominal suffix attached to a noun or preposition is in the genitive case, the second member of a construct phrase or the object of a preposition, respectively. A pronominal suffix attached to a verb can only be in the accusative case, object of the verb. The accusative suffixes are identical with the genitive suffixes except in the first person singular, where the accusative form is ...نِي rather than ي... (see Chapter XII, section II, 8, note B; also below, Chapter XVIII, section I, 8).

8. The verb حَسُنَ is of the root pattern فَعُلَ (see II, 5, above).

The combination عَيْنُه is a construct phrase made up of the noun عَيْن and the pronominal suffix ....هُ. However, this pronominal suffix has changed to ...هِ under the influence of the preceding kasrah.

NOTE A: In the suffixes ...هِ ...هِما ...هِمْ ...هِنَّ the dammahs change into kasrahs following ...ـِ... or ...ِي or ...ِي.

NOTE B: The conjugation of the perfect singular, Form I, is as follows:[1]

3rd M	فَعَلَ
3rd F	فَعَلَتْ
2nd M	فَعَلْتَ
2nd F	فَعَلْتِ
1st	فَعَلْتُ

III. PRACTICE TEXT

1. My dear 'Umar.

١. عَزِيزِي عُمَرُ.

2. I went to Baghdad in the [season of] spring.

٢. ذَهَبْتُ إِلَى بَغْدَادَ فِي فَصْلِ الرَّبِيعِ.

3. And my sister went with me.

٣. وَذَهَبَتْ أُخْتِي مَعِي.

[1] For the conjugation of all verb forms, consult paradigms, Appendix I.

4. And I stopped at the Tigris Hotel.

٤. وَنَزَلْتُ فِي فُنْدُقِ دِجْلَةَ.

5. Where you yourself stopped last year.

٥. حَيْثُ نَزَلْتَ أَنْتَ فِي ٱلسَّنَةِ ٱلْمَاضِيَةِ.

6. And my sister visited the famous tomb of King Fayṣal.

٦. وَزَارَتْ أُخْتِي قَبْرَ ٱلْمَلِكِ فَيْصَلٍ ٱلْمَشْهُورَ.

7. And on the second day I, myself, set out for

the mosque of al-Kāẓimayn, and I saw its golden dome.

٧. وَفِي ٱلْيَوْمِ ٱلثَّانِي قَصَدْتُ أَنَا جَامِعَ ٱلْكَاظِمَيْنِ وَرَأَيْتُ قُبَّتَهُ ٱلذَّهَبِيَّةَ.

8. And Baghdad is really a great city.

٨. وَبَغْدَادُ فِي ٱلْحَقِيقَةِ مَدِينَةٌ عَظِيمَةٌ.

9. Your friend, 'Ali.

٩. صَدِيقُكَ عَلِيٌّ.

IV. EXERCISES

Translate into English:

١. ذَهَبْتُ إِلَى ٱلْجَامِعَةِ وَأَخَذْتُ ٱبْنِي مَعِي.

٢. وَدَخَلَ ٱبْنِي غُرْفَةَ ٱللُّغَةِ ٱلْعَرَبِيَّةِ وَحَضَرَ ٱلدَّرْسَ.

٣. لَقِيَ ٱلْمَلِكُ ٱلْعَظِيمُ شَعْبَهُ بِحُبٍّ شَدِيدٍ.

٤. قَصَدَتْ أُمِّي ٱلْجَبَلَ حَيْثُ ٱلْجَوُّ جَافٌّ.

٥. أَنْتَ رَأَيْتَ ٱلْهِلَالَ فَوْقَ ٱلْقَرْيَةِ وَأَنَا رَأَيْتُهُ.

Translate into Arabic:

1. I set out for my mother's house, but I met her in the house of her sister.
2. You took my book from my room.
3. My sister attended a class at the university.
4. My friend 'Umar went to Riyadh and visited 'Abd al-'Azīz ibn al-Su'ūd.
5. I went to the top [head] of the mountain and saw the large wadi.

RELATIVE PRONOUNS. ADVERBS.
إِنَّ AND ITS "SISTERS"

I. ILLUSTRATIVE TEXT

1. There came (the news) from Damascus today that

١. جَاءَ عَنْ دِمَشْقَ ٱلْيَوْمَ أَنَّ

2. 'Abd al-Raḥmān (*literally* the servant of the Merciful) Azzām Pasha, the Secretary

٢. عَبْدَ ٱلرَّحْمٰنِ عَزَّامًا¹ بَاشَا ٱلْأَمِينَ

3. General of the Arab League, who

٣. ٱلْعَامَّ لِلْجَامِعَةِ ٱلْعَرَبِيَّةِ ٱلَّذِي

4. visited Syria recently, spoke at the [house of the]

٤. زَارَ سُورِيَّةَ أَخِيرًا قَدْ خَطَبَ فِي دَارِ

5. Arab club saying: "[Indeed] the Arab

٥. ٱلنَّادِي ٱلْعَرَبِيِّ قَائِلًا "اِنَّ ٱلْأُمَّةَ

6. nation, which has an ancient glory,

٦. ٱلْعَرَبِيَّةَ ٱلَّتِي لَهَا مَجْدٌ قَدِيمٌ

7. failed in the Palestine war because of its weakness and lack of unity."

٧. قَدْ فَشِلَتْ فِي حَرْبِ فِلَسْطِينَ

لِضَعْفِهَا وَعَدَمِ وَحْدَتِهَا."

II. GRAMMATICAL ANALYSIS

1. In item 1 the verb جَاءَ is a hollow verb the final radical of which is a hamzah without a chair.

The word دَمَشْقَ is diptote.

أَلْيَوْمَ, literally *the day*, means *today*. It is an adverb of time and, therefore, like adverbs in general, is in the accusative.

أَنَّ is a subordinate conjunction which is best translated as *that*. It always introduces a nominal sentence. The subject of a sentence intro-

---

¹ Although this book consistently vocalizes all proper names, modern practice usually omits inflection except where the name is made up of a construct phrase.

duced by it is in the accusative, and the predicate of such a sentence is in the nominative.

2. In item 2 the word عَبْد is the subject of the sentence introduced by أَنَّ and, therefore, is in the accusative. The sign of the accusative is the final faṭḥa. There is no nūnation because the word is definite, being the first member of a construct phrase.

The word اَلرَّحْمٰن is of the adjectival pattern فَعْلَانْ, but in this particular word the long alif is usually replaced by a 'dagger' alif.

The name عَزَّامَا is in the accusative because it is in apposition with عَبْد which in itself is in the accusative.

NOTE: A word in apposition takes the same case as the word with which it is in apposition.

The words بَاشَا (invariable) and اَلْأَمِين are also in apposition with عَبْد.

3. In item 3 اَلْعَامّ is an adjective modifying اَلْأَمِين. It is of the active participle pattern فَاعِل from the verb عَمَّ (< *عَمَمَ). It will be noted that the assimilation of the two mīms persists in the active participle.

The combination لِلْجَامِعَة consists of the preposition لِ..., the definite article اَلْ..., and the noun, جَامِعَة. It will be noticed that the waṣlah and its chair have in this case dropped out. See Chapter XIII, footnote 2.

اَلَّذِي is the masculine singular relative pronoun. It introduces the relative clause اَلَّذِي زَارَ سُورِيَّة أَخِيرًا, which modifies عَبْد. The relative pronoun is only used when the noun modified is definite.

4. أَخِيرًا, which is formed on the adjectival pattern of فَعِيل, is here used as an adverb of time and is, therefore, accusative.

The particle قَد, when used before the perfect, asserts the completion of the action and may be translated by *really*, *verily*, or *indeed*; however, it may frequently be omitted in translation.

5. قَائِلًا is used as an adverb of manner and tells *how* the action of the verb خَطَبَ took place. Like other adverbs, the adverb of manner is in the accusative. It is used a great deal in Arabic and is frequently of the active participle pattern. The word قَائِلًا is formed on the active participle pattern of فَاعِل from the hollow verb قَالَ 'to say'. The middle radical of

56

hollow verbs changes into hamzah in the active participle form. The sentence, إِنَّ...فَشَلَتْ, is, as a whole, the direct object of the active participle قَائِلًا. Active participles, though nouns, retain enough verbal force to take a direct object.

إِنَّ is an assertive particle which introduces a nominal sentence. The subject of a sentence introduced by it is in the accusative, and the predicate is in the nominative as is the case with sentences introduced by its "sister" أَنَّ. It is best translated by *verily* or *indeed*, but the translation may frequently be omitted.

ٱلْأُمَّةُ is the subject of a sentence introduced by إِنَّ.

6. ٱلَّتِي is the feminine singular relative pronoun. It introduces the relative clause ٱلَّتِي لَهَا مَجْدٌ قَدِيمٌ.

The total syntax of this verbal sentence may be best explained by the following diagram in which only the essentials of the sentence appear:

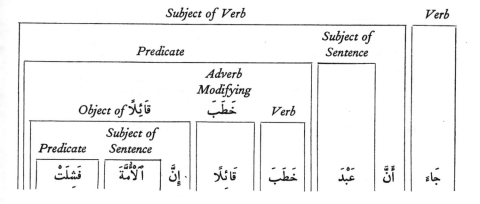

NOTE A: The most important relative pronouns are as follows:

	Singular		Dual		Plural	
	M	*F*	*M*	*F*	*M*	*F*
Nom.	ٱلَّذِي	ٱلَّتِي	ٱللَّذَانِ	ٱللَّتَانِ	ٱلَّذِينَ	ٱللَّوَاتِي
Acc.	,,	,,	ٱللَّذَيْنِ	ٱللَّتَيْنِ	,,	,,
Gen.	,,	,,	,,	,,	,,	,,

Other pronouns used as relatives are:

مَنْ   he who

مَا   that which, what

NOTE: The particles which cause the subject of a nominal sentence to be in the accusative and its predicate to be in the nominative (i.e. إِنَّ and its so-called "sisters") are:

إِنَّ	verily	لٰكِنَّ	but
أَنَّ	that	لَيْتَ	would that
كَأَنَّ	as if	لَعَلَّ	perhaps
لِأَنَّ	because		

III. PRACTICE TEXT

1. And he added to that, saying

١. وَزَادَ عَلَى ذٰلِكَ قَائِلًا

that he had sought from the president

إِنَّهُ طَلَبَ إِلَى رَئِيسِ

of the political committee the holding of a meeting

ٱللَّجْنَةِ ٱلسِّيَاسِيَّةِ عَقْدَ جَلْسَةٍ

immediately to look into this matter which had occupied

حَالًا لِلنَّظَرِ فِي هٰذَا ٱلْأَمْرِ ٱلَّذِي شَغَلَ

the attention of the Arabs for a long time.

بَالَ ٱلْعَرَبِ مُدَّةً طَوِيلَةً.

IV. EXERCISES

Translate into English:

١. إِنَّ عُنْوَانَ[2] رَئِيسِ دَوْلَةِ أَمْرِيكَا مَشْهُورٌ فِي ٱلْعَالَمِ.

٢. وَهٰذَا ٱلْعُنْوَانُ هُوَ ٱلْبَيْتُ ٱلْأَبْيَضُ فِي ٱلْعَاصِمَةِ.

[2] This word means *address* as well as *title*.

٣. إِنِّي رَأَيْتُ ٱلرَّئِيسَ ٱلْيَوْمَ نَازِلًا مِنْ غُرْفَتِهِ ٱلَّتِي فِي ٱلْبَيْتِ ٱلْأَبْيَضِ.

٤. وَذَهَبَ إِلَى ٱلْمَدِينَةِ قَاصِدًا قَبْرَ أَمِيرِ ٱلْبَحْرِ ٱلْمَشْهُورِ "دُوِي" (Dewey) حَيْثُ خَطَبَ عَنْ حُبِّ "دُوِي" لِأُمَّتِهِ.

Translate into Arabic:

1. Al-Azhar is today the oldest university in the world.
2. Recently I went to it seeking extensive knowledge.
3. I entered the room of the rector, whom I had met [him] before, and he said to me that studying the Arabic language in al-Azhar is better than studying it in any university in America.

CHAPTER XVII

THE DERIVED FORMS OF THE VERB

I. ILLUSTRATIVE TEXT

1. Napoleon left Egypt

١. خَرَجَ نَابُلْيُونُ مِنْ مِصْرَ

2. and headed his army toward Palestine,

٢. وَوَجَّهَ جَيْشَهُ إِلَى فِلَسْطِينَ

3. and the Turkish army met him,

٣. وَقَابَلَهُ ٱلْجَيْشُ ٱلتُّرْكِيُّ

4. (the army) which al-Jazzār had sent [it] to Jaffa.

٤. ٱلَّذِي أَرْسَلَهُ ٱلْجَزَّارُ إِلَى يَافَا .

5. Napoleon's army advanced on the Turkish army

٥. تَقَدَّمَ جَيْشُ نَابُلْيُونَ إِلَى ٱلْجَيْشِ ٱلتُّرْكِيِّ

6. and exchanged fire with it.

٦. وَتَبَادَلَ ٱلنَّارَ مَعَهُ .

7. Then the Turkish army broke,

٧. فَٱنْكَسَرَ ٱلْجَيْشُ ٱلتُّرْكِيُّ

8. and Napoleon occupied the city and killed every

man who had fallen as a prisoner into his hand,

٨. وَٱحْتَلَّ نَابُلْيُونُ ٱلْمَدِينَةَ وَقَتَلَ كُلَّ رَجُلٍ وَقَعَ أَسِيرًا فِي يَدِهِ

9. and the ground reddened with blood. Then Napoleon

crept forward to Acre

٩. فَٱحْمَرَّتِ ٱلْأَرْضُ مِنَ ٱلدَّمِ . ثُمَّ زَحَفَ نَابُلْيُونُ إِلَى عَكَّا

10. and resumed the war there.

But he was not able to conquer (literally, the opening of) the city, and finally he

١٠. وَٱسْتَأْنَفَ ٱلْحَرْبَ هُنَاكَ . وَلَكِنَّهُ مَا ٱسْتَطَاعَ فَتْحَ ٱلْمَدِينَةِ وَأَخِيرًا

| withdrew from Palestine and returned to Egypt a failure. | اِنْسَحَبَ مِنْ فِلَسْطِينَ وَرَجَعَ إِلَى مِصْرَ فَاشِلًا. |

II. GRAMMATICAL ANALYSIS

2. In this verbal sentence the verb وَجَّهَ is formed by "doubling" the middle radical of the root form وَجَهَ. Verbs formed in this way are known as Form II verbs or as verbs of the فَعَّلَ form.

A verb of Form II modifies the meaning of the root form so as to express the idea of a causative or intensive action.

3. The verb قَابَلَ is formed by inserting an alif between the first and second radicals of the root form قَبَلَ. Verbs formed in this way are known as Form III verbs or as verbs of the فَاعَلَ form.

Verbs of Form III modify the meaning of the root form either by expressing mutuality of action or by relating the action to another entity. Thus here, for example, the root form قَبَلَ means *to draw near*, and Form III قَابَلَ relates the action of drawing near to an entity, *him*.

4. In this clause the verb أَرْسَلَ is formed by prefixing a hamzah fatḥah (أَ) to the root form رَسَلَ and by eliminating its initial vowel. Verbs formed in this way are called Form IV verbs or verbs of the أَفْعَلَ form.

Form IV verbs modify the meaning of the root form by rendering it causative.

NOTE: The pronoun ـهُ... suffixed to أَرْسَلَ refers back to الَّذِي. A relative clause must contain a pronoun which refers back to the relative pronoun. It may be either expressed as in I, 4, above or hidden as is the case in Chapter XVI, section I, 3–4. (See Chapter XXV, section II, 6, note.)

5. The verb تَقَدَّمَ is formed by prefixing ...تَ to Form II. Verbs of this type are called Form V or تَفَعَّلَ form verbs.

Form V verbs are, in meaning, the reflexive Form II verbs. Thus, for example, قَدِمَ means *to go forward*, قَدَّمَ means *to cause to go forward*, and تَقَدَّمَ means *to cause oneself to go forward*.

6. The verb تَبَادَلَ is formed by prefixing ....تَ to Form III. Verbs of this type are called Form VI or تَفَاعَلَ form verbs.

Form VI verbs are in meaning the reflexive of Form III verbs. Reciprocity is emphasized.

7. The verb إِنْكَسَرَ is formed by prefixing ....إِنْ to the root form كَسَرَ. Verbs of this type are called Form VII or إِنْفَعَلَ form verbs.

Form VII verbs modify the meaning of the root form by making it reflexive or by giving it a passive sense. Thus, for example, كَسَرَ means *to break* (transitive), whereas إِنْكَسَرَ means *to break* (*by itself*).

8. The verb إِحْتَلَّ is formed from حَلَّ by prefixing إِ, infixing ....تَ.... after the first radical, and eliminating the vowel of the first radical. Verbs of this type are called Form VIII or إِفْتَعَلَ form verbs. It will be noticed that the root form of إِحْتَلَّ is a doubled verb (see Chapter XII, section II, 6).

Form VIII verbs modify the meaning of the root form by making it reflexive in the sense of doing a thing for one's self or, less often, by rendering it reciprocal. The verb إِحْتَلَّ exemplifies the first modification. The root form حَلَّ means *to alight at*; إِحْتَلَّ, *to alight at a place for one's self* > *to occupy*.

The noun كُلّ means *every* or *all* depending on whether the noun with which it is in construct is, respectively, indefinite or definite. كُلُّ ٱلرَّجُلِ would mean *all of the man*.

The word أَسِيرًا is here used as an adverb of manner.

9. The verb إِحْمَرَّ is formed from حَمِرَ by prefixing إِ, by omitting the vowel of the first radical, and by 'doubling' the final radical. Verbs of this type are called Form IX or إِفْعَلَّ form verbs.

Form IX verbs are used to express the action of assuming a color or defect.

أَحْمَرَّتْ is feminine because the subject of the verb ٱلْأَرْضُ is feminine. ٱلْأَرْضُ is one of a number of nouns which are feminine without a feminine ending. Normally, a third person feminine singular verb ends in تْ....

Here, however, the verb is followed by the definite article ...اَلْ whose hamzah must be elided. In order to make this elision possible, therefore, a helping kasrah is added, thus: ...تِ (see Chapter VI, section III).

10. The verb إِسْتَأْنَفَ is formed by prefixing إِسْتَ... to the root form and by omitting the vowel of the first radical. Verbs of this type are called Form X or إِسْتَفْعَلَ form verbs.

Form X verbs modify the meaning of the root form by adding to it the idea of desiring, asking, esteeming, feigning. Thus إِسْتَأْنَفَ means *to desire to renew > to resume*.

The adverb هُنَاكَ is invariable.

مَا is the negative particle normally used before the perfect tense.

إِسْتَطَاعَ is Form X of the hollow verb طَاعَ.

The active participle فَاشِلاً is used as an adverb of manner.

NOTE A: 1. The hamzah of Form IV is always أ, whereas the hamzahs of Forms VII, VIII, IX, and X become ا unless initial.

2. The conjugation of derived verbs in the perfect is the same as that of the root form (for paradigms, consult Appendix I).

NOTE B: The presentation of verb forms given above needs some amplification:

1. Not all forms of any single verb are used.

2. In some cases derived forms may be in use although the root form is not.

3. Although at one time derived forms may have followed more consistently the semantic modifications outlined above, many have diverged to such an extent that the relationship is hardly apparent. The student must, therefore, treat derived forms as separate vocabulary units.

III. PRACTICE TEXT

1. The political committee of the Arab League met today.

١. إِجْتَمَعَتِ ٱللَّجْنَةُ ٱلسِّيَاسِيَّةُ لِلْجَامِعَةِ ٱلْعَرَبِيَّةِ فِي هٰذَا ٱلْيَوْمِ.

2. It resumed the study of the affair of Greater Syria.

٢. وَٱسْتَأْنَفَتْ بَحْثَ أَمْرِ سُورِيَّةَ ٱلْكُبْرَى.

3. Nūri Pasha al-Sa'īd, the head of the Iraqi government, spoke in this session.

٣. وَقَدْ تَكَلَّمَ نُورِي بَاشَا ٱلسَّعِيدُ، رَئِيسُ ٱلْحُكُومَةِ ٱلْعِرَاقِيَّةِ، فِي هٰذِهِ ٱلْجَلْسَةِ.

4. He said that Arab unity is a real fact,

٤. فَقَالَ إِنَّ ٱلْوَحْدَةَ ٱلْعَرَبِيَّةَ هِيَ حَقِيقَةٌ وَاقِعَةٌ.

5. and that perhaps the love for it in the soul of the people is mightier than

٥. وَلَعَلَّ حُبَّهَا فِي نَفْسِ ٱلشَّعْبِ أَعْظَمُ مِنْ

their love for life itself.

حُبِّهِ لِلْحَيَاةِ نَفْسِهَا.

IV. EXERCISES

Translate into English:

١. لَقِيَتِ ٱلْحُكُومَةُ ٱلْعَادِلَةُ حُبًّا عَظِيمًا مِنَ ٱلشَّعْبِ.

٢. إِنْسَحَبْتُ مِنَ ٱلنَّادِي فِي ٱلسَّنَةِ ٱلْمَاضِيَةِ.

٣. وَقَعْتُ فِي ٱلْوَادِي فَٱنْكَسَرَتْ يَدِي.

٤. قَابَلْتُ صَدِيقِي عُمَرَ ٱلْكَاتِبَ ٱلْقَدِيرَ فِي ٱلسُّوقِ فَقَالَ لِي إِنَّهُ أَرْسَلَ إِلَى ٱلْجَامِعَةِ عَدَدًا مِنْ مَجَلَّتِهِ ٱلْجَدِيدَةِ.

٥. إِحْتَلَّ ٱلْأَمِيرُ فَيْصَلُ مَدِينَةَ دِمَشْقَ فِي ٱلْحَرْبِ ٱلْعَالَمِيَّةِ وَدَخَلَهَا رَاكِبًا عَلَى فَرَسِهِ ٱلْمَحْبُوبَةِ.

Translate into Arabic:

1. 'Umar sent Khālid to Iraq, but after a short time Khālid directed his army to Syria.

2. He advanced on Damascus and was able to conquer it.

3. Before 'Umar occupied Jerusalem (al-Quds), he held a meeting with the governor of Jerusalem and spoke to him about the conquest of the city.

4. Then 'Umar returned to Medina.

64

WEAK VERBS IN THE PERFECT.
SUBORDINATE CONJUNCTIONS

I. ILLUSTRATIVE TEXT

1. I got up in the morning.

٠١ قُمْتُ صَبَاحًا.

2. Then I immediately turned my face towards the *qiblah*,

٠٢ فَحَوَّلْتُ وَجْهِي حَالاً نَحْوَ ٱلْقِبْلَةِ

3. and performed the morning prayer.

٠٣ وَأَقَمْتُ صَلَاةَ ٱلصَّبَاحِ.

4. Then my father prayed, and my sister prayed after him.

٠٤ ثُمَّ صَلَّى وَالِدِي وَصَلَّتْ أُخْتِي بَعْدَهُ.

5. After I had fulfilled this duty,

٠٥ وَبَعْدَ أَنْ أَدَّيْتُ هٰذَا ٱلْوَاجِبَ

6. I went down to the bazaar and bought the necessit(ies) of the house.

٠٦ نَزَلْتُ إِلَى ٱلسُّوقِ وَٱبْتَعْتُ حَاجَةَ ٱلْبَيْتِ.

7. Then I contacted my friend Ḥasan on the telephone,

٠٧ ثُمَّ ٱتَّصَلْتُ بِصَدِيقِي حَسَنٍ تَلَفُونِيًّا

8. and he invited (*literally*, called) me to his house.

٠٨ فَدَعَانِي إِلَى بَيْتِهِ.

II. GRAMMATICAL ANALYSIS

1. In this sentence the verb قُمْتُ is the first person singular perfect of the hollow verb قَامَ (< ‫*قَوَمَ‬).

A hollow verb is a verb whose second radical is one of the weak letters و or ي.

The word قُمْتُ reveals one of the irregularities in the conjugation of hollow verbs, for it will be noticed that its middle radical has disappeared. These irregularities may be summarized as follows:

(*a*) In the perfect of Forms I, IV, VII, VIII, and X the weak letter و or ي changes into an alif in the third person, masculine and feminine except in the case of the third person feminine plural where it is dropped.

(b) In the perfect of Forms I, IV, VII, VIII, and X the weak letter disappears in the first and second persons and in the third person feminine plural.

(c) In all other cases the original و or ي is retained.

(d) In those cases in Form I where the middle radical disappears (i.e. in 1 (b) above) the vowel of the first radical is ـُ if the original weak letter was و and ـ if the original weak letter was ي.

NOTE: Like most rules, the preceding one has exceptions (e.g. خِفْتُ < خَافَ < خَوِفَ* 'to be afraid'). The student is advised to master paradigms.

2. In the verb حَوَّلْتُ the original و is retained in accordance with the explanation given above.

3. In the verb أَقَمْتُ the original و has disappeared as explained above.

4. The words صَلَّى and صَلَّتْ are respectively the third person masculine singular and the third person feminine singular of Form II of the theoretical root form صَلَوَ* which is a weak-lām verb. A weak-lām verb is one whose third radical is either و or ي. The conjugation of weak-lām verbs is more complex than that of the hollow verbs and may best be grasped by a thorough familiarity with the paradigms.

5. أَنْ is a subordinate conjunction which is best translated as *that*. It always introduces a verbal sentence (cf. أَنَّ, Chapter XVI, section II, 1). For a list of subordinate conjunctions see below, II, 8, note.

أَدَّيْتُ is the first person singular of Form II of the weak-lām root form أَدَّى (< أَدَيَ*).

6. اِبْتَعْتُ is the first person singular of Form VIII of the hollow verb بَاعَ (< بَيِعَ*). The weak letter has disappeared in accordance with the explanation given above in II, 1.

7. اِتَّصَلْتُ is the first person singular of إِتَّصَلَ which is Form VIII of the root form وَصَلَ—a weak-fā' verb. A weak-fā' verb is one which begins with و or ي. The conjugation of the perfect of weak-fā' verbs is regular except for Form VIII. In Form VIII, for purposes of euphony, the first radical is replaced by a ت which is written together with the ت of Form VIII forming a ...تّ.

تَلَفُونِيًّا is a nisbah formed from the loan word تَلَفُون and is here in the accusative as an adverb of manner.

8. دَعَا (< ‎*‎دَعَوَ) is a weak-lām verb. It is followed by the accusative pronominal suffix of the first person singular, ‎ـنِي....

NOTE: The most common subordinate conjunctions are the following:

أَنَّ	that (with nominal sentence)	إِذْ	since, because, after, when
أَنْ	that (with verbal sentence)	لَمَّا	when
لِ...	so that	فِيمَا	while
إِذَا	if, when	عِنْدَمَا	when
لَوْ	if	بَعْدَمَا	after
مُنْذُ	since	قَبْلَمَا	before
إِلَّا	except	(لِ)كَيْ	in order that
غَيْرَ أَنَّ	however	لِأَنَّ	because
أَمَّا... فَ...	as for	بَيْنَمَا	while
حَتَّى	until, so that	كَأَنَّ	as if
إِنْ	if, whether		

Many of these conjunctions need special consideration and will be dealt with as they occur.

III. PRACTICE TEXT

1. Muḥammad ‘Ali the Great assumed the rule in the land of Egypt after the

   departure of Napoleon from it.

٢. He set up in Egypt a government which undertook

   the rule of the Egyptian people in a more modern way.

١. وَلِيَ مُحَمَّدُ عَلِيٌّ الْكَبِيرُ الْحُكْمَ فِي أَرْضِ مِصْرَ بَعْدَ خُرُوجِ نَابِلْيُونَ مِنْهَا.

٢. وَقَدْ أَقَامَ فِي مِصْرَ حُكُومَةً تَوَلَّتْ حُكْمَ الشَّعْبِ الْمِصْرِيِّ عَلَى طَرِيقَةٍ أَحْدَثَ.

67

3. He sent to the West a scientific mission

which rendered a great service to Egypt.

٣. وَوَجَّهَ إِلَى ٱلْغَرْبِ بَعْثَةً عِلْمِيَّةً

أَدَّتْ خِدْمَةً كَبِيرَةً لِمِصْرَ.

4. He sent his son Ibrāhīm Pasha to Syria, and he conquered it.

٤. وَأَرْسَلَ ٱبْنَهُ إِبْرَاهِيمَ بَاشَا إِلَى سُورِيَّةَ فَٱسْتَوْلَى عَلَيْهَا.

5. But in view of the pressure of Britain, his father agreed with her on departing

from Syria. Then Ibrāhīm returned to Egypt.

٥. وَلَكِنْ نَظَرًا لِضَغْطِ بَرِيطَانِيَا ٱتَّفَقَ وَالِدُهُ مَعَهَا عَلَى ٱلْخُرُوجِ

مِنْ سُورِيَّةَ فَرَجَعَ إِبْرَاهِيمُ إِلَى مِصْرَ.

IV. EXERCISES

Translate into English:

١. مَا ٱسْتَطَعْتُ ٱلسَّفَرَ إِلَى ٱلرِّيَاضِ لِأَنَّ ٱلسَّفَرَ إِلَيْهَا فِي ٱلْحَقِيقَةِ صَعْبٌ.

٢. إِبْتَعْتُ كِتَابَ ٱللُّغَةِ ٱلْعَرَبِيَّةِ مِنْ صَدِيقٍ لِي.

٣. خِدْمَةُ ٱلْوَطَنِ وَاجِبٌ عَلَى كُلِّ مَنْ وَلِيَ ٱلْحُكْمَ.

٤. إِسْتَوْلَى ٱبْنُ ٱلسُّعُودِ عَلَى نَجْدٍ بَعْدَ أَنْ وَقَعَ حَاكِمُ مَدِينَةِ ٱلرِّيَاضِ أَسِيرًا فِي يَدِهِ.

Translate into Arabic:

1. I contacted my sister who is in Damascus on the telephone, and she told me that my father had gone to Baghdad.
2. The political committee of the Arab League agreed to study the best way for (achieving) Arab unity.
3. The Arab Club invited me to its (club)house, so I spoke there about the Arab conquest of Egypt.
4. In the year 1918 the Arab army advanced under the Amīr Fayṣal from the Arabian peninsula to Damascus and occupied Syria.

CHAPTER XIX

MAṢDARS

I. ILLUSTRATIVE TEXT

1. The parliament held a meeting last night.

١. عَقَدَ ٱلْبَرْلَمَانُ ٱجْتِمَاعاً ٱللَّيْلَةَ ٱلْمَاضِيَةَ .

2. It studied the question of the agreement between the

government and the oil company, concerning the concession which

the company had sought, and exchanged opinion(s) about it.

٢. وَدَرَسَ أَمْرَ ٱلِاتِّفَاقِ بَيْنَ ٱلْحُكُومَةِ وَشَرِكَةِ ٱلزَّيْتِ بِشَأْنِ ٱلِامْتِيَازِ ٱلَّذِي طَلَبَتْهُ ٱلشَّرِكَةُ وَتَبَادَلَ ٱلرَّأْيَ فِيهِ .

3. A deputy from the city of Homs spoke,

٣. وَتَكَلَّمَ نَائِبٌ مِنْ مَدِينَةِ حِمْصَ

4. and he said in his speech that this concession (was)

against the interest of the country and its true independence.

٤. وَقَالَ فِي خِطَابِهِ إِنَّ هٰذَا ٱلِامْتِيَازَ هُوَ ضِدُّ مَصْلَحَةِ ٱلْوَطَنِ وَٱسْتِقْلَالِهِ ٱلصَّحِيحِ .

5. His speech caused a split in the parliament,

٥. فَسَبَّبَ كَلَامُهُ ٱنْشِقَاقًا فِي ٱلْبَرْلَمَانِ

6. but the minister of national economy said,

٦. وَلٰكِنَّ وَزِيرَ ٱلِاقْتِصَادِ ٱلْوَطَنِيِّ قَالَ :

7. "The negotiation(s) are proceeding with the company in

a spirit of co-operation and sincerity,

٧. " إِنَّ ٱلْمُفَاوَضَةَ جَارِيَةٌ مَعَ ٱلشَّرِكَةِ بِرُوحِ ٱلتَّعَاوُنِ وَٱلْإِخْلَاصِ ،

8. and the company has come forward with an undertaking for

٨. وَإِنَّ ٱلشَّرِكَةَ قَدْ تَقَدَّمَتْ بِتَعَهُّدٍ

the realization of every national demand."

لِتَحْقِيقِ كُلِّ مَطْلَبٍ وَطَنِيٍّ. "

II. GRAMMATICAL ANALYSIS

1. ٱلْبَرْلَمَانُ is a loan word from French *parlement*. ٱجْتِمَاعًا is derived from the verb ٱجْتَمَعَ on the pattern of إِفْتِعَالٌ. This is the gerund or *maṣdar* of the Form VIII verb. A maṣdar is an abstract noun expressing the action of the corresponding verb. Thus ٱجْتَمَعَ 'to meet together' > ٱجْتِمَاعٌ 'a meeting.' At least one maṣdar may be derived from each verb form.

2. ٱلٱتِّفَاقُ is the maṣdar of إِتَّفَقَ which itself is Form VIII of the root form وَفَقَ. إِتَّفَقَ means *to agree*; إِتِّفَاقٌ means *agreeing*, i.e. *agreement*.

ٱلْحُكُومَة 'government' is a maṣdar of the root form حَكَمَ 'to rule' on the pattern of فُعُولَةٌ.

شَرِكَةٌ 'company' is a maṣdar of the root form شَرِكَ 'to become a partner' on the pattern of فَعِلَةٌ.

شَأْنٌ 'matter,' 'affair' is a maṣdar of the root form شَأَنَ on the pattern of فَعْلٌ.

ٱلٱمْتِيَاز is the maṣdar of Form VIII of مَازَ (< مَيَزَ*).

ٱلرَّأْيُ 'opinion' is a maṣdar of the root form رَأَى 'to see' on the pattern of فَعْلٌ.

4. خِطَابٌ is a maṣdar of the root form خَطَبَ on the pattern of فَعَالٌ.

مَصْلَحَة is derived from the root form صَلُحَ on the maṣdar pattern of مَفْعَلَةٌ. Some maṣdars are formed from the root forms on the patterns مَفْعَلٌ and مَفْعَلَةٌ. This type of maṣdar is called a *maṣdar mīmī* because of the prefixed mīm. Maṣdar mīmis are also formed from the derived verb forms (see Chapter XX, section II, 5, and Chapter XXI, section II, 10, note).

ٱسْتِقْلَال is the maṣdar of the Form X verb إِسْتَقَلَّ 'to be independent' on the pattern of إِسْتِفْعَالٌ.

5. كَلَام 'speech' is a maṣdar of the root form كَلَمَ 'to speak' on the pattern of فَعَالٌ.

إِنْشِقَاقًا is the maṣdar of the Form VII verb إِنْشَقَّ 'to be split' on the pattern of إِنْفِعَالٌ.

6. اَلْاِقْتِصَاد 'economy,' 'economics' is the maṣdar of the Form VIII verb إِقْتَصَدَ 'to be thrifty.'

7. اَلْمُفَاوَضَة is a maṣdar of the Form III verb فَاوَضَ 'to negotiate' on the pattern of مُفَاعَلَةٌ.

اَلتَّعَاوُن is the maṣdar of the Form VI verb تَعَاوَنَ, 'to co-operate' on the pattern of تَفَاعُلٌ.

اَلْإِخْلَاص is the maṣdar of the Form IV verb أَخْلَصَ 'to be sincere' on the pattern of إِفْعَالٌ.

8. تَعَهُّد is the maṣdar of the Form V verb تَعَهَّدَ 'to undertake' on the pattern of تَفَعُّلٌ.

تَحْقِيق is a maṣdar of the Form II verb حَقَّقَ 'to realize,' 'carry out' on the pattern of تَفْعِيلٌ.

مَطْلَب is a maṣdar mīmi of the root form طَلَبَ 'to demand' on the pattern of مَفْعَلٌ.

NOTE A: The hamzah of the maṣdar of Form IV verbs is always إِ, whereas the hamzahs of Forms VII, VIII, IX, and X become ٱ unless initial (see Chapter XVII, section II, 10, note A).

NOTE B: The maṣdars of the root form are numerous. Some of them have been used prior to this lesson, such as:

وَخُرُوج, سِيَاسَة, خِدْمَة, وَحْدَة, سَفَر, حَبّ, دَرْس, عِلْم, حُكُومَة.

The most commonly used maṣdar patterns of the root form are the following:

فَعَلٌ	فِعْلٌ
فَعَلٌ	فُعْلٌ

فَعَلٌ	فَعَالٌ
فُعَلٌ	فِعَالٌ
فِعْلَةٌ	فُعَالٌ
فُعْلَةٌ	فَعَالَةٌ
فَعْلَةٌ	فِعَالَةٌ
فَعَلَةٌ	فُعُولٌ
فِعْلَةٌ	فُعُولَةٌ

NOTE C: The most commonly used maṣdars of the derived forms are as follows:

II.	تَفْعِيلٌ and تَفْعِلَةٌ	VII.	إِنْفِعَالٌ
III.	مُفَاعَلَةٌ and فِعَالٌ	VIII.	إِفْتِعَالٌ
IV.	إِفْعَالٌ	IX.	إِفْعِلَالٌ
V.	تَفَعُّلٌ	X.	إِسْتِفْعَالٌ
VI.	تَفَاعُلٌ		

III. PRACTICE TEXT

1. General Slim arrived in Cairo by [way of] air.

١. وَصَلَ إِلَى ٱلْقَاهِرَةِ بِطَرِيقِ ٱلْجَوِّ ٱلْجَنَرَالُ "سليم."

2. He came for negotiation(s) with the Egyptian govern-

ment about the affair of amending the military

agreement for the defense of the Suez Canal.

٢. وَقَدْ جَاءَ لِلْمُفَاوَضَةِ مَعَ ٱلْحُكُومَةِ ٱلْمِصْرِيَّةِ بِشَأْنِ تَعْدِيلِ ٱلِاتِّفَاقِ ٱلْعَسْكَرِيِّ لِلدِّفَاعِ عَنْ قَنَاةِ ٱلسُّوَيْسِ.

3. This agreement is a part of the Anglo-Egyptian treaty.

٣. وَهَذَا ٱلِاتِّفَاقُ هُوَ قِسْمٌ مِنَ ٱلْمُعَاهَدَةِ ٱلْمِصْرِيَّةِ ٱلْبَرِيطَانِيَّةِ.

4. The negotiation(s) began in a cordial atmosphere.

٤. وَقَدِ ابْتَدَأَتِ ٱلْمُفَاوَضَةُ فِي جَوٍّ وَدِّيٍّ .

5. But the insistence of the British army on not

٥. وَلٰكِنَّ إِصْرَارَ ٱلْجَيْشِ ٱلْبَرِيطَانِيِّ عَلَى عَدَمِ

withdrawing from the Suez Canal caused the cutting

ٱلِانْسِحَابِ مِنْ قَنَاةِ ٱلسُّوِيْسِ سَبَّبَ

off of negotiation(s).

قَطْعَ ٱلْمُفَاوَضَةِ .

6. And so General Slim immediately returned to London.

٦. فَرَجَعَ ٱلْجَنَرَالُ "سليم" حَالاً إِلَى لُنْدُنَ .

IV. EXERCISES

Translate into English:

١. إِجْتَمَعَ ٱلْمَلِكُ بِوَزِيرِ ٱلِاقْتِصَادِ ٱلْوَطَنِيِّ وَطَلَبَ إِلَيْهِ ٱلنَّظَرَ فِي أَمْرِ ٱمْتِيَازِ ٱلزَّيْتِ .

٢. زُرْتُ ٱلْبَرْلَمَانَ وَحَضَرْتُ جَلْسَةَ ٱلصَّبَاحِ حَيْثُ جَرَى ٱلْبَحْثُ فِي قَطْعِ ٱلْمُفَاوَضَةِ بِشَأْنِ سُورِيَّةَ ٱلْكُبْرَى .

٣. إِنَّ ٱلتَّعَاوُنَ بَيْنَ ٱلْبَرْلَمَانِ وَٱلْحُكُومَةِ وَاجِبٌ لِمَصْلَحَةِ ٱلْوَطَنِ .

٤. وَجَّهَتِ ٱلْحُكُومَةُ ٱلْمِصْرِيَّةُ بَعْثَةً سِيَاسِيَّةً وَعَسْكَرِيَّةً إِلَى لُنْدُنَ لِتَعْدِيلِ ٱلْمُعَاهَدَةِ .

Translate into Arabic:

1. The government presented an undertaking to the people for the realization of every just demand.

2. The independence of Lebanon began with the withdrawal of the British army from its soil.

3. The insistence of Iraq on cutting off the oil from Palestine caused a split between Iraq and Britain.

4. The realization of the unity of the Arab nation is a duty for every Arab government.

PARTICIPLES. كَانَ AND ITS SISTERS.
APPOSITION

I. ILLUSTRATIVE TEXT

1. Sa'd Zaghlūl was an Egyptian patriot (*literally*, struggler) devoted to the service of (his) country and the realization of its true independence.

١. كَانَ سَعْدُ زَغْلُولُ مُجَاهِدًا مِصْرِيًّا مُتَفَانِيًا فِي خِدْمَةِ ٱلْوَطَنِ وَتَحْقِيقِ ٱسْتِقْلَالِهِ ٱلصَّحِيحِ .

2. He began his active life (as) a government employee—

as an editor of the *Official Journal.*

٢. إِبْتَدَأَ حَيَاتَهُ ٱلْعَمَلِيَّةَ مُوَظَّفًا فِي ٱلْحُكُومَةِ كَمُحَرِّرٍ لِلْجَرِيدَةِ ٱلرَّسْمِيَّةِ .

3. Then he became an assistant in the Ministry of the Interior, then Minister of Education, then Minister of Justice.

٣. ثُمَّ أَصْبَحَ مُعَاوِنًا فِي وِزَارَةِ ٱلدَّاخِلِيَّةِ فَوَزِيرًا لِلتَّرْبِيَةِ فَوَزِيرًا لِلْعَدْلِ .

4. But he disagreed with the Khedive 'Abbās Ḥilmi, and so he left his post and became the leader of the opposition.

٤. وَلكِنَّهُ ٱخْتَلَفَ مَعَ ٱلْخَدِيْوِيِّ عَبَّاسٍ حِلْمِيٍّ فَتَرَكَ وَظِيفَتَهُ وَصَارَ زَعِيمَ ٱلْمُعَارَضَةِ .

5. After the First World War he headed (*literally*, marched at the head of)

٥. بَعْدَ ٱلْحَرْبِ ٱلْعَالَمِيَّةِ ٱلْأُولَى سَارَ عَلَى رَأْسِ

a delegation (which) went to the British High

وَفْدٍ قَصَدَ ٱلْمَنْدُوبَ ٱلسَّامِيَ ٱلْبَرِيطَانِيَّ

Commissioner and sought permission to attend the

وَطَلَبَ إِذْنًا لِحُضُورِ

peace conference, the holding of which took place

مُؤْتَمَرِ ٱلصُّلْحِ ٱلَّذِي جَرَى عَقْدُهُ

in Paris.

فِي بَارِيسَ .

6. Sa'd was striving to assure the future of Egypt and to

٦. وَكَانَ سَعْدٌ مُجْتَهِدًا فِي تَأْمِينِ مُسْتَقْبِلِ مِصْرَ

change it from a colonized land into an independent

وَتَحْوِيلِهَا مِنْ أَرْضٍ مُسْتَعْمَرَةٍ إِلَى دَوْلَةٍ

state; the story of his life is the story of the

مُسْتَقِلَّةٍ ، فَقِصَّةُ حَيَاتِه هِيَ قِصَّةُ

independence of Egypt.

ٱسْتِقْلَالِ مِصْرَ .

II. GRAMMATICAL ANALYSIS

1. The verb كَانَ 'to be' is third person masculine singular.

زَغْلُولٌ is in the nominative case because it is in apposition with سَعْدٌ, the subject of the verb. Any word in apposition takes the same case as that of the word with which it is in apposition.

The noun مُجَاهِدًا is an active participle (see Chapter VIII, section II, 2) of the Form III verb جَاهَدَ 'to struggle.' It is formed on the pattern of مُفَاعِلٌ.

مُجَاهِدًا is in the accusative because it is the predicate of the verb كَانَ. The predicate of كَانَ, unlike that of the verb *to be* in English, is always in the accusative. Certain other similar verbs (see below, II, 6, note B) also take a predicate in the accusative.

مِصْرِيًّا is in the accusative because it is a nisbah adjective modifying مُجَاهِدًا.

مُتَقَانِيًا is also in the accusative because it is used as an adjective modifying مُجَاهِدًا. It is an active participle of the Form VI verb تَقَانَى 'to devote oneself' on the pattern of مُتَفَاعِل.

2. مُوَظَّفًا is a passive participle of the Form II verb وَظَّفَ 'to employ' on the pattern of مُفَعَّل. Here مُوَظَّفًا is used as an adverb of manner.

مُحَرِّر is an active participle of the Form II verb حَرَّرَ 'to edit' on the pattern of مُفَعِّل.

3. The verb أَصْبَحَ 'to become,' like كَانَ, takes a predicate in the accusative.

مُعَاوِنًا is an active participle of the Form III verb عَاوَنَ 'to assist.' It is the predicate of أَصْبَحَ, and, therefore, in the accusative.

وِزَارَة is a maṣdar of the root form وَزَرَ.

اَلتَّرْبِيَة is a maṣdar of the Form II verb رَبَّى 'to bring up,' 'educate,' on the pattern of تَفْعِلَة.

4. The verb صَارَ 'to become,' like كَانَ, takes a predicate in the accusative; hence, the final fatḥah on the predicate زَعِيم.

5. اَلْأُولَى is the feminine of اَلْأَوَّل and is used here because it agrees with اَلْحَرْب which is feminine. (For the pattern فُعْلَى see Chapter XIV, section II, 3, note.)

It is to be noticed that the relative clause beginning with قَصَدَ is not introduced by a relative pronoun because the noun which it modifies is indefinite (see Chapter XVI, section II, 3).

مُؤْتَمَر is a maṣdar mīmi (see Chapter XIX, section II, 4) of the Form VIII verb إِنْتَمَرَ 'to confer.' It should be pointed out, however, that it is identical in pattern (مُفْتَعَل) with the passive participle of a Form VIII verb.

NOTE: The mīmi maṣdars of all derived forms are identical with the corresponding passive participles.

6. مُجْتَهِدًا is an active participle of the Form VIII verb إِجْتَهَدَ 'to endeavor,' 'strive' on the pattern of مُفْتَعِل.

76

مُسْتَقْبَل is an active participle of the Form X verb إِسْتَقْبَلَ 'to come forward' on the pattern of مُسْتَفْعَل.

مُسْتَعْمَرَة is a passive participle of the Form X verb إِسْتَعْمَرَ 'to colonize' on the pattern of مُسْتَفْعَل.

مُسْتَقِلَّة is an active participle of the Form X verb إِسْتَقَلَّ 'to be independent.'

NOTE A: The participles are as follows:

	Active	Passive
I.	فَاعِل	مَفْعُول
II.	مُفَعِّل	مُفَعَّل
III.	مُفَاعِل	مُفَاعَل
IV.	مُفْعِل	مُفْعَل
V.	مُتَفَعِّل	مُتَفَعَّل
VI.	مُتَفَاعِل	مُتَفَاعَل
VII.	مُنْفَعِل	مُنْفَعَل
VIII.	مُفْتَعِل	مُفْتَعَل
IX.	مُفْعَلّ	—
X.	مُسْتَفْعِل	مُسْتَفْعَل

NOTE B: The most frequently used verbs which take a predicate in the accusative are:

كَانَ   to be

لَيْسَ   not to be (which may also take a predicate with the preposition بِ....)

بَقِيَ   to remain

دَامَ   to continue

مَا زَالَ   not to cease, continue

صَارَ   to become

أَصْبَحَ   to become

أَمْسَى   to become

بَاتَ   to become

III. PRACTICE TEXT

1. The Wafd party was the biggest party in Egypt,
   and it assumed power more than once (*literally*, other than a time).

١. كَانَ حِزْبُ ٱلْوَفْدِ أَكْبَرَ حِزْبٍ فِي مِصْرَ وَقَدْ تَوَلَّى ٱلْحُكْمَ غَيْرَ مَرَّةٍ .

2. Its first leader was Saʻd Zaghlūl.

٢. وَكَانَ زَعِيمُهُ ٱلْأَوَّلُ سَعْدًا زَغْلُولًا .

3. As for its second leader, he was Muṣṭafa al-Naḥḥās Pasha.

٣. أَمَّا زَعِيمُهُ ٱلثَّانِي فَكَانَ مُصْطَفَى ٱلنَّحَّاسَ بَاشَا .

4. He is descended from a poor family (*literally*, house).

٤. وَهُوَ مُتَحَدِّرٌ مِنْ بَيْتٍ فَقِيرٍ .

5. But he was industrious, so he went to Cairo
   college and became a lawyer.

٥. وَلٰكِنَّهُ كَانَ مُجْتَهِدًا فَقَصَدَ كُلِّيَّةَ ٱلْقَاهِرَةِ وَأَصْبَحَ مُحَامِيًا .

6. Then the government appointed him a judge.

٦. ثُمَّ عَيَّنَتْهُ ٱلْحُكُومَةُ قَاضِيًا .

7. After that he became a minister and head of the Wafd.

٧. وَبَعْدَ ذٰلِكَ صَارَ وَزِيرًا وَرَئِيسَ ٱلْوَفْدِ .

8. He led a delegation to the Montreux Conference,
   where the agreement took place for abolishing

٨. وَقَادَ وَفْدًا إِلَى مُؤْتَمَرِ " مُونْترو " حَيْثُ جَرَى ٱلِٱتِّفَاقُ عَلَى إِلْغَاء

| every foreign concession (i.e. capitulation) in the land of Egypt. | كُلِّ ٱمْتِيَازٍ أَجْنَبِيٍّ فِي أَرْضِ مِصْرَ. |
| 9. President Muḥammad Najīb dissolved the Wafd party in the year 1952. | ٩. وَقَدْ حَلَّ ٱلرَّئِيسُ مُحَمَّدُ نَجِيبُ حِزْبَ ٱلْوَفْدِ سَنَةَ ١٩٥٢. |

IV. EXERCISES

Translate into English:

١. كَانَ "مُصْطَفَى كَمَالٌ" ٱلزَّعِيمُ ٱلتُّرْكِيُّ مُجَاهِدًا لِٱسْتِقْلَالِ ٱلْوَطَنِ.

٢. مِصْرُ أَوَّلُ دَوْلَةٍ عَرَبِيَّةٍ أَصْبَحَتْ مُسْتَقِلَّةً فِي ٱلْعَالَمِ ٱلْعَرَبِيِّ بَعْدَ مُعَاهَدَةِ ٱلصُّلْحِ.

٣. عَقَدَتْ مِصْرُ مُعَاهَدَةً وَدِّيَّةً مَعَ بَرِيطَانِيَا، وَفِي ٱلْمُعَاهَدَةِ تَعَهُّدُ بَرِيطَانِيَا بِتَحْقِيقِ مَطْلَبِ مِصْرَ وَهُوَ ٱلْٱنْسِحَابُ مِنَ ٱلْقَاهِرَةِ.

٤. حَوَّلَ مُحَمَّدُ عَلِيٌّ وَجْهَ مِصْرَ نَحْوَ ٱلْغَرْبِ.

٥. بَعْدَ ٱلْحَرْبِ ٱلْعَالَمِيَّةِ ٱلثَّانِيَةِ عَيَّنَتْ أَمْرِيكَا مَنْدُوبًا سَامِيًا فِي أَلْمَانِيَا.

Translate into Arabic:

1. The magazine editor's assistant is an able writer.
2. The governor of the colony of Aden ('Adan) is descended from a famous house.
3. The lawyer resigned from the ministry of the interior, and the king appointed him minister of justice.
4. Every employee in the ministry is devoted to serving the future of the country.
5. The co-operation between the opposition party and the party of the government continued for the period of the war.

NOUNS OF INSTRUMENT.
NOUNS OF PLACE AND TIME.
EMPHATIC NOUNS. DIMINUTIVES.
ABSTRACT NISBAHS

I. ILLUSTRATIVE TEXT

1. Dr. Ṭaha Ḥusayn is an Egyptian scholar and a famous writer.

١. أَلدُّكْتُورُ طَه حُسَيْنْ عَلَّامَةٌ مِصْرِيٌّ وَكَاتِبٌ مَشْهُورٌ.

2. He occupied the position of Minister of Education in the government of al-Naḥḥās Pasha.

٢. وَقَدْ شَغَلَ مَنْصِبَ وَزِيرِ ٱلتَّرْبِيَةِ فِي حُكُومَةِ ٱلنَّحَّاسِ بَاشَا.

3. He is from a poor family, for his father was a farmer who lived in the country.

٣. وَهُوَ مِنْ بَيْتٍ فَقِيرٍ فَقَدْ كَانَ وَالِدُهُ فَلَّاحًا سَكَنَ ٱلرِّيفَ.

4. He studied in the village school, in the Azhar mosque, and the Egyptian university.

٤. وَقَدْ دَرَسَ فِي مَدْرَسَةِ ٱلْقَرْيَةِ وَفِي ٱلْجَامِعِ ٱلْأَزْهَرِ وَٱلْجَامِعَةِ ٱلْمِصْرِيَّةِ.

5. Then he travelled to Paris where he stayed a long time to study Western literature.

٥. ثُمَّ سَافَرَ إِلَى بَارِيسَ حَيْثُ أَقَامَ مُدَّةً طَوِيلَةً لِدِرَاسَةِ ٱلْأَدَبِ ٱلْغَرْبِيِّ.

6. Upon his return to Egypt he became professor of classical history, then of Arabic literature.

٦. وَعِنْدَ رُجُوعِهِ إِلَى مِصْرَ أَصْبَحَ أُسْتَاذَ ٱلتَّأْرِيخِ ٱلْكَلَاسِيكِيِّ فَأُسْتَاذَ ٱلْأَدَبِ ٱلْعَرَبِيِّ.

7. Thus he is a true mirror of what is good in the East and the West. ٧. لِذٰلِكَ فَهُوَ مِرْآةٌ صَحِيحَةٌ لِمَا هُوَ حَسَنٌ فِي ٱلشَّرْقِ وَٱلْغَرْبِ.

8. For he has brought together the spirit of Western civilization with the spirit of Eastern civilization. ٨. فَقَدْ جَمَعَ بَيْنَ رُوحِ ٱلْمَدَنِيَّةِ ٱلْغَرْبِيَّةِ وَرُوحِ ٱلْمَدَنِيَّةِ ٱلشَّرْقِيَّةِ.

9. He has weighed with the scale of reason every matter which he has investigated [it]. ٩. وَوَزَنَ بِمِيزَانِ ٱلْعَقْلِ كُلَّ أَمْرٍ بَحَثَ فِيهِ.

10. He is without doubt the greatest personality in the modern Arabic literary movement. ١٠. وَهُوَ بِدُونِ شَكٍّ أَعْظَمُ شَخْصِيَّةٍ فِي ٱلْحَرَكَةِ ٱلْأَدَبِيَّةِ ٱلْعَرَبِيَّةِ ٱلْحَدِيثَةِ.

II. GRAMMATICAL ANALYSIS

1. أَلدُّكْتُور is a loan word. The proper noun طَهَ is Koranic. It is invariable.

The proper noun حُسَيْن is a diminutive of حَسَن on the pattern of فُعَيْل. This pattern is used to form the diminutive of any triliteral noun. Diminutives are used to express littleness, endearment, and sometimes contempt.

The emphatic noun عَلَّامَة is formed from the verb عَلِمَ on the pattern of فَعَّال. This pattern denotes one who does something intensively and by extension one who follows a particular trade. The pattern فَعَّال is frequently further strengthened by suffixing ـَة... as in the case of عَلَّامَة.

The pattern فَعَّالَة need not be feminine. It can be either masculine or feminine depending upon the person it refers to. When referring to things, it is always feminine (e.g. طَيَّارَة in III, 2, below).

2. The noun مَنْصَب is formed from the verb نَصَبَ 'to set up' on the pattern of مَفْعَل. This pattern, together with مَفْعِل and مَفْعَلَة, denotes

81

the place or time of an action. Here, therefore, مَنْصِب means *a place where some one is set up* or *a position*.

The proper noun ٱلنَّحَّاس is of the pattern فَعَّال and as a common noun means *coppersmith*.

3. فَلَّاحًا is also of the pattern فَعَّال and means *farmer*.

4. مَدْرَسَة is a noun of place formed from the verb دَرَس.

6. أُسْتَاذ is a loan word from Persian.

ٱلْكَلَاسِيكِيّ is a loan word from French *classique*.

7. The noun مِرْآة (*مِرْأَية> < *مِرْأَاة>) is formed from the verb رَأَى 'to see' on the pattern of مِفْعَلَة. This pattern, together with مِفْعَال and مِفْعَل, denotes an instrument. Here, therefore, مِرْآة denotes *an instrument for seeing*, hence *a mirror*.

8. ٱلْمَدَنِيَّة is a feminine nisbah (see Chapter XI, section II, 6) formed from مَدِينَة. Note that the yā' of مَدِينَة has dropped in the formation of the nisbah.

The feminine nisbah frequently denotes an abstraction of the noun from which it is formed. Thus مَدِينَة 'city,' مَدَنِيَّة 'civilization.'

9. مِيزَان (*مُوزَان>) is a noun of instrument formed from the verb وَزَن on the pattern of مِفْعَال.

10. شَخْصِيَّة is a feminine nisbah formed from شَخْص 'a person.' Hence it has the abstract meaning, *personality*.

NOTE: The nouns of place and time of the derived verbs are identical in form with the passive participles and the mīmī maṣdars of the derived forms (see Chapter XX, section II, 5).

III. PRACTICE TEXT

Cairo, March 2—by the special
correspondent of *al-Ahrām*:

أَلْقَاهِرَةُ فِي ٢ مَارِس—لِمُرَاسِل
''ٱلْأَهْرَامِ'' ٱلْخَاصّ:

1. (His) Excellency Riyāḍ Bey al-Ṣulḥ, Lebanese Prime Minister, arrived this morning at Cairo airport to attend the Council of the Arab League.

١. وَصَلَ صَبَاحَ ٱلْيَوْمِ إِلَى مَطَارِ ٱلْقَاهِرَة دَوْلَةُ رِيَاضِ بِكَ ٱلصُّلْحِ رَئِيسِ ٱلْوِزَارَة ٱللُّبْنَانِيَّة لِحُضُورِ مَجْلِسِ ٱلْجَامِعَةِ ٱلْعَرَبِيَّةِ.

2. A little before his arrival, the plane of His Highness Prince Fayṣal landed at the airport coming from Jidda.

٢. وَقَبِيلَ وُصُوله نَزَلَتْ فِي ٱلْمَطَارِ طَيَّارَةُ سُمُوِّ ٱلْأَمِيرِ فَيْصَلٍ قَادِمَةً مِنْ جُدَّة.

3. It was delayed beyond its appointed time of arrival for the period of an hour.

٣. وَقَدْ تَأَخَّرَتْ عَنْ مَوْعِد وُصُولِهَا مُدَّةَ سَاعَة.

4. His Excellency Riyāḍ Bey said that the stand of Lebanon towards amending the covenant of the Arab League continues as it was.

٤. وَقَدْ قَالَ دَوْلَةُ رِيَاضِ بِكَ إِنَّ مَوْقِفَ لُبْنَانَ مِنْ تَعْدِيلِ مِيثَاقِ ٱلْجَامِعَةِ ٱلْعَرَبِيَّةِ مَا زَالَ عَلَى مَا كَانَ عَلَيْهِ.

5. He added [saying] that a great responsibility now (rests) on the Arab League in preserving the unity of the Arab nation.

٥. وَزَادَ قَائِلًا إِنَّ عَلَى ٱلْجَامِعَةِ ٱلْعَرَبِيَّةِ ٱلْآنَ مَسْؤُولِيَّةً كُبْرَى فِي حِفْظِ وَحْدَةِ ٱلْأُمَّةِ ٱلْعَرَبِيَّةِ.

IV. EXERCISES

Translate into English:

١. صُورَةُ رَئِيسِ حِزْبِ ٱلْمُعَارَضَة عَلَى ٱلصَّفْحَةِ ٱلْأُولَى مِنَ ٱلْجَرِيدَة.

٢. عَقَدَ مَجْلِسُ ٱلْكُلِّيَّة جَلْسَةً صَبَاحَ ٱلْيَوْمِ تَكَلَّمَ فِيهَا عَلَّامَةٌ قَدِمَ مِنْ أَمْرِيكَا عَنْ مَسْؤُولِيَّة ٱلْحُكُومَة نَحْوَ ٱلْفَقِيرِ وَٱلْفَلَّاحِ.

٣. طَلَبَتِ ٱلْوِزَارَةُ مِنَ ٱلْمَجْلِسِ إِلْغَاءَ مَنْصِبِ أُسْتَاذِ ٱللُّغَةِ ٱلْأَلْمَانِيَّةِ فِي ٱلْجَامِعَةِ ٱلْوَطَنِيَّةِ.

٤. عَيَّنَتِ ٱلْحُكُومَةُ شَخْصِيَّةً رَسْمِيَّةً كَمَنْدُوبٍ عَنْهَا فِي ٱلْمُؤْتَمَرِ ٱلْأَدَبِيِّ ٱلَّذِي ٱجْتَمَعَ فِي ٱلْقَاهِرَةِ.

٥. إِنِّي عَلَى مَوْعِدٍ مَعَ مُوَظَّفٍ فِي وِزَارَةِ ٱلتَّرْبِيَةِ لِبَحْثِ حَاجَةِ ٱلْمَدِينَةِ لِمَدْرَسَةٍ جَدِيدَةٍ وَبَيْتٍ لِرَئِيسِهَا.

٦. إِنَّ صَدِيقِي حُسَيْنًا شَخْصِيَّةٌ كَبِيرَةٌ. فَقَدْ كَانَ مُحَامِيًا كَبِيرًا ثُمَّ أَصْبَحَ قَاضِيًا فِي دِمَشْقَ. وَهُوَ ٱلْآنَ فِي وَظِيفَةِ مُعَاوِنٍ لِوَزِيرِ ٱلْعَدْلِ. وَهُوَ فَوْقَ كُلِّ هٰذَا كَاتِبٌ مَشْهُورٌ.

Translate into Arabic:

1 The covenant of the Arab League is a mirror of the unity of the Arabs.

2. On every nation (rests) responsibility for world peace.

3. The airplane which landed at the London airport today is the biggest airplane in the world.

4. President Roosevelt was a beloved personality.

5. A little before the morning prayer the farmer got up and went to the village mosque.

THE DUAL

I. ILLUSTRATIVE TEXT

1. The two friends, Jamīl and Ḥusayn, went to

   Damascus and stopped at the Hotel Umayyah and

   visited the Umawi mosque.

١. ذَهَبَ ٱلصَّدِيقَانِ جَمِيلٌ وَحُسَيْنٌ إِلَى دِمَشْقَ وَنَزَلَا فِي فُنْدُقِ أُمَيَّةَ وَزَارَا ٱلْجَامِعَ ٱلْأُمَوِيَّ .

2. Then the two rented an automobile to Baalbek

   where they stayed two days.

٢. ثُمَّ ٱسْتَأْجَرَا سَيَّارَةً إِلَى بَعْلَبَكَّ حَيْثُ بَقِيَا يَوْمَيْنِ .

3. They passed their two days in visiting the town and

   the Roman temple.

٣. وَقَدْ قَضَيَا يَوْمَيْهِمَا فِي زِيَارَةِ ٱلْبَلْدَةِ وَٱلْمَعْبَدِ ٱلرُّومَانِيِّ .

4. On the third day they travelled to Beirut.

٤. وَفِي ٱلْيَوْمِ ٱلثَّالِثِ سَافَرَا إِلَى بَيْرُوتَ .

5. On their way they passed by two beautiful towns,

   Zaḥlah and Ṣawfar.

٥. وَمَرَّا فِي طَرِيقِهِمَا بِبَلْدَتَيْنِ جَمِيلَتَيْنِ، زَحْلَةَ وَصَوْفَرَ .

6. These two are the two large towns for summering

   in Lebanon.

٦. وَهُمَا بَلْدَتَا ٱلْاِصْطِيَافِ ٱلْكَبِيرَتَانِ فِي لُبْنَانَ .

II. GRAMMATICAL ANALYSIS

1. In this verbal sentence the subject of the verb ٱلصَّدِيقَانِ 'the two friends' is dual. It is formed in the nominative case by omitting the case ending of the singular (ٱلصَّدِيقُ) and by suffixing ـَانِ....

The verb ذَهَبَ remains singular despite the fact that the subject of the verb is dual. This situation obtains because the subject of the verb is expressed.

NOTE: Whenever the subject of a verb is expressed, the verb is in the singular. If the subject of the verb is not expressed, the verb agrees in number with the unexpressed subject unless that subject is a plural not referring to rational beings, in which case the verb is feminine singular. (See Chapter XXIV, section II, 2.)

جَمِيل and حُسَين are both nominative because they are in apposition with الصَّدِيقان.

The verbs نَزَلَا and زَارَا are both third person masculine dual perfect. They are dual because the dual subject of the verb is not expressed in either case.

The nisbah الأُمَوِيّ is formed from the proper noun أُمَيَّة. The change, أُمَوِيّ > *أُمَيِيّ, is for purposes of euphony.

2. The tenth form verb اسْتَأْجَرَا is dual because the dual subject of the verb is not expressed.

سَيَّارَة is formed from the verb سَارَ 'to go' on the emphatic, or intensive, pattern of فَعَّال and is further strengthened by suffixing ة.... Thus, سَيَّارَة literally means *something which goes a great deal*, i.e. *an automobile*.

يَوْمَيْن is dual and is in the accusative because it is an adverb of time. The accusative of the dual is formed by omitting the case ending of the singular (يَوْم) and by suffixing يْن....

3. يَوْمَيْهِما consists of two words: the dual accusative يَوْمَيْن and the dual pronominal suffix هِما.... However, the final ن of يَوْمَيْن has been omitted because يَوْمَيْن is in construct with هِما....

NOTE: Regardless of case, when a dual is in construct, its final ن is omitted.

5. بَلْدَتَيْن is dual and is in the genitive case, object of the preposition بِـ.... The genitive of the dual is identical with the accusative.

جَمِيلَتَيْن is dual because adjectives modifying dual nouns agree with them in number.

86

6. The nominative, dual noun بَلْدَتَا has lost its final ن because it is in construct.

اَلْاصْطِيَاف is the maṣdar of the Form VIII verb إِصْطَاف (< ‏*إِصْتَاف) which is derived from the root form صَاف. The change from ت to ط takes place under the influence of the velarized letter ص.

NOTE A: If the first radical of a Form VIII verb is one of the emphatic letters ض ص or ط, the ت changes into a ط.

NOTE B: For conjugation of the dual, consult paradigms, Appendix I.

III. PRACTICE TEXT

1. Qays and Layla are the two personalities of

Arabic literature famous for great love.

١. قَيْسٌ وَلَيْلَى شَخْصِيَّتَا اَلْأَدَبِ اَلْعَرَبِيِّ اَلْمَشْهُورَتَانِ بِالْحُبِّ اَلْعَظِيمِ.

2. The story of their love has become an example

for every lover.

٢. وَقَدْ أَمْسَتْ قِصَّةُ حُبِّهِمَا مِثَالًا لِكُلِّ مُحِبٍّ.

3. Qays had loved Layla since childhood, and

they decided on marriage.

٣. وَقَدْ أَحَبَّ قَيْسٌ لَيْلَى مُنْذُ الطُّفُولَةِ وَعَزَمَا عَلَى الزَّوَاجِ.

4. But in view of the appearance of the love poetry

which Qays had composed about his beloved Layla,

her father forbade them from marrying.

٤. وَلَكِنْ نَظَرًا لِظُهُورِ الشِّعْرِ الْغَزَلِيِّ اَلَّذِي نَظَمَهُ قَيْسٌ فِي حَبِيبَتِهِ لَيْلَى فَإِنَّ وَالِدَهَا مَنَعَهُمَا مِنَ الزَّوَاجِ.

5. Then Qays became a madman and wandered in the distant

desert bewildered [on his face], and his name became Majnūn Layla.

٥. فَأَمْسَى قَيْسٌ مَجْنُونًا وَطَافَ فِي الصَّحْرَاءِ[1] الْبَعِيدَةِ هَائِمًا عَلَى وَجْهِهِ وَصَارَ اسْمُهُ "مَجْنُونَ لَيْلَى."

[1] For this pattern see Chapter XXV, section II, 8, note B, 2.

6. As for the two lovers, they continued their love until death.

٦. أَمَّا ٱلْحَبِيبَانِ فَقَدْ بَقِيَا عَلَى حُبِّهِمَا حَتَّى ٱلْمَوْتِ.

IV. EXERCISES

Translate into English:

١. عِنْدِي سَيَّارَةٌ وَعِنْدَ أُخْتِي ٱلْكُبْرَى سَيَّارَتَانِ.

٢. لِلْجَامِعِ قُبَّتَانِ جَمِيلَتَانِ مِنْ ذَهَبٍ، أَصْغَرُهُمَا أَجْمَلُهُمَا.

٣. حَضَرْتُ ٱلْيَوْمَ ٱجْتِمَاعَيْنِ جَرَى عَقْدُهُمَا فِي ٱلْمَدِينَةِ.

٤. كَانَتْ يَدَا ٱلرَّجُلِ فَوْقَ رَأْسِهِ لَمَّا وَقَعَ أَسِيرًا.

٥. إِنَّ مَطْلَبَيْ مِصْرَ هُمَا ٱنْسِحَابُ ٱلْجَيْشِ ٱلْبَرِيطَانِيِّ مِنْ قَنَاةِ ٱلسُّوَيْسِ وَوَحْدَةُ وَادِي ٱلنِّيلِ (Nile).

٦. ذَهَبَ مَنْدُوبُ ٱلْمَلِكِ ٱبْنِ ٱلسُّعُودِ إِلَى ٱلْبَحْرَيْنِ بِٱلطَّيَّارَةِ وَبَحَثَ مَعَ سُمُوِّ شَيْخِهَا أَمْرَ ٱلزَّيْتِ تَحْتَ ٱلْبَحْرِ ٱلْوَاقِعِ بَيْنَ دَوْلَتَيْهِمَا، وَمَوْقِفَ هَاتَيْنِ ٱلدَّوْلَتَيْنِ مِنْهُ.

Translate into Arabic:

1. When I was in Beirut, I visited its two universities.
2. Ḥusayn and Fayṣal the Second are two Hāshimi kings.
3. Suʿūd and Fayṣal, the two sons of King ʿAbd al-ʿAzīz, have two big positions in the state.
4. America and Britain fought Germany in two world wars.
5. Layla, the beloved of Qays, had [two] beautiful eyes.

CHAPTER XXIII

PERFECT VERBS IN THE PLURAL
SOUND PLURAL NOUNS

I. ILLUSTRATIVE TEXT

1. When I was a teacher in the National College and

   my wife was also a teacher in it,

   ١. لَمَّا كُنْتُ مُعَلِّمًا فِي ٱلْكُلِّيَّةِ ٱلْوَطَنِيَّةِ

   وَكَانَتْ زَوْجَتِي مُعَلِّمَةً فِيهَا أَيْضًا،

2. we went with a group, in which were (both) teachers (m.) and teachers (f.), to visit the city of Damascus.

   ٢. ذَهَبْنَا مَعَ فَرِيقٍ فِيهِ مُعَلِّمُونَ

   وَمُعَلِّمَاتٌ لِزِيَارَةِ مَدِينَةِ دَمَشْقَ.

3. The group stayed in the Hotel Umayyah. Then they divided into two sections.

   ٣. وَقَدْ نَزَلَ ٱلْجَمِيعُ فِي فُنْدُقِ أُمَيَّةَ

   وَثُمَّ ٱنْقَسَمُوا إِلَى قِسْمَيْنِ.

4. The teachers (f.) went out to al-Ḥamīdīyah Sūq and

   bought from it what they needed and what pleased their eye.

   ٤. فَٱلْمُعَلِّمَاتُ خَرَجْنَ إِلَى ٱلسُّوقِ ٱلْحَمِيدِيَّةِ

   وَٱبْتَعْنَ مِنْهَا حَاجَتَهُنَّ وَمَا حَلَا فِي عَيْنَيْهِنَّ.

5. As for the teachers (m.), they went to the Umawi mosque. Then they visited the tomb of Ṣalāḥ al-Dīn (*literally*, rectitude of the religion).

   ٥. أَمَّا ٱلْمُعَلِّمُونَ فَقَصَدُوا ٱلْجَامِعَ ٱلْأَمَوِيَّ.

   ثُمَّ زَارُوا قَبْرَ صَلَاحِ ٱلدِّينِ.

6. When the group met in the hotel in the afternoon, and the teachers (f.) learned that the teachers (m.) had

   ٦. وَلَمَّا ٱلْتَقَى ٱلْجَمِيعُ فِي ٱلْفُنْدُقِ بَعْدَ

   ٱلظُّهْرِ وَعَلِمَتِ ٱلْمُعَلِّمَاتُ أَنَّ ٱلْمُعَلِّمِينَ

89

visited that famous mosque without them, they became angry and said to the teachers (m.):

زَارُوا ذٰلِكَ ٱلْجَامِعَ ٱلْمَشْهُورَ بِدُونِهِنَّ غَضِبْنَ وَقُلْنَ لِلْمُعَلِّمِينَ :

7. "You went to the Umawi mosque without us despite the fact

٧. '' إِنَّكُمْ ذَهَبْتُمْ إِلَى ٱلْجَامِعِ ٱلْأُمَوِيِّ بِدُونِنَا مَعَ أَنَّهُ

that the visiting of it was our desire . . . !"

كَانَتْ بِوُدِّنَا نَحْنُ زِيَارَتُهُ . . . ! ''

8. When their anger had subsided, the group headed

٨. وَلَمَّا سَكَتَ عَنْهُنَّ ٱلْغَضَبُ تَوَجَّهَ ٱلْجَمِيعُ

towards al-Ẓāhirīyah library and saw the old manuscripts in it.

إِلَى ٱلْمَكْتَبَةِ ٱلظَّاهِرِيَّةِ وَشَاهَدُوا ٱلْمَخْطُوطَاتِ ٱلْقَدِيمَةَ فِيهَا .

9. After the employees of the library had offered them

٩. وَبَعْدَ أَنْ قَدَّمَ لَهُمْ مُوَظَّفُو ٱلْمَكْتَبَةِ

[the] coffee, they returned to the hotel where they spent the night [there].

ٱلْقَهْوَةَ رَجَعُوا إِلَى ٱلْفُنْدُقِ حَيْثُ قَضَوْا لَيْلَتَهُمْ هُنَاكَ .

II. GRAMMATICAL ANALYSIS

1. أَيْضًا 'also' is an adverb.

2. The verb ذَهَبْنَا is first person plural perfect. ذَهَبْنَا is in the plural because the plural subject of the verb is not expressed. It is to be noted that there is no dual for the first person. The plural is used instead.

The subject of the nominal clause فِيهِ مُعَلِّمُونَ وَمُعَلِّمَاتٌ is مُعَلِّمُونَ 'teachers' (m.), the plural of مُعَلِّم. It is formed in the nominative case by omitting the case ending of the singular and by suffixing ـُونَ..... This type of plural, which is regular in its formation, is called the sound masculine plural.

90

مُعَلَّمَاتٌ is co-ordinate with مُعَلَّمُونَ and is, therefore, in the nominative case also. It is the plural of مُعَلَّمَة. It is formed by omitting the tā' mar-būṭah of the singular and by suffixing اتُ.... This type of plural is called the sound feminine plural. Many feminine nouns ending with tā' mar-būṭah take the sound feminine plural.

3. اِنْقَسَمُوا is third person masculine plural perfect of the Form VII verb اِنْقَسَمَ. The final alif of the third person masculine plural of verbs is not pronounced and is only added to prevent confusion of the و of the plural with the conjunction وَ 'and.'

4. The verb خَرَجْنَ is third person feminine plural perfect. It is in the plural because the plural subject of the verb is not expressed.

The verb اِبْتَعْنَ is third person feminine plural of Form VIII of the hollow verb بَاعَ. For loss of the middle radical see Chapter XVIII, section II, 1, (a) and (b).

عَيْنَيْنِ is composed of two words, عَيْن and the pronominal suffix هِنَّ.... (< هِنَّ..., see Chapter XV, section II, 8, note A).

6. The verb عَلِمَتْ is in the singular because the subject of the verb is expressed. It is feminine because the subject of the verb is feminine.

اَلْمُعَلِّمِينَ is in the accusative because it is the subject of a sentence intro-duced by أَنَّ. The accusative of the sound masculine plural is formed by omitting the case ending of the singular and by suffixing يـنَ....

The verb قُلْنَ is third person feminine plural perfect of the hollow verb قَالَ.

(أَ)اَلْمُعَلِّمِينَ is in the genitive because it is object of the preposition لِ.... The genitive and the accusative of the sound masculine plural are iden-tical.

7. إِنَّكُمْ is composed of two words, إِنَّ and the second person masculine plural pronominal suffix كُمْ.... The suffix كُمْ... is in the accusative because it is the subject of a sentence introduced by إِنَّ. It is invariable.

The verb ذَهَبْتُمْ is second person masculine plural perfect.

مَعَ أَنَّ is an idiom meaning *although*. The pronominal suffix ـهُ... in أَنَّهُ is the subject of أَنَّ.

The particles إِنَّ and أَنَّ require a subject; if none is found, the pronominal suffix ـهُ... is introduced to act as such. This pronoun anticipates and represents a subsequent clause which forms the predicate of the sentence introduced by the particle. Thus in this sentence كَانَتْ...زِيَارَتُهُ is the predicate.

بِوُدِّنَا is composed of three words: the preposition ...بِ, the maṣdar وُدّ, and the first person plural pronominal suffix ...نَا.

نَحْنُ 'ourselves' is added for emphasis.

8. ٱلْمَخْطُوطَات is the sound feminine plural of مَخْطُوطَة and is in the accusative case, object of the verb شَاهَدُوا. The sign of the accusative is the final kasrah. Sound feminine plurals take kasrah in the accusative as well as in the genitive.

ٱلْقَدِيمَة is an adjective modifying ٱلْمَخْطُوطَات. It is to be noticed that the adjective is singular although the noun that it modifies is plural.

Adjectives modifying sound feminine plural nouns are feminine singular unless the noun refers to people, in which case the adjective may be either singular or plural.

9. مُوَظَّفُو is the sound masculine plural of مُوَظَّف. The final نْ has been omitted because مُوَظَّفُونَ is in construct with ٱلْمَكْتَبَة.

NOTE A: When a sound masculine plural, regardless of case, is in construct, the final نْ is omitted. (See Chapter XXII, section II, note, for the similar process in the dual.)

The verb قَضَوْا (*قَضَيُوا >) is third person masculine plural perfect of the weak-lām verb قَضَى. In this type of verb the final radical is omitted, and the fatḥah of the medial radical forms a dipthong with the و of the plural.

NOTE B: The most important uses of the sound masculine plural are to form the plurals of:

1. All participles which refer to people.

2. All nisbahs which refer to people.

3. Nouns of the form فَعَّال which refer to people.

4. Adjectives which modify nouns in one of the above categories (optional; broken plurals are also used; see Chapter XXV).

The most important uses of the sound feminine plural are to form the plurals of:

1. Many words ending in ة.

2. Maṣdars of derived verb forms. (The maṣdars of Form II may also take broken plurals.)

3. Nouns of foreign origin.

4. Adjectives modifying a sound feminine plural referring to people (optional; see above, analysis of sentence 8).

III. PRACTICE TEXT

1. In the year known as the year of the Hijrah the Prophet emigrated with a group of Muslims from Mecca to Yathrib.

١. فِي ٱلسَّنَةِ ٱلْمَعْرُوفَةِ بِعَامِ ٱلْهِجْرَةِ هَاجَرَ ٱلنَّبِيُّ مَعَ فَرِيقٍ مِنَ ٱلْمُسْلِمِينَ مِنْ مَكَّةَ إِلَى يَثْرِبَ .

2. After that its name became Medina, that is, the city of the Prophet.

٢. فَأَصْبَحَ ٱسْمُهَا بَعْدَ ذَلِكَ "ٱلْمَدِينَةَ" أَيْ مَدِينَةَ ٱلنَّبِيِّ .

3. The people of Medina called these Meccans, both believers (m.) and believers (f.), who had emigrated with the Prophet, the Emigrants.

٣. وَدَعَا أَهْلُ ٱلْمَدِينَةِ هٰؤُلَاءِ ٱلْمَكِّيِّينَ ٱلَّذِينَ هَاجَرُوا مَعَ ٱلنَّبِيِّ مِنْ مُؤْمِنِينَ وَمُؤْمِنَاتٍ ٱلْمُهَاجِرِينَ .

4. These Emigrants lived as good citizens in Medina.

٤. وَعَاشَ هٰؤُلَاءِ ٱلْمُهَاجِرُونَ مُوَاطِنِينَ صَالِحِينَ فِي ٱلْمَدِينَةِ .

5. They co-operated with its people under the leadership

٥. فَتَعَاوَنُوا مَعَ أَهْلِهَا تَحْتَ قِيَادَةِ

of the Prophet in preserving
Islam from attack by the

Meccans until the signing of a
treaty with them took place.

ٱلنَّبِيّ فِي حِفْظِ ٱلْإِسْلَامِ مِنْ مُهَاجَمَةِ

ٱلْمَكِّيِّينَ حَتَّى جَرَى تَوْقِيعُ مُعَاهَدَةٍ

مَعَهُمْ.

IV. EXERCISES

Translate into English:

١. حَضَرَ ٱلْمُعَلِّمُونَ وَزَوْجَاتُهُمُ ٱجْتِمَاعًا خَطَبَ فِيهِ ٱلدُّكْتُورُ طَهَ حُسَيْنٌ زَعِيمُ ٱلْحَرَكَةِ ٱلْأَدَبِيَّةِ ٱلْحَدِيثَةِ عَنْ تَأْرِيخِ ٱلْأَدَبِ ٱلْعَرَبِيِّ فَحَلَا كَلَامُهُ فِي عَيْنِهِمْ.

٢. فِي ٱلشَّرْقِ ٱلْأَوْسَطِ عَدَدٌ مِنَ ٱلشَّرِكَاتِ ٱلْكَبِيرَةِ لِلزَّيْتِ.

٣. رَأَيْنَا مَعْبَدَ ٱلرُّومَانِيِّينَ فِي بَلْدَةِ بَعْلَبَكَّ وَرَأَيْنَا مَا بَقِيَ مِنْ قُبَّتِهِ.

٤. قَصَدَ لُبْنَانَ بِالطَّيَّارَةِ فَرِيقٌ مِنَ ٱلْمِصْرِيِّينَ لِلِٱصْطِيَافِ فِيهِ وَقَالُوا إِنَّ مَطَارَ بَيْرُوتَ هُوَ أَفْضَلُ مَطَارٍ فِي ٱلشَّرْقِ ٱلْأَوْسَطِ.

٥. ذَهَبَ فَرِيقٌ مِنَ ٱلْمُسْلِمِينَ إِلَى مَكَّةَ وَطَافُوا حَوْلَ ٱلْكَعْبَةِ (Kaaba) قِبْلَةِ ٱلْإِسْلَامِ.

٦. قَالَ مُرَاسِلُ "ٱلْأَهْرَامِ" ٱلْخَاصُّ إِنَّ مَنْدُوبِي ٱلْعِرَاقِ وَمِصْرَ وَسُورِيَّةَ ٱخْتَلَفُوا فِي ٱلرَّأْيِ حَوْلَ سُورِيَّةَ ٱلْكُبْرَى وَحَوْلَ إِصْرَارِ ٱلْمَلِكِ عَبْدِ ٱللهِ عَلَى تَحْقِيقِهَا.

Translate into Arabic:

1. In America there are many Muslims, and they are good citizens.
2. In the past the editors of *al-Ahrām* were Lebanese.
3. The newspaper *al-Miṣri* has correspondents in every great capital in the world.
4. Today I studied Arabic for many hours.
5. Arabic study(es) are among the most recent in the American universities.
6. The teachers (m.) of the school are more numerous than its teachers (f.).

94

CHAPTER XXIV

THE IMPERFECT. THE DOUBLED VERB

I. ILLUSTRATIVE TEXT

1. Shamm al-Nasīm (*literally,* smelling the breeze) is an Egyptian national

   holiday in which the people rejoice and become merry

   because of the appearance of the summer season.

١. "شَمُّ ٱلنَّسِيم" عِيدٌ وَطَنِيٌّ مِصْرِيٌّ

يَفْرَحُ فِيهِ ٱلشَّعْبُ وَيَبْتَهِجُ

لِظُهُورِ فَصْلِ ٱلصَّيْفِ.

2. During it you see [the] families leaving the city

   and heading toward the country where they spend

   a whole day.

٢. وَأَنْتَ تُشَاهِدُ ٱلْعَائِلَاتِ تَخْرُجُ فِيهِ مِنَ

ٱلْمَدِينَةِ وَتَتَوَجَّهُ نَحْوَ ٱلرِّيفِ حَيْثُ تَصْرِفُ

يَوْمًا كَامِلًا.

3. And you see [the] peasants leaving their

   work. Then they play and exchange talk (i.e.

   converse) with the people of their village.

٣. وَتُشَاهِدُ ٱلْفَلَّاحِينَ يَتْرُكُونَ

عَمَلَهُمْ فَيَلْعَبُونَ وَيَتَبَادَلُونَ ٱلْكَلَامَ

مَعَ أَهْلِ قَرْيَتِهِمْ.

4. As for this holiday, it is old, for the

   Egyptians knew it before Islam.

٤. أَمَّا هٰذَا ٱلْعِيدُ فَهُوَ قَدِيمٌ إِذْ

كَانَ ٱلْمِصْرِيُّونَ يَعْرِفُونَهُ قَبْلَ ٱلْإِسْلَامِ.

5. We do not doubt that this festival and the people's

   love for it will last for a long time.

٥. وَنَحْنُ لَا نَشُكُّ فِي أَنَّ هٰذَا ٱلْعِيدَ وَحُبَّ

ٱلشَّعْبِ لَهُ سَوْفَ يَسْتَمِرَّانِ طَوِيلًا.

II. GRAMMATICAL ANALYSIS

1. The verb يَفْرَحُ is third person masculine singular, imperfect of the root form فَرِحَ. The word *imperfect*, as used in reference to the tense of an Arabic verb, means that the action of such a verb has not been completed (see Chapter XV, section II, 1). In this sentence the imperfect corresponds to the present in English.

The conjugation of imperfect verbs is regular except for the vowel of the medial radical of Form I, which is either − − or −́. To ascertain this, a dictionary must be consulted.[1]

NOTE: For the conjugation of imperfect verbs consult Appendix I. يَبْتَهِجُ is third person masculine singular imperfect of the Form VIII verb إِبْتَهَجَ.

It is to be noticed that the relative clause that starts with the verb يَفْرَحُ is not introduced by a relative pronoun because the noun عِيد, which the clause modifies, is indefinite (see Chapter XVI, section II, 3).

2. تُشَاهِدُ is second person masculine singular imperfect of the Form III verb شَاهَدَ. It is to be noticed that the vowel of the prefix تُ... is ḍammah. Any imperfect of a verb whose third person masculine singular perfect has four letters (i.e. Forms II, III, IV) takes ḍammah on the prefix of the imperfect. All other Forms take fatḥah.

The imperfect verb تَخْرُجُ is third person feminine singular. It forms a subordinate clause expressing an act that continues during the time of the main verb تُشَاهِدُ and is best translated by an active participle. When an imperfect follows another verb without an intervening conjunction, this situation usually obtains.

تَخْرُجُ is singular because it does not refer to rational beings. (See Chapter XXII, section II, 1, note.)

تَتَوَجَّهُ is third person feminine singular imperfect of the Form V verb تَوَجَّهَ.

---

[1] J. G. Hava, *Arabic-English Dictionary* (Beirut: Catholic Press, 1951) indicates the medial vowel of the imperfect by putting an *a*, an *i*, or an *o* immediately after the root.

3. The verb يُتْرَكُونَ is a subordinate clause of the same type as تَخْرُجَ in II, 2 above. However, in this case the verb is plural because it refers to rational beings.

يَتَبَادَلُونَ is third person masculine plural imperfect of the Form VI verb تَبَادَلَ.

4. In the verbal sentence introduced by كَانَ the subject of كَانَ is ٱلْمِصْرِيُّونَ and its predicate is يَعْرِفُونَهُ قَبْلَ ٱلْإِسْلَامِ.

This combination of the perfect of كَانَ and the imperfect of another verb gives the idea of continuous or habitual action in the past.

5. لَا is a negative particle which negates an imperfect verb but may not negate a perfect verb.

نَشُكُّ is first person plural imperfect of the doubled verb شَكَّ (< شَكَكَ*). A doubled verb is one in which the second and third radicals are the same and in which the second radical has no vowel. The two radicals are, therefore, written together with shaddah. In the imperfect the vowel which would have been on the second radical is shifted to the first (which in a regular verb would have had sukūn).

سَوْفَ and its contraction, the prefix ...ـَ, are particles used with the imperfect to indicate futurity.

يَسْتَمِرَّانِ is third person masculine dual imperfect of Form X of the doubled verb مَرَّ.

III. PRACTICE TEXT

1. We, the Muslims, consider the glorious Koran the Book of God.	١. نَحْنُ ٱلْمُسْلِمُونَ نَعْتَبِرُ ٱلْقُرْآنَ ٱلْكَرِيمَ كِتَابَ ٱللهِ.
2. We sanctify it, and we recite it on many occasions.	٢. فَنَحْنُ نُقَدِّسُهُ وَنَقْرَأُهُ فِي مُنَاسَبَاتٍ عَدِيدَةٍ.
3. It accompanies us in school when (we are) learning Arabic.	٣. وَهُوَ يُرَافِقُنَا فِي ٱلْمَدْرَسَةِ عِنْدَ دِرَاسَةِ ٱلْعَرَبِيَّةِ.
4. We use it at prayer.	٤. وَنَسْتَعْمِلُهُ عِنْدَ ٱلصَّلَاةِ.

97

5. It forms the primary foundation for Islamic law.

٥. وَيُشَكِّلُ ٱلْأَسَاسَ ٱلْأَوَّلَ لِلشَّرِيعَةِ ٱلْإِسْلَامِيَّةِ.

6. We believe in its uncreatedness because it

is a copy of the Mother of the Book, that is,

the tablet preserved in heaven.

٦. وَنَحْنُ نَعْتَقِدُ بِعَدَمِ خَلْقِهِ لِأَنَّهُ

نُسْخَةٌ عَنْ أُمِّ ٱلْكِتَابِ — أَيِ

ٱللَّوْحِ ٱلْمَحْفُوظِ فِي ٱلسَّمَاءِ.

7. As for the Mu'tazilah (school), it believed in its creation.

٧. أَمَّا ٱلْمُعْتَزِلَةُ فَكَانَتْ تَعْتَقِدُ بِخَلْقِهِ.

IV. EXERCISES

Translate into English:

١. مِنَ ٱلْمَعْرُوفِ أَنَّ ٱلْمُسْلِمِينَ يَتَّفِقُونَ ٱلْيَوْمَ عَلَى عَدَمِ خَلْقِ ٱلْقُرْآنِ، وَلَكِنَّهُمْ كَانُوا يَخْتَلِفُونَ فِي ٱلرَّأْيِ حَوْلَ هَذَا ٱلْأَمْرِ فِي ٱلْمَاضِي.

٢. يَجْمَعُ ٱلْإِسْلَامُ بَيْنَ ٱلْمَلِكِ وَٱلْفَقِيرِ، وَيَعْتَبِرُ كُلَّ رَجُلٍ كَالثَّانِي.

٣. يَتَوَجَّهُ ٱلْمُسْلِمُونَ مَرَّةً فِي ٱلسَّنَةِ إِلَى مَكَّةَ.

٤. إِنِّي أَفْرَحُ وَتَبْتَهِجُ نَفْسِي عِنْدَ ظُهُورِ فَصْلِ ٱلرَّبِيعِ.

٥. سَوْفَ نَجْمَعُ فَرِيقًا مِنَ ٱلْمُوَاطِنِينَ هَذِهِ ٱللَّيْلَةَ وَنَبْتَهِجُ لِأَنَّ ٱلْيَوْمَ هُوَ يَوْمُ زَوَاجِ زَعِيمِ ٱلْبَلْدَةِ.

Translate into Arabic:

1. Co-operation between a man and his wife is a great responsibility.
2. Their army is withdrawing in the desert under violent pressure from our airplanes.
3. The Koran begins with "al-Fātiḥah," which every Muslim uses in his prayer.
4. Western civilization is advancing rapidly in science because it sanctifies personal responsibility.
5. I shall see the minister of interior upon his return from summering in Lebanon.

BROKEN PLURALS. OTHER DIPTOTES.
OTHER FEMININE ENDINGS

I. ILLUSTRATIVE TEXT

1. In recent days a delegation of leaders who

   represent the Egyptian opposition parties was formed.

١. تَأَلَّفَ فِي ٱلْأَيَّامِ ٱلْأَخِيرَةِ وَفْدٌ مِنْ زُعَمَاءَ يُمَثِّلُونَ ٱلْأَحْزَابَ ٱلْمِصْرِيَّةَ ٱلْمُعَارِضَةَ.

2. It went to the royal palace in protest against

   the irregular actions which the President of the Council

   of Ministers carried out

٢. وَقَصَدَ ٱلْقَصْرَ ٱلْمَلَكِيَّ مُحْتَجًّا عَلَى أَعْمَالٍ خَرْقَاءَ قَامَ بِهَا رَئِيسُ مَجْلِسِ ٱلْوُزَرَاءِ

3. when he expelled the senators belonging to the

   opposition parties from the senate,

٣. لَمَّا أَخْرَجَ ٱلشُّيُوخَ ٱلتَّابِعِينَ لِلْأَحْزَابِ ٱلْمُعَارِضَةِ مِنْ مَجْلِسِ ٱلشُّيُوخِ.

4. and appointed other senators from among friends

   and protégés who had aided him in the elections.

٤. وَعَيَّنَ شُيُوخًا آخَرِينَ مِنْ أَصْدِقَاءَ وَمَحَاسِيبَ سَاعَدُوهُ فِي ٱلْٱنْتِخَابَاتِ.

5. At (the time of) the exit of the delegation from the palace

   a number of newspaper correspondents met it,

٥. وَعِنْدَ خُرُوجِ ٱلْوَفْدِ مِنَ ٱلْقَصْرِ قَابَلَهُ عَدَدٌ مِنْ مُرَاسِلِي ٱلْجَرَائِدِ،

6. and they asked it about the matters around which the

   discussion had especially revolved.

٦. فَسَأَلُوهُ عَنِ ٱلشُّؤُونِ ٱلَّتِي دَارَ حَوْلَهَا ٱلْبَحْثُ خَاصَّةً.

99

7. One of the leaders said that His Majesty the King

٧. فَقَالَ أَحَدُ ٱلزُّعَمَاءِ إِنَّ جَلَالَةَ ٱلْمَلِك

had agreed to most of the well-known demands of the opposition,

يُوَافِقُ عَلَى مُعْظَمِ مَطَالِبِ ٱلْمُعَارَضَةِ ٱلْمَعْرُوفَةِ،

8. and that he would study all the ways which would aid in solving this problem amicably.

٨. وَإِنَّهُ سَوْفَ يَدْرُسُ جَمِيعَ ٱلطُّرُقِ ٱلَّتِي تُسَاعِدُ عَلَى حَلٍّ وَدِّيٍّ لِهٰذِهِ ٱلْمُشْكِلَةِ.

II. GRAMMATICAL ANALYSIS

1. اَلْأَيَّام is the broken plural of يَوْم formed on the pattern of أَفْعَال (أَيَّام > *أَيْوَام).

Broken plurals are different from sound plurals (see Chapter XXIII) in that they are not formed by the addition of regular endings to the singular. Rather, they are formed by internal changes and/or additions to the singular, according to some thirty patterns, the most important of which are listed below in II, 8, note A. Broken plurals occur much more frequently than sound plurals and are used for all situations not governed by the rules for sound plurals (see Chapter XXIII, section II, 9, NOTE B).

It is to be noticed that certain singular patterns tend to take certain broken plural patterns. There are, however, so many exceptions to these tendencies that it is advisable to learn the plural of each word individually.

اَلْأَخِيرَة is an adjective modifying اَلْأَيَّام. It is to be noted that this adjective is feminine singular although it modifies a plural.

Broken plurals are treated grammatically as feminine singulars unless they refer to people in which case they may be treated either as feminine singulars, or as masculine or feminine plurals depending on the gender of the people.

زُعَمَاء is the broken plural of زَعِيم formed on the pattern of فُعَلَاء. Broken plurals of this pattern are diptote (see above, Chapter XIV, section II, 1; for a list of other patterns which are diptote see below, II, 8, note B).

اَلْأَحْزَاب is the broken plural of حِزْب on the pattern of أَفْعَال.

2. خَرْقَاء is the feminine of أَخْرَق formed on the فَعْلَاء pattern. This pattern is used for the feminine of those words of the أَفْعَل pattern which denote colors and defects but not of comparatives and superlatives. Feminines of this pattern are diptote.

The feminine is used in this case because the adjective modifies a broken plural.

The broken plural أَلْوُزَرَاء, although of the فُعَلَاء pattern, is treated as a triptote because it is definite (see Chapter XIV, section II, 1).

3. أَلشُّيُوخ is the broken plural of شَيْخ on the pattern of فُعُول (cf. خُرُوج in I, 5, above which is a maṣdar).

4. أَصْدِقَاء is the broken plural of صَدِيق on the pattern of أَفْعِلَاء which is diptote.

مَحَاسِيب is the broken plural of مَحْسُوب on the pattern of فَعَالِيل which is diptote.

5. أَلْجَرَائِد is the broken plural of جَرِيدَة on the pattern of فَعَائِل which is diptote when indefinite.

6. The feminine singular relative pronoun أَلَّتِي is here used because it refers to a broken plural.

The pronominal suffix ‫ـهَا‬... in حَوْلَهَا refers to أَلشُّؤُون and is feminine singular because أَلشُّؤُون is a broken plural.

NOTE: A relative clause in Arabic always needs an additional pronoun which refers back to the antecedent. This pronoun, called 'ā'id, is either expressed or implied. It is expressed in a relative clause whose subject (in a nominal clause) or the subject of whose verb (in a verbal clause) is other than the antecedent. It is implied in a relative clause whose subject or the subject of whose verb is the same as the antecedent (as was the case in Chapter XVI, section I, 3 and 4).

7. مَطَالِب is the broken plural of مَطْلَب formed on the pattern of فَعَالِل.

8. أَلطُّرُق is the broken plural of طَرِيق formed on the pattern of فُعُل.

تُسَاعِد is the third person feminine singular because its subject refers to a broken plural (أَلطُّرُق).

NOTE A: The most common broken plural patterns are the following:

أَفْعَالُ	فُعَلٌ
فُعُولٌ	فُعَّالٌ
فُعَلَاءُ	أَفْعِلَةٌ
فِعَالٌ	فَعْلَى
أَفْعِلَاءُ	فُعْلَانٌ
(أَفَاعِيلُ، تَفَاعِيلُ، مَفَاعِيلُ) فَعَالِيلُ	(الْفَعَالِي) فَعَالٍ
(فَوَاعِلُ، أَفَاعِلُ، تَفَاعِلُ، مَفَاعِلُ، فَعَائِلُ) فَعَالِلُ	فَعَالَى
فُعُلٌ	
أَفْعُلٌ	
فُعْلَانٌ	

For a complete list of broken plural patterns consult William Wright, *A Grammar of the Arabic Language* (Cambridge: The University Press, 1896), I, pp. 199–233.

NOTE B: In addition to the words which are diptote because they are foreign proper nouns or of the أَفْعَلُ pattern (see Chapter XIV, section II, 1), the following are the most common diptotes:

1. Broken plurals of the patterns أَفْعِلَاءُ، فَعَالِلُ، فَعَالِيلُ، فُعَلَاءُ.
2. The feminine pattern فَعْلَاءُ[1].
3. Some adjectives of the فَعْلَانُ pattern.
4. All proper names that end in tā' marbūṭah.

For a more thorough discussion of diptotes consult G. W. Thatcher, *Arabic Grammar* (Heidelberg: Julius Groos, 1927), pp. 274–277.

---

[1] In fact it may be said that any noun ending in ـَاءُ... in which the hamzah is not a radical is diptote.

III. PRACTICE TEXT

1. Among the important matters which the men of

   education in the Arab countries are studying

   is the plan of unifying education in them.

2. However, there are many problems which block the

   path of this unification.

3. Among them is (the fact) that the Arab world is

   divided into numerous states,

4. and thus unification of the methods of education

   and the organization of schools in them on a common foundation is difficult.

5. But there are many encouraging things,

6. among which is (the fact) that schools in (both)

   cities and villages have improved,

7. and that the budgets of departments of education

   in those countries which were under mandate or (were)

   colonies have increased since the withdrawal of

   the foreigners.

١. مِنَ ٱلْأُمُورِ ٱلْمُهِمَّةِ ٱلَّتِي يَدْرُسُهَا

رِجَالُ ٱلتَّرْبِيَةِ فِي ٱلْبِلَادِ ٱلْعَرَبِيَّةِ

مَشْرُوعُ تَوْحِيدِ ٱلتَّعْلِيمِ فِيهَا .

٢. غَيْرَ أَنَّ هُنَالِكَ مَشَاكِلَ كَثِيرَةً تَعْتَرِضُ

سَبِيلَ هٰذَا ٱلتَّوْحِيدِ .

٣. مِنْهَا أَنَّ ٱلْعَالَمَ ٱلْعَرَبِيَّ

مُنْقَسِمٌ إِلَى دُوَلٍ عَدِيدَةٍ،

٤. وَلِذٰلِكَ يَصْعُبُ تَوْحِيدُ طُرُقِ ٱلتَّعْلِيمِ

وَتَنْظِيمُ ٱلْمَدَارِسِ فِيهَا عَلَى أَسَاسٍ مُشْتَرَكٍ .

٥. وَلٰكِنَّ هُنَالِكَ أُمُورًا كَثِيرَةً مُشَجِّعَةً،

٦. مِنْهَا أَنَّ ٱلْمَدَارِسَ فِي

ٱلْمُدُنِ وَٱلْقُرَى تَحَسَّنَتْ،

٧. وَأَنَّ مِيزَانِيَّاتِ دَوَائِرِ ٱلتَّرْبِيَةِ

فِي تِلْكَ ٱلْبُلْدَانِ ٱلَّتِي كَانَتْ تَحْتَ ٱلْٱنْتِدَابِ

أَوْ مُسْتَعْمَرَاتٍ قَدْ زَادَتْ مُنْذُ ٱنْسِحَابِ

ٱلْأَجَانِبِ .

IV. EXERCISES

Translate into English:

١. في رَأْي ٱلْأَجَانِبِ أَنَّ تَنْظِيمَ ٱلْمُدُنِ وَٱلْقُرَى فِي ٱلْبُلْدَانِ ٱلْعَرَبِيَّةِ لَا يَتْبَعُ ٱلطُّرُقَ ٱلْغَرْبِيَّةَ.

٢. لِي أَصْدِقَاءُ كَثِيرُونَ فِي ٱلدَّوَائِرِ ٱلْحُكُومِيَّةِ؛ أَحَدُهُمْ يَشْغَلُ وَظِيفَةَ رَئِيسٍ لِلْمِيزَانِيَّةِ.

٣. إِنَّ تَعَاوُنَ ٱلْبِلَادِ ٱلْعَرَبِيَّةِ فِي ٱلشُّؤُونِ ٱلْعَسْكَرِيَّةِ وَٱلْاقْتِصَادِيَّةِ يُشَجِّعُ عَلَى تَأْمِينِ مُسْتَقْبِلٍ أَحْسَنَ مِنَ ٱلْمَاضِي.

٤. إِجْتَمَعَ رَئِيسُ ٱلْوُزَرَاءِ بِفَرِيقٍ مِنْ مُحَرِّرِي ٱلْجَرَائِدِ وَزُعَمَاءِ أَحْزَابِ ٱلْمُعَارَضَةِ مَرَّاتٍ عَدِيدَةً فِي ٱلْأَيَّامِ ٱلْأَخِيرَةِ وَبَحَثَ مَعَهُمْ مَطَالِبَهُمُ ٱلْمُهِمَّةَ وَقَدَّمَ لَهُمْ تَعَهُّدًا بِتَحْقِيقِهَا.

Translate into Arabic:

1. The Arab states face today many problems which were caused by the World War.

2. After the last election the new ministry expelled many of the protégés of His Majesty the King.

3. The men who accompanied the Prophet in the emigration from Mecca to Medina were strugglers for the cause of (along the path of) God.

4. The affairs of state are a great responsibility for the men of authority.

CHAPTER XXVI

REVIEW

١. جَلَالَةُ مَلِكِ مِصْرَ مُتَحَدِّرٌ مِنْ عَائِلَةٍ أَجْنَبِيَّةٍ .

٢. فِي ٱلْحَرْبِ ٱلْعَالَـمِيَّةِ ٱلْأُولَى جَرَى تَحْوِيلٌ لِٱسْمِ ٱلْحَاكِمِ فِي مِصْرَ مِنْ " خُدَيْوِيٍّ " إِلَى " سُلْطَانٍ ". ثُمَّ جَرَى تَحْوِيلُ هٰذَا ٱلِٱسْمِ إِلَى " مَلِكٍ " بَعْدَ تِلْكَ ٱلْحَرْبِ .

٣. قَادَ ٱلْجَنَرَالُ " أَيْزِنْهَاوَرْ " (Eisenhower) جَيْشَ ٱلدَّ فَاعِ ٱلتَّابِعَ لِلدُّوَلِ ٱلْغَرْبِيَّةِ .

٤. جَرَى فَتْحُ قَنَاةٍ بَحْرِيَّةٍ فِي أَرْضِ " بَنَامَا " (Panama) وَهِيَ دَوْلَةٌ فِي أَمْرِيكَا ٱلْوُسْطَى .

٥. لَمَّا سَافَرْتُ إِلَى لُبْنَانَ ٱلْتَقَيْتُ بِمُوَاطِنٍ فَلَّاحٍ فَقِيرٍ يَسْكُنُ تَحْتَٱلسَّمَاءِ فَأَخَذْتُهُ إِلَى بَيْتِي وَقَدَّمْتُ لَهُ حَاجَتَهُ وَسَاعَدْتُهُ فِي أُمُورٍ عَدِيدَةٍ غَيْرِهَا فَفَرِحَ وَٱبْتَهَجَ .

٦. إِنَّ مَوْقِفَ مِصْرَ فِي ٱلْإِصْرَارِ عَلَى مَطْلَبِهَا ، أَيْ وَحْدَةِ وَادِي ٱلنَّيلِ ، رَاجِعٌ إِلَى ضَغْطِ ٱلشَّعْبِ ٱلْمِصْرِيِّ لِخُرُوجِ ٱلْأَجَانِبِ مِنْ ذٰلِكَ ٱلْوَادِي وَلِتَحْقِيقِ ٱلِٱسْتِقْلَالِ ٱلْكَامِلِ .

٧. بِمُنَاسَبَةِ ٱلِٱنْتِخَابَاتِ زَادَ جَلَالَةُ ٱلْمَلِكِ عَبْدِ ٱللهِ عَدَدَ ٱلشُّيُوخِ فِي ٱلْمَجْلِسِ لِأَنَّ ٱلِٱنْتِخَابَاتِ جَرَتْ فِي شَرْقِ ٱلْأُرْدُنِّ (Jordan) وَغَرْبِهِ أَيْضًا .

٨. إِبْتَدَأَ ٱلِٱنْتِدَابُ ٱلْبَرِيطَانِيُّ عَلَى ٱلْعِرَاقِ بَعْدَ تَوْقِيعِ ٱلْمُعَاهَدَةِ ٱلْمَعْرُوفَةِ بِمُعَاهَدَةِ " قَرْسَايَ " (Versailles).

٩. لَيْسَ ٱلشِّعْرُ ٱلْغَزَلِيُّ ٱلْعَرَبِيُّ غَيْرَ مِرْآةٍ لِرُوحِ حَيَاةِ ٱلصَّحْرَاءِ ٱلْعَرَبِيَّةِ ٱلَّتِي شَكَّلَتْ ذٰلِكَ ٱلشِّعْرَ.

١٠. سَأَلَ نَائِبٌ فِي ٱلْبَرْلَمَانِ ٱلْبَرِيطَانِيِّ بَعْدَ ظُهْرِ ٱلْيَوْمِ وَزِيرَ ٱلدَّاخِلِيَّةِ عَنِ ٱلِٱجْتِمَاعِ ٱلَّذِي دَعَا إِلَيْهِ حِزْبُ ٱلْحُكُومَةِ لِبَحْثِ عَقْدِ ٱنْتِخَابَاتٍ عَامَّةٍ فِي هٰذَا ٱلْعَامِ وَٱعْتَرَضَ عَلَى ذٰلِكَ ٱلِٱجْتِمَاعِ.

١١. عَلَمُ ٱلْأُمَّةِ هُوَ مِثَالٌ لِمَجْدِهَا، وَمَا دَامَ[1] ٱلشَّعْبُ يُقَدِّمُ لَهُ ٱلْحُبَّ وَٱلْإِخْلَاصَ يَسْتَمِرُّ مَحْفُوظًا.

١٢. إِتَّصَلَ ٱبْنِي بِي بِٱلتِّلِفُونِ بَعْدَ ٱلظُّهْرِ وَطَلَبَ إِذْنًا بِٱلْخُرُوجِ إِلَى ٱلرِّيفِ مَعَ أَصْدِقَائِهِ لِحُضُورِ عِيدِ شَمِّ ٱلنَّسِيمِ. فَٱسْتَأْجَرَ هُوَ وَأَصْدِقَاؤُهُ سَيَّارَةً فَرَكِبُوهَا وَطَافُوا بِهَا فِي ٱلطُّرُقِ ٱلرِّيفِيَّةِ ٱلْبَعِيدَةِ وَلَعِبُوا مُدَّةَ سَاعَةٍ.

١٣. تَقُولُ ٱلدَّوَائِرُ ٱلرَّسْمِيَّةُ إِنَّ ٱلْقِيَادَةَ ٱلْعَسْكَرِيَّةَ وَجَّهَتْ جَيْشًا لِمُهَاجَمَةِ ٱلْعَاصِمَةِ، فَٱنْقَسَمَ ٱلْجَيْشُ سَرِيعًا إِلَى قِسْمَيْنِ زَحَفَ أَحَدُهُمَا إِلَى ٱلْعَاصِمَةِ نَفْسِهَا وَتَقَدَّمَ مِنْهَا وَدَارَ ٱلثَّانِي حَوْلَهَا فَٱحْتَلَّ جَمِيعَ ٱلطُّرُقِ ٱلَّتِي تَخْرُجُ مِنْهَا فَمَنَعَ أَهْلَهَا مِنَ ٱلْخُرُوجِ مِنْهَا وَوَقَعَ ٱلْمَلِكُ أَسِيرًا فِي يَدِهِ.

١٤. وَجَّهَ مُحَمَّدٌ عَلِيٌّ ٱبْنَهُ إِبْرَاهِيمَ إِلَى سُورِيَّةَ فَجَرَى فَتْحُهَا عَلَى يَدِهِ وَأَخْرَجَ ٱلْحُكُومَةَ ٱلتُّرْكِيَّةَ مِنْهَا.

١٥. فِي مَكْتَبَتِي مَخْطُوطَةٌ تُمَثِّلُ أَقْدَمَ نُسْخَةٍ لِكِتَابٍ عَنِ ٱلشَّرِيعَةِ ٱلْإِسْلَامِيَّةِ، وَعُنْوَانُهَا عَلَى صَفْحَتِهَا ٱلْأُولَى مَكْتُوبٌ بِمَاءِ ٱلذَّهَبِ.

١٦. كَانَتِ ٱلْكَعْبَةُ مَعْبَدًا لِلْعَرَبِ قَبْلَ ٱلْإِسْلَامِ.

---

[1] The verb دَامَ preceded by مَا means *as long as.*

WEAK VERBS IN THE IMPERFECT

I. ILLUSTRATIVE TEXT

1. The traveller from Beirut to Damascus passes by

   several summer-resort villages spread out on

   both sides of the road in the mountains.

٠١ إِنَّ ٱلْمُسَافِرَ مِنْ بَيْرُوتَ إِلَى ٱلشَّامِ[1] يَمُرُّ بِعِدَّةِ قُرًى لِلْٱصْطِيَافِ مُنْتَشِرَةٍ عَلَى جَانِبَيِ ٱلطَّرِيقِ فِي ٱلْجِبَالِ.

2. When he reaches Ẓahr al-Baydar and begins to look (*literally*,

   changes his looking) to the east, he sees the fertile plain of al-Biqāʿ stretch-

   ing from north to south.

٠٢ وَعِنْدَمَا يَصِلُ إِلَى ظَهْرِ ٱلْبَيْدَرِ وَيُحَوِّلُ نَظَرَهُ إِلَى ٱلشَّرْقِ يَرَى سَهْلَ ٱلْبِقَاعِ ٱلْخَصِيبَ مُمْتَدًّا مِنَ ٱلشَّمَالِ إِلَى ٱلْجَنُوبِ.

3. In front of him the town of Shutūrah appears with

   its beautiful gardens.

٠٣ وَتَبْدُو أَمَامَهُ بَلْدَةُ شَتُورَةَ بِجَنَائِنِهَا ٱلْجَمِيلَةِ.

4. From a distance looms the head of a white mountain—Mount Hermon.

٠٤ وَيَلُوحُ مِنْ بُعْدٍ رَأْسُ جَبَلٍ أَبْيَضَ وَهُوَ جَبَلُ ٱلشَّيْخِ.

5. When the traveller resumes his journeying beyond that

   town in the anti-Lebanon mountains, he almost thinks

   himself in the desert because of the extreme dryness.

٠٥ وَإِذْ يَسْتَأْنِفُ ٱلْمُسَافِرُ سَيْرَهُ بَعْدَ تِلْكَ ٱلْبَلْدَةِ فِي جِبَالِ لُبْنَانَ ٱلشَّرْقِيَّةِ يَكَادُ يَظُنُّ نَفْسَهُ فِي ٱلصَّحْرَاءِ لِشِدَّةِ ٱلْجَفَافِ.

[1] The word ٱلشَّامُ (or ٱلشَّامُ) is used both for Syria and for Damascus, its capital; see above, Chapter XIV, footnote 1.

6. But when he draws near the city of Damascus, he finds the trees, orchards, and gardens which the Barada river waters.

٦. وَلٰكِنَّهُ عِنْدَمَا يَقْتَرِبُ مِنْ مَدِينَةِ ٱلشَّأْمِ يَجِدُ ٱلْأَشْجَارَ وَٱلْبَسَاتِينَ وَٱلْجَنَائِنَ ٱلَّتِي يَرْوِيهَا نَهْرُ بَرَدَى.

7. His soul is rested (because) of them.

٧. فَتَسْتَرِيحُ نَفْسُهُ لَهَا.

8. Then he sees a broad street which leads to the heart of the city, which (heart) is right next to the river.

٨. ثُمَّ يَرَى شَارِعًا عَرِيضًا يُؤَدِّي إِلَى قَلْبِ ٱلْمَدِينَةِ ٱلَّذِي يَلِي ٱلنَّهْرَ.

II. GRAMMATICAL ANALYSIS

1. The word قُرًى is in the genitive case. Any indefinite word which ends in alif has fatḥah tanwīn over the preceding letter regardless of case.

2. يَصِلُ is the third person masculine singular imperfect of وَصَلَ. Most verbs whose first radical is wāw lose the wāw in the imperfect.

يَرَى is third person masculine singular imperfect of رَأَى. In this verb, which occurs frequently, the hamzah is dropped in the imperfect and in the Form IV perfect.

مُمْتَدًّا is the active participle of the Form VIII verb إِمْتَدَّ.

3. تَبْدُو is the third person feminine singular imperfect of بَدَا.

In the imperfect indicative of weak-lām verbs the final radical may be determined from the vowel of the middle radical.[2] If the vowel of the middle radical is ḍammah, as in the case of تَبْدُو, the final radical is an unvowelled wāw. If the vowel of the middle radical is fatḥah, the final radical is alif maqṣūrah, as in يَبْقَى. If the vowel of the middle radical is kasrah, the final radical is an unvowelled yā', as in يَجْرِي.

In the imperfect indicative of the derived forms of weak-lām verbs the final syllable is ...ِي (e.g. يَسْتَدْعِي) except in Forms V and VI where it is ...َى (e.g. يَتَدَاعَى).

[2] For determination of the vowel of the middle radical of the imperfect see Chapter XXIV, section II, 1.

If, however, inflection of the imperfect weak-lām verb also occurs at the end of the word, as in the plural, the final radical frequently drops out (for which see Appendix I).

4. يَلُوحُ is third person masculine singular of the hollow verb لَاحَ.

In the imperfect indicative of underived hollow verbs the middle radical becomes the letter which prolongs the vowel that would be present on the middle radical if the verb were conjugated as a sound verb. It gives up its vowel to the normally unvowelled first radical. Thus يَكَادُ > *يَكْوَدُ > (*كَوَدَ <) كَادَ . Similarly يَلُوحُ > *يَلْوُحُ > (*لَوَحَ <) لَاحَ and يَصِيرُ > *يَصْيِرُ > (*صِيرَ <) صَارَ .

Hollow verbs of Forms II, III, V, VI, and IX are conjugated regularly in the imperfect.

The middle radical of hollow verbs of Forms IV and X is always yā' in accordance with the principle stated above for the underived hollow verb.

The middle radical of hollow verbs of Forms VII and VIII is always a lengthening alif.

5. يَكَادُ is third person masculine singular imperfect of the hollow verb كَادَ. The verb كَادَ may be thought of as an auxiliary verb which adds to the meaning of the main verb (in this case يَظُنُّ) the sense of "almost."

6. يَجِدُ is third person masculine singular imperfect of وَجَدَ.

يَرْوِي is third person masculine singular imperfect of the Form IV verb أَرْوَى.

7. تَسْتَرِيحُ is third person feminine singular imperfect of the Form X verb إِسْتَرَاحَ.

8. يُؤَدِّي is third person masculine singular imperfect of the Form II verb أَدَّى.

يَلِي is third person masculine singular imperfect of the doubly weak verb وَلِيَ. Its conjugation combines the characteristics of both the weak-fā' and the weak-lām verbs.

III. PRACTICE TEXT

1. Dhu al-Ḥijjah is the month of pilgrimage
in Islam.

١. ذُو ٱلْحِجَّةِ هُوَ شَهْرُ ٱلْحَجِّ
فِي ٱلْإِسْلَامِ.

2. In it every Muslim who is able sets out
on the pilgrimage to Mecca the Honored, whatever
the distance from his country might be.

٢. فَفِيهِ يَتَوَجَّهُ كُلُّ مُسْلِمٍ قَادِرٍ
عَلَى ٱلْحَجِّ إِلَى مَكَّةَ ٱلْمُكَرَّمَةِ مَهْمَا
كَانَ بُعْدُ بِلَادِهِ.

3. He enters that city in a sanctified state and
circumambulates the Kaaba and prays thereat.

٣. وَيَدْخُلُ تِلْكَ ٱلْمَدِينَةَ مُحْرِمًا
وَيَطُوفُ بِٱلْكَعْبَةِ وَيُصَلِّي عِنْدَهَا.

4. The pilgrimage begins with the march to Mount 'Arafāt
where the *wuqūf* (halting) takes place.

٤. وَيَبْتَدِئُ ٱلْحَجُّ بِٱلسَّيْرِ إِلَى جَبَلِ عَرَفَاتٍ
حَيْثُ يَجْرِي ٱلْوُقُوفُ.

5. On the tenth day of the month the feast of
al-Aḍḥā occurs. The people rejoice

٥. وَفِي ٱلْيَوْمِ ٱلْعَاشِرِ مِنَ ٱلشَّهْرِ يَكُونُ
عِيدُ ٱلْأَضْحَى. فَيَفْرَحُ ٱلنَّاسُ

6. and every Muslim who is able sacrifices a
sacrificial animal and gives it to the people.

٦. وَيُضَحِّي كُلُّ مُسْلِمٍ قَادِرٍ
ضَحِيَّةً وَيُعْطِيهَا لِلنَّاسِ.

7. Then he undertakes a visit to Medina the
Illuminated, the seat of the Messenger's tomb.

٧. ثُمَّ يَقُومُ بِزِيَارَةِ ٱلْمَدِينَةِ
ٱلْمُنَوَّرَةِ مَرْكَزِ قَبْرِ ٱلرَّسُولِ.

IV. EXERCISES

Translate into English:

١. يَكَادُ يَكُونُ ٱلْمُعَلِّمُ رَسُولًا.

٢. يُضَحِّي ٱلْمُجَاهِدُ بِنَفْسِهِ فِي سَبِيلِ وَطَنِهِ حَتَّى ٱلْمَوْتِ.

٣. مَكَّةُ ٱلْمُكَرَّمَةُ هِيَ ٱلْمَدِينَةُ ٱلْمُهِمَّةُ ٱلْمُقَدَّسَةُ فِي ٱلْإِسْلَامِ وَتَلِيهَا ٱلْمَدِينَةُ ٱلْمُنَوَّرَةُ ٱلْوَاقِعَةُ إِلَى ٱلشَّمَالِ مِنْهَا.

٤. إِنَّ عَدَمَ ٱلْمَسْؤُولِيَّةِ فِي ٱلْحُكْمِ مُشْكِلَةٌ تُؤَدِّي إِلَى أَعْمَالٍ خَرْقَاءَ لَا تَحْلُو لِلشَّعْبِ.

٥. يَعِيشُ ٱلْمُسْلِمُ ٱلصَّالِحُ مُحِبًّا لِلهِ وَرَسُولِهِ بِكُلِّ قَلْبِهِ وَمُجْتَهِدًا فِي خِدْمَةِ ٱلدِّينِ مِنَ ٱلطُّفُولَةِ حَتَّى ٱلْمَوْتِ.

٦. تَقُومُ ٱلْحُكُومَةُ ٱلْيَوْمَ بِحَلِّ جَمِيعِ ٱلْمَشَاكِلِ ٱلدَّاخِلِيَّةِ ٱلْمَعْرُوفَةِ ٱلَّتِي ٱعْتَرَضَتْهَا فِي تَحْقِيقِ ٱلْمَطَالِبِ ٱلْوَطَنِيَّةِ.

Translate into Arabic:

1. Although a new government has come to power, the fundamental problems of the country remain.

2. In summer the people of Cairo rest in the afternoon, but they remain at their work until a late hour.

3. The Iraqi-British treaty gives concessions to the British in the territory of Iraq.

4. The man of the desert lives a poor life economically.

5. The president of the club calls for a meeting once a month.

PARTICIPLES AND MAṢDARS OF WEAK VERBS. ADVERB OF PURPOSE

I. ILLUSTRATIVE TEXT

1. In the year 1929 the late Shaykh Ḥasan

   al-Bannā' founded the society known as the

   Muslim Brethren because he believed that Egypt

   was in need of it.

١. في سَنَة ١٩٢٩ أَسَّسَ ٱلْمَرْحومُ ٱلشَّيْخُ حَسَن ٱلْبَنَّاءُ ٱلْجَمْعِيَّةَ ٱلْمَعْروفَةَ بِٱلْإِخْوانِ ٱلْمُسْلِمِينَ لِأَنَّهُ ٱعْتَقَدَ أَنَّ مِصْرَ كانَتْ مُحْتاجَةً إِلَيْها .

2. That society had, upon its foundation, a

   religious character which called for faith in God and

   obedience to His orders and the orders of His Messenger,

٢. وَكانَتْ تِلْكَ ٱلْجَمْعِيَّةُ عِنْدَ تَأْسِيسِها ذاتَ صِفَةٍ دِينِيَّةٍ تَدْعو إِلَى ٱلْإِيمانِ بِٱللّٰهِ وَٱلِٱنْقِياد لِأَوامِرِهِ وَأَوامِرِ رَسولِهِ

3. and for uprightness in action and for national

   education.

٣. وَإِلَى ٱلِٱسْتِقامَةِ في ٱلْعَمَلِ وَٱلتَّرْبِيَةِ ٱلْوَطَنِيَّةِ .

4. It was founded in answer to the intense desire of some

   Egyptians for the plan of building nationalism on the

   basis of the Islamic religion.

٤. وَقَدْ تَأَسَّسَتْ إِجابَةً لِشِدَّةِ ٱلرَّغْبَةِ لَدَى بَعْضِ ٱلْمِصْرِيِّينَ في مَشْروعِ بِناءِ قَوْمِيَّةٍ عَلَى أَساسِ ٱلدّينِ ٱلْإِسْلامِيِّ .

5. After its confidence in itself grew strong, it

   took on a political character, so it established

٥. وَبَعْدَما ٱشْتَدَّتْ ثِقَتُها بِنَفْسِها ٱتَّخَذَتْ صِفَةً سِياسِيَّةً فَأَقامَتْ

connections with men in
other parties in the
country.

صِلاتٍ مَعَ رِجالِ ٱلْأَحْزابِ ٱلْأُخْرَى في
ٱلْبِلادِ .

6. The result was that the
Muslim Brethren Society
entered the political field,
with the aim of seizing
power, or participating in it,
by methods (which were) not
straight and far from
moderation.

٦. وَكانَتِ ٱلنَّتِيجَةُ أَنْ دَخَلَتْ جَمْعِيَّةُ ٱلْإِخْوانِ
ٱلْمُسْلِمينَ ٱلْمَيْدانَ ٱلسِّياسِيَّ وَمُرادُها
ٱلْإِسْتيلاءُ عَلَى ٱلْحُكْمِ أَوِ ٱلْإِشْتِراكُ فيهِ
بِطُرُقٍ غَيْرِ مُسْتَقيمَةٍ بَعيدَةٍ عَنِ
ٱلْإِعْتِدالِ .

7. But that was not possible
because the government
became angry at it and dissolved it, as it would
dissolve any organization
calling for revolution
against it.

٧. وَلٰكِنَّ ذٰلِكَ ما كانَ بِٱلْمُسْتَطاعِ لِأَنَّ
ٱلْحُكومَةَ
غَضِبَتْ عَلَيْها وَحَلَّتْها كَما
تَحُلُّ أَيَّ مُنْتَدًى داعٍ إِلَى ٱلثَّوْرَةِ
ضِدَّها .

8. After some disturbances the
assassination of its
founder and the manager of
its affairs, Shaykh Ḥasan
al-Bannā', took place. He
passed away a martyr for
his belief. Then Mr. Ḥasan
al-Huḍaybi assumed the
directorship of it. He had
previously occupied a
position as a judge.

٨. وَبَعْدَ بَعْضِ ٱلْإِضْطِراباتِ جَرَى ٱغْتِيالُ
مُؤَسِّسِها وَمُديرِ شُؤُونِها ٱلشَّيْخِ حَسَنِ
ٱلْبَنّاءِ فَذَهَبَ ضَحِيَّةً
إيمانِهِ . ثُمَّ تَوَلَّى إِدارَتَها ٱلْأُسْتاذُ
حَسَنْ ٱلْهُضَيْبِيُّ وَقَدْ شَغَلَ
وَظيفَةَ قاضٍ قَبْلًا .

II. GRAMMATICAL ANALYSIS

1. ٱلْبَنَّاء is formed on the pattern of فَعَّال (see Chapter XXI, section II, 1 and 3) from the root بَنَى. It will be noticed that the weak final radical has changed into a hamzah. In all nouns derived from weak-lām verbs, if the final weak letter is preceded by an alif, it changes into hamzah.

مُحْتَاجَة is active participle of the Form VIII verb إِحْتَاج < حَاج < (حَوَجَ*). It will be noticed that the weak middle radical appears as alif. The passive participle of a Form VIII hollow verb is identical in form with the active participle. The participles of Form VII hollow verbs behave in the same way.

2. ذَات means *owner of, possessor of.* It is the feminine of ذُو (see Chapter XXXII, section II, 7).

صِفَة is a maṣdar of the verb وَصَف. Verbs which have an initial wāw and drop it in the imperfect may form maṣdars on the pattern of عِلَة.

ٱلْإِيمَان is the maṣdar of the Form IV verb آمَن (< أَأْمَنَ*). In verbs whose initial radical is hamzah or wāw, the initial hamzah or wāw changes into yā' under the influence of the preceding kasrah in Form IV maṣdars.

ٱلْٱنْقِيَاد is the maṣdar of the Form VII verb إِنْقَاد. In the maṣdars of the VIIᵗʰ and VIIIᵗʰ Forms of hollow verbs the wāw changes into yā' under the influence of the preceding kasrah.

3. ٱسْتِقَامَة is the maṣdar of the Form X verb إِسْتَقَام. The maṣdars of Forms IV and X of hollow verbs drop the middle radical and suffix tā' marbūṭah.

ٱلتَّرْبِيَة is the maṣdar of the Form II verb رَبَّى, formed on the pattern of تَفْعِلَة (see Chapter XIX, section II, 8, note c). Weak-lām verbs and verbs whose third radical is hamzah always form their maṣdars on this pattern in Form II. It may, however, also be used with sound verbs.

4. إِجَابَة is the maṣdar of the Form IV verb أَجَاب; see II, 3, above.

إِجَابَةً is an adverb of purpose and shows the purpose or motive for which the action was performed. Like other adverbs, the adverb of purpose is in the accusative case.

بِنَاءٌ is a maṣdar of the root form بَنَى formed on the pattern of فَعَالٌ. For the change of the final radical into hamzah, see II, 1, above.

5. ثِقَةٌ is a maṣdar of the verb وَثِقَ formed on the عِلَة pattern.

أَتَّخَذَتْ is third person feminine singular perfect Form VIII of the root أَخَذَ. Note that in Form VIII of أَخَذَ the hamzah is assimilated by the following tā'.

صِلَاتٌ is the plural of another maṣdar of the عِلَة pattern, formed from وَصَلَ.

6. ٱلْمَيْدَانُ is the maṣdar of the verb مَادَ 'to sway', 'to quiver' on the pattern of فَعْلَانٌ. The meaning of ٱلْمَيْدَانُ as *field, arena, public square* is derived from *swaying* or *quivering* > the place where such movements take place.

مُرَادٌ is the passive participle of the Form IV verb أَرَادَ. It will be noticed that the weak middle radical appears as an alif. This change always takes place in the passive participles of hollow verbs of Forms IV and X.

ٱسْتِيلَاءٌ is the maṣdar of the Form X verb إِسْتَوْلَى. The wāw has changed into a yā' under the influence of the preceding kasrah. In the maṣdars of Forms IV and X of weak-fā' verbs the wāw always changes into yā'. In addition, in the word إِسْتِيلَاءٌ the weak third radical has changed into hamzah following the principle explained in II, 1, above.

مُسْتَقِيمَة is the feminine of مُسْتَقِيم, the active participle of the Form X verb إِسْتَقَامَ. It will be noticed that the weak middle radical appears as a yā'. This change always occurs in the active participles of hollow verbs of Forms IV and X.

7. ٱلْمُسْتَطَاعُ is the passive participle of the Form X verb إِسْتَطَاعَ. The middle radical has changed into alif following the principle explained in II, 6, above.

أَيُّ is a noun meaning *any*. It is in construct with the word that it qualifies.

مُنْتَدَى, which is in the genitive case, is the passive participle of the Form VIII verb إِنْتَدَى. Passive participles of derived forms of weak-lām verbs always end in alif maqṣūrah. Since the alif is unvowelled, the preceding fatḥah is nūnated when the word is indefinite. The fatḥah, not being a case ending, does not change, regardless of case.

دَاعٍ is the active participle of the weak-lām verb دَعَا. In certain instances the active participles of weak-lām verbs lose their final radical, and the kasrah of the second radical is nūnated. This is the case whether the participles are of root or derived forms. For the conjugation of these participles, see II, 8, note A, below.

8. اَلْإِضْطِرَابَات is the plural of إِضْطِرَاب, the maṣdar of the Form VIII verb إِضْطَرَب (> اِضْتَرَبَ*). It is to be noticed that the infixed tā' of Form VIII has changed into ṭā' under the influence of the preceding emphatic, ḍād.[1]

مُدِير is the active participle of the Form IV verb أَدَارَ; see discussion under مُسْتَقِيم in II, 6, above.

NOTE A: The declension of the active participle of a weak-lām verb is as follows:

	INDEFINITE		DEFINITE	
	Singular	*Plural*	*Singular*	*Plural*
Nom.	دَاعٍ	دَاعُونَ	اَلدَّاعِي	اَلدَّاعُونَ
Acc.	دَاعِيًا	دَاعِينَ	اَلدَّاعِيَ	اَلدَّاعِينَ
Gen.	دَاعٍ	دَاعِينَ	اَلدَّاعِي	اَلدَّاعِينَ

NOTE B: Most of the irregular participles and maṣdars of weak verbs have been included in sections I and II of this lesson. By and large other participles and maṣdars of weak verbs are regular. For a complete list of them see the paradigms at the end of the volume.

---

[1] For other changes of this type in Form VIII, consult G. W. Thatcher, *Arabic Grammar* (Heidelberg: Julius Groos, 1927), p. 113.

III. PRACTICE TEXT

1. In the year 1943 the Lebanese parliament

   ١. في عام ١٩٤٣ ٱتَّخَذَ ٱلْبَرْلَمانُ ٱللُّبْنانِيُّ

   adopted a resolution amending the constitution

   قَرارًا بِتَعْدِيلِ ٱلدُّسْتُورِ

   and abolishing French authority so that the

   وَبِإِلْغاءِ ٱلسُّلْطَةِ ٱلْفَرَنْسِيَّةِ بِحَيْثُ

   country became independent of foreign administration.

   أَصْبَحَتِ ٱلْبِلادُ مُسْتَقِلَّةً عَنِ ٱلْإِدارَةِ ٱلْأَجْنَبِيَّةِ.

2. But the French government immediately protested this

   ٢. وَلٰكِنَّ ٱلْحُكُومَةَ ٱلْفَرَنْسِيَّةَ ٱحْتَجَّتْ عَلَى هٰذا

   plan and announced that it was not within the power

   ٱلْمَشْرُوعِ حالًا وَأَعْلَنَتْ أَنَّهُ لَيْسَ بِٱسْتِطاعَةِ

   of Lebanon to do that without consulting it (the French government).

   لُبْنانَ عَمَلُ ذٰلِكَ دُونَ ٱسْتِشارَتِها.

3. One black day the French High Commissioner dissolved

   ٣. وَفِي يَوْمٍ أَسْوَدَ حَلَّ ٱلْمَنْدُوبُ ٱلسّامِي

   the Lebanese government and for a short while

   ٱلْفَرَنْسِيُّ ٱلْحُكُومَةَ ٱللُّبْنانِيَّةَ

   imprisoned Shaykh Bishārah al-Khūri, the President of

   وَسَجَنَ ٱلشَّيْخَ بِشارَةَ ٱلْخُورِيَّ رَئِيسَ

   the Republic, and most of the ministers, desiring

   ٱلْجُمْهُورِيَّةِ وَمُعْظَمَ ٱلْوُزَراءِ لِمُدَّةٍ قَصِيرَةٍ

   (thereby) to kill the nationalist spirit.

   رَغْبَةً فِي قَتْلِ ٱلرُّوحِ ٱلْقَوْمِيَّةِ.

4. That action caused revolution, disturbances,

   ٤. وَسَبَّبَ ذٰلِكَ ٱلْعَمَلُ ثَوْرَةً وَٱضْطِراباتٍ

   strikes and assassinations in the country.

   وَإِضْراباتٍ وَٱغْتِيالاتٍ فِي ٱلْبِلادِ.

5. Then the confidence of the Lebanese in themselves

   ٥. فَزادَتْ ثِقَةُ ٱللُّبْنانِيِّينَ بِأَنْفُسِهِمْ

increased, and their faith in
their case was strengthened.

وَٱشْتَدَّ إِيمَانُهُمْ بِقَضِيَّتِهِمْ.

6. They began preparing for de-
scent into the arena of
holy struggle in defense of the
fatherland.

٦. وَأَخَذُوا[2] يَسْتَعِدُّونَ لِلنُّزُولِ إِلَى مَيْدانِ ٱلْجِهادِ ٱلْمُقَدَّسِ دِفاعاً عَنِ ٱلْوَطَنِ.

7. But the French backed down
because of Anglo-American
pressure, and followed the
road of moderation. Then
the anger of the Leban-
ese quieted down, the
country
obtained its independence,
and the people lived in peace.

٧. وَلٰكِنَّ ٱلْفَرَنْسِيِّينَ تَراجَعُوا بِسَبَبِ ٱلضَّغْطِ ٱلْإِنْكِليزِيِّ وَٱلْأَمْرِيكِيِّ وَتَبِعُوا طَرِيقَ ٱلْإِعْتِدالِ فَسَكَتَ غَضَبُ ٱللُّبْنانِيِّينَ وَنالَتِ ٱلْبِلادُ ٱسْتِقْلالَها وَعاشَ ٱلنَّاسُ بِسَلامٍ.

IV. EXERCISES

Translate into English:

١. أَظُنُّ أَنَّ والِدي أَسَّسَ ٱلْمُنْتَدَى ٱلْأَدَبِيَّ قَبْلَ ٱسْتيلاءِ ٱلْإِنْكَليزِ عَلَى ٱلْبِلادِ بِمُدَّةٍ قَصيرَةٍ.

٢. تَحْتاجُ ٱلْجُمْهُورِيَّةُ إِلَى دُسْتُورٍ تَكُونُ ثِقَةُ ٱلشَّعْبِ وَإِيمانُهُ بِهِ شَديدَيْنِ.

٣. أَعْلَنَتْ لَجْنَةُ ٱلْمُعَلِّمِينَ ٱلْإِضْرابَ وَٱتَّخَذَتْ قَراراً بِذٰلِكَ مُحْتَجَّةً عَلَى مُديرِ ٱلْمَدْرَسَةِ وَأَوامِرِهِ ٱلْخَرْقاءِ ٱلْعَديدَةِ.

٤. إِنْتَشَرَ ٱلْقَتْلُ وَٱلْإِغْتِيالُ فِي جَنُوبِ ٱلْمُسْتَعْمَرَةِ وَشَمالِها بَعْدَما سَجَنَتِ ٱلْحُكُومَةُ زُعَماءَ ٱلثَّوْرَةِ ٱلْقَوْمِيِّينَ.

---

[2] For this usage see Chapter XXXV, section II, 6.

٥. لَيْسَ بِالْمُسْتَطَاعِ ٱنْقِيَادُ مُعْظَمِ ٱلشَّعْبِ لِأَوَامِرِ مَحَاسِيبِ ٱلدُّوَلِ ٱلْأَجْنَبِيَّةِ ٱلَّتِي لَهَا صِلَاتٌ مَعَنَا.

٦. قَصَدْتُ إِدَارَةَ ٱلْجَامِعَةِ بَعْدَ ٱلظُّهْرِ لِٱسْتِشَارَتِهَا بِشَأْنِ أُمُورِ ٱلدِّرَاسَةِ فِي ٱلسَّنَةِ ٱلثَّانِيَةِ.

Translate into Arabic:

1. The assassination of Shaykh Ḥasan al-Bannā' caused disturbances in Egypt.

2. The French High Commissioner expelled the Lebanese Prime Minister from his post.

3. The Arab League met and discussed the case for amending the covenant.

4. The director of the Economic Co-operation Administration is an upright man.

5. The government obtained the confidence of the parliament.

JUSSIVE. SUBJUNCTIVE.
INTERROGATIVE

I. ILLUSTRATIVE TEXT

1. Farīd: Do you believe that the United Nations

   has it within its power to preserve world peace?

١. فَرِيدٌ : هَلْ تَعْتَقِدُ أَنَّ ٱلْأُمَمَ ٱلْمُتَّحِدَةَ بِٱسْتِطَاعَتِها أَنْ تُحَافِظَ عَلَى ٱلسَّلَامِ ٱلْعَالَمِيِّ؟

2. Saʿīd: I, personally, do not believe that, because

   the states participating in it have not granted it

   sufficient authority. Therefore, I expect the

   occurrence of another world war.

٢. سَعِيدٌ : إِنَّنِي أَنا شَخْصِيًّا لا أَعْتَقِدُ ذٰلِكَ بِسَبَبِ أَنَّ ٱلدُّوَلَ ٱلْمُشْتَرِكَةَ فِيها لَمْ تَمْنَحْها ٱلسُّلْطَةَ ٱلْكَافِيَةَ. لِذٰلِكَ فَإِنِّي أَنْتَظِرُ أَنْ تَقَعَ حَرْبٌ عَالَمِيَّةٌ أُخْرَى.

3. Farīd: I implore you; don't say that, and don't

   forget that the United Nations, the *qiblah* of the whole world, has already solved various world problems by its resolutions.

٣. فَرِيدٌ : أَرْجُوكَ لا تَنْطِقْ بِمِثْلِ هٰذا، ثُمَّ لا تَنْسَ أَنَّ ٱلْأُمَمَ ٱلْمُتَّحِدَةَ قِبْلَةَ ٱلْعالَمِ كُلِّهِ قَدْ حَلَّتْ مَشاكِلَ عالَمِيَّةً مُخْتَلِفَةً بِقَرارَاتِها.

4. Saʿīd: What are those problems and when did it solve them? I am confident that the United Nations'

٤. سَعِيدٌ : ما هِيَ تِلْكَ ٱلْمَشاكِلُ وَمَتَى حَلَّتْها؟ أَنا وَاثِقٌ بِأَنَّ مَنْدُوبِي ٱلْأُمَمِ

delegates will never solve a problem of importance.	ٱلْمُتَّحِدَة لَنْ يَحُلُّوا مُشْكِلَةً ذاتَ شَأْنٍ .
5. Farīd: Do you not agree with me that its existence	٥. فَرِيدٌ : أَلا تُوافِقُني عَلَى أَنَّ وُجودَها
is better than its non-existence and that it	أَفْضَلُ مِنْ عَدَمِهِ وَأَنَّها
represents the first step in the evolution towards	تَمَثَّلُ أَوَّلَ دَرَجَةٍ في ٱلتَّطَوُّرِ نَحْوَ
peace?	ٱلسَّلامِ؟
6. Sa'īd: Yes, but it is necessary that it have,	٦. سَعيدٌ : نَعَمْ، وَلٰكِنْ يَجِبُ أَنْ يَكونَ لَها
in its charter, greater authority in order for it	في ميثاقِها سُلْطَةٌ أَكْبَرُ لِكَيْ
to be able to preserve peace.	تَسْتَطيعَ أَنْ تُحافِظَ عَلَى ٱلسَّلامِ .

II. GRAMMATICAL ANALYSIS

1. هَلْ is a particle which introduces interrogative sentences. أَنْ is a particle equivalent to the English subordinate conjunction *that*. When an imperfect verb follows this particle, the verb is put in the subjunctive mood.

تُحافِظَ is third person feminine singular Form III subjunctive. The sign of the subjunctive for all persons in the singular (except the second person feminine, see paradigm in II, 6, note B, below) and for the first person plural is a final fatḥah. For the subjunctive plural see II, 4, below and paradigm in II, 6, note B, below. There is no perfect subjunctive.

The combination of أَنْ and the subjunctive may always be replaced by the maṣdar of the verb.

2. إِنَّني is an alternate form of إِنِّي.

لَمْ is a negative particle which always introduces the jussive mood, which like the subjunctive occurs only in the imperfect. However, a jussive verb after لَمْ is always perfect in meaning.

تَمْنَحْ is third person feminine singular jussive of the verb مَنَحَ. The sign of the jussive in this case is the final sukūn. The jussive has the same forms as the subjunctive except that where the third radical is the last letter, it takes sukūn instead of fatḥah (see paradigm in II, 6, note c, below). There is no perfect jussive.

3. تَنْطِقْ is second person masculine singular jussive of the verb نَطَقَ. Whenever the second person jussive follows the negative particle لَا, the significance is negative imperative.

تَنْسَ is second person masculine singular jussive of the weak-lām verb نَسِيَ. The sign of the jussive in this case is the omission of the final weak letter. In the jussive singular (except the second person feminine) and first person plural of weak-lām verbs the weak letter is omitted. In other cases the nūn of the indicative is omitted where such omission takes place in the jussive of sound verbs (including the second person feminine singular).

NOTE. In the jussive of hollow verbs, whenever the third radical has a sukūn (see paradigm in II, 6, note c), the weak letter is omitted. Thus, the jussive of يَكُونُ is يَكُنْ.

4. مَا is used here as an interrogative pronoun and means *what*?

مَتَى is used here as an interrogative adverb and means *when*?

لَنْ is a particle which negates the future absolutely. It is followed by a verb in the subjunctive.

يَحُلُّوا is third person masculine plural subjunctive of the verb حَلَّ. The characteristic of the subjunctive in the dual and plural is the omission of the final nūn of the indicative; however, the second and third person feminine plural are identical with the indicative (see paradigm in II, 6, note B, below).

5. The initial أَ in this sentence is an interrogative particle identical in meaning with هَلْ. It is to be noted that neither of these particles is used if there is another interrogative in the sentence.

6. لِكَيْ is a conjunction meaning *so that*. It is followed by a verb in the subjunctive.

CHAPTER XXIX

NOTE A: The subjunctive is used after the following conjunctions:

أَنْ	that	لِكَيْ	so that
أَلَّا (< أَنْ لَا)	that not	لِئَلَّا (< لِأَنْ لَا)	lest
لِـ...	so that	حَتَّى	so that
لِأَنْ	so that	لَنْ	will never
كَيْ	so that		

NOTE B:

CONJUGATION OF SUBJUNCTIVE

	Singular	Dual	Plural
3rd m.	يَـفْعَلَ	يَـفْعَلَا	يَـفْعَلُوا
3rd f.	تَـفْعَلَ	تَـفْعَلَا	يَـفْعَلْنَ
2nd m.	تَـفْعَلَ	تَـفْعَلَا	تَـفْعَلُوا
2nd f.	تَـفْعَلِي	تَـفْعَلَا	تَـفْعَلْنَ
1st	أَفْعَلَ	—	نَـفْعَلَ

NOTE C:

CONJUGATION OF JUSSIVE

	Singular	Dual	Plural
3rd m.	يَـفْعَلْ	يَـفْعَلَا	يَـفْعَلُوا
3rd f.	تَـفْعَلْ	تَـفْعَلَا	يَـفْعَلْنَ
2nd m.	تَـفْعَلْ	تَـفْعَلَا	تَـفْعَلُوا
2nd f.	تَـفْعَلِي	تَـفْعَلَا	تَـفْعَلْنَ
1st	أَفْعَلْ	—	نَـفْعَلْ

NOTE D: The jussive is used in the following cases:

1. After لَمْ.
2. With the negative imperative after لَا.

3. After the lām of the imperative (see Chapter XXX, section II, 11).

4. In conditional sentences (see Chapter XXXIV, section I, 6 to end).

NOTE E: In addition to the particles هَلْ and أَ, the following interrogatives are commonly used:

Pronouns		*Adjectives*		*Adverbs*	
مَنْ	who?	أَيُّ	what?	كَيْفَ	how?
مَا	what?	أَيُّ	which?	مَتَى	when?
مَاذَا	what?			أَيْنَ	where?
أَيُّ	which?			لِمَاذَا	why?
				كَمْ	how many?

III. PRACTICE TEXT

1. His late Majesty King ʿAbd al-ʿAzīz ibn-al-

   Suʿūd was a great and upright king in the

   Arabian peninsula (*literally*, island).

١. كَانَ ٱلْمَرْحُومُ جَلَالَةُ ٱلْمَلِكِ عَبْدِ ٱلْعَزِيزِ بْنِ ٱلسُّعُودِ مَلِكًا عَظِيمًا مُسْتَقِيمًا فِي ٱلْجَزِيرَةِ ٱلْعَرَبِيَّةِ .

2. But when he was young, his family did not have

   (any) power in the peninsula.

٢. وَلَكِنْ لَمَّا كَانَ صَغِيرًا لَمْ يَكُنْ لِعَائِلَتِهِ سُلْطَةٌ فِي ٱلْجَزِيرَةِ .

3. Rather, that family, (which was) descended

   from a noble origin, had emigrated to Kuwait,

٣. بَلْ كَانَتْ تِلْكَ ٱلْعَائِلَةُ ٱلْمُتَحَدِّرَةُ مِنْ أَصْلٍ كَرِيمٍ مُهَاجِرَةً فِي ٱلْكُوَيْتِ ،

4. for ibn-Rashīd had seized its capital, Riyadh, and

   did not permit the Suʿūds or their men to return to

   their country.

٤. فَٱبْنُ رَشِيدٍ كَانَ مُسْتَوْلِيًا عَلَى عَاصِمَتِهَا ٱلرِّيَاضِ وَلَمْ يَأْذَنْ لِلسُّعُودِيِّينَ وَلَا لِرِجَالِهِمْ بِٱلرُّجُوعِ إِلَى بِلَادِهِمْ .

5. Do you think that 'Abd al-'Azīz was satisfied

with this situation?

٥. أَتَظُنُّ أَنَّ عَبْدَ ٱلْعَزيزِ كَانَ راضِيًا

بِهٰذِهِ ٱلْحالَةِ؟

6. No. He was very desirous of seizing the country of

his fathers and grandfathers.

٦. لا، إِنَّهُ كَانَ شَديدَ ٱلرَّغْبَةِ في ٱلٱسْتيلاءِ

عَلَى بِلادِ آبائِهِ وَأَجْدادِهِ .

7. So he advanced on Riyadh with a small group

of his devoted men,

٧. فَزَحَفَ عَلَى ٱلرِّياضِ مَعَ فَريقٍ صَغيرٍ

مِنْ رِجالِهِ ٱلْمُخْلِصينَ ،

8. and approached it at night resolving to expel ibn-

Rashīd from it, and to change it for the second

(time) into a Su'ūdi capital.

٨. وَتَقَدَّمَ إِلَيْها في ٱللَّيْلِ عازِمًا عَلَى أَنْ

يُخْرِجَ ٱبْنَ رَشيدٍ مِنْها وَأَنْ يُحَوِّلَها ثانِيَةً

إِلَى عاصِمَةٍ سُعوديَّةٍ .

9. It was not but a few hours until he seized the city

and restored peace to it.

٩. وَما هِيَ إِلَّا ساعاتٌ مَعْدودَةٌ حَتَّى

ٱسْتَوْلَى عَلَى ٱلْمَدينَةِ وَأَعادَ إِلَيْها ٱلسَّلامَ .

IV. EXERCISES

Translate into English:

١. لَمْ تَرْضَ زَوْجَتي بِأَنْ نَسْتَأْجِرَ بَيْتًا في جِبالِ ٱلْجَنوبِ لِلٱصْطِيافِ لِأَنَّنا لَمْ نَسْتَرِحْ هُناكَ في ٱلصَّيْفِ ٱلْماضي وَلَمْ نَلْتَقِ بِأَصْدِقائِنا .

٢. يَجِبُ عَلَى ٱلرَّجُلِ أَنْ يَتْرُكَ عائِلَتَهُ وَيَتْبَعَ زَوْجَتَهُ وَيَثِقَ بِها فَهِيَ مَسْؤوليَّتُهُ ٱلْأولَى كَما تَجِبُ ٱسْتِشارَتُها في كُلِّ مُشْكِلَةٍ .

٣. هَلْ بِاسْتِطاعَتِكَ أَنْ تَجِدَ فِي ٱلْمَكْتَبَةِ نُسْخَةً مِنْ مَخْطوطَةِ " عُنْوانُ ٱلْمَجْدِ فِي تَأْريخِ نَجْدٍ " ؟ أَرْجو أَنْ تُعْطِيَها لي فَإِنَّني مُحْتاجٌ إِلَى عِدَّةِ صَفَحاتٍ مِنْها لأَنَّها تَدورُ حَوْلَ قَضِيَّةٍ أَبْحَثُ فيها وَسَوْفَ أُعيدُها إِلَيْكَ فيما بَعْدُ.

٤. مَتى تَأَسَّسَتْ هٰذِهِ ٱلْجَمْعِيَّةُ ٱلأَجْنَبِيَّةُ وَأَيْنَ دُسْتورُها وَمَنْ كانَ مُؤَسِّسُها؟

٥. يُحِبُّ ٱلْعَرَبُ أَنْ يَنْظِموا ٱلشِّعْرَ وَأَنْ يَسْتَعْمِلوهُ في كَلامِهِمْ كَيْ يَكونَ ٱلْقَوْلُ جَميلاً.

Translate into Arabic:

1. Do you believe that the Arab League will find a way for unifying the Arabs?

2. God said: "Thou shalt not kill."

3. I did not agree in the past, and I shall never agree in the future to this solution of the problem.

4. How was Muḥammad 'Ali able to conquer Syria and when was that?

5. The strike will continue in all parts of the country so that the people will obtain their demands.

THE IMPERATIVE

I. ILLUSTRATIVE TEXT

1. The deposit, Mr. So-and-So, delivered in the parliament yesterday a speech which revolved around the emancipation of women. In it occurred the following:

١. أَلْقَى ٱلنَّائِبُ ٱلسَّيِّدُ فُلانُ ٱلْفُلانِيُّ خِطابًا في مَجْلِسِ ٱلْبَرْلَمانِ يَوْمَ أَمْسِ دارَ حَوْلَ تَحْريرِ ٱلْمَرْأَةِ، وجاء فيه ما يَلي :

2. "O reactionary conservative, open your heart and your eyes to the light, descend from your high (horse), look at the reality of the world around you where woman occupies her place in society and judge it, and be just in your judgement.

٢. "أَيُّها ٱلْمُحافِظُ ٱلرَّجْعيُّ، إِفْتَحْ قَلْبَكَ وَعَيْنَيْكَ لِلنُّورِ، إِنْزِلْ مِنْ عَلْيائِكَ، أُنْظُرْ إِلَى حَقيقَةِ ٱلْعالَمِ حَوْلَكَ حَيْثُ تَحْتَلُّ ٱلْمَرْأَةُ مَكانَها في ٱلْمُجْتَمَعِ وَٱحْكُمْ عَلَيْهِ وَكُنْ عادِلًا في حُكْمِكَ .

3. Liberate your daughter.

٣. حَرِّرِ ٱبْنَتَكَ،

4. Treat her as you treat your son and defend her rights.

٤. عامِلْها كَما تُعامِلُ ٱبْنَكَ وَدافِعْ عَنْ حُقوقِها .

5. Send her to schools to improve her condition,

٥. أَرسِلْها إِلَى ٱلْمَدارِسِ لِإِصْلاحِ حالِها

grant her your complete love, and give her

whatever she needs.

وَٱمْنَحْها حُبَّكَ ٱلْكامِلَ وَأَعْطِها ما تَحْتاجُ إِلَيْهِ .

6. Speak to her kindly.

٦. تَكَلَّمْ إِلَيْها بِرِفْقٍ .

7. O reformers, co-operate with women in the reform

of society and the solution of its problems.

٧. أَيُّها ٱلْمُصْلِحونَ : تَعاوَنوا مَعَ ٱلْمَرْأَةِ في إِصْلاحِ ٱلْمُجْتَمَعِ وَحَلِّ مَشاكِلِهِ .

8. Desist from belittling her position

٨. إِنْصَرِفوا عَنِ ٱلتَّخْفيضِ مِنْ مَقامِها

9. and rely on her in public life, and do not stand in

her way.

٩. وَٱعْتَمِدوا عَلَيْها في ٱلْحَياةِ ٱلْعامَّةِ وَلا تَعْتَرِضوا سَبيلَها .

10. Make her serve in offices and factories and in

every post which suits her naturally, and do not cut

her off from public life, for we need her very much.

١٠. وَٱسْتَخْدِموها في ٱلْمَكاتِبِ وَٱلْمَعامِلِ وَفي كُلِّ مَنْصِبٍ يُناسِبُها طَبيعِيًّا وَلا تَقْطَعوها عَنِ ٱلْحَياةِ ٱلْعامَّةِ فَإِنَّنا مُحْتاجونَ إِلَيْها كَثيرًا .

11. Let each of us do his duty in this cause (*literally*, path)

١١. لِيَعْمَلْ كُلٌّ مِنَّا واجِبَهُ في هٰذا ٱلسَّبيلِ

12. so that we may take her out of her black night into the

light of morning."

١٢. حَتَّى نُخْرِجَها مِنْ لَيْلِها ٱلْأَسْوَدِ إِلَى نورِ ٱلصَّباحِ . "

II. GRAMMATICAL ANALYSIS

1. اَلسَّيِّدُ is of the faʿīl pattern from the verb سَادَ in accordance with the following progression:

$$ سَيِّدٌ > * سَيْيِدٌ > * سِيِيدٌ > * سَوِيدٌ $$

The invariable word أَمْسِ always ends with kasrah and is not nūnated.

2. أَيُّهَا is a vocative particle meaning *O*. It is used only before nouns having the definite article.

إِفْتَحْ is the masculine singular imperative of the verb فَتَحَ.

NOTE: The imperative is formed from the second person jussive singular, dual, and plural, by omitting the prefix; however, since in Forms I, VII, VIII, IX, and X this process produces an unpronounceable initial sukūn, a hamzat al-waṣl is prefixed. In Forms II, III, V, and VI no hamzah is necessary. In Form I the prefixed hamzah takes the vowel — when the second radical has either — or —, but takes — when the second radical has —. In Forms VII, VIII, IX, and X the hamzat al-waṣl takes kasrah. Form IV takes hamzat al-qatʿ bearing fatḥah.

Since the middle radical of يَفْتَحْ is —, the vowel of the hamzat al-waṣl of the imperative is — (> إِفْتَحْ).

إِنْزِلْ is the masculine singular imperative of the verb نَزَلَ. Since the vowel of the middle radical of يَنْزِلْ is —, the vowel of the hamzat al-waṣl of the imperative is —.

أُنْظُرْ is the masculine singular imperative of the verb نَظَرَ. Since the vowel of the middle radical of يَنْظُرْ is —, the vowel of the hamzat al-waṣl of the imperative is —.

كُنْ is the masculine singular imperative of the hollow verb كَانَ. No initial hamzah is added in this case because when the prefix of the jussive is omitted, the first letter has a vowel and is pronounceable: thus,

$$ كُنْ > تَكُنْ > تَكُونُ . $$

3. حَرِّرْ is masculine singular imperative of the Form II verb حَرَّرَ. In verbs of Form II, III, V, and VI the imperative is formed merely by omitting the prefix of the jussive.

4. عَامِلْ is the masculine singular imperative of the Form III verb عَامَلَ. (See II, 3, above.)

5. أَرْسِلْ is the masculine singular imperative of the Form IV verb أَرْسَلَ. In the imperative of Form IV verbs the prefixed hamzah is a hamzat al-qaṭʻ.

أَعْطِ is the masculine singular imperative of the Form IV verb أَعْطَى (imperfect indicative يُعْطِي, jussive يُعْطِ). It will be noted that the final weak radical has disappeared. In the imperative of weak-lām verbs (all Forms) the final weak radical drops out in the singular and masculine plural.

6. تَكَلَّمْ is the masculine singular imperative of the Form V verb تَكَلَّمَ. (See II, 3, above.)

7. تَعَاوَنُوا is the masculine plural imperative of the Form VI verb تَعَاوَنَ. (See II, 3, above.)

8. إِنْصَرِفُوا is the masculine plural imperative of the Form VII verb إِنْصَرَفَ. (See II, 2, note, above.)

9. أَعْتَمِدُوا is the masculine plural imperative of the Form VIII verb إِعْتَمَدَ. (See II, 2, note, above.)

10. أَسْتَخْدِمُوا is the masculine plural imperative of the Form X verb إِسْتَخْدَمَ. (See II, 2, note, above.)

11. لِيَعْمَلْ is composed of two words: the particle لِ... and the jussive verb يَعْمَلْ. The particle لِ... in this usage is called the lām of the imperative because it signifies a command. The lām of the imperative must be followed by the jussive. This construction occurs in the first or, more frequently, third person and may best be translated "Let him (her, etc.)...."

NOTE: The conjugation of the Form I imperative is as follows:

	Singular	Dual	Plural
2nd m.	إِفْعَلْ	إِفْعَلَا	إِفْعَلُوا
2nd f.	إِفْعَلِي	إِفْعَلَا	إِفْعَلْنَ

III. PRACTICE TEXT

1. The commander delivered a speech to the army

   yesterday in the presence of the representative of

   the President of the Republic and the Chief

   of Staff (*literally*, chief of the columns *or* pillars) and said in his speech:

١. أَلْقَى ٱلْقَائِدُ خِطَابًا يَوْمَ أَمْسِ فِي ٱلْجَيْشِ

بِحُضُورِ مُمَثِّلِ

رَئِيسِ ٱلْجُمْهُورِيَّةِ وَرَئِيسِ

ٱلْأَرْكَانِ فَقَالَ فِي خِطَابِهِ :

2. "Know that you, in your defense of your country,

   are defending your homes and families.

٢. "إِعْلَمُوا أَنَّكُمْ فِي دِفَاعِكُمْ عَنْ وَطَنِكُمْ تُدَافِعُونَ عَنْ بُيُوتِكُمْ وَعَائِلَاتِكُمْ .

3. Be ready for struggle and black death in the

   field, for the sake (*literally*, in the path) of your cause and faith.

٣. إِسْتَعِدُّوا لِلْجِهَادِ وَلِلْمَوْتِ ٱلْأَسْوَدِ فِي ٱلْمَيْدَانِ فِي سَبِيلِ قَضِيَّتِكُمْ وَإِيمَانِكُمْ .

4. Do not retreat from your place during the

   attack, but be an example of tenacity, of

   courage and of following orders.

٤. لَا تَتَرَاجَعُوا مِنْ مَكَانِكُمْ عِنْدَ ٱلْمُهَاجَمَةِ بَلْ كُونُوا مِثَالًا لِلشِّدَّةِ وَٱلشَّجَاعَةِ وَٱلٱنْقِيَادِ لِلْأَوَامِرِ .

5. Let every one of you encourage the other,

and let him be a helper to him.

٥. لِيُشَجِّعْ كُلٌّ مِنْكُمُ ٱلْآخَرَ وَلْيَكُنْ ¹
مُعَاوِنًا لَهُ .

6. And if you should meet a woman, safeguard her

chastity (*literally*, inviolability), and if you should chance upon a

child, treat him with kindness and moderation.

٦. وَإِذَا ² قَابَلْتُمُ ٱمْرَأَةً حَافِظُوا عَلَى
حُرْمَتِهَا وَإِذَا لَقِيتُمْ وَلَدًا
عَامِلُوهُ بِٱلرِّفْقِ وَٱلْٱعْتِدَالِ .

7. Do not steal a thing belonging to others.

٧. وَلَا تَسْرِقُوا شَيْئًا لِغَيْرِكُمْ .

8. Call upon God in your prayer; and go forth with

His blessing; then you will never fail."

٨. أُدْعُوا ٱللّٰهَ فِي صَلَاتِكُمْ وَسِيرُوا عَلَى
بَرَكَتِهِ فَلَنْ تَفْشَلُوا ."

IV. EXERCISES

Translate into English:

١. إِقْرَأْ كِتَابَكَ وَشَاهِدِ ٱلصُّورَةَ ذَاتَ ٱلشَّكْلِ ٱلْجَمِيلِ ٱلَّتِي فِي أَوَّلِهِ .

٢. أُسْكُتْ أَيُّهَا ٱلْوَلَدُ ٱلْكَسْلَانُ أَيْ لَا تَنْطِقْ ، وَٱقْتَرِبْ مِنْ هٰذَا ٱلْمَكَانِ حَتَّى
تُشَاهِدَ مَا أَعْمَلُهُ فَإِنَّهُ يُسَاعِدُكَ فِي عَمَلِكَ .

٣. ثِقْ بِنَفْسِكَ أَيُّهَا ٱلرَّجُلُ فِي أَيِّ مُجْتَمَعٍ وَكُنْ مُسْتَعِدًّا لِهٰذِهِ ٱلْحَيَاةِ ٱلصَّعْبَةِ
وَلِحَلِّ مَشَاكِلِهَا ، فَسِرْ فِي طَرِيقِكَ بِشَجَاعَةٍ وَلَا تَتَرَاجَعْ .

---

¹ The kasrah of the lām of the imperative drops out when it is preceded by the
conjunctions ...فَ or وَ....

² For this conditional particle, see Chapter XXXIV, section II, 12.

٤. إِعْمَلْ عَمَلَكَ ٱلْيَوْمَ وَلَا تَتَأَخَّرْ، وَلَا تَعْتَمِدْ عَلَى قَوْلِ زُعَمَاءِ ٱلْإِضْرَاب بَلْ تَعَاوَنْ مَعَ ٱلْمُخْلِصِينَ مِنْ إِخْوَانِكَ .

٥. أَحِبَّ لِغَيْرِكَ مَا تُحِبُّ لِنَفْسِكَ وَٱكْرَهْ لَهُ مَا تَكْرَهُهُ لَها.

٦. ضَحُّوا بِأَنْفُسِكُمْ فِي سَبِيلِ أُمَّتِكُمْ.

٧. إِفْتَحْ بَابَ غُرْفَتِكَ حَتَّى يَدْخُلَ ٱلنّورُ.

Translate into Arabic:

1. Tell the teacher that the lesson was very difficult.

2. Announce to the army that the hour for attacking has come.

3. Contact your friend and agree with him on a meeting place.

4. Do your duty in the service of your country.

5. Open the door and get out of the house.

CHAPTER XXXI

THE PASSIVE

I. ILLUSTRATIVE TEXT

1. The late Riyāḍ Bey al-Ṣulḥ was born in the year

   1894, and it has (also) been said in the year 1893.

١. وُلِدَ المَرْحُومُ رِيَاض بِك الصُّلْحُ سَنةَ ١٨٩٤ وَقِيلَ سَنةَ ١٨٩٣ .

2. After he had studied in the schools of Beirut, he

   was sent to Istanbul to study law and to become

   a lawyer.

٢. وَبَعْدَ أَنْ دَرَسَ في مَدارِسِ بَيْروت أُرْسِلَ إلى إسْطَمْبولَ لِيَدْرُسَ الشَّريعَة ويمسِيَ مُحامِيًا .

3. In the first World War he was punished by (*literally*, from the side of) the Turkish authorities for

   his participation in the movement of Arab struggle

   for liberty by being sentenced to death.

٣. وَفي الحَرْبِ العالَميّة الأولى عوقِبَ مِنْ جانِبِ السُّلَطات التُّرْكيّة لاشْتِراكِه في حَرَكة الجِهاد العَرَبيّ لِلْحُرّية بِأَنْ حُكِمَ عَلَيْه بِالإعْدام .

4. But that sentence was commuted to banishment

   to Asia Minor.

٤. وَلَكِنَّ ذلكَ الحُكْمَ اُسْتُبْدِلَ بِالنَّفْي إلى آسِيا الصُّغْرى .

5. He was appointed a representative of southern

   Lebanon in the Syrian Congress which was convened

   for swearing fealty to Fayṣal.

٥. وَقَدْ عُيِّنَ مُمَثِّلاً عَنْ لُبْنانَ الجَنوبيّ في المُؤْتَمَرِ السّوريّ الّذي عُقِدَ لِمُبايَعة فَيْصَلٍ .

6. When the French occupied Syria, he was obliged to leave the country. Then he returned to Lebanon.

٦. وَعِنْدَما اَحْتَلَّ الفَرَنْسِيُّونَ سوريّةَ اَضْطُرَّ إلى الخُروجِ مِنَ البِلادِ ثُمَّ عادَ إلى لُبْنانَ.

7. In the year 1936 he was invited to accompany the Syrian delegation to the Paris conference as a consultant for the negotiations concerning a treaty with France.

٧. وَفي سَنَةِ ١٩٣٦ دُعِيَ لِيُرافِقَ الوَفْدَ السّوريَّ إلى مُؤْتَمَرِ باريسَ كَمُسْتَشارٍ لِلْمُفاوَضَةِ بِشَأْنِ مُعاهَدَةٍ مَعَ فَرَنْسا.

8. After the amending of the constitution, he was appointed the first premier of the independent Lebanese Republic.

٨. وَبَعْدَ تَعْديلِ الدُّستورِ عُيِّنَ أَوَّلَ رَئيسِ وُزَراءَ لِلْجُمْهوريّةِ اللُّبْنانيّةِ المُسْتَقِلَّةِ.

9. He was killed by assassination in Amman in the summer of 1951.

٩. وَقُتِلَ اَغْتيالاً في عَمّانَ في صَيْفِ ١٩٥١.

10. He is considered to be, fundamentally, among the Arab patriots, and it is said that he became an advocate of Lebanese independence during the Second World War.

١٠. وَيُعَدُّ أَصْلاً مِنَ الوَطَنِيِّينَ العَرَبِ، وَيُقالُ إنَّهُ أَصْبَحَ داعِيًا لِلاِسْتِقْلالِ اللُّبْنانيِّ في الحَرْبِ العالَمِيّةِ الثّانِية.

11. It is believed that he was one of the pillars of that independence and one of those who sacrificed (a great deal) in its cause.

١١. وَيُعْتَقَدُ أَنَّهُ كانَ مِنْ أَرْكانِ ذلكَ الاِسْتِقْلالِ وَمِنَ الَّذينَ ضَحَّوْا في سَبيلِه.

12. Therefore, his name is honored and preserved

١٢. لِذلكَ فَإنَّ اَسْمَهُ يُكْرَمُ وَيُحْفَظُ

as a sincere and able leader
in recognition of

his service to his country.

كَقَائِدٍ مُخْلِصٍ قَدِيرٍ اِعْتِرَافًا

بِخِدْمَتِهِ لِبِلَادِهِ.

II. GRAMMATICAL ANALYSIS

1. The verb وُلِدَ is third person masculine singular perfect passive of the root وَلَدَ. The perfect passive of any trisyllabic verb[1] is formed by changing the first vowel of the perfect active to a ḍammah and the second vowel to a kasrah.

The verb قِيلَ is third person masculine singular perfect passive of the root قَالَ. In the perfect passive of hollow verbs of Forms I, IV, VII, VIII, and X the middle radical is always a ي preceded by a kasrah.

2. The verb أُرْسِلَ is third masculine singular perfect passive of the Form IV verb أَرْسَلَ. Since the active has three syllables, the passive is formed in accordance with the principle mentioned in II, 1, above. The hamzah of Form IV verbs is hamzat al-qaṭʻ in the passive as well as in the active.

3. The verb عُوقِبَ is third masculine singular perfect passive of the Form III verb عَاقَبَ. Note that in Forms III and VI the alif is changed into a wāw under the influence of the preceding ḍammah.

4. The verb أُسْتُبْدِلَ is third person masculine singular perfect passive of the Form X verb إِسْتَبْدَلَ. The perfect passive of any quadrisyllabic verb is formed by changing the first two vowels of the perfect active to ḍammahs and the third vowel to a kasrah.

5. The verb عُيِّنَ is third person masculine singular perfect passive of the Form II verb عَيَّنَ.

6. The verb أُضْطُرَّ < *أُضْطُرِرَ is third person masculine singular perfect passive of the Form VIII verb إِضْطَرَّ. Note that since this is a doubled

---

[1] That is, any perfect verb which has three syllables regardless of Form.

verb, the kasrah of the third syllable is assimilated by the shaddah. (For the tā' > ṭā' change see Chapter XXVIII, section II, 8.)

7. The verb دُعِيَ is third person masculine singular perfect passive of the weak-lām verb دَعَا. In the perfect passive of weak-lām verbs the third radical always becomes a consonantal yā' and carries fatḥah. This applies in all Forms.

10. The verb يُعَدُّ (< يُعْدَدُ *) is third person masculine singular imperfect passive of عَدَّ. The imperfect passive is formed by changing the vowel of the prefix to ḍammah and the vowel of the second radical to fatḥah. Note that since this is a doubled verb, the vowel which would have been on the middle radical has shifted to the first (as in the active; see Chapter XXIV, section II, 5).

The verb يُقَالُ is third person masculine singular imperfect passive of the hollow verb قَالَ. In the imperfect passive of Forms I, IV, VII, VIII, and X of hollow verbs, the fatḥah which would be expected on the middle radical (in accordance with the rule in the preceding paragraph) is shifted to the first radical, and the middle radical reverts to alif. (Cf. the perfect of hollow verbs.)

11. The verb يُعْتَقَد is third person masculine singular imperfect passive of the Form VIII verb إِعْتَقَد.

12. The verb يُكْرَم is third person masculine singular imperfect passive of the Form IV verb أَكْرَمَ. Note that the imperfect passives of Forms I and IV are identical in form.

NOTE: In the imperfect passive of weak-fā' verbs of Forms I and IV the first radical is always a lengthening wāw. In other Forms the first radical behaves regularly.

In the imperfect passive of weak-lām verbs of all Forms the last radical is alif maqṣūrah.

III. PRACTICE TEXT

1. The newspaper *al-Ahrām* was founded in the year

   1875 in Alexandria. Its founders were Messrs.

   Salīm and Bishārah Taqla.

١. أُسِّسَتْ جَرِيدَةُ ''الأَهْرام'' سَنَةَ ١٨٧٥ في الإسْكَنْدَرِيّةِ. وَمُؤَسِّساها هُما الأُسْتاذانِ سَلِيمٌ وَبِشارَةُ تَقْلا.

2. They had been obliged, a little before that, to

   emigrate from their original country, that is

   Lebanon, after they had been prevented, because

   of the intensity of Turkish pressure, from

   working freely in journalism.

٢. وَكانا قَدْ اضْطُرّا قُبَيْلَ ذلِكَ إلى أَنْ يُهاجِرا مِنْ بِلادِهِما الأَصْلِيّةِ أَيْ لُبْنانَ بَعْدَ أَنْ مُنِعا مِنَ العَمَلِ في الصِّحافةِ بِحُرِّيّةٍ بِسَبَبِ شِدّةِ الضَّغْطِ التُّرْكِيِّ.

3. The headquarters of the newspaper was moved in

   the year 1900 to Cairo, and it improved greatly.

٣. وَنُقِلَ مَرْكَزُ الجَرِيدةِ سَنَةَ ١٩٠٠ إلى القاهِرةِ وَتَحَسَّنَتْ كَثيراً.

4. When Bishārah Taqla died, his wife assumed the

   direction of the newspaper's affairs until

   her son, Gabriel, should be taught those affairs.

٤. وَلَمّا تُوُفِّيَ بِشارةُ تَقْلا تَوَلَّتْ زَوْجَتُهُ إدارةَ شُؤُونِ الجَرِيدةِ حَتّى يَتَعَلَّمَ ابْنُها جِبْرائيلُ تِلْكَ الشُّؤُونَ.

5. When Gabriel took over the administration,

   offices were opened in all the important cities

   and correspondents of the paper were appointed in

   them to transmit accurate news.

٥. وَعِنْدَما تَوَلّى جِبْرائيلُ الإدارةَ فُتِحَتْ مَكاتِبُ في كُلِّ المُدُنِ المُهِمّةِ وَعُيِّنَ مُراسِلونَ لِلْجَرِيدةِ فيها لِيَنْقُلوا الأَخْبارَ الصَّحيحةَ.

6. The photographic picture was used on a wide basis, and the linotype was employed for the first time in the Arab countries.

٦. وَٱسْتُعْمِلَتِ الصّورةُ الفُوتوغرافِيّةُ عَلى أَساسٍ واسِعٍ وَٱسْتُخْدِمَ اللّينوتَيْبُ لِأَوّلِ مَرّةٍ في البُلْدانِ العَرَبِيّةِ.

7. Then al-Ahrām came to be considered the greatest newspaper in the Arab World.

٧. فَصارَتِ "الأهْرامُ" تُعَدُّ أَكْبَرَ الجَرائِدِ في العالَمِ العَرَبِيِّ.

8. Gabriel died in the year 1943 (leaving) a son and two daughters.

٨. وَتُوُفِّيَ جِبْرائيلُ سَنَةَ ١٩٤٣ عَنِ ٱبْنٍ وَٱبْنَتَيْنِ.

9. As for the son, whose name was also Bishārah, he has spent a short time in North America, establishing connections with American journalism and studying the administration of newspapers so that he may become an editor who can be relied on in that job, and in whom there is confidence.

٩. أمّا الإبْنُ وَٱسْمُهُ بِشارةُ أَيْضًا فَقَدْ صَرَفَ وَقْتًا قَصيرًا في أمْريكا الشّمالِيّةِ وَهُوَ يُقيمُ الصّلاتِ مَعَ الصّحافةِ الأَمْريكِيّةِ وَيَدْرُسُ إدارةَ الجَرائِدِ كَيْ يُصْبِحَ مُحَرّرًا يُعْتَمَدُ عَلَيْهِ في ذٰلِكَ المَنْصِبِ وَيوثَقُ بِهِ.

IV. EXERCISES

Translate into English:

١. شوهِدَ الهِلالُ في ٱلسّماءِ بادِيًا مِنْ بُعْدٍ وَراءَ ٱلْجِبالِ لَيْلَةَ أَمْسِ فَٱبْتَدَأَ العيدُ وَٱبْتَهَجَ الشّعْبُ.

٢. تُعْرَفُ يَثْرِبُ الآنَ بِٱسْمِ المَدينةِ وَيُقالُ إنّها ٱتَّخَذَتْ ذٰلِكَ الإسْمَ بَعْدَ هِجْرةِ النّبِيِّ إلَيْها.

139

٣. زَحَفَ الجَيْشُ الإِسْلامِيُّ عَلَى الشَّامِ وَاقْتَرَبَ مِنْها فَفُتِحَتْ في أَيَّامِ عُمَرَ تَحْتَ قِيادَةِ "خَالِدٍ" وَعِنْدَ الاِسْتِيلاءِ عَلَيْها أُكْرِمَ أَهْلُها وَقُدِّمَ إِلَيْهِمْ تَعَهُّدٌ بِحِفْظِ حَياتِهِمْ وَعَدَمِ قَتْلِهِمْ وَعُومِلوا بِرِفْقٍ وَحوفِظَ عَلَى حُرْمَةِ بُيوتِهِمْ وَتَحَسَّنَتْ حالَتُهُمْ.

٤. تُعْتَبَرُ الشَّجاعَةُ مِنْ أَفْضَلِ الصِّفاتِ الَّتِي تُرافِقُ الرَّجُلَ وَخاصَّةً في الحَرْبِ.

٥. يُسْتَأْنَفُ العَمَلُ قَبْلَ ظُهْرِ اليَوْمِ في المَعامِلِ بَعْدَ أَنْ مَرَّ عَلَى الإِضْرابِ ضِدَّ الشَّرِكَةِ شَهْرٌ كامِلٌ. وَقَدِ اتَّفَقَتْ لَجْنَةُ المُوَظَّفينَ مَعَ مُحامِي الشَّرِكَةِ وَمُديرِها عَلَى ساعاتِ العَمَلِ وَعَلَى تَحْقيقِ المَطالِبِ الأُخْرى.

٦. تَقولُ الأَخْبارُ إِنَّهُ أُعْلِنَ في عاصِمَةِ الجُمْهورِيَّةِ أَنَّ حُكومَةً جَديدَةً شُكِّلَتِ اليَوْمَ بِقِيادَةِ نائِبٍ قَديرٍ هُوَ رَئيسُ الحِزْبِ الوَطَنِيِّ. وَيَبْدو أَنَّ هَذِهِ الحُكومَةَ تَتَأَلَّفُ مِنْ زُعَماءَ مُخْلِصينَ يَحْكُمونَ بِالعَدْلِ وَالاِسْتِقامَةِ وَيَتَعاوَنونَ لِمَصْلَحَةِ الأُمَّةِ، وَلَيْسَتْ كَالحُكومَةِ الرَّجْعِيَّةِ الماضِيَةِ، وَلِذَلِكَ مِنَ المُنْتَظَرِ أَنْ تَنالَ ثِقَةَ المَجْلِسِ.

Translate into Arabic:

1. After the revolution the prime minister was expelled from the country, and it was demanded of him that he not return.

2. The city was conquered and many of the people were imprisoned.

3. The men of the press were permitted to meet the minister of interior in order to present their demands.

4. Al-Azhar was founded in the year 972 and it is believed to be the oldest university in the world.

5. Aḥmad was elected president of the Royal Society for Historical Studies.

CHAPTER XXXII

ACCUSATIVES IN GENERAL

I. ILLUSTRATIVE TEXT

1. The story of Jabalah ibn-al-Ayham represents the Caliph 'Umar's pursuit of justice and uprightness in governing.

١. إِنَّ قِصَّةَ جَبَلَةَ بْنِ الأَيْهَمِ تُمَثِّلُ تَتَبُّعَ الْخَلِيفَةِ عُمَرَ الْعَدْلَ وَالاِسْتِقَامَةَ فِي الْحُكْمِ.

2. Jabalah was a Christian prince in Syria.

٢. كَانَ جَبَلَةُ أَمِيرًا نَصْرَانِيًّا فِي الشَّامِ.

3. When he embraced the religion of Islam, he went to "the mother of towns," that is Mecca the Honored, in order to (perform) the pilgrimage.

٣. وَلَمَّا دَخَلَ فِي دِينِ الإِسْلَامِ ذَهَبَ إِلَى أُمِّ الْقُرَى أَيْ مَكَّةَ الْمُكَرَّمَةِ لِلْحَجِّ.

4. And while he was circumambulating the Kaaba (*literally*, the house), a Bedouin stepped

on his waistband and untied it.

٤. وَبَيْنَمَا كَانَ يَطُوفُ بِالْبَيْتِ دَعَسَ بَدَوِيٌّ إِزَارَهُ فَحَلَّهُ.

5. Jabalah looked at him in anger and slapped him [a slapping] in order to reprimand him

for untying the waistband.

٥. فَنَظَرَ إِلَيْهِ جَبَلَةُ غَاضِبًا وَلَطَمَهُ لَطْمًا تَوْبِيخًا لَهُ عَلَى حَلِّ الإِزَارِ.

6. The Bedouin protested to 'Umar,

٦. فَاحْتَجَّ الْبَدَوِيُّ لِعُمَرَ،

7. so 'Umar called Jabalah before him and asked him saying,

٧. فَدَعَا عُمَرُ جَبَلَةَ أَمَامَهُ وَسَأَلَهُ قَائِلًا:

141

"O Jabalah, why did you slap your brother?"

8. He said, "O Commander of the Faithful, is there no preference to me over this Bedouin? Am I not higher in position than he?"

9. He said, "O Jabalah, Islam has made you both equal (*literally*, brought you together)."

10. The result was that Jabalah went out of the Abode of Islam and returned to the country of the Byzantines approving his previous religion.

"يا جَبَلَةُ لِماذا لَطَمْتَ أَخاكَ؟"

٨. قالَ: "يا أَميرَ المُؤْمِنينَ أَلا اَمْتيازَ لي عَلى هٰذا البَدَويِّ؟ أَلَسْتُ أَنا أَكْبَرَ مَقامًا مِنْهُ؟"

٩. قالَ: "يا جَبَلَةُ لَقَدْ جَمَعَكُما الإِسْلامُ."

١٠. وَكانَتِ النَتيجَةُ أَنْ خَرَجَ جَبَلَةُ مِنْ دارِ الإِسْلامِ وَعادَ إِلى بِلادِ الرومِ مُسْتَحْسِنًا دينَهُ القَديمَ.

II. GRAMMATICAL ANALYSIS

NOTE: This lesson is intended to review the uses of the accusative case already presented and to present a few new uses.

1. The noun قِصَّة is in the accusative because it is the subject of a sentence introduced by إِنَّ. (Chapter XVI, section II, 2.)

When the word اِبْن occurs between the name of son and father, the waṣlah and its chair drop out. (See Chapter XIII, section II, footnote 2, for similar usage with ...لِ and the definite article.)

The maṣdar تَتَبُّع is in the accusative because it is the direct object of the verb تَمَثَّل. (Chapter XV, section II, 3.) Yet this same maṣdar takes اَلْعَدْلَ for an object because of the verbal element in it. This maṣdar-object relationship obtains in modern Arabic only when the maṣdar as first member of a construct is separated from the object by the second member of the same construct. If the object follows the maṣdar immediately it is no more object but a second member of a construct in the genitive.

2. The noun أَمِيرًا is in the accusative because it is the predicate of the verb كَانَ. (Chapter XX, section II, 1.)

نَصْرَانِيًّا is in the accusative because it is an adjective which modifies a noun in the accusative, i.e. أَمِيرًا. (Chapter XI, section II, 1.)

5. غَاضِبًا is in the accusative because it is an adverb of manner. (Chapter XVI, section II, 5.)

لَطْمًا is in the accusative because it is the object of the verb لَطَمَ. It is to be noticed that the object is a maṣdar of the verb of which it is an object. Whenever this situation obtains, the object is called an absolute object. Its purpose is to give added force to the verb.

تَوْبِيخًا is in the accusative because it is an adverb of purpose. (Chapter XXVIII, section II, 4.)

7. أَمَامَ is an adverb of place used as a preposition. (Chapter XIII, section II, 1 and 5, note.)

يَا is a vocative particle equivalent to the English vocative particle, *O*. The noun which follows it cannot have the definite article. If this following noun is not in construct, it is nominative but without nūnation (as in this example). If it is in construct it is accusative (as in II, 8, below).

NOTE: In addition to يَا there are other vocative particles of which the most frequently used is أَيُّهَا or the combination يَا أَيُّهَا. In either of these latter two cases the noun following must be defined by the definite article. (Chapter XXX, section II, 2.)

أَخَاكَ is composed of two words, the noun أَخ and the pronominal suffix كَ.... أَخ is one of the "five nouns" which nouns, when in construct, show their case by a lengthening of the usual case ending. If they are not in construct, they behave like other nouns. Of the five, أَب, أَخ, 'father,' and ذُو 'owner of,' 'possessor of'—(this word occurs only in construct) are the commonest.

8. أَمِيرَ is accusative because it follows the vocative particle يَا and is in construct (see II, 7, above).

أَلَا is composed of two words, the interrogative particle, أَ, and the particle of complete negation, لَا.

143

The word اِمْتِيَازَ is in the accusative without nūnation because it immediately follows the لَا of complete negation, and is negated by it. Such nouns are always in the accusative without nūnation.

لَسْتُ is the first person singular of لَيْسَ (see Chapter XX, section II, 6, note B; for paradigm see II, 10, note, below).

أَكْبَرَ is accusative because it is the predicate of لَيْسَ, a sister of كَانَ.

مَقَامًا specifies in regard to what Jabalah is higher. This usage requires an indefinite accusative which is called accusative of specification. Insertion of the phrase "in regard to" before the accusative is a rough means of identifying the usage.

10. مُسْتَحْسِنًا is in the accusative because it is an adverb of manner.

دِينَ is in the accusative because it is the direct object of the active participle مُسْتَحْسِنًا. Active participles retain sufficient verbal force to take a direct object. (Chapter XVI, section II, 5.)

NOTE: The conjugation of لَيْسَ, which verb is perfect in form but imperfect in meaning, is as follows:

	Singular	Dual	Plural
3rd m.	لَيْسَ	لَيْسَا	لَيْسُوا
3rd f.	لَيْسَتْ	لَيْسَتَا	لَسْنَ
2nd m.	لَسْتَ	لَسْتُمَا	لَسْتُمْ
2nd f.	لَسْتِ	لَسْتُمَا	لَسْتُنَّ
1st	لَسْتُ		لَسْنَا

III. PRACTICE TEXT

1. Yesterday Arab unity was a beautiful, golden theory, far from realization (that was espoused) by the Arab nation.

١. كَانَتِ الْوَحْدَةُ الْعَرَبِيَّةُ بِالْأَمْسِ نَظَرِيَّةً ذَهَبِيَّةً جَمِيلَةً بَعِيدَةَ التَّحْقِيقِ لَدَى الْأُمَّةِ الْعَرَبِيَّةِ.

2. But today that theory has become something

of a reality, in answer to the desire of the nationalists—by

their establishing the Arab League in

the year 1945.

٢. وَلكِنَّ تِلْكَ النَّظَرِيَّةَ أَمْسَتِ اليَوْمَ حَقيقةً

بَعْضَ الشَّيْءِ إِجابةً لِرَغْبَةِ القَوْمِيِّينَ

وَذٰلِكَ عِنْدَ تَأْسِيسِهِمِ الجامِعَةَ العَرَبِيَّةَ

عامَ ١٩٤٥.

3. The signing of the charter of the League represents

the first step in the evolution towards unification

very soundly, for it was formed for the defense of

the independence of the Arab states, for the

assurance of co-operation between them politically, and for the

organization of their economic life.

٣. وَيُمَثِّلُ التَّوْقِيعُ عَلى مِيثاقِ الجامِعَةِ

الدَّرَجَةَ الأُولى في التَّطَوُّرِ نَحْوَ التَّوْحِيدِ

تَمْثِيلًا صَحِيحًا إِذْ أَنَّها شُكِّلَتْ لِلدِّفاعِ

عَنِ اسْتِقْلالِ الدُّوَلِ العَرَبِيَّةِ

وَتَأْمِينِ التَّعاوُنِ بَيْنَها سِياسيًّا

وَتَنْظِيمِ حَياتِها الإِقْتِصادِيَّةِ.

4. The League took Cairo as its center in

recognition of the importance of Egypt.

٤. وَقَدِ اتَّخَذَتِ الجامِعَةُ القاهِرَةَ مَرْكَزًا لَها

اعْتِرافًا بِأَهَمِّيَّةِ مِصْرَ.

5. The Secretary-General of the League is the most

important employee in it, for it has no president.

٥. وَالأَمِينُ العامُّ لِلجامِعَةِ هُوَ أَكْبَرُ

مُوَظَّفٍ فِيها إِذْ لا رَئِيسَ لَها.

6. As for its future, God only knows, because it is

evidencing some weakness in the functioning of its

activities and also in its influence on world

٦. أَمّا مُسْتَقْبِلُها فَعِلْمُهُ عِنْدَ اللهِ لِأَنَّها

مُبْدِيَةٌ بَعْضَ الضَّعْفِ في سَيْرِ أَعْمالِها

وَفي تَأْثِيرِها في السِّياسةِ العالَمِيَّةِ

politics, although the Arabs still expect much

أَيْضًا مَعَ أَنَّ الْعَرَبَ لَا يَزَالُونَ يَنْتَظِرُونَ

from it.

الْكَثِيرَ مِنْهَا .

IV. EXERCISES

Translate into English:

١. بَقِيَ الْقَائِدُ مُجَاهِدًا وَمُدَافِعًا عَنْ مَرْكَزِهِ فِي وَطَنِ الْآبَاءِ وَالْأَجْدَادِ كَأَنَّ الْحَرْبَ مَا زَالَتْ مُسْتَمِرَّةً وَكَأَنَّ السَّلَامَ غَيْرُ مَوْجُود .

٢. بِمُبَايَعَةِ الْمُسْلِمِينَ "أَبَا بَكْرٍ" تَحَسَّنَتْ حَالَةُ الْمُهَاجِرِينَ الَّذِينَ رَافَقُوا الرَّسُولَ إِلَى الْمَدِينَةِ تَحَسُّنًا سَرِيعًا وَاشْتَدَّتْ ثِقَتُهُمْ بِنَفْسِهِمْ .

٣. إِجَابَةً لِرَغْبَةِ الْعَدِيدِينَ مِنَ الْأَجَانِبِ فِي أَنْ يَدْرُسُوا اللُّغَةَ الْعَرَبِيَّةَ وَأَنْ يَنْطِقُوا بِهَا بِطَرِيقَةٍ لَا مُشْكِلَةَ فِيهَا اضْطُرِرْنَا إِلَى أَنْ نَكْتُبَ هٰذَا الْكِتَابَ بَعْدَ اسْتِشَارَةِ الْعَلَّامَةِ فُلَان . وَإِنَّنَا نَرْجُو أَنْ يَرْضَوْا عَنْهُ وَعَنْ شَكْلِهِ وَأَنْ يَكُونَ كَافِيًا لِحَاجَتِهِمْ وَأَنْ يَسْتَعْمِلُوهُ فِي دَرْسِهِمْ فَيُكْرِمُوا كَاتِبَيْه .

٤. لَاحَتِ السَّيَّارَةُ السَّرِيعَةُ ذَاتُ اللَّوْنِ الْأَخْضَرِ مِنْ بُعْدٍ مُرْسِلَةً نُورَهَا إِلَى شَارِعٍ عَرِيضٍ مُسْتَقِيمٍ امْتَدَّ أَمَامَهَا ثُمَّ مَرَّتْ بِنَا كَأَنَّهَا طَيَّارَةٌ فَاضْطُرِرْنَا إِلَى أَنْ نَنْتَظِرَ سَيَّارَةً أُخْرَى .

٥. لَا شَكَّ فِي أَنَّ الرَّجُلَ أَكْثَرُ شَجَاعَةً مِنَ الْمَرْأَةِ وَأَشَدُّ تَأْثِيرًا فِي الْمُجْتَمَعِ وَأَسْمَى مَقَامًا فِي الْحَيَاةِ الْعَامَّةِ أَيْضًا . وَلٰكِنَّ الْمَرْأَةَ الْمَشْهُورَةَ بِالضَّعْفِ تُعْتَبَرُ أَشَدَّ مِنْهُ إِخْلَاصًا وَاسْتِقَامَةً بِدَرَجَاتٍ كَثِيرَة .

Translate into Arabic:

1. O people of the Book, why do you say that Jesus ('Īsa) is God?
2. The Arabian prophet Muḥammad came announcing a new religion.
3. Ibn-Rashīd was the ruler of Nejd before ibn-Su'ūd seized power there.
4. There is not any water in the desert.
5. The government agreed on the abolition of political parties in order to preserve peace in the country.

THE NUMERALS

"The numerals are the nightmare of a bankrupt financier."[1]

I. ILLUSTRATIVE TEXT

1. The month consists of thirty or thirty-one

   days except the month of February.

١. يَتَأَلَّفُ الشَّهْرُ مِنْ ثَلاثِينَ يَوْمًا أَوْ واحِدٍ وَثَلاثِينَ إِلَّا شَهْرَةَ فِبْرايِرَ.[2]

2. It has twenty-eight days in every three

   of four years.

٢. فَهُوَ ثَمانِيَةٌ وَعِشْرُونَ يَوْمًا فِي كُلِّ ثَلاثٍ مِنْ أَرْبَعِ سَنَواتٍ.

3. But in the fourth year it has twenty-nine days.

٣. أَمَّا فِي السَّنةِ الرّابِعةِ فَهُوَ تِسْعةٌ وَعِشْرُونَ يَوْمًا.

4. The year has twelve months; it thus consists

   of three hundred and sixty-five and one-

   fourth days.

٤. وَفِي السَّنةِ اثْنا عَشَرَ شَهْرًا، فَتَتَأَلَّفُ السَّنةُ إِذًا مِنْ ثَلاثِ مِئةٍ وَخَمْسةٍ وَسِتِّينَ يَوْمًا وَرُبْعِ اليَوْمِ.

5. Every day has twenty-four hours; the hour is

   divided into sixty minutes.

٥. وَفِي كُلِّ يَوْمٍ أَرْبَعٌ وَعِشْرُونَ ساعةً، وَتَنْقَسِمُ الساعةُ الى سِتِّينَ دَقيقةً.

---

[1] A. S. Tritton, *Teach Yourself Arabic* (Philadelphia: David McKay Co., n.d.) p. 171.

[2] The exceptive particle إِلَّا is sometimes followed by a noun in the accusative. On this intricate point see Wright, *op. cit.*, II, 335 ff.

147

6. Thirty minutes are called half an hour; twenty minutes are one-third of an hour; fifteen minutes are one-fourth of an hour; forty-five minutes are three-fourths of an hour.

٦. فَتُسَمَّى الثَلاثُونَ دَقيقةً نِصْفَ ساعةٍ والعِشرُونَ دَقيقةً ثُلُثَ ساعةٍ والخَمْسَ عَشْرَةَ دَقيقةً رُبْعَ ساعةٍ والخَمْسُ والأَرْبَعونَ دَقيقةً ثَلاثةَ أَرْباعِ الساعةِ.

7. The seasons of the year are: first, the season of spring, which begins in the third month of the year;

٧. أَمّا فُصولُ السَنة فَهِيَ: أَوَّلاً فَصْلُ الرَبيعِ ويَبْتَدىءُ في الشَهْرِ الثالثِ من السَنةِ،

8. second, the season of summer, which begins in the sixth month;

٨. ثانيًا فَصْلُ الصَيْفِ ويَبْتَدىءُ في الشَهْرِ السادِسِ.

9. third, the season of autumn, which begins in the ninth month;

٩. ثالثًا فَصْلُ الخَريفِ ويَبْتَدىءُ في الشَهْرِ التاسِعِ،

10. fourth, the season of winter, which begins in the twelfth month.

١٠. رابِعًا فَصْلُ الشِتاءِ ويَبْتَدىءُ في الشَهْرِ الثانِيَ عَشَرَ.

II. GRAMMATICAL ANALYSIS

The morphology and syntax of numerals do not readily lend themselves to inductive analysis, and therefore the following analysis is deductive; however, whenever possible examples are cited from the above text.

Cardinals

ONE:

	Masculine	*Feminine*	
I	وَاحِدٌ	وَاحِدَةٌ	The ordinary cardinal, which is a fully declined adjective agreeing, like any other, with the noun it modifies, e.g. لَيْلَةٌ ،يَوْمٌ وَاحِدٌ, وَاحِدَةٌ.
	أَحَدٌ	إِحْدَى	An alternative cardinal used as a pronoun, e.g. لَمْ أَجِدْ أَحَدًا 'I did not find anyone.'

TWO:

	Masculine	*Feminine*	
2	إِثْنَانِ	إِثْنَتَانِ	Seldom used adjectivally because a noun in the dual is sufficient, e.g. لَيْلَتَانِ، يَوْمَانِ. It is usually used as a pronoun and is declined like a dual (which it is).

THREE THROUGH TEN:

	Masculine	*Feminine*	
3	ثَلَاثَةٌ	ثَلَاثٌ	The numerals 3 through 10 have ة— in the masculine and no ة— in the feminine. This reversal of normal gender endings is called polarity and is found in other Semitic languages. The gender of the *singular* of the counted noun determines the gender of the numeral.
4	أَرْبَعَةٌ	أَرْبَعٌ	
5	خَمْسَةٌ	خَمْسٌ	
6	سِتَّةٌ	سِتٌّ	
7	سَبْعَةٌ	سَبْعٌ	
8	ثَمَانِيَةٌ	ثَمَانٍ[3]	These numerals are declined regularly. They are in construct with the counted noun which is in the *genitive plural*.
9	تِسْعَةٌ	تِسْعٌ	
10	عَشْرَةٌ	عَشْرٌ	

[3] Declined like دَاعٍ; see Chapter XXVIII, section II, 8, note A.

EXAMPLES:

أَرْبَعَ سَنَوَاتٍ (see I, 2, above)

ثَلَاثَةَ أَرْبَاعٍ (see I, 6, above)

NOTE: The cardinals from 3 through 10 may follow the thing counted as an adjective does, but the principle of polarity still obtains, e.g. رِجَالٌ ثَلَاثَةٌ.

ELEVEN:

	Masculine	Feminine	
11	أَحَدَ عَشَرَ	إِحْدَى عَشْرَةَ	11 is indeclinable.

TWELVE:

	Masculine	Feminine	
12	إِثْنَا عَشَرَ	إِثْنَتَا عَشْرَةَ	

The first element of 12, being a dual in construct, forms Genitive-Accusative إِثْنَيْ عَشَرَ (masc.) and إِثْنَتَيْ عَشْرَةَ (fem.). The second element is indeclinable.

THIRTEEN THROUGH NINETEEN:

	Masculine	Feminine
13	ثَلَاثَةَ عَشَرَ	ثَلَاثَ عَشْرَةَ
14	أَرْبَعَةَ عَشَرَ	أَرْبَعَ عَشْرَةَ
15	خَمْسَةَ عَشَرَ	خَمْسَ عَشْرَةَ
16	سِتَّةَ عَشَرَ	سِتَّ عَشْرَةَ
17	سَبْعَةَ عَشَرَ	سَبْعَ عَشْرَةَ
18	ثَمَانِيَةَ عَشَرَ	ثَمَانِيَ عَشْرَةَ
19	تِسْعَةَ عَشَرَ	تِسْعَ عَشْرَةَ

These numerals are indeclinable. It is to be noted that the principle of polarity does *not* extend to the عَشَر of the " teens."

TWENTY THROUGH NINETY-NINE:

	Masculine	Feminine
20	عِشْرُونَ	Same
21	وَاحِدٌ وَعِشْرُونَ	إِحْدَى وَعِشْرُونَ
22	إِثْنَانِ وَعِشْرُونَ	إِثْنَتَانِ وَعِشْرُونَ
23	ثَلَاثَةٌ وَعِشْرُونَ	ثَلَاثٌ وَعِشْرُونَ
30	ثَلَاثُونَ	Same
40	أَرْبَعُونَ	,,
50	خَمْسُونَ	,,
60	سِتُّونَ	,,
70	سَبْعُونَ	,,
80	ثَمَانُونَ	,,
90	تِسْعُونَ	,,

The tens, which do not vary with the gender of the thing counted, are declined as sound masculine plurals. Note that the compound numerals are formed on the "four-and-twenty black-birds" principle and that polarity applies to the units (from three through nine).

NOTE: The numerals from 11 to 99 are followed by the noun in the *accusative singular*, which is considered an accusative of specification:

EXAMPLES:

مِنْ ثَلَاثِينَ يَوْمًا   (see I, 1, above)

ثَمَانِيَةٌ وَعِشْرُونَ يَوْمًا   (see I, 2, above)

إِثْنَا عَشَرَ شَهْرًا   (see I, 4, above)

أَرْبَعٌ وَعِشْرُونَ سَاعَةً   (see I, 5, above)

خَمْسَ عَشْرَةَ دَقِيقَةً   (see I, 6, above)

ONE HUNDRED AND ABOVE:

Masculine and Feminine

100	مِئَةٌ or مائَةٌ[1]
200	مِئَتانِ
300	ثَلاثُ مِئَةٍ
400	أَرْبعُ مِئَةٍ
500	خَمْسُ مِئَةٍ
600	سِتُّ مِئَةٍ
700	سَبْعُ مِئَةٍ
800	ثَمانِي مِئَةٍ
900	تِسْعُ مِئَةٍ
1,000	أَلْفٌ
2,000	أَلْفانِ
3,000	ثَلاثَةُ آلافٍ
11,000	أَحَدَ عَشَرَ أَلْفاً
100,000	مِئَةُ أَلْفٍ
1,000,000	مَلْيُونٌ
2,000,000	مَلْيُونانِ
3,000,000	ثَلاثَةُ مَلايِينَ

It is to be noted that the words مِئَةٌ and أَلْفٌ and مَلْيُونٌ are considered to be nouns counted in multiples such as 300, 6,000, 20,000 or 5,000,000. However, مِئَةٌ remains singular in multiples from 300 to 900 and not plural as one would expect following the numbers 3 through 9.

In even hundreds, thousands, and millions (e.g. 100, 300, 1,000, 3,000,000) the words مِئَةٌ and أَلْفٌ and مَلْيُونٌ are in construct with the thing counted, which is in the genitive singular.

In compound numerals above 100 the last numeral mentioned determines the case and grammatical number of the thing counted in accordance with the principles outlined above.

In modern Arabic the word order of compound numerals above 100 is that the highest number comes first except that the units precede the tens on the "four-and-twenty blackbirds" principle. Each digit is linked to the other by the conjunction وَ.

EXAMPLE:

فَتَتَأَلَّفُ السَّنَةُ إِذاً مِنْ ثَلاثِ مِئَةٍ وَخَمْسَةٍ وَسِتِّينَ يَوْماً (see I, 4, above)

NOTE: In this example the word ثَلاث has no ة because مِئَة is feminine. The word مِئَة is genitive singular even though one would expect genitive

[1] The alif in this spelling is not pronounced.

plural after ثَلَاث. The word خَمْسَة has ة because يَوْمًا is masculine. The word يَوْمًا is accusative singular because the last number mentioned is سِتِّينَ, one of the numbers from 11 to 99.

Ordinals

	Masculine	Feminine	
1st	أَوَّل	أُولَى	The ordinal for *first* is of the أَفْعَل pattern, though nūnated. The ordinals from 2 through 10 are of the فَاعِل pattern. They are regular adjectives, fully declined, following the noun they modify. The principle of polarity does not apply to the ordinals, and they take ة in the feminine (except for the anomaly أُولَى). Note that the two ت's of the cardinal سِتَّة (6) have become د and س in the ordinal. These ordinals are not necessarily indefinite.
2nd	ثَانٍ¹		
3rd	ثَالِث		
4th	رَابِع		
5th	خَامِس		
6th	سَادِس		
7th	سَابِع		
8th	ثَامِن		
9th	تَاسِع		
10th	عَاشِر		
the 11th	الْحَادِي عَشَر	الْحَادِيَة عَشْرَة	The ordinals from 11 through 19 are indeclinable. Note that حَادِي is an artificially formed فَاعِل pattern from وَحَد < * حَدَا > حَدَ; the ordinal أَوَّل is not used in higher ordinals. The feminines are all like the feminine of "11th" shown in the list.
the 12th	الثَّانِي عَشَر		
the 13th	الثَّالِث عَشَر		
etc. through 19th			For round tens (20th, 30th, etc.) the cardinals are used. They do not vary according to gender, and are declined as sound masculine plurals.
the 20th	الْعِشْرُونَ		
the 21st	الْحَادِي وَالْعِشْرُونَ		

¹ Declined like دَاعٍ; see Chapter XXVIII, section II, 8, note A.

153

 أَلْحَادِيَةُ وَٱلْعِشْرُونَ

the 22nd   أَلثَّانِي وَٱلْعِشْرُونَ

the 23rd   أَلثَّالِثُ وَٱلْعِشْرُونَ

the 100th   أَلْمِئَةُ

For compound ordinals consisting of tens and units, the ordinals of the units are joined to the cardinals of the tens (as in English). Only the units vary according to gender. If the unit has the definite article, the ten must also have it.

NOTE A: Sometimes the ordinals are used in construct with a following noun, e.g. أُوَّلُهُمْ 'the first of them,' سَادِسُ رَجُلٍ 'the sixth man.'

NOTE B: The numeral adverbs, "firstly, secondly," etc., are expressed by putting indefinite ordinals in the accusative, e.g. ثَانِيًا, أَوَّلًا.

EXAMPLES:

فِي ٱلسَّنَةِ ٱلرَّابِعَةِ   (see I, 3, above)

أَمَّا فُصُولُ ٱلسَّنَةِ فَهِيَ أَوَّلًا   (see I, 7, above)

فِي ٱلشَّهْرِ ٱلثَّالِثِ   (see I, 7, above)

فِي ٱلشَّهْرِ ٱلثَّانِيَ عَشَرَ   (see I, 10, above)

Fractions

The fractions from ⅓ through ¹⁄₁₀ are of the فُعْل (less often فُعُل) pattern. Their plurals are of the أَفْعَال pattern. The fractions are in construct with the noun following them.

½	نِصْف	(pl. أَنْصَاف)
⅓	ثُلْث	(pl. أَثْلَاث)
¼	رُبْع	etc.
⅕	خُمْس	
⅙	سُدْس	
⅐	سُبْع	
⅛	ثُمْن	
⅑	تُسْع	
¹⁄₁₀	عُشْر	

Fractions with higher denominators are usually expressed by a circumlocution such as: خَمْسَةُ أَجْزَاءٍ مِنْ سِتَّةٍ وَعِشْرِينَ جُزْءًا '5 parts out of 26 parts' $= \frac{5}{26}$.

Percentage is expressed as follows: أَرْبَعُونَ بِٱلْمِئَةِ مِنَ ٱلشَّعْبِ '40 in the hundred of the people' $= 40\%$ of the people.

EXAMPLES:

وَتُسَمَّى ... نِصْفَ ساعةٍ   (see I, 6, above)

وَتُسَمَّى ... ثُلُثَ سَاعَةٍ   (see I, 6, above)

وَتُسَمَّى ... رُبْعَ سَاعَةٍ   (see I, 6, above)

وَتُسَمَّى ... ثَلَاثَةَ أَرْبَاعِ ٱلسَّاعَةِ   (see I, 6, above)

Analysis of Other Points

Two points not relating to numerals require specific treatment.

1. In I, 2, above, the word سَنَوَات is a sound feminine plural of سَنَةٌ. It is to be observed that a و has been added in the formation of this plural. Actually this و was originally the third radical of the root, سَنَا. Thus سَنَةٌ is a contraction of سَنْوَةٌ* and the و reappears in the sound feminine plural. Other examples of this phenomenon are: أَخَوَاتٌ plural of أُخْتٌ and شَفَوَاتٌ plural of شَفَةٌ.

2. In I, 4, above, the word إِذًا (alternative spelling إِذَنْ) is a conjunctive adverb meaning *therefore*.

III. PRACTICE TEXT

1. These are the months of the Nativity (i.e.

Christian) year as they are known in the Fertile

Crescent: January, February, March, April,

١. هٰذِهِ هِيَ أَشْهُرُ السَّنةِ المِيلادِيَّةِ

كَمَا تُعْرَفُ في الهِلالِ الخَصِيبِ:

كانونُ الثاني، شُباطُ، آذارُ، نيسانُ،

| May, June, July, August, September, October, | أَيَّارُ، حَزيرانُ، تَمّوزُ، آبُ، أَيلولُ، |
| November, December. | تِشرينُ الأَوَّلُ، تِشرينُ الثاني، كانونُ الأَوَّلُ. |

2. These months are called in Egypt and

some other countries (as follows): January, February, etc.

٢. وتُسَمَّى هٰذِه الأَشْهُرُ في مِصْرَ وبَعْضِ البُلْدانِ الأُخْرى: يَنايِرُ، فِبْرايِرُ، مارِسُ، أَبْريلُ، مايو، يونْيو، يولْيو، أَغْسُطُسُ، سِبْتِمبِرُ، أَكْتوبِرُ، نوفِمبِرُ، ديسِمبِرُ.

3. These are the months of the Hijrah year:

al-Muḥarram, Ṣafar, etc.

٣. أَمّا أَشْهُرُ السَنةِ الهِجْريّةِ فتُقسَمُ: المُحَرَّمُ، صَفَرُ، رَبيعُ الأَوَّلُ، رَبيعُ الثاني، جُمادَى الأُولَى، جُمادَى الآخِرَةُ، رَجَبُ، شَعْبانُ، رَمَضانُ، شَوَّالُ، ذو القَعْدَةِ، ذو الحِجّةِ.

4. As for the days of the week, they are: Sunday,

Monday, etc.

٤. أَمّا أَيّامُ الأُسْبوعِ فهِيَ: يَوْمُ الأَحَدِ، يَوْمُ الإِثْنَينِ، يَوْمُ الثلاثاءِ، يَوْمُ الأَرْبِعاءِ، يَوْمُ الخَميسِ، يَوْمُ الجُمْعةِ، يَوْمُ السَبْتِ.

5. Dates are written or read in this way:

٥. ويُكْتَبُ التّأْريخُ أَوْ يُقْرَأُ على هٰذِه الطَّريقةِ:

Tuesday, the seventeenth of February in the year

يَوْمُ الثلاثاءِ في السابعَ عَشَرَ مِن (شَهْرِ) فِبْرايِرَ سَنةَ

one thousand nine hundred and fifty-three A.D., that is

أَلْفٍ وتِسْعِ مِئةٍ وثَلاثٍ وخَمْسينَ ميلاديّةٍ أَيْ

the third of Jumāda al-Ākhirah in the year

أَليَوْمُ الثّالِثُ مِن (شَهْرِ) جُمادَى الآخِرةِ سَنةَ

one thousand three hundred
and seventy-two A.H.

أَلْف وَثَلاثِ مِئَةٍ وَاثْنَتَيْنِ وَسَبْعِينَ هِجْرِيَّةً.

IV. EXERCISES

Translate into English:

١. في الشَّريعة الإسلاميّة تُعْطَى المَرْأَةُ نِصْفَ ما يَنالُهُ الرَجُلُ، ويَقولُ البَعْضُ إنَّ ذلكَ كافٍ لَها.

٢. لِمِصْرَ خَمْسَةَ عَشَرَ مُمَثِّلًا في الأُمَم المُتَّحِدة لَهُمْ صِفَةٌ رَسْمِيَّةٌ يَحْضُرُ بَعْضُهُمُ الجَلَسات بَيْنَما يَعْمَلُ البَعْضُ الآخَرُ في عِدَّة مَكاتِبَ كَمُستشارينَ يَبْحَثونَ في القَرارات المُخْتَلِفة، ويَقومُ هؤُلاءِ بِتَنْظيم شُؤون الوَفْد.

٣. الصَلاةُ والحَجُّ مِن أَرْكانِ الإسْلام الخَمْسة، ويَجِبُ على المسلِم القادِرِ أَنْ يَقومَ بِهما.

٤. في لُنْدُنَ يُوجَدُ كَثيرٌ من الجَنائِن العامّة التي تَمْتَدُّ الواحِدةُ منها بَعْدَ الأُخْرى. ولَعَلَّ عَدَدَها أَكْثَرُ من المِئَة. ولِمُعْظَم البُيوتِ في مُدُنٍ بَريطانيا بَساتينُ او جَنائِنُ خاصَّةٌ.

٥. وَصَلَ كُولُمْبُوسُ (Columbus) الى أَمْريكا قادِمًا من إسْبانيا (Spain) سَنَةَ أَلْفٍ وأَرْبَعِ مِئَةٍ وَاثْنَتَيْنِ وَتِسْعينَ فَأَسَّسَ مستعمَرةً إسْبانيَّةً، وفي العام نَفْسِه اضْطُرَّ الإسْبانُ العَرَبَ الى الخُروجِ من إسْبانيا التي سَمّاها العَرَبُ الأَنْدَلُسَ.

٦. خَلَقَ (created) اللهُ السَّمواتِ الواسِعةَ والأَرْضَ وكُلَّ ما في الوُجودِ في سِتّةِ أَيّامٍ واسْتَراحَ في اليَوْم السابع.

٧. يَلوحُ لي أَنَّ الأُسْتاذَ فُلانًا الفُلانيَّ يَكادُ لا يَعْرِفُ كَمْ هُوَ ثُلْثُ الثَلاثة.

٨. تَتَأَلَّفُ البَعْثةُ الدِراسيَّةُ العراقيَّةُ من ثَلاثِ مِئَةِ طالِبٍ قَدِموا من جَميع أَجْزاء العِراقِ وَانْتَشَروا في جامعات أَمْريكا الكُبْرى وهُمْ يَسْتَعِدّونَ لِخِدْمَة أُمَّتِهِمْ وتحقيق مَجْدِها ومَدَنِيَّتِها.

Translate into Arabic:

1. The Umayyads had fourteen caliphs.

2. The people of Kuwait are more than one hundred and fifty thousand.

3. The fifth Umayyad caliph was 'Abd al-Malik, who built Qubbat al-Ṣakhrah.

4. The employees presented four demands to the manager and said they would continue their strike until the realization of their demands.

5. The existence of the Arab League represents a step towards co-operation among the nine Arab states.

6. The British occupied Egypt in the year one thousand eight hundred and eighty-two.

QUADRILITERAL VERBS. CONDITIONAL SENTENCES

I. ILLUSTRATIVE TEXT

١. بَرْهَنَ العُلَماء أَنَّ شَريعة حَمُورَابِي

1. Scholars have proved that the law of Hammurabi,

التي تُرْجِمَتْ إلى كُلِّ لُغات

which has been translated into all languages of the

العالَم كانَتْ نتيجة تَطَوّرٍ دامَ

world, was the result of a development which lasted

مُدَّةً طويلةً .

a long time.

٢. وقد اطْمَأَنَّ الناسُ إليها

2. The people looked with favor at it, and it

وبَقِيَتْ معمولاً بها حَتَّى اضْمَحَلَّتْ

remained in force until the state of Babylon faded away.

دَوْلةُ بَابِلَ .

٣. ويَبْدو أَنَّ العِبْرانِيين عند خُروجِهِم

3. It appears that the Hebrews, upon their emergence from

من الصَّحْراء ووُصولِهِم إلى الهِلال الخصيب

the desert and their arrival in the Fertile

أقامُوا الصِلات مع أَهْلِ بَابِلَ

Crescent, established connections with the people

وتَتَلْمَذوا عليهم وأَخَذوا

of Babylon, became their students, and took the

الشريعة عنهم .

law from them.

٤. فَخَلَقَ ذلك جَوّا مناسبا لظُهُورِ أَنْبِياء

4. That (situation) created a suitable atmosphere for

طَلَبوا إلى الناس

the appearance of prophets who sought from the people

159

that they believe in the existence of God, that they

draw near to Him, that they eschew Satan, who whispers in their

breasts, and that they follow the straight path.

أَنْ يَعْتَقِدوا بِوُجودِ الله

وَأَنْ يَقْتَرِبوا منه وَيَتْرُكوا

الشَّيْطانَ الذي يُوَسْوِسُ في صُدورِهم
وَيَتْبَعوا الطريقَ المستقيمَ.

5. There occurred in that law what follows:

٥. وقد جاء في تلك الشريعة ما يَلي :

6. If a person pulls out the eye of another, his eye

shall be pulled out.

٦. إِنْ يَقْلَعْ إِنْسانٌ عَيْنَ آخَرَ

تُقْلَعْ عَيْنُه.

7. If a person breaks the tooth of another, his

tooth shall be broken.

٧. إِنْ يَكْسِرْ إِنْسانٌ سِنَّ آخَرَ

فَسِنُّه تُكْسَرْ.

8. He who kills, shall be killed.

٨. مَنْ يَقْتُلْ يُقْتَلْ.

9. If a person steals a thing belonging to

another, he shall return it and the like of it.

٩. إِنْ يَسْرِقْ إِنْسانٌ شَيْئًا لِغَيْرِه

أَعادَه وأَعادَ مِثْلَه.

10. If a person is a highway robber (*literally*, cuts the road), he shall be

killed by drowning.

١٠. إِنْ قَطَعَ إِنسانٌ الطريقَ

قُتِلَ غَرَقا.

11. It is said that had these Babylonians not reached a

great degree of civilization, they would not have had a law like this.

١١. وَيُقالُ لَوْ أَنَّ هؤلاء البابِلِيينَ
ما وَصَلوا
إلى دَرَجةٍ كَبيرةٍ من المَدَنية لَما
كانَتْ لَدَيْهم شريعةٌ مِثْلُ هذه.

12. If the world should follow the spirit of this law, it

١٢. فَإِذا تَبِعَ العالَمُ روحَ تلك الشريعة

would be in a happier condition and more able to
solve its problems.

كانَ أَسْعَدَ حالاً وأَقْدَرَ على حَلِّ

مشاكِله .

II. GRAMMATICAL ANALYSIS

1. The verb بَرْهَنَ is third person masculine singular perfect of a quadriliteral verb, i.e. one composed of four radicals. Quadriliteral verbs are said to be of the فَعْلَلَ pattern. فَعْلَلَ is the simple, underived quadriliteral verb and is conjugated like Form II (فَعَّلَ) of the triliteral verb. (For the conjugation see paradigms, Appendix I.) The active and passive participles are also like those of فَعَّلَ. The maṣdar is of the فَعْلَلَة (or فِعْلَلَة) pattern.

The verb تُرْجِمَتْ is third person feminine singular perfect passive of the Form I quadriliteral verb تَرْجَمَ.

2. The verb إِطْمَأَنَّ is third person masculine singular perfect of Form IV of the quadriliteral root form طَمْأَنَ. Form IV of quadriliteral verbs is of the pattern إِفْعَلَلَّ. The participles are of the patterns مُفْعَلِلّ and مُفْعَلَلّ. The maṣdar is of the pattern إِفْعِلّالّ. (For the conjugation, see paradigm in Appendix I.)

Form IV of quadriliteral verbs modifies the meaning of the root form by making it intransitive and intensive, thus طَمْأَنَ 'to rest (a thing),' إِطْمَأَنَّ 'to be thoroughly at rest,' 'to be assured.'

The verb إِضْمَحَلَّتْ is third person feminine singular perfect of Form IV of the quadriliteral ضَمْحَلَ.

3. The verb تَتَلْمَذُوا is third person masculine plural perfect of Form II of the quadriliteral root form تَلْمَذَ. Form II of quadriliteral verbs is of the pattern تَفَعْلَلَ and is conjugated like Form V (تَفَعَّلَ) of the triliteral. The participles and maṣdars are also formed like those of تَفَعَّلَ. (For the conjugation see paradigms, Appendix I.)

Form II of quadriliteral verbs modifies the meaning of the root form in the same way that Form V modifies the meaning of the triliteral root form.

NOTE: Form III of the quadriliteral (إِفْعَنْلَلَ) is very rare; there are no other derived forms.

4. The verb يُوَسْوِسُ is third person masculine singular imperfect of the quadriliteral root form وَسْوَسَ.

It may be observed that the verb وَسْوَسَ is an onomatopoetic word formed by repeating a biliteral syllable. There are many such verbs indicating repetition of a sound or movement.

Another type of quadriliteral is the denominative, from nouns of more than three letters, such as تَلْمَذَ (> تِلْمِيذ 'student').

6. The word إِنْ is a conditional particle introducing the *if*-clause or *sharṭ* ('condition') of a conditional sentence in which the hypothesis is possible or plausible.[1] Usually the if-clause precedes the main clause or *jawāb* ('answer'). In this type of conditional sentence either the jussive or the perfect may be used in either the sharṭ or the jawāb (as is shown in I, 6, 7, 8, and 9) with a present or future sense.

7. In this sentence it will be noted that the jawāb is introduced by the conjunction فَ.... which must be used when the jawāb is a nominal sentence or an imperative. It will also be noted that the verb of the jawāb is imperfect indicative. In a nominal jawāb the verb is imperfect indicative.

8. In this sentence the relative pronoun مَنْ has a force similar to that of إِنْ. Therefore, the clause مَنْ يَقْتُلْ is a sharṭ and يُقْتَلْ is a jawāb.

NOTE: Some other words which, like مَنْ, introduce a sharṭ are:

مَا	whatever
أَيْنَمَا	wherever
مَتَى	when
مَهْمَا	whatever
أَيُّ	whoever, whichever
حَيْثُمَا	wherever

[1] For a thorough treatment of conditional sentences consult M. Gaudefroy-Demombynes and R. Blachère, *Grammaire de l'Arabe classique*, 3rd ed. (Paris: Editions G. P. Maisonneuve et Cie., 1952), pp. 450–468.

11. The word لَوْ is a conditional particle introducing the sharṭ of a conditional sentence in which the hypothesis is impossible. If the sharṭ is a nominal sentence, لَوْ أَنَّ is used. In this type of conditional sentence the perfect is commonly used in both sharṭ and jawāb although the imperfect indicative may be used.

The particle of affirmation لَ... commonly introduces the jawāb when the sharṭ is introduced by لَوْ but not if the jawāb precedes the sharṭ.

12. The word إِذَا is a conditional particle introducing the sharṭ of a conditional sentence indicating an eventuality which is likely to occur. The jawāb tells what will happen when it does occur. There is a weak temporal sense in the word إِذَا and it may frequently be translated by *when*.

Conditional sentences introduced by إِذَا commonly have the perfect in both sharṭ and jawāb.

III. PRACTICE TEXT

1. Yesterday I received a letter from my girl

friend in which she said:

١. أَخَذْتُ أَمْسِ كِتابا من صديقتي

قالَتْ فيه :

2. "My dear: It was not within my power to

visit you last week in accordance with our

appointment.

٢. "حبيبي : إِنَّني لَمْ يَكُنْ باستطاعتي

زيارتُك في الأُسْبوعِ الماضي كما كانَ

مَوْعِدُنا .

3. I want to say to you that if I had had

sufficient time, I would have visited you and

talked to you at length about an important

matter—the matter of our marriage.

٣. وأُريدُ أَنْ أَقولَ لك إِنَّه لَوْكانَ لديَّ

الوَقْتُ الكافي لَزُرْتُك

وتَكَلَّمْتُ إِليك طويلا في أَمْرٍ ذي

أَهَمِّيَّةٍ هو أَمْرُ زَواجِنا.

4. If I have time in this month, I will come to

visit you on the fifth, to be at your side and to

spend with you a whole week.

٤. وَإِذَا كَانَ لَدَيَّ الوَقْتُ في هذا الشَّهْر

جِئْتُ لِأَزُورَك في الخامِسِ منه لِأَكُونَ

بِجانِبِك وَأَصْرِفَ معك أُسْبوعا كامِلا .

5. If the airplane is late, I will arrive on the

sixth.

٥. وَإِذَا تَأَخَّرَتِ الطَّيَّارَةُ وَصَلْتُ عندك في

السادس منه .

6. If you would wait for me at the airport at the time

of my arrival, I would consider it a kindness from you.

٦. وَإِنْ تَنْتَظِرْني في المطارِ وَقْتَ

وُصولي عَدَدْتُ ذلك كَرَما منك .

7. You will see that I still love you, and that you are

still the qiblah of my heart;

٧. إنَّك سَتَرَى أَنَّني لا أَزالُ أُحِبُّك

وأنَّك لا تَزالُ قِبْلَةَ قَلْبي ،

8. for whatever you do, I will do; wherever you go, I will

go; and whomever you visit, I will visit so that you

will be satisfied and relaxed about me.

٨. فَمَهْما تَعْمَلْ أَعْمَلْ ، وحيثما تَذْهَبْ

أَذْهَبْ ، وأيّا تَزُرْ أَزُرْ حَتَّى تَكونَ

راضِيا عنّي ومستريحا إِلَيَّ .

9. My actions will prove my sincerity.

٩. وَسَوْفَ تُبَرْهِنُ أَعْمالي عن إِخْلاصي .

10. So I hope, therefore, that your mind rests easy about

me, and don't rely on the talk of those people who

whisper about me and who convey to you untrue and

unweighed information.

١٠. فَأَرْجو إِذًا أَنْ يَطْمَئِنَّ بالُك عنّي ،

ولا تَعْتَمِدْ على قَوْلِ الذين

يُوَسْوِسونَ عنّي من الناسِ ويَنْقُلونَ إليك

الأَخْبارَ غَيْرَ الصحيحة ولا الموزونة .

11. Sincerely, your beloved, Layla."

١١. المخلِصة حبيبتك لَيْلَى . "

CHAPTER XXXIV

IV. EXERCISES

Translate into English:

١. إِنْ تُوَافِقِ الجامعةُ العَرَبيّةُ على ميثاقِ الدفاعِ اطْمَأَنَّ بالُ العَرَبِ في الشَّرْقِ الأوْسَطِ على مستقبِلِهم وتأمينِ مَصْلَحتِهم وحِفْظِ وَحْدَتِهم وتحويلِ ضَعْفِهم إلى شِدّةٍ .

٢. مَنْ عامَلَ الناسَ بِرِفْقٍ وإخلاصٍ عُوبِلَ بِمِثْلِهما .

٣. إذا التَقَيْتَ بِأخي أو أبي أرْجو أَنْ تَسْأَلَهما أَنْ يَتَّصِلا بي حالا في النادي كَيْ أَطْمَئِنَّ عن حالِهما وأَنْقُلَ إليهما أَخْبارَ والدتي .

٤. لَوْلا أَنَّ اللهَ يُريدُ مَصْلَحةَ الناسِ لَما أَرْسَلَ اليهم الأَنْبِياءَ ومَنَحَهم البَرَكاتِ .

٥. كُنْ مِمَّنْ (مِنْ مَنْ) إذا قالَ فَعَلَ .

٦. مَنْ يُتَرْجِمْ كتابا من لُغَةٍ إلى أُخْرى يُكْرَمْ وَيَنَلْ بَرَكاتِ العُلَماءِ ويُصْبِحْ أَسْمى مَقاما وأَعْظَمَ أَهَمِّيَّةً في نَظَرِ مواطنيه .

٧. إِنْ تَسْجِنِ الحُكومةُ إِنْسانا بدونِ وُجودِ سَبَبٍ تَدْعَسْ على حُرّيّةٍ أساسِيةٍ مقدَّسةٍ للناسِ وتَفْشَلْ في واجبِها للدفاعِ عن حُرمتِهم وتَخْلُقْ في أَنْفُسِهم عَدَمَ الثِّقةِ بها وَتَكَدْ تُشَجِّعُهم على الثَّورةِ وخَلْقِ الإضطراباتِ .

Translate into Arabic:

1. If a man does not defend his faith, he has no faith.
2. If you need anything from the city, tell me before I go.
3. If a general fears war, he must resign before his weakness spreads to the army.
4. Had I known you were a great scholar in this field, I would have become your student.
5. If there were no oil in the Arab world, the economic situation would be more difficult.

165

CHAPTER XXXV

POTPOURRI

I. ILLUSTRATIVE TEXT

1. The great Muslim reformer, the scholar, Shaykh

   Muḥammad 'Abduh was born in the year 1849 of a

   poor family which was living in the Mudīrīyah

   (administrative district) of al-Buḥayrah. He spent

   his childhood as his father[s] and grandfathers had spent

   theirs in the Egyptian countryside.

2. No sooner had he reached the thirteenth (year) of his life,

   than he read and memorized the Koran. Then he headed

   for the religious school of Tanta to study the Koranic "sciences."

3. But he did not stay in it long; on the contrary he

   left it, despairing of studying in it.

4. However, some one interested him in continuing (his)

١. وُلِدَ المُصلِحُ الإسلامي الكبير الشيخ العلّامة

محمدٌ عبدُهُ عامَ ١٨٤٩ في عائلة فقيرة تَسكُنُ مديرية البحيرة . وقضى طفولتَه كما قضاها آباؤُه وأجدادُه في الريف المصري .

٢. وما أن بلغ الثالثةَ عشرةَ من عمره حتى قرأ القرآنَ وحفظه . فقصد مدرسةَ طنطا الدينيةَ يَدْرُسُ العلومَ القرآنية .

٣. ولكنه لم يَدُمْ فيها طويلا ، بل تركها وهو يائسٌ من الدرس فيها .

٤. غير أن أحدَهم حبّب اليه أن يستمرّ

study; the result was that he returned to the Tanta school.

في الدرس فكانت النتيجةُ أن عاد الى مدرسة طنطا.

5. Then in the following year (1866) he headed for al-Azhar

٥. ثم في السنة التالية (١٨٦٦) قصد

in which a new spirit had spread, it being recognition

الأزهرَ حيث كانت روحٌ جديدة قد انتشرت

of the importance of history and the natural sciences.

فيه ، وهي الاعترافُ بأهمّية التأريخ والعلوم الطبيعية.

6. During this period Shaykh Muḥammad ʿAbduh began to tend

٦. وفي هذه المدة أخذ الشيخُ محمد عبده

toward asceticism and to leave the affairs of this life.

يميل الى الزُهْد ويتركُ أمورَ هذه الحياة.

7. His condition continued thus until he contacted a great

٧. وبقي حالُه كذلك حتى اتصل بمعلّم

teacher. The name of this teacher was Sayyid Jamāl

كبير. وهذا المعلّمُ اسمُه السيّد جمال

al-Dīn al-Afghāni, (who) had arrived in Egypt. He

الدين الافغاني، وكان وصل الى مصر

interested him in modern Islamic and Egyptian affairs.

فحبّب اليه الأمورَ الإسلامية والمصرية الحديثة.

8. In the following ten years he was either teaching in

٨. وفي السنوات العشر التالية كان إمّا يُعلّم

Dār al-ʿUlūm College or working in journalism as

في كلّية دار العلوم أو يعمل في الصحافة

editor of *al-Waqāʾiʿ al-Miṣrīyah*, a gazette

كمحرّر لمجلّة " الوقائعُ المصرية " ذاتِ

of official character.

الصفة الرسمية.

9. It is thought that he participated in the rebellion

٩. ويُظنّ أنه اشترك في الثورة

led by al-ʿArābi in the year 1882, against the

التي قادها العرابي سنة ١٨٨٢ ضدَّ

167

Egyptian government, but the degree of his participation

الحكومة المصرية ولكنْ لا تُعرف درجةُ

is not known. There is no doubt that he

ذلك الاشتراك. ومّما لا شكّ فيه أنه

advocated moderation in it since he sincerely believed

كان يدعو الى الاعتدال فيها اذ كان يعتقد

in evolution, [he is] unlike Sayyid Jamāl al-Dīn, who believed

مُخلصا بالتطوُّر وهو ليسَ مثلَ السيّد جمال الدين

in jihad and revolution.

الذى كان يعتقد بالجهاد والثورة.

10. After the rebellion had failed, he was sentenced to

١٠ وبعدما فشلت الثورةُ حُكمَ عليه

banishment from Egypt— this is what usually happens to

بالنفي من مصر — وهذا هو ما يجري عامّةً

sincere reformers. Then he traveled to Beirut, and then

للمُصلحينَ المؤمنينَ. فسافر الى بيروت

Paris, where he spent some time and established with

فباريس حيث صرف بعضَ الوقت وأسّس مع

his teacher, Jamāl al-Dīn, the magazine, al-'Urwah

استاذه جمال الدين مجلّةَ '' العروةُ الوثقى ''

al-Wuthqa, in which they defended the Islamic cause.

فدافعا فيها عن القضية الإسلامية.

Then he returned to Beirut and lived in it until the

ثم عاد الى بيروت وسكنها حتى أذنت

Egyptian government permitted him to return to

له الحكومةُ المصرية بالرجوع الى

his country. He returned seeking to teach.

بلاده. فعاد اليها يطلُبُ التعليمَ فيها.

11. That was not allowed him, but he was appointed a

١١. فلم يُؤذَنْ له بذلك بل عُيّن

judge, then *conseiller* in the court of appeals, and

قاضيا فمستشارا في محكمة الاستئناف،

finally *mufti* of Egypt.

فمُفتيَ مصر.

168

12. He led the reform movement in al-Azhar, which caused

violent opposition on the part of the reactionary

and conservative circles; and between him and them

there were sharp disputes, but he did not retreat from

his position; in fact his insistence on it increased.

13. He said that his program stood on the following

matters or pillars: first, reform of the Muslim religion

and returning it to its original condition;

second, reform of the Arabic language; and third, recognition

of the rights of the people vis-à-vis the government.

14. And he declared war on "traditionalism"; in fact

he appealed for freedom of ijtihād and for a new ijmā',

(just) as he wanted the common good to be the basis

of law, for he gave it precedence over the literal

text. He always weighed matters in the scale of

reason on the basis of his extensive knowledge.

١٢. وقد قاد حركةَ الإصلاحات في الأزهر ممّا

سبّب معارضةً شديدة بين الدوائر الرَجعية

والمُحافظة . فكان بينه وبينها

مناقشاتٌ شديدة ولكنه لم يتراجعْ عن موقفه

بل اشتدَّ إصرارُه عليه .

١٣. وقال ان مشروعَه يقوم على الأمور

أو الأركان التالية : أولا إصلاحُ الدين الإسلامي والرجوعُ به الى حالته الأصلية؛

ثانيا إصلاحُ اللغة العربية؛ وثالثا

الاعترافُ بحقوق الشعب مُقابلَ الحكومة .

١٤. وقد أعلن الحربَ على التقليد، بل

دعا الى حرّية الاجتهاد والى إجماع جديد

كما أراد أن تكون المصلحةُ أساسَ الشريعة فقدّمها على النصّ الحرفي .

وكان دائما يزن الأمورَ بميزان العقل

على أساس علمه الواسع .

15. Shaykh Muḥammad ‘Abduh, may God have mercy on him, died

in the year 1905.

١٥. وتوفّيَ الشيخُ محمدٍ عبده، رحمَهُ اللهُ

سنةَ ١٩٠٥.

16. There is no doubt that he has had to date a great

influence in the Muslim world because he is con-

sidered to be an example for reformers; but will this

influence last, or will it cease? This is what history

will prove.

١٦. وممّا لا شكَّ فيه أنه كان له حتى الآن

تأثيرٌ كبير في العالم الإسلامي لأنه

يُعْتَبَرُ مثالا للمصلحين، ولكنْ هل

يدوم هذا التأثيرُ أَمْ أنه يزول؟

هذا ما سيُبرهنه التأريخُ.

II. GRAMMATICAL ANALYSIS

1. The verb تَسْكُنْ, although imperfect, has here a past continuous signification. Imperfect verbs acquire the force of the past when they follow a perfect verb without an intervening conjunction. Imperfect verbs have the force of the past:

(a) In relative clauses (as is the case with تَسْكُنْ in this item), best translated by the past continuous.

(b) When the imperfect verb has the force of an accusative of purpose (as in قَصَدَ....يَدْرُس in II, 2, below), best translated by the infinitive.

(c) After the verb كَانَ (as in كَانَ....يُعَلِّمُ in II, 8, below), best translated by the past progressive or frequently by translating كَانَ as *used to*.

(d) When the imperfect verb has the force of an adverb of manner (as in عَادَ....يَطْلُبُ in II, 10, below), best translated by the active participle.

The verb قَضَى in "قَضَاهَا" is necessarily translated by the past perfect since its action took place before the action of another perfect verb قَضَى.

2. The idiom حَتَّى....بَلَغَ أَنْ مَا.... (the أَنْ is optional; بَلَغَ is not part of the idiom; any verb may be used) means literally, *not (that) he reached...until...*, and may be translated *no sooner had he reached ...than....*

The adjective الدِيـنِيَّة modifies the word مَدْرَسَة, not the word طَنْطَا. An adjective modifying either the first or the second member of a construct phrase must follow the second. In such a case one must depend on the context in order to know which noun the adjective modifies.

For use of the imperfect verb يَدْرُس, consult II, 1 (b), above.

3. The conjunctive particle بَلْ when used after a negative statement introduces a rectification of the original statement with the idea of opposition and may be translated by *but* or *on the contrary*. (For use of بَلْ after a positive statement, see II, 14, below.)

The clause وَهْوَ يَائِس is the equivalent of the adverb of manner يَائِسًا. Such nominal clauses are called "manner clauses" (Arabic singular جُمْلَة حَالِيَّة) and are always introduced by the conjunction وَ which is in this usage called the "wāw of manner" (Arabic وَاوُ ٱلْحَال). Such clauses are to be distinguished from that usage of the imperfect explained in II, 1 (d), above (where يَطْلُب also has the force of an adverb of manner) by the presence of the wāw of manner introducing a nominal clause. In some cases the two usages are interchangeable.

4. The combination غَيْرَ أَنَّ expresses in modern Arabic the sense of *however*.

The conjunction ...فَ, as in فَكَانَ, denotes an immediate sequence.

5. The conjunction ثُمَّ denotes a less immediate sequence than does ...فَ.

The sequence كَانَتْ...ٱنْتَشَرَتْ exemplifies the Arabic method of expressing the past perfect, i.e. the perfect of كَانَ plus the perfect of another verb. The subject (here رُوح) is often placed between the two verbs.

6. In the sequence أَخَذَ يَمِيلُ the verb أَخَذَ means *to begin*. The verbs أَخَذَ 'to take,' صَارَ 'to become,' and جَعَلَ 'to make,' when followed by a verb in the imperfect mean *to begin*.

7. In the sentence هٰذَا ٱلْمُعَلِّمُ ٱسْمُهُ جَمَالُ ٱلدِّين the subject of the sentence is ٱلْمُعَلِّمُ and the predicate is ٱسْمُهُ جَمَالُ ٱلدِّين. The predicate itself is a nominal sentence in which ٱسْمُ is the subject and جَمَالُ is the

predicate. Such a construction, in which the subject of the predicate is a different entity from the subject of the sentence but related to it by a pronoun, though unusual in Indo-European languages, is common in Arabic.

8. The sequence كَانَ ... يَعْلَمُ exemplifies the Arabic method of expressing the past progressive, i.e. the perfect of كَانَ plus the imperfect of another verb. (See II, 1 (c), above.)

The sequence of conjunctions إِمَّا ... أَوْ is the equivalent of *either . . . or.* An alternative sequence is إِمَّا ... وَإِمَّا.

9. The imperfect passive verb يُظَنُّ exemplifies one of the uses of the imperfect which is to signify an act that was started in the past and continued through the present. The same is true of the imperfect passive verb تُعْرَفُ.

The idiom مِمَّا لَا شَكَّ فِيه (literally, *among those things about which there is no doubt*) is frequently used in modern Arabic and means *there is no doubt.* مِمَّا is an assimilation of مِنْ and مَا.

10. The imperfect verb يَجْرِي exemplifies another use of the imperfect, the signification of which is that the action endures or is likely to happen repeatedly.

For the use of the imperfect verb يَطْلُبُ consult II, 1 (d), above.

12. In the last sentence of I, 12, it is to be noted that the prepositional adverb بَيْن 'between' is repeated. This always happens when at least one of the two words dependent on بَيْن is a pronoun.

13. It is to be noted that after the verb قَالَ the particle إِنَّ (normal meaning, *verily*) is used instead of the particle أَنَّ (normal meaning, *that*) to express the conjunction *that* which introduces indirect speech. Direct and indirect speech are not clearly distinguished in Arabic.

14. The conjunctive particle بَلْ, when used after a positive statement, introduces a rectification of the original statement with the idea of completing it or even going farther along the lines suggested by it. It may be translated by *in fact, rather, better still,* or *more exactly.*

15. The verb رَحِم, though perfect and therefore basically signifying a completed and definite action, has here an optative force because it ex-

presses a hope that something be done. For wishes, prayers, and curses, the perfect is used instead of the imperfect to give the wish, prayer, or curse the character of definiteness or actual happening by implying that it has already been realized.

16. The perfect verb كَانَ here exemplifies a use of the perfect which is the equivalent of the English present perfect tense, i.e. the action has already been completed at the moment of speaking.

The particle أَمْ is always used in alternative questions to signify *or* instead of the particle أَوْ.

The imperfect verb يَدُومُ here exemplifies the imperfect used with a future meaning.

APPENDICES

PARADIGMS

Twelve triliteral verbs have been used in the main body of these paradigms to illustrate the major verbal types in the Arabic language. They are conjugated in parallel columns in order to show the modifications of each type of weak verb vis-à-vis the sound verb. Each page is devoted to a single mood of a single verb. As samples, the verbs have been presented in all Forms in which verbs of their particular type may appear regardless of whether or not the sample verbs themselves do in fact make use of all the Forms. The dictionary should be consulted to ascertain the actual Forms which any verb, including these samples, assumes. The sample verbs and the types which they illustrate are as follows:

Number	*Verb*	*Type of Verb*
1	فَعَلَ	Sound
2	رَدَّ	Doubled
3	وَضَعَ	Weak-fā'
4	قَامَ	Hollow, original medial wāw preserved in the imperfect
5	نَامَ	Hollow, medial wāw or yā', but takes alif in imperfect
6	سَارَ	Hollow, original medial yā' preserved in the imperfect
7	نَدَا	Weak-lām, original final wāw preserved in the imperfect
8	رَمَى	Weak-lām, original final yā' preserved in the imperfect
9	رَضِيَ	Weak-lām, original final yā' of the فَعَلَ type, takes alif maqṣūrah in the imperfect
10	أَسَرَ	Initial hamzah
11	بَؤُسَ	Medial hamzah
12	قَرَأَ	Final hamzah

The numbers at the top of the columns in the paradigms refer to the numbers in the preceding list and thus indicate which verb is being conjugated in each column. In the derived forms where the conjugation of hollow and of weak-lām verbs of different types are identical, only the first verb of the type is conjugated. The numbers of the other verbs of that type are, however, shown in the column heading. The same process is followed in listing the maṣdars and active and passive participles of such verbs.

In Form IX only the sound verb is conjugated because there are no variants.

In the passive all types are given, but synopsized: third person masculine and feminine and second person masculine in the perfect, in the imperfect third masculine singular only. No subjunctives or jussives of the passive are shown.

Participles of all Forms and maṣdars of derived Forms are self explanatory as are conjugations of the imperative and of the quadriliteral verb.

It will be noted that some variants, such as weak-fā' verbs beginning with yā', have been omitted; and that in some cases where alternate choices exist an arbitrary choice has been made. Also some purely hypothetical forms have been shown.

A table of contents for the paradigms follow:

ACTIVE, FORM I, PERFECT

Singular

	1	2	3	4	5	6	7	8	9	10	11	12
3 M	فَعَلَ	رَدَّ	وَضَعَ	قَامَ	خَافَ	سَارَ	نَدَا	رَمَى	رَضِيَ	أَسَرَ	بَقِيَ	قَرَأَ
3 F	فَعَلَتْ	رَدَّتْ	وَضَعَتْ	قَامَتْ	خَافَتْ	سَارَتْ	نَدَتْ	رَمَتْ	رَضِيَتْ	أَسَرَتْ	بَقِيَتْ	قَرَأَتْ
2 M	فَعَلْتَ	رَدَدْتَ	وَضَعْتَ	قُمْتَ	خِفْتَ	سِرْتَ	نَدَوْتَ	رَمَيْتَ	رَضِيتَ	أَسَرْتَ	بَقِيتَ	قَرَأْتَ
2 F	فَعَلْتِ	رَدَدْتِ	وَضَعْتِ	قُمْتِ	خِفْتِ	سِرْتِ	نَدَوْتِ	رَمَيْتِ	رَضِيتِ	أَسَرْتِ	بَقِيتِ	قَرَأْتِ
1	فَعَلْتُ	رَدَدْتُ	وَضَعْتُ	قُمْتُ	خِفْتُ	سِرْتُ	نَدَوْتُ	رَمَيْتُ	رَضِيتُ	أَسَرْتُ	بَقِيتُ	قَرَأْتُ

Dual

	1	2	3	4	5	6	7	8	9	10	11	12
3 M	فَعَلَا	رَدَّا	وَضَعَا	قَامَا	خَافَا	سَارَا	نَدَوَا	رَمَيَا	رَضِيَا	أَسَرَا	بَقِيَا	قَرَآ
3 F	فَعَلَتَا	رَدَّتَا	وَضَعَتَا	قَامَتَا	خَافَتَا	سَارَتَا	نَدَتَا	رَمَتَا	رَضِيَتَا	أَسَرَتَا	بَقِيَتَا	قَرَأَتَا
2	فَعَلْتُمَا	رَدَدْتُمَا	وَضَعْتُمَا	قُمْتُمَا	خِفْتُمَا	سِرْتُمَا	نَدَوْتُمَا	رَمَيْتُمَا	رَضِيتُمَا	أَسَرْتُمَا	بَقِيتُمَا	قَرَأْتُمَا

Plural

	1	2	3	4	5	6	7	8	9	10	11	12
3 M	فَعَلُوا	رَدُّوا	وَضَعُوا	قَامُوا	خَافُوا	سَارُوا	نَدَوْا	رَمَوْا	رَضُوا	أَسَرُوا	بَقُوا	قَرَأُوا
3 F	فَعَلْنَ	رَدَدْنَ	وَضَعْنَ	قُمْنَ	خِفْنَ	سِرْنَ	نَدَوْنَ	رَمَيْنَ	رَضِينَ	أَسَرْنَ	بَقِينَ	قَرَأْنَ
2 M	فَعَلْتُمْ	رَدَدْتُمْ	وَضَعْتُمْ	قُمْتُمْ	خِفْتُمْ	سِرْتُمْ	نَدَوْتُمْ	رَمَيْتُمْ	رَضِيتُمْ	أَسَرْتُمْ	بَقِيتُمْ	قَرَأْتُمْ
2 F	فَعَلْتُنَّ	رَدَدْتُنَّ	وَضَعْتُنَّ	قُمْتُنَّ	خِفْتُنَّ	سِرْتُنَّ	نَدَوْتُنَّ	رَمَيْتُنَّ	رَضِيتُنَّ	أَسَرْتُنَّ	بَقِيتُنَّ	قَرَأْتُنَّ
1	فَعَلْنَا	رَدَدْنَا	وَضَعْنَا	قُمْنَا	خِفْنَا	سِرْنَا	نَدَوْنَا	رَمَيْنَا	رَضِينَا	أَسَرْنَا	بَقِينَا	قَرَأْنَا

ACTIVE, FORM I, IMPERFECT INDICATIVE

	12	11	10	9	8	7	6	5	4	3	2	1	
Singular													
3 M	يَقْرَأُ	يَبْغُضُ	يَأْسِرُ	يَرْضَى	يَرْمِي	يَبْدُو	يَيْسِرُ	يَبَانُ	يَقُولُ	يَفْصِمُ	يَرُدُّ	يَفْعُلُ	3 M
3 F	تَقْرَأُ	تَبْغُضُ	تَأْسِرُ	تَرْضَى	تَرْمِي	تَبْدُو	تَيْسِرُ	تَبَانُ	تَقُولُ	تَفْصِمُ	تَرُدُّ	تَفْعُلُ	3 F
2 M	تَقْرَأُ	تَبْغُضُ	تَأْسِرُ	تَرْضَى	تَرْمِي	تَبْدُو	تَيْسِرُ	تَبَانُ	تَقُولُ	تَفْصِمُ	تَرُدُّ	تَفْعُلُ	2 M
2 F	تَقْرَئِينَ	تَبْغُضِينَ	تَأْسِرِينَ	تَرْضَيْنَ	تَرْمِينَ	تَبْدِينَ	تَيْسِرِينَ	تَبَانِينَ	تَقُولِينَ	تَفْصِمِينَ	تَرُدِّينَ	تَفْعُلِينَ	2 F
1	أَقْرَأُ	أَبْغُضُ	أَأْسِرُ	أَرْضَى	أَرْمِي	أَنْدُو	أَيْسِرُ	أَبَانُ	أَقُولُ	أَفْصِمُ	أَرُدُّ	أَفْعُلُ	1
Dual													
3 M	يَقْرَآنِ	يَبْغُضَانِ	يَأْسِرَانِ	يَرْضَيَانِ	يَرْمِيَانِ	يَبْدُوَانِ	يَيْسِرَانِ	يَبَانَانِ	يَقُولَانِ	يَفْصِمَانِ	يَرُدَّانِ	يَفْعُلَانِ	3 M
3 F	تَقْرَآنِ	تَبْغُضَانِ	تَأْسِرَانِ	تَرْضَيَانِ	تَرْمِيَانِ	تَبْدُوَانِ	تَيْسِرَانِ	تَبَانَانِ	تَقُولَانِ	تَفْصِمَانِ	تَرُدَّانِ	تَفْعُلَانِ	3 F
2	تَقْرَآنِ	تَبْغُضَانِ	تَأْسِرَانِ	تَرْضَيَانِ	تَرْمِيَانِ	تَبْدُوَانِ	تَيْسِرَانِ	تَبَانَانِ	تَقُولَانِ	تَفْصِمَانِ	تَرُدَّانِ	تَفْعُلَانِ	2
Plural													
3 M	يَقْرَؤُونَ	يَبْغُضُونَ	يَأْسِرُونَ	يَرْضَوْنَ	يَرْمُونَ	يَبْدُونَ	يَيْسِرُونَ	يَبَانُونَ	يَقُولُونَ	يَفْصِمُونَ	يَرُدُّونَ	يَفْعُلُونَ	3 M
3 F	يَقْرَأْنَ	يَبْغُضْنَ	يَأْسِرْنَ	يَرْضَيْنَ	يَرْمِينَ	يَبْدُونَ	يَيْسِرْنَ	يَبَنَّ	يَقُلْنَ	يَفْصِمْنَ	يَرْدُدْنَ	يَفْعُلْنَ	3 F
2 M	تَقْرَؤُونَ	تَبْغُضُونَ	تَأْسِرُونَ	تَرْضَوْنَ	تَرْمُونَ	تَبْدُونَ	تَيْسِرُونَ	تَبَانُونَ	تَقُولُونَ	تَفْصِمُونَ	تَرُدُّونَ	تَفْعُلُونَ	2 M
2 F	تَقْرَأْنَ	تَبْغُضْنَ	تَأْسِرْنَ	تَرْضَيْنَ	تَرْمِينَ	تَبْدُونَ	تَيْسِرْنَ	تَبَنَّ	تَقُلْنَ	تَفْصِمْنَ	تَرْدُدْنَ	تَفْعُلْنَ	2 F
1	نَقْرَأُ	نَبْغُضُ	نَأْسِرُ	نَرْضَى	نَرْمِي	نَبْدُو	نَيْسِرُ	نَبَانُ	نَقُولُ	نَفْصِمُ	نَرُدُّ	نَفْعُلُ	1

182

ACTIVE, FORM I, SUBJUNCTIVE

	1	2	3	4	5	6	7	8	9	10	11	12	
						Singular							
3 M	يَفْعَلَ	يَرُدَّ	يَمْضِيَ	يَقُومَ	يَنَامَ	يَسِيرَ	يَنْدُو	يَرْمِيَ	يَرْضَى	يَأْسِرَ	يَبْؤُسَ	يَقْرَأَ	3 M
3 F	تَفْعَلَ	تَرُدَّ	تَمْضِيَ	تَقُومَ	تَنَامَ	تَسِيرَ	تَنْدُو	تَرْمِيَ	تَرْضَى	تَأْسِرَ	تَبْؤُسَ	تَقْرَأَ	3 F
2 M	تَفْعَلَ	تَرُدَّ	تَمْضِيَ	تَقُومَ	تَنَامَ	تَسِيرَ	تَنْدُو	تَرْمِيَ	تَرْضَى	تَأْسِرَ	تَبْؤُسَ	تَقْرَأَ	2 M
2 F	تَفْعَلِي	تَرُدِّي	تَمْضِي	تَقُومِي	تَنَامِي	تَسِيرِي	تَنْدِي	تَرْمِي	تَرْضَي	تَأْسِرِي	تَبْؤُسِي	تَقْرَئِي	2 F
1	أَفْعَلَ	أَرُدَّ	أَمْضِيَ	أَقُومَ	أَنَامَ	أَسِيرَ	أَنْدُو	أَرْمِيَ	أَرْضَى	أَأْسِرَ	أَبْؤُسَ	أَقْرَأَ	1
						Dual							
3 M	يَفْعَلَا	يَرُدَّا	يَمْضِيَا	يَقُومَا	يَنَامَا	يَسِيرَا	يَنْدُوَا	يَرْمِيَا	يَرْضَيَا	يَأْسِرَا	يَبْؤُسَا	يَقْرَآ	3 M
3 F	تَفْعَلَا	تَرُدَّا	تَمْضِيَا	تَقُومَا	تَنَامَا	تَسِيرَا	تَنْدُوَا	تَرْمِيَا	تَرْضَيَا	تَأْسِرَا	تَبْؤُسَا	تَقْرَآ	3 F
2	تَفْعَلَا	تَرُدَّا	تَمْضِيَا	تَقُومَا	تَنَامَا	تَسِيرَا	تَنْدُوَا	تَرْمِيَا	تَرْضَيَا	تَأْسِرَا	تَبْؤُسَا	تَقْرَآ	2
						Plural							
3 M	يَفْعَلُوا	يَرُدُّوا	يَمْضُوا	يَقُومُوا	يَنَامُوا	يَسِيرُوا	يَنْدُوا	يَرْمُوا	يَرْضَوْا	يَأْسِرُوا	يَبْؤُسُوا	يَقْرَؤُوا	3 M
3 F	يَفْعَلْنَ	يَرْدُدْنَ	يَمْضِينَ	يَقُمْنَ	يَنَمْنَ	يَسِرْنَ	يَنْدُونَ	يَرْمِينَ	يَرْضَيْنَ	يَأْسِرْنَ	يَبْؤُسْنَ	يَقْرَأْنَ	3 F
2 M	تَفْعَلُوا	تَرُدُّوا	تَمْضُوا	تَقُومُوا	تَنَامُوا	تَسِيرُوا	تَنْدُوا	تَرْمُوا	تَرْضَوْا	تَأْسِرُوا	تَبْؤُسُوا	تَقْرَؤُوا	2 M
2 F	تَفْعَلْنَ	تَرْدُدْنَ	تَمْضِينَ	تَقُمْنَ	تَنَمْنَ	تَسِرْنَ	تَنْدُونَ	تَرْمِينَ	تَرْضَيْنَ	تَأْسِرْنَ	تَبْؤُسْنَ	تَقْرَأْنَ	2 F
1	نَفْعَلَ	نَرُدَّ	نَمْضِيَ	نَقُومَ	نَنَامَ	نَسِيرَ	نَنْدُو	نَرْمِيَ	نَرْضَى	نَأْسِرَ	نَبْؤُسَ	نَقْرَأَ	1

ACTIVE, FORM I, JUSSIVE

	1	2	3	4	5	6	7	8	9	10	11	12	
Singular													
3 M	يَفْعُلْ	يَرْدُدْ	يَقْضِ	يَقُمْ	يَجِدْ	يَسِرْ	يَبْدُ	يَرِثْ	يَرْضَ	يَأْسُرْ	يَبْقُسْ	يَقْرَأْ	3 M
3 F	تَفْعُلْ	تَرْدُدْ	تَقْضِ	تَقُمْ	تَجِدْ	تَسِرْ	تَبْدُ	تَرِثْ	تَرْضَ	تَأْسُرْ	تَبْقُسْ	تَقْرَأْ	3 F
2 M	تَفْعُلْ	تَرْدُدْ	تَقْضِ	تَقُمْ	تَجِدْ	تَسِرْ	تَبْدُ	تَرِثْ	تَرْضَ	تَأْسُرْ	تَبْقُسْ	تَقْرَأْ	2 M
2 F	تَفْعُلِي	تَرْدُدِي	تَقْضِي	تَقُومِي	تَجِدِي	تَسِيرِي	تَبْدَي	تَرِثِي	تَرْضَي	تَأْسِرِي	تَبْقُسِي	تَقْرَئِي	2 F
1	أَفْعُلْ	أَرْدُدْ	أَقْضِ	أَقُمْ	أَجِدْ	أَسِرْ	أَبْدُ	أَرِثْ	أَرْضَ	أَأْسُرْ	أَبْقُسْ	أَقْرَأْ	1
Dual													
3 M	يَفْعُلَا	يَرْدُدَا	يَقْضِيَا	يَقُومَا	يَجِدَا	يَسِيرَا	يَبْدُوَا	يَرِثَا	يَرْضَيَا	يَأْسُرَا	يَبْقُسَا	يَقْرَآ	3 M
3 F	تَفْعُلَا	تَرْدُدَا	تَقْضِيَا	تَقُومَا	تَجِدَا	تَسِيرَا	تَبْدُوَا	تَرِثَا	تَرْضَيَا	تَأْسُرَا	تَبْقُسَا	تَقْرَآ	3 F
2	تَفْعُلَا	تَرْدُدَا	تَقْضِيَا	تَقُومَا	تَجِدَا	تَسِيرَا	تَبْدُوَا	تَرِثَا	تَرْضَيَا	تَأْسُرَا	تَبْقُسَا	تَقْرَآ	2
Plural													
3 M	يَفْعُلُوا	يَرْدُدُوا	يَقْضُوا	يَقُومُوا	يَجِدُوا	يَسِيرُوا	يَبْدُوا	يَرِثُوا	يَرْضَوْا	يَأْسُرُوا	يَبْقُسُوا	يَقْرَؤُوا	3 M
3 F	يَفْعُلْنَ	يَرْدُدْنَ	يَقْضِينَ	يَقُمْنَ	يَجِدْنَ	يَسِرْنَ	يَبْدُونَ	يَرِثْنَ	يَرْضَيْنَ	يَأْسُرْنَ	يَبْقُسْنَ	يَقْرَأْنَ	3 F
2 M	تَفْعُلُوا	تَرْدُدُوا	تَقْضُوا	تَقُومُوا	تَجِدُوا	تَسِيرُوا	تَبْدُوا	تَرِثُوا	تَرْضَوْا	تَأْسُرُوا	تَبْقُسُوا	تَقْرَؤُوا	2 M
2 F	تَفْعُلْنَ	تَرْدُدْنَ	تَقْضِينَ	تَقُمْنَ	تَجِدْنَ	تَسِرْنَ	تَبْدُونَ	تَرِثْنَ	تَرْضَيْنَ	تَأْسُرْنَ	تَبْقُسْنَ	تَقْرَأْنَ	2 F
1	نَفْعُلْ	نَرْدُدْ	نَقْضِ	نَقُمْ	نَجِدْ	نَسِرْ	نَبْدُ	نَرِثْ	نَرْضَ	نَأْسُرْ	نَبْقُسْ	نَقْرَأْ	1

184

ACTIVE, FORM II, PERFECT

	1	2	3	4 and 5	6	7, 8, and 9	10	11	12
Singular									
3 M	فَعَّلَ	رَدَّدَ	وَضَّحَ	قَوَّمَ	سَيَّرَ	نَدَّى	أَسَّرَ	بَأَّسَ	قَرَّأَ
3 F	فَعَّلَتْ	رَدَّدَتْ	وَضَّحَتْ	قَوَّمَتْ	سَيَّرَتْ	نَدَّتْ	أَسَّرَتْ	بَأَّسَتْ	قَرَّأَتْ
2 M	فَعَّلْتَ	رَدَّدْتَ	وَضَّحْتَ	قَوَّمْتَ	سَيَّرْتَ	نَدَّيْتَ	أَسَّرْتَ	بَأَّسْتَ	قَرَّأْتَ
2 F	فَعَّلْتِ	رَدَّدْتِ	وَضَّحْتِ	قَوَّمْتِ	سَيَّرْتِ	نَدَّيْتِ	أَسَّرْتِ	بَأَّسْتِ	قَرَّأْتِ
1	فَعَّلْتُ	رَدَّدْتُ	وَضَّحْتُ	قَوَّمْتُ	سَيَّرْتُ	نَدَّيْتُ	أَسَّرْتُ	بَأَّسْتُ	قَرَّأْتُ
Dual									
3 M	فَعَّلَا	رَدَّدَا	وَضَّحَا	قَوَّمَا	سَيَّرَا	نَدَّيَا	أَسَّرَا	بَأَّسَا	قَرَّآ
3 F	فَعَّلَتَا	رَدَّدَتَا	وَضَّحَتَا	قَوَّمَتَا	سَيَّرَتَا	نَدَّتَا	أَسَّرَتَا	بَأَّسَتَا	قَرَّأَتَا
2	فَعَّلْتُمَا	رَدَّدْتُمَا	وَضَّحْتُمَا	قَوَّمْتُمَا	سَيَّرْتُمَا	نَدَّيْتُمَا	أَسَّرْتُمَا	بَأَّسْتُمَا	قَرَّأْتُمَا
Plural									
3 M	فَعَّلُوا	رَدَّدُوا	وَضَّحُوا	قَوَّمُوا	سَيَّرُوا	نَدَّوْا	أَسَّرُوا	بَأَّسُوا	قَرَّؤُوا
3 F	فَعَّلْنَ	رَدَّدْنَ	وَضَّحْنَ	قَوَّمْنَ	سَيَّرْنَ	نَدَّيْنَ	أَسَّرْنَ	بَأَّسْنَ	قَرَّأْنَ
2 M	فَعَّلْتُمْ	رَدَّدْتُمْ	وَضَّحْتُمْ	قَوَّمْتُمْ	سَيَّرْتُمْ	نَدَّيْتُمْ	أَسَّرْتُمْ	بَأَّسْتُمْ	قَرَّأْتُمْ
2 F	فَعَّلْتُنَّ	رَدَّدْتُنَّ	وَضَّحْتُنَّ	قَوَّمْتُنَّ	سَيَّرْتُنَّ	نَدَّيْتُنَّ	أَسَّرْتُنَّ	بَأَّسْتُنَّ	قَرَّأْتُنَّ
1	فَعَّلْنَا	رَدَّدْنَا	وَضَّحْنَا	قَوَّمْنَا	سَيَّرْنَا	نَدَّيْنَا	أَسَّرْنَا	بَأَّسْنَا	قَرَّأْنَا

ACTIVE, FORM II, IMPERFECT INDICATIVE

	12	11	10	7, 8, and 9	6	4 and 5	3	2	1	
					Singular					
يُبَرِّي	يُبَيِّنُ	يُقَوِّرُ	يُبَنِّي	يُيَسِّرُ	يُقَوِّمُ	يُوَصِّي	يُرَدِّدُ	يُفَعِّلُ	3 M
تُبَرِّي	تُبَيِّنُ	تُقَوِّرُ	تُبَنِّي	تُيَسِّرُ	تُقَوِّمُ	تُوَصِّي	تُرَدِّدُ	تُفَعِّلُ	3 F
تُبَرِّي	تُبَيِّنُ	تُقَوِّرُ	تُبَنِّي	تُيَسِّرُ	تُقَوِّمُ	تُوَصِّي	تُرَدِّدُ	تُفَعِّلُ	2 M
تُبَرِّينَ	تُبَيِّنِينَ	تُقَوِّرِينَ	تُبَنِّينَ	تُيَسِّرِينَ	تُقَوِّمِينَ	تُوَصِّينَ	تُرَدِّدِينَ	تُفَعِّلِينَ	2 F
أُبَرِّي	أُبَيِّنُ	أُقَوِّرُ	أُبَنِّي	أُيَسِّرُ	أُقَوِّمُ	أُوَصِّي	أُرَدِّدُ	أُفَعِّلُ	1
					Dual					
يُبَرِّيَانِ	يُبَيِّنَانِ	يُقَوِّرَانِ	يُبَنِّيَانِ	يُيَسِّرَانِ	يُقَوِّمَانِ	يُوَصِّيَانِ	يُرَدِّدَانِ	يُفَعِّلَانِ	3 M
تُبَرِّيَانِ	تُبَيِّنَانِ	تُقَوِّرَانِ	تُبَنِّيَانِ	تُيَسِّرَانِ	تُقَوِّمَانِ	تُوَصِّيَانِ	تُرَدِّدَانِ	تُفَعِّلَانِ	3 F
تُبَرِّيَانِ	تُبَيِّنَانِ	تُقَوِّرَانِ	تُبَنِّيَانِ	تُيَسِّرَانِ	تُقَوِّمَانِ	تُوَصِّيَانِ	تُرَدِّدَانِ	تُفَعِّلَانِ	2
					Plural					
يُبَرُّونَ	يُبَيِّنُونَ	يُقَوِّرُونَ	يُبَنُّونَ	يُيَسِّرُونَ	يُقَوِّمُونَ	يُوَصُّونَ	يُرَدِّدُونَ	يُفَعِّلُونَ	3 M
يُبَرِّينَ	يُبَيِّنَّ	يُقَوِّرْنَ	يُبَنِّينَ	يُيَسِّرْنَ	يُقَوِّمْنَ	يُوَصِّينَ	يُرَدِّدْنَ	يُفَعِّلْنَ	3 F
تُبَرُّونَ	تُبَيِّنُونَ	تُقَوِّرُونَ	تُبَنُّونَ	تُيَسِّرُونَ	تُقَوِّمُونَ	تُوَصُّونَ	تُرَدِّدُونَ	تُفَعِّلُونَ	2 M
تُبَرِّينَ	تُبَيِّنَّ	تُقَوِّرْنَ	تُبَنِّينَ	تُيَسِّرْنَ	تُقَوِّمْنَ	تُوَصِّينَ	تُرَدِّدْنَ	تُفَعِّلْنَ	2 F
نُبَرِّي	نُبَيِّنُ	نُقَوِّرُ	نُبَنِّي	نُيَسِّرُ	نُقَوِّمُ	نُوَصِّي	نُرَدِّدُ	نُفَعِّلُ	1

ACTIVE, FORM II, SUBJUNCTIVE

	1	2	3	4 and 5	6	7, 8, and 9	10	11	12	
					Singular					
3 M	يَفْعِل	يُرَدِّد	يُوَقِّي	يُقَوِّي	يُسَيِّر	يُبَدِّى	يُقَوِّر	يُحَيِّى	يُقَرِّى	3 M
3 F	تَفْعِل	تُرَدِّد	تُوَقِّي	تُقَوِّي	تُسَيِّر	تُبَدِّى	تُقَوِّر	تُحَيِّى	تُقَرِّى	3 F
2 M	تَفْعِل	تُرَدِّد	تُوَقِّي	تُقَوِّي	تُسَيِّر	تُبَدِّى	تُقَوِّر	تُحَيِّى	تُقَرِّى	2 M
2 F	تَفْعِلي	تُرَدِّدي	تُوَقِّي	تُقَوِّي	تُسَيِّري	تُبَدِّى	تُقَوِّري	تُحَيِّى	تُقَرِّى	2 F
1	أَفْعِل	أُرَدِّد	أُوَقِّي	أُقَوِّي	أُسَيِّر	أُبَدِّى	أُقَوِّر	أُحَيِّى	أُقَرِّى	1
					Dual					
3 M	يَفْعِلا	يُرَدِّدا	يُوَقِّيا	يُقَوِّيا	يُسَيِّرا	يُبَدِّيا	يُقَوِّرا	يُحَيِّيا	يُقَرِّيا	3 M
3 F	تَفْعِلا	تُرَدِّدا	تُوَقِّيا	تُقَوِّيا	تُسَيِّرا	تُبَدِّيا	تُقَوِّرا	تُحَيِّيا	تُقَرِّيا	3 F
2	تَفْعِلا	تُرَدِّدا	تُوَقِّيا	تُقَوِّيا	تُسَيِّرا	تُبَدِّيا	تُقَوِّرا	تُحَيِّيا	تُقَرِّيا	2
					Plural					
3 M	يَفْعِلوا	يُرَدِّدوا	يُوَقِّوا	يُقَوِّوا	يُسَيِّروا	يُبَدّوا	يُقَوِّروا	يُحَيّوا	يُقَرّوا	3 M
3 F	يَفْعِلنَ	يُرَدِّدنَ	يُوَقِّينَ	يُقَوِّينَ	يُسَيِّرنَ	يُبَدِّينَ	يُقَوِّرنَ	يُحَيِّينَ	يُقَرِّينَ	3 F
2 M	تَفْعِلوا	تُرَدِّدوا	تُوَقِّوا	تُقَوِّوا	تُسَيِّروا	تُبَدّوا	تُقَوِّروا	تُحَيّوا	تُقَرّوا	2 M
2 F	تَفْعِلنَ	تُرَدِّدنَ	تُوَقِّينَ	تُقَوِّينَ	تُسَيِّرنَ	تُبَدِّينَ	تُقَوِّرنَ	تُحَيِّينَ	تُقَرِّينَ	2 F
1	نَفْعِل	نُرَدِّد	نُوَقِّي	نُقَوِّي	نُسَيِّر	نُبَدِّى	نُقَوِّر	نُحَيِّى	نُقَرِّى	1

187

ACTIVE, FORM II, JUSSIVE

	1	2	3	4 and 5	6	7, 8, and 9	10	11	12
					Singular				
3 M									
3 F									
2 M									
2 F									
1									
					Dual				
3 M									
3 F									
2									
					Plural				
3 M									
3 F									
2 M									
2 F									
1									

188

ACTIVE, FORM III, PERFECT

	1	2	3	4 and 5	6	7, 8, and 9	10	11	12	
Singular										
3 M	فاعَلَ	رادَّ	واضَعَ	قاوَمَ	سايَرَ	نادى	آسَرَ	ياسى	قارَأَ	3 M
3 F	فاعَلَتْ	رادَّتْ	واضَعَتْ	قاوَمَتْ	سايَرَتْ	نادَتْ	آسَرَتْ	ياسَتْ	قارَأَتْ	3 F
2 M	فاعَلْتَ	رادَدْتَ	واضَعْتَ	قاوَمْتَ	سايَرْتَ	نادَيْتَ	آسَرْتَ	ياسَيْتَ	قارَأْتَ	2 M
2 F	فاعَلْتِ	رادَدْتِ	واضَعْتِ	قاوَمْتِ	سايَرْتِ	نادَيْتِ	آسَرْتِ	ياسَيْتِ	قارَأْتِ	2 F
1	فاعَلْتُ	رادَدْتُ	واضَعْتُ	قاوَمْتُ	سايَرْتُ	نادَيْتُ	آسَرْتُ	ياسَيْتُ	قارَأْتُ	1
Dual										
3 M	فاعَلا	رادّا	واضَعا	قاوَما	سايَرا	نادَيا	آسَرا	ياسَيا	قارَآ	3 M
3 F	فاعَلَتا	رادَّتا	واضَعَتا	قاوَمَتا	سايَرَتا	نادَتا	آسَرَتا	ياسَتا	قارَأَتا	3 F
2	فاعَلْتُما	رادَدْتُما	واضَعْتُما	قاوَمْتُما	سايَرْتُما	نادَيْتُما	آسَرْتُما	ياسَيْتُما	قارَأْتُما	2
Plural										
3 M	فاعَلوا	رادّوا	واضَعوا	قاوَموا	سايَروا	نادَوْا	آسَروا	ياسَوْا	قارَؤوا	3 M
3 F	فاعَلْنَ	رادَدْنَ	واضَعْنَ	قاوَمْنَ	سايَرْنَ	نادَيْنَ	آسَرْنَ	ياسَيْنَ	قارَأْنَ	3 F
2 M	فاعَلْتُم	رادَدْتُم	واضَعْتُم	قاوَمْتُم	سايَرْتُم	نادَيْتُم	آسَرْتُم	ياسَيْتُم	قارَأْتُم	2 M
2 F	فاعَلْتُنَّ	رادَدْتُنَّ	واضَعْتُنَّ	قاوَمْتُنَّ	سايَرْتُنَّ	نادَيْتُنَّ	آسَرْتُنَّ	ياسَيْتُنَّ	قارَأْتُنَّ	2 F
1	فاعَلْنا	رادَدْنا	واضَعْنا	قاوَمْنا	سايَرْنا	نادَيْنا	آسَرْنا	ياسَيْنا	قارَأْنا	1

ACTIVE, FORM III, IMPERFECT INDICATIVE

	1	2	3	4 and 5	6	7, 8, and 9	10	11	12	
					Singular					
3 M	يُفَاعِلُ	يُرَادِدُ	يُوَاضِحُ	يُقَاوِمُ	يُسَايِرُ	يُنَادِي	يُقَاسِرُ	يُبَاتِسُ	يُقَارِي	3 M
3 F	تُفَاعِلُ	تُرَادِدُ	تُوَاضِحُ	تُقَاوِمُ	تُسَايِرُ	تُنَادِي	تُقَاسِرُ	تُبَاتِسُ	تُقَارِي	3 F
2 M	تُفَاعِلُ	تُرَادِدُ	تُوَاضِحُ	تُقَاوِمُ	تُسَايِرُ	تُنَادِي	تُقَاسِرُ	تُبَاتِسُ	تُقَارِي	2 M
2 F	تُفَاعِلِينَ	تُرَادِدِينَ	تُوَاضِحِينَ	تُقَاوِمِينَ	تُسَايِرِينَ	تُنَادِينَ	تُقَاسِرِينَ	تُبَاتِسِينَ	تُقَارِينَ	2 F
1	أُفَاعِلُ	أُرَادِدُ	أُوَاضِحُ	أُقَاوِمُ	أُسَايِرُ	أُنَادِي	أُقَاسِرُ	أُبَاتِسُ	أُقَارِي	1
					Dual					
3 M	يُفَاعِلَانِ	يُرَادِدَانِ	يُوَاضِحَانِ	يُقَاوِمَانِ	يُسَايِرَانِ	يُنَادِيَانِ	يُقَاسِرَانِ	يُبَاتِسَانِ	يُقَارِيَانِ	3 M
3 F	تُفَاعِلَانِ	تُرَادِدَانِ	تُوَاضِحَانِ	تُقَاوِمَانِ	تُسَايِرَانِ	تُنَادِيَانِ	تُقَاسِرَانِ	تُبَاتِسَانِ	تُقَارِيَانِ	3 F
2	تُفَاعِلَانِ	تُرَادِدَانِ	تُوَاضِحَانِ	تُقَاوِمَانِ	تُسَايِرَانِ	تُنَادِيَانِ	تُقَاسِرَانِ	تُبَاتِسَانِ	تُقَارِيَانِ	2
					Plural					
3 M	يُفَاعِلُونَ	يُرَادِدُونَ	يُوَاضِحُونَ	يُقَاوِمُونَ	يُسَايِرُونَ	يُنَادُونَ	يُقَاسِرُونَ	يُبَاتِسُونَ	يُقَارُونَ	3 M
3 F	يُفَاعِلْنَ	يُرَادِدْنَ	يُوَاضِحْنَ	يُقَاوِمْنَ	يُسَايِرْنَ	يُنَادِينَ	يُقَاسِرْنَ	يُبَاتِسْنَ	يُقَارِينَ	3 F
2 M	تُفَاعِلُونَ	تُرَادِدُونَ	تُوَاضِحُونَ	تُقَاوِمُونَ	تُسَايِرُونَ	تُنَادُونَ	تُقَاسِرُونَ	تُبَاتِسُونَ	تُقَارُونَ	2 M
2 F	تُفَاعِلْنَ	تُرَادِدْنَ	تُوَاضِحْنَ	تُقَاوِمْنَ	تُسَايِرْنَ	تُنَادِينَ	تُقَاسِرْنَ	تُبَاتِسْنَ	تُقَارِينَ	2 F
1	نُفَاعِلُ	نُرَادِدُ	نُوَاضِحُ	نُقَاوِمُ	نُسَايِرُ	نُنَادِي	نُقَاسِرُ	نُبَاتِسُ	نُقَارِي	1

ACTIVE, FORM III, SUBJUNCTIVE

	1	2	3	4 and 5	6	7, 8, and 9	10	11	12	
					Singular					
3 M	يُقاتِلَ	يُرَاوِدَ	يُوَاضِحَ	يُقَاوِمَ	يُسَايِرَ	يُنَادِيَ	يُقَاسِرَ	يُبَايِنَ	يُرَاقِيَ	3 M
3 F	تُقاتِلَ	تُرَاوِدَ	تُوَاضِحَ	تُقَاوِمَ	تُسَايِرَ	تُنَادِيَ	تُقَاسِرَ	تُبَايِنَ	تُرَاقِيَ	3 F
2 M	تُقاتِلَ	تُرَاوِدَ	تُوَاضِحَ	تُقَاوِمَ	تُسَايِرَ	تُنَادِيَ	تُقَاسِرَ	تُبَايِنَ	تُرَاقِيَ	2 M
2 F	تُقاتِلِي	تُرَاوِدِي	تُوَاضِحِي	تُقَاوِمِي	تُسَايِرِي	تُنَادِي	تُقَاسِرِي	تُبَايِنِي	تُرَاقِي	2 F
1	أُقاتِلَ	أُرَاوِدَ	أُوَاضِحَ	أُقَاوِمَ	أُسَايِرَ	أُنَادِيَ	أُقَاسِرَ	أُبَايِنَ	أُرَاقِيَ	1
					Dual					
3 M	يُقاتِلا	يُرَاوِدا	يُوَاضِحا	يُقَاوِما	يُسَايِرا	يُنَادِيا	يُقَاسِرا	يُبَايِنا	يُرَاقِيا	3 M
3 F	تُقاتِلا	تُرَاوِدا	تُوَاضِحا	تُقَاوِما	تُسَايِرا	تُنَادِيا	تُقَاسِرا	تُبَايِنا	تُرَاقِيا	3 F
2	تُقاتِلا	تُرَاوِدا	تُوَاضِحا	تُقَاوِما	تُسَايِرا	تُنَادِيا	تُقَاسِرا	تُبَايِنا	تُرَاقِيا	2
					Plural					
3 M	يُقاتِلوا	يُرَاوِدوا	يُوَاضِحوا	يُقَاوِموا	يُسَايِروا	يُنَادُوا	يُقَاسِروا	يُبَايِنوا	يُرَاقُوا	3 M
3 F	يُقاتِلْنَ	يُرَاوِدْنَ	يُوَاضِحْنَ	يُقَاوِمْنَ	يُسَايِرْنَ	يُنَادِينَ	يُقَاسِرْنَ	يُبَايِنَّ	يُرَاقِينَ	3 F
2 M	تُقاتِلوا	تُرَاوِدوا	تُوَاضِحوا	تُقَاوِموا	تُسَايِروا	تُنَادُوا	تُقَاسِروا	تُبَايِنوا	تُرَاقُوا	2 M
2 F	تُقاتِلْنَ	تُرَاوِدْنَ	تُوَاضِحْنَ	تُقَاوِمْنَ	تُسَايِرْنَ	تُنَادِينَ	تُقَاسِرْنَ	تُبَايِنَّ	تُرَاقِينَ	2 F
1	نُقاتِلَ	نُرَاوِدَ	نُوَاضِحَ	نُقَاوِمَ	نُسَايِرَ	نُنَادِيَ	نُقَاسِرَ	نُبَايِنَ	نُرَاقِيَ	1

	12	11	10	7, 8, and 9	6	4 and 5	3	2	1	
				Singular						
3 M	يُقَاوِرْ	يُبَاسِرْ	يُقَاسِرْ	يُنَادِ	يُسَايِرْ	يُقَاوِمْ	يُوَاضِحْ	يُرَادِدْ	يُقَاعِلْ	3 M
3 F	تُقَاوِرْ	تُبَاسِرْ	تُقَاسِرْ	تُنَادِ	تُسَايِرْ	تُقَاوِمْ	تُوَاضِحْ	تُرَادِدْ	تُقَاعِلْ	3 F
2 M	تُقَاوِرْ	تُبَاسِرْ	تُقَاسِرْ	تُنَادِ	تُسَايِرْ	تُقَاوِمْ	تُوَاضِحْ	تُرَادِدْ	تُقَاعِلْ	2 M
2 F	تُقَاوِرِي	تُبَاسِرِي	تُقَاسِرِي	تُنَادِي	تُسَايِرِي	تُقَاوِمِي	تُوَاضِحِي	تُرَادِدِي	تُقَاعِلِي	2 F
1	أُقَاوِرْ	أُبَاسِرْ	أُقَاسِرْ	أُنَادِ	أُسَايِرْ	أُقَاوِمْ	أُوَاضِحْ	أُرَادِدْ	أُقَاعِلْ	1
				Dual						
3 M	يُقَاوِرَا	يُبَاسِرَا	يُقَاسِرَا	يُنَادِيَا	يُسَايِرَا	يُقَاوِمَا	يُوَاضِحَا	يُرَادِدَا	يُقَاعِلَا	3 M
3 F	تُقَاوِرَا	تُبَاسِرَا	تُقَاسِرَا	تُنَادِيَا	تُسَايِرَا	تُقَاوِمَا	تُوَاضِحَا	تُرَادِدَا	تُقَاعِلَا	3 F
2	تُقَاوِرَا	تُبَاسِرَا	تُقَاسِرَا	تُنَادِيَا	تُسَايِرَا	تُقَاوِمَا	تُوَاضِحَا	تُرَادِدَا	تُقَاعِلَا	2
				Plural						
3 M	يُقَاوِرُوا	يُبَاسِرُوا	يُقَاسِرُوا	يُنَادُوا	يُسَايِرُوا	يُقَاوِمُوا	يُوَاضِحُوا	يُرَادِدُوا	يُقَاعِلُوا	3 M
3 F	يُقَاوِرْنَ	يُبَاسِرْنَ	يُقَاسِرْنَ	يُنَادِينَ	يُسَايِرْنَ	يُقَاوِمْنَ	يُوَاضِحْنَ	يُرَادِدْنَ	يُقَاعِلْنَ	3 F
2 M	تُقَاوِرُوا	تُبَاسِرُوا	تُقَاسِرُوا	تُنَادُوا	تُسَايِرُوا	تُقَاوِمُوا	تُوَاضِحُوا	تُرَادِدُوا	تُقَاعِلُوا	2 M
2 F	تُقَاوِرْنَ	تُبَاسِرْنَ	تُقَاسِرْنَ	تُنَادِينَ	تُسَايِرْنَ	تُقَاوِمْنَ	تُوَاضِحْنَ	تُرَادِدْنَ	تُقَاعِلْنَ	2 F
1	نُقَاوِرْ	نُبَاسِرْ	نُقَاسِرْ	نُنَادِ	نُسَايِرْ	نُقَاوِمْ	نُوَاضِحْ	نُرَادِدْ	نُقَاعِلْ	1

ACTIVE, FORM IV, PERFECT

	1	2	3	4, 5, and 6	7, 8, and 9	10	11	12	
Singular									
3 M	أَفْعَلَ	أَرَدَّ	أَوْضَحَ	أَقَامَ	أَلْقَى	أَسَرَّ	أَبَاسَ	أَقْرَأَ	3 M
3 F	أَفْعَلَتْ	أَرَدَّتْ	أَوْضَحَتْ	أَقَامَتْ	أَلْقَتْ	أَسَرَّتْ	أَبَاسَتْ	أَقْرَأَتْ	3 F
2 M	أَفْعَلْتَ	أَرْدَدْتَ	أَوْضَحْتَ	أَقَمْتَ	أَلْقَيْتَ	أَسْرَرْتَ	أَبَسْتَ	أَقْرَأْتَ	2 M
2 F	أَفْعَلْتِ	أَرْدَدْتِ	أَوْضَحْتِ	أَقَمْتِ	أَلْقَيْتِ	أَسْرَرْتِ	أَبَسْتِ	أَقْرَأْتِ	2 F
1	أَفْعَلْتُ	أَرْدَدْتُ	أَوْضَحْتُ	أَقَمْتُ	أَلْقَيْتُ	أَسْرَرْتُ	أَبَسْتُ	أَقْرَأْتُ	I
Dual									
3 M	أَفْعَلَا	أَرَدَّا	أَوْضَحَا	أَقَامَا	أَلْقَيَا	أَسَرَّا	أَبَاسَا	أَقْرَآ	3 M
3 F	أَفْعَلَتَا	أَرَدَّتَا	أَوْضَحَتَا	أَقَامَتَا	أَلْقَتَا	أَسَرَّتَا	أَبَاسَتَا	أَقْرَأَتَا	3 F
2	أَفْعَلْتُمَا	أَرْدَدْتُمَا	أَوْضَحْتُمَا	أَقَمْتُمَا	أَلْقَيْتُمَا	أَسْرَرْتُمَا	أَبَسْتُمَا	أَقْرَأْتُمَا	2
Plural									
3 M	أَفْعَلُوا	أَرَدُّوا	أَوْضَحُوا	أَقَامُوا	أَلْقَوْا	أَسَرُّوا	أَبَاسُوا	أَقْرَؤُوا	3 M
3 F	أَفْعَلْنَ	أَرْدَدْنَ	أَوْضَحْنَ	أَقَمْنَ	أَلْقَيْنَ	أَسْرَرْنَ	أَبَسْنَ	أَقْرَأْنَ	3 F
2 M	أَفْعَلْتُمْ	أَرْدَدْتُمْ	أَوْضَحْتُمْ	أَقَمْتُمْ	أَلْقَيْتُمْ	أَسْرَرْتُمْ	أَبَسْتُمْ	أَقْرَأْتُمْ	2 M
2 F	أَفْعَلْتُنَّ	أَرْدَدْتُنَّ	أَوْضَحْتُنَّ	أَقَمْتُنَّ	أَلْقَيْتُنَّ	أَسْرَرْتُنَّ	أَبَسْتُنَّ	أَقْرَأْتُنَّ	2 F
1	أَفْعَلْنَا	أَرْدَدْنَا	أَوْضَحْنَا	أَقَمْنَا	أَلْقَيْنَا	أَسْرَرْنَا	أَبَسْنَا	أَقْرَأْنَا	I

ACTIVE, FORM IV, IMPERFECT INDICATIVE

	1	2	3	4, 5, and 6	7, 8, and 9	10	11	12	
				Singular					
3 M	يُفْعِلُ	يَرُدُّ	يُوصِي	يَقُومُ	يُنْدِي	يُبِيرُ	يُبْنِي	يُقْرِي	3 M
3 F	تُفْعِلُ	تَرُدُّ	تُوصِي	تَقُومُ	تُنْدِي	تُبِيرُ	تُبْنِي	تُقْرِي	3 F
2 M	تُفْعِلُ	تَرُدُّ	تُوصِي	تَقُومُ	تُنْدِي	تُبِيرُ	تُبْنِي	تُقْرِي	2 M
2 F	تُفْعِلِينَ	تَرُدِّينَ	تُوصِينَ	تَقُومِينَ	تُنْدِينَ	تُبِيرِينَ	تُبْنِينَ	تُقْرِينَ	2 F
1	أُفْعِلُ	أَرُدُّ	أُوصِي	أَقُومُ	أُنْدِي	أُبِيرُ	أُبْنِي	أُقْرِي	1
				Dual					
3 M	يُفْعِلَانِ	يَرُدَّانِ	يُوصِيَانِ	يَقُومَانِ	يُنْدِيَانِ	يُبِيرَانِ	يُبْنِيَانِ	يُقْرِيَانِ	3 M
3 F	تُفْعِلَانِ	تَرُدَّانِ	تُوصِيَانِ	تَقُومَانِ	تُنْدِيَانِ	تُبِيرَانِ	تُبْنِيَانِ	تُقْرِيَانِ	3 F
2	تُفْعِلَانِ	تَرُدَّانِ	تُوصِيَانِ	تَقُومَانِ	تُنْدِيَانِ	تُبِيرَانِ	تُبْنِيَانِ	تُقْرِيَانِ	2
				Plural					
3 M	يُفْعِلُونَ	يَرُدُّونَ	يُوصُونَ	يَقُومُونَ	يُنْدُونَ	يُبِيرُونَ	يُبْنُونَ	يُقْرُونَ	3 M
3 F	يُفْعِلْنَ	يَرْدُدْنَ	يُوصِينَ	يَقُمْنَ	يُنْدِينَ	يُبِرْنَ	يُبْنِينَ	يُقْرِينَ	3 F
2 M	تُفْعِلُونَ	تَرُدُّونَ	تُوصُونَ	تَقُومُونَ	تُنْدُونَ	تُبِيرُونَ	تُبْنُونَ	تُقْرُونَ	2 M
2 F	تُفْعِلْنَ	تَرْدُدْنَ	تُوصِينَ	تَقُمْنَ	تُنْدِينَ	تُبِرْنَ	تُبْنِينَ	تُقْرِينَ	2 F
1	نُفْعِلُ	نَرُدُّ	نُوصِي	نَقُومُ	نُنْدِي	نُبِيرُ	نُبْنِي	نُقْرِي	1

194

	1	2	3	4, 5, and 6	7, 8, and 9	10	11	12	
Singular									
3 M	يَفْعَلَ	يَرُدَّ	يُرْضِيَ	يُقِيمَ	يَبْدُ، يَبْدُوَ	يُوسِرَ	يُنْسِيَ	يَقْوَى	3 M
3 F	تَفْعَلَ	تَرُدَّ	تُرْضِيَ	تُقِيمَ	تَبْدُ، تَبْدُوَ	تُوسِرَ	تُنْسِيَ	تَقْوَى	3 F
2 M	تَفْعَلَ	تَرُدَّ	تُرْضِيَ	تُقِيمَ	تَبْدُ، تَبْدُوَ	تُوسِرَ	تُنْسِيَ	تَقْوَى	2 M
2 F	تَفْعَلِي	تَرُدِّي	تُرْضِي	تُقِيمِي	تَبْدِي	تُوسِرِي	تُنْسِي	تَقْوَيْ	2 F
1	أَفْعَلَ	أَرُدَّ	أُرْضِيَ	أُقِيمَ	أَبْدُ، أَبْدُوَ	أُوسِرَ	أُنْسِيَ	أَقْوَى	1
Dual									
3 M	يَفْعَلَا	يَرُدَّا	يُرْضِيَا	يُقِيمَا	يَبْدُوَا	يُوسِرَا	يُنْسِيَا	يَقْوَيَا	3 M
3 F	تَفْعَلَا	تَرُدَّا	تُرْضِيَا	تُقِيمَا	تَبْدُوَا	تُوسِرَا	تُنْسِيَا	تَقْوَيَا	3 F
2	تَفْعَلَا	تَرُدَّا	تُرْضِيَا	تُقِيمَا	تَبْدُوَا	تُوسِرَا	تُنْسِيَا	تَقْوَيَا	2
Plural									
3 M	يَفْعَلُوا	يَرُدُّوا	يُرْضُوا	يُقِيمُوا	يَبْدُوا	يُوسِرُوا	يُنْسُوا	يَقْوَوْا	3 M
3 F	يَفْعَلْنَ	يَرْدُدْنَ	يُرْضِينَ	يُقِمْنَ	يَبْدِينَ	يُوسِرْنَ	يُنْسِينَ	يَقْوَيْنَ	3 F
2 M	تَفْعَلُوا	تَرُدُّوا	تُرْضُوا	تُقِيمُوا	تَبْدُوا	تُوسِرُوا	تُنْسُوا	تَقْوَوْا	2 M
2 F	تَفْعَلْنَ	تَرْدُدْنَ	تُرْضِينَ	تُقِمْنَ	تَبْدِينَ	تُوسِرْنَ	تُنْسِينَ	تَقْوَيْنَ	2 F
1	نَفْعَلَ	نَرُدَّ	نُرْضِيَ	نُقِيمَ	نَبْدُ، نَبْدُوَ	نُوسِرَ	نُنْسِيَ	نَقْوَى	1

ACTIVE, FORM IV, JUSSIVE

	1	2	3	4, 5, and 6	7, 8, and 9	10	11	12	
				Singular					
3 M	يُفْعِلْ	يَرْدِدْ	يُوضِعْ	يُقِمْ	يُنْدِ	يُؤْسِرْ	يُبْئِسْ	يُقْرِئْ	3 M
3 F	تُفْعِلْ	تَرْدِدْ	تُوضِعْ	تُقِمْ	تُنْدِ	تُؤْسِرْ	تُبْئِسْ	تُقْرِئْ	3 F
2 M	تُفْعِلْ	تَرْدِدْ	تُوضِعْ	تُقِمْ	تُنْدِ	تُؤْسِرْ	تُبْئِسْ	تُقْرِئْ	2 M
2 F	تُفْعِلِي	تُرْدِدِي	تُوضِعِي	تُقِيمِي	تُنْدِي	تُؤْسِرِي	تُبْئِسِي	تُقْرِئِي	2 F
1	أُفْعِلْ	أُرْدِدْ	أُوضِعْ	أُقِمْ	أُنْدِ	أُوسِرْ	أُبْئِسْ	أُقْرِئْ	1
				Dual					
3 M	يُفْعِلَا	يُرِدَّا	يُوضِعَا	يُقِيمَا	يُنْدِيَا	يُؤْسِرَا	يُبْئِسَا	يُقْرِئَا	3 M
3 F	تُفْعِلَا	تُرِدَّا	تُوضِعَا	تُقِيمَا	تُنْدِيَا	تُؤْسِرَا	تُبْئِسَا	تُقْرِئَا	3 F
2	تُفْعِلَا	تُرِدَّا	تُوضِعَا	تُقِيمَا	تُنْدِيَا	تُؤْسِرَا	تُبْئِسَا	تُقْرِئَا	2
				Plural					
3 M	يُفْعِلُوا	يُرِدُّوا	يُوضِعُوا	يُقِيمُوا	يُنْدُوا	يُؤْسِرُوا	يُبْئِسُوا	يُقْرِئُوا	3 M
3 F	يُفْعِلْنَ	يُرْدِدْنَ	يُوضِعْنَ	يُقِمْنَ	يُنْدِينَ	يُؤْسِرْنَ	يُبْئِسْنَ	يُقْرِئْنَ	3 F
2 M	تُفْعِلُوا	تُرِدُّوا	تُوضِعُوا	تُقِيمُوا	تُنْدُوا	تُؤْسِرُوا	تُبْئِسُوا	تُقْرِئُوا	2 M
2 F	تُفْعِلْنَ	تُرْدِدْنَ	تُوضِعْنَ	تُقِمْنَ	تُنْدِينَ	تُؤْسِرْنَ	تُبْئِسْنَ	تُقْرِئْنَ	2 F
1	نُفْعِلْ	نُرْدِدْ	نُوضِعْ	نُقِمْ	نُنْدِ	نُؤْسِرْ	نُبْئِسْ	نُقْرِئْ	1

196

ACTIVE, FORM V, PERFECT

	1	2	3	4 and 5	6	7, 8, and 9	10	11	12	
					Singular					
3 M	تَفَعَّلَ	تَرَدَّدَ	تَوَضَّعَ	تَقَوَّمَ	تَيَسَّرَ	تَنَدّى	تَأَسَّرَ	تَأَسَّسَ	تَقَرَّأَ	3 M
3 F	تَفَعَّلَتْ	تَرَدَّدَتْ	تَوَضَّعَتْ	تَقَوَّمَتْ	تَيَسَّرَتْ	تَنَدَّتْ	تَأَسَّرَتْ	تَأَسَّسَتْ	تَقَرَّأَتْ	3 F
2 M	تَفَعَّلْتَ	تَرَدَّدْتَ	تَوَضَّعْتَ	تَقَوَّمْتَ	تَيَسَّرْتَ	تَنَدَّيْتَ	تَأَسَّرْتَ	تَأَسَّسْتَ	تَقَرَّأْتَ	2 M
2 F	تَفَعَّلْتِ	تَرَدَّدْتِ	تَوَضَّعْتِ	تَقَوَّمْتِ	تَيَسَّرْتِ	تَنَدَّيْتِ	تَأَسَّرْتِ	تَأَسَّسْتِ	تَقَرَّأْتِ	2 F
1	تَفَعَّلْتُ	تَرَدَّدْتُ	تَوَضَّعْتُ	تَقَوَّمْتُ	تَيَسَّرْتُ	تَنَدَّيْتُ	تَأَسَّرْتُ	تَأَسَّسْتُ	تَقَرَّأْتُ	1
					Dual					
3 M	تَفَعَّلَا	تَرَدَّدَا	تَوَضَّعَا	تَقَوَّمَا	تَيَسَّرَا	تَنَدَّيَا	تَأَسَّرَا	تَأَسَّسَا	تَقَرَّأَا	3 M
3 F	تَفَعَّلَتَا	تَرَدَّدَتَا	تَوَضَّعَتَا	تَقَوَّمَتَا	تَيَسَّرَتَا	تَنَدَّيَتَا	تَأَسَّرَتَا	تَأَسَّسَتَا	تَقَرَّأَتَا	3 F
2	تَفَعَّلْتُمَا	تَرَدَّدْتُمَا	تَوَضَّعْتُمَا	تَقَوَّمْتُمَا	تَيَسَّرْتُمَا	تَنَدَّيْتُمَا	تَأَسَّرْتُمَا	تَأَسَّسْتُمَا	تَقَرَّأْتُمَا	2
					Plural					
3 M	تَفَعَّلُوا	تَرَدَّدُوا	تَوَضَّعُوا	تَقَوَّمُوا	تَيَسَّرُوا	تَنَدَّوْا	تَأَسَّرُوا	تَأَسَّسُوا	تَقَرَّأُوا	3 M
3 F	تَفَعَّلْنَ	تَرَدَّدْنَ	تَوَضَّعْنَ	تَقَوَّمْنَ	تَيَسَّرْنَ	تَنَدَّيْنَ	تَأَسَّرْنَ	تَأَسَّسْنَ	تَقَرَّأْنَ	3 F
2 M	تَفَعَّلْتُمْ	تَرَدَّدْتُمْ	تَوَضَّعْتُمْ	تَقَوَّمْتُمْ	تَيَسَّرْتُمْ	تَنَدَّيْتُمْ	تَأَسَّرْتُمْ	تَأَسَّسْتُمْ	تَقَرَّأْتُمْ	2 M
2 F	تَفَعَّلْتُنَّ	تَرَدَّدْتُنَّ	تَوَضَّعْتُنَّ	تَقَوَّمْتُنَّ	تَيَسَّرْتُنَّ	تَنَدَّيْتُنَّ	تَأَسَّرْتُنَّ	تَأَسَّسْتُنَّ	تَقَرَّأْتُنَّ	2 F
1	تَفَعَّلْنَا	تَرَدَّدْنَا	تَوَضَّعْنَا	تَقَوَّمْنَا	تَيَسَّرْنَا	تَنَدَّيْنَا	تَأَسَّرْنَا	تَأَسَّسْنَا	تَقَرَّأْنَا	1

197

ACTIVE, FORM V, IMPERFECT INDICATIVE

	1	2	3	4 and 5	6	7, 8, and 9	10	11	12
Singular									
3 M	يَتَفَعَّل	يَتَرَدَّد	يَتَوَضَّح	يَتَقَوَّم	يَتَسَيَّر	يَتَدَلَّى	يَتَأَسَّر	يَتَأَسَّس	يَتَقَرَّأ
3 F	تَتَفَعَّل	تَتَرَدَّد	تَتَوَضَّح	تَتَقَوَّم	تَتَسَيَّر	تَتَدَلَّى	تَتَأَسَّر	تَتَأَسَّس	تَتَقَرَّأ
2 M	تَتَفَعَّل	تَتَرَدَّد	تَتَوَضَّح	تَتَقَوَّم	تَتَسَيَّر	تَتَدَلَّى	تَتَأَسَّر	تَتَأَسَّس	تَتَقَرَّأ
2 F	تَتَفَعَّلِينَ	تَتَرَدَّدِينَ	تَتَوَضَّحِينَ	تَتَقَوَّمِينَ	تَتَسَيَّرِينَ	تَتَدَلَّيْنَ	تَتَأَسَّرِينَ	تَتَأَسَّسِينَ	تَتَقَرَّئِينَ
1	أَتَفَعَّل	أَتَرَدَّد	أَتَوَضَّح	أَتَقَوَّم	أَتَسَيَّر	أَتَدَلَّى	أَتَأَسَّر	أَتَأَسَّس	أَتَقَرَّأ
Dual									
3 M	يَتَفَعَّلانِ	يَتَرَدَّدانِ	يَتَوَضَّحانِ	يَتَقَوَّمانِ	يَتَسَيَّرانِ	يَتَدَلَّيانِ	يَتَأَسَّرانِ	يَتَأَسَّسانِ	يَتَقَرَّآنِ
3 F	تَتَفَعَّلانِ	تَتَرَدَّدانِ	تَتَوَضَّحانِ	تَتَقَوَّمانِ	تَتَسَيَّرانِ	تَتَدَلَّيانِ	تَتَأَسَّرانِ	تَتَأَسَّسانِ	تَتَقَرَّآنِ
2	تَتَفَعَّلانِ	تَتَرَدَّدانِ	تَتَوَضَّحانِ	تَتَقَوَّمانِ	تَتَسَيَّرانِ	تَتَدَلَّيانِ	تَتَأَسَّرانِ	تَتَأَسَّسانِ	تَتَقَرَّآنِ
Plural									
3 M	يَتَفَعَّلونَ	يَتَرَدَّدونَ	يَتَوَضَّحونَ	يَتَقَوَّمونَ	يَتَسَيَّرونَ	يَتَدَلَّوْنَ	يَتَأَسَّرونَ	يَتَأَسَّسونَ	يَتَقَرَّؤونَ
3 F	يَتَفَعَّلْنَ	يَتَرَدَّدْنَ	يَتَوَضَّحْنَ	يَتَقَوَّمْنَ	يَتَسَيَّرْنَ	يَتَدَلَّيْنَ	يَتَأَسَّرْنَ	يَتَأَسَّسْنَ	يَتَقَرَّأْنَ
2 M	تَتَفَعَّلونَ	تَتَرَدَّدونَ	تَتَوَضَّحونَ	تَتَقَوَّمونَ	تَتَسَيَّرونَ	تَتَدَلَّوْنَ	تَتَأَسَّرونَ	تَتَأَسَّسونَ	تَتَقَرَّؤونَ
2 F	تَتَفَعَّلْنَ	تَتَرَدَّدْنَ	تَتَوَضَّحْنَ	تَتَقَوَّمْنَ	تَتَسَيَّرْنَ	تَتَدَلَّيْنَ	تَتَأَسَّرْنَ	تَتَأَسَّسْنَ	تَتَقَرَّأْنَ
1	نَتَفَعَّل	نَتَرَدَّد	نَتَوَضَّح	نَتَقَوَّم	نَتَسَيَّر	نَتَدَلَّى	نَتَأَسَّر	نَتَأَسَّس	نَتَقَرَّأ

ACTIVE, FORM V, SUBJUNCTIVE

	1	2	3	4 and 5	6	7, 8, and 9	10	11	12
Singular									
3 M	يَتَفَعَّل	يَتَرَدَّد	يَتَوَضَّح	يَتَقَوَّل	يَتَيَسَّر	يَتَنَدَّى	يَتَأَسَّر	يَتَأَسَّى	يَتَقَرَّأ
3 F	تَتَفَعَّل	تَتَرَدَّد	تَتَوَضَّح	تَتَقَوَّل	تَتَيَسَّر	تَتَنَدَّى	تَتَأَسَّر	تَتَأَسَّى	تَتَقَرَّأ
2 M	تَتَفَعَّل	تَتَرَدَّد	تَتَوَضَّح	تَتَقَوَّل	تَتَيَسَّر	تَتَنَدَّى	تَتَأَسَّر	تَتَأَسَّى	تَتَقَرَّأ
2 F	تَتَفَعَّلِي	تَتَرَدَّدِي	تَتَوَضَّحِي	تَتَقَوَّلِي	تَتَيَسَّرِي	تَتَنَدَّيْ	تَتَأَسَّرِي	تَتَأَسَّيْ	تَتَقَرَّئِي
1	أَتَفَعَّل	أَتَرَدَّد	أَتَوَضَّح	أَتَقَوَّل	أَتَيَسَّر	أَتَنَدَّى	أَتَأَسَّر	أَتَأَسَّى	أَتَقَرَّأ
Dual									
3 M	يَتَفَعَّلَا	يَتَرَدَّدَا	يَتَوَضَّحَا	يَتَقَوَّلَا	يَتَيَسَّرَا	يَتَنَدَّيَا	يَتَأَسَّرَا	يَتَأَسَّيَا	يَتَقَرَّآ
3 F	تَتَفَعَّلَا	تَتَرَدَّدَا	تَتَوَضَّحَا	تَتَقَوَّلَا	تَتَيَسَّرَا	تَتَنَدَّيَا	تَتَأَسَّرَا	تَتَأَسَّيَا	تَتَقَرَّآ
2	تَتَفَعَّلَا	تَتَرَدَّدَا	تَتَوَضَّحَا	تَتَقَوَّلَا	تَتَيَسَّرَا	تَتَنَدَّيَا	تَتَأَسَّرَا	تَتَأَسَّيَا	تَتَقَرَّآ
Plural									
3 M	يَتَفَعَّلُوا	يَتَرَدَّدُوا	يَتَوَضَّحُوا	يَتَقَوَّلُوا	يَتَيَسَّرُوا	يَتَنَدَّوْا	يَتَأَسَّرُوا	يَتَأَسَّوْا	يَتَقَرَّؤُوا
3 F	يَتَفَعَّلْنَ	يَتَرَدَّدْنَ	يَتَوَضَّحْنَ	يَتَقَوَّلْنَ	يَتَيَسَّرْنَ	يَتَنَدَّيْنَ	يَتَأَسَّرْنَ	يَتَأَسَّيْنَ	يَتَقَرَّأْنَ
2 M	تَتَفَعَّلُوا	تَتَرَدَّدُوا	تَتَوَضَّحُوا	تَتَقَوَّلُوا	تَتَيَسَّرُوا	تَتَنَدَّوْا	تَتَأَسَّرُوا	تَتَأَسَّوْا	تَتَقَرَّؤُوا
2 F	تَتَفَعَّلْنَ	تَتَرَدَّدْنَ	تَتَوَضَّحْنَ	تَتَقَوَّلْنَ	تَتَيَسَّرْنَ	تَتَنَدَّيْنَ	تَتَأَسَّرْنَ	تَتَأَسَّيْنَ	تَتَقَرَّأْنَ
1	نَتَفَعَّل	نَتَرَدَّد	نَتَوَضَّح	نَتَقَوَّل	نَتَيَسَّر	نَتَنَدَّى	نَتَأَسَّر	نَتَأَسَّى	نَتَقَرَّأ

ACTIVE, FORM V, JUSSIVE

	1	2	3	4 and 5	6	7, 8, and 9	10	11	12	
					Singular					
3 M	يَتَفَعَّلْ	يَتَرَدَّدْ	يَتَوَضَّأْ	يَتَقَوَّمْ	يَتَبَسَّرْ	يَتَبَدَّلْ	يَتَأَسَّرْ	يَتَأَسَّ	يَتَقَرَّ	3 M
3 F	تَتَفَعَّلْ	تَتَرَدَّدْ	تَتَوَضَّأْ	تَتَقَوَّمْ	تَتَبَسَّرْ	تَتَبَدَّلْ	تَتَأَسَّرْ	تَتَأَسَّ	تَتَقَرَّ	3 F
2 M	تَتَفَعَّلْ	تَتَرَدَّدْ	تَتَوَضَّأْ	تَتَقَوَّمْ	تَتَبَسَّرْ	تَتَبَدَّلْ	تَتَأَسَّرْ	تَتَأَسَّ	تَتَقَرَّ	2 M
2 F	تَتَفَعَّلِي	تَتَرَدَّدِي	تَتَوَضَّئِي	تَتَقَوَّمِي	تَتَبَسَّرِي	تَتَبَدَّلِي	تَتَأَسَّرِي	تَتَأَسَّي	تَتَقَرَّي	2 F
1	أَتَفَعَّلْ	أَتَرَدَّدْ	أَتَوَضَّأْ	أَتَقَوَّمْ	أَتَبَسَّرْ	أَتَبَدَّلْ	أَتَأَسَّرْ	أَتَأَسَّ	أَتَقَرَّ	1
					Dual					
3 M	يَتَفَعَّلَا	يَتَرَدَّدَا	يَتَوَضَّآ	يَتَقَوَّمَا	يَتَبَسَّرَا	يَتَبَدَّلَا	يَتَأَسَّرَا	يَتَأَسَّا	يَتَقَرَّا	3 M
3 F	تَتَفَعَّلَا	تَتَرَدَّدَا	تَتَوَضَّآ	تَتَقَوَّمَا	تَتَبَسَّرَا	تَتَبَدَّلَا	تَتَأَسَّرَا	تَتَأَسَّا	تَتَقَرَّا	3 F
2	تَتَفَعَّلَا	تَتَرَدَّدَا	تَتَوَضَّآ	تَتَقَوَّمَا	تَتَبَسَّرَا	تَتَبَدَّلَا	تَتَأَسَّرَا	تَتَأَسَّا	تَتَقَرَّا	2
					Plural					
3 M	يَتَفَعَّلُوا	يَتَرَدَّدُوا	يَتَوَضَّؤُوا	يَتَقَوَّمُوا	يَتَبَسَّرُوا	يَتَبَدَّلُوا	يَتَأَسَّرُوا	يَتَأَسَّوْا	يَتَقَرَّوْا	3 M
3 F	يَتَفَعَّلْنَ	يَتَرَدَّدْنَ	يَتَوَضَّأْنَ	يَتَقَوَّمْنَ	يَتَبَسَّرْنَ	يَتَبَدَّلْنَ	يَتَأَسَّرْنَ	يَتَأَسَّيْنَ	يَتَقَرَّيْنَ	3 F
2 M	تَتَفَعَّلُوا	تَتَرَدَّدُوا	تَتَوَضَّؤُوا	تَتَقَوَّمُوا	تَتَبَسَّرُوا	تَتَبَدَّلُوا	تَتَأَسَّرُوا	تَتَأَسَّوْا	تَتَقَرَّوْا	2 M
2 F	تَتَفَعَّلْنَ	تَتَرَدَّدْنَ	تَتَوَضَّأْنَ	تَتَقَوَّمْنَ	تَتَبَسَّرْنَ	تَتَبَدَّلْنَ	تَتَأَسَّرْنَ	تَتَأَسَّيْنَ	تَتَقَرَّيْنَ	2 F
1	نَتَفَعَّلْ	نَتَرَدَّدْ	نَتَوَضَّأْ	نَتَقَوَّمْ	نَتَبَسَّرْ	نَتَبَدَّلْ	نَتَأَسَّرْ	نَتَأَسَّ	نَتَقَرَّ	1

200

ACTIVE, FORM VI, PERFECT

	1	2	3	4 and 5	6	7, 8, and 9	10	11	12
Singular									
3 M	تَفَاعَلَ	تَرَادَّ	تَوَاضَعَ	تَقَاوَمَ	تَسَايَرَ	تَنَادَى	تَأَسَّرَ	تَيَاسَرَ	تَقَارَأَ
3 F	تَفَاعَلَتْ	تَرَادَّتْ	تَوَاضَعَتْ	تَقَاوَمَتْ	تَسَايَرَتْ	تَنَادَتْ	تَأَسَّرَتْ	تَيَاسَرَتْ	تَقَارَأَتْ
2 M	تَفَاعَلْتَ	تَرَادَدْتَ	تَوَاضَعْتَ	تَقَاوَمْتَ	تَسَايَرْتَ	تَنَادَيْتَ	تَأَسَّرْتَ	تَيَاسَرْتَ	تَقَارَأْتَ
2 F	تَفَاعَلْتِ	تَرَادَدْتِ	تَوَاضَعْتِ	تَقَاوَمْتِ	تَسَايَرْتِ	تَنَادَيْتِ	تَأَسَّرْتِ	تَيَاسَرْتِ	تَقَارَأْتِ
1	تَفَاعَلْتُ	تَرَادَدْتُ	تَوَاضَعْتُ	تَقَاوَمْتُ	تَسَايَرْتُ	تَنَادَيْتُ	تَأَسَّرْتُ	تَيَاسَرْتُ	تَقَارَأْتُ
Dual									
3 M	تَفَاعَلَا	تَرَادَّا	تَوَاضَعَا	تَقَاوَمَا	تَسَايَرَا	تَنَادَيَا	تَأَسَّرَا	تَيَاسَرَا	تَقَارَآ
3 F	تَفَاعَلَتَا	تَرَادَّتَا	تَوَاضَعَتَا	تَقَاوَمَتَا	تَسَايَرَتَا	تَنَادَتَا	تَأَسَّرَتَا	تَيَاسَرَتَا	تَقَارَأَتَا
2	تَفَاعَلْتُمَا	تَرَادَدْتُمَا	تَوَاضَعْتُمَا	تَقَاوَمْتُمَا	تَسَايَرْتُمَا	تَنَادَيْتُمَا	تَأَسَّرْتُمَا	تَيَاسَرْتُمَا	تَقَارَأْتُمَا
Plural									
3 M	تَفَاعَلُوا	تَرَادُّوا	تَوَاضَعُوا	تَقَاوَمُوا	تَسَايَرُوا	تَنَادَوْا	تَأَسَّرُوا	تَيَاسَرُوا	تَقَارَؤُوا
3 F	تَفَاعَلْنَ	تَرَادَدْنَ	تَوَاضَعْنَ	تَقَاوَمْنَ	تَسَايَرْنَ	تَنَادَيْنَ	تَأَسَّرْنَ	تَيَاسَرْنَ	تَقَارَأْنَ
2 M	تَفَاعَلْتُمْ	تَرَادَدْتُمْ	تَوَاضَعْتُمْ	تَقَاوَمْتُمْ	تَسَايَرْتُمْ	تَنَادَيْتُمْ	تَأَسَّرْتُمْ	تَيَاسَرْتُمْ	تَقَارَأْتُمْ
2 F	تَفَاعَلْتُنَّ	تَرَادَدْتُنَّ	تَوَاضَعْتُنَّ	تَقَاوَمْتُنَّ	تَسَايَرْتُنَّ	تَنَادَيْتُنَّ	تَأَسَّرْتُنَّ	تَيَاسَرْتُنَّ	تَقَارَأْتُنَّ
1	تَفَاعَلْنَا	تَرَادَدْنَا	تَوَاضَعْنَا	تَقَاوَمْنَا	تَسَايَرْنَا	تَنَادَيْنَا	تَأَسَّرْنَا	تَيَاسَرْنَا	تَقَارَأْنَا

ACTIVE, FORM VI, IMPERFECT INDICATIVE

Singular

	1	2	3	4 and 5	6	7, 8, and 9	10	11	12	
3 M	يَتَفَاعَلُ	يَتَرَادُّ	يَتَوَاطَأُ	يَتَقَاوَمُ	يَتَسَايَرُ	يَتَنَادَى	يَتَآسَرُ	يَتَنَاسَى	يَتَقَارَأُ	3 M
3 F	تَتَفَاعَلُ	تَتَرَادُّ	تَتَوَاطَأُ	تَتَقَاوَمُ	تَتَسَايَرُ	تَتَنَادَى	تَتَآسَرُ	تَتَنَاسَى	تَتَقَارَأُ	3 F
2 M	تَتَفَاعَلُ	تَتَرَادُّ	تَتَوَاطَأُ	تَتَقَاوَمُ	تَتَسَايَرُ	تَتَنَادَى	تَتَآسَرُ	تَتَنَاسَى	تَتَقَارَأُ	2 M
2 F	تَتَفَاعَلِينَ	تَتَرَادِّينَ	تَتَوَاطَئِينَ	تَتَقَاوَمِينَ	تَتَسَايَرِينَ	تَتَنَادَيْنَ	تَتَآسَرِينَ	تَتَنَاسَيْنَ	تَتَقَارَئِينَ	2 F
1	أَتَفَاعَلُ	أَتَرَادُّ	أَتَوَاطَأُ	أَتَقَاوَمُ	أَتَسَايَرُ	أَتَنَادَى	أَتَآسَرُ	أَتَنَاسَى	أَتَقَارَأُ	1

Dual

	1	2	3	4 and 5	6	7, 8, and 9	10	11	12	
3 M	يَتَفَاعَلَانِ	يَتَرَادَّانِ	يَتَوَاطَأَانِ	يَتَقَاوَمَانِ	يَتَسَايَرَانِ	يَتَنَادَيَانِ	يَتَآسَرَانِ	يَتَنَاسَيَانِ	يَتَقَارَأَانِ	3 M
3 F	تَتَفَاعَلَانِ	تَتَرَادَّانِ	تَتَوَاطَأَانِ	تَتَقَاوَمَانِ	تَتَسَايَرَانِ	تَتَنَادَيَانِ	تَتَآسَرَانِ	تَتَنَاسَيَانِ	تَتَقَارَأَانِ	3 F
2	تَتَفَاعَلَانِ	تَتَرَادَّانِ	تَتَوَاطَأَانِ	تَتَقَاوَمَانِ	تَتَسَايَرَانِ	تَتَنَادَيَانِ	تَتَآسَرَانِ	تَتَنَاسَيَانِ	تَتَقَارَأَانِ	2

Plural

	1	2	3	4 and 5	6	7, 8, and 9	10	11	12	
3 M	يَتَفَاعَلُونَ	يَتَرَادُّونَ	يَتَوَاطَؤُونَ	يَتَقَاوَمُونَ	يَتَسَايَرُونَ	يَتَنَادَوْنَ	يَتَآسَرُونَ	يَتَنَاسَوْنَ	يَتَقَارَؤُونَ	3 M
3 F	يَتَفَاعَلْنَ	يَتَرَادَدْنَ	يَتَوَاطَأْنَ	يَتَقَاوَمْنَ	يَتَسَايَرْنَ	يَتَنَادَيْنَ	يَتَآسَرْنَ	يَتَنَاسَيْنَ	يَتَقَارَأْنَ	3 F
2 M	تَتَفَاعَلُونَ	تَتَرَادُّونَ	تَتَوَاطَؤُونَ	تَتَقَاوَمُونَ	تَتَسَايَرُونَ	تَتَنَادَوْنَ	تَتَآسَرُونَ	تَتَنَاسَوْنَ	تَتَقَارَؤُونَ	2 M
2 F	تَتَفَاعَلْنَ	تَتَرَادَدْنَ	تَتَوَاطَأْنَ	تَتَقَاوَمْنَ	تَتَسَايَرْنَ	تَتَنَادَيْنَ	تَتَآسَرْنَ	تَتَنَاسَيْنَ	تَتَقَارَأْنَ	2 F
1	نَتَفَاعَلُ	نَتَرَادُّ	نَتَوَاطَأُ	نَتَقَاوَمُ	نَتَسَايَرُ	نَتَنَادَى	نَتَآسَرُ	نَتَنَاسَى	نَتَقَارَأُ	1

ACTIVE, FORM VI, SUBJUNCTIVE

Singular

	1	2	3	4 and 5	6	7, 8, and 9	10	11	12	
3 M	يتَفاعَلْ	يَتَدارَدْ	يتَواضَعا	يتَقاوَمْ	يتَسايَرْ	يتَنادَ	يتَآسَرْ	يتَناءَسْ	يتَقارَأْ	3 M
3 F	تَتَفاعَلْ	تتَدارَدْ	تتَواضَعا	تتَقاوَمْ	تتَسايَرْ	تتَنادَ	تتَآسَرْ	تتَناءَسْ	تتَقارَأْ	3 F
2 M	تتَفاعَلْ	تتَدارَدْ	تتَواضَعا	تتَقاوَمْ	تتَسايَرْ	تتَنادَ	تتَآسَرْ	تتَناءَسْ	تتَقارَأْ	2 M
2 F	تتَفاعَلي	تتَدارَدي	تتَواضَعي	تتَقاوَمي	تتَسايَري	تتَنادَيْ	تتَآسَري	تتَناءَسي	تتَقارَئي	2 F
1	أتَفاعَلْ	أتَدارَدْ	أتَواضَعا	أتَقاوَمْ	أتَسايَرْ	أتَنادَ	أتَآسَرْ	أتَناءَسْ	أتَقارَأْ	1

Dual

	1	2	3	4 and 5	6	7, 8, and 9	10	11	12	
3 M	يتَفاعَلا	يتَدارَدا	يتَواضَعا	يتَقاوَما	يتَسايَرا	يتَنادَيا	يتَآسَرا	يتَناءَسا	يتَقارَآ	3 M
3 F	تتَفاعَلا	تتَدارَدا	تتَواضَعا	تتَقاوَما	تتَسايَرا	تتَنادَيا	تتَآسَرا	تتَناءَسا	تتَقارَآ	3 F
2	تتَفاعَلا	تتَدارَدا	تتَواضَعا	تتَقاوَما	تتَسايَرا	تتَنادَيا	تتَآسَرا	تتَناءَسا	تتَقارَآ	2

Plural

	1	2	3	4 and 5	6	7, 8, and 9	10	11	12	
3 M	يتَفاعَلوا	يتَدارَدوا	يتَواضَعوا	يتَقاوَموا	يتَسايَروا	يتَنادَوْا	يتَآسَروا	يتَناءَسوا	يتَقارَؤوا	3 M
3 F	يتَفاعَلْنَ	يتَدارَدْنَ	يتَواضَعْنَ	يتَقاوَمْنَ	يتَسايَرْنَ	يتَنادَيْنَ	يتَآسَرْنَ	يتَناءَسْنَ	يتَقارَأْنَ	3 F
2 M	تتَفاعَلوا	تتَدارَدوا	تتَواضَعوا	تتَقاوَموا	تتَسايَروا	تتَنادَوْا	تتَآسَروا	تتَناءَسوا	تتَقارَؤوا	2 M
2 F	تتَفاعَلْنَ	تتَدارَدْنَ	تتَواضَعْنَ	تتَقاوَمْنَ	تتَسايَرْنَ	تتَنادَيْنَ	تتَآسَرْنَ	تتَناءَسْنَ	تتَقارَأْنَ	2 F
1	نتَفاعَلْ	نتَدارَدْ	نتَواضَعا	نتَقاوَمْ	نتَسايَرْ	نتَنادَ	نتَآسَرْ	نتَناءَسْ	نتَقارَأْ	1

ACTIVE, FORM VI, JUSSIVE

	1	2	3	4 and 5	6	7, 8, and 9	10	11	12	
					Singular					
3 M	يَتَقَاعَلْ	يَتَرَادَدْ	يَتَوَاضَعْ	يَتَقَاوَمْ	يَتَسَايَرْ	يَتَنَادَ	يَتَأَسَرْ	يَتَيَاسَرْ	يَتَقَارَأْ	3 M
3 F	تَتَقَاعَلْ	تَتَرَادَدْ	تَتَوَاضَعْ	تَتَقَاوَمْ	تَتَسَايَرْ	تَتَنَادَ	تَتَأَسَرْ	تَتَيَاسَرْ	تَتَقَارَأْ	3 F
2 M	تَتَقَاعَلْ	تَتَرَادَدْ	تَتَوَاضَعْ	تَتَقَاوَمْ	تَتَسَايَرْ	تَتَنَادَ	تَتَأَسَرْ	تَتَيَاسَرْ	تَتَقَارَأْ	2 M
2 F	تَتَقَاعَلِي	تَتَرَادَدِي	تَتَوَاضَعِي	تَتَقَاوَمِي	تَتَسَايَرِي	تَتَنَادَي	تَتَأَسَرِي	تَتَيَاسَرِي	تَتَقَارَئِي	2 F
1	أَتَقَاعَلْ	أَتَرَادَدْ	أَتَوَاضَعْ	أَتَقَاوَمْ	أَتَسَايَرْ	أَتَنَادَ	أَتَأَسَرْ	أَتَيَاسَرْ	أَتَقَارَأْ	1
					Dual					
3 M	يَتَقَاعَلَا	يَتَرَادَدَا	يَتَوَاضَعَا	يَتَقَاوَمَا	يَتَسَايَرَا	يَتَنَادَيَا	يَتَأَسَرَا	يَتَيَاسَرَا	يَتَقَارَآ	3 M
3 F	تَتَقَاعَلَا	تَتَرَادَدَا	تَتَوَاضَعَا	تَتَقَاوَمَا	تَتَسَايَرَا	تَتَنَادَيَا	تَتَأَسَرَا	تَتَيَاسَرَا	تَتَقَارَآ	3 F
2	تَتَقَاعَلَا	تَتَرَادَدَا	تَتَوَاضَعَا	تَتَقَاوَمَا	تَتَسَايَرَا	تَتَنَادَيَا	تَتَأَسَرَا	تَتَيَاسَرَا	تَتَقَارَآ	2
					Plural					
3 M	يَتَقَاعَلُوا	يَتَرَادَدُوا	يَتَوَاضَعُوا	يَتَقَاوَمُوا	يَتَسَايَرُوا	يَتَنَادَوْا	يَتَأَسَرُوا	يَتَيَاسَرُوا	يَتَقَارَؤُوا	3 M
3 F	يَتَقَاعَلْنَ	يَتَرَادَدْنَ	يَتَوَاضَعْنَ	يَتَقَاوَمْنَ	يَتَسَايَرْنَ	يَتَنَادَيْنَ	يَتَأَسَرْنَ	يَتَيَاسَرْنَ	يَتَقَارَأْنَ	3 F
2 M	تَتَقَاعَلُوا	تَتَرَادَدُوا	تَتَوَاضَعُوا	تَتَقَاوَمُوا	تَتَسَايَرُوا	تَتَنَادَوْا	تَتَأَسَرُوا	تَتَيَاسَرُوا	تَتَقَارَؤُوا	2 M
2 F	تَتَقَاعَلْنَ	تَتَرَادَدْنَ	تَتَوَاضَعْنَ	تَتَقَاوَمْنَ	تَتَسَايَرْنَ	تَتَنَادَيْنَ	تَتَأَسَرْنَ	تَتَيَاسَرْنَ	تَتَقَارَأْنَ	2 F
1	نَتَقَاعَلْ	نَتَرَادَدْ	نَتَوَاضَعْ	نَتَقَاوَمْ	نَتَسَايَرْ	نَتَنَادَ	نَتَأَسَرْ	نَتَيَاسَرْ	نَتَقَارَأْ	1

	1	2	3	4, 5, and 6	7, 8, and 9	10	11	12
Singular								
3 M	اِنْفَعَلَ	اِرَدَّ	اِبْوَصَحَ	اِقْتَا	اِنْدَى	اِنْأَسَرَ	اِنْبَاسَ	اِقْرَأَ
3 F	اِنْفَعَلَتْ	اِرَدَّتْ	اِبْوَصَحَتْ	اِقْتَاتْ	اِنْدَتْ	اِنْأَسَرَتْ	اِنْبَاسَتْ	اِقْرَأَتْ
2 M	اِنْفَعَلْتَ	اِرْدَدْتَ	اِبْوَصَحْتَ	اِقْتَتْ	اِنْدَيْتَ	اِنْأَسَرْتَ	اِنْبَاسْتَ	اِقْرَأْتَ
2 F	اِنْفَعَلْتِ	اِرْدَدْتِ	اِبْوَصَحْتِ	اِقْتَتِ	اِنْدَيْتِ	اِنْأَسَرْتِ	اِنْبَاسْتِ	اِقْرَأْتِ
1	اِنْفَعَلْتُ	اِرْدَدْتُ	اِبْوَصَحْتُ	اِقْتَتُ	اِنْدَيْتُ	اِنْأَسَرْتُ	اِنْبَاسْتُ	اِقْرَأْتُ
Dual								
3 M	اِنْفَعَلَا	اِرَدَّا	اِبْوَصَحَا	اِقْتَا	اِنْدَيَا	اِنْأَسَرَا	اِنْبَاسَا	اِقْرَآ
3 F	اِنْفَعَلَتَا	اِرَدَّتَا	اِبْوَصَحَتَا	اِقْتَاتَا	اِنْدَتَا	اِنْأَسَرَتَا	اِنْبَاسَتَا	اِقْرَأَتَا
2	اِنْفَعَلْتُمَا	اِرْدَدْتُمَا	اِبْوَصَحْتُمَا	اِقْتَتُمَا	اِنْدَيْتُمَا	اِنْأَسَرْتُمَا	اِنْبَاسْتُمَا	اِقْرَأْتُمَا
Plural								
3 M	اِنْفَعَلُوا	اِرَدُّوا	اِبْوَصَحُوا	اِقْتَاوْا	اِنْدَوْا	اِنْأَسَرُوا	اِنْبَاسُوا	اِقْرَؤُوا
3 F	اِنْفَعَلْنَ	اِرْدَدْنَ	اِبْوَصَحْنَ	اِقْتَيْنَ	اِنْدَيْنَ	اِنْأَسَرْنَ	اِنْبَاسْنَ	اِقْرَأْنَ
2 M	اِنْفَعَلْتُمْ	اِرْدَدْتُمْ	اِبْوَصَحْتُمْ	اِقْتَتُمْ	اِنْدَيْتُمْ	اِنْأَسَرْتُمْ	اِنْبَاسْتُمْ	اِقْرَأْتُمْ
2 F	اِنْفَعَلْتُنَّ	اِرْدَدْتُنَّ	اِبْوَصَحْتُنَّ	اِقْتَتُنَّ	اِنْدَيْتُنَّ	اِنْأَسَرْتُنَّ	اِنْبَاسْتُنَّ	اِقْرَأْتُنَّ
1	اِنْفَعَلْنَا	اِرْدَدْنَا	اِبْوَصَحْنَا	اِقْتَنَا	اِنْدَيْنَا	اِنْأَسَرْنَا	اِنْبَاسْنَا	اِقْرَأْنَا

ACTIVE, FORM VII, IMPERFECT INDICATIVE

	1	2	3	4, 5, and 6	7, 8, and 9	10	11	12	
Singular									
3 M	يَنْفَعِلُ	يَرْتَدُّ	يَفْوَضِحُ	يَقْتَالُ	يَبْدِي	يَأْسِرُ	يَنْتَمِي	يَتَّقِّي	3 M
3 F	تَنْفَعِلُ	تَرْتَدُّ	تَفْوَضِحُ	تَقْتَالُ	تَبْدِي	تَأْسِرُ	تَنْتَمِي	تَتَّقِّي	3 F
2 M	تَنْفَعِلُ	تَرْتَدُّ	تَفْوَضِحُ	تَقْتَالُ	تَبْدِي	تَأْسِرُ	تَنْتَمِي	تَتَّقِّي	2 M
2 F	تَنْفَعِلِينَ	تَرْتَدِّينَ	تَفْوَضِحِينَ	تَقْتَالِينَ	تَبْدِينَ	تَأْسِرِينَ	تَنْتَمِينَ	تَتَّقِّينَ	2 F
1	أَنْفَعِلُ	أَرْتَدُّ	أَفْوَضِحُ	أَقْتَالُ	أَبْدِي	أَأْسِرُ	أَنْتَمِي	أَتَّقِّي	1
Dual									
3 M	يَنْفَعِلَانِ	يَرْتَدَّانِ	يَفْوَضِحَانِ	يَقْتَالَانِ	يَبْدِيَانِ	يَأْسِرَانِ	يَنْتَمِيَانِ	يَتَّقِّيَانِ	3 M
3 F	تَنْفَعِلَانِ	تَرْتَدَّانِ	تَفْوَضِحَانِ	تَقْتَالَانِ	تَبْدِيَانِ	تَأْسِرَانِ	تَنْتَمِيَانِ	تَتَّقِّيَانِ	3 F
2	تَنْفَعِلَانِ	تَرْتَدَّانِ	تَفْوَضِحَانِ	تَقْتَالَانِ	تَبْدِيَانِ	تَأْسِرَانِ	تَنْتَمِيَانِ	تَتَّقِّيَانِ	2
Plural									
3 M	يَنْفَعِلُونَ	يَرْتَدُّونَ	يَفْوَضِحُونَ	يَقْتَالُونَ	يَبْدُونَ	يَأْسِرُونَ	يَنْتَمُونَ	يَتَّقُّونَ	3 M
3 F	يَنْفَعِلْنَ	يَرْتَدِدْنَ	يَفْوَضِحْنَ	يَقْتَالْنَ	يَبْدِينَ	يَأْسِرْنَ	يَنْتَمِينَ	يَتَّقِّينَ	3 F
2 M	تَنْفَعِلُونَ	تَرْتَدُّونَ	تَفْوَضِحُونَ	تَقْتَالُونَ	تَبْدُونَ	تَأْسِرُونَ	تَنْتَمُونَ	تَتَّقُّونَ	2 M
2 F	تَنْفَعِلْنَ	تَرْتَدِدْنَ	تَفْوَضِحْنَ	تَقْتَالْنَ	تَبْدِينَ	تَأْسِرْنَ	تَنْتَمِينَ	تَتَّقِّينَ	2 F
1	نَنْفَعِلُ	نَرْتَدُّ	نَفْوَضِحُ	نَقْتَالُ	نَبْدِي	نَأْسِرُ	نَنْتَمِي	نَتَّقِّي	1

	1	2	3	4, 5, and 6	7, 8, and 9	10	11	12	
				Singular					
3 M	يَنْفَعِلْ	يَرْدُدْ	يَتَوَضَّحْ	يَنْقَا	يَبْدِيَ	يَأْسِرْ	يَنْتُسِرْ	يَتَقْرَى	3 M
3 F	تَنْفَعِلْ	تَرْدُدْ	تَتَوَضَّحْ	تَنْقَا	تَبْدِيَ	تَأْسِرْ	تَنْتُسِرْ	تَتَقْرَى	3 F
2 M	تَنْفَعِلْ	تَرْدُدْ	تَتَوَضَّحْ	تَنْقَا	تَبْدِيَ	تَأْسِرْ	تَنْتُسِرْ	تَتَقْرَى	2 M
2 F	تَنْفَعِلِي	تَرْدُدِي	تَتَوَضَّحِي	تَنْقَايِ	تَبْدِيَ	تَأْسِرِي	تَنْتُسِي	تَتَقْرَيِ	2 F
1	أَنْفَعِلْ	أَرْدُدْ	أَتَوَضَّحْ	أَنْقَا	أَبْدِيَ	آسِرْ	أَنْتُسِرْ	أَتَقْرَى	1
				Dual					
3 M	يَنْفَعِلَا	يَرْدُدَا	يَتَوَضَّحَا	يَنْقَا	يَبْدِيَا	يَأْسِرَا	يَنْتُسِرَا	يَتَقْرَيَا	3 M
3 F	تَنْفَعِلَا	تَرْدُدَا	تَتَوَضَّحَا	تَنْقَا	تَبْدِيَا	تَأْسِرَا	تَنْتُسِرَا	تَتَقْرَيَا	3 F
2	تَنْفَعِلَا	تَرْدُدَا	تَتَوَضَّحَا	تَنْقَا	تَبْدِيَا	تَأْسِرَا	تَنْتُسِرَا	تَتَقْرَيَا	2
				Plural					
3 M	يَنْفَعِلُوا	يَرْدُدُوا	يَتَوَضَّحُوا	يَنْقَاوُا	يَبْدُوا	يَأْسِرُوا	يَنْتُسِرُوا	يَتَقْرَوُا	3 M
3 F	يَنْفَعِلْنَ	يَرْدُدْنَ	يَتَوَضَّحْنَ	يَنْقَيْنَ	يَبْدِينَ	يَأْسِرْنَ	يَنْتُسِرْنَ	يَتَقْرَيْنَ	3 F
2 M	تَنْفَعِلُوا	تَرْدُدُوا	تَتَوَضَّحُوا	تَنْقَاوُا	تَبْدُوا	تَأْسِرُوا	تَنْتُسِرُوا	تَتَقْرَوُا	2 M
2 F	تَنْفَعِلْنَ	تَرْدُدْنَ	تَتَوَضَّحْنَ	تَنْقَيْنَ	تَبْدِينَ	تَأْسِرْنَ	تَنْتُسِرْنَ	تَتَقْرَيْنَ	2 F
1	نَنْفَعِلْ	نَرْدُدْ	نَتَوَضَّحْ	نَنْقَا	نَبْدِيَ	نَأْسِرْ	نَنْتُسِرْ	نَتَقْرَى	1

ACTIVE, FORM VII, JUSSIVE

	1	2	3	4, 5, and 6	7, 8, and 9	10	11	12	
				Singular					
3 M	يَنْقَتِلْ	يَرْدُدْ	يَنْقَضِ	يَنْقَمْ	يَبِدْ	يَأْسِرْ	يَنْغَمِسْ	يَنْقَرِ	3 M
3 F	تَنْقَتِلْ	تَرْدُدْ	تَنْقَضِ	تَنْقَمْ	تَبِدْ	تَأْسِرْ	تَنْغَمِسْ	تَنْقَرِ	3 F
2 M	تَنْقَتِلْ	تَرْدُدْ	تَنْقَضِ	تَنْقَمْ	تَبِدْ	تَأْسِرْ	تَنْغَمِسْ	تَنْقَرِ	2 M
2 F	تَنْقَتِلِي	تَرْدُدِي	تَنْقَضِي	تَنْقَمِّي	تَبِدِي	تَأْسِرِي	تَنْغَمِسِي	تَنْقَرِي	2 F
1	أَنْقَتِلْ	أَرْدُدْ	أَنْقَضِ	أَنْقَمْ	أَبِدْ	أَأْسِرْ	أَنْغَمِسْ	أَنْقَرِ	1
				Dual					
3 M	يَنْقَتِلَا	يَرْدُدَا	يَنْقَضِيَا	يَنْقَمَّا	يَبِدَا	يَأْسِرَا	يَنْغَمِسَا	يَنْقَرِيَا	3 M
3 F	تَنْقَتِلَا	تَرْدُدَا	تَنْقَضِيَا	تَنْقَمَّا	تَبِدَا	تَأْسِرَا	تَنْغَمِسَا	تَنْقَرِيَا	3 F
2	تَنْقَتِلَا	تَرْدُدَا	تَنْقَضِيَا	تَنْقَمَّا	تَبِدَا	تَأْسِرَا	تَنْغَمِسَا	تَنْقَرِيَا	2
				Plural					
3 M	يَنْقَتِلُوا	يَرْدُدُوا	يَنْقَضُوا	يَنْقَمُّوا	يَبِدُوا	يَأْسِرُوا	يَنْغَمِسُوا	يَنْقَرُوا	3 M
3 F	يَنْقَتِلْنَ	يَرْدُدْنَ	يَنْقَضِينَ	يَنْقَمِّنَ	يَبِدْنَ	يَأْسِرْنَ	يَنْغَمِسْنَ	يَنْقَرِينَ	3 F
2 M	تَنْقَتِلُوا	تَرْدُدُوا	تَنْقَضُوا	تَنْقَمُّوا	تَبِدُوا	تَأْسِرُوا	تَنْغَمِسُوا	تَنْقَرُوا	2 M
2 F	تَنْقَتِلْنَ	تَرْدُدْنَ	تَنْقَضِينَ	تَنْقَمِّنَ	تَبِدْنَ	تَأْسِرْنَ	تَنْغَمِسْنَ	تَنْقَرِينَ	2 F
1	نَنْقَتِلْ	نَرْدُدْ	نَنْقَضِ	نَنْقَمْ	نَبِدْ	نَأْسِرْ	نَنْغَمِسْ	نَنْقَرِ	1

ACTIVE, FORM VIII, PERFECT

	1	2	3	4, 5, and 6	7, 8, and 9	10	11	12	
				Singular					
3 M	اِفْتَعَلَ	اِرْتَدَّ	اِتَّخَمَ	اِقْتَانَ	اِتَّدَى	اِبْتَسَرَ	اِبْتَاسَ	اِقْتَرَّ	3 M
3 F	اِفْتَعَلَتْ	اِرْتَدَّتْ	اِتَّخَمَتْ	اِقْتَانَتْ	اِتَّدَتْ	اِبْتَسَرَتْ	اِبْتَاسَتْ	اِقْتَرَّتْ	3 F
2 M	اِفْتَعَلْتَ	اِرْتَدَدْتَ	اِتَّخَمْتَ	اِقْتَنْتَ	اِتَّدَيْتَ	اِبْتَسَرْتَ	اِبْتَاسْتَ	اِقْتَرَرْتَ	2 M
2 F	اِفْتَعَلْتِ	اِرْتَدَدْتِ	اِتَّخَمْتِ	اِقْتَنْتِ	اِتَّدَيْتِ	اِبْتَسَرْتِ	اِبْتَاسْتِ	اِقْتَرَرْتِ	2 F
1	اِفْتَعَلْتُ	اِرْتَدَدْتُ	اِتَّخَمْتُ	اِقْتَنْتُ	اِتَّدَيْتُ	اِبْتَسَرْتُ	اِبْتَاسْتُ	اِقْتَرَرْتُ	1
				Dual					
3 M	اِفْتَعَلَا	اِرْتَدَّا	اِتَّخَمَا	اِقْتَانَا	اِتَّدَيَا	اِبْتَسَرَا	اِبْتَاسَا	اِقْتَرَّا	3 M
3 F	اِفْتَعَلَتَا	اِرْتَدَّتَا	اِتَّخَمَتَا	اِقْتَانَتَا	اِتَّدَتَا	اِبْتَسَرَتَا	اِبْتَاسَتَا	اِقْتَرَّتَا	3 F
2	اِفْتَعَلْتُمَا	اِرْتَدَدْتُمَا	اِتَّخَمْتُمَا	اِقْتَنْتُمَا	اِتَّدَيْتُمَا	اِبْتَسَرْتُمَا	اِبْتَاسْتُمَا	اِقْتَرَرْتُمَا	2
				Plural					
3 M	اِفْتَعَلُوا	اِرْتَدُّوا	اِتَّخَمُوا	اِقْتَانُوا	اِتَّدَوْا	اِبْتَسَرُوا	اِبْتَاسُوا	اِقْتَرُّوا	3 M
3 F	اِفْتَعَلْنَ	اِرْتَدَدْنَ	اِتَّخَمْنَ	اِقْتَنَّ	اِتَّدَيْنَ	اِبْتَسَرْنَ	اِبْتَاسْنَ	اِقْتَرَرْنَ	3 F
2 M	اِفْتَعَلْتُمْ	اِرْتَدَدْتُمْ	اِتَّخَمْتُمْ	اِقْتَنْتُمْ	اِتَّدَيْتُمْ	اِبْتَسَرْتُمْ	اِبْتَاسْتُمْ	اِقْتَرَرْتُمْ	2 M
2 F	اِفْتَعَلْتُنَّ	اِرْتَدَدْتُنَّ	اِتَّخَمْتُنَّ	اِقْتَنْتُنَّ	اِتَّدَيْتُنَّ	اِبْتَسَرْتُنَّ	اِبْتَاسْتُنَّ	اِقْتَرَرْتُنَّ	2 F
1	اِفْتَعَلْنَا	اِرْتَدَدْنَا	اِتَّخَمْنَا	اِقْتَنَّا	اِتَّدَيْنَا	اِبْتَسَرْنَا	اِبْتَاسْنَا	اِقْتَرَرْنَا	1

209

ACTIVE, FORM VIII, IMPERFECT INDICATIVE

Singular

	1	2	3	4, 5, and 6	7, 8, and 9	10	11	12	
3 M	يَفْتَعِلُ	يَرْتَدُّ	يَخْتَصِمُ	يَقْتَانُ	يَبْتَدِي	يَأْتَسِرُ	يَنْتَهِي	يَقْتَرِي	3 M
3 F	تَفْتَعِلُ	تَرْتَدُّ	تَخْتَصِمُ	تَقْتَانُ	تَبْتَدِي	تَأْتَسِرُ	تَنْتَهِي	تَقْتَرِي	3 F
2 M	تَفْتَعِلُ	تَرْتَدُّ	تَخْتَصِمُ	تَقْتَانُ	تَبْتَدِي	تَأْتَسِرُ	تَنْتَهِي	تَقْتَرِي	2 M
2 F	تَفْتَعِلِينَ	تَرْتَدِّينَ	تَخْتَصِمِينَ	تَقْتَانِينَ	تَبْتَدِينَ	تَأْتَسِرِينَ	تَنْتَهِينَ	تَقْتَرِينَ	2 F
1	أَفْتَعِلُ	أَرْتَدُّ	أَخْتَصِمُ	أَقْتَانُ	أَبْتَدِي	آتَسِرُ	أَنْتَهِي	أَقْتَرِي	1

Dual

	1	2	3	4, 5, and 6	7, 8, and 9	10	11	12	
3 M	يَفْتَعِلَانِ	يَرْتَدَّانِ	يَخْتَصِمَانِ	يَقْتَانَانِ	يَبْتَدِيَانِ	يَأْتَسِرَانِ	يَنْتَهِيَانِ	يَقْتَرِيَانِ	3 M
3 F	تَفْتَعِلَانِ	تَرْتَدَّانِ	تَخْتَصِمَانِ	تَقْتَانَانِ	تَبْتَدِيَانِ	تَأْتَسِرَانِ	تَنْتَهِيَانِ	تَقْتَرِيَانِ	3 F
2	تَفْتَعِلَانِ	تَرْتَدَّانِ	تَخْتَصِمَانِ	تَقْتَانَانِ	تَبْتَدِيَانِ	تَأْتَسِرَانِ	تَنْتَهِيَانِ	تَقْتَرِيَانِ	2

Plural

	1	2	3	4, 5, and 6	7, 8, and 9	10	11	12	
3 M	يَفْتَعِلُونَ	يَرْتَدُّونَ	يَخْتَصِمُونَ	يَقْتَانُونَ	يَبْتَدُونَ	يَأْتَسِرُونَ	يَنْتَهُونَ	يَقْتَرُونَ	3 M
3 F	يَفْتَعِلْنَ	يَرْتَدِدْنَ	يَخْتَصِمْنَ	يَقْتَانَّ	يَبْتَدِينَ	يَأْتَسِرْنَ	يَنْتَهِينَ	يَقْتَرِينَ	3 F
2 M	تَفْتَعِلُونَ	تَرْتَدُّونَ	تَخْتَصِمُونَ	تَقْتَانُونَ	تَبْتَدُونَ	تَأْتَسِرُونَ	تَنْتَهُونَ	تَقْتَرُونَ	2 M
2 F	تَفْتَعِلْنَ	تَرْتَدِدْنَ	تَخْتَصِمْنَ	تَقْتَانَّ	تَبْتَدِينَ	تَأْتَسِرْنَ	تَنْتَهِينَ	تَقْتَرِينَ	2 F
1	نَفْتَعِلُ	نَرْتَدُّ	نَخْتَصِمُ	نَقْتَانُ	نَبْتَدِي	نَأْتَسِرُ	نَنْتَهِي	نَقْتَرِي	1

ACTIVE, FORM VIII, SUBJUNCTIVE

	1	2	3	4, 5, and 6	7, 8, and 9	10	11	12
Singular								
3 M	يَفْتَعِلْ	يَرْتَدَّ	يَنْخَصِمْ	يَقْتَضِ	يَبْتَدِ	يَأْتَسِرْ	يَبْتَصِ	يَقْتَرِيَ
3 F	تَفْتَعِلْ	تَرْتَدَّ	تَنْخَصِمْ	تَقْتَضِ	تَبْتَدِ	تَأْتَسِرْ	تَبْتَصِ	تَقْتَرِيَ
2 M	تَفْتَعِلْ	تَرْتَدَّ	تَنْخَصِمْ	تَقْتَضِ	تَبْتَدِ	تَأْتَسِرْ	تَبْتَصِ	تَقْتَرِيَ
2 F	تَفْتَعِلِي	تَرْتَدِّي	تَنْخَصِمِي	تَقْتَضِي	تَبْتَدِي	تَأْتَسِرِي	تَبْتَصِي	تَقْتَرِي
1	أَفْتَعِلْ	أَرْتَدَّ	أَنْخَصِمْ	أَقْتَضِ	أَبْتَدِ	أَتَسِرْ	أَبْتَصِ	أَقْتَرِيَ
Dual								
3 M	يَفْتَعِلَا	يَرْتَدَّا	يَنْخَصِمَا	يَقْتَضِيَا	يَبْتَدِيَا	يَأْتَسِرَا	يَبْتَصِيَا	يَقْتَرِيَا
3 F	تَفْتَعِلَا	تَرْتَدَّا	تَنْخَصِمَا	تَقْتَضِيَا	تَبْتَدِيَا	تَأْتَسِرَا	تَبْتَصِيَا	تَقْتَرِيَا
2	تَفْتَعِلَا	تَرْتَدَّا	تَنْخَصِمَا	تَقْتَضِيَا	تَبْتَدِيَا	تَأْتَسِرَا	تَبْتَصِيَا	تَقْتَرِيَا
Plural								
3 M	يَفْتَعِلُوا	يَرْتَدُّوا	يَنْخَصِمُوا	يَقْتَضُوا	يَبْتَدُوا	يَأْتَسِرُوا	يَبْتَصُوا	يَقْتَرُوا
3 F	يَفْتَعِلْنَ	يَرْتَدِدْنَ	يَنْخَصِمْنَ	يَقْتَضِينَ	يَبْتَدِينَ	يَأْتَسِرْنَ	يَبْتَصِينَ	يَقْتَرِينَ
2 M	تَفْتَعِلُوا	تَرْتَدُّوا	تَنْخَصِمُوا	تَقْتَضُوا	تَبْتَدُوا	تَأْتَسِرُوا	تَبْتَصُوا	تَقْتَرُوا
2 F	تَفْتَعِلْنَ	تَرْتَدِدْنَ	تَنْخَصِمْنَ	تَقْتَضِينَ	تَبْتَدِينَ	تَأْتَسِرْنَ	تَبْتَصِينَ	تَقْتَرِينَ
1	نَفْتَعِلْ	نَرْتَدَّ	نَنْخَصِمْ	نَقْتَضِ	نَبْتَدِ	نَأْتَسِرْ	نَبْتَصِ	نَقْتَرِيَ

ACTIVE, FORM VIII, JUSSIVE

	12	11	10	7, 8, and 9	4, 5, and 6	3	2	1	
				Singular					
3 M	يَقْتَرِ	يَبْتَسِ	يَأْتَسِرْ	يَنْتَدِ	يَقْتَمِ	يَخْتَصِ	يَرْتَدِدْ	يَفْتَعِلْ	3 M
3 F	تَقْتَرِ	تَبْتَسِ	تَأْتَسِرْ	تَنْتَدِ	تَقْتَمِ	تَخْتَصِ	تَرْتَدِدْ	تَفْتَعِلْ	3 F
2 M	تَقْتَرِ	تَبْتَسِ	تَأْتَسِرْ	تَنْتَدِ	تَقْتَمِ	تَخْتَصِ	تَرْتَدِدْ	تَفْتَعِلْ	2 M
2 F	تَقْتَرِي	تَبْتَسِي	تَأْتَسِرِي	تَنْتَدِي	تَقْتَمِي	تَخْتَصِي	تَرْتَدِّي	تَفْتَعِلِي	2 F
1	أَقْتَرِ	أَبْتَسِ	أَأْتَسِرْ	أَنْتَدِ	أَقْتَمِ	أَخْتَصِ	أَرْتَدِدْ	أَفْتَعِلْ	1
				Dual					
3 M	يَقْتَرِيَا	يَبْتَسِيَا	يَأْتَسِرَا	يَنْتَدِيَا	يَقْتَمِيَا	يَخْتَصِيَا	يَرْتَدَّا	يَفْتَعِلَا	3 M
3 F	تَقْتَرِيَا	تَبْتَسِيَا	تَأْتَسِرَا	تَنْتَدِيَا	تَقْتَمِيَا	تَخْتَصِيَا	تَرْتَدَّا	تَفْتَعِلَا	3 F
2	تَقْتَرِيَا	تَبْتَسِيَا	تَأْتَسِرَا	تَنْتَدِيَا	تَقْتَمِيَا	تَخْتَصِيَا	تَرْتَدَّا	تَفْتَعِلَا	2
				Plural					
3 M	يَقْتَرُوا	يَبْتَسُوا	يَأْتَسِرُوا	يَنْتَدُوا	يَقْتَمُوا	يَخْتَصُوا	يَرْتَدُّوا	يَفْتَعِلُوا	3 M
3 F	يَقْتَرِينَ	يَبْتَسِينَ	يَأْتَسِرْنَ	يَنْتَدِينَ	يَقْتَمِينَ	يَخْتَصِينَ	يَرْتَدِدْنَ	يَفْتَعِلْنَ	3 F
2 M	تَقْتَرُوا	تَبْتَسُوا	تَأْتَسِرُوا	تَنْتَدُوا	تَقْتَمُوا	تَخْتَصُوا	تَرْتَدُّوا	تَفْتَعِلُوا	2 M
2 F	تَقْتَرِينَ	تَبْتَسِينَ	تَأْتَسِرْنَ	تَنْتَدِينَ	تَقْتَمِينَ	تَخْتَصِينَ	تَرْتَدِدْنَ	تَفْتَعِلْنَ	2 F
1	نَقْتَرِ	نَبْتَسِ	نَأْتَسِرْ	نَنْتَدِ	نَقْتَمِ	نَخْتَصِ	نَرْتَدِدْ	نَفْتَعِلْ	1

ACTIVE, FORM IX, SOUND VERB ONLY

	PERFECT	IMPERFECT INDICATIVE	SUBJUNCTIVE	JUSSIVE	
			Singular		
3 M	إِفْعَلَّ	يَفْعَلُّ	يَفْعَلَّ	(يَفْعَلِلْ) يَفْعَلَّ	3 M
3 F	إِفْعَلَّتْ	تَفْعَلُّ	تَفْعَلَّ	(تَفْعَلِلْ) تَفْعَلَّ	3 F
2 M	إِفْعَلَلْتَ	تَفْعَلُّ	تَفْعَلَّ	(تَفْعَلِلْ) تَفْعَلَّ	2 M
2 F	إِفْعَلَلْتِ	تَفْعَلِّينَ	تَفْعَلِّي	تَفْعَلِّي	2 F
1	إِفْعَلَلْتُ	أَفْعَلُّ	أَفْعَلَّ	(أَفْعَلِلْ) أَفْعَلَّ	1
			Dual		
3 M	إِفْعَلَّا	يَفْعَلَّانِ	يَفْعَلَّا	يَفْعَلَّا	3 M
3 F	إِفْعَلَّتَا	تَفْعَلَّانِ	تَفْعَلَّا	تَفْعَلَّا	3 F
2	إِفْعَلَلْتُمَا	تَفْعَلَّانِ	تَفْعَلَّا	تَفْعَلَّا	2
			Plural		
3 M	إِفْعَلُّوا	يَفْعَلُّونَ	يَفْعَلُّوا	يَفْعَلُّوا	3 M
3 F	إِفْعَلَلْنَ	يَفْعَلِلْنَ	يَفْعَلِلْنَ	يَفْعَلِلْنَ	3 F
2 M	إِفْعَلَلْتُمْ	تَفْعَلُّونَ	تَفْعَلُّوا	تَفْعَلُّوا	2 M
2 F	إِفْعَلَلْتُنَّ	تَفْعَلِلْنَ	تَفْعَلِلْنَ	تَفْعَلِلْنَ	2 F
1	إِفْعَلَلْنَا	نَفْعَلُّ	نَفْعَلَّ	(نَفْعَلِلْ) نَفْعَلَّ	1

ACTIVE, FORM X, PERFECT

Singular

	1	2	3	4, 5, and 6	7, 8, and 9	10	11	12
3 M	اِسْتَفْعَلَ	اِسْتَرَدَّ	اِسْتَوْضَحَ	اِسْتَقالَ	اِسْتَهْدى	اِسْتَأْنَسَ	اِسْتَسْأَسَ	اِسْتَقْرَأَ
3 F	اِسْتَفْعَلَتْ	اِسْتَرَدَّتْ	اِسْتَوْضَحَتْ	اِسْتَقالَتْ	اِسْتَهْدَتْ	اِسْتَأْنَسَتْ	اِسْتَسْأَسَتْ	اِسْتَقْرَأَتْ
2 M	اِسْتَفْعَلْتَ	اِسْتَرْدَدْتَ	اِسْتَوْضَحْتَ	اِسْتَقَلْتَ	اِسْتَهْدَيْتَ	اِسْتَأْنَسْتَ	اِسْتَسْأَسْتَ	اِسْتَقْرَأْتَ
2 F	اِسْتَفْعَلْتِ	اِسْتَرْدَدْتِ	اِسْتَوْضَحْتِ	اِسْتَقَلْتِ	اِسْتَهْدَيْتِ	اِسْتَأْنَسْتِ	اِسْتَسْأَسْتِ	اِسْتَقْرَأْتِ
1	اِسْتَفْعَلْتُ	اِسْتَرْدَدْتُ	اِسْتَوْضَحْتُ	اِسْتَقَلْتُ	اِسْتَهْدَيْتُ	اِسْتَأْنَسْتُ	اِسْتَسْأَسْتُ	اِسْتَقْرَأْتُ

Dual

	1	2	3	4, 5, and 6	7, 8, and 9	10	11	12
3 M	اِسْتَفْعَلا	اِسْتَرَدّا	اِسْتَوْضَحا	اِسْتَقالا	اِسْتَهْدَيا	اِسْتَأْنَسا	اِسْتَسْأَسا	اِسْتَقْرَأا
3 F	اِسْتَفْعَلَتا	اِسْتَرَدَّتا	اِسْتَوْضَحَتا	اِسْتَقالَتا	اِسْتَهْدَتا	اِسْتَأْنَسَتا	اِسْتَسْأَسَتا	اِسْتَقْرَأَتا
2	اِسْتَفْعَلْتُما	اِسْتَرْدَدْتُما	اِسْتَوْضَحْتُما	اِسْتَقَلْتُما	اِسْتَهْدَيْتُما	اِسْتَأْنَسْتُما	اِسْتَسْأَسْتُما	اِسْتَقْرَأْتُما

Plural

	1	2	3	4, 5, and 6	7, 8, and 9	10	11	12
3 M	اِسْتَفْعَلوا	اِسْتَرَدّوا	اِسْتَوْضَحوا	اِسْتَقالوا	اِسْتَهْدَوْا	اِسْتَأْنَسوا	اِسْتَسْأَسوا	اِسْتَقْرَأوا
3 F	اِسْتَفْعَلْنَ	اِسْتَرْدَدْنَ	اِسْتَوْضَحْنَ	اِسْتَقَلْنَ	اِسْتَهْدَيْنَ	اِسْتَأْنَسْنَ	اِسْتَسْأَسْنَ	اِسْتَقْرَأْنَ
2 M	اِسْتَفْعَلْتُمْ	اِسْتَرْدَدْتُمْ	اِسْتَوْضَحْتُمْ	اِسْتَقَلْتُمْ	اِسْتَهْدَيْتُمْ	اِسْتَأْنَسْتُمْ	اِسْتَسْأَسْتُمْ	اِسْتَقْرَأْتُمْ
2 F	اِسْتَفْعَلْتُنَّ	اِسْتَرْدَدْتُنَّ	اِسْتَوْضَحْتُنَّ	اِسْتَقَلْتُنَّ	اِسْتَهْدَيْتُنَّ	اِسْتَأْنَسْتُنَّ	اِسْتَسْأَسْتُنَّ	اِسْتَقْرَأْتُنَّ
1	اِسْتَفْعَلْنا	اِسْتَرْدَدْنا	اِسْتَوْضَحْنا	اِسْتَقَلْنا	اِسْتَهْدَيْنا	اِسْتَأْنَسْنا	اِسْتَسْأَسْنا	اِسْتَقْرَأْنا

ACTIVE, FORM X, IMPERFECT INDICATIVE

	1	2	3	4, 5, and 6	7, 8, and 9	10	11	12
Singular								
3 M	يَسْتَفْعِلُ	يَسْتَرِدُّ	يَسْتَرْضِعُ	يَسْتَبْقِمُ	يَسْتَبْقِى	يُسْتَاسِرُ	يَسْتَبْقِى	يَسْتَقْرِى
3 F	تَسْتَفْعِلُ	تَسْتَرِدُّ	تَسْتَرْضِعُ	تَسْتَبْقِمُ	تَسْتَبْقِى	تُسْتَاسِرُ	تَسْتَبْقِى	تَسْتَقْرِى
2 M	تَسْتَفْعِلُ	تَسْتَرِدُّ	تَسْتَرْضِعُ	تَسْتَبْقِمُ	تَسْتَبْقِى	تُسْتَاسِرُ	تَسْتَبْقِى	تَسْتَقْرِى
2 F	تَسْتَفْعِلِينَ	تَسْتَرِدِّينَ	تَسْتَرْضِعِينَ	تَسْتَبْقِمِينَ	تَسْتَبْقِينَ	تُسْتَاسِرِينَ	تَسْتَبْقِينَ	تَسْتَقْرِينَ
1	أَسْتَفْعِلُ	أَسْتَرِدُّ	أَسْتَرْضِعُ	أَسْتَبْقِمُ	أَسْتَبْقِى	أُسْتَاسِرُ	أَسْتَبْقِى	أَسْتَقْرِى
Dual								
3 M	يَسْتَفْعِلَانِ	يَسْتَرِدَّانِ	يَسْتَرْضِعَانِ	يَسْتَبْقِمَانِ	يَسْتَبْقِيَانِ	يُسْتَاسِرَانِ	يَسْتَبْقِيَانِ	يَسْتَقْرِيَانِ
3 F	تَسْتَفْعِلَانِ	تَسْتَرِدَّانِ	تَسْتَرْضِعَانِ	تَسْتَبْقِمَانِ	تَسْتَبْقِيَانِ	تُسْتَاسِرَانِ	تَسْتَبْقِيَانِ	تَسْتَقْرِيَانِ
2	تَسْتَفْعِلَانِ	تَسْتَرِدَّانِ	تَسْتَرْضِعَانِ	تَسْتَبْقِمَانِ	تَسْتَبْقِيَانِ	تُسْتَاسِرَانِ	تَسْتَبْقِيَانِ	تَسْتَقْرِيَانِ
Plural								
3 M	يَسْتَفْعِلُونَ	يَسْتَرِدُّونَ	يَسْتَرْضِعُونَ	يَسْتَبْقِمُونَ	يَسْتَبْقُونَ	يُسْتَاسِرُونَ	يَسْتَبْقُونَ	يَسْتَقْرُونَ
3 F	يَسْتَفْعِلْنَ	يَسْتَرْدِدْنَ	يَسْتَرْضِعْنَ	يَسْتَبْقِمْنَ	يَسْتَبْقِينَ	يُسْتَاسِرْنَ	يَسْتَبْقِينَ	يَسْتَقْرِينَ
2 M	تَسْتَفْعِلُونَ	تَسْتَرِدُّونَ	تَسْتَرْضِعُونَ	تَسْتَبْقِمُونَ	تَسْتَبْقُونَ	تُسْتَاسِرُونَ	تَسْتَبْقُونَ	تَسْتَقْرُونَ
2 F	تَسْتَفْعِلْنَ	تَسْتَرْدِدْنَ	تَسْتَرْضِعْنَ	تَسْتَبْقِمْنَ	تَسْتَبْقِينَ	تُسْتَاسِرْنَ	تَسْتَبْقِينَ	تَسْتَقْرِينَ
1	نَسْتَفْعِلُ	نَسْتَرِدُّ	نَسْتَرْضِعُ	نَسْتَبْقِمُ	نَسْتَبْقِى	نُسْتَاسِرُ	نَسْتَبْقِى	نَسْتَقْرِى

ACTIVE, FORM X, SUBJUNCTIVE

	12	11	10	7, 8, and 9	4, 5, and 6	3	2	1	
				Singular					
3 M	يَسْتَكْبِرَ	يَسْتَفْعِلَ	يَسْتَنَاسِرَ	يَسْتَنَادِيَ	يَسْتَكْفِرَ	يَسْتَخْرِجَ	يَسْتَرْدِدَ	يَسْتَفْعِلَ	3 M
3 F	تَسْتَكْبِرَ	تَسْتَفْعِلَ	تَسْتَنَاسِرَ	تَسْتَنَادِيَ	تَسْتَكْفِرَ	تَسْتَخْرِجَ	تَسْتَرْدِدَ	تَسْتَفْعِلَ	3 F
2 M	تَسْتَكْبِرَ	تَسْتَفْعِلَ	تَسْتَنَاسِرَ	تَسْتَنَادِيَ	تَسْتَكْفِرَ	تَسْتَخْرِجَ	تَسْتَرْدِدَ	تَسْتَفْعِلَ	2 M
2 F	تَسْتَكْبِرِي	تَسْتَفْعِلِي	تَسْتَنَاسِرِي	تَسْتَنَادِي	تَسْتَكْفِرِي	تَسْتَخْرِجِي	تَسْتَرْدِدِي	تَسْتَفْعِلِي	2 F
1	أَسْتَكْبِرَ	أَسْتَفْعِلَ	أَسْتَنَاسِرَ	أَسْتَنَادِيَ	أَسْتَكْفِرَ	أَسْتَخْرِجَ	أَسْتَرْدِدَ	أَسْتَفْعِلَ	1
				Dual					
3 M	يَسْتَكْبِرَا	يَسْتَفْعِلَا	يَسْتَنَاسِرَا	يَسْتَنَادِيَا	يَسْتَكْفِرَا	يَسْتَخْرِجَا	يَسْتَرْدِدَا	يَسْتَفْعِلَا	3 M
3 F	تَسْتَكْبِرَا	تَسْتَفْعِلَا	تَسْتَنَاسِرَا	تَسْتَنَادِيَا	تَسْتَكْفِرَا	تَسْتَخْرِجَا	تَسْتَرْدِدَا	تَسْتَفْعِلَا	3 F
2	تَسْتَكْبِرَا	تَسْتَفْعِلَا	تَسْتَنَاسِرَا	تَسْتَنَادِيَا	تَسْتَكْفِرَا	تَسْتَخْرِجَا	تَسْتَرْدِدَا	تَسْتَفْعِلَا	2
				Plural					
3 M	يَسْتَكْبِرُوا	يَسْتَفْعِلُوا	يَسْتَنَاسِرُوا	يَسْتَنَادُوا	يَسْتَكْفِرُوا	يَسْتَخْرِجُوا	يَسْتَرْدِدُوا	يَسْتَفْعِلُوا	3 M
3 F	يَسْتَكْبِرْنَ	يَسْتَفْعِلْنَ	يَسْتَنَاسِرْنَ	يَسْتَنَادِينَ	يَسْتَكْفِرْنَ	يَسْتَخْرِجْنَ	يَسْتَرْدِدْنَ	يَسْتَفْعِلْنَ	3 F
2 M	تَسْتَكْبِرُوا	تَسْتَفْعِلُوا	تَسْتَنَاسِرُوا	تَسْتَنَادُوا	تَسْتَكْفِرُوا	تَسْتَخْرِجُوا	تَسْتَرْدِدُوا	تَسْتَفْعِلُوا	2 M
2 F	تَسْتَكْبِرْنَ	تَسْتَفْعِلْنَ	تَسْتَنَاسِرْنَ	تَسْتَنَادِينَ	تَسْتَكْفِرْنَ	تَسْتَخْرِجْنَ	تَسْتَرْدِدْنَ	تَسْتَفْعِلْنَ	2 F
1	نَسْتَكْبِرَ	نَسْتَفْعِلَ	نَسْتَنَاسِرَ	نَسْتَنَادِيَ	نَسْتَكْفِرَ	نَسْتَخْرِجَ	نَسْتَرْدِدَ	نَسْتَفْعِلَ	1

ACTIVE, FORM X, JUSSIVE

	1	2	3	4, 5, and 6	7, 8, and 9	10	11	12	
Singular									
3 M	يَسْتَفْعِلْ	يَسْتَرْدِدْ	يَسْتَوْضِحْ	يَسْتَفِنّ	يَسْتَبْدِلْ	يَسْتَأْسِرْ	يَسْتَبْنِسْ	يَسْتَقْوِ	3 M
3 F	تَسْتَفْعِلْ	تَسْتَرْدِدْ	تَسْتَوْضِحْ	تَسْتَفِنّ	تَسْتَبْدِلْ	تَسْتَأْسِرْ	تَسْتَبْنِسْ	تَسْتَقْوِ	3 F
2 M	تَسْتَفْعِلْ	تَسْتَرْدِدْ	تَسْتَوْضِحْ	تَسْتَفِنّ	تَسْتَبْدِلْ	تَسْتَأْسِرْ	تَسْتَبْنِسْ	تَسْتَقْوِ	2 M
2 F	تَسْتَفْعِلِي	تَسْتَرْدِدِي	تَسْتَوْضِحِي	تَسْتَفِنِّي	تَسْتَبْدِلِي	تَسْتَأْسِرِي	تَسْتَبْنِسِي	تَسْتَقْوِي	2 F
1	أَسْتَفْعِلْ	أَسْتَرْدِدْ	أَسْتَوْضِحْ	أَسْتَفِنّ	أَسْتَبْدِلْ	أَسْتَأْسِرْ	أَسْتَبْنِسْ	أَسْتَقْوِ	1
Dual									
3 M	يَسْتَفْعِلَا	يَسْتَرْدِدَا	يَسْتَوْضِحَا	يَسْتَفِنَّا	يَسْتَبْدِلَا	يَسْتَأْسِرَا	يَسْتَبْنِسَا	يَسْتَقْوِيَا	3 M
3 F	تَسْتَفْعِلَا	تَسْتَرْدِدَا	تَسْتَوْضِحَا	تَسْتَفِنَّا	تَسْتَبْدِلَا	تَسْتَأْسِرَا	تَسْتَبْنِسَا	تَسْتَقْوِيَا	3 F
2	تَسْتَفْعِلَا	تَسْتَرْدِدَا	تَسْتَوْضِحَا	تَسْتَفِنَّا	تَسْتَبْدِلَا	تَسْتَأْسِرَا	تَسْتَبْنِسَا	تَسْتَقْوِيَا	2
Plural									
3 M	يَسْتَفْعِلُوا	يَسْتَرْدِدُوا	يَسْتَوْضِحُوا	يَسْتَفِنُّوا	يَسْتَبْدِلُوا	يَسْتَأْسِرُوا	يَسْتَبْنِسُوا	يَسْتَقْوُوا	3 M
3 F	يَسْتَفْعِلْنَ	يَسْتَرْدِدْنَ	يَسْتَوْضِحْنَ	يَسْتَفْنِنَ	يَسْتَبْدِلْنَ	يَسْتَأْسِرْنَ	يَسْتَبْنِسْنَ	يَسْتَقْوِينَ	3 F
2 M	تَسْتَفْعِلُوا	تَسْتَرْدِدُوا	تَسْتَوْضِحُوا	تَسْتَفِنُّوا	تَسْتَبْدِلُوا	تَسْتَأْسِرُوا	تَسْتَبْنِسُوا	تَسْتَقْوُوا	2 M
2 F	تَسْتَفْعِلْنَ	تَسْتَرْدِدْنَ	تَسْتَوْضِحْنَ	تَسْتَفْنِنَ	تَسْتَبْدِلْنَ	تَسْتَأْسِرْنَ	تَسْتَبْنِسْنَ	تَسْتَقْوِينَ	2 F
1	نَسْتَفْعِلْ	نَسْتَرْدِدْ	نَسْتَوْضِحْ	نَسْتَفِنّ	نَسْتَبْدِلْ	نَسْتَأْسِرْ	نَسْتَبْنِسْ	نَسْتَقْوِ	1

PASSIVE, FORMS I–IV, PERFECT

	1	2	3	4 and 5	6	7, 8, and 9	10	11	12	
				Form I, Singular						
3 M	قُتِلَ	رُدَّ	وُضِعَ	قِيلَ	سِيرَ	نُدِيَ	أُسِرَ	بُنِيَ	قُوِيَ	3 M
3 F	قُتِلَتْ	رُدَّتْ	وُضِعَتْ	قِيلَتْ	سِيرَتْ	نُدِيَتْ	أُسِرَتْ	بُنِيَتْ	قُوِيَتْ	3 F
2 M	قُتِلْتَ	رُدِدْتَ	وُضِعْتَ	قِلْتَ	سِرْتَ	نُدِيتَ	أُسِرْتَ	بُنِيتَ	قُوِيتَ	2 M
				Form II, Singular						
3 M	قُتِّلَ	رُدِّدَ	وُضِّعَ	قُوِّلَ	سُيِّرَ	نُدِّيَ	أُسِّرَ	بُنِّيَ	قُوِّيَ	3 M
3 F	قُتِّلَتْ	رُدِّدَتْ	وُضِّعَتْ	قُوِّلَتْ	سُيِّرَتْ	نُدِّيَتْ	أُسِّرَتْ	بُنِّيَتْ	قُوِّيَتْ	3 F
2 M	قُتِّلْتَ	رُدِّدْتَ	وُضِّعْتَ	قُوِّلْتَ	سُيِّرْتَ	نُدِّيتَ	أُسِّرْتَ	بُنِّيتَ	قُوِّيتَ	2 M
				Form III, Singular						
3 M	قُوتِلَ	رُودِدَ	وُوضِعَ	قُووِلَ	سُويِرَ	نُودِيَ	أُوسِرَ	بُوني	قُووِيَ	3 M
3 F	قُوتِلَتْ	رُودِدَتْ	وُوضِعَتْ	قُووِلَتْ	سُويِرَتْ	نُودِيَتْ	أُوسِرَتْ	بُونِيَتْ	قُووِيَتْ	3 F
2 M	قُوتِلْتَ	رُودِدْتَ	وُوضِعْتَ	قُووِلْتَ	سُويِرْتَ	نُودِيتَ	أُوسِرْتَ	بُونِيتَ	قُووِيتَ	2 M
				Form IV, Singular						
3 M	أُقْتِلَ	أُرِدَّ	أُوضِعَ	أُقِيلَ	أُسِيرَ	أُنْدِيَ	أُوسِرَ	أُبْنِيَ	أُقْوِيَ	3 M
3 F	أُقْتِلَتْ	أُرِدَّتْ	أُوضِعَتْ	أُقِيلَتْ	أُسِيرَتْ	أُنْدِيَتْ	أُوسِرَتْ	أُبْنِيَتْ	أُقْوِيَتْ	3 F
2 M	أُقْتِلْتَ	أُرْدِدْتَ	أُوضِعْتَ	أُقِلْتَ	أُسِرْتَ	أُنْدِيتَ	أُوسِرْتَ	أُبْنِيتَ	أُقْوِيتَ	2 M

	1	2	3	4 and 5	6	7, 8, and 9	10	11	12	
				Form V, Singular						3 M
3 M	تُفُعِّل	تُرُدِّد	تُوُضِّح	تُقُوِّم	تُسِيِّر	تُنُدِّي	تُقُوِّس	تُنُشِّى	تَقُرِّى	
3 F	تُفُعِّلَت	تُرُدِّدَت	تُوُضِّحَت	تُقُوِّمَت	تُسِيِّرَت	تُنُدِّيَت	تُقُوِّسَت	تُنُشِّيَت	تَقُرِّيَت	3 F
2 M	تُفُعِّلت	تُرُدِّدت	تُوُضِّحت	تُقُوِّمت	تُسِيِّرت	تُنُدِّيت	تُقُوِّست	تُنُشِّيت	تَقُرِّيت	2 M
				Form VI, Singular						3 M
3 M	تُفُوعِل	تُرُودِد	تُوُوضِح	تُقُووِم	تُسُويِر	تُنُودِي		تُنُوشِى	تَقُورِى	
3 F	تُفُوعِلَت	تُرُودِدَت	تُوُوضِحَت	تُقُووِمَت	تُسُويِرَت	تُنُودِيَت	تُقُووِسَت	تُنُوشِيَت	تَقُورِيَت	3 F
2 M	تُفُوعِلت	تُرُودِدت	تُوُوضِحت	تُقُووِمت	تُسُويِرت	تُنُودِيت	تُقُووِست	تُنُوشِيت	تَقُورِيت	2 M
				Form VII, Singular						3 M
3 M	اُنْفُعِل	اُنْرُدِد	اُنْوُضِح	اُنْقُوِم	اُنْسِيِر	اُنْدُلِى	اُنْقُوِس	اُنْتُشِى	اُنْقُرِى	
3 F	اُنْفُعِلَت	اُنْرُدِدَت	اُنْوُضِحَت	اُنْقُوِمَت	اُنْسِيِرَت	اُنْدُلِيَت	اُنْقُوِسَت	اُنْتُشِيَت	اُنْقُرِيَت	3 F
2 M	اُنْفُعِلت	اُنْرُدِدت	اُنْوُضِحت	اُنْقُوِمت	اُنْسِيِرت	اُنْدُلِيت	اُنْقُوِست	اُنْتُشِيت	اُنْقُرِيت	2 M
				Form VIII, Singular						3 M
3 M	اُفْتُعِل	اُرْتُدِد	اُتُّضِح	اُقْتُوِم	اُسْتُيِر	اُنْتُدِى	اُقْتُوِس	اُنْتُشِى	اُقْتُرِى	
3 F	اُفْتُعِلَت	اُرْتُدِدَت	اُتُّضِحَت	اُقْتُوِمَت	اُسْتُيِرَت	اُنْتُدِيَت	اُقْتُوِسَت	اُنْتُشِيَت	اُقْتُرِيَت	3 F
2 M	اُفْتُعِلت	اُرْتُدِدت	اُتُّضِحت	اُقْتُوِمت	اُسْتُيِرت	اُنْتُدِيت	اُقْتُوِست	اُنْتُشِيت	اُقْتُرِيت	2 M

PASSIVE, FORM X, PERFECT

Form X, Singular

	I	2	3	4 and 5	6	7, 8, and 9	10	11	12	
3 M	أُسْتُفْعِلَ	اُسْتُرِدَّ	اُسْتُوخِمَ	اُسْتُفِمَّ	اُسْتُسِرَ	اُسْتُدْعِيَ	اُسْتُقْوِسَ	اُسْتُأْسِيَ	اُسْتُقْرِئَ	3 M
3 F	أُسْتُفْعِلَتْ	اُسْتُرِدَّتْ	اُسْتُوخِمَتْ	اُسْتُفِمَّتْ	اُسْتُسِرَتْ	اُسْتُدْعِيَتْ	اُسْتُقْوِسَتْ	اُسْتُأْسِيَتْ	اُسْتُقْرِئَتْ	3 F
2 M	أُسْتُفْعِلْتَ	اُسْتُرِدَدْتَ	اُسْتُوخِمْتَ	اُسْتُفِمْتَ	اُسْتُسِرْتَ	اُسْتُدْعِيتَ	اُسْتُقْوِسْتَ	اُسْتُأْسِيتَ	اُسْتُقْرِئْتَ	2 M

PASSIVE, ALL FORMS, IMPERFECT INDICATIVE

Third Masculine Singular Only

	I	2	3	4 and 5	6	7, 8, and 9	10	11	12	
I	يُفْعَلُ	يُرَدُّ	يُوخَمُ	يُقَامُ	يُسَارُ	يُدْعَى	يُقْوَسُ	يُأْسَى	يُقْرَأُ	I
II	يُفَعَّلُ	يُرَدَّدُ	يُوَخَّمُ	يُقَوَّمُ	يُسَيَّرُ	يُدَعَّى	يُقَوَّسُ	يُأَسَّى	يُقَرَّئُ	II
III	يُفَاعَلُ	يُرَادُّ	يُوَاخَمُ	يُقَاوَمُ	يُسَايَرُ	يُدَاعَى	يُقَاوَسُ	يُؤَاسَى	يُقَارَئُ	III
IV	يُفْعَلُ	يُرَدُّ	يُوخَمُ	يُقَامُ	يُسَارُ	يُدْعَى	يُقْوَسُ	يُأْسَى	يُقْرَأُ	IV
V	يُتَفَعَّلُ	يُتَرَدَّدُ	يُتَوَخَّمُ	يُتَقَوَّمُ	يُتَسَيَّرُ	يُتَدَعَّى	يُتَقَوَّسُ	يُتَأَسَّى	يُتَقَرَّئُ	V
VI	يُتَفَاعَلُ	يُتَرَادُّ	يُتَوَاخَمُ	يُتَقَاوَمُ	يُتَسَايَرُ	يُتَدَاعَى	يُتَقَاوَسُ	يُتَأَاسَى	يُتَقَارَئُ	VI
VII	يُنْفَعَلُ	يُنْرَدُّ	يُنْوَخَمُ	يُنْقَامُ	يُنْسَارُ	يُنْدَعَى	يُنْقَاسُ	يُنْأَاسُ	يُنْقَرَئُ	VII
VIII	يُفْتَعَلُ	يُرْتَدُّ	يُوتَخَمُ	يُقْتَامُ	يُسْتَارُ	يُدْتَعَى	يُقْتَاسُ	يُأْتَاسُ	يُقْتَرَئُ	VIII
X	يُسْتَفْعَلُ	يُسْتَرَدُّ	يُسْتَوْخَمُ	يُسْتَقَامُ	يُسْتَسَارُ	يُسْتَدْعَى	يُسْتَقَاسُ	يُسْتَأْاسُ	يُسْتَقْرَئُ	X

DERIVED FORM MASDARS

	1	2	3	4 and 5	6	7, 8, and 9	10	11	12
II	تَفْعِيل / تَفْعِلَة	تَرْدِيد	تَوْضِيع	تَقْوِيم	تَسْيِير	تَنْدِيب	تَأْسِير	تَأْنِيس	تَقْرِئَة / تَقْرِيء
III	فِعَال / مُفَاعَلَة	رِدَاد	وِضَاع	قِوَام / مُقَاوَمَة	سِيَار	نِدَاب	إِسَار	إِنَاس	قِرَاء / مُقَارَأَة
IV	إِفْعَال	إِرْدَاد	إِيضَاع	إِقَامَة	إِسَارة	إِنْدَاب	إِيسَار	إِينَاس	إِقْرَاء
V	تَفَعُّل	تَرَدُّد	تَوَضُّع	تَقَوُّم	تَسَيُّر	تَنَدُّب	تَأَسُّر	تَأَنُّس	تَقَرُّؤ
VI	تَفَاعُل	تَرَادّ	تَوَاضُع	تَقَاوُم	تَسَايُر	تَنَادُب	تَآسُر	تَآنُس	تَقَارُؤ
VII	اِنْفِعَال	اِرْدِدَاد	اِنْوِضَاع	اِنْقِيَام	اِنْسِيَار	اِنْدِدَاب	اِنْئِسَار	اِنْئِنَاس	اِنْقِرَاء
VIII	اِفْتِعَال	اِرْتِدَاد	اِتِّضَاع	اِقْتِيَام	اِسْتِيَار	اِنْتِدَاب	اِتِّسَار	اِتِّنَاس	اِقْتِرَاء
IX	اِفْعِلَال			اِقْوِيَام					
X	اِسْتِفْعَال	اِسْتِرْدَاد	اِسْتِيضَاع	اِسْتِقَامَة	اِسْتِسَارة	اِسْتِنْدَاب	اِسْتِئْسَار	اِسْتِئْنَاس	اِسْتِقْرَاء

ACTIVE PARTICIPLES, ALL FORMS

	1	2	3	4 and 5	6	7, 8, and 9	10	11	12
I	فاعل	رادّ	واعٍ	قائم	سائر	قاضٍ	آسٍ	باسٍ	قاوٍ
II	مُفَعِّل	مُرَدِّد	مُوَعٍّ	مُقَوِّم	مُسَيِّر	مُقَضٍّ	مُؤَسٍّ	مُبَسٍّ	مُقَوٍّ
III	مُفَاعِل	مُرَادّ	مُوَاعٍ	مُقَاوِم	مُسَايِر	مُقَاضٍ	مُؤَاسٍ	مُبَاسٍ	مُقَاوٍ
IV	مُفْعِل	مُرِدّ	مُوعٍ	مُقِيم	مُسِير	مُقْضٍ	مُؤْسٍ	مُبْسٍ	مُقْوٍ
V	مُتَفَعِّل	مُتَرَدِّد	مُتَوَعٍّ	مُتَقَوِّم	مُتَسَيِّر	مُتَقَضٍّ	مُتَأَسٍّ	مُتَبَسٍّ	مُتَقَوٍّ
VI	مُتَفَاعِل	مُتَرَادّ	مُتَوَاعٍ	مُتَقَاوِم	مُتَسَايِر	مُتَقَاضٍ	مُتَآسٍ	مُتَبَاسٍ	مُتَقَاوٍ
VII	مُنْفَعِل	مُنْرَدّ	مُنْوَعٍ	مُنْقَاوِم	مُنْسَار	مُنْقَضٍّ	مُنْقَضٍّ	مُنْبَاسٍ	مُنْقَوٍ
VIII	مُفْتَعِل	مُرْتَدّ	مُتَّعٍ	مُقْتَاوِم	مُسْتَار	مُنْتَدٍ	مُقْتَضٍ	مُبْتَاسٍ	مُقْتَوٍ
IX									
X	مُسْتَفْعِل	مُسْتَرِدّ	مُسْتَوْعٍ	مُسْتَقِيم	مُسْتَسِير	مُسْتَقْضٍ	مُسْتَآسٍ	مُسْتَبْسٍ	مُسْتَقْوٍ

222

	I	2	3	4 and 5	6	7	8 and 9	10	11	12	
I	مَفْعُول	مَرْدُود	مَوْضُوع	مَقُول	مَبِيع	مَلْوِيّ	مَرْمِيّ	مَسُور	مَدْعُوّ	مَقْرُوء	I
II	مُفَعَّل	مُرَدَّد	مُوَضَّح	مُقَوَّم	مُسَيَّر	مُنَدَّى	مُرَبَّى	مُؤَسَّس	مُنَبَّس	مُقَرَّأ	II
III	مُفَاعَل	مُرَادّ	مُوَاضَح	مُقَاوَم	مُسَايَر	مُنَادَى	مُرَاءَى	مُقَاسَر	مُبَاس	مُقَارَأ	III
IV	مُفْعَل	مُرَدّ	مُوَضَح	مُقَام	مُسَار	مُنْدَى	مُرْمَى	مُقَوَّسَر	مُبَاس	مُقَارَأ	IV
V	مُتَفَعَّل	مُتَرَدَّد	مُتَوَضَّح	مُتَقَوَّم	مُتَسَيَّر	مُتَنَدَّى	مُتَرَبَّى	مُتَقَاسَر	مُتَنَبَّس	مُتَقَرَّأ	V
VI	مُتَفَاعَل	مُتَرَادّ	مُتَوَاضَح	مُتَقَاوَم	مُتَسَايَر	مُتَنَادَى	مُتَرَاءَى	مُتَقَاسَر	مُتَبَاس	مُتَقَارَأ	VI
VII	مُنْفَعَل	مُنْرَدّ	مُنْوَضَح	مُنْقَام	مُنْسَار	مُنْدَى	مُنْرَمَى	مُنْقَاس	مُنْبَاس	مُنْقَرَأ	VII
VIII	مُفْتَعَل	مُرْتَدّ	مُتَّضَح	مُتَّقَام	مُتَّسَار	مُتَّدَى	مُرْتَمَى	مُتَّقَاس	مُتَّبَاس	مُتَّقَرَأ	VIII
IX	مُفْعَلّ										IX
X	مُسْتَفْعَل	مُسْتَرَدّ	مُسْتَوْضَح	مُسْتَقَام	مُسْتَسَار	مُسْتَنْدَى	مُسْتَرْمَى	مُسْتَقَاسَر	مُسْتَنْبَس	مُسْتَقْرَأ	X

IMPERATIVE, FORMS I–IV

	1	2	3	4	5	6

Form I

	1	2	3	4	5	6
Sing. M	إِقْعُلْ	أُرْدُدْ	ضَعْ	قُمْ	نَمْ	سِرْ
F	إِقْعُلِي	أُرْدُدِي	ضَعِي	قُومِي	نَامِي	سِيرِي
Dual M–F	إِقْعُلَا	أُرْدُدَا	ضَعَا	قُومَا	نَامَا	سِيرَا
Plural M	إِقْعُلُوا	أُرْدُدُوا	ضَعُوا	قُومُوا	نَامُوا	سِيرُوا
F	إِقْعُلْنَ	أُرْدُدْنَ	ضَعْنَ	قُمْنَ	نَمْنَ	سِرْنَ

Form II

	1	2	3	4	5	6
Sing. M	فَعِّلْ	رَدِّدْ	وَضِّعْ	قَوِّمْ	نَوِّمْ	سَيِّرْ
F	فَعِّلِي	رَدِّدِي	وَضِّعِي	قَوِّمِي	نَوِّمِي	سَيِّرِي
Dual M–F	فَعِّلَا	رَدِّدَا	وَضِّعَا	قَوِّمَا	نَوِّمَا	سَيِّرَا
Plural M	فَعِّلُوا	رَدِّدُوا	وَضِّعُوا	قَوِّمُوا	نَوِّمُوا	سَيِّرُوا
F	فَعِّلْنَ	رَدِّدْنَ	وَضِّعْنَ	قَوِّمْنَ	نَوِّمْنَ	سَيِّرْنَ

Form III

	1	2	3	4	5	6
Sing. M	فَاعِلْ	رَادِدْ	وَاضِعْ	قَاوِمْ	نَاوِمْ	سَايِرْ
F	فَاعِلِي	رَادِدِي	وَاضِعِي	قَاوِمِي	نَاوِمِي	سَايِرِي
Dual M–F	فَاعِلَا	رَادِدَا	وَاضِعَا	قَاوِمَا	نَاوِمَا	سَايِرَا
Plural M	فَاعِلُوا	رَادِدُوا	وَاضِعُوا	قَاوِمُوا	نَاوِمُوا	سَايِرُوا
F	فَاعِلْنَ	رَادِدْنَ	وَاضِعْنَ	قَاوِمْنَ	نَاوِمْنَ	سَايِرْنَ

Form IV

	1	2	3	4	5	6
Sing. M	أَقْعِلْ	أَرْدِدْ	أَوْضِعْ	أَقِمْ	أَنِمْ	أَسِرْ
F	أَقْعِلِي	أَرْدِدِي	أَوْضِعِي	أَقِيمِي	أَنِيمِي	أَسِيرِي
Dual M–F	أَقْعِلَا	أَرْدِدَا	أَوْضِعَا	أَقِيمَا	أَنِيمَا	أَسِيرَا
Plural M	أَقْعِلُوا	أَرْدِدُوا	أَوْضِعُوا	أَقِيمُوا	أَنِيمُوا	أَسِيرُوا
F	أَقْعِلْنَ	أَرْدِدْنَ	أَوْضِعْنَ	أَقِمْنَ	أَنِمْنَ	أَسِرْنَ

7	8	9	10	11	12	
			Form I			
أُنْدُ	إِرْم	إِرْضْ	إِيسِرْ	أُبْؤُسْ	إِقْرَأْ	*Sing.* M
أُنْدِي	إِرْمِي	إِرْضَيْ	إِيسِرِي	أُبْؤُسِي	إِقْرَئِي	F
أُنْدُوَا	إِرْمِيَا	إِرْضَيَا	إِيسِرَا	أُبْؤُسَا	إِقْرَآ	*Dual* M–F
أُنْدُوا	إِرْمُوا	إِرْضَوْا	إِيسِرُوا	أُبْؤُسُوا	إِقْرَؤُوا	*Plural* M
أُنْدُونَ	إِرْمِينَ	إِرْضَيْنَ	إِيسِرْنَ	أُبْؤُسْنَ	إِقْرَأْنَ	F
			Form II			
نَدِّ	رَمِّ	رَضِّ	أَسِّرْ	بَسِّسْ	قَرِّئْ	*Sing.* M
نَدِّي	رَمِّي	رَضِّي	أَسِّرِي	بَسِّسِي	قَرِّئِي	F
نَدِّيَا	رَمِّيَا	رَضِّيَا	أَسِّرَا	بَسِّسَا	قَرِّئَا	*Dual* M–F
نَدُّوا	رَمُّوا	رَضُّوا	أَسِّرُوا	بَسِّسُوا	قَرِّئُوا	*Plural* M
نَدِّينَ	رَمِّينَ	رَضِّينَ	أَسِّرْنَ	بَسِّسْنَ	قَرِّئْنَ	F
			Form III			
نَادِ	رَامِ	رَاضِ	آسِرْ	بَائِسْ	قَارِئْ	*Sing.* M
نَادِي	رَامِي	رَاضِي	آسِرِي	بَائِسِى	قَارِئِي	F
نَادِيَا	رَامِيَا	رَاضِيَا	آسِرَا	بَائِسَا	قَارِئَا	*Dual* M–F
نَادُوا	رَامُوا	رَاضُوا	آسِرُوا	بَائِسُوا	قَارِئُوا	*Plural* M
نَادِينَ	رَامِينَ	رَاضِينَ	آسِرْنَ	بَائِسْنَ	قَارِئْنَ	F
			Form IV			
أَنْدِ	أَرْمِ	أَرْضِ	آسِرْ	أَبْئِسْ	أَقْرِئْ	*Sing.* M
أَنْدِي	أَرْمِي	أَرْضِي	آسِرِي	أَبْئِسِي	أَقْرِئِي	F
أَنْدِيَا	أَرْمِيَا	أَرْضِيَا	آسِرَا	أَبْئِسَا	أَقْرِئَا	*Dual* M–F
أَنْدُوا	أَرْمُوا	أَرْضُوا	آسِرُوا	أَبْئِسُوا	أَقْرِئُوا	*Plural* M
أَنْدِينَ	أَرْمِينَ	أَرْضِينَ	آسِرْنَ	أَبْئِسْنَ	أَقْرِئْنَ	F

IMPERATIVE, FORMS V–VIII

	1	2	3	4	5	6

Form V

	1	2	3	4	5	6
Sing. M	تَفَعَّلْ	تَرَدَّدْ	تَوَضَّعْ	تَقَوَّمْ	تَنَوَّمْ	تَسَيَّرْ
F	تَفَعَّلِي	تَرَدَّدِي	تَوَضَّعِي	تَقَوَّمِي	تَنَوَّمِي	تَسَيَّرِي
Dual M–F	تَفَعَّلَا	تَرَدَّدَا	تَوَضَّعَا	تَقَوَّمَا	تَنَوَّمَا	تَسَيَّرَا
Plural M	تَفَعَّلُوا	تَرَدَّدُوا	تَوَضَّعُوا	تَقَوَّمُوا	تَنَوَّمُوا	تَسَيَّرُوا
F	تَفَعَّلْنَ	تَرَدَّدْنَ	تَوَضَّعْنَ	تَقَوَّمْنَ	تَنَوَّمْنَ	تَسَيَّرْنَ

Form VI

	1	2	3	4	5	6
Sing. M	تَفَاعَلْ	تَرَادَدْ	تَوَاضَعْ	تَقَاوَمْ	تَنَاوَمْ	تَسَايَرْ
F	تَفَاعَلِي	تَرَادِّي	تَوَاضَعِي	تَقَاوَمِي	تَنَاوَمِي	تَسَايَرِي
Dual M–F	تَفَاعَلَا	تَرَادَّا	تَوَاضَعَا	تَقَاوَمَا	تَنَاوَمَا	تَسَايَرَا
Plural M	تَفَاعَلُوا	تَرَادُّوا	تَوَاضَعُوا	تَقَاوَمُوا	تَنَاوَمُوا	تَسَايَرُوا
F	تَفَاعَلْنَ	تَرَادَدْنَ	تَوَاضَعْنَ	تَقَاوَمْنَ	تَنَاوَمْنَ	تَسَايَرْنَ

Form VII

	1	2	3	4	5	6
Sing. M	إِنْفَعِلْ	إِنْرَدِدْ	إِنْوَضِعْ	إِنْقَمْ	إِنَّمْ	إِنْسَرْ
F	إِنْفَعِلِي	إِنْرَدِّي	إِنْوَضِعِي	إِنْقَامِي	إِنَّامِي	إِنْسَارِي
Dual M–F	إِنْفَعِلَا	إِنْرَدَّا	إِنْوَضِعَا	إِنْقَامَا	إِنَّامَا	إِنْسَارَا
Plural M	إِنْفَعِلُوا	إِنْرَدُّوا	إِنْوَضِعُوا	إِنْقَامُوا	إِنَّامُوا	إِنْسَارُوا
F	إِنْفَعِلْنَ	إِنْرَدِدْنَ	إِنْوَضِعْنَ	إِنْقَمْنَ	إِنَّمْنَ	إِنْسَرْنَ

Form VIII

	1	2	3	4	5	6
Sing. M	إِقْتَعِلْ	إِرْتَدِدْ	إِتَّضِعْ	إِقْتَمْ	إِنْتَمْ	إِسْتَرْ
F	إِقْتَعِلِي	إِرْتَدِّي	إِتَّضِعِي	إِقْتَامِي	إِنْتَامِي	إِسْتَارِي
Dual M–F	إِقْتَعِلَا	إِرْتَدَّا	إِتَّضِعَا	إِقْتَامَا	إِنْتَامَا	إِسْتَارَا
Plural M	إِقْتَعِلُوا	إِرْتَدُّوا	إِتَّضِعُوا	إِقْتَامُوا	إِنْتَامُوا	إِسْتَارُوا
F	إِقْتَعِلْنَ	إِرْتَدِدْنَ	إِتَّضِعْنَ	إِقْتَمْنَ	إِنْتَمْنَ	إِسْتَرْنَ

IMPERATIVE, FORMS V–VIII

Form V

7	8	9	10	11	12	
تَنَدَّ	تَرَمَّ	تَرَضَّ	تَأَسَّرْ	تَبَأَّسْ	تَقَرَّأُ	Sing. M
تَنَدِّي	تَرَمِّي	تَرَضِّي	تَأَسَّرِي	تَبَأَّسِي	تَقَرَّئِي	F
تَنَدَّيَا	تَرَمَّيَا	تَرَضَّيَا	تَأَسَّرَا	تَبَأَّسَا	تَقَرَّآ	Dual M–F
تَنَدَّوْا	تَرَمَّوْا	تَرَضَّوْا	تَأَسَّرُوا	تَبَأَّسُوا	تَقَرَّؤُوا	Plural M
تَنَدَّيْنَ	تَرَمَّيْنَ	تَرَضَّيْنَ	تَأَسَّرْنَ	تَبَأَّسْنَ	تَقَرَّأْنَ	F

Form VI

7	8	9	10	11	12	
تَنَادَ	تَرَامَ	تَرَاضَ	تَأَسَرْ	تَبَاءَسْ	تَقَارَأُ	Sing. M
تَنَادَيْ	تَرَامَيْ	تَرَاضِي	تَأَسَرِي	تَبَاءَسِي	تَقَارَئِي	F
تَنَادَيَا	تَرَامَيَا	تَرَاضَيَا	تَأَسَرَا	تَبَاءَسَا	تَقَارَآ	Dual M–F
تَنَادَوْا	تَرَامَوْا	تَرَاضَوْا	تَأَسَرُوا	تَبَاءَسُوا	تَقَارَؤُوا	Plural M
تَنَادَيْنَ	تَرَامَيْنَ	تَرَاضَيْنَ	تَأَسَرْنَ	تَبَاءَسْنَ	تَقَارَأْنَ	F

Form VII

7	8	9	10	11	12	
إِنَّدَّ	إِنْرَمَّ	إِنْرَضَّ	إِنْأَسَرْ	إِنْبَئِسْ	إِنْقَرِئُ	Sing. M
إِنَّدِّي	إِنْرَمِّي	إِنْرَضِّي	إِنْأَسَرِي	إِنْبَئِسِي	إِنْقَرِئِي	F
إِنَّدِّيَا	إِنْرَمِّيَا	إِنْرَضِّيَا	إِنْأَسَرَا	إِنْبَئِسَا	إِنْقَرِئَا	Dual M–F
إِنَّدُّوا	إِنْرَمُّوا	إِنْرَضُّوا	إِنْأَسَرُوا	إِنْبَئِسُوا	إِنْقَرِئُوا	Plural M
إِنَّدِّينَ	إِنْرَمِّينَ	إِنْرَضِّينَ	إِنْأَسَرْنَ	إِنْبَئِسْنَ	إِنْقَرِئْنَ	F

Form VIII

7	8	9	10	11	12	
إِرْتَدَّ	إِرْتَمَّ	إِرْتَضَّ	إِيتَسَرْ	إِبْتَئِسْ	إِقْتَرِئُ	Sing. M
إِرْتَدِّي	إِرْتَمِّي	إِرْتَضِّي	إِيتَسَرِي	إِبْتَئِسِي	إِقْتَرِئِي	F
إِرْتَدِّيَا	إِرْتَمِّيَا	إِرْتَضِّيَا	إِيتَسَرَا	إِبْتَئِسَا	إِقْتَرِئَا	Dual M–F
إِرْتَدُّوا	إِرْتَمُّوا	إِرْتَضُّوا	إِيتَسَرُوا	إِبْتَئِسُوا	إِقْتَرِئُوا	Plural M
إِرْتَدِّينَ	إِرْتَمِّينَ	إِرْتَضِّينَ	إِيتَسَرْنَ	إِبْتَئِسْنَ	إِقْتَرِئْنَ	F

	1	2	3	4	5	6

Form IX

	1	2	3	4	5	6
Sing. M	إِفْعَلِلْ					
F	إِفْعَلِّي					
Dual M–F	إِفْعَلَّا					
Plural M	إِفْعَلُّوا					
F	إِفْعَلِلْنَ					

Form X

	1	2	3	4	5	6
Sing. M	إِسْتَفْعِلْ	إِسْتَرْدِدْ	إِسْتَوْضِعْ	إِسْتَقِمْ	إِسْتَنِمْ	إِسْتَسِرْ
F	إِسْتَفْعِلِي	إِسْتَرِدِّي	إِسْتَوْضِعِي	إِسْتَقِيمِي	إِسْتَنِيمِي	إِسْتَسِيرِي
Dual M–F	إِسْتَفْعِلَا	إِسْتَرِدَّا	إِسْتَوْضِعَا	إِسْتَقِيمَا	إِسْتَنِيمَا	إِسْتَسِيرَا
Plural M	إِسْتَفْعِلُوا	إِسْتَرِدُّوا	إِسْتَوْضِعُوا	إِسْتَقِيمُوا	إِسْتَنِيمُوا	إِسْتَسِيرُوا
F	إِسْتَفْعِلْنَ	إِسْتَرْدِدْنَ	إِسْتَوْضِعْنَ	إِسْتَقِمْنَ	إِسْتَنِمْنَ	إِسْتَسِرْنَ

7	8	9	10	11	12	

Form IX

						Sing. M
						F
						Dual M–F
						Plural M
						F

Form X

7	8	9	10	11	12	
إِسْتَنِدْ	إِسْتَرِمْ	إِسْتَرْضِ	إِسْتَأْسِرْ	إِسْتَبْئِسْ	إِسْتَقْرِئُ	Sing. M
إِسْتَنِدِي	إِسْتَرِمِي	إِسْتَرْضِي	إِسْتَأْسِرِي	إِسْتَبْئِسِي	إِسْتَقْرِئِي	F
إِسْتَنِدِيَا	إِسْتَرِمِيَا	إِسْتَرْضِيَا	إِسْتَأْسِرَا	إِسْتَبْئِسَا	إِسْتَقْرِئَا	Dual M–F
إِسْتَنِدُوا	إِسْتَرِمُوا	إِسْتَرْضُوا	إِسْتَأْسِرُوا	إِسْتَبْئِسُوا	إِسْتَقْرِئُوا	Plural M
إِسْتَنِدِينَ	إِسْتَرِمِينَ	إِسْتَرْضِينَ	إِسْتَأْسِرْنَ	إِسْتَبْئِسْنَ	إِسْتَقْرِئْنَ	F

QUADRILITERAL, FORM I (تَرْجَمَ)

	PERFECT	IMPERFECT INDICATIVE	SUBJUNCTIVE	JUSSIVE	PERFECT PASSIVE	IMPERFECT PASSIVE	IMPERATIVE		DERIVED NOUNS
				Singular					*Active Participle*
3 M	تَرْجَمَ	يُتَرْجِمُ	يُتَرْجِمَ	يُتَرْجِمْ	تُرْجِمَ	يُتَرْجَمُ		3 M	مُتَرْجِم
3 F	تَرْجَمَتْ	تُتَرْجِمُ	تُتَرْجِمَ	تُتَرْجِمْ	تُرْجِمَتْ	تُتَرْجَمُ		3 F	*Passive Participle*
2 M	تَرْجَمْتَ	تُتَرْجِمُ	تُتَرْجِمَ	تُتَرْجِمْ	تُرْجِمْتَ	تُتَرْجَمُ	تَرْجِمْ	2 M	مُتَرْجَم
2 F	تَرْجَمْتِ	تُتَرْجِمِينَ	تُتَرْجِمِي	تُتَرْجِمِي	تُرْجِمْتِ	تُتَرْجَمِينَ	تَرْجِمِي	2 F	*Maṣdar*
1	تَرْجَمْتُ	أُتَرْجِمُ	أُتَرْجِمَ	أُتَرْجِمْ	تُرْجِمْتُ	أُتَرْجَمُ		1	تَرْجَمَة
				Dual					
3 M	تَرْجَمَا	يُتَرْجِمَانِ	يُتَرْجِمَا	يُتَرْجِمَا	تُرْجِمَا	يُتَرْجَمَانِ		3 M	
3 F	تَرْجَمَتَا	تُتَرْجِمَانِ	تُتَرْجِمَا	تُتَرْجِمَا	تُرْجِمَتَا	تُتَرْجَمَانِ		3 F	
2	تَرْجَمْتُمَا	تُتَرْجِمَانِ	تُتَرْجِمَا	تُتَرْجِمَا	تُرْجِمْتُمَا	تُتَرْجَمَانِ	تَرْجِمَا	2	
				Plural					
3 M	تَرْجَمُوا	يُتَرْجِمُونَ	يُتَرْجِمُوا	يُتَرْجِمُوا	تُرْجِمُوا	يُتَرْجَمُونَ		3 M	
3 F	تَرْجَمْنَ	يُتَرْجِمْنَ	يُتَرْجِمْنَ	يُتَرْجِمْنَ	تُرْجِمْنَ	يُتَرْجَمْنَ		3 F	
2 M	تَرْجَمْتُمْ	تُتَرْجِمُونَ	تُتَرْجِمُوا	تُتَرْجِمُوا	تُرْجِمْتُمْ	تُتَرْجَمُونَ	تَرْجِمُوا	2 M	
2 F	تَرْجَمْتُنَّ	تُتَرْجِمْنَ	تُتَرْجِمْنَ	تُتَرْجِمْنَ	تُرْجِمْتُنَّ	تُتَرْجَمْنَ	تَرْجِمْنَ	2 F	
1	تَرْجَمْنَا	نُتَرْجِمُ	نُتَرْجِمَ	نُتَرْجِمْ	تُرْجِمْنَا	نُتَرْجَمُ		1	

230

QUADRILITERAL, FORM II (تَتَلْتَلَ)

	PERFECT	IMPERFECT INDICATIVE	SUB-JUNCTIVE	JUSSIVE	PERFECT PASSIVE	IMPERFECT PASSIVE	IMPERA-TIVE		DERIVED NOUNS
				Singular					*Active Participle*
3 M	تَتَلْتَلَ	يَتَتَلْتَلُ	يَتَتَلْتَلَ	يَتَتَلْتَلْ	تُتُلْتِلَ	يُتَتَلْتَلُ		3 M	مُتَتَلْتِل
3 F	تَتَلْتَلَتْ	تَتَتَلْتَلُ	تَتَتَلْتَلَ	تَتَتَلْتَلْ	تُتُلْتِلَتْ	تُتَتَلْتَلُ		3 F	*Passive Participle* مُتَتَلْتَل
2 M	تَتَلْتَلْتَ	تَتَتَلْتَلُ	تَتَتَلْتَلَ	تَتَتَلْتَلْ	تُتُلْتِلْتَ	تُتَتَلْتَلُ	تَتَلْتَلْ	2 M	مُتَتَلْتَل
2 F	تَتَلْتَلْتِ	تَتَتَلْتَلِينَ	تَتَتَلْتَلِي	تَتَتَلْتَلِي	تُتُلْتِلْتِ	تُتَتَلْتَلِينَ	تَتَلْتَلِي	2 F	*Maṣdar*
1	تَتَلْتَلْتُ	أَتَتَلْتَلُ	أَتَتَلْتَلَ	أَتَتَلْتَلْ	تُتُلْتِلْتُ	أُتَتَلْتَلُ		1	تَتَلْتُل
				Dual					
3 M	تَتَلْتَلَا	يَتَتَلْتَلَانِ	يَتَتَلْتَلَا	يَتَتَلْتَلَا	تُتُلْتِلَا	يُتَتَلْتَلَانِ		3 M	
3 F	تَتَلْتَلَتَا	تَتَتَلْتَلَانِ	تَتَتَلْتَلَا	تَتَتَلْتَلَا	تُتُلْتِلَتَا	تُتَتَلْتَلَانِ		3 F	
2	تَتَلْتَلْتُمَا	تَتَتَلْتَلَانِ	تَتَتَلْتَلَا	تَتَتَلْتَلَا	تُتُلْتِلْتُمَا	تُتَتَلْتَلَانِ	تَتَلْتَلَا	2	
				Plural					
3 M	تَتَلْتَلُوا	يَتَتَلْتَلُونَ	يَتَتَلْتَلُوا	يَتَتَلْتَلُوا	تُتُلْتِلُوا	يُتَتَلْتَلُونَ		3 M	
3 F	تَتَلْتَلْنَ	يَتَتَلْتَلْنَ	يَتَتَلْتَلْنَ	يَتَتَلْتَلْنَ	تُتُلْتِلْنَ	يُتَتَلْتَلْنَ		3 F	
2 M	تَتَلْتَلْتُمْ	تَتَتَلْتَلُونَ	تَتَتَلْتَلُوا	تَتَتَلْتَلُوا	تُتُلْتِلْتُمْ	تُتَتَلْتَلُونَ	تَتَلْتَلُوا	2 M	
2 F	تَتَلْتَلْتُنَّ	تَتَتَلْتَلْنَ	تَتَتَلْتَلْنَ	تَتَتَلْتَلْنَ	تُتُلْتِلْتُنَّ	تُتَتَلْتَلْنَ	تَتَلْتَلْنَ	2 F	
1	تَتَلْتَلْنَا	نَتَتَلْتَلُ	نَتَتَلْتَلَ	نَتَتَلْتَلْ	تُتُلْتِلْنَا	نُتَتَلْتَلُ		1	

231

QUADRILITERAL, FORM IV (اطْمَأَنَّ)

	PERFECT	IMPERFECT INDICATIVE	SUBJUNCTIVE	JUSSIVE	IMPERATIVE		DERIVED NOUNS
			Singular				*Active Participle* مُطْمَئِنٌّ
3 M	اطْمَأَنَّ	يَطْمَئِنُّ	يَطْمَئِنَّ	يَطْمَئِنَّ (يَطْمَأْنِنْ)		3 M	
3 F	اطْمَأَنَّتْ	تَطْمَئِنُّ	تَطْمَئِنَّ	تَطْمَئِنَّ (تَطْمَأْنِنْ)		3 F	*Maṣdar*
2 M	اطْمَأْنَنْتَ	تَطْمَئِنُّ	تَطْمَئِنَّ	تَطْمَئِنَّ (تَطْمَأْنِنْ)	اطْمَئِنَّ	2 M	اطْمِئْنانٌ
2 F	اطْمَأْنَنْتِ	تَطْمَئِنِّينَ	تَطْمَئِنِّي	تَطْمَئِنِّي	اطْمَئِنِّي	2 F	
1	اطْمَأْنَنْتُ	أَطْمَئِنُّ	أَطْمَئِنَّ	أَطْمَئِنَّ (اطْمَأْنِنْ)		1	
			Dual				
3 M	اطْمَأَنّا	يَطْمَئِنّانِ	يَطْمَئِنّا	يَطْمَئِنّا		3 M	
3 F	اطْمَأَنَّتا	تَطْمَئِنّانِ	تَطْمَئِنّا	تَطْمَئِنّا		3 F	
2	اطْمَأْنَنْتُما	تَطْمَئِنّانِ	تَطْمَئِنّا	تَطْمَئِنّا	اطْمَئِنّا	2	
			Plural				
3 M	اطْمَأَنّوا	يَطْمَئِنّونَ	يَطْمَئِنّوا	يَطْمَئِنّوا		3 M	
3 F	اطْمَأْنَنَّ	يَطْمَأْنِنَّ	يَطْمَأْنِنَّ	يَطْمَأْنِنَّ		3 F	
2 M	اطْمَأْنَنْتُمْ	تَطْمَئِنّونَ	تَطْمَئِنّوا	تَطْمَئِنّوا	اطْمَئِنّوا	2 M	
2 F	اطْمَأْنَنْتُنَّ	تَطْمَأْنِنَّ	تَطْمَأْنِنَّ	تَطْمَأْنِنَّ	اطْمَأْنِنَّ	2 F	
1	اطْمَأْنَنّا	نَطْمَئِنُّ	نَطْمَئِنَّ	نَطْمَئِنَّ (نَطْمَأْنِنْ)		1	

232

APPENDIX II

VERBS AND THEIR PREPOSITIONS

This appendix is intended to present, in simple form, verbs which take one or more prepositions. These include all such verbs used in this book and, in addition, all other such verbs occurring in the first 2,000 words of M. Brill's *The Basic Word List of the Arabic Daily Newspaper* (Jerusalem: The Hebrew University Press Association, 1940). A few common verbal idioms are also included.

The verbs are listed alphabetically in Arabic, *not* by roots, but as they are spelled. In alphabetizing, hamzah precedes alif, maddah is treated as hamzah-alif, and shaddah is disregarded.

The following abbreviations and specialized usages have been employed (except when obvious): s. = some, o. = one, th. = thing, فلان = any one, الشيء = a concrete thing, الامر = an action (= a maṣdar), كذا = a person or a thing, الخ = etc. In some cases where specific nouns or concepts are almost always used with a verb or idiom, that noun or a sample of the concept is given between parentheses. In other cases, words in English in parentheses specify the subject of the verb.

Closely related English meanings are separated by commas, and the *to* of the infinitive is not repeated. Where meanings are more divergent, they are separated by semicolons and *to* is repeated.

to punish s.o. for; to blame s.o. for	آخَذَ فلانا ب او على	to agree	إتَّفَقَ
to protect s.o.	آمَنَ فلانا	to agree with s.o. on s.th.	—— مع فلان على الشيء
to believe in, have faith in	—— ب	to influence	أَثَّرَ في
to come	أَتَى	to answer	أَجَابَ
to finish, complete s.th.	—— على الشيء	to answer s.o. about a question	—— فلانا عن السؤال او اليه
to bring s.o. *or* s.th.	—— بكذا	to meet, assemble	إجْتَمَعَ
to present, offer s.th. to s.o.	—— فلانا بالشيء	to unite against	—— على
		to meet s.o.	—— بفلان
to contact; to be connected with	إتَّصَلَ ب	to agree on; to resolve upon	أَجْمَعَ على

to surround	أَحَاطَ ب
to be in need of	إِحْتَاجَ الى
to protest to s.o. about s.th.	إِحْتَجَّ الى فلان على الامر
to keep, preserve s.th.	إِحْتَفَظَ الشيء او به
to flock in, congregate, assemble	إِحْتَفَلَ
to celebrate	ب ——
to take care of; to welcome	—— ب او في
to comprise, include s.th.	إِحْتَوَى الشيء او عليه
to inform s.o. of s.th.	أَخْبَرَ فلانا الشيء او به
to take	أَخَذَ
to begin, start s.th.	—— في الامر
to study (a science) under s.o.	—— (العلمَ) عن فلان
to pay, discharge, settle	أَدَّى
to lend to; to result in	—— الى
to turn, cause to revolve; to manage, govern	أَدَارَ
to divert s.o. from	—— فلانا عن
to induce s.o. toward	—— فلانا على
to claim as a right; to pretend	إِدَّعَى الشيء او به
to enter an action against, sue	—— على
to give an ear or listen to	أَذِنَ الى
to allow, permit s.o. to	—— لفلان ب

to get ready for, prepare for	إِسْتَعَدَّ ل
to find s.th. little; to be independent	إِسْتَقَلَّ
to be independent of	—— عن
to be alone in	—— ب
to seize, occupy (country)	إِسْتَوْلَى على (البلاد)
to unveil	أَسْفَرَ
to result in	—— عن
to praise	أَشَادَ ب
to contain, include, comprise; to consist of	إِشْتَمَلَ على
to supervise (a work)	أَشْرَفَ على (العمل)
to overlook (a place)	—— على (المكان)
to be on the point of (death)	—— على (الموت)
to strike a mark, hit; to be right, correct; to obtain, attain, get	أَصَابَ
to strike s.o. with the evil eye	—— فلانا بالعين
to pay attention to; to give ear to	أَصْغَى الى
to entertain (a guest); to add, join, annex	أَضَافَ
to add to	—— الى
to cease doing; to go on strike by refusing to do s.th.	أَضْرَبَ عن الامر
to force s.o. to do s.th.	إِضْطَرَّ فلانا الى الشيء

to be forced to	أُضْطُرَّ الى	to remain in (a place)	أَقَامَ ب (مكان)
to see; to know	إطَّلَعَ على	to approach, draw near	أَقْبَلَ
to feel assured, confident	إطْمَأَنَّ	to come on *or* to	―― الى او على
to have confidence in	―― الى	to begin to do s.th.; to welcome	―― على
to consider, esteem	إعْتَبَرَ	to prosper	أَقْبَلَتْ عليه الدنيا
to learn a lesson from	―― ب	to approach, come near to	إقْتَرَبَ من
to trespass on; to assault, commit aggression against	إعْتَدَى على	to suggest	إقْتَرَحَ
to be in the way of	إعْتَرَضَ	to suggest to	―― على
to prevent, preclude, debar	―― ل	to be limited to	إقْتَصَرَ على
to object to, remonstrate with, protest against	―― على	to meet together	إلْتَقَى
		to meet s.o.	―― بفلان
to acknowledge	إعْتَرَفَ ب	to tame, domesticate; to write; to compose, form	أَلَّفَ
to confess to (priest)	―― الى (الكاهن)		
to arabicize	أعْرَبَ	to harmonize, join, bring together	―― بين كذا وكذا
to explain	―― عن	to deliver (a speech) to (people)	أَلْقَى (خطابا) في (الناس)
to parse (a sentence)	―― (الجملة)		
to inform s.o. about s.th.	أعْلَمَ فلانا الشيءَ او بالشيء	to order s.o. to do s.th.	أَمَرَ فلانا بالامر
to lead s.o. to	أفْضَى بفلان الى	to clear up, become plain	إنْجَلَى
to reveal s.th. to s.o.	―― الى فلان بالشيء	to end in, result in s.th.	―― عن الشيء
to set up, raise; to establish	أَقَامَ	to leave, depart	إنْصَرَفَ
to perform prayer	―― الصلاة	to abandon, give up	―― عن
to continue; to stick to (opinion)	―― على	to join s.o. *or* s.th., be connected with	إنْضَمَّ الى كذا
to set s.o. over, appoint s.o. over	―― فلانا على	to include, comprise	―― على
		to be cut, broken	انْقَطَعَ

235

to cease, desist from s.th.	إِنْقَطَعَ عن الامر
to concentrate on, be devoted to s.th.	—— الى الامر
to interest oneself in, concern oneself with s.th.	إِهْتَمَّ بالشيء
to bequeath s.th. to s.o.	أَوْصَى لفلان بالشيء
to charge s.o. with s.th.	—— فلانا بالشيء
to order s.o. to do s.th.	—— فلانا بِعَمَلِ شيءٍ
to recommend s.o.; to praise s.o.	—— بفلان
to study, investigate, discuss s.th.	بَحَثَ في
to look or search for	—— عن
to send, dispatch s.o. or s.th.; to delegate	بَعَثَ كذا او بكذا
to awaken, stir up	بَعَثَ
to raise from the dead, resurrect	—— من الموت
to incite s.o. to	بَعَثَ فلانا على
to be moved, influenced by	تَأَثَّرَ ب
to be affected by; to be hurt by (feelings)	—— من
to become certain	تَأَكَّدَ
to ascertain, be certain of	—— من
to be composed	تَأَلَّفَ
to be composed of	—— من
to become the student of, study under s.o.	تَتَلْمَذَ على فلان او له

to go beyond, exceed; to trespass on	تَجَاوَزَ
to overlook; to forgo, relinquish	—— عن
to talk about s.th.	تَحَدَّثَ بالشيء او عنه
to be saved from; to get rid of	تَخَلَّصَ من
to be arranged, set in order	تَرَتَّبَ
to be a consequence of	—— على
to participate in a demonstration	تَظَاهَرَ
to feign s.th.	—— بالشيء
to hang down, dangle	تَعَلَّقَ
to cling to; to belong or pertain to	ب
to precede; to advance, proceed, come forward	تَقَدَّمَ
to surpass	—— على
to be firmly fixed	تَمَكَّنَ
to master s.th.; to be able to do s.th.	—— من الامر
to stop, halt, pause	تَوَقَّفَ
to abstain from	—— عن
to be decided on the basis of, depend on	—— على
to come	جَاءَ
to bring	—— ب
to strip s.o. of s.th.; to take s.th. from s.o.	جَرَّدَ فلانا من الشيء
to collect, gather	جَمَعَ
to bring together	—— بين

to preserve, defend; to observe (a custom)	حَافَظَ على
to come between	حَالَ (يَحُولُ) بين
to prevent, stand in the way of	—— دون
to interest s.o. in s.th.; to render s.th. lovable to s.o.	حَبَّبَ الشيء الى فلان
to happen, take place, occur	حَصَلَ
to obtain, acquire, get	—— على
to happen to, befall	—— لكذا
to rule, govern; to judge, decide	حَكَمَ
to pass a judgment against, sentence	—— على فلان
to give judgment in favor of	—— لفلان
to judge against or for s.o. concerning s.th.	حَكَمَ على او لفلان بالشيء
to sentence s.o. to death	—— على فلان بالإعْدَام
to untie, solve; to alight at, to be lawful	حَلَّ
to settle in (a place)	—— ب (مكان)
for s.th. to befall or happen to s.o.	—— بفلان الامرُ
to protect, defend	حَمَى
to protect s.o. or s.th. against or from	—— كذا من
to carry, bear	حَمَلَ
to induce s.o. to do s.th.	—— فلانا على الامر
to raid, charge s.o. or s.th.	حَمَلَ على كذا
to take s.th. upon one's self	—— الشيء على عاتقه
to displace; to turn; to change	حَوَّلَ
to divert, turn aside from	—— عن
to go out	خَرَجَ
to go out from	—— من
to go for, attack	—— على فلان
to rebel against (a governor)	—— على (الحاكم)
to secede from	—— عن
to fear, dread	خَشِيَ
to fear for s.o.	—— على فلان
to make s.th. available only to s.o.	خَصَّ فلانا بالشيء
to speak or orate to (a group)	خَطَبَ في (القوم)
to defend s.o. or s.th.	دَافَعَ عن كذا
to call	دَعَا
to urge s.o. to do s.th.; to appeal to s.o. for s.th.; to invite s.o. to (a party)	—— فلانا الى الامر
to curse, wish evil to s.o. or s.th.	—— على كذا
to bless, wish good to s.o. or s.th.	—— لكذا
to push, drive back, repel; to refute; to pay	دَفَعَ
to drive, urge, compel, induce s.o. to do s.th.	—— فلانا الى الامر

237

to ward off دَفَعَ عن فلان الشيء s.th. from s.o., defend s.o. from s.th.	to shun, avoid رَغِبَ عن
	to implore s.o. الى فلان ----
to direct دَلَّ فلانا على الامر او اليه or guide s.o. to s.th., indicate s.th. to s.o.	to raise, lift; to erect رَفَعَ
	to submit الشيء الى فلان ---- s.th. to s.o.
to go away, depart ذَهَبَ	to remove الشيء عن كذا ---- s.th. from s.o. or s.th.
to take s.o. or s.th. بكذا ---- away	to throw رَمَى
to go to a place الى ----	to aim at الى ----
to hold الى الامر او الى أنَّ ---- the opinion that, think that	to shake off عن ----
to return رَجَعَ	to accuse s.o. فلانا بالامر ---- of s.th.
to return to الى ----	to increase زَادَ
to return from من ----	to exceed عن كذا بالشيء ---- s.o. or s.th. in s.th.
to have الى كذا في الامر ---- recourse to s.o. or s.th. in deciding s.th.	to add to s.th. على الشيء ----
to retreat from; to desist عن ----	to creep forward; to زَحَفَ الى advance on (army)
to welcome s.o. رَحَّبَ بكذا or s.th.	to go, be in motion سَارَ (يَسِيرُ)
to return, send or give رَدَّ back; to repel	to conduct, lead, go بفلان ---- with s.o.
to answer s.o. or على كذا ---- s.th., refute	to march on على ----
to dissuade فلانا عن الامر ---- s.o. from s.th.	to help, aid, assist سَاعَدَ
to avert s.th. الامرَ عن فلان ---- from s.o.	to conduce to, على ---- promote
to accept, رَضِيَ الشيء او به او فيه agree to; to be satisfied with	to leave behind, outstrip سَبَقَ
to be pleased عن فلان او عليه ---- with, approve of	to precede, go before سَبَقَ الى
to wish for, desire رَغِبَ في	to go about, walk, سَعَى move; to act
	to proceed or go الى ---- toward
	to endeavour to do للامر ----

to exert one's self in s.th.	سَعَى في الامر	to turn the back upon	صَدَّ عن كذا
to break off speech, be silent	سَكَتَ	to avert s.o. or s.th. from s.o. or s.th.	—— كذا عن كذا
his anger subsided	—— عنه الغَضَبُ	to happen, occur	صَدَرَ
to name	سَمَّى	to proceed or emanate from; to result from	—— عن او من
to name s.o. s.th.; call s.o. by such-and-such a name	—— فلانا الشيء او بالشيء	to declare, avow; to clarify	صَرَّح الامرَ او بالامر
to permit s.o. to do s.th.	سَمَح له بالامر	to dismiss	صَرَف
to hear	سَمِع	to deter s.o. from; to dissuade	—— فلانا عن
to hear of s.o. or s.th.	—— بكذا	to disregard	—— النظرَ عن
to hear, listen to; to obey	—— من فلان او له	to be good	صَلُح
to dominate, rule over	سَيْطَرَ على	to suit or fit s.o. or s.th.	—— لكذا
to perceive s.th.	شَعَرَ بالشيء	to sacrifice s.th.	ضَحَّى بالشيء
to witness, be present; to testify, bear witness	شَهِدَ	to strike, hit	ضَرَبَ
to testify concerning, certify	—— بالامر	to strike s.o. with, shoot at with (weapon)	—— فلانا ب
to testify in favor of s.o.	—— لفلان	to multiply a number by another	—— عددا في آخر
to testify against s.o.	—— على فلان	to avoid, disregard s.o.	—— عن فلان
to happen; to become	صَارَ (يَصِيرُ)	to incline toward s.o.	—— الى فلان
for something to happen to s.o.	—— لفلان كذا	to prevent; to interdict (legal)	ضَرَبَ على يَدِ فلان
to end in s.th.	—— الى الامر	to gather, collect; to amalgamate	ضَمَّ
to begin to do	—— يَفْعَل	to add to; to annex	—— الى
to check, restrain, stop, oppose	صَدَّ	to embrace, hug (his son)	—— اليه او الى صدره (ابنَهُ)

to walk around s.th.	طَافَ (يَطُوفُ) حول الشيء او به
to ramble around in (a country)	—— في (البلاد)
to demand s.th. from s.o.	طَالَب فلانا بالشيء
to seek, look or search for; to summon	طَلَبَ كذا
to beg, entreat s.o.	—— الى فلان
to appeal to s.o. for, request s.o. to	—— من فلان الامرَ
to covet s.th. eagerly	طَمِع في الشيء او به
to think, suppose	ظَنَّ
to suspect s.o.	—— بفلان
to appear; to become known	ظَهَرَ
to overcome, conquer, surmount	—— على
to return, come back	عَادَ
to resume s.th.	—— الى الامر
to benefit s.o.	—— على فلان بالشيء
to express s.th.	عَبَّر عن الامر
to trip, stumble	عَثَرَ
to stumble upon, discover	—— على
the times are against s.o.	—— بفلان الزمانُ
to be unable to do s.th.	عَجَز عن الامر
to straighten; to act justly	عَدَلَ
to deviate from, give up s.th.	—— عن الامر

to be known as	عُرِفَ ب
to resolve on s.th. or on doing s.th.	عَزَم الامرَ او عليه
to suspend, hang; to keep in abeyance	عَلَّق
to hang s.th. on s.th.	—— الشيء بالشيء
to attach importance to	—— أهميةٌ على
to comment on s.th.	—— على الامر
to make; to do; to work; to act	عَمِلَ
to act upon, affect s.o. or s.th.	—— في كذا
to work toward; to be efficacious in	—— على
to act according to s.th.	—— بالامر
to mean, signify	عَنَى
to be concerned with or about s.th.	عُنِيَ بالامر
to look after, see to, attend to; to know; to fulfil (a promise)	عَهَدَ
to entrust s.o. with s.th., commit s.th. to s.o.	—— الى فلان بالامر
to win s.th.; to obtain s.th.	قَازَ بالشيء
to escape from	—— من
to open; to disclose; to conquer; to begin	فَتَحَ
for God to grant success or victory to s.o.	—— اللهُ على فلان

to inspect, investigate	فَتَّشَ	to rise *or* revolt against s.o.	قَامَ على فلان
to seek, look for	ـــــ عن	to superintend s.th.	ـــــ على الشيء
to be empty	فَرِغَ	to grasp, hold s.th.	قَبَضَ الشيء او عليه او به
to finish, complete	ـــــ من		
to devote one's self entirely to s.th.	ـــــ للامر او اليه	to arrest, seize s.o.	ـــــ على فلان
for patience to run out, lose patience	ـــــ الصبرُ	to be able	قَدِرَ
to prefer s.o. *or* s.th. to	فَضَّلَ كذا على كذا	to be able to; to gain mastery over	ـــــ على
to think about *or* reflect on s.th.	فَكَّرَ في الامر	to evaluate	قَدَّرَ
to encounter, confront, face; to be in front of, opposite to; to meet	قَابَلَ	to measure s.o. *or* s.th. against	ـــــ كذا بكذا
to compare s.o. *or* s.th. with	ـــــ كذا بكذا	for God to decree *or* destine s.th. for s.o.	ـــــ اللّهُ على فلانٍ الامرَ
to return evil with evil	ـــــ الشرَّ بالشرّ	to allot s.th. to s.o.	ـــــ الامرَ لفلان
to associate with	قَارَنَ	to advance, bring forward	قَدَّمَ
to compare s.o. *or* s.th. with	ـــــ كذا بكذا	to present s.o. to s.o.	ـــــ فلانا الى فلان
to say, speak, utter	قَالَ	to furnish s.th. to s.o.	ـــــ الشيء لفلان
to say to s.o., tell s.o.	ـــــ لفلان	to prefer s.o. *or* s.th. to	ـــــ كذا على كذا
to profess a doctrine	ـــــ بالامر	to execute, carry out, perform; to decide	قَضَى
to speak against	ـــــ على كذا		
to give an opinion about	ـــــ في كذا	to exterminate, do away with	ـــــ على
to relate (*hadīth*) on the authority of s.o.	ـــــ عن فلان	to sentence s.o. to s.th.	ـــــ على فلان بالامر
it is said about s.o. *or* s.th. that	يُقَالُ عن كذا أَنَّ	to give a judgment to s.o. regarding s.th.	ـــــ لفلان بالامر
to rise, stand up	قَامَ	to make a judicial ruling that s.th. be done	ـــــ بالامر
to undertake	ـــــ بالامر	to cut	قَطَعَ

to deprive of	قَطَعَ عن
to affirm	—— في القول
to write	كَتَبَ
to write to s.o. about s.th.	—— الى فلان بالامر
to bequeath s.th. to s.o.	—— لفلان الشيء
for God to decree s.th. for s.o.	—— اللّهُ على فلان الامر
for s.o. to conclude a marriage contract with s.o.; to marry	—— فلانٌ كتابَه على فلانة
to uncover, disclose, expose, discover, unveil; to examine	كَشَفَ الشيءَ او عنه
to charge s.o. with s.th.	كَلَّفَ فلانا بالامر
to take refuge in; to resort to	لَجَأَ الى
to play, sport, frolic; to joke	لَعِبَ
to play with s.o.	—— مع فلان
to play with s.th.	—— بالشيء
to turn, bend, twist	لَفَتَ
to divert s.o. from	—— فلانا عن
to draw s.o.'s attention to	—— نَظَرَ فلانٍ الى
for s.o. not to be (old)	لَيْسَ فلانٌ (كبيرا) او (بكبير)
to incline, lean	مَالَ (يَمِيلُ)
to incline toward s.th.	—— الى الشيء
to deviate, turn away from s.th.	—— عن الشيء

to lean on s.o. or s.th.	مَالَ على كذا
to compare; to represent, portray, take the place of; to exemplify	مَثَّلَ
to make an example of s.o.; to mutilate s.o.	—— بفلان
to pass, go by; to depart; to elapse	مَرَّ
to pass by s.th. (or place)	—— بالشيء او عليه
to travel through	—— من
to pass through (as in flight)	—— في
to go, go away; to expire; to pass	مَضَى
to carry out or execute s.th.; to carry s.th. through to the end	—— على الامر
for time to pass or elapse when such and such is the situation	—— على كذا وقتُ
to continue s.th. or proceed in it	—— في الامر
to prevent, forbid	مَنَعَ
to deny s.o. s.th.; to forbid s.o. to	—— فلانا الامرَ او منه او عنه
to call out to; to summon	نَادَى
to announce, proclaim	—— بالامر
to proclaim s.o. king	—— بفلان ملكا
to obtain, get, acquire	نَالَ (يَنَالُ نَيْلاً)
to affect s.o.; to produce an effect on s.o.	—— من فلان

to defame s.o.	نَالَ من عِرض فلان
for s.o. to acquire s.th.	‌—— فلانا شيءٌ
to make known	نَدَّد
to criticize; to revile; to expose s.o.	‌—— بفلان
to remove, take off; to depose	نَزَعَ
to take s.th. away from s.o.	‌—— الشيء من فلان
to strip or peel s.th. off s.o. or s.th.	‌—— الشيء عن كذا
to incline towards s.th.	‌—— الى الشيء
to shy away from s.th.	‌—— عن الشيء
to go down, descend	نَزَلَ
to alight from, dismount, get off or out of (mare, car, etc.)	‌—— عن (الفرس او السيّارة الخ)
to forgo a right	‌—— عن حق
to take the field	‌—— الى الميدان
to fall on; to attack	‌—— على
to stay with a group of people	‌—— على القوم او بهم
to do what s.o. wants one to do	‌—— عند إرادة فلان
for s.th. to happen to s.o.	‌—— بفلان الامرُ
to stop or stay at a place	‌—— في المكان
to determine, define	نَصَّ
to provide (law) s.th.	‌—— القانونُ على

to advise s.o. to	نَصَح فلانا او له بكذا
to articulate, speak	نَطَقَ
to say a word	‌—— بكلمة
to pronounce sentence	‌—— بالحُكم
to see	نَظَرَ
to look at	‌—— الى كذا
to look into, examine	‌—— في
to judge between	‌—— بين
to make s.th. pierce; to carry through, execute	نَفَّذَ
to send, forward, dispatch to	‌—— الى
to decrease, diminish; to be lacking	نَقَصَ
to fall short of	‌—— عن
for s.o. to lack s.th.	‌—— فلانا الشيءُ
to transfer, remove, transmit, transport; to move; to copy	نَقَلَ
to quote, cite from	‌—— عن فلان
to translate	‌—— من لغة الى أخرى
to fall desperately in love with	هامَ (يَهِيمُ) بكذا
to wander, roam about aimlessly	‌—— على وَجْهِه
to congratulate s.o. on s.th.	هَنَّأ فلانا بكذا
to concur with s.o.; to fit; to suit s.o.	وَافَقَ فلانا
to agree with s.o. upon s.th.	‌—— فلانا في الامر او عليه

to have confidence in; وَثِقَ بِكَذَا
to trust

to be necessary وَجَبَ

to be incumbent ‏—— عَلَى فلان
on s.o.

to send s.o. or وَجَّهَ كَذَا الى
s.th. to

to come to (water); to وَرَدَ
reach, arrive at

for ‏—— الشيءَ فلانا او عليه او اليه
a thing to reach s.o.

to occur in (a في (الكِتَاب) ——
book)

to reach, وَصَلَ المَكَانَ او اليه
arrive at a place

to connect ‏—— الشيءَ بالشيءِ
s.th. with s.th.

to put, place, lay; to make وَضَعَ
(law); to give birth

to drop s.th. الشيءَ من يده ——
from one's hand

to impose الشيءَ على فلان ——
(a tax) on s.o.

to write, compile, الكِتَابَ ——
compose a book

to fabricate الحديثَ ——
traditions from the Prophet

to keep in نُصْبَ عَيْنَيْهِ ——
view, bear in mind

to put one's يَدَه على الشيءِ ——
hand on; to take possession of
s.th.

to disparage s.o. وَضَعَ من قَدْرِ فلان

to promise; to threaten وَعَدَ

to ‏—— فلانا الامرَ او بالامرِ
promise s.o. s.th.

to come; to وَفَدَ على او الى
reach, arrive at

to adapt, render fit وَفَّقَ

to reconcile, conciliate ‏—— بين

for God to grant اللّٰهُ فلانا ——
success to s.o.

to fall, drop; to take place وَقَعَ

for s.th. to لفلان الامرُ ——
happen to or befall s.o.

‏—— الامرُ من فلان مَوْقِعا حسنا for
s.th. to please s.o.

for a الكلامُ في او من نفسه ——
speech to make an impression on
s.o.

‏—— الامرُ عند فلان مَوْقِعَ الرِّضَى
for something to please s.o.

for s.o. to الحقُّ على فلان ——
be at fault

to stop, stand still; وَقَفَ
to stand up

to ‏—— أمامَ فلانٍ او في وجهِه
obstruct, oppose, resist s.o.

to understand, على الامرِ ——
comprehend; to know; to ascertain s.th.

to make s.th. الامرَ على كذا ——
depend on

to endow property for a purpose	وَقَفَ المالَ على كذا
to take a stand	—— موقفا
to suspend operations	—— عن العمل

to be adjacent, close to; to follow s.o. *or* s.th. immediately	وَلِيَ
to rule s.o. *or* s.th.; to take charge of s.th.	—— كذا او عليه
to despair of s.th.	يَئِسَ من الامر

ENGLISH-ARABIC VOCABULARY

NOTE: There are various deliberate omissions: certain common prepositions and conjunctions, various pronouns, names of months, days of the week, personal names, minor geographical names, most numbers.

Various common broken plurals not used in the text are supplied. Plurals are indicated by ج (= جمع 'plural'). Quotation marks indicate literal meanings. In some cases the meanings are limited to contextual usages.

In addition to the more obvious abbreviations, the following have been used: s.o. = someone; s.th. = something.

A

able	قَدِير	agree	إِتَّفَقَ، وَافَقَ عَلَى او فِي
be able	إِسْتَطَاعَ	agreement	إِتِّفَاق
abolition	إِلْغَاء	aid (*v.*)	سَاعَدَ
absence of	عَدَم	aim	مُرَاد
accompany	رَافَقَ	airplane	طَيَّارَة
Acre	عَكَّا	airport	مَطَار
act (*v.*)	عَمِلَ (يَعْمَل)	Alexandria	الإِسْكَنْدَرِيَّة
action	عَمَل ج أَعْمَال	all	جَمِيع، كُلّ
active	عَمَلِيّ	almost (*auxiliary v.*)	كَادَ (يَكَاد)
add	زَادَ (يَزِيد)	amending	تَعْدِيل
address (*n.*)	عُنْوَان	America	أَمْرِيكَا
admiral	أَمِير الْبَحْر	ancient	قَدِيم
advance (*v.*)	تَقَدَّمَ	anger	غَضَب
advocate (*v.*)	دَعَا (يَدْعُو)	angry	غَاضِب
advocate (*n.*)	دَاعٍ (الدَّاعِي)	become angry	غَضِبَ (يَغْضَب)

Ankara	أَنْقَرَة	attend	حَضَرَ (يَحْضُرُ)
announce	أَعْلَنَ	attention	بَال
answer (n.)	إِجَابَة	authority	سُلْطَة
apostle	رَسُول	automobile	سَيَّارَة
appear	بَدَا (يَبْدُو)	autumn	خَرِيف
appearance	ظُهُور		
appoint	عَيَّنَ	**B**	
appointed time	مَوْعِد	Babylon	بَابِل
approach (v.)	تَقَدَّمَ	back down (v.)	تَرَاجَعَ
approving	مُسْتَحْسِن	Baghdad	بَغْدَاد
Arabia	أَلْجَزِيرَة ٱلْعَرَبِيَّة	banishment	نَفْي
Arabian	عَرَبِيّ	basis	أَسَاس
Arabic (language)	أَلْعَرَبِيَّة	bazaar	سُوق
Arabs	عَرَب	bear (a child)	وَلَدَ (يَلِدُ)
army	جَيْش	beautiful	جَمِيل
arrival	وُصُول	become	أَصْبَحَ ، أَمْسَى ، صَارَ
arrive	وَصَلَ (يَصِلُ)		(يَصِيرُ) ، بَاتَ (يَبِيتُ)
asceticism	زُهْد	Bedouin	بَدَوِيّ
Asia Minor	آسِيَا ٱلصُّغْرَى	(before) a little before	قَبِيل
ask	سَأَلَ (يَسْأَلُ)	begin	إِبْتَدَأَ
assassination	إِغْتِيَال	Beirut	بَيْرُوت
assistant	مُعَاوِن	believe	إِعْتَقَدَ
assume rule	تَوَلَّى ٱلْحُكْمَ	believer	مُؤْمِن
assuring (n.)	تَأْمِين	belittling	تَخْفِيض
atmosphere	جَوّ	belonger (act. part.)	تَابِع
attack (n.)	مُهَاجَمَة	beloved	حَبِيب ، مَحْبُوب
		bewildered	هَائِم

Bey (*title*)	بِكْ	call (*v.*) (i.e. name)	سَمَّى
big	كَبِير	call s.o.	دَعَا
black	أَسْوَد	caller	دَاعٍ، اَلدَّاعِي
block (*v.*)	إِعْتَرَضَ	canal	قَنَاة
blood	دَم	capital (city)	عَاصِمَة
book	كِتَاب ج كُتُب	carry out (i.e. finish)	قَضَى (يَقْضِي)
boy	وَلَد ج أَوْلَاد	case (i.e. cause, question)	قَضِيَّة
break (*trans.*)	كَسَرَ (يَكْسُر)	cause (*v.*)	سَبَّبَ
break (*intrans.*)	إِنْكَسَرَ	cause (i.e. reason)	سَبَب ج أَسْبَاب
breast (i.e. chest)	صَدْر	cause ("path," "way")	سَبِيل
breeze	نَسِيم	cause (i.e. case)	قَضِيَّة
bring	جَاءَ (يَجِيءُ) بِ	cavalier	فَارِس
bring together	جَمَعَ (يَجْمَعُ) بَيْنَ	cease	زَالَ (يَزَالُ)
Britain	بِرِيطَانِيَا	changing (*n.*)	تَحْوِيل
broad	عَرِيض	character(istic)	صِفَة
brother	أَخ ج إِخْوَان	charter	مِيثَاق
budget	مِيزَانِيَّة	chief	رَئِيس ج رُؤَسَاء
building	بِنَاء	childhood	طُفُولَة
but	لٰكِنْ، لٰكِنَّ	Christian ("Nazarene")	نَصْرَانِيّ
butcher	جَزَّار	Christian (era)	مِيلَادِيّ
buy	إِبْتَاعَ	circle	دَائِرَة ج دَوَائِر
Byzantines	اَلرُّوم	circumambulate	طَافَ (يَطُوفُ) بِ
C		citizen	مُوَاطِن
Cairo	اَلْقَاهِرَة	city	مَدِينَة ج مُدُن
caliph	خَلِيفَة	civilization	مَدَنِيَّة

classical	كَلَاسِيكِيٌّ
club	نَادٍ (النَّادِي)
coffee	قَهْوَةٌ
college	كُلِّيَّةٌ
colonized	مُسْتَعْمَرٌ
colony	مُسْتَعْمَرَةٌ
color	لَوْنٌ ج أَلْوَانٌ
column	رُكْنٌ ج أَرْكَانٌ
come	جَاءَ (يَجِيءُ) ؛ قَدِمَ (يَقْدُمُ)
command (n.)	أَمْرٌ ج أَوَامِرُ
commander	قَائِدٌ
commissioner	مَنْدُوبٌ
committee	لَجْنَةٌ
common	مُشْتَرَكٌ
commute (a sentence)	إِسْتَبْدَلَ
company	شَرِكَةٌ
complete (adj.)	كَامِلٌ
compose (i.e. put together)	نَظَّمَ (يَنْظِمُ)
concession	إِمْتِيَازٌ
condition	حَالٌ ج أَحْوَالٌ ؛ حَالَةٌ
conference	مُؤْتَمَرٌ
confidence	ثِقَةٌ
confident	وَاثِقٌ
congress	مُؤْتَمَرٌ
connection	صِلَةٌ

conquer	إِسْتَوْلَى عَلَى، فَتَحَ (يَفْتَحُ)
conquering (n.)	فَتْحٌ ج فُتُوحٌ
conservative	مُحَافِظٌ
consider	عَدَّ (يَعُدُّ) ؛ إِعْتَبَرَ
consist	تَأَلَّفَ
constitution	دُسْتُورٌ
consultant	مُسْتَشَارٌ
consultation	إِسْتِشَارَةٌ
contact (v.)	إِتَّصَلَ
continue	لَايَزَالُ
convene	عَقَدَ (يَعْقِدُ)
convey	نَقَلَ (يَنْقُلُ)
co-operate	تَعَاوَنَ
co-operation	تَعَاوُنٌ
copy (n.)	نُسْخَةٌ ج نُسَخٌ
cordial	وَدِّيٌّ
correspondent	مُرَاسِلٌ
council	مَجْلِسٌ ج مَجَالِسُ
country	بِلَادٌ، وَطَنٌ ج أَوْطَانٌ
country(side)	رِيفٌ
courage	شَجَاعَةٌ
covenant	مِيثَاقٌ
create	خَلَقَ (يَخْلُقُ)
creation	خَلْقٌ
creep	زَحَفَ (يَزْحَفُ)
crescent	هِلَالٌ

current	جَارٍ (أَلْجَارِي)	despair of	يَئِسَ (يَيْأَسُ) مِن
be current	جَرَى (يَجْرِي)	devil	شَيْطَانٌ
cut	قَطَعَ (يَقْطَعُ)	devoted (i.e.	مُتَفَانٍ (أَلْمُتَفَانِي)
D		self-sacrificing)	
Damascus	دِمَشْقُ ، أَلشَّأْمُ	devoted (i.e. sincere)	مُخْلِصٌ
daughter	إِبْنَةٌ	Dhu al-Ḥijjah	ذُو ٱلْحِجَّةِ
day	يَوْمٌ ج أَيَّامٌ	die	تُوُفِّيَ
dear	عَزِيزٌ	differ	إِخْتَلَفَ
death	مَوْتٌ	difficult	صَعْبٌ
decide	عَزَمَ (يَعْزِمُ)	be difficult	صَعُبَ (يَصْعُبُ)
defend	دَافَعَ	director	مُدِيرٌ
defense	دِفَاعٌ	directorship	إِدَارَةٌ
(delay) be delayed	تَأَخَّرَ	disagree	إِخْتَلَفَ
delegation	وَفْدٌ ج وُفُودٌ	discussion	بَحْثٌ ج بُحُوثٌ وَأَبْحَاثٌ
delicious	لَذِيذٌ	disliked	مَكْرُوهٌ
deliver (speech)	أَلْقَى	dispute	مُنَاقَشَةٌ
demand	مَطْلَبٌ ج مَطَالِبُ	dissolve	حَلَّ (يَحُلُّ)
department	دَائِرَةٌ ج دَوَائِرُ	distance	بُعْدٌ
departure	خُرُوجٌ	distant	بَعِيدٌ
deputy	نَائِبٌ ج نُوَّابٌ	disturbance	إِضْطِرَابٌ
descend	نَزَلَ (يَنْزِلُ)	divide into (*intrans.*)	إِنْقَسَمَ إِلَى
descended (lineally)	مُتَحَدِّر	divided	مُنْقَسِم
descent	نُزُولٌ	do	عَمِلَ (يَعْمَلُ) ؛ فَعَلَ (يَفْعَلُ)
desert	صَحْرَاءُ	doctor	دُكْتُورٌ
desire	رَغْبَةٌ ، وَدٌّ	dog	كَلْبٌ ج كِلَابٌ
desist	إِنْصَرَفَ عَنْ	dome	قُبَّةٌ

door	بَابْ ج أَبْوَابْ	enter	دَخَلَ (يَدْخُلُ)
doubt (v.)	شَكَّ (يَشُكُّ)	establish	أَسَّسَ، أَقَامَ
doubt (n.)	شَكّ	establishing	تَأْسِيس
draw near	إِقْتَرَبَ مِنْ	every	كُلّ
drowning (n.)	غَرَق	evidencing	مَبْدِ (الْمَبْدِي)
dry	جَافّ	evolution	تَطَوُّر
dryness	جَفَافْ	example	مِثَالْ
duty	وَاجِبْ	(excellency) His Excellency	دَوْلَة

E

		except	غَيْر
east (n.)	شَرْق	exchange	تَبَادَلَ
economy	إِقْتِصَادْ	execution (i.e. capital punishment)	إِعْدَامْ
editor	مُحَرِّر	existence	وُجُودْ
education	تَرْبِيَة ، تَعْلِيم	expect	إِنْتَظَرَ
Egypt	مِصْر	expel	أَخْرَجَ
Egyptian	مِصْرِيّ	extensive	وَاسِع
elect	إِنْتَخَبَ	extremeness	شِدَّة
election	إِنْتِخَابْ	eye	عَيْنْ ج عُيُونْ

F

emancipation	تَحْرِير		
emergence	خُرُوج	face (n.)	وَجْهْ ج وُجُوه
emigrant	مُهَاجِر	factory	مَعْمَلْ ج مَعَامِل
emigrate	هَاجَرَ	fade away	إِضْمَحَلَّ
employ	إِسْتَخْدَمَ	fail	فَشَلَ (يَفْشَلُ)
encourage	شَجَّعَ	failure (act. part.)	فَاشِلْ
encouraging	مُشَجِّعَة	faith	إِيمَانْ
enjoyable	لَذِيذْ	faithful	أَمِينْ

English	Arabic	English	Arabic
fall	وَقَعَ (يَقَعُ)	form (n.)	شَكْل
family	عَائِلَة، بَيْت	format	شَكْل
famous	مَشْهُور	found (v.)	أَسَّس
farmer	فَلَّاح	be founded	تَأَسَّس
fast (adj.)	سَرِيع	foundation	أَسَاس، تَأْسِيس
father	وَالِد	founder	مُؤَسِّس
favor (i.e. view with favor)	إِطْمَأَنَّ إِلَى	fourth (ordinal)	رَابِع
		fourth (fraction)	رُبْع
feast	عِيد	friend	صَدِيق ج أَصْدِقَاء
fertile	خَصِيب	fulfill	أَدَّى
few	مَعْدُود	functioning (i.e. operation)	سَيْر
field	مَيْدَان	future	مُسْتَقْبَل
fire	نَار		
first	أَوَّل	**G**	
flag	عَلَم ج أَعْلَام	garden	جُنَيْنَة ج جَنَائِن
follow	تَبِعَ	general (adj.)	عَامّ
follow (i.e. be immediately after)	وَلِيَ (يَلِي)؛ تَلَا (يَتْلُو)	generous	كَرِيم
following (immediately after)	تَالٍ (أَلتَّالِي)	Germany	أَلْمَانِيَا
		get up	قَامَ (يَقُوم)
forbid	مَنَعَ (يَمْنَعُ)	girl	بِنْت ج بَنَات
(force) in force	مَعْمُول ب	girl friend	صَدِيقَة
foreign	أَجْنَبِيّ	give	أَعْطَى
foreigner	أَجْنَبِيّ ج أَجَانِب	glorious	كَرِيم
forget	نَسِيَ (يَنْسَى)	glory	مَجْد
form (trans.)	شَكَّل	go	قَصَدَ (يَقْصِد)؛ ذَهَبَ (يَذْهَب)
be formed	تَأَلَّف	God	أَللّٰه

gold	ذَهَب	holding (e.g. meeting)	عَقْد
golden	ذَهَبِيّ	holiday	عيد ج أَعْيَاد
good	حَسَن	holy	مُقَدَّس
governing (n.)	حُكْم	Homs	حِمْص
government	حُكُومَة	honor (trans.)	أَكْرَم
grand	عَظِيم	honored	مُكَرَّم
grandfather	جَدّ ج أَجْدَاد	hope (v.)	رَجَا (يَرْجُو)
grant (v.)	مَنَح (يَمْنَح)	hotel	فُنْدُق
green	أَخْضَر	hour	سَاعَة
ground (n.)	أَرْض	house	بَيْت ج بُيُوت ؛ دَار
group	فَرِيق	however	غَيْرَ أَنَّ
		hundred	مِئَة
H		husband	زَوْج
halt (n.)	وُقُوف		
hand	يَد	**I**	
happen	جَرَى (يَجْرِي)	ijmāʿ	إِجْمَاع
happy	سَعِيد	ijtihād	إِجْتِهَاد
head (intrans.)	تَوَجَّه	illuminated	مُنَوَّر
head (n.)	رَأْس ج رُؤُوس	immediately	حَالاً
heart	قَلْب ج قُلُوب	importance	شَأْن ؛ ج شُؤُون أَهَمِّيَّة
heaven	سَمَاء ج سَمٰوَات	important	مُهِمّ
Hebrew (n. or adj.)	عِبْرَانِيّ	imprison	سَجَن (يَسْجُن)
high	سَامٍ (أَلسَّامِي)	improve	تَحَسَّن
highness	سُمُوّ	improvement	إِصْلَاح
Hijrah	هِجْرَة	increase (i.e. grow stronger)	إِشْتَدَّ
history	تَأْرِيخ	independence	إِسْتِقْلَال
hold (e.g. meeting)	عَقَد (يَعْقِد)	independent	مُسْتَقِلّ

English	Arabic	English	Arabic
industrious	مُجْتَهِدٌ	just	عَادِلٌ
influence	تَأْثِيرٌ	justice	عَدْلٌ
inhabit	سَكَنَ (يَسْكُنُ)	**K**	
insistence	إِصْرَارٌ	Kaaba	كَعْبَةٌ
intention	مُرَادٌ	Khedive	خَدِيوِيٌّ
interest (i.e. benefit)	مَصْلَحَةٌ	kill	قَتَلَ (يَقْتُلُ)
interest s.o. in	حَبَّبَ إِلَى	killed	مَقْتُولٌ
interior	دَاخِلِيٌّ	kindness	رِفْقٌ
interpret	تَرْجَمَ	king	مَلِكٌ ج مُلُوكٌ
inviolability	حُرْمَةٌ	know	عَرَفَ (يَعْرِفُ) ؛ عَلِمَ (يَعْلَمُ)
invite	دَعَا (يَدْعُو)	knower	عَالِمٌ ج عُلَمَاءُ
Iraq	ٱلْعِرَاقُ	knowledge	عِلْمٌ ج عُلُومٌ
irregular	أَخْرَقُ	known	مَعْرُوفٌ
Islam	ٱلْإِسْلَامُ	Koran	قُرْآنٌ
Islamic	إِسْلَامِيٌّ	Koranic	قُرْآنِيٌّ
island	جَزِيرَةٌ ج جَزَائِرُ وَجُزُرٌ	Kuwait	ٱلْكُوَيْتُ
Istanbul	إِسْطَمْبُولُ	**L**	
		lack	عَدَمٌ
J		lake	بُحَيْرَةٌ
Jaffa	يَافَا	land	أَرْضٌ، بِلَادٌ
job	مَنْصِبٌ ج مَنَاصِبُ	language	لُغَةٌ
journalism	صِحَافَةٌ	last (v.)	إِسْتَمَرَّ، دَامَ (يَدُومُ)
journey	سَيْرٌ	last (adj.)	مَاضٍ (ٱلْمَاضِي)
judge (v.)	حَكَمَ (يَحْكُمُ)	late (i.e. deceased)	مَرْحُومٌ
judge (n.)	قَاضٍ (ٱلْقَاضِي) ج قُضَاةٌ	law	شَرِيعَةٌ
judgment	حُكْمٌ ج أَحْكَامٌ	lawyer	مُحَامٍ (ٱلْمُحَامِي)

lazy	كَسْلَانُ	love (v.)	أَحَبَّ
lead to	أَدَّى إِلَى	love (n.)	حُبٌّ
lead (v.)	قَادَ (يَقُودُ)	love (adj. of poetry)	غَزَلِيٌّ
leader	زَعِيمٌ ج زُعَمَاءُ ؛ قَائِدٌ ج قُوَّادٌ	lover	مُحِبٌّ
leadership	قِيَادَةٌ		

M

learned	عَالِمٌ ج عُلَمَاءُ	madman	مَجْنُونٌ
leave	خَرَجَ (يَخْرُجُ)	magazine	مَجَلَّةٌ
Lebanon	لُبْنَانُ	majesty	جَلَالَةٌ
lesson	دَرْسٌ ج دُرُوسٌ	man (i.e. human being)	إِنْسَانٌ
liberate	حَرَّرَ	man	رَجُلٌ ج رِجَالٌ
liberty	حُرِّيَّةٌ	manager	مُدِيرٌ
library	مَكْتَبَةٌ	mandate	إِنْتِدَابٌ
life	عُمْرٌ، حَيَاةٌ	manuscript	مَخْطُوطَةٌ
light (n.)	نُورٌ	march (v.)	سَارَ (يَسِيرُ)
light (in weight)	خَفِيفٌ	mare	فَرَسٌ
liked	مَحْبُوبٌ	market	سُوقٌ ج أَسْوَاقٌ
likeness	مِثْلٌ	marriage	زَوَاجٌ
linotype	لِينُوتِيبٌ	matter	شَأْنٌ ج شُوُونٌ ؛ أَمْرٌ ج أُمُورٌ
lion	أَسَدٌ	meet (i.e. assemble)	إِجْتَمَعَ
literal	حَرْفِيٌّ	meet (together)	إِلْتَقَى
literature	أَدَبٌ ج آدَابٌ	meet s.o.	قَابَلَ، لَقِيَ (يَلْقَى)؛ إِلْتَقَى بِ
live (v.)	عَاشَ (يَعِيشُ)	meeting	جَلْسَةٌ، إِجْتِمَاعٌ
long	طَوِيلٌ	Merciful (i.e. God)	رَحْمَنٌ
look (v.)	نَظَرَ (يَنْظُرُ)	be merciful	رَحِمَ (يَرْحَمُ)
looking (n.)	نَظَرٌ	(merry) become merry	إِبْتَهَجَ
loom (v.)	لَاحَ (يَلُوحُ)	messenger	رَسُولٌ

English	Arabic
middle	أَوْسَطُ
mighty	عَزِيزٌ
military	عَسْكَرِيٌّ
mind	بَالٌ
minister (in government)	وَزِيرٌ ج وُزَرَاءُ
ministry	وِزَارَةٌ
minute	دَقِيقَةٌ ج دَقَائِقُ
mirror	مِرْآةٌ
mission	بَعْثَةٌ
mister	سَيِّدٌ، أُسْتَاذٌ ج أَسَاتِذَةٌ
moderation	إِعْتِدَالٌ
modern	حَدِيثٌ
month	شَهْرٌ ج أَشْهُرٌ
morning	صَبَاحٌ
mosque	جَامِعٌ ج جَوَامِعُ
most	مُعْظَمٌ
mother	أُمٌّ ج أُمَّهَاتٌ
mountain	جَبَلٌ ج جِبَالٌ
move (v.) (i.e. transfer)	نَقَلَ (يَنْقُلُ)
movement	حَرَكَةٌ
mudīrīyah (i.e. adm. district)	مُدِيرِيَّةٌ
mufti	مُفْتٍ (الْمُفْتِي)
Muslim	مُسْلِمٌ
Mu'tazilah	مُعْتَزِلَةٌ

N

name (v.)	سَمَّى
name (n.)	إِسْمٌ ج أَسْمَاءُ
nation	أُمَّةٌ
nationalism	قَوْمِيَّةٌ
natural	طَبِيعِيٌّ
(necessary) be necessary	وَجَبَ (يَجِبُ)
necessity	حَاجَةٌ
need (v.)	إِحْتَاجَ
needy	مُحْتَاجٌ
negotiation	مُفَاوَضَةٌ
Nejd	نَجْد
Nejdi	نَجْدِيٌّ
new	جَدِيدٌ
newspaper	جَرِيدَةٌ ج جَرَائِدُ
night	لَيْلَةٌ ج لَيَالٍ (الْلَّيَالِي)
noble	كَرِيمٌ
north	شَمَالٌ
number	عَدَدٌ ج أَعْدَادٌ
numerous	عَدِيدٌ

O

obedience	إِنْقِيَادٌ
oblige to	إِضْطَرَّ إِلَى
obtain	نَالَ (يَنَالُ)
occasion	مُنَاسَبَةٌ

257

occupy (e.g. territory)	إِحْتَلَّ	Palestine	فَلَسْطِينُ
occupy (e.g. attention or position)	شَغَلَ (يَشْغَلُ)	Paris	بَارِيس
offer	قَدَّمَ	parliament	بَرْلَمَانٌ
office	مَكْتَبٌ ج مَكَاتِبُ	part	قِسْمٌ ج أَقْسَامٌ
official (adj.)	رَسْمِيٌّ	participant	مُشْتَرِكٌ
official (n.)	مُوَظَّفٌ	participate	إِشْتَرَكَ
oil	زَيْتٌ	participation	إِشْتِرَاكٌ
old ("big"; of animate beings)	كَبِيرٌ	party (political)	حِزْبٌ ج أَحْزَابٌ
old (of inanimate things)	قَدِيمٌ	pasha	بَاشَا
old man	شَيْخٌ ج شُيُوخٌ	pass (by)	مَرَّ (يَمُرُّ)
one possessing or having	ذُو	pass (i.e. spend time)	قَضَى (يَقْضِي)
open	فَتَحَ (يَفْتَحُ)	path	سَبِيلٌ
opening	فَتْحٌ	patriot	مُجَاهِدٌ
opinion	رَأْيٌ ج آرَاءٌ	peace	سَلَامٌ
opposition	مُعَارَضَةٌ	people (sing.)	شَعْبٌ ج شُعُوبٌ ؛ قَوْمٌ ، أَهْلٌ
orchard	بُسْتَانٌ ج بَسَاتِينُ		
order (n.) (i.e. command)	أَمْرٌ ج أَوَامِرُ	perform prayer	أَقَامَ ٱلصَّلَاةَ
organization (e.g. club)	مُنْتَدًى	period (time)	مُدَّةٌ
organization (i.e. systematization)	تَنْظِيمٌ	permission	إِذْنٌ
		permit (v.)	أَذِنَ ، يَأْذَنُ
origin	أَصْلٌ ج أُصُولٌ	personal	شَخْصِيٌّ
original	أَصْلِيٌّ	personality	شَخْصِيَّةٌ
other	آخَرُ ، غَيْرُ	photographic	فُوتُوغْرَافِيٌّ
P			
page	صَفْحَةٌ	picture	صُورَةٌ ج صُوَرٌ
palace	قَصْرٌ ج قُصُورٌ	pilgrimage	حَجٌّ

258

pillar	رُكْنٌ ج أَرْكَانٌ	prepare	إِسْتَعَدَّ
place	مَكَانٌ، مَحَلٌّ، مَقَامٌ	presence	حُضُورٌ
plain (n.)	سَهْلٌ ج سُهُولٌ	preservation	حِفْظٌ
plan	مَشْرُوعٌ	preserve	حَفِظَ (يَحْفَظُ) ؛ حَافَظَ عَلَى
play (v.)	لَعِبَ (يَلْعَبُ)	preserved (pass. part.)	مَحْفُوظَةٌ
playful	لَعُوبٌ	president	رَئِيسٌ ج رُؤَسَاءُ
please (i.e. be fine, good)	حَسُنَ (يَحْسُنُ)	pressure	ضَغْطٌ
please (i.e. be sweet)	حَلَا (يَحْلُو)	prevent	مَنَعَ (يَمْنَعُ)
poetry	شِعْرٌ	prime minister	رَئِيسُ الْوُزَرَاءِ
policy	سِيَاسَةٌ	prince	أَمِيرٌ ج أُمَرَاءُ
political	سِيَاسِيٌّ	princess	أَمِيرَةٌ
politics	سِيَاسَةٌ	prisoner	أَسِيرٌ
poor	فَقِيرٌ	problem	مُشْكِلَةٌ
position	مَقَامٌ، مَوْقِفٌ	proceed	جَرَى (يَجْرِي)
position (i.e. job)	مَنْصِبٌ ج مَنَاصِبُ ؛ وَظِيفَةٌ ج وَظَائِفُ	professor	أُسْتَاذٌ ج أَسَاتِذَةٌ
		program (i.e. plan)	مَشْرُوعٌ
possible	مُسْتَطَاعٌ	prophet	نَبِيٌّ ج أَنْبِيَاءُ
power (i.e. ability)	إِسْتِطَاعَةٌ، مُسْتَطَاعٌ	protégé	مَحْسُوبٌ ج مَحَاسِيبُ
power (i.e. rule)	حُكْمٌ	protest (v.)	إِحْتَجَّ، إِعْتَرَضَ على
pray	صَلَّى	protester	مُحْتَجٌّ
prayer	صَلَاةٌ ج صَلَوَاتٌ	prove	بَرْهَنَ
(precedence) give precedence to	قَدَّمَ عَلَى	public (adj.)	عَامٌّ
		pull out	قَلَعَ (يَقْلَعُ)
preference	إِمْتِيَازٌ	punish	عَاقَبَ
		pursuit	تَتَبُّعٌ
premier	رَئِيسُ الْوُزَرَاءِ	pyramid	هَرَمٌ ج أَهْرَامٌ

Q

qiblah	قِبْلَةٌ
quiet down (*v.*)	سَكَتَ
queen	مَلِكَةٌ

R

reach (i.e. attain)	بَلَغَ (يَبْلُغُ)
reactionary	رَجْعِيٌّ
read	قَرَأَ (يَقْرَأُ)
real	وَاقِعٌ، حَقِيقِيٌّ
reality	حَقِيقَةٌ ج حَقَائِقُ
realization	تَحْقِيقٌ
reason (i.e. mind)	عَقْلٌ ج عُقُولٌ
reason (i.e. cause)	سَبَبٌ ج أَسْبَابٌ
receive (<"get" <"take")	أَخَذَ (يَأْخُذُ)
recent	أَخِيرٌ
recite	قَرَأَ (يَقْرَأُ)
recognition	إِعْتِرَافٌ
recognize	إِعْتَرَفَ
rectitude	صَلَاحٌ
redden	إِحْمَرَّ
reform (*n.*)	إِصْلَاحٌ
reformer	مُصْلِحٌ
rejoice	فَرِحَ (يَفْرَحُ)
relaxed	مُسْتَرِيحٌ
religion	دِينٌ ج أَدْيَانٌ

religious	دِينِيٌّ
rely	إِعْتَمَدَ
remain	بَقِيَ (يَبْقَى)؛ مَازَالَ (لَا يَزَالُ)
render	أَدَّى
rent (*v.*)	إِسْتَأْجَرَ
reporter	مُرَاسِلٌ
represent	مَثَّلَ
representation	تَمْثِيلٌ
representative	مُمَثِّلٌ
reprimand (*n.*)	تَوْبِيخٌ
republic	جُمْهُورِيَّةٌ
request (*v.*)	طَلَبَ (يَطْلُبُ)
resolution	قَرَارٌ
resolved	عَازِمٌ
responsibility	مَسْؤُولِيَّةٌ
rest (*n.*)	إِسْتِرَاحَةٌ
restore	أَعَادَ
result (*n.*)	نَتِيجَةٌ ج نَتَائِجُ
resume	إِسْتَأْنَفَ
retreat (*v.*)	تَرَاجَعَ
return (*n.*)	رُجُوعٌ
return (*intrans.*)	عَادَ (يَعُودُ)؛ رَجَعَ (يَرْجِعُ)
return (*trans.*)	أَعَادَ
revolution	ثَوْرَةٌ

260

revolve	دَارَ (يَدُورُ)	scholar	عَلَّامَةٌ
rice	أُرْزٌّ	school	مَدْرَسَةٌ ج مَدَارِسُ
rider	رَاكِبٌ	sea	بَحْرٌ ج أَبْحُرٌ
right (n.)	حَقٌّ ج حُقُوقٌ	season	فَصْلٌ ج فُصُولٌ
river	نَهْرٌ ج أَنْهَارٌ	seat (i.e. center)	مَرْكَزٌ ج مَرَاكِزُ
Riyadh	الرِّيَاضُ	second (ordinal)	ثَانٍ (الثَّانِي)
rob (highway)	قَطَعَ (يَقْطَعُ) الطَّرِيقَ	see	رَأَى (يَرَى)
		see (i.e. witness)	شَاهَدَ
Roman	رُومَانِيٌّ	seek	طَلَبَ (يَطْلُبُ)
room	غُرْفَةٌ	seizer	مُسْتَوْلٍ (الْمُسْتَوْلِي) عَلَى
rule (n.)	حُكْمٌ	seizure	إِسْتِيلَاءٌ
ruler	حَاكِمٌ ج حُكَّامٌ	self	نَفْسٌ ج أَنْفُسٌ
run	جَرَى (يَجْرِي)	senator	شَيْخٌ ج شُيُوخٌ
		send	أَرْسَلَ
S		sentence (legal)	حُكْمٌ ج أَحْكَامٌ
sacrifice s.th.	ضَحَّى بِ	(serve) make s.o. serve	إِسْتَخْدَمَ
sacrificial offering	ضَحِيَّةٌ	service	خِدْمَةٌ
safeguard (v.)	حَافَظَ عَلَى	set out for	قَصَدَ (يَقْصِدُ)
sanctified (on pilgrimage)	مُحْرِمٌ	sharp (i.e. intense)	شَدِيدٌ
sanctify	قَدَّسَ	short	قَصِيرٌ
Samarkand	سَمَرْقَنْدُ	side	جَانِبٌ
satisfied	رَاضٍ (الرَّاضِي)	signing	تَوْقِيعٌ
Saudi	سَعُودِيٌّ	sincere	مُخْلِصٌ
say	قَالَ (يَقُولُ)	sincerity	إِخْلَاصٌ
sayer	قَائِلٌ	sister	أُخْتٌ ج أَخَوَاتٌ
scales	مِيزَانٌ		

English	Arabic	English	Arabic
sitting (i.e. session)	جَلْسَة	spring (season)	رَبِيع
slap (v.)	لَطَم (يَلْطِم)	spring (water)	عَيْن ج عُيُون
slapping	لَطْم	square (i.e. in a city)	مَيْدَان ج مَيَادِين
small	صَغِير	stand (n.)	مَوْقِف ج مَوَاقِف
smell	شَمّ	state (i.e. nation)	دَوْلَة ج دُوَل
so-and-so	فُلان	steal	سَرَق (يَسْرِق)
society (i.e. organization)	جَمْعِيَّة	step (as in stairs, scale)	دَرَجَة
society (i.e. human environment)	مُجْتَمَع	step on	دَعَس (يَدْعَس)
solution	حَلّ	stop at	نَزَل (يَنْزِل) في
solve	حَلَّ (يَحُلّ)	story	قِصَّة ج قِصَص
son	إِبْن ج بَنُون	straight	مُسْتَقِيم
south	جَنُوب	street	شَارِع ج شَوَارِع
southern	جَنُوبِيّ	(strengthen) be strengthened	إِشْتَدّ
speak	تَكَلَّم، نَطَق (يَنْطِق)	stretching (act. part.)	مُمْتَدّ
speak (i.e. make a speech)	خَطَب (يَخْطُب)	strike (n.)	إِضْرَاب
special	خَاصّ	striver	مُجَاهِد، مُجْتَهِد
speech (i.e. oration)	خِطَاب	strong	شَدِيد
spend (time)	قَضَى (يَقْضِي)	grow strong(er)	إِشْتَدّ
spend (time, money, effort, etc.)	صَرَف (يَصْرِف)	struggle	جِهَاد
spirit	نَفْس ج أَنْفُس ونُفُوس؛ رُوح ج أَرْوَاح	student	طَالِب ج طُلَّاب وطَلَبَة
split (n.)	إِنْشِقَاق	study (n.)	بَحْث ج أَبْحَاث؛ دِرَاسَة؛ دَرْس
spread (intrans.)	إِنْتَشَر	study (v.)	دَرَس
spread out	مُنْتَشِر	study under (become student of)	تَتَلْمَذَ عَلَى

English	Arabic
subside (e.g. anger)	سَكَتَ (يَسْكُتُ)
Suez	سُوَيْس
sufficient	كَافٍ (أَلْكَافِي)
suit (v.)	نَاسَبَ
suitable	مُنَاسِب
summer	صَيْف
summering (n.)	إِصْطِيَاف
swearing fealty	مُبَايَعَة
Syria	سُورِيَّة

T

tablet	لَوْح
take	أَخَذَ (يَأْخُذُ)
take on (i.e. adopt)	إِتَّخَذَ
tall	طَوِيل
talk (n.)	قَوْل ، كَلَام
Ṭanṭa (town in Nile Delta)	طَنْطَا
teach	عَلَّمَ
teacher	مُعَلِّم
teaching (n.)	تَعْلِيم
telephone (n.)	تِلِفُون
temple	مَعْبَد ج مَعَابِد
tenacity	شِدَّة
tend (i.e. incline)	مَالَ (يَمِيلُ)
tenth (ordinal)	عَاشِر
text	نَصّ ج نُصُوص

English	Arabic
theory	نَظَرِيَّة
think	ظَنَّ (يَظُنُّ)
third (fraction)	ثُلْث
tie (n.) (i.e. bond)	عُرْوَة
Tigris	دِجْلَة
time (i.e. a time)	مَرَّة
title	عُنْوَان
today	أَلْيَوْم
tomb	قَبْر ج قُبُور
tooth	سِنّ ج أَسْنَان
town	بَلْدَة
traditionalism	تَقْلِيد
translate	تَرْجَمَ
transport (v.)	نَقَلَ (يَنْقُلُ)
travel (v.)	سَافَرَ
traveler	مُسَافِر
treat with	عَامَلَ
treaty	مُعَاهَدَة
tree	شَجَرَة
true	صَحِيح
truth (i.e. fact)	حَقِيقَة ج حَقَائِق
Turkey	تُرْكِيَّا
turn (i.e. change direction)	حَوَّلَ
turn s.o. towards	وَجَّهَ إِلَى

U

undertaking (i.e. covenant)	تَعَهُّد

English	Arabic	English	Arabic
unification	تَوْحِيدٌ	weakness	ضَعْفٌ
united	مُتَّحِدٌ	week	أُسْبُوعٌ ج أَسَابِيعُ
unity	وَحْدَةٌ	weigh (i.e. on scales)	وَزَنَ (يَزِنُ)
university	جَامِعَةٌ	weighed	مَوْزُونٌ
untie	حَلَّ (يَحُلُّ)	west (n.)	غَرْبٌ
uprightness	إِسْتِقَامَةٌ	whatever	مَهْمَا
use (v.)	إِسْتَعْمَلَ	wherever	حَيْثُمَا
usually	عَامَّةً	whisper (v.)	وَسْوَسَ
		white	أَبْيَضُ
V		whoever	أَيٌّ
valley	وَادٍ (الْوَادِي)	whole	كَامِلٌ
various	مُخْتَلِفٌ	wide	وَاسِعٌ
village	قَرْيَةٌ ج قُرًى	wife	زَوْجَةٌ
violent	شَدِيدٌ	winter	شِتَاءٌ
vis-à-vis	مُقَابِلَ	withdraw	إِنْسَحَبَ
visit (n.)	زِيَارَةٌ	withdrawal	إِنْسِحَابٌ
visit (v.)	زَارَ (يَزُورُ)	woman	مَرْأَةٌ، إِمْرَأَةٌ
W		work (i.e. occupy a position)	شَغَلَ (يَشْغَلُ)
wādī	وَادٍ (الْوَادِي)	world	عَالَمٌ
waistband	إِزَارٌ	writer	كَاتِبٌ ج كُتَّابٌ
wander	طَافَ (يَطُوفُ)	**Y**	
want (v.) (i.e. desire)	أَرَادَ	Yathrib	يَثْرِبُ
war	حَرْبٌ ج حُرُوبٌ	year	سَنَةٌ ج سَنَوَاتٌ؛ عَامٌ ج أَعْوَامٌ
water (v.)	أَرْوَى	yesterday	أَمْسِ
water (n.)	مَاءٌ ج مِيَاهٌ	young	صَغِيرٌ
way	طَرِيقٌ		

ARABIC-ENGLISH VOCABULARY

NOTE: There are various deliberate omissions: certain very common particles, personal pronouns, pronominal suffixes, vocative particles, names of months, days of the week, personal names, minor geographical names, most numbers, words occurring only in Section II of a given Chapter.

Alphabetization is by separate words; participles, maṣdars, broken plurals, etc., are, therefore, treated separately. In alphabetizing, hamzah precedes alif; maddah is treated as hamzah-alif; vowels, shaddah, and the definite article are disregarded; tā' marbūṭah is considered as the last letter of the alphabet. Quotation marks indicate the literal meanings of words.

Contextual meanings are always given; in addition, other important usages are added at the authors' discretion. Some singulars are entered though only the broken plural occurs in the text.

In addition to the more obvious abbreviations, the following have been used: s.o. =someone; s.th. =something.

interrogative particle	أ	white	أَبْيَض
fathers	آبَاء	take on, adopt	إِتَّخَذَ
other	آخَر	contact (*v.*)	إِتَّصَلَ
Asia Minor	آسِيَا الصُّغْرَى	agreement	إِتِّفَاق
now	أَلْآنَ	agree	إِتَّفَقَ
father	أَب	answer (*n.*)	إِجَابَة
buy	إِبْتَاعَ	foreigners	أَجَانِب
begin	إِبْتَدَأَ	convene, meet (*intrans.*)	إِجْتَمَعَ
become merry	إِبْتَهَج	*ijtihād* (legal interpretation); endeavoring	إِجْتِهَاد
son	إِبْن	grandfathers, forefathers	أَجْدَاد
daughter	إِبْنَة	parts, sections; volumes	أَجْزَاء

ijmā' (consenus)	إِجْمَاعٌ	therefore	إِذَنْ
foreign; foreigner	أَجْنَبِيٌّ	permit (*v.*)	أَذِنَ
love (*v.*)	أَحَبَّ	permission	إِذْنٌ
need (*v.*)	إِحْتَاجَ	want, desire (*v.*)	أَرَادَ
protest (*v.*)	إِحْتَجَّ	rice	أَرُزٌّ
occupy	إِحْتَلَّ	send	أَرْسَلَ
parties (*political*)	أَحْزَابٌ	ground, land, earth	أَرْضٌ
better, best	أَحْسَنُ	pillars, columns, supports	أَرْكَانٌ
redden	إِحْمَرَّ	general staff	أَرْكَان حَرْب
brother	أَخٌ	water, irrigate	أَرْوَى
news	أَخْبَارٌ	waistband	إِزَارٌ
sister	أُخْتٌ	foundation, basis	أَسَاسٌ
disagree, differ	إِخْتَلَفَ	Spaniards	إِسْبَانٌ
take; receive	أَخَذَ	Spain	إِسْبَانِيَا
other (*f.*)	أُخْرَى	week	أُسْبُوعٌ
expel	أَخْرَجَ	rent (*v.*)	إِسْتَأْجَرَ
irregular, aberrant	أَخْرَقُ	resume	إِسْتَأْنَفَ
green	أَخْضَرُ	professor; mister	أُسْتَاذٌ
sincerity	إِخْلَاصٌ	commute (a sentence); exchange	إِسْتَبْدَلَ
brothers, brethren	إِخْوَانٌ		
recently	أَخِيرًا	make s.o. serve, employ; use	إِسْتَخْدَمَ
directorship, administration	إِدَارَةٌ	rest, relax	إِسْتَرَاحَ
fulfil, discharge; pay, render	أَدَّى	consultation	إِسْتِشَارَةٌ
literature; good breeding	أَدَبٌ	be able	إِسْتَطَاعَ
since; when	إِذْ	ability, power	إِسْتِطَاعَةٌ
if; when	إِذَا	prepare	إِسْتَعَدَّ
therefore	إِذًا		

266

use (v.)	إِسْتَعْمَلَ	original	أَصْلِيّ
uprightness	إِسْتِقَامَةٌ	strike (labor)	إِضْرَابٌ
independence	إِسْتِقْلَالٌ	oblige, force	إِضْطَرَّ إِلَى
last, continue	إِسْتَمَرَّ	disturbance	إِضْطِرَابٌ
conquer	إِسْتَوْلَى عَلَى	fade away	إِضْمَحَلَّ
seizure	إِسْتِيلَاءٌ	be assured	إِطْمَأَنَّ
lion	أَسَدٌ	restore, return, give back	أَعَادَ
found (v.)	أَسَّسَ	consider	إِعْتَبَرَ
Istanbul	إِسْطَمْبُولُ	moderation	إِعْتِدَالٌ
Alexandria	الْإِسْكَنْدَرِيَّةُ	recognition	إِعْتِرَافٌ
Islam	الْإِسْلَامُ	block, oppose	إِعْتَرَضَ
Islamic	إِسْلَامِيّ	recognize	إِعْتَرَفَ
name; noun	إِسْم	believe	إِعْتَقَدَ
black	أَسْوَدُ	rely on	إِعْتَمَدَ
prisoner	أَسِيرٌ	execution (i.e. capital punishment)	إِعْدَامٌ
grow stronger	إِشْتَدَّ	give	أَعْطَى
participation, joining; subscription	إِشْتِرَاكٌ	announce	أَعْلَنَ
participate, join; subscribe	إِشْتَرَكَ	deeds, actions	أَعْمَالٌ
		assassination	إِغْتِيَالٌ
months	أَشْهُر	better, best	أَفْضَلُ
become	أَصْبَحَ	set up, establish	أَقَامَ
friends	أَصْدِقَاءُ	perform prayer	أَقَامَ الصَّلَاةَ
insistence	إِصْرَارٌ	draw near to	إِقْتَرَبَ مِنْ
summering, estivage	إِصْطِيَافٌ	economy; economics	إِقْتِصَادٌ
origin, root	أَصْلٌ	honor (v.)	أَكْرَمَ
improvement, reform	إِصْلَاحٌ	except	إِلَّا

English	Arabic	English	Arabic
to	إِلَى	that (*conjunct.*)	أَنْ
meet (*v.*)	اِلْتَقَى	if (*conjunct.*)	إِنْ
who, which (*f.*)	اَلَّتِي	that (*conjunct.*)	أَنَّ
who, which (*m.*)	اَلَّذِي	verily; that (*conjunct.*)	إِنَّ
abolition	إِلْغَاء	prophets	أَنْبِيَاء
thousand	أَلْف	election	إِنْتِخَاب
deliver (e.g. speech)	أَلْقَى	elect	إِنْتَخَب
God	اَللّٰه	mandate	إِنْتِدَاب
Germany	اَلْمَانِيَا	spread (*v.*)	إِنْتَشَر
or	أَمْ	expect, await	إِنْتَظَر
mother	أُمّ	Andalusia	اَلْأَنْدَلُس
as for	أَمَّا	man (*generic*)	إِنْسَان
either	إِمَّا	withdrawal	إِنْسِحَاب
in front of	أَمَام	withdraw	إِنْسَحَب
concesion; preference	اِمْتِيَاز	split (*n.*)	إِنْشِقَاق
matter; order, command	أَمْر	leave; desist	إِنْصَرَفَ عَنْ
America	أَمْرِيكَا	spirits, souls, selves	أَنْفُس
yesterday	أَمْس	Ankara	أَنْقَرَة
become	أَمْسَى	divide (*intrans.*)	إِنْقَسَم
nations	أُمَم	obedience	إِنْقِيَاد
affairs, matters, things	أُمُور	break (*intrans.*)	إِنْكَسَر
prince; commander	أَمِير	English; an Englishman	إِنْكَلِيزِيّ
admiral	أَمِير الْبَحْر	pyramids	أَهْرَام
princess	أَمِيرَة	importance	أَهَمِّيَّة
faithful	أَمِين	orders, commands	أَوَامِر
nation	أُمَّة	middle, central	أَوْسَط

first (*m.*)	أَوَّلُ	orchard	بُسْتَانْ
first (*f.*)	أُولَى	mission (i.e. delegated body)	بَعْثَةُ
that is	أَيْ	after	بَعْدَ
whoever; any	أَيُّ	distance	بُعْدُ
days	أَيَّامُ	some; part	بَعْضُ
also	أَيْضًا	to some extent	بَعْضُ الشَّيْءِ
faith	إِيمَانْ	Baalbek	بَعْلَبَكَّ
where	أَيْنَ	distant, far	بَعِيدْ
wherever	أَيْنَمَا	Baghdad	بَغْدَادُ
ب		Biqāʿ (plain in Lebanon)	ٱلْبِقَاعُ
door, gate	بَابْ	remain	بَقِيَ (يَبْقَى)
Babylon	بَابِلُ	Bey (*title*)	بَكْ
Paris	بَارِيسُ	country, countries	بِلَادْ
pasha	بَاشَا	countries	بُلْدَانْ
mind, attention	بَالْ	town	بَلْدَةْ
study, investigation, discussion	بَحْثْ	reach, attain	بَلَغَ (يَبْلُغُ)
sea	بَحْرْ	building	بِنَاءْ
lake; name of an Egyptian *mudīrīyah*	بُحَيْرَةْ	girl, daughter	بِنْتْ
appear	بَدَا (يَبْدُو)	house	بَيْتْ
Bedouin	بَدَوِيّْ	Beirut	بَيْرُوتُ
Barada (river in Damascus)	بَرَدَى	between	بَيْنَ
blessing (*n.*)	بَرَكَةْ	while	بَيْنَمَا
parliament	بَرْلَمَانْ	houses	بُيُوتْ
prove	بَرْهَنَ	**ت**	
Britain	بَرِيطَانِيَا	influence	تَأْثِيرْ
orchards	بَسَاتِينْ	be delayed	تَأَخَّرَ

history	تَأْرِيخ	amending, amendment	تَعْدِيل
be founded	تَأَسَّس	education, instruction	تَعْلِيم
foundation, establishment	تَأْسِيس	undertaking; covenant	تَعَهُّد
consist of	تَأَلَّف مِنْ	advance, approach (v.)	تَقَدَّم
assuring, surety; insurance	تَأْمِين	traditionalism	تَقْلِيد
following, belonging to	تَابِع	speak	تَكَلَّم
following, coming after	تَالٍ (أَلتَّالِي)	telephone (n.)	تَلَفُون
exchange (v.)	تَبَادَل	that (demonstrative, f., s.)	تِلْكَ
follow	تَبِعَ (يَتْبَعُ)	representation	تَمْثِيل
pursuit	تَتَبُّع	organization	تَنْظِيم
study under, be student of	تَتَلْمَذَ عَلَى	reprimand (n.)	تَوْبِيخ
under, below	تَحْتَ	head (v., intrans.)	تَوَجَّه
emancipation, liberation	تَحْرِير	unification	تَوْحِيد
improve (intrans.)	تَحَسَّن	die	تُوُفِّي
realization; investigation	تَحْقِيق	signing	تَوْقِيع
changing (n.)	تَحْوِيل	assume rule	تَوَلَّى ٱلْحُكْمَ
belittling	تَخْفِيض	**ث**	
retreat (v.)	تَرَاجَع	second (ordinal)	ثَانٍ (أَلثَّانِي)
education	تَرْبِيَة	confidence	ثِقَة
translate, interpret	تَرْجَم	third (fraction)	ثُلْث
Turkey	تُرْكِيَّا	revolution, revolt	ثَوْرَة
evolution	تَطَوُّر	**ج**	
co-operate	تَعَاوَن	come	جَاءَ (يَجِيءُ)
co-operation	تَعَاوُن	current, proceeding	جَارٍ (أَلْجَارِي)
		dry	جَافّ

English	Arabic		English	Arabic
mosque	جَامِع		garden	جُنَيْنَة
university; league (i.e. confederation)	جَامِعَة		struggle, *jihād*	جِهَاد
side	جَانِب		atmosphere	جَوّ
mountains	جِبَال		army	جَيْش
mountain	جَبَل		**ح**	
grandfather	جَدّ		necessity, need	حَاجَة
new	جَدِيد		preserve, safeguard	حَافَظَ عَلَى
run, be current; happen	جَرَى (يَجْرِي)		ruler, governor	حَاكِم
newspapers	جَرَائِد		situation, state, condition	حَال
newspaper	جَرِيدَة		immediately	حَالاً
part, section; volume	جُزْء		condition	حَالَة
butcher	جَزَّار		love	حُبّ
island	جَزِيرَة		interest s.o. in	حَبَّ إِلَى
dryness	جَفَاف		dear, beloved	حَبِيب
majesty	جَلَالَة		until; so that; even	حَتَّى
sitting, session, meeting	جَلْسَة		pilgrimage	حَجّ
collect, gather	جَمَع (يَجْمَع)		modern; tradition of Muḥammad	حَدِيث
society (i.e. organization)	جَمْعِيَة		war	حَرْب
republic	جُمْهُورِيَة		liberate	حَرَّر
all, totality	جَمِيع		literal	حَرْفِيّ
beautiful	جَمِيل		movement	حَرَكَة
gardens	جَنَائِن		inviolability	حُرْمَة
south	جَنُوب		liberty	حُرِّيَة
southern	جَنُوبِيّ		party (*political*)	حِزْب
			be fine, pleasing	حَسُن (يَحْسُن)
			good, fine; handsome	حَسَن

English	Arabic	English	Arabic
attend, be present at	حَضَرَ (يَحْضُرُ)	autumn	خَرِيفٌ
presence, attendence	حُضُورٌ	fertile	خَصِيبٌ
preserve, protect; memorize	حَفِظَ (يَحْفَظُ)	speech, ovation	خِطَابٌ
preservation	حِفْظٌ	speak (i.e. make a speech)	خَطَبَ (يَخْطُبُ)
right; truth	حَقٌّ	light (adj., of weight)	خَفِيفٌ
rights, laws	حُقُوقٌ	create	خَلَقَ (يَخْلُقُ)
truth, fact, reality	حَقِيقَةٌ	creation	خَلْقٌ
judge; rule (v.)	حَكَمَ (يَحْكُمُ)	caliph	خَلِيفَةٌ
rule, government; judgement	حُكْمٌ		
government	حُكُومَةٌ	**د**	
dissolve, untie	حَلَّ (يَحُلُّ)	circle; department	دَائِرَةٌ
untying	حَلٌّ	interior (adj.)	دَاخِلِيٌّ
be sweet, please	حَلَا (يَحْلُو)	revolve	دَارَ (يَدُورُ)
Homs	حِمْصُ	house	دَارٌ
around, about	حَوْلَ	caller, advocate	دَاعٍ (الدَّاعِي)
turn, change	حَوَّلَ	defend	دَافَعَ
life	حَيَاةٌ	last, endure	دَامَ (يَدُومُ)
where	حَيْثُ	Tigris	دِجْلَةُ
wherever	حَيْثُمَا	enter, go into	دَخَلَ (يَدْخُلُ)
خ		step, degree, stage	دَرَجَةٌ
special	خَاصٌّ	study (n.)	دِرَاسَةٌ
service	خِدْمَةٌ	study (v.)	دَرَسَ (يَدْرُسُ)
Khedive (title)	خَدِيوِيٌّ	lesson	دَرْسٌ
leave, go out	خَرَجَ (يَخْرُجُ)	constitution	دُسْتُورٌ
irregular (f.)	خَرْقَاءُ	call, invite, advocate	دَعَا (يَدْعُو)
departure, emergence, exit	خُرُوجٌ	step on	دَعَسَ (يَدْعَسُ)

defense	دِفَاع	prime minister, premier	رَئِيسُ ٱلْوُزَرَاء
minute	دَقِيقَة	fourth (*ordinal*)	رَابِع
doctor	دُكْتُور	satisfied	رَاضٍ (ٱلرَّاضِي)
blood	دَم	accompany	رَافَقَ
Damascus	دِمَشْق	rider	رَاكِب
departments; circles	دَوَائِر	fourth (*fraction*)	رُبْع
states (i.e. nations)	دُوَل	spring (season)	رَبِيع
state (i.e. nation); Excellency	دَوْلَة	hope (*v.*)	رَجَا (يَرْجُو)
without; below	دُونَ	men	رِجَال
religion	دِين	return (*v.*)	رَجَعَ (يَرْجِعُ)
religious	دِينِيّ	reactionary	رَجْعِيّ
ذ		man	رَجُل
one possessing *or* having (*f.*); essence	ذَاتُ	return (*n.*)	رُجُوع
that (*demonstrative, m., s.*)	ذٰلِكَ	have mercy	رَحِمَ (يَرْحَمُ)
go	ذَهَبَ (يَذْهَبُ)	Merciful (i.e. God)	رَحْمٰن
gold	ذَهَب	official (*adj.*)	رَسْمِيّ
golden	ذَهَبِيّ	messenger, apostle	رَسُول
one possessing *or* having (*m.*)	ذُو	desire	رَغْبَة
Dhu al-Ḥijjah	ذُو ٱلْحِجَّة	kindness	رِفْق
ر		pillar, column	رُكْن
see	رَأَى (يَرَى)	spirit	رُوح
head (*n.*)	رَأْس	Byzantines	ٱلرُّوم
opinion	رَأْي	Roman	رُومَانِيّ
president	رَئِيس	Riyadh	ٱلرِّيَاض
chief of staff	رَئِيسُ أَرْكَانٍ	country, rural area	رِيف

happy	سَعِيدٌ		ز
become quiet, subside	سَكَتَ (يَسْكُتُ)	add	زَادَ (يَزِيدُ)
inhabit	سَكَنَ (يَسْكُنُ)	visit (v.)	زَارَ (يَزُورُ)
peace	سَلَامٌ	cease	زَالَ (يَزَالُ)
sultan	سُلْطَانٌ	creep; advance (v.)	زَحَفَ (يَزْحَفُ)
authority, power	سُلْطَةٌ	leaders	زُعَمَاءُ
name (v.)	سَمَّى	leader	زَعِيمٌ
heaven	سَمَاءٌ	asceticism	زُهْد
Samarkand	سَمَرْقَنْدُ	marriage	زَوَاج
highness	سُمُوّ	husband	زَوْج
tooth	سِنّ	wife	زَوْجَةٌ
year	سَنَةٌ	visit, visiting	زِيَارَةٌ
plain	سَهْل	oil	زَيْت
Syria	سُورِيَّةٌ		س
future particle	سَوْفَ	ask, question (v.)	سَأَلَ (يَسْأَلُ)
market, bazaar	سُوق	march (v.)	سَارَ (يَسِيرُ)
Suez	سُوِيس	aid (v.)	سَاعَدَ
automobile	سَيَّارَةٌ	hour	سَاعَةٌ
political	سِيَاسِيّ	travel (v.)	سَافَرَ
politics, policy	سِيَاسَةٌ	high	سَامٍ (السَّامِي)
master; mister	سَيِّدٌ	cause (v.)	سَبَّبَ
journey, course; functioning	سَيْر	"way," "path"; cause (i.e. sake)	سَبِيل
	ش	imprison	سَجَنَ (يَسْجُنُ)
Damascus	أَلشَّامُ	steal	سَرَقَ (يَسْرِقُ)
matter, affair; importance	شَأْن	fast, quick	سَرِيع
matters, affairs	شُؤُون	Saudi	سَعُودِيّ

street	شَارِعٌ	devil	شَيْطَانٌ
see, witness (*v.*)	شَاهَدَ	old men; senators	شُيُوخٌ
winter	شِتَاءٌ	**ص**	
courage	شَجَاعَةٌ	become	صَارَ (يَصِيرُ)
trees (*collect.*)	شَجَرٌ	morning	صَبَاحٌ
tree	شَجَرَةٌ	friend	صَدِيقٌ
encourage	شَجَّعَ	journalism	صِحَافَةٌ
personal	شَخْصِيٌّ	desert	صَحْرَاءُ
personality	شَخْصِيَّةٌ	true, accurate, sound	صَحِيحٌ
strong, violent, sharp	شَدِيدٌ	breast, chest	صَدْرٌ
extremeness, violence, tenacity	شِدَّةٌ	breasts, chests	صُدُورٌ
east	شَرْقٌ	girl friend	صَدِيقَةٌ
company	شَرِكَةٌ	spend (time, money, effort, *etc.*)	صَرَفَ (يَصْرِفُ)
law	شَرِيعَةٌ	be difficult	صَعُبَ (يَصْعُبُ)
people (*collect.*)	شَعْبٌ	difficult	صَعْبٌ
poetry	شِعْرٌ	younger, youngest; smaller, smallest (*f.*)	صُغْرَى
work (i.e. occupy a position)	شَغَلَ (يَشْغَلُ)	young, small	صَغِيرٌ
doubt (*v.*)	شَكَّ (يَشُكُّ)	page	صَفْحَةٌ
doubt (*n.*)	شَكٌّ	character, characteristic (*n.*)	صِفَةٌ
form (*v., trans.*)	شَكَّلَ	pray	صَلَّى
form, format, shape	شَكْلٌ	rectitude	صَلَاحٌ
smelling	شَمٌّ	prayer	صَلَاةٌ
north	شَمَالٌ	connection	صِلَةٌ
month	شَهْرٌ	picture	صُورَةٌ
old man, shaykh; senator	شَيْخٌ	summer	صَيْفٌ

	ض	live	عَاشَ (يَعِيشُ)
sacrifice s. th.	ضَحَّى بِ	tenth (*ordinal*)	عَاشِرٌ
sacrificial offering	ضَحِيَّةٌ	capital (of a country)	عَاصِمَةٌ
against, opposed to	ضِدَّ	punish	عَاقَبَ
weakness	ضَعْفٌ	world	عَالَمٌ
pressure	ضَغْطٌ	learned, knower, scholar	عَالِمٌ
	ط	year	عَامٌ
wander	طَافَ (يَطُوفُ)	general, common, public	عَامٌّ
circumambulate s.th.	طَافَ بِ	treat with	عَامَلَ
student	طَالِبٌ	usually	عَامَّةً
natural	طَبِيعِيٌّ	'Abd al-'Azīz	عَبْدُ الْعَزِيز
ways, roads; methods	طُرُقٌ	'Abdullāh	عَبْدُ اللهِ
way, road	طَرِيقٌ	Hebrew	عِبْرَانِيٌّ
childhood	طُفُولَةٌ	consider, count	عَدَّ (يَعُدُّ)
seek, ask, request	طَلَبَ (يَطْلُبُ)	number	عَدَدٌ
Ṭanṭa (town in Nile Delta)	طَنْطَا	justice	عَدْلٌ
long, tall	طَوِيلٌ	lack of, absence of	عَدَمٌ
airplane	طَيَّارَةٌ	numerous	عَدِيدٌ
	ظ	Iraq	أَلْعِرَاقُ
think	ظَنَّ (يَظُنُّ)	Arabs	عَرَبٌ
appearance	ظُهُورٌ	an Arab, Arabian, Arabic	عَرَبِيٌّ
	ع	Arabic language	أَلْعَرَبِيَّةُ
family	عَائِلَةٌ	know	عَرَفَ (يَعْرِفُ)
return, go back	عَادَ (يَعُودُ)	tie, bond	عُرْوَةٌ
just	عَادِلٌ	broad, wide	عَرِيضٌ
one resolved, one who wills	عَازِمٌ عَلَى		

will, decide, resolve	عَزَمَ (يَعْزِمُ) عَلَى	title; address	عُنْوَانٌ
dear; mighty	عَزِيزٌ	holiday, feast	عِيدٌ
military	عَسْكَرِيٌّ	appoint	عَيَّنَ
grand, magnificent	عَظِيمٌ	eye; spring of water	عَيْنٌ
tie, hold; convene	عَقَدَ (يَعْقِدُ)	**غ**	
tying, holding (e.g. meeting)	عَقْدٌ	angry	غَاضِبٌ
reason, intelligence	عَقْلٌ	west	غَرْبٌ
Acre	عَكَّا	room	غُرْفَةٌ
on, over	عَلَى	drown	غَرِقَ (يَغْرَقُ)
scholar	عَلَّامَةٌ	love (*adj.* of poetry)	غَزَلِيٌّ
know	عَلِمَ (يَعْلَمُ)	become angry	غَضِبَ (يَغْضَبُ)
teach	عَلَّمَ	anger	غَضَبٌ
flag	عَلَمٌ	other, except	غَيْرٌ
knowledge, science	عِلْمٌ	**ف**	
scholars, ulema	عُلَمَاءٌ	cavalier, knight	فَارِسٌ
sciences, disciplines	عُلُومٌ	failure (*act. part.*)	فَاشِلٌ
high position	عَلْيَاءُ	Fāḍil (*man's name*)	فَاضِلٌ
Amman	عَمَّانُ	open; conquer	فَتَحَ (يَفْتَحُ)
life (span)	عُمْرٌ	opening; conquest	فَتْحٌ
act, do	عَمِلَ (يَعْمَلُ)	rejoice	فَرِحَ (يَفْرَحُ)
action, deed	عَمَلٌ	mare	فَرَسٌ
active	عَمَلِيٌّ	group	فَرِيقٌ
from; concerning; away from	عَنْ	fail	فَشِلَ (يَفْشَلُ)
chez; with; at	عِنْدَ	season; division, section; chapter	فَصْلٌ
when	عِنْدَمَا		

seasons; divisions, sections; chapters	فُصُول	a little before	قُبَيْلَ
poor	فَقِير	kill	قَتَلَ (يَقْتُلُ)
farmer, peasant	فَلَّاح	before (*place*)	قُدَّام
so-and-so	فُلَان	sanctify	قَدَّسَ
Palestine	فَلَسْطِين	offer, present (*v.*)	قَدَّمَ
hotel	فُنْدُق	able	قَدِير
photographic	فُوتُوغْرَافِيّ	old (*of inanimate objects*), ancient	قَدِيم
in; concerning	فِي	read, recite	قَرَأَ (يَقْرَأُ)
while	فِيمَا	Koran	قُرْآن
		Koranic	قُرْآنِيّ
ق		resolution; decree	قَرَار
commander	قَائِد	village	قَرْيَة
sayer, saying	قَائِل	part, section	قِسْم
meet	قَابَلَ	set out for, head towards	قَصَدَ (يَقْصِدُ)
lead (*v.*)	قَادَ (يَقُودُ)	palace	قَصْر
able, capable	قَادِر	short	قَصِير
comer, coming	قَادِم	story	قِصَّة
judge	قَاضٍ (ٱلْقَاضِي)	decide, judge; spend (time); carry out	قَضَى (يَقْضِي)
say	قَالَ (يَقُولُ)	case, cause	قَضِيَّة
get up, stand up	قَامَ (يَقُومُ)		
Cairo	ٱلْقَاهِرَة	cut off	قَطَعَ (يَقْطَعُ)
tomb	قَبْر	heart	قَلْب
dome	قُبَّة	pull out	قَلَعَ (يَقْلَعُ)
before	قَبْلَ	canal	قَنَاة
before (*conjunct.*)	قَبْلَمَا	coffee	قَهْوَة
qiblah (direction of prayer)	قِبْلَة	talk, what is said	قَوْل

278

nationalism	قَوْمِيَّة	Kuwait	ٱلْكُوَيْت
leadership	قِيَادَة	in order that	كَيْ
		how?	كَيْفَ

ك

ل

as if	كَأَنَّ	because	لِأَنَّ
writer, scribe, clerk	كَاتِب	no, not	لَا
almost (*auxiliary verb*)	كَادَ (يَكَادُ)	continue ("not cease")	لَا يَزَالُ
al-Kāzimayn	ٱلْكَاظِمَيْن	loom (*v.*)	لَاحَ (يَلُوحُ)
sufficient	كَافٍ (ٱلْكَافِي)	Lebanon	لُبْنَان
whole, complete	كَامِل	committee	لَجْنَة
bigger, biggest; older, oldest (*f.*)	كُبْرَى	with, *chez*	لَدَى
		enjoyable, delicious	لَذِيذ
big; old	كَبِير	slap, strike (*v.*)	لَطَمَ (يَلْطِمُ)
book; letter	كِتَاب	play (*v.*)	لَعِبَ (يَلْعَبُ)
generous; glorious, noble	كَرِيم	playful	لَعُوب
break (*trans.*)	كَسَرَ (يَكْسِرُ)	language	لُغَة
lazy	كَسْلَان	meet; find	لَقِيَ (يَلْقَى)
Kaaba	كَعْبَة	but	لَكِنْ، لَكِنَّ
all; every	كُلّ	in order that	لِكَيْ
classical	كَلَاسِيكِيّ	not	لَمْ
talk	كَلَام	when	لَمَّا
dog	كَلْب	why?	لِمَاذَا
whenever	كُلَّمَا	will never	لَنْ
college; totality	كُلِّيَّة	London	لَنْدُن
how much? how many?	كَمْ	if	لَوْ
as	كَمَا	tablet	لَوْح

279

color	لَوْنٌ
would that!	لَيْتَ
not to be	لَيْسَ
night	لَيْلٌ
night, evening, eye	لَيْلَةٌ
linotype	لِينُوتِيبٌ

م

conference, congress	مُؤْتَمَرٌ
founder	مُؤَسِّسٌ
believer	مُؤْمِنٌ
hundred	مِئَةٌ
what (*relative*); not	مَا
water	مَاءٌ
past, last	مَاضٍ (اَلْمَاضِي)
tend, incline	مَالَ (يَمِيلُ)
act of swearing fealty	مُبَايَعَةٌ
showing, evidencing	مُبْدٍ (اَلْمُبْدِي)
when?; when (*conjunct.*)	مَتَى
united	مُتَّحِدٌ
lineally descended	مُتَحَدِّرٌ
devoted, self-sacrificing	مُتَفَانٍ (اَلْمُتَفَانِي)
example	مِثَالٌ
represent	مَثَّلَ
likeness	مِثْلٌ

patriot, striver	مُجَاهِدٌ
society (i.e. human environment)	مُجْتَمَعٌ
striver	مُجْتَهِدٌ
glory	مَجْدٌ
council, assembly	مَجْلِسٌ
magazine	مَجَلَّةٌ
madman, mad	مَجْنُونٌ
protégés	مَحَاسِيبُ
conservative; governor	مُحَافِظٌ
lawyer	مُحَامٍ (اَلْمُحَامِي)
lover	مُحِبٌّ
beloved, liked	مَحْبُوبٌ
needy	مُحْتَاجٌ
protester	مُحْتَجٌّ
editor; liberator	مُحَرِّرٌ
sanctified (*on pilgrimage*)	مُحْرِمٌ
protégé	مَحْسُوبٌ
preserved	مَحْفُوظٌ
various, varying	مُخْتَلِفٌ
manuscript	مَخْطُوطَةٌ
sincere, devoted	مُخْلِصٌ
schools	مَدَارِسُ
school	مَدْرَسَةٌ
cities	مُدُنٌ

civilization	مَدَنِيَّة	straight; upright	مُسْتَقِيم
manager, director	مُدِير	seizer	مُسْتَوْلٍ (الْمُسْتَوْلِي) عَلَى
directorate; province (Egyptian adm. district)	مُدِيرِيَّة	Muslim	مُسْلِم
city	مَدِينَة	problems	مَشَاكِل
Medina	الْمَدِينَة	common, shared	مُشْتَرَك
period (of time)	مُدَّة	participant; subscriber	مُشْتَرِك
pass (v.)	مَرَّ (يَمُرُّ)	encouraging	مُشَجِّع
woman	مَرْأَة	plan, project, program	مَشْرُوع
mirror	مِرْآة	problem	مُشْكِلَة
aim, intention	مُرَاد	famous	مَشْهُور
reporter, correspondent	مُرَاسِل	Egypt	مِصْر
late, deceased	مَرْحُوم	Egyptian	مِصْرِيّ
center, seat	مَرْكَز	reformer	مُصْلِح
time (i.e. a time)	مَرَّة	interest, benefit	مَصْلَحَة
responsibility	مَسْؤُولِيَّة	airport	مَطَار
traveler	مُسَافِر	demands	مَطَالِب
approving	مُسْتَحْسِن	demand (n.)	مَطْلَب
relaxed	مُسْتَرِيح	with	مَعَ
consultant, advisor; chancellor	مُسْتَشَار	although	مَعَ أَنَّ
possible	مُسْتَطَاع	opposition	مُعَارَضَة
colonialized	مُسْتَعْمَر	factories	مَعَامِل
colony	مُسْتَعْمَرَة	treaty	مُعَاهَدَة
future	مُسْتَقْبِل	assistant	مُعَاوِن
independent	مُسْتَقِلّ	temple	مَعْبَد

Mu'tazilah school of thought	مُعْتَزِلَة	occasion	مُنَاسَبَة
numbered, limited, few	مَعْدُود	dispute, debate	مُنَاقَشَة
known	مَعْرُوف	organization, club	مُنْتَدًى
most, majority	مُعْظَم	spread out (adj.)	مُنْتَشِر
teacher	مُعَلِّم	grant (v.)	مَنَح (يَمْنَح)
factory	مَعْمَل	commissioner, representative	مَنْدُوب
in force	مَعْمُول ب	since	مُنْذُ
negotiation	مُفَاوَضَة	position, job, post	مَنْصِب
mufti	مُفْتٍ (الْمُفْتِي)	forbid, prevent	مَنَع (يَمْنَع)
vis-à-vis	مُقَابِل	divided	مُنْقَسِم
position, place	مَقَام	illuminated	مُنَوَّر
killed	مَقْتُول	emigrant	مُهَاجِر
holy	مُقَدَّس	attack (n.)	مُهَاجَمَة
offices	مَكَاتِب	important	مُهِمّ
place	مَكَان	whatever	مَهْمَا
office	مَكْتَب	citizen	مُوَاطِن
library	مَكْتَبَة	death	مَوْت
honored	مُكَرَّم	weighed (adj.)	مَوْزُون
disliked	مَكْرُوه	employee	مُوَظَّف
king	مَلِك	appointed time, appointment	مَوْعِد
stretching	مُمْتَدّ	stand, position	مَوْقِف
representative	مُمَثِّل	covenant, charter	مِيثَاق
from, of, among	مِنْ	field, square (i.e. in a city)	مَيْدَان
he who, whoever	مَنْ	scales, balance	مِيزَان
suitable	مُنَاسِب	budget	مِيزَانِيَّة
		Christian (era)	مِيلَادِيّ

ن

deputy, member of parliament	نَائِب
club	نَادٍ (اَلنَّادِي)
fire	نَارُ
people	نَاس
suit (*v.*)	نَاسَبَ
obtain	نَالَ (يَنَالُ)
prophet	نَبِيُّ
result	نَتِيجَةُ
Nejd	نَجْد
Nejdi	نَجْدِيُّ
towards; approximately	نَحْوَ
descend, alight, stop	نَزَلَ (يَنْزِلُ)
descent	نُزُولُ
copy (*n.*)	نُسْخَةُ
forget	نَسِيَ (يَنْسَى)
breeze	نَسِيم
text	نَصّ
Christian ("Nazarene")	نَصْرَانِيُّ
speak, utter	نَطَقَ (يَنْطِقُ)
look at	نَظَرَ (يَنْظُرُ)
looking (*n.*)	نَظَر
theory	نَظَرِيَّةُ
compose (e.g. poetry), put together	نَظَّمَ (يَنْظِمُ)
yes	نَعَمْ

spirit, soul, self	نَفْس
banishment	نَفْي
transport, move, convey; translate	نَقَلَ (يَنْقُلُ)
river	نَهْر
light	نُور
Nile	اَلنِّيل

these	هٰؤُلَاءِ
bewildered	هَائِم
these (*dual, f.*)	هَاتَانِ، هَاتَيْنِ
emigrate	هَاجَرَ
this (*m.*)	هٰذَا
this (*f.*)	هٰذِهِ
Hijrah	هِجْرَةُ
interrogative particle	هَلْ
crescent	هِلَال
there	هُنَاكَ، هُنَالِكَ
Hind (girl's name)	هِنْد

و

confident, sure	وَاثِق
duty	وَاجِب
wadi, valley, gulch	وَادٍ (اَلْوَادِي)
wide, extensive	وَاسِع
agree with	وَافَقَ
real, actual	وَاقِع

father	وَالِدٌ	arrival	وُصُولٌ
stronger, strongest; indissoluble (f.)	وُثْقَى	country, homeland	وَطَنٌ
be necessary, be incumbent on	وَجَبَ (يَجِبُ) عَلَى	post, position, job	وَظِيفَةٌ
direct s.th. towards	وَجَّهَ	delegation	وَفْدٌ
face (n.)	وَجْهٌ	events	وَقَائِعُ
existence	وُجُودٌ	fall; occur	وَقَعَ (يَقَعُ)
unity	وَحْدَةٌ	halt (n.)	وُقُوفٌ
desire, liking, affection	وُدٌّ	bear, beget	وَلَدَ (يَلِدُ)
cordial	وُدِّيٌّ	boy; child	وَلَدٌ
behind	وَرَاءَ	follow (i.e. be immediately after)	وَلِيَ (يَلِي)
ministry (in government)	وِزَارَةٌ		
ministers (in government)	وُزَرَاءُ	ي	
weigh	وَزَنَ (يَزِنُ)	despair (v.)	يَئِسَ (يَيْأَسُ)
minister (in government)	وَزِيرٌ	Jaffa	يَافَا
middle, central (f.)	وُسْطَى	Yathrib	يَثْرِبُ
whisper (v.)	وَسْوَسَ	hand	يَدٌ
arrive; connect	وَصَلَ (يَصِلُ)	day	يَوْمٌ

284

ENGLISH INDEX

Under the entry, Verb, the main sub-entries are italicized and are immediately followed by the items subordinate to the sub-entry.

'Ā' id, 55, 61, 101
Abstract nisbah, 82
Absolute object, 143
Accent: of word, 10, 19; in sentences, 19
Accusative: sign of, 52; for object of verb, 52; for subject of sentence introduced by *inna*, 55–56, 57, 58; adverbs, 55, 56, 62, 63, 67, 76, 86, 114, 143; for object of active participle, 57, 144; for predicate of *kāna* and its sisters, 74–78, 143; of dual, 86; of sound masculine plural, 91; of sound feminine plural, 92; of purpose, 114, 143; imperfect verb used as accusative of purpose, 170; for absolute object, 143; for object of *maṣdar*, 142; after vocative, 143; of specification, 144; after *lā* of complete negation, 144; after *illā*, 147 n. 2. *See also* Adverb
Active participle: 22, 27; used as proper name, 30; used adjectivally, 36; of doubled verb, 40, 56; of hollow verb, 56–57; of hollow verb, Form X, 115; verbal force of, 57, 144; direct object of, 57, 144; of derived forms, 75–77, 77 (list), 115; of weak lām verb, 116; of quadriliteral verb, 161
Adjective: 22, 26, 35–37, 56; used as noun, 27, 29; agreement with

singular nouns, 35, 36, 52; patterns, 37; nisbah, 36, 44, 82, 86; formation of nisbah with tā' marbūṭah word, 36; feminine of nisbah, 82; comparative, 47–48; superlative, 48; agreement with plural noun, 92, 100; of hollow verbs, 129; position in construct phrase, 171
Adverb: of time or place, used as preposition, 44, 45 (list), 143; invariable, 52, 63. *See also* Accusative, 90; of time, 55, 56; of time in dual, 86; of manner, 56, 62, 63, 67, 76, 143; of purpose, 114, 143; imperfect verb used as adverb of purpose, 170; conjunctive, 155; imperfect verb as adverb of manner, 170; nominal clause as adverb of manner, 171
Adverbs, 22–23, 44
Affirmation, particle of, 163. *See also* Particle, assertive
Agreement: of adjective with noun, 35, 36, 52; of verb with subject, 86, 91, 96–97; of adjective with sound feminine plural, 92; of adjective with broken plural, 100; of verb with broken plural, 101
Alif: as chair for hamzah, 3 n. 1, 14–15; "dagger", 15, 56; with maddah, 15; final, 16; maqṣūrah, 16; alif at end of plural verb, 91
Alphabet, the Arabic, 3, 8–9

Relative clause: 55, 56, 57, 96, 101; with indefinite antecedent, 43–44; use of 'ā'id in, 61; imperfect verb in, 170

Relative pronoun, 57–58 (list), 162

Reflexive verbs, 61, 62

Root: triconsonantal, 20; quadriliteral, 161–162

Repeated action, 172

Sentence: conditional, 124, 162–163; used as adverb of manner, 171; nominal, see Nominal sentence; verbal, see Verbal sentence

Sentence structure, 23–24

Shaddah, 11, 17

Sharṭ of conditional sentences, 162–163

Sisters of kāna, 75–76, 77–78 (list), 144

Sisters of inna, 58 (list)

Specification, accusative of, 144

Subject of nominal sentence: 23–24, 26, 29, 30, 32, 35, 36, 39; following predicate, 24 and n. 6, 43, 44; introduced by subordinate conjunction, 55–56, 91; introduced by assertive particle, 57

Subject of verb, see Sentence, verbal, subject of

Subjunctive mood: 121; of dual and plural, 122; conjugation, Form I, 123; conjunctions requiring, 123 (list)

Subordinate conjunction, see Conjunction, subordinate

Sukūn, 7

"Sun" letters, 17, 18

Superlative, 48

Syllable: open, 10; closed, 10; with

vowel lengthener, 12; diphthong as, 13; accent with, 19

Syntax, see Sentence structure

Tā' marbūṭah: 6, 29, 30; in nisbah adjective, 36; followed by pronominal suffix, 40

Tanwīn, see Nūnation

Tense, see Imperfect tense, Perfect tense, Past, and Aspect

Terminology, grammatical, 20–21

To be, absence of in declarative sentence, 26

To begin, auxiliary verbs used to mean, 171

Triconsonantal root, 20

Triptotes, 47–48

Verb: 21; derived forms, 21, 61–63; perfect of derived forms, 65–66; maṣdars of derived forms, 72 (list); derived forms of weak-lām verbs, 108–109; derived forms of hollow verbs, 109; imperative of derived forms, 129–130; perfect passive of derived forms, 136–137; doubled, 40, 62, 97, 136–137; active participle of doubled, 56; imperfect passive of doubled, 137; subject of, 23–24, 51–53, 86; hidden subject of, 52, 53; transitive, 52; object of transitive, 52; hollow, 52, 55, 65–66, 109; active participle of hollow, 56–57; underived hollow, 109; conjugation of derived hollow, 109; maṣdars of hollow verbs of Forms IV, VII, VIII, X, 114–115; active and passive participles of hollow verbs of Forms IV, X, 114–115; jussive of hollow, 122; adjectival

ARABIC INDEX

Words are alphabetized according to spelling, not by root. Left hand column precedes right. In alphabetizing, hamzah precedes alif, ـَى is treated as yā'; shaddah is disregarded; where the consonants are the same, the arrangement of words is based on the vowel order: a i u. Items cited in terms of فعل may refer either to the pattern *per se* or to a derivation on that pattern from a weak root.

تم الكتاب بعونه تعالى

A CATALOG OF SELECTED
DOVER BOOKS
IN ALL FIELDS OF INTEREST

A CATALOG OF SELECTED DOVER
BOOKS IN ALL FIELDS OF INTEREST

CONCERNING THE SPIRITUAL IN ART, Wassily Kandinsky. Pioneering work by father of abstract art. Thoughts on color theory, nature of art. Analysis of earlier masters. 12 illustrations. 80pp. of text. 5⅜ x 8½. 23411-8

ANIMALS: 1,419 Copyright-Free Illustrations of Mammals, Birds, Fish, Insects, etc., Jim Harter (ed.). Clear wood engravings present, in extremely lifelike poses, over 1,000 species of animals. One of the most extensive pictorial sourcebooks of its kind. Captions. Index. 284pp. 9 x 12. 23766-4

CELTIC ART: The Methods of Construction, George Bain. Simple geometric techniques for making Celtic interlacements, spirals, Kells-type initials, animals, humans, etc. Over 500 illustrations. 160pp. 9 x 12. (Available in U.S. only.) 22923-8

AN ATLAS OF ANATOMY FOR ARTISTS, Fritz Schider. Most thorough reference work on art anatomy in the world. Hundreds of illustrations, including selections from works by Vesalius, Leonardo, Goya, Ingres, Michelangelo, others. 593 illustrations. 192pp. 7⅛ x 10¼. 20241-0

CELTIC HAND STROKE-BY-STROKE (Irish Half-Uncial from "The Book of Kells"): An Arthur Baker Calligraphy Manual, Arthur Baker. Complete guide to creating each letter of the alphabet in distinctive Celtic manner. Covers hand position, strokes, pens, inks, paper, more. Illustrated. 48pp. 8¼ x 11. 24336-2

EASY ORIGAMI, John Montroll. Charming collection of 32 projects (hat, cup, pelican, piano, swan, many more) specially designed for the novice origami hobbyist. Clearly illustrated easy-to-follow instructions insure that even beginning papercrafters will achieve successful results. 48pp. 8¼ x 11. 27298-2

THE COMPLETE BOOK OF BIRDHOUSE CONSTRUCTION FOR WOODWORKERS, Scott D. Campbell. Detailed instructions, illustrations, tables. Also data on bird habitat and instinct patterns. Bibliography. 3 tables. 63 illustrations in 15 figures. 48pp. 5¼ x 8½. 24407-5

BLOOMINGDALE'S ILLUSTRATED 1886 CATALOG: Fashions, Dry Goods and Housewares, Bloomingdale Brothers. Famed merchants' extremely rare catalog depicting about 1,700 products: clothing, housewares, firearms, dry goods, jewelry, more. Invaluable for dating, identifying vintage items. Also, copyright-free graphics for artists, designers. Co-published with Henry Ford Museum & Greenfield Village. 160pp. 8¼ x 11. 25780-0

HISTORIC COSTUME IN PICTURES, Braun & Schneider. Over 1,450 costumed figures in clearly detailed engravings—from dawn of civilization to end of 19th century. Captions. Many folk costumes. 256pp. 8⅜ x 11¾. 23150-X

CATALOG OF DOVER BOOKS

PERSPECTIVE FOR ARTISTS, Rex Vicat Cole. Depth, perspective of sky and sea, shadows, much more, not usually covered. 391 diagrams, 81 reproductions of drawings and paintings. 279pp. 5⅜ x 8½. 22487-2

DRAWING THE LIVING FIGURE, Joseph Sheppard. Innovative approach to artistic anatomy focuses on specifics of surface anatomy, rather than muscles and bones. Over 170 drawings of live models in front, back and side views, and in widely varying poses. Accompanying diagrams. 177 illustrations. Introduction. Index. 144pp. 8⅜ x11¼. 26723-7

GOTHIC AND OLD ENGLISH ALPHABETS: 100 Complete Fonts, Dan X. Solo. Add power, elegance to posters, signs, other graphics with 100 stunning copyright-free alphabets: Blackstone, Dolbey, Germania, 97 more—including many lower-case, numerals, punctuation marks. 104pp. 8⅛ x 11. 24695-7

HOW TO DO BEADWORK, Mary White. Fundamental book on craft from simple projects to five-bead chains and woven works. 106 illustrations. 142pp. 5⅜ x 8. 20697-1

THE BOOK OF WOOD CARVING, Charles Marshall Sayers. Finest book for beginners discusses fundamentals and offers 34 designs. "Absolutely first rate . . . well thought out and well executed."—E. J. Tangerman. 118pp. 7¾ x 10⅝. 23654-4

ILLUSTRATED CATALOG OF CIVIL WAR MILITARY GOODS: Union Army Weapons, Insignia, Uniform Accessories, and Other Equipment, Schuyler, Hartley, and Graham. Rare, profusely illustrated 1846 catalog includes Union Army uniform and dress regulations, arms and ammunition, coats, insignia, flags, swords, rifles, etc. 226 illustrations. 160pp. 9 x 12. 24939-5

WOMEN'S FASHIONS OF THE EARLY 1900s: An Unabridged Republication of "New York Fashions, 1909," National Cloak & Suit Co. Rare catalog of mail-order fashions documents women's and children's clothing styles shortly after the turn of the century. Captions offer full descriptions, prices. Invaluable resource for fashion, costume historians. Approximately 725 illustrations. 128pp. 8⅜ x 11¼. 27276-1

THE 1912 AND 1915 GUSTAV STICKLEY FURNITURE CATALOGS, Gustav Stickley. With over 200 detailed illustrations and descriptions, these two catalogs are essential reading and reference materials and identification guides for Stickley furniture. Captions cite materials, dimensions and prices. 112pp. 6½ x 9¼. 26676-1

EARLY AMERICAN LOCOMOTIVES, John H. White, Jr. Finest locomotive engravings from early 19th century: historical (1804–74), main-line (after 1870), special, foreign, etc. 147 plates. 142pp. 11⅜ x 8¼. 22772-3

THE TALL SHIPS OF TODAY IN PHOTOGRAPHS, Frank O. Braynard. Lavishly illustrated tribute to nearly 100 majestic contemporary sailing vessels: Amerigo Vespucci, Clearwater, Constitution, Eagle, Mayflower, Sea Cloud, Victory, many more. Authoritative captions provide statistics, background on each ship. 190 black-and-white photographs and illustrations. Introduction. 128pp. 8⅞ x 11¾. 27163-3

LITTLE BOOK OF EARLY AMERICAN CRAFTS AND TRADES, Peter Stockham (ed.). 1807 children's book explains crafts and trades: baker, hatter, cooper, potter, and many others. 23 copperplate illustrations. 140pp. 4⅝ x 6. 23336-7

VICTORIAN FASHIONS AND COSTUMES FROM HARPER'S BAZAR, 1867–1898, Stella Blum (ed.). Day costumes, evening wear, sports clothes, shoes, hats, other accessories in over 1,000 detailed engravings. 320pp. 9⅜ x 12¼. 22990-4

GUSTAV STICKLEY, THE CRAFTSMAN, Mary Ann Smith. Superb study surveys broad scope of Stickley's achievement, especially in architecture. Design philosophy, rise and fall of the Craftsman empire, descriptions and floor plans for many Craftsman houses, more. 86 black-and-white halftones. 31 line illustrations. Introduction 208pp. 6½ x 9¼. 27210-9

THE LONG ISLAND RAIL ROAD IN EARLY PHOTOGRAPHS, Ron Ziel. Over 220 rare photos, informative text document origin (1844) and development of rail service on Long Island. Vintage views of early trains, locomotives, stations, passengers, crews, much more. Captions. 8⅞ x 11¾. 26301-0

VOYAGE OF THE LIBERDADE, Joshua Slocum. Great 19th-century mariner's thrilling, first-hand account of the wreck of his ship off South America, the 35-foot boat he built from the wreckage, and its remarkable voyage home. 128pp. 5⅜ x 8½. 40022-0

TEN BOOKS ON ARCHITECTURE, Vitruvius. The most important book ever written on architecture. Early Roman aesthetics, technology, classical orders, site selection, all other aspects. Morgan translation. 331pp. 5⅜ x 8½. 20645-9

THE HUMAN FIGURE IN MOTION, Eadweard Muybridge. More than 4,500 stopped-action photos, in action series, showing undraped men, women, children jumping, lying down, throwing, sitting, wrestling, carrying, etc. 390pp. 7⅞ x 10⅝. 20204-6 Clothbd.

TREES OF THE EASTERN AND CENTRAL UNITED STATES AND CANADA, William M. Harlow. Best one-volume guide to 140 trees. Full descriptions, woodlore, range, etc. Over 600 illustrations. Handy size. 288pp. 4½ x 6⅜. 20395-6

SONGS OF WESTERN BIRDS, Dr. Donald J. Borror. Complete song and call repertoire of 60 western species, including flycatchers, juncoes, cactus wrens, many more—includes fully illustrated booklet. Cassette and manual 99913-0

GROWING AND USING HERBS AND SPICES, Milo Miloradovich. Versatile handbook provides all the information needed for cultivation and use of all the herbs and spices available in North America. 4 illustrations. Index. Glossary. 236pp. 5⅜ x 8½. 25058-X

BIG BOOK OF MAZES AND LABYRINTHS, Walter Shepherd. 50 mazes and labyrinths in all—classical, solid, ripple, and more—in one great volume. Perfect inexpensive puzzler for clever youngsters. Full solutions. 112pp. 8⅛ x 11. 22951-3

PIANO TUNING, J. Cree Fischer. Clearest, best book for beginner, amateur. Simple repairs, raising dropped notes, tuning by easy method of flattened fifths. No previous skills needed. 4 illustrations. 201pp. 5⅜ x 8½. 23267-0

HINTS TO SINGERS, Lillian Nordica. Selecting the right teacher, developing confidence, overcoming stage fright, and many other important skills receive thoughtful discussion in this indispensible guide, written by a world-famous diva of four decades' experience. 96pp. 5⅜ x 8½. 40094-8

THE COMPLETE NONSENSE OF EDWARD LEAR, Edward Lear. All nonsense limericks, zany alphabets, Owl and Pussycat, songs, nonsense botany, etc., illustrated by Lear. Total of 320pp. 5⅜ x 8½. (Available in U.S. only.) 20167-8

VICTORIAN PARLOUR POETRY: An Annotated Anthology, Michael R. Turner. 117 gems by Longfellow, Tennyson, Browning, many lesser-known poets. "The Village Blacksmith," "Curfew Must Not Ring Tonight," "Only a Baby Small," dozens more, often difficult to find elsewhere. Index of poets, titles, first lines. xxiii + 325pp. 5⅝ x 8¼. 27044-0

DUBLINERS, James Joyce. Fifteen stories offer vivid, tightly focused observations of the lives of Dublin's poorer classes. At least one, "The Dead," is considered a masterpiece. Reprinted complete and unabridged from standard edition. 160pp. 5$\frac{3}{16}$ x 8¼. 26870-5

GREAT WEIRD TALES: 14 Stories by Lovecraft, Blackwood, Machen and Others, S. T. Joshi (ed.). 14 spellbinding tales, including "The Sin Eater," by Fiona McLeod, "The Eye Above the Mantel," by Frank Belknap Long, as well as renowned works by R. H. Barlow, Lord Dunsany, Arthur Machen, W. C. Morrow and eight other masters of the genre. 256pp. 5⅜ x 8½. (Available in U.S. only.) 40436-6

THE BOOK OF THE SACRED MAGIC OF ABRAMELIN THE MAGE, translated by S. MacGregor Mathers. Medieval manuscript of ceremonial magic. Basic document in Aleister Crowley, Golden Dawn groups. 268pp. 5⅜ x 8½. 23211-5

NEW RUSSIAN-ENGLISH AND ENGLISH-RUSSIAN DICTIONARY, M. A. O'Brien. This is a remarkably handy Russian dictionary, containing a surprising amount of information, including over 70,000 entries. 366pp. 4½ x 6⅛. 20208-9

HISTORIC HOMES OF THE AMERICAN PRESIDENTS, Second, Revised Edition, Irvin Haas. A traveler's guide to American Presidential homes, most open to the public, depicting and describing homes occupied by every American President from George Washington to George Bush. With visiting hours, admission charges, travel routes. 175 photographs. Index. 160pp. 8¼ x 11. 26751-2

NEW YORK IN THE FORTIES, Andreas Feininger. 162 brilliant photographs by the well-known photographer, formerly with *Life* magazine. Commuters, shoppers, Times Square at night, much else from city at its peak. Captions by John von Hartz. 181pp. 9¼ x 10¾. 23585-8

INDIAN SIGN LANGUAGE, William Tomkins. Over 525 signs developed by Sioux and other tribes. Written instructions and diagrams. Also 290 pictographs. 111pp. 6⅛ x 9¼. 22029-X

ANATOMY: A Complete Guide for Artists, Joseph Sheppard. A master of figure drawing shows artists how to render human anatomy convincingly. Over 460 illustrations. 224pp. 8⅜ x 11¼.   27279-6

MEDIEVAL CALLIGRAPHY: Its History and Technique, Marc Drogin. Spirited history, comprehensive instruction manual covers 13 styles (ca. 4th century through 15th). Excellent photographs; directions for duplicating medieval techniques with modern tools. 224pp. 8⅜ x 11¼.   26142-5

DRIED FLOWERS: How to Prepare Them, Sarah Whitlock and Martha Rankin. Complete instructions on how to use silica gel, meal and borax, perlite aggregate, sand and borax, glycerine and water to create attractive permanent flower arrangements. 12 illustrations. 32pp. 5⅜ x 8½.   21802-3

EASY-TO-MAKE BIRD FEEDERS FOR WOODWORKERS, Scott D. Campbell. Detailed, simple-to-use guide for designing, constructing, caring for and using feeders. Text, illustrations for 12 classic and contemporary designs. 96pp. 5⅜ x 8½.
25847-5

SCOTTISH WONDER TALES FROM MYTH AND LEGEND, Donald A. Mackenzie. 16 lively tales tell of giants rumbling down mountainsides, of a magic wand that turns stone pillars into warriors, of gods and goddesses, evil hags, powerful forces and more. 240pp. 5⅜ x 8½.   29677-6

THE HISTORY OF UNDERCLOTHES, C. Willett Cunnington and Phyllis Cunnington. Fascinating, well-documented survey covering six centuries of English undergarments, enhanced with over 100 illustrations: 12th-century laced-up bodice, footed long drawers (1795), 19th-century bustles, 19th-century corsets for men, Victorian "bust improvers," much more. 272pp. 5⅜ x 8¼.   27124-2

ARTS AND CRAFTS FURNITURE: The Complete Brooks Catalog of 1912, Brooks Manufacturing Co. Photos and detailed descriptions of more than 150 now very collectible furniture designs from the Arts and Crafts movement depict davenports, settees, buffets, desks, tables, chairs, bedsteads, dressers and more, all built of solid, quarter-sawed oak. Invaluable for students and enthusiasts of antiques, Americana and the decorative arts. 80pp. 6½ x 9¼.   27471-3

WILBUR AND ORVILLE: A Biography of the Wright Brothers, Fred Howard. Definitive, crisply written study tells the full story of the brothers' lives and work. A vividly written biography, unparalleled in scope and color, that also captures the spirit of an extraordinary era. 560pp. 6⅛ x 9¼.   40297-5

THE ARTS OF THE SAILOR: Knotting, Splicing and Ropework, Hervey Garrett Smith. Indispensable shipboard reference covers tools, basic knots and useful hitches; handsewing and canvas work, more. Over 100 illustrations. Delightful reading for sea lovers. 256pp. 5⅜ x 8½.   26440-8

FRANK LLOYD WRIGHT'S FALLINGWATER: The House and Its History, Second, Revised Edition, Donald Hoffmann. A total revision—both in text and illustrations—of the standard document on Fallingwater, the boldest, most personal architectural statement of Wright's mature years, updated with valuable new material from the recently opened Frank Lloyd Wright Archives. "Fascinating"—*The New York Times*. 116 illustrations. 128pp. 9¼ x 10¾.   27430-6

CATALOG OF DOVER BOOKS

THE STORY OF THE TITANIC AS TOLD BY ITS SURVIVORS, Jack Winocour (ed.). What it was really like. Panic, despair, shocking inefficiency, and a little heroism. More thrilling than any fictional account. 26 illustrations. 320pp. 5⅜ x 8½. 20610-6

FAIRY AND FOLK TALES OF THE IRISH PEASANTRY, William Butler Yeats (ed.). Treasury of 64 tales from the twilight world of Celtic myth and legend: "The Soul Cages," "The Kildare Pooka," "King O'Toole and his Goose," many more. Introduction and Notes by W. B. Yeats. 352pp. 5⅜ x 8½. 26941-8

BUDDHIST MAHAYANA TEXTS, E. B. Cowell and others (eds.). Superb, accurate translations of basic documents in Mahayana Buddhism, highly important in history of religions. The Buddha-karita of Asvaghosha, Larger Sukhavativyuha, more. 448pp. 5⅜ x 8½. 25552-2

ONE TWO THREE . . . INFINITY: Facts and Speculations of Science, George Gamow. Great physicist's fascinating, readable overview of contemporary science: number theory, relativity, fourth dimension, entropy, genes, atomic structure, much more. 128 illustrations. Index. 352pp. 5⅜ x 8½. 25664-2

EXPERIMENTATION AND MEASUREMENT, W. J. Youden. Introductory manual explains laws of measurement in simple terms and offers tips for achieving accuracy and minimizing errors. Mathematics of measurement, use of instruments, experimenting with machines. 1994 edition. Foreword. Preface. Introduction. Epilogue. Selected Readings. Glossary. Index. Tables and figures. 128pp. 5⅜ x 8½. 40451-X

DALÍ ON MODERN ART: The Cuckolds of Antiquated Modern Art, Salvador Dalí. Influential painter skewers modern art and its practitioners. Outrageous evaluations of Picasso, Cézanne, Turner, more. 15 renderings of paintings discussed. 44 calligraphic decorations by Dalí. 96pp. 5⅜ x 8½. (Available in U.S. only.) 29220-7

ANTIQUE PLAYING CARDS: A Pictorial History, Henry René D'Allemagne. Over 900 elaborate, decorative images from rare playing cards (14th–20th centuries): Bacchus, death, dancing dogs, hunting scenes, royal coats of arms, players cheating, much more. 96pp. 9¼ x 12¼. 29265-7

MAKING FURNITURE MASTERPIECES: 30 Projects with Measured Drawings, Franklin H. Gottshall. Step-by-step instructions, illustrations for constructing handsome, useful pieces, among them a Sheraton desk, Chippendale chair, Spanish desk, Queen Anne table and a William and Mary dressing mirror. 224pp. 8⅛ x 11¼. 29338-6

THE FOSSIL BOOK: A Record of Prehistoric Life, Patricia V. Rich et al. Profusely illustrated definitive guide covers everything from single-celled organisms and dinosaurs to birds and mammals and the interplay between climate and man. Over 1,500 illustrations. 760pp. 7½ x 10⅛. 29371-8

Paperbound unless otherwise indicated. Available at your book dealer, online at **www.doverpublications.com**, or by writing to Dept. GI, Dover Publications, Inc., 31 East 2nd Street, Mineola, NY 11501. For current price information or for free catalogues (please indicate field of interest), write to Dover Publications or log on to **www.doverpublications.com** and see every Dover book in print. Dover publishes more than 500 books each year on science, elementary and advanced mathematics, biology, music, art, literary history, social sciences, and other areas.